AMERICAN SCHOOL OF PREHISTORIC RESEARCH

PEABODY MUSEUM • HARVARD UNIVERSITY

BULLETIN NO. 37

EXCAVATION OF THE
ABRI PATAUD
LES EYZIES (DORDOGNE)

Hallam L. Movius, Jr.
General Editor and Director of Excavations

Harvey M. Bricker
Volume Editor

THE NOAILLIAN (LEVEL 4) ASSEMBLAGES AND THE NOAILLIAN CULTURE IN WESTERN EUROPE

by
Nicholas David

PEABODY MUSEUM OF ARCHAEOLOGY AND ETHNOLOGY
Harvey University, Cambridge, Massachusetts
1985
Distributed by Harvard University Press

Contents

Figures

Tables

xiv

Preface

This monograph is based upon a dissertation completed in 1966, revised for publication in 1972, and revised again in 1983–1984. The original aims were to develop a form of descriptive attribute analysis applicable to the study of Upper Palaeolithic stone tools (and by extension to assemblages of other periods and other materials). By this means, I would test Denis Peyrony's (1933) formulation of Upper Périgordian systematics, initially through the study of a part of the Upper Périgordian series from the Abri Pataud. The analytical results gave good grounds for arguing that the Périgordian Vc with Noailles burins, which I was to rename the Noaillian,* did not form part of the classic Upper Périgordian but stemmed from a separate cultural tradition. In order to test this hypothesis, I then broadened my horizons to investigate all the series from France, Italy, and even further afield that I knew to include or were claimed to include diagnostically Noaillian artifacts. This enabled me to define the Noaillian as an archaeological culture in terms of its chronology and environment (on which data were then very sketchy indeed), its regional and areal facies as expressed in typological variation, and a very preliminary outline of its historical development.

The attribute system, with modifications, improvements, and additions by H. M. Bricker and R. B. Clay, was published as Bulletin No. 26 of the American School of Prehistoric Research (Movius et al. 1968). It will not be repeated below. The descriptive attribute analysis of materials from the Abri Pataud and other sites will be presented in abbreviated form in support of the hypotheses of independence of the Noaillian tradition and of its regional differentiation into distinctive facies. In the intervening years typological methods have themselves developed, and it is for the reader to judge whether the absence of some new ideas and manipulative techniques and procedures invalidate my results. In my view it does not; the general approach employed is very close to that recently characterized by J. R. Sackett (1982) as "isochrestic."

Besides Sackett's formulation of a model of style that is generally (although perhaps with some modification) applicable in archaeology, there have of course been many other developments that took place while the 1972 version of this monograph lay "in press" for lack of funds to pub-

lish. In 1971 I used the information I had gathered in conjunction with ethnographic and ecological data to offer a theory of the dynamics of culture change among Upper Palaeolithic hunters of reindeer (David 1973). This has recently come under fire from Arthur Spiess (1979), whose information on caribou and their hunters and whose criticisms, discussed in chapter XVIII, have led me to modify my views in detail but not in substance. Several new sites have been published; these I have attempted to incorporate in the body of the work. The most significant are those of Provence (Onoratini 1982) and of Spain, the latter studied by Major McCollough (1971), who has kindly contributed an authoritative note to chapter XII on the Noaillian of the Pyrenees.

Much new information has also become available on the Upper Palaeolithic environment and, more particularly, on that of the Abri Pataud through the work of several specialists (Movius, ed., 1975). This is also briefly discussed with special reference to the Upper Périgordian and Noaillian period in chapter XVIII. But perhaps the most fundamental advance over the past decade has been the synthesis of the chrono-stratigraphic record by Laville, Rigaud, and Sackett (1980). Unfortunately, their conclusions and mine are in profound disagreement regarding the correlations of sites that have given Noaillian assemblages, so much so that if they are correct, not only is my reading of Noaillian and Périgordian relationships totally at sea but, I think it fair to say, archaeologists will be required to rethink some of their most basic beliefs about the nature and significance of stylistic variation. Our differences are considered in detail and tentative alternative correlations suggested in part 2.

The foregoing is not intended in any way to excuse the manifold deficiencies of the present text (how, for example, even in the early 1960s, can I have avoided study of core reduction techniques?), but to give the reader some idea of the circumstances under which it came, over a span of twenty years, to be engendered.

---

* An innovator in many aspects of Upper Palaeolithic studies, Mme de Sonneville-Bordes (1954, p. 216n) should also be given the credit for first proposing, ironically, the term "Noaillian."

Acknowledgments

First and foremost I give profound thanks to Professor Hallam L. Movius, Jr., who trained me as a practical archaeologist and directed my research, providing unfailing support and encouragement during our long association, including the benefit of his encyclopedic knowledge of the field. A demanding taskmaster, he gave his students that most precious of all gifts, the freedom to question all authorities and to follow our research to whatever conclusions it might lead. He was also a severe critic and the hardest to convince of the reality of an independent Noaillian tradition.

I would like to express special thanks to the Wenner-Gren Foundation, which appointed me as a Pre-Doctoral Fellow in 1964.

I owe much to James R. Sackett, who initiated me into the Pataud team and from and with whom I developed my analytical approach. I owe more to Harvey M. Bricker, without whom this, I hope, final version could not have been written. He assisted me in the processing of the Abri Pataud data and made many valuable suggestions during our long discussions of the Upper Périgordian. As my editor, he has not only carried out the normal duties of that office but has written draft sections on some of the Pataud materials that I did not study and on some sites published since 1966. He also reanalysed the backed tools from the Noaillian level according to his improved methods and has allowed me to make free use of his magisterial but as yet unpublished work on the classic Upper Périgordian (Bricker 1973). Especially in the final phases of writing and rewriting he has been a tower of strength, providing me with materials not otherwise available in Calgary and also with the benefits of his criticism. I hasten to add that opinions expressed herein are my own and any errors the fault of the word processor.

I have pleasure in acknowledging an intellectual debt to Mme Denise de Sonneville-Bordes, without whose pioneering systematization of the Upper Palaeolithic of the Périgord my work would not have been feasible. Many prehistorians and museum directors opened their collections to me and provided me with facilities for their study. M. Henri Delporte, Mme la Comtesse de Saint-Périer, and Dr. Louis Pradel allowed me to impose myself on them for considerable periods, offering me every hospitality while I worked on the important materials in their care. At a very late stage Bill Farrand gave me valuable advice, not all of which I took, on the geochronological sequence, and M. Gérard Onoratini kindly supplied me with his thesis and other information on the Noaillian of Provence which has allowed me tentatively to identify the culture ancestral to the Noaillian of Aquitaine. From them and from my colleagues in Italy and Czechoslovakia I learnt much archaeology and also how to receive and look after a guest. The late Professor Lothar Zotz and Professor Gisela Freund of the Universität Erlangen-Nürnberg kindly gave me the run of the Institut für Ur- und Frühgeschichte and room to work in peace during the winter of 1964–1965.

I am proud that the Abri Pataud artifact illustrations are the work of Pierre Laurent, lineal descendant of the great Upper Palaeolithic artists. I also thank Ursula Naber, who inked my drawings of tools from other sites; Hilke Hennig, who fresh from completion of her own doctorate undertook the typing of the first draft of an excessively lengthy thesis from my execrable handwriting; and Christine Davies, who volunteered similar assistance at a later stage.

During the long winter evenings in Tursac, Daphne and the late and most regretted Heinz Henghes made me welcome at their home and provided a much appreciated antidote to the niggling intricacies of burin typology. The Bouyssou family of Lespinasse went far beyond their duties as landlords and endeavored to enculturate me as a latter-day Périgordian. I am happy to count them and many other Tursacois as my friends.

Lastly I would thank the many students, now almost all professional archaeologists, who sweated through the Dordogne summers to provide the primary data.

I dedicate this work to François Bordes, Heinz Henghes, and Gabriel Bouyssou.

PART 1. LEVEL 4 AND LEVEL 4a SERIES

The Périgordian Vc, or Noaillian, Assemblages: Introduction and Preliminary Overview

The stratigraphy of the Abri Pataud is summarized by Movius (1975, pp. 7–18), and the reader is referred to a detailed account by the same author (1977) of the stratigraphy of the Upper Périgordian and intervening éboulis deposits and of the nature of the successive settlements. Movius's summary figure showing the sequence of levels and inferred climatic sequence is reproduced here as figure 1. Before proceeding to the analysis of what, in anticipation of my findings, I shall throughout refer to as the Noaillian, rather than Périgordian Vc, assemblages, certain points relevant to their evaluation deserve emphasis.

First, the site is vast. The shelter, or shelter complex, extends some 90 m along the cliff overlooking the Vézère River, and the Noaillian horizons of Level 4 have been shown to extend uninterruptedly for 32 m along it and to continue both north and south. If, on the evidence of the stratigraphy of the main excavation, we assess the mean depth of the shelter in Noaillian times conservatively at 10 m, the occupied area may still have exceeded half a hectare—excluding the much larger area of talus that slopes down to the west onto the river terrace. Level 4 deposits were recovered over approximately 85 m^2 within the main excavation, but the artifact samples analyzed in the following chapters are drawn from only about 37 m^2, or that part of the site combining good preservation of the integrity of the various minor levels or lenses with the finest stratigraphic control (i.e., Trench III, Squares D–F and part of G; Trench IV, Squares C–F and part of G; and Trench V(North), Squares A–C and part of D). We may therefore claim to have studied a fair sample only of those materials discarded under the shelter overhang.

Second, in the southwestern portion of the excavated area a large portion of the shelter roof had collapsed, terminating the Périgordian IV occupation of Level 5. It continued to affect the Noaillian habitat on account of its bulk and because the retreat of the overhang allowed increased amounts of water to enter the shelter, whether as driven rain or from new drip lines. Water ran off the rockfall into natural and in some cases artificial channels and into features such as the N-1/2 ditch in the MIDDLE subdivision and the O-2b pit in the LOWER that may have served as a sump. These

contributed directly and indirectly to redeposition of sediments and to the incorporation of materials of differing ages into some excavated lenses (Movius 1977, pp. 58–74, figs. 13–17, 22–27). In spite of the most painstaking excavation, there is some inherent mixture that must tend to blur the distinctiveness of the series from the various major and minor subdivisions. Thus, for example, Lens M-la at the top of Level 4 and the "éboulis a" above did not exist when the shelter was abandoned at the end of the main Noaillian occupation, but in the process of their formation came to incorporate M-1, M-2, and locally perhaps even earlier materials.

Third, Professor Movius and I disagree about the nature of the series from Level 4a, a thin and discontinuous zone lying at or near the contact between the Éboulis 3-4: Tan and Red subdivisions. In his view (ibid., p. 56), this represents a Terminal Noaillian occupation; while this is by no means impossible, I believe that the weight of the evidence favors interpretation of the 4a materials as a *mixture* of more or less contemporaneous Terminal Noaillian and late Upper Périgordian assemblages. This will be argued below in chapter VII.

Information on the environment of the Noaillian occupation is provided by several contributors to Movius (ed.) 1975 and by Spiess (1979). The summary information given in figure 1 is sufficient for present purposes. My aim in part 1 is to describe the Level 4 and Level 4a series and to argue that they are culturally distinct from the Upper Périgordian proper, represented at the Abri Pataud by the Périgordian IV of Level 5 and the Périgordian VI of Level 3. Part 2 extends the study to other sites in France, Spain, and Italy in order to establish the time-space systematics of the culture and its place in the Last Glacial sequence that are prerequisite to the drawing of inferences about Noaillian ethnography. The final chapter of part 2 attempts a reconstruction of limited aspects of Noaillian life.

ASSEMBLAGE OVERVIEW

The artifact samples studied are taken, as noted above, from those parts of the excavation over which we have the finest

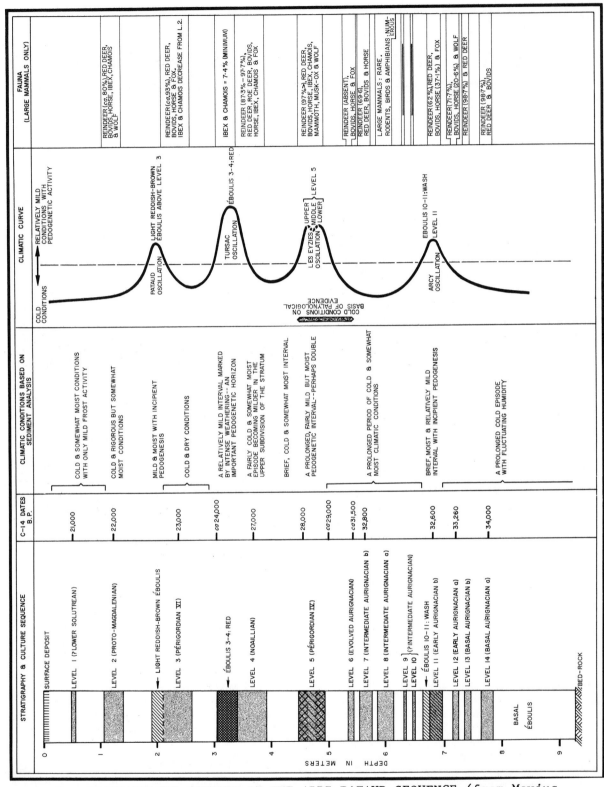

Figure 1.   DIAGRAMMATIC SUMMARY OF THE ABRI PATAUD SEQUENCE (from Movius 1977, p. 163, fig. j).

Table 1

DISTRIBUTION OF THE TABULATED ASSEMBLAGES FROM LEVEL 4

Artifact Category	LOWER	MIDDLE	UPPER	Total
Flint Tools Shown on Cumulative Graph	2307	1193	1718	5218
Miscellaneous Slightly Retouched and/or Utilized Blades and Flakes	482	66	90	638
Nuclei, Slightly Worked Nodules, and Flint Chunks	173	127	100	400
Artifacts of Stone Other than Flint	50	157	104	311
Perforated Shells	–	27	29	56
Artifacts of Tooth, Bone, Antler, and Ivory	58	83	104	245
Total Tabulated Assemblage	3070	1653	2145	6868

stratigraphic control. They are designated and correlate with the excavated lenses as follows:

Major Subdivision	Minor Subdivision	Lens
UPPER	UPPER-1a	Éboulis a, M-la
	UPPER-1	M-1
	UPPER-2	M-2
MIDDLE	MIDDLE-1	N-1, N-2, N-3
	MIDDLE-2	N-4
LOWER	REAR: LOWER	O-1, O-2 (hut, circle), O-2a, O-2b (pit)
	FRONT: LOWER-1	O-1a, O-2c
	FRONT: LOWER-2	O-3a, O-3, O-4

Over 11,000 cataloged artifacts were recovered from Level 4 in the area of the main excavation. Our samples include 6,868, or roughly 60%, of that total, distributed unequally among the LOWER, MIDDLE, and UPPER major subdivisions (table 1). The full series also includes untabulated quantities of river stones brought to the site for use in cooking and heating and of *débitage* flakes resulting from the manufacture of flint tools.

The contents of the great majority of the flint industry are summarized for each subdivision in table 2. The 92-type list established for the French Upper Palaeolithic by de Sonneville-Bordes and Perrot (1954–1956) is employed for this purpose. Percentage frequencies for the three subdivisions are shown also as cumulative graphs drawn in the standard format in figures 2, 3, and 4. The graph for LOWER (fig. 2) shows also the curve for the Périgordian IV assemblages of the later units of Level 5 (i.e., REAR plus FRONT:UPPER), the archaeological horizons underlying Level 4. Similarly, the UPPER graph (fig. 4) includes the curve for the Périgordian VI assemblage of the overlying

Level 3. Various typological indices based on the tool type frequencies are also given in table 2 (de Sonneville-Bordes 1954, pp. 200–201; 1960, pp. 28–29). Noailles burins are included in the truncation burin index.

The use of the de Sonneville-Bordes/Perrot type list and the cumulative graphs will serve to introduce the flint industry of Level 4 in terms that are comparable with a larger body of published material on French Upper Palaeolithic sites. The major tool classes—scrapers, burins, backed tools, truncated pieces, and marginally retouched pieces—are also subjected to extensive analyses which constitute a principal part of this study. For this reason, introductory comment on these tools is brief, and specific reference to the illustrated specimens is not made in this chapter. Tools of lesser importance in the assemblage—e.g., notched pieces, picks—are not subjected to attribute analysis; they are discussed only in this chapter, and references to illustrations are included (figs. 5; 6).

It is important to note, as has already been done for Levels 5 and 3, that tabulation of the flint industry in terms of the de Sonneville-Bordes/Perrot typology and the attribute analyses presented in the following chapters are separate operations with quite different requirements. Insofar as possible, the 92-type list includes all flint tools, complete or broken, in good condition or damaged. Tools that are too fragmentary or badly damaged must, however, be excluded from the attribute analyses. Also, tools which fit the definition of a single type in a typology designed to permit the comparison of a variety of industries may be assigned to different typological entities in the analysis of a single culture. The reverse case also occurs, where the "standard" typology employed in the construction of cumulative curves arbitrarily divides into separate types tools that attribute analysis demonstrates are variants of a single entity. The two ways of describing the flint industry are designed for different analytical purposes and do not provide directly comparable results.

Table 2

DISTRIBUTION OF TOOL TYPES AND INDICES OF TOOL GROUPS FROM LEVEL 4
SHOWN IN THE CUMULATIVE GRAPHS

Type No.	Type	LOWER		MIDDLE		UPPER	
		n	%	n	%	n	%
1	End-Scraper	85	3.68	69	5.78	66	3.84
2	Atypical End-Scraper	51	2.21	24	2.01	21	1.22
3	Double End-Scraper	5	0.22	2	0.17	4	0.23
4	Ogival End-Scraper	31	1.34	33	2.77	29	1.69
5	End-Scraper on Retouched Blade or Flake	21	0.91	26	2.18	27	1.57
6	End-Scraper on Aurignacian Blade	-	-	1	0.08	-	-
7	Fan-Shaped End-Scraper	13	0.56	6	0.50	2	0.12
8	Discoidal Scraper	1	0.04	1	0.08	-	-
9	Circular Scraper	1	0.04	-	-	-	-
10	Thumbnail Scraper	-	-	-	-	-	-
11	Carinate Scraper	-	-	-	-	-	-
12	Atypical Carinate Scraper	-	-	-	-	-	-
13	Thick Nose-Shaped Scraper	-	-	-	-	-	-
14	Flat Nose-Shaped or Shouldered End-Scraper	-	-	-	-	-	-
15	Nucleiform Scraper	-	-	-	-	-	-
16	Rabot or Plane	-	-	-	-	-	-
17	End-Scraper + Burin	26	1.13	18	1.51	42	2.44
18	End-Scraper + Truncated Piece	1	0.04	5	0.42	6	0.35
19	Burin + Truncated Piece	4	0.17	6	0.50	11	0.64
20	Perforator + Truncated Piece	2	0.09	-	-	-	-
21	Perforator + End-Scraper	1	0.04	-	-	-	-
22	Perforator + Burin	3	0.13	2	0.17	7	0.41
23	Perforator	16	0.69	7	0.59	11	0.64
24	Bec or Atypical Perforator	12	0.52	7	0.59	20	1.16
25	Multiple Perforator or Bec	-	-	-	-	1	0.06
26	Microperforator	-	-	-	-	-	-
27	Symmetrical Dihedral Burin	97	4.20	59	4.95	62	3.61
28	Asymmetrical Dihedral Burin	156	6.76	68	5.70	50	2.91
29	Transverse or Transverse/Oblique Dihedral Burin	13	0.56	9	0.75	5	0.29
30a	Burin on Broken Surface	52	2.25	48	4.02	62	3.61
30b	Burin on Unretouched Edge or End of Flake or Blade	17	0.74	4	0.34	9	0.52
31	Multiple Burin associating Types 27 to 30	43	1.86	34	2.85	25	1.46
32	Busked Burin	-	-	-	-	-	-
33	Parrot Beak Burin	-	-	-	-	-	-
34	Burin on Straight, Right-Angle Truncation	8	0.35	2	0.17	8	0.47
35	Burin on Straight, Oblique Truncation	89	3.86	105	8.80	159	9.25

Table 2 (continued)

Type No.	Type	LOWER		MIDDLE		UPPER	
		n	%	n	%	n	%
36	Burin on Concave Truncation	76	3.29	67	5.67	144	8.38
37	Burin on Convex Truncation	13	0.56	26	2.18	25	1.46
38	Transverse Burin on Straight or Convex Lateral Truncation	1	0.04	-	-	2	0.12
39	Transverse Burin on Concave Lateral Truncation	2	0.09	3	0.25	1	0.06
40	Multiple Burin associating Types 34 to 39	7	0.30	60	5.03	96	5.59
41	Mixed Multiple Burin, Types 27-30 + Types 34-39	27	1.17	35	2.93	64	3.73
42	Noailles Burin	869	37.67	109	9.14	42	2.44
43	Nucleiform Burin	2	0.09	-	-	-	-
44	Flat-Faced Burin	27	1.17	77	6.45	202	11.76
45	Abri Audi Knife	-	-	-	-	-	-
46	Châtelperron Point	-	-	-	-	-	-
47	Atypical Châtelperron Point	-	-	-	-	-	-
48	Gravette Point	11	0.48	2	0.17	3	0.17
49	Atypical Gravette Point	4	0.17	3	0.25	2	0.12
50	Les Vachons Point	-	-	-	-	-	-
51	Micro-Gravette Point	31	1.34	1	0.08	1	0.06
52	Font-Yves Point	-	-	-	-	-	-
53	Gibbous Backed Piece	2	0.09	-	-	1	0.06
54	Fléchette	-	-	-	-	-	-
55	Tanged Point	-	-	-	-	-	-
56	Périgordian Shouldered Point	-	-	-	-	-	-
57	Shouldered Piece	4	0.17	-	-	-	-
58	Completely Backed Blade	-	-	-	-	-	-
59	Partially Backed Blade	-	-	-	-	-	-
60	Piece with Straight, Right-Angle Truncation	6	0.26	6	0.50	11	0.64
61	Piece with Straight, Oblique Truncation	27	1.17	15	1.26	21	1.22
62	Piece with Concave Truncation	43	1.86	21	1.76	34	1.98
63	Piece with Convex Truncation	1	0.04	2	0.17	2	0.12
64	Bitruncated Piece	1	0.04	-	-	-	-
65	Piece with Continuous Retouch on One Edge	118	5.12	77	6.45	186	10.83
66	Piece with Continuous Retouch on Both Edges	68	2.95	52	4.36	153	8.91
67	Aurignacian Blade	-	-	-	-	-	-
68	Strangled Blade	-	-	-	-	-	-
69-72	Solutrean Tools	-	-	-	-	-	-
73	Pick	6	0.26	-	-	1	0.06
74	Notched Piece	178	7.72	60	5.03	59	3.43
75	Denticulate Piece	15	0.65	6	0.50	13	0.76
76	Splintered Piece	5	0.22	20	1.68	17	0.99

Table 2 (continued)

Type No.	Type	LOWER n	LOWER %	MIDDLE n	MIDDLE %	UPPER n	UPPER %
77	Side-Scraper	2	0.09	1	0.08	3	0.17
78	Raclette	–	–	–	–	–	–
79–83	Geometric Pieces	–	–	–	–	–	–
84	Truncated Bladelet	–	–	–	–	–	–
85	Backed Bladelet	1	0.04	1	0.08	–	–
86	Truncated Backed Bladelet	1	0.04	–	–	–	–
87	Denticulate Backed Bladelet	–	–	–	–	–	–
88	Denticulate Bladelet	–	–	–	–	–	–
89	Notched Bladelet	–	–	–	–	–	–
90	Dufour Bladelet	–	–	–	–	1	0.06
91	Azilian Point	–	–	–	–	–	–
92	Other Tools, not included in Types 1 to 91	11	0.48	13	1.09	6	0.35
	Totals	2307	99.96	1193	100.04	1718	100.02

Indices:

IG	(Scraper Index, Types 1–15)	9.02	13.58	8.67
IB	(Burin Index, Types 27–44)	64.98	59.18	55.65
IBd	(Dihedral Burin Index, Types 27–31)	16.38	18.61	12.40
IBt	(Truncation Burin Index, Types 34–37, 40, 42)	46.03	30.93	27.59
IP	(Perforator Index, Types 23–25)	1.21	1.17	1.86
GP	(Périgordian Characteristic Group Index, Types 45–64, 84–87)	5.72	4.28	4.37

Several general explanatory remarks are needed about the attribute analyses discussed in later sections of this report. Unless otherwise indicated, the attribute systems used here to describe the lithic artifacts are those explained in detail in Movius, David, Bricker, and Clay (1968). It was the wish of the Abri Pataud project director, Hallam L. Movius, Jr., to include in this report as large a sample as possible of the attribute data on which the study of the Pataud artifacts is based. After having experimented with several different techniques of presentation, Movius decided to present many of the attribute data for the illustrated examples of the major classes of flint tools in the form of detailed figure captions. Although the data in the captions are not, of course, sufficient for reanalysis by other workers, they should offer a clear understanding of the way the attribute systems were used in practice. The numbers appearing within parentheses immediately following the object numbers in the figure captions to the artifact illustrations are the original catalog numbers of the artifacts in question, e.g., the catalog number

of the retouched point shown in figure 5, number 1, is "5710." Finally, the enclosure within parentheses of some percentage values appearing in the attribute distribution tables indicates that they are based on samples of less than 50 objects; percentages of larger samples are shown without parentheses.

DISCUSSION OF THE CUMULATIVE GRAPHS

Scrapers

The scraper index (IG) in Level 4 varies between subdivisions and does not change regularly through time. All values are much lower than that for the underlying later Level 5 (IG = 21.80). The highest scraper index in Level 4 is in MIDDLE (IG = 13.58); this is almost identical with the value for the overlying Level 3 (IG = 13.76).

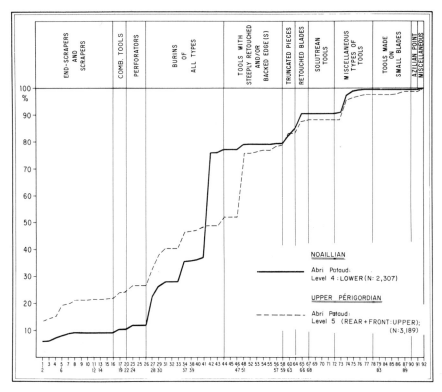

Figure 2. CUMULATIVE GRAPHS OF THE LATER LEVEL 5 AND LEVEL 4: LOWER ASSEMBLAGES.

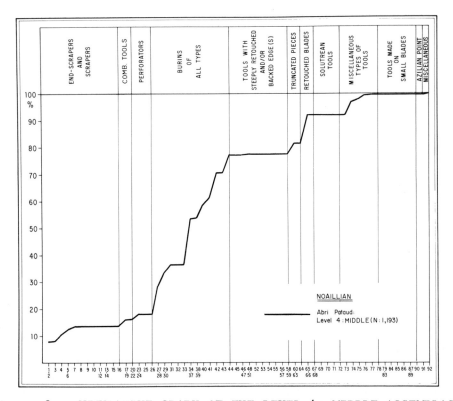

Figure 3. CUMULATIVE GRAPH OF THE LEVEL 4: MIDDLE ASSEMBLAGE.

Double end-scrapers are very infrequent throughout the level. Ogival end-scrapers, most common in MIDDLE, are slightly more frequent than in Levels 5 or 3. End-scrapers on retouched blades or flakes are very rare in LOWER, but frequencies increase in MIDDLE and UPPER. This reflects a general increase in marginal retouch through time in Level 4 that is best shown by the marginally retouched pieces, Types 65 and 66. Fan-shaped end-scrapers are infrequent in LOWER and MIDDLE, with percentages comparable to later Level 5, and virtually absent in UPPER. The end-scrapers of Level 4 differ from those of later Level 5 and Level 3 in various ways that do not register on the cumulative graphs or 92-type lists. These will be treated in the attribute analysis below, but one difference obvious from casual examination of the illustrations is in blank morphology. Discoidal scrapers are of no quantitative importance in Level 4, a clear difference from both Levels 5 and 3. Aurignacian scrapers are absent.

Combination Tools

Combination tools are infrequent throughout Level 4; as in Levels 5 and 3, the most frequently associated tools are end-scrapers and burins.

Perforators

The perforator index increases between the MIDDLE and UPPER subdivisions. The UPPER value (IP = 1.86) is comparable to that of Level 3, but it is less than that for later Level 5 (IP = 2.51). Although most of the perforators and *becs* are made on small, usually flake blanks (fig. 5:4), a small number of well-made examples are on larger blanks (fig. 5:5).

Burins

The most marked characteristics of Level 4 assemblages are their very high burin indices. Even the lowest value, for UPPER (IB = 55.65), is much higher than that for Level 3 (IB = 31.39) or later Level 5 (IB = 25.74). In the LOWER subdivision, burins account for 65% of all graphed tools. The principal factor accounting for the decrease in the burin index through time in the level is the drop in frequency of Noailles burins. The dihedral burin index (IBd) is always heavily dominated by the truncation burin index (IBt). This is like Level 3, although in later Level 5 dihedral burins are always more numerous than truncation burins. The difference is even greater than the indices seem to suggest, because break burins and unretouched edge/end burins are included in the dihedral burin index. The true dihedral burins are predominantly median or asymmetrical; transverse or transverse oblique examples are extremely rare.

Truncation burins which are not Noailles burins or flat-faced burins (i.e., Types 34–40) differ greatly in frequency between LOWER (8.50%), on the one hand, and MIDDLE (22.05%) and UPPER (25.32%), on the other. As flat-faced burins are very infrequent in LOWER, this points up again

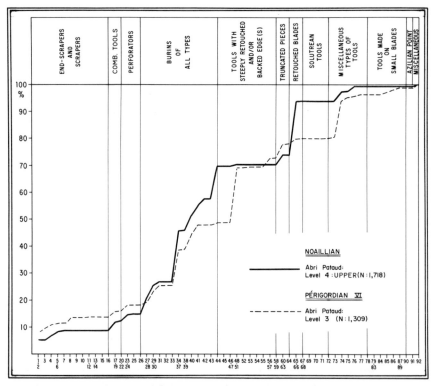

Figure 4.   CUMULATIVE GRAPHS OF THE LEVEL 4: UPPER AND LEVEL 3 ASSEMBLAGES.

the overwhelming contribution Noailles burins make to the LOWER series. Straight, right-angle truncations are rare, and convex truncations are infrequent. The most numerous truncation shapes are straight oblique and concave, the former being slightly more common. The dominance of oblique truncations is found also in later Level 5, but not in Level 3. Transverse truncation burins are very rare and do not constitute a distinct morphological variant as they do in Level 3.

Noailles burins are exceedingly frequent in the LOWER subdivision, where they account for 37.67% of all graphed tools. The frequency declines radically in MIDDLE (9.14%) and becomes even smaller in UPPER (2.44%). This striking decrease through time is accompanied by an increase in the frequencies of flat-faced burins, from 1.17% in LOWER to 6.45% in MIDDLE to 11.76% in UPPER. These percentages do not, however, do justice to the typological realities of the Level 4 burin series. Many, but not all, of the pieces tabulated as flat-faced burins (Type 44) are representatives of a special category of burin, dealt with at some length in the analysis below, called Raysse burins (Movius and David 1970). The frequency increase of Raysse burins through time in Level 4, paralleling the frequency decrease of Noailles burins, is more marked than can be seen simply from the percentages of Type 44. Not all flat-faced burins are Raysse burins, and some Raysse burins, forming parts of double or mixed burins, are tabulated as Types 40 or 41.

Another special category of burin, discussed in the analysis section as the burin-point (ibid.), is not distinguished in the 92-type list. These burins, which are most often truncation or dihedral burins, are not as frequent as Noailles or Raysse burins, but their distinctiveness and their pattern of change through time make them a very significant component of the burin series.

Backed Tools (fig. 5:11–14, 16–27)

Backed tools of any kind are extremely infrequent in Level 4; this is a clear and very important difference between the Noaillian, on the one hand, and the Périgordian IV and VI, on the other. Backed tools are least uncommon in LOWER (2.34%); they are virtually absent in MIDDLE (0.59%) and UPPER (0.41%). Gravette points and Micro-Gravette points make up the bulk of the backed tool series. Evidence will be presented in the attribute analysis which follows that the Gravette/Micro-Gravette points of Level 4 are qualitatively different from those of Levels 5 and 3, as well as being much less numerous. *Fléchettes*, Font-Robert points, and Périgordian shouldered points are all absent from the assemblages.

Truncated Pieces (fig. 5:6–9)

Truncated pieces constitute a small component of the assemblage in all subdivisions (LOWER = 3.38%; MIDDLE = 3.69%; UPPER = 3.96%). These frequencies are very slightly lower than those for later Level 5 (4.42%) and Level 3 (4.89%). Pieces with concave truncation are most numerous throughout the level, followed by those with straight oblique truncations. Bitruncated pieces are virtually absent.

The Périgordian Characteristic Group Index (GP), including all backed tools and truncated pieces, is low for all subdivisions of Level 4. The index values for the Périgordian IV of later Level 5 (GP = 31.17) and the Périgordian VI of Level 3 (GP = 30.94) are approximately six times greater. The significance of this index is less than clear, but if one accepts it as a useful criterion of cultural affiliation, Level 4 is certainly not Périgordian in the same sense as Levels 5 and 3.

Marginally Retouched Pieces (fig. 6:1–8)

Marginally retouched pieces are quantitatively important in Level 4, and they become increasingly so from LOWER (8.06%) to MIDDLE (10.81%) to UPPER (19.73%). Even in LOWER, this is a real difference from the lesser frequencies in later Level 5 (5.14%) and especially in Level 3 (2.45%). In UPPER, where marginally retouched pieces account for almost one-fifth of all graphed tools, the difference is of major importance. The majority of pieces bear marginal retouch on one edge only. The most frequent kind of retouch in LOWER is fine; that in MIDDLE and UPPER is scaled.

Various Pieces

There are seven picks in Level 4, six of which come from the LOWER subdivision. The series of notched (fig. 6:9, 12–14) and denticulate pieces calls for no special comment. Splintered pieces, especially in MIDDLE and UPPER, are slightly more numerous than in Levels 5 or 3 (fig. 5:15). There is one Dufour bladelet from the UPPER subdivision. Twenty of the 30 tools assigned to Type 92 are retouched points. These are made on both blades (fig. 5:1) and flakes (fig. 5:2); one on a narrow blade has invasive and stepped, inverse retouch at the point (fig. 5:3). Also included in Type 92 are: three "nosed pieces," one *pointe burinante*, one chopper, one disc, one quartz flake, and two microblade cores with dihedral burin removals.

ARTIFACTS NOT SHOWN ON THE CUMULATIVE GRAPH

Miscellaneous slightly retouched and/or utilized blades and flakes are pieces that have been slightly modified after their removal from the core. The modification, although visible to the naked eye, is, however, neither extensive nor regular enough to permit the assignment of the piece to a more formal tool category. The other artifacts shown in table 1—nuclei, slightly worked nodules, flint chunks, artifacts of stone other than flint, perforated shells, and artifacts of

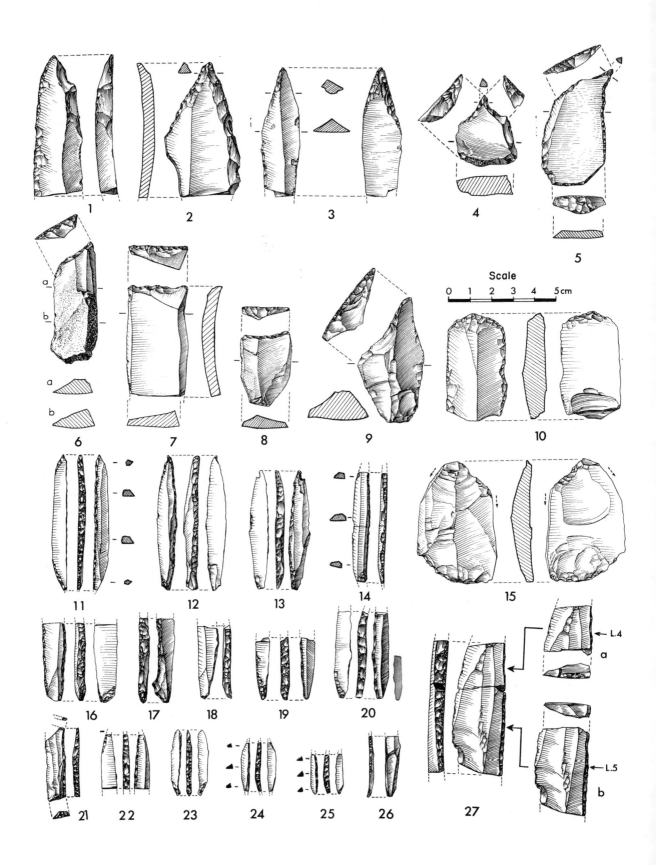

Scale
0 1 2 3 4 5 cm

Figure 5. POINTS, PERFORATORS, TRUNCATED BLADES, SPLINTERED PIECES, AND GRAVETTE POINTS

1 (5710): UPPER-1: Median point with continuous medium and scaled retouch on the left side.
2 (8459): UPPER-1: Asymmetrical point (right) with partial heavy retouch on the left side and continuous very heavy retouch on the right side.
3 (7614): LOWER-2: Median point with flat inverse retouch at the distal extremity.
4 (6748): UPPER-2: Median perforator with heavy steep retouch along the concavities on both sides of the perforator projection.
5 (9538): MIDDLE-1: Asymmetrical perforator (right) with partial fine and medium retouch on the left side, heavy steep retouch at the distal extremity, and continuous medium retouch on the right side. Note heavy steep retouch at the proximal extremity.
6 (8903): UPPER-1: Steeply retouched truncated blade with slightly concave/oblique truncation at the distal extremity.
7 (8951): UPPER-1: Steeply retouched truncated blade with straight truncation at the distal extremity; proximal portion broken.
8 (7387): MIDDLE-1: Steeply retouched truncated blade with slightly concave/straight truncation at the distal extremity.
9 (10,311): MIDDLE-1: Steeply retouched truncated blade with concave/ very oblique truncation at the distal extremity.
10 (10,335): MIDDLE-1: Broken and splintered end-scraper (distal extremity); fine and scaled retouch on the left side; continuous scaled retouch on the right side. Note splinter removals on bulbar surface of both extremities.
11 (14,650): LOWER-2: Complete Gravette point; IIa (IIa+IIB+IIIb+IVb); utilized edge opposite the backing. Point: Inverse-1. Butt: Inverse-3a.
12 (10,516a+b): MIDDLE-2: Complete Gravette point; IIIb (IIIb+Vb); utilized edge opposite the backing. Point: Obverse. Butt: Obverse-4. This piece was found in an area of Lens 4 in Trench IV, Square F, directly overlying Level 5; it may have derived therefrom.
13 (11,043): LOWER-2: Complete Gravette point; Ia (Ia+IIb+IIIb); utilized edge opposite the backing. Point: Inverse-1. Butt: Unretouched-1.
14 (13,034): LOWER-1: Almost complete Gravette point; IVb; utilized edge opposite the backing. Butt: Unretouched-2.
15 (6314): UPPER-1: Splintered piece with removals off both extremities of bulbar surface.
16 (4004): UPPER-1a: Gravette point butt; IIIb; continuous obverse retouch on edge opposite the backing. Butt: Inverse-3b.
17 (6979): LOWER-2b: Gravette point butt; Ia (Ia+IIIb+IVb); utilized edge opposite the backing. Butt: Unretouched-1. Note gibbosity on backed edge near proximal extremity.
18 (11,297): UPPER-1a: Gravette point butt; IIb; utilized edge opposite the backing. Butt: Unretouched-1.
19 (13,208): LOWER-1: Gravette point butt; IIa (IIa+IIb); utilized edge opposite backing. Butt: Inverse-3a.

Figure 5 (continued)

20 (8308): UPPER-2: Gravette point butt; IIb (IIb+IVb); utilized edge
    opposite the backing. Butt: Inverse-3a.
21 (13,774): LOWER-1: Almost complete *lamelle à dos tronquée*; IVb;
    utilized edge opposite the backing.
22 (505): LOWER: Gravette point with backing on the left; IIa (IIa+IIb);
    unretouched and unutilized edge opposite the backing.
23 (4740): LOWER: Complete Gravette point; Ib. This piece, found in
    one of the test trenches, was not studied.
24 (14,513): LOWER-2: Almost complete Gravette point; Ib; utilized edge
    opposite the backing. Point: Inverse-1. butt: Inverse-3a.
25 (14,705): LOWER-2: Almost complete Gravette point; Ia (Ia+Ic);
    utilized edge opposite the backing. Butt: Inverse-2a.
26 (11,190): MIDDLE-2: Partially backed bladelet; butt; Vb.
27a (12,950): LOWER-1: Segment of Gravette point; IVa (IVa+IVb);
    utilized edge opposite the backing. Note slight retouch on broken
    proximal extremity; fits #3161 from Level 5.
27b (3161): *Level 5*: REAR:UPPER: Segment of Gravette point; IVa
    (IVa+Vb); utilized edge opposite the backing. Note removal on right
    margin of broken distal extremity; fits #12,950 from Level 4.

Figure 6.   RETOUCHED BLADES, FLAKES, FLAKE/BLADES, AND NOTCHED PIECES

 1 (8754): UPPER-1: Flake/blade with continuous heavy (medium) retouch
    on the left side; partial fine retouch on the right side.
 2 (5911): UPPER-1a: Blade with continuous scaled retouch on the left
    side; proximal portion.
 3 (8494): UPPER-1: Blade with continuous heavy and scaled retouch on
    the left side and on the proximal portion of the right side.
 4 (11,155): UPPER-1: Blade with continuous fine to medium scaled
    retouch on the right side; continuous medium to heavy scaled retouch
    on the left side.
 5 (10,244): MIDDLE-1: Blade with partial medium scaled retouch on the
    right side; continuous fine to medium retouch on the left side.
 6 (3304): UPPER-2: Blade with continuous medium to heavy scaled retouch
    on the left side; partial medium to heavy scaled retouch on the right
    side. Note fine retouch on the proximal portion of the right side.
 7 (2115): UPPER-2: Blade with continuous fine and scaled retouch on
    the left side; slight fine retouch on the right side; proximal
    extremity broken; distal portion.
 8 (9559): MIDDLE-1: Blade with continuous medium to heavy scaled
    retouch on the right side; partial fine retouch on the left side.
    Note heavy scaled retouch on the proximal portion of the left side.
 9 (6550): UPPER-1a: Blade with notch and partial fine retouch on the
    left side; irregular edge chipping resulting from use on the right
    side; both extremities broken.
10 (8616): MIDDLE-2: Flake with discontinuous irregular retouch on the
    right side.
11 (9754): MIDDLE-1: Flake with partial heavy retouch on the right side.
12 (10,282): MIDDLE-1: Flake with partial fine inverse retouch and
    inversely retouched notch on the right side.

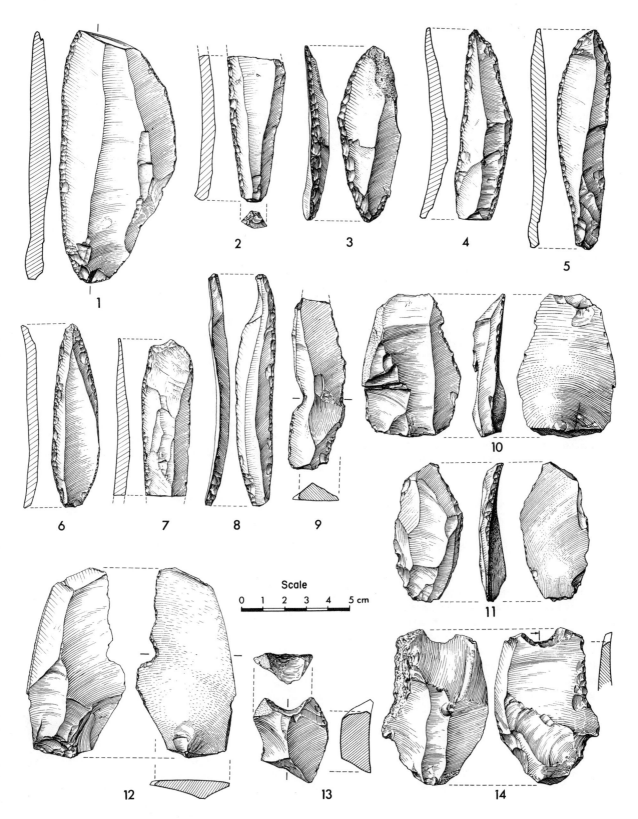

13 (10,322): MIDDLE-1: Irregular flake with broad notch at the distal extremity.

14 (9336): MIDDLE-1: Flake with inversely retouched notch at the distal extremity and partial heavy scaled retouch on the left side.

tooth, bone, antler, and ivory—are all discussed below in chapters that follow the attribute analysis of the flint tools. Of special note here are the large series of artifacts of stone other than flint and those of organic materials. The majority of the former are small river pebbles, water-rolled and sometimes polished, that were brought to the site for unknown purposes. The assemblage also includes a series of distinctive antler armatures (sagaies) characteristic of the Noaillian. Both these groups of artifacts are best represented in the MIDDLE and UPPER subdivisions.

DISCUSSION

The most distinctive tool class in the Level 4 assemblage and the one which most obviously differentiates it from the assemblages of Levels 5 and 3 is that of the burins. Unfortunately, this is also the class for which the de Sonneville-Bordes/Perrot list is least adequate for characterizing the particular typological features of the assemblage in question. Certain things are, however, quite clear from the graph, type list, and indices. Over half the graphed tools are burins (IB = 55.65 to 64.98); burins do not approach this quantitative importance in either Level 5 or Level 3. The overwhelming dominance of truncation burins over burins of other kinds, especially in the LOWER subdivisions, is the reverse of the situation found in later Level 5. The relative frequencies of truncation and dihedral burins in Level 4 are like those of Level 3, but the heavy contributors to the truncation burin index in Level 4—i.e., Noailles burins and Raysse burins—are not found in Level 3. The extraordinary wealth of Noailles burins in the LOWER subdivision—37.67% of all graphed tools—is well illustrated by the graph. The quantitative importance of the Raysse burins and burin-points and their changes through time are shown below by attribute analysis.

Another major characteristic of the Level 4 assemblage is the paucity of backed tools. On this basis alone, the Level 4 assemblage is clearly differentiated from those of Levels 5 and 3. With a high of just over 2% and a low of less than one-half of 1%, backed tools do not constitute a quantitatively significant component of the Level 4 assemblage.

The Level 4 scrapers are predominantly end-scrapers; the discoidal scrapers and other scrapers made on flakes that are characteristic of Level 3 and later Level 5 are not quantitatively important in Level 4. The most important differences between the Level 4 end-scrapers and those of the other two levels do not appear in the cumulative graphs.

The greater incidence of marginal retouch on end-scrapers and marginally retouched pieces is, however, reflected in the graphs. In addition to the frequency differences, the kinds of marginal retouch, particularly in MIDDLE and UPPER, are distributed differently than in Levels 5 and 3.

A third major characteristic of the Level 4 series is the marked typological change through time within the level. This is clearly seen by comparing the graph for LOWER with that for UPPER. This change is, however, not regular. The graphs for MIDDLE and UPPER are very similar except for differences in frequencies of Noailles burins, flat-faced burins, and pieces with marginal retouch. All three differences reflect trends that are discussed more fully below. The graphs for MIDDLE and LOWER are quite different; although the same tools are involved as for MIDDLE versus UPPER, the magnitude of the difference is greater. The great majority of the graphed tools from MIDDLE are from MIDDLE-1, the MIDDLE-2 sample being very small. Therefore, the similarity shown by the graphs is primarily between UPPER and MIDDLE-1 as contrasted with LOWER (plus, as is shown later, MIDDLE-2). The typological discontinuity shown here is explored in much greater detail by attribute analysis; its repeated appearance in various tool classes has permitted the recognition of "Early Noaillian" (LOWER and MIDDLE-2) and "Late Noaillian" (MIDDLE-1 and UPPER) phases.

The radical quantitative differences between the Level 4 assemblages and those of Levels 5 and 3 are certainly shown by the cumulative graphs and the type lists, and qualitative differences are also indicated by the presence and absence in the various levels of certain highly characterized types. In the succeeding chapters we shall demonstrate that there are also recurrent, standardized, qualitative differences between the major tool types present in both Noaillian and Upper Périgordian assemblages and that these require the attribution of such assemblages to two independent cultural traditions.

Unless otherwise specified, the definition of attributes and the techniques and procedures used in their study follow those described by Movius, David, Bricker, and Clay (1968) and exemplified by Bricker and David in their monograph (1984) on the Périgordian VI of the Abri Pataud. Only a selection of the tools shown in Pierre Laurent's superb drawings is referred to in the text. Figure captions include detailed information on the pieces, including catalog numbers, provenience by subdivision, and attribute data.

Attribute Analysis of End-Scrapers and Other Scrapers in Level 4

END-SCRAPERS

End-scrapers are proportionately less frequent in Level 4 than in Levels 5 and 3. They are studied by the UPPER (n = 177), MIDDLE (n = 168) and LOWER (n = 223) major subdivisions. Big differences separate the Périgordian and Noaillian series. These differences are expressed in almost every attribute, in those reflecting primary reduction techniques, as well as in minor stylistic features. If end-scrapers are to be considered as a banal element in the Upper Palaeolithic tool kit, as part of a common substrate, then on the evidence of the end-scrapers alone the Noaillian should be considered a cultural tradition independent of the Périgordian IV and VI.

The Level 4 end-scrapers appear on inspection more variable than their later Level 5 and Level 3 counterparts. The analysis does not, however, support typological subdivision of the sample, although a possible case of incipient specialization will be discussed below with reference to blunt point end-scrapers.

Nature of the Blank

As in later Level 5 and Level 3, end-scrapers made on other than regular blades are rare; the same variations from the regular blade blank, including corner platforms, are present. Noaillian blades are, however, less regular in outline, dorsal ridge pattern, and thickness. We have not attempted to quantify this variation or to study in detail the immediately obvious difference in the basic blade technology (figs. 7–9). It is possible that many Level 4 blades classed as regular would, in a late Level 5 context, lie on the borderline of irregular blades. In the MIDDLE and UPPER subdivisions, the blanks are definitely more regular than in the LOWER.

A minor consequence of the decreased regularity and parallel-sidedness of blades in Level 4 is an increased difficulty in delimitation of the retouch forming the scraping edge and thus in the measurement of end-scrapers. This is apparent in the measurement of arc end-scrapers (see below). A morphological variant, possibly intentional or perhaps a direct consequence of lesser parallel-sidedness, is seen in the presence of fan-shaped end-scrapers (*grattoirs*

en éventail), on which the scraping edge is at the widest portion of the blank, the margins diverging more-or-less regularly from the butt toward the scraping edge (fig. 9:4–6). The number of fan-shaped end-scrapers is highest in the LOWER subdivision (n = 13; 7.07% of all single end-scrapers), decreasing regularly in MIDDLE (n = 6; 4.58%) and UPPER (n = 2; 1.55%). This is congruent with our impression of an improvement in blade technology from LOWER to MIDDLE to UPPER.

Length, Scraping Edge Width, and Scraping Edge Thickness

The distributions of blank length for all complete single end-scrapers and scraping edge width and thickness for all end-scrapers are shown in table 3. There is a wide internal variation in length among the samples, the LOWER subdivision being characterized by much shorter blanks than the MIDDLE and UPPER subdivisions. There is little variation in scraping edge width and thickness, though the scraping edges of UPPER are slightly narrower and thinner than those of LOWER and MIDDLE. Size appears, consequently, of limited value as a typological indicator of cultural change and likeness, depending on basic technological factors that we are unable to control, and reflecting and being influenced by the total range of blanks produced and the tools made upon them. Thus a specialization in some other section of the tool kit may entrain with it variations in size of other tools.

The mean lengths of end-scrapers in LOWER and MIDDLE are clearly lower than in the later units of Level 5 or Level 3, but that of UPPER is closely comparable. Scraping edge width and thickness in all three subdivisions are smaller than in later Level 5 and Level 3, which, for their part, are quite similar.

Scraping Edge Contour

The distribution of scraping edge contour is shown for the three subdivisions in table 4. The arc-of-circle contour (e.g., fig. 7:1–14) is found on a majority of end-scrapers through-

Table 3

DISTRIBUTION OF LENGTH OF COMPLETE SINGLE END-SCRAPERS
AND SCRAPING EDGE WIDTH AND THICKNESS OF ALL END-SCRAPERS IN LEVEL 4

	LOWER	MIDDLE	UPPER
Length (mm)			
$\bar{X} \pm s_{\bar{X}}$	53.18 ± 1.30	62.53 ± 2.70	66.97 ± 3.18
Range	24–83	32–101	35–116
s	12.27	16.63	18.58
n	89	38	34
Scraping Edge Thickness (mm)			
$\bar{X} \pm s_{\bar{X}}$	21.80 ± 0.41	21.70 ± 0.46	20.12 ± 0.46
Range	7–43	8–37	6–38
s	6.15	5.96	6.08
n	223	168	177
Scraping Edge Thickness (mm)			
$\bar{X} \pm s_{\bar{X}}$	6.76 ± 0.19	7.21 ± 0.19	6.59 ± 0.18
Range	2–16	3–16	2–14
s	2.84	2.45	2.38
n	223	168	177

Note: Sample values shown are mean ($\bar{X}$), standard error of the mean ($s_{\bar{X}}$), and standard deviation (s).

Table 4

DISTRIBUTIONS OF SCRAPING EDGE CONTOUR OF END-SCRAPERS
IN LATER LEVEL 5, LEVEL 4, AND LEVEL 3

Scraping Edge Contour	Later Level 5 %	Level 4 LOWER n	%	MIDDLE n	%	UPPER n	%	Level 3 %
Arc	48.71	113	50.67	89	52.98	92	51.98	33.33
Blunt Point	5.47	36	16.14	39	23.21	46	25.99	9.74
Asymmetrical	19.77	15	6.73	12	7.14	10	5.65	23.59
Flattened	4.66	3	1.35	4	2.38	5	2.83	8.72
Irregular	19.77	56	25.11	24	14.29	24	13.56	24.62
N	622	223		168		177		195

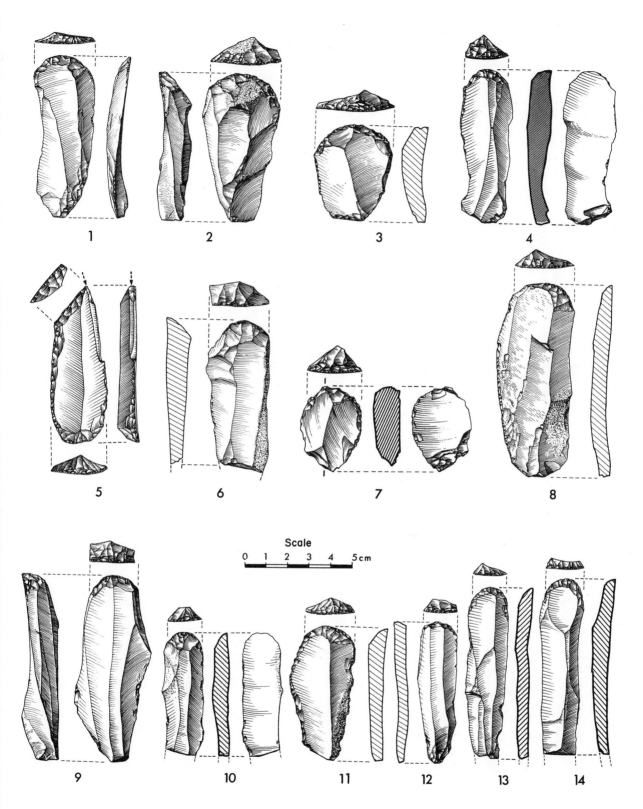

Figure 7. END-SCRAPERS

Figure 7. END-SCRAPERS

SHAPE OF END

Arc of Circle

```
 1  (6127):  UPPER-1a:  120°; 1.5 cm
 2  (8585):  UPPER-1a:  140°; 1.75 cm
 3  (6811):  UPPER-1:   120°; 2 cm
 4  (8450):  UPPER-1:   140°; 1 cm
 5  (5548):  UPPER-1:   140°; 1.25 cm
 6  (5746):  UPPER-2:   90°; 1.25 cm
 7  (5712):  UPPER-2:   170°; 1.25 cm
 8  (6514):  UPPER-2:   140°; 1.5 cm
 9  (9497):  MIDDLE-1:  130°; 1.25 cm
10  (9410):  MIDDLE-1:  140°; 0.75 cm
11  (10,305): MIDDLE-1:  130°; 1.25 cm
12  (10,822): LOWER-1:   100°; 1 cm
13  (9718):  MIDDLE-1:  140°; 0.75 cm
14  (10,215): MIDDLE-1:  170°; 0.75 cm
```

RETOUCH ANGLE

Acute	Medium	Steep	Perpendicular
1 (6127)	2 (8585)	3 (6811)	7 (5712)
13 (9718)	5 (5548)	4 (8450)	12 (10,822)
	6 (5746)	9 (9497)	
	8 (6514)		
	10 (9410)		
	11 (10,305)		
	14 (10,215)		

RETOUCH PATTERN

Convergent	Semi-Convergent	Non-Convergent
4 (8450)	7 (5712)	1 (6127)
5 (5548)	8 (6514)	2 (8585)
10 (9410)	13 (9718)	3 (6811)
11 (10,305)		6 (5746)
		9 (9497)
		12 (10,822)
		14 (10,215)

MISCELLANEOUS

```
 7  (5712):  Note splinter removals from bulbar surface
10  (9410):  Broken distal portion
13  (9718):  Broken distal portion
14  (10,215): Broken distal portion
```

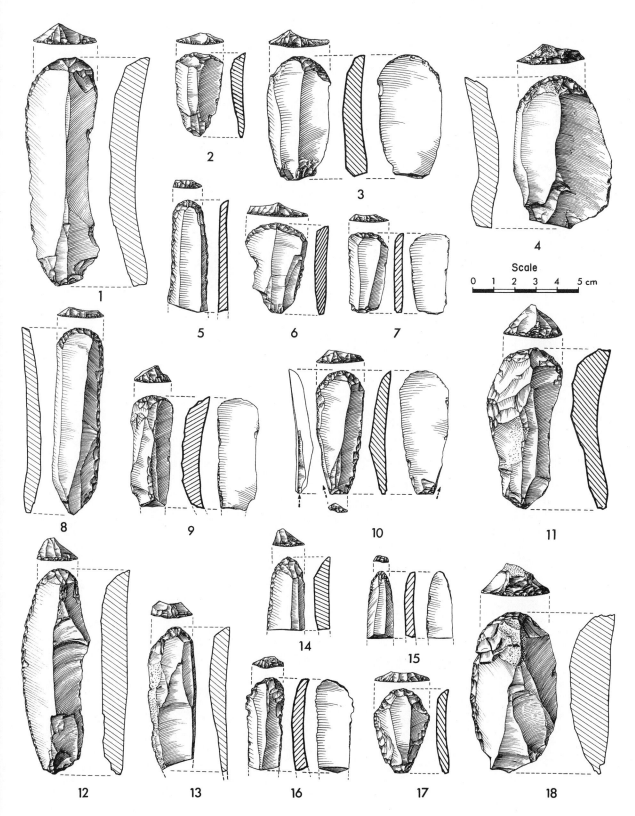

Scale
0 1 2 3 4 5 cm

Figure 8. END-SCRAPERS

Figure 8. END-SCRAPERS

SHAPE OF END

Arc of Circle   Blunt Point

 1 (9652):   MIDDLE-1: 120°; 1.25 cm   12 (7329):   MIDDLE-1: Asymmetrical
 2 (10,438): MIDDLE-1: 90°; 1.05 cm   13 (6944):   UPPER-2: Ogival
 3 (9599):   MIDDLE-1: 140°; 1.05 cm   14 (9510):   MIDDLE-1: Ogival
 4 (10,473): MIDDLE-2: 130°; 1.75 cm   15 (12,998): LOWER-1: Ogival
 5 (9863):   MIDDLE-1: 180°; 0.75 cm   16 (9490):   MIDDLE-1: Ogival
 6 (14,483): LOWER-2: 110°; 1.75 cm   17 (14,638): LOWER-1: Ogival
 7 (6876):   LOWER-2: 100°; 1.25 cm   18 (6245):   LOWER-2a: Asymmetrical
 8 (10,720): LOWER-1: 140°; 1.25 cm
 9 (10,932): LOWER-2: 100°; 1.25 cm
10 (6999):   LOWER-2: 160°; 1 cm
11 (14,651): LOWER-2: 140°; 1.05 cm

RETOUCH ANGLE

Acute   Medium   Steep   Perpendicular

 4 (10,473)   1 (9652)   3 (9599)   16   (9490)
 5 (9863)   2 (10,438)   6 (14,483)
 9 (10,932)   7 (6876)   11 (14,651)
10 (6999)   8 (10,720)   15 (12,998)
14 (9510)   12 (7329)   18 (6245)
                 13 (6944)
                 17 (14,638)

Convergent   Semi-Convergent   Non-Convergent

 1 (9652)   3 (9599)   2 (10,438)
 4 (10,473)   5 (9863)   15 (12,998)
12 (7329)   6 (14,483)   16 (9490)
14 (9510)   7 (6876)   18 (6245)
                  8 (10,720)
                  9 (10,932)
                 10 (6999)
                 11 (14,651)
                 13 (6944)
                 17 (14,638)

ASSOCIATIONS, COMBINATIONS, AND MISCELLANEOUS

 6 (14,483): Fan-shaped
10 (6999): Broken truncation burin at proximal extremity
17 (14,638): Fan-shaped; continuous retouch left and right

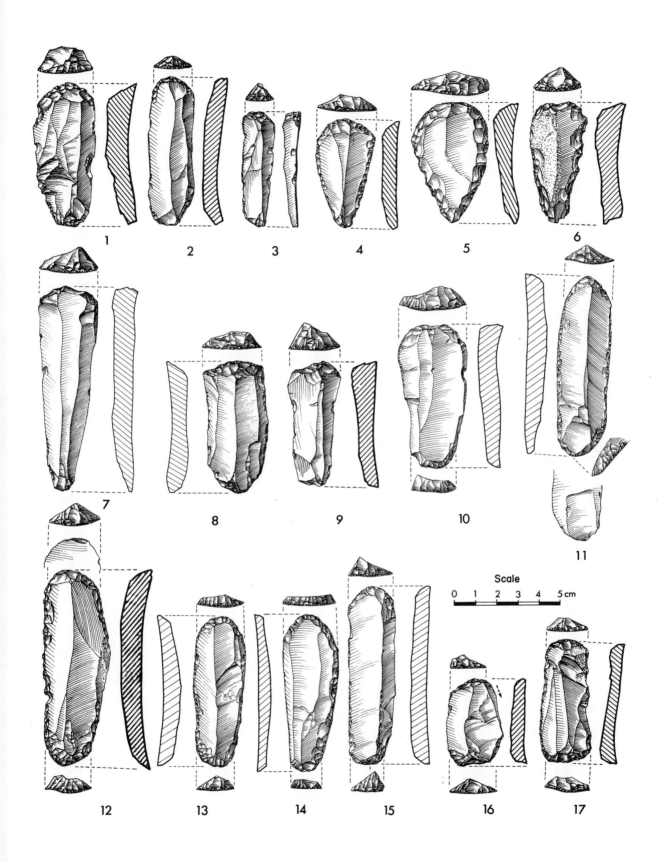

Figure 9.   END-SCRAPERS

Figure 9. END-SCRAPERS

SHAPE OF END

Arc of Circle

10 (9832): MIDDLE-1: Proximal
    extremity: 150°; 1 cm; Distal
    extremity: 130°; 1.25 cm
12 (9970): MIDDLE-1: Distal
    extremity: 160°; 1.25 cm
13 (8663): UPPER-1: Distal
    extremity: 120°; 1 cm
14 (4476): UPPER-1a: Proximal
    extremity: 140°; 0.75 cm
17 (6981): LOWER-2a: 100°; 1.25 cm

Blunt Point

1   (14,076): LOWER-2: Asymmetrical
2   (10,826): LOWER-1: Asymmetrical
11 (9420): MIDDLE-1: Distal
    extremity; ogival
12 (9970): MIDDLE-1: Proximal
    extremity; ogival
13 (8663): UPPER-1: Proximal
    extremity; asymmetrical
14 (4476): UPPER-1a: Distal
    extremity; ogival
15 (10,176): MIDDLE-1: Distal
    extremity; asymmetrical

Asymmetrical

3   (7009): LOWER-2
4   (12,935): LOWER-1
5   (13,457): LOWER-1
11 (9420): MIDDLE-1:
    Proximal extremity

Flattened

15 (10,176): MIDDLE-1:
    Proximal extremity
17 (6981): MIDDLE-1

Irregular

6   (13,384): LOWER-1
7   (9394): MIDDLE-1
8   (6260): UPPER-1
9   (13,320): LOWER-1
16 (10,465): MIDDLE-1:
    Both extremities

RETOUCH ANGLE

Acute

1   (14,076): LOWER-2
12 (9970): MIDDLE-1:
    Proximal extremity
13 (8663): UPPER-1:
    Proximal extremity
15 (10,176): MIDDLE-1:
    Proximal extremity

Medium

4   (12,935): LOWER-1
5   (13,457): LOWER-1
8   (6260): UPPER-1
9   (13,320): LOWER-1
10 (9832): MIDDLE-1:
    Both extremities
11 (9420): MIDDLE-1:
    Proximal extremity
13 (8663): UPPER-1:
    Distal extremity
14 (4476): UPPER-1a:
    Both extremities
17 (6981): LOWER-1a:
    Distal extremity

Steep

2   (10,826): LOWER-1
3   (7009): LOWER-2
11 (9420): MIDDLE-1:
    Distal extremity
12 (9970): MIDDLE-1:
    Distal extremity
15 (10,176): MIDDLE-1:
    Distal extremity
16 (10,465): MIDDLE-1:
    Proximal extremity
17 (6981): LOWER-1a:
    Proximal extremity

Perpendicular

6   (13,384): LOWER-2
7   (9394): MIDDLE-1
16 (10,465): MIDDLE-1:
    Distal extremity

Figure 9 (continued).

RETOUCH PATTERN

Convergent	Semi-Convergent	Non-Convergent
9 (13,320): LOWER-1	2 (10,816): LOWER-1	1 (14,076): LOWER-2
11 (9420): MIDDLE-1: Distal extremity	3 (7009): LOWER-2	4 (12,935): LOWER-1
12 (9970): MIDDLE-1: Distal extremity	10 (9832): MIDDLE-1: Distal extremity	5 (13,457): LOWER-1
15 (10,176): MIDDLE-1: Distal extremity	12 (9970): MIDDLE-1: Proximal extremity	6 (13,384): LOWER-1
17 (6881): LOWER-2a: Distal extremity	13 (8663): UPPER-1: Distal and proximal extremities	7 (9394): MIDDLE-1
	15 (10,176): MIDDLE-1: Proximal extremity	8 (6260): UPPER-1
	16 (10,465): MIDDLE-1: Proximal extremity	10 (9832): MIDDLE-1: Proximal extremity
		11 (9420): MIDDLE-1: Proximal extremity
		14 (4476): UPPER-1a: Both extremities
		16 (10,465): MIDDLE-1: Distal extremity
		17 (6981): LOWER-2a: Proximal extremity

ASSOCIATION: DOUBLE END-SCRAPERS

10 (9832)
11 (9420)
12 (9970)
13 (8663)
14 (4476)
15 (10,176)
16 (10,465)
17 (6981)

MISCELLANEOUS

4 (12,935): LOWER-1: Fan-shaped
5 (13,457): LOWER-1: Fan-shaped
6 (13,384): LOWER-1: Fan-shaped

out the level, and frequencies are extremely stable. In UPPER and MIDDLE, the blunt point contour (e.g., fig. 8:12–18) is next most frequent, accounting for about one-quarter of the series, followed by irregular examples (e.g., fig. 9:6–9, 16). These relationships are reversed in LOWER, where irregular dominates blunt point. Although the blunt point frequencies of MIDDLE and UPPER contrast collectively with that of LOWER, there is in fact a trend of increasing blunt point proportions through time. Asymmetrical and flattened contours are of little quantitative importance throughout.

The picture presented by Level 4 differs markedly from those of later Level 5 and Level 3 (fig. 10). Relative arc-of-circle frequency for later Level 5 is essentially identical to those of Level 4, but in Level 3 is much lower. Major differences occur in the asymmetrical and blunt point categories, where Levels 5 and 3, themselves very similar, contrast with all subdivisions of Level 4. End-scrapers with a regular asymmetrical contour, of major importance in Levels 5 and 3, account for less than 8% of any Level 4 series. On the other hand, blunt point contours, a miscellaneous and residual category in Levels 5 and 3, play an important and patterned role in the Level 4 end-scraper series. Flattened contours seem also more important in Levels 5 and 3 than in Level 4. We consider differences in shapes and proportions of scraping edge contours to be real and important indicators of cultural likeness and difference, reflecting manufacturing norms, motor habits, and perhaps functional differences in the use of tools. There is another suggestion of differences in the use of Level 4 end-scrapers. Slightly over 5% of the end-scrapers have one or more flat removals, or *écailles*, off the ventral surface of the piece at the scraping edge (e.g., figs. 5:10; 7:7). Such removals appear to be the products of sharp shocks received in use, not of intentional working of the ventral surface. They occur only in isolated instances in later Level 5 and Level 3. The general homogeneity (arc end-scrapers excepted) of the Périgordian IV and VI, with its implied persistence and conservatism in end-scraper manufacture, becomes more remarkable when contrasted with the very different picture of the stratigraphically intervening Noaillian series.

The blunt point end-scraper has been defined in terms of its variation from an arc, i.e., the foremost projection of the scraping edge falls beyond the arc described by the sides. This description is valid for Level 4, but the Level 4 blunt point end-scrapers are nonetheless qualitatively different from those of Levels 5 and 3, varying away from the arc to a form in which the sides leading to the blunt point are almost straight (fig. 9:14). They tend also to be more definitely pointed than in Levels 5 and 3 (figs. 8:14; 9:11; 28:13), approximating the "ogival" end-scraper of de Sonneville-Bordes and Perrot (1954, p. 328).

A morphological variant not present in Levels 5 or 3 is the shouldered end-scraper (*grattoir à épaulement*). In its extreme form, the scraping edge is degaged from the blank and its width reduced by the retouch forming the shoulders (fig. 8:17). A shoulder may be at one or both sides and is sometimes instrumental in forming a blunt point end-scraper.

There is no defined class of shouldered end-scrapers and no discernable break between shouldered and nonshouldered pieces. Even on the specimens which we have counted as shouldered, the characteristic is recognizable more as a tendency than a discrete stylistic element. At least one of the extreme examples of the shouldered variant is made on a comparatively thick blade; in an Aurignacian context, it would probably be considered to be a broad nose-ended scraper. Where on extreme examples there appears to have been a definite intention to delimit the edge, we have measured the scraping edge so delimited. Where the shouldering is minor, the whole edge has been measured and the variation noted separately. The incidence of shouldered forms increases from 4 in LOWER to 5 in MIDDLE to 22 in UPPER.

Radius of Circle and Degrees of Arc

It is more difficult to take accurate measurements of the degrees of arc of end-scrapers in Level 4 than in Levels 5 and 3. The greater irregularity of the Level 4 blades is in part responsible, as is the presence of shouldered forms, both of which make the delimitation of the scraping retouch harder to determine. But the difficulty is caused mainly by the presence of small rounded specimens on which measurement of degrees of arc by 10° classes is impracticable.

Cross-tabulations of radius of circle and degrees of arc are shown for each subdivision in table 5, and the parameters of these attributes are shown in table 6. Within Level 4

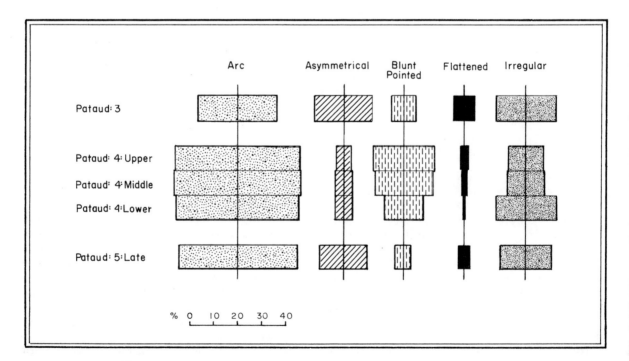

Figure 10.   BAR GRAPH SHOWING THE DISTRIBUTION OF LATER LEVEL 5, LEVEL 4, AND LEVEL 3 END-SCRAPERS BY SCRAPING EDGE CONTOUR.

Table 5

CROSS-TABULATION OF RADIUS OF CIRCLE AND DEGREES OF ARC OF ARC END-SCRAPERS IN LEVEL 4

Radius of Circle (cm)	Degrees of Arc														n
	50	60	70	80	90	100	110	120	130	140	150	160	170	180	
LOWER															
2.25		1													1
2.00	1						1	1							3
1.75				2	1	1	2	1	1	1					9
1.50				2	1	2	2	4	3	3		1			18
1.25				1	1	9	6	7	5	9	2		3	3	46
1.00				1	1	4	1	1	4	5	3	4	1		25
0.75						2	2		2	1		2			9
0.50		1							1						2
0.25															–
Total	1	2	–	6	4	18	14	14	16	19	5	7	4	3	113
MIDDLE															
2.25					1										1
2.00		1	1												2
1.75				2	1		1	1	2			1			8
1.50					2	3	2	1	1	1	2	1			13
1.25	1					2		4	6		2	4			19
1.00					1		1	1	1	6	3	3		2	18
0.75							5	3	1	3	4	3	3	1	23
0.50									1	2		1			4
0.25												1			1
Total	1	1	1	2	5	5	9	10	12	12	11	14	3	3	89
UPPER															
2.25															–
2.00								1							1
1.75				1		1		1	1	2					6
1.50					1		1	1	3	2	1	2			11
1.25			2			1	4	1	3	1	2	1	2		19
1.00					1			3	8	3	4	1	2	1	24
0.75				1	1	4		3	2	6	4	1		1	23
0.50				1			2		1	2	1				7
0.25														1	1
Total	–	–	2	3	3	10	5	19	10	17	7	9	4	3	92

there is a progressive decrease in mean radius. Mean degrees of arc increases significantly (the scraping edge becomes more rounded) from LOWER to MIDDLE. As with contour shapes, the UPPER and MIDDLE subdivisions are more similar to each other than to the LOWER.

The mean values of radius of circle and degrees of arc in later Level 5 are somewhat different from those of Level 3, but the Level 4 values are different from both. Mean radius is lower, and mean degrees of arc is higher. Together with the lesser mean scraping edge width in Level 4, this indicates that the Level 4 end-scrapers have smaller, much more rounded scraping edges than the end-scrapers of either later Level 5 or Level 3.

In the course of measurement, irregular end-scrapers were classed, where this distinction was at all meaningful, as very shallow, shallow, medium, or rounded. The distribution of the irregular pieces reflects that of the arc end-scrapers except in LOWER, where there are proportionately fewer rounded-irregular than rounded-arc end-scrapers.

Retouch Angle

The retouch angle is, demonstrably in many cases and presumptively in others, closely correlated with the thickness of the blank and resharpening of the end-scraper, which may terminate, if the piece is worked out, in a stepped overhanging edge (e.g., figs. 7:17; 9:7). The retouch angle may therefore represent only the degree to which an end-scraper was used before it was thrown away. Indirectly it also reflects interaction between the availability of raw material and the skill of the knapper.

Table 6
DISTRIBUTION OF RADIUS OF CIRCLE AND DEGREES OF ARC
OF ARC END-SCRAPERS IN LEVEL 4

	LOWER	MIDDLE	UPPER
Radius (cm)			
$\bar{X} \pm s_{\bar{X}}$	1.25 ± 0.03	1.13 ± 0.04	1.06 ± 0.04
Range	0.50–2.25	0.25–2.25	0.25–2.00
s	0.33	0.40	0.36
n	113	89	92
Degrees of Arc			
$\bar{X} \pm s_{\bar{X}}$	122.65 ± 2.30	131.01 ± 2.93	129.02 ± 2.61
Range	50–180	50–180	70–180
s	26.52	27.68	25.06
n	113	89	92

Table 7
DISTRIBUTION OF RETOUCH ANGLE OF END-SCRAPERS

Retouch Angle	Later Level 5 %	LOWER n	LOWER %	MIDDLE n	MIDDLE %	UPPER n	UPPER %	Level 3 %
Perpendicular/ Overhanging	10.77	17	7.62	20	11.90	16	9.04	13.85
Steep	18.97	53	23.77	36	21.43	30	16.95	25.13
Medium	55.63	129	57.85	78	46.43	89	50.28	47.18
Acute	14.63	24	10.76	34	20.24	42	23.73	13.85
N	622	223		168		177		195

The study produced strong confirmation of the hypothesis that retouch angle increases with reworking of the piece. All perpendicular specimens showed reworking, also common in the steep group but found on only a few of the medium specimens. It should be noted that this argument is faulty. We recognize reworking either by the presence of a stepped front to the tool or, if there is no marked step, by the presence of old facets on the dorsal surface of the scraper, the proximal ends of which have been removed by later retouch. These facets, if projected to meet the plane of the ventral surface, would form a more acute angle than that formed by the later retouch on the underside. But what about reworking that does not leave these traces? There is

no reason why the angle on these specimens should change significantly, although *if* the tool gets thicker away from the scraping edge, there may be a tendency toward an increase in angle. Thus, by reworked specimens we mean those detectably or perhaps unsuccessfully reworked. In spite of the flawed argument, it does point out an important correlation.

The distribution of retouch angle is shown in table 7 for the Level 4, later Level 5, and Level 3 end-scrapers. A medium angle (e.g., fig. 7:2, 5, 6, 8, 10, 11, 14) is dominant in all the Level 4 subdivisions, and scraping edges duller than medium are more frequent than those sharper than medium. There is a clear contrast between the LOWER and the other subdivisions in the incidence of acute retouch angles (e.g., fig. 7:1, 13), the simplest explanation for which is that the later Noaillian artisans were less concerned to conserve flint, and discarded end-scrapers more freely.

A comparison of the Level 4 distributions with those of later Level 5 and Level 3 supports the general proposition that the retouch angle is, in itself, not of importance as a cultural indicator. In spite of these similarities, the investigation of retouch angle versus scraping edge contour shows very different patterns of internal variation in the two groups of samples. In Level 5 as well as in Level 3, there are no significant differences between arc and asymmetrical contours in distribution of scraping retouch angle. Both of these contours are, however, significantly sharper than irregular ones. The positions of blunt point and flattened contours are not clear because of small sample sizes, but it is likely that in Level 5 at least some of the (poorly characterized) blunt point contours behave like a somewhat special kind of irregular contour. In Level 4, on the other hand, arc *and* blunt point contours are significantly sharper than other contours. Thus blunt point forms, in addition to being relatively more numerous in Level 4, show qualitative differences. Irregular contours are, as always, blunter than expected were there no association between variables; so are flattened ones. In Level 4 it is the flattened and not the blunt point contour that is a variant of irregular. The position of the assymmetrical contour is not clear, though it appears to be a variant of the arc.

We might interpret the different behavior of blunt point forms in one of three ways. First, it might be suggested that they form a separate tool type not connected with arc end-scrapers, but there is no support for this hypothesis since there is no morphological discontinuity between the forms and since they behave, insofar as the angle of retouch is concerned, like arc end-scrapers. Second, this might be considered a case of incipient specialization, the blunt point form being in process of dissociating itself from other end-scrapers, becoming more pointed and more acute. If and when Noaillian sites chronologically later than the UPPER subdivision of Level 4 at the Abri Pataud are studied by attribute analysis, this hypothesis may be tested. The explanation that appears most reasonable in the light of present evidence is that, in the Noaillian, the end-scraper norm is less firmly centered on the arc-asymmetrical combination of the Périgordian IV and VI and is closer to the blunt point contour. The shift is along a dimension of variation, that of scraping edge contour, which cannot be perfectly controlled by our geometrically based system of contour measurement, although this happened to be an effective and appropriate instrument in the case of the end-scrapers from Levels 5 and 3. Its lesser suitability when applied to Noaillian end-scrapers is in itself evidence of their cultural differentiation. It may also be responsible for some increase in *apparent* variability of the Level 4 samples. But even assuming equal *real* variability of samples in the Levels 5, 3, and 4 assemblages, a difference in norm or mental template does account for the increased variation away from

the arc and asymmetrical forms toward more pointed contours, including the extreme ogival variants.

Blank Cross-Section

The proportions of triangular, trapezoidal, and amorphous cross-sections vary within Level 4 (table 8), the break coming again between the LOWER and MIDDLE subdivisions, with an increase in the proportions of triangular and amorphous blanks and a corresponding decrease in trapezoidal blanks. The Level 4 samples are differentiated from those of later Level 5 by their much higher proportions of triangular cross-sections and from that of Level 3 by their lower proportion of amorphous sections. Frequencies of triangular sections differ greatly between Levels 5 and 3, and in this respect Level 4 closely resembles the latter.

Retouch Pattern

The distribution of retouch pattern is shown for each subdivision in table 8. Non-convergent retouch is dominant throughout, and convergent retouch is least common. The LOWER subdivision is similar to the later units of Level 5, but MIDDLE and UPPER have more convergent and semi-convergent retouch than the latter. The very low proportion of pieces with convergent retouch in Level 3 differentiates it clearly from the Level 4 samples.

Retouch pattern is very closely related to the form of the blank and in particular to the pattern of dorsal ridges (*arêtes*). The relationship is finer than this study can show, but may be described as follows: there is a general tendency toward convergent retouch, but achievement of true convergence is constrained by the width, thickness, and dorsal ridges of the blank and is also affected by irregularities produced by resharpening. A piece with a broad trapezoidal cross-section is likely to show two distinct convergences toward the ridges, while on a piece with an essentially triangular cross-section modified by a minor ridge, the minor ridge is likely to be ignored. It may, however, be sufficient to prevent convergence.

In Levels 5 and 3 convergent and semi-convergent retouch are positively associated with triangular cross-section, an association in part determined by the nature of flint and flint working. The same association exists in Level 4, as shown by Chi-square testing (P<0.005).[1]

Marginal Retouch

The distribution of marginal retouch on all end-scrapers not part of combination tools is shown in table 9. Frequencies

1. We also tested for relationship between retouch angle and retouch pattern and between retouch pattern and scraping edge contour, finding associations of non-convergent retouch with irregular contour and with perpendicular retouch angle. These are both by-products of unsuccessful reworking.

Table 8

CROSS-TABULATION OF BLANK CROSS-SECTION AND SCRAPER RETOUCH PATTERN
OF END-SCRAPERS IN LEVEL 4

	Triangular	Trapezoidal	Amorphous	n	%
UPPER					
Convergent	29	1	–	30	16.95
Semi-Convergent	45	12	6	63	35.59
Non-Convergent	30	38	16	84	47.46
Total	104	51	22	177	
%	58.76	28.81	12.43		100.00
MIDDLE					
Convergent	37	5	–	42	25.00
Semi-Convergent	38	17	4	59	35.12
Non-Convergent	29	25	13	67	39.88
Total	104	47	17	168	
%	61.90	27.98	10.12		100.00
LOWER					
Convergent	27	3	–	30	13.45
Semi-Convergent	44	30	2	76	34.08
Non-Convergent	37	65	15	117	52.47
Total	108	98	17	223	
%	48.43	43.95	7.62		100.00

increase through time, but LOWER contrasts clearly with MIDDLE and UPPER, which are similar. The frequencies in all Level 4 subdivisions are much higher than that of all single end-scrapers in Level 3. The later Level 5 data are not directly comparable, because in Level 5 a piece was accepted as being marginally retouched if one-sixth (as opposed to one-fourth in Levels 4 and 3) of the blank circumference bore retouch. An average percentage frequency of all single end-scrapers with marginal retouch in later Level 5 is ca. 23%, comparable to Level 4: LOWER. In spite of the differences in the attribute definitions employed, it is clear that on the end-scrapers of Level 4 marginal retouch is more common than on those of either later Level 5 or Level 3.

Scaled retouch is the most frequent type throughout Level 4, contrasting clearly with Level 3, where fine retouch on end-scrapers is dominant. In later Level 5, frequencies of scaled and fine retouch are generally close, with one or the other dominating in various units. The percentage frequencies of scaled retouch in Level 4 are, however, greater—often much greater—than in either Level 5 or Level 3. Within Level 4, scaled retouch (e.g., fig. 8:11) becomes

more common through time, and while proportionately the more frequent in LOWER (42.50%), it is absolutely dominant in MIDDLE (60.00%) and UPPER (73.17%).

Double End-Scrapers and Combination Tools (figs. 8:10–17; 40)

Double end-scrapers (table 10) are comparatively rare in Level 4 except in the MIDDLE subdivision. End-scrapers on combination tools are more frequent throughout than in Levels 5 or 3.

Conclusions

We have attempted in the foregoing analysis to describe the Level 4 end-scrapers in terms of their attributes and to distinguish between those attributes and attribute interactions that strongly reflect style and those that are substantially affected by mechanical contingencies. End-scraper contour, for example, in Level 4 differs from that in Levels 5 and 3 in ways that are clearly stylistic, although imperfect re-

Table 9

DISTRIBUTION OF MARGINAL RETOUCH

ON ALL END-SCRAPERS NOT PART OF COMBINATION TOOLS IN LEVEL 4

	Continuous Both Sides	Continuous One Side	Partial	Totals
UPPER				
Fine	1	2	–	
Heavy	–	3	2	
Scaled	3	15	12	
Mixed	3	–	–	
				41 (30.83%)[b]
MIDDLE				
Fine	–	1	5	
Heavy	1	4[a]	3[a]	
Scaled	5	9	10	
Mixed	1	–	1	
				40 (28.17%)[b]
LOWER				
Fine	1	5	6	
Heavy	3	4	2	
Scaled	3	9	5	
Mixed	2	–	–	
				40 (21.28%)[b]

a.   Includes one piece with Aurignacian retouch.
b.   Percentage of all end-scrapers not part of combination tools.

sharpening tends to reduce the distinction. An understanding of the nature of attribute interaction is a prerequisite for proper evaluation of cultural likeness and difference, their loci and expression. To take an obvious example, variation in the frequencies of convergent and semi-convergent retouch between series need not reflect stylistic differentiation. Before such a claim can be made it must first be shown that: (a) the series compared have similar porportions of triangular and other cross-sections; and (b) the extent of resharpening (itself an indirect measure of the economizing of flint resources) is also comparable. If the latter condition holds but not the former, then a stylistic difference between series may exist, but its locus is most likely to lie not in the retouching but in core reduction techniques and choice of blanks for end-scraper manufacture.

This being said, it is indeed apparent that, in spite of the imperfections of our measuring instruments, the Level 4 end-scrapers can all be considered as variants of a single emic type, the characteristics of which nonetheless change from major subdivision to major subdivision, and that the type is stylistically differentiated from those characteristic of the later Level 5 and Level 3 series. The differences between the latter types are such as may most reasonably be interpreted as arising from developmental changes within one cultural tradition. End-scrapers are by no means insensitive indicators of cultural relationships.

In virtually every attribute considered, the expressions of which are determined primarily by style, the differences between the later Level 5 and Level 3 samples are less than those between any of these samples and any from Level 4. The chronological ordering of the series according to the site stratigraphy has no equivalence in similar seriation of end-scraper attributes. The changes found within and between the Level 4 samples are not such as can under any circumstances be considered a reflection of the evolution of a later Périgordian IV type norm toward that of the Périgordian VI. On the contrary, Périgordian Vc, or Noaillian, end-scrapers appear as a stratigraphically intrusive element, typologically foreign to the Périgordian IV–VI continuum.

The Level 4 samples appear more variable than those of later Level 5 or Level 3. This increase in variability may be in part an artifact of our analytical method, which we have suggested is less congruent with the norms of the Noaillian than with those of the Périgordian IV and VI.

Table 10

ASSOCIATION OF END-SCRAPERS IN LEVEL 4

	LOWER		MIDDLE		UPPER	
	Both Studied	One End Studied	Both Studied	One End Studied	Both Studied	One End Studied
Double End-Scraper (= pieces)	3	1	9	2	4	–
	Studied	Unstudied	Studied	Unstudied	Studied	Unstudied
Combination Tool: End-Scraper +						
Truncation Burin	6	2	4	6	13	1
Dihedral Burin	10	2	2	1	7	2
Break Burin	2	–	2	–	3	3
Other Burin	2	1	1	–	7	1
Other Tool	2	–	1	–	2	1
Total	27[a]		17[b]		40[c]	

a. Includes two Noailles burins.
b. Includes three Raysse burins.
c. Includes three burin-points and 11 Raysse burins.

Some portion of the variability may be attributed to the lesser emphasis placed upon these tools, indicated by their lower proportional frequency in the assemblage. If we interpret this to mean that end-scrapers were made less often, a decrease in standardization is to be expected. But apart from this general increase in variability—which may be attributed to either, or more probably both, of these factors—there is a major locus of variability in Level 4 that cannot be explained in these terms. This is the differentiation, recognized in the majority of end-scraper attributes, of the LOWER subdivision from the MIDDLE and UPPER subdivisions, which appear to be more closely affiliated with each other.

The significance of this typological hiatus, if we may term it such, is difficult to interpret; the order of magnitude is not such as might justify the affiliation of the LOWER subdivision with a divergent tradition. On the other hand, the break, apparent in other tool types as well, suggests that there is some cultural discontinuity between the LOWER and MIDDLE subdivisions. This discontinuity represents either an actual hiatus in the occupation of the site or the advent of a new Noaillian group. In studies of other sites, the answer to this problem may eventually be found; in

studies of other tool classes from Level 4 at the Abri Pataud, the problem will be stated in other terms.

OTHER FORMS OF SCRAPER IN LEVEL 4

Scrapers other than end-scrapers are virtually absent in Level 4, a clear and important difference between the Noaillian and the Périgordian IV and VI. The few examples which are present are noted below:

Three side-scrapers.

End-and-side scrapers. There are three pieces, one crude and irregularly worked, one fragment, and one that is rather a double side-scraper with an end-scraper worked at the extremity. Since the retouch is clearly distinguished from the retouch down the sides, it was included in the studied end-scraper series.

Miscellaneous scrapers. There is one steep Aurignacioid scraper or microblade nucleus.

There are no circular or subcircular scrapers or *coupoirs*.

Table 12a
DISTRIBUTION OF ATTRIBUTES OF BACKING TYPOLOGY
OF GRAVETTE POINTS IN LEVELS 4 AND 4a

Attribute	Level 4		Level 4a	
	n	%	n	%
Priority Backing Type				
Ia	12	20.00	7	(31.82)
Ib	10	16.67	4	(18.18)
IIa	4	6.67	3	(13.64)
IIb	10	16.67	3	(13.64)
IIIb	14	23.33	4	(18.18)
IVb	3	5.00	1	(4.55)
Vb	5	8.33	–	–
VIb	2	3.33	–	–
Total	60	100.00	22	(100.01)
Extent of Backing				
Heavy	36	60.00	17	(77.27)
Medium	17	28.33	5	(22.73)
Light	7	11.67	–	–
Backing Direction				
Bidirectional	16	26.67	10	(45.45)
From Ventral	44	73.33	12	(54.55)
From Dorsal	–	–	–	–
Cross-Section				
Triangular	41	68.33	15	(68.18)
Trapezoidal	19	31.67	7	(31.82)

Table 12b
DISTRIBUTION OF STATE OF EDGE OPPOSITE BACKING
OF GRAVETTE POINTS IN LEVELS 4 AND 4a

	Level 4		Level 4a	
	n	%	n	%
State of Edge Opposite Backing				
Unretouched and Unutilized	10	16.67	6	(27.27)
Utilized	39	65.00	6	(27.27)
Retouched	11	18.33	10	(45.45)
Extent of Retouch				
Partial	5		4	
Continuous	6		6	
Kind of Retouch				
Obverse	8		10	
Inverse	3		–	
Obverse/Inverse	–		–	

Table 13

DISTRIBUTION OF ATTRIBUTES OF BUTT TYPOLOGY
OF GRAVETTE POINTS IN LEVELS 4 AND 4a

Butt Class	Level 4		Level 4a	
	n	Vachons[a]	n	Vachons[a]
Unretouched-1	7		1	
Unretouched-2	4		–	
Obverse-1	1		–	
Obverse-2a	1		–	
Obverse-2b	2		–	
Obverse-3a	2		1	
Obverse-3b	1		–	
Obverse-4	3		2	
Inverse-1	1		–	
Inverse-2a	3		1	
Inverse-2b	3	(1)	1	
Inverse-3a	5	(1)	1	
Inverse-3b	2	(1)	2	
Inverse-4	2	(1)	1	(1)
Obverse/Inverse	–		3	(3)
Total	37		13	
All Butts				
Unretouched	9	(24.32)	1	(7.69)
Obverse	7	(18.92)	3	(23.08)
Inverse	13	(35.14)	6	(46.15)
Obverse/Inverse	–	–	3	(23.08)
Vachons	4	(10.81)	4	(30.77)
Retouched Butts				
Obverse	7	(35.00)	3	(25.00)
Inverse	13	(65.00)	6	(50.00)
Obverse/Inverse	–	–	3	(25.00)
Shape 2	8		2	
Shape 3	7		4	
Shape a	7		3	
Shape b	8		3	

a. Included in n.

form. This is also true for Level 5, with only minor exceptions late in the sequence. In Level 4a Vachons retouch is found on four butts (fig. 11:6, 10), and in three cases it is of the classic kind. The value for Level 3 is 21.57%, with a diminished frequency of classic Vachons examples.

The frequency of points in both series is too small for analysis.

The original broken length of fragmentary Gravettes in Level 4 was predicted from the following partial regression equation based on only eight complete and almost complete pieces:

Length = 8.15 Width − 2.20 Thickness − 2.21

The multiple correlation coefficient of length, width, and thickness is 0.91 (0.01 > P > 0.001), and the standard

Table 14

DISTRIBUTION OF LENGTH, WIDTH, AND THICKNESS OF GRAVETTE POINTS
IN LEVELS 4 AND 4a, WITH VALUES OF LENGTH/WIDTH AND WIDTH/THICKNESS INDICES

	Level 4	Level 4a
Length (mm)		
$\overline{X} \pm s_{\overline{X}}$	42.29 ± 1.96	–
Range	20–79	–
s	15.03	–
Width (mm)		
$\overline{X} \pm s_{\overline{X}}$	6.50 ± 0.37	9.73 ± 0.60
Range	3–22	5–17
s	2.86	2.81
Thickness (mm)		
$\overline{X} \pm s_{\overline{X}}$	3.00 ± 0.15	4.18 ± 0.34
Range	1–7	3–10
s	1.14	1.59
$\overline{L} \times 100/\overline{W}$	651	–
$\overline{W} \times 100/\overline{Th}$	217	233
n	60	22

error of the estimate is 7.04 mm. This is not a satisfactory prediction equation, as seen from the fact that increasing thickness results in decreasing length. The mean length resulting from it is presented here, but it is not regarded as sufficiently accurate to attempt identification of subgroups. The distributions of the metrical dimensions of the two series are shown in table 14.

The Level 4 Gravettes are smaller in all dimensions than those of Level 5: REAR; they are closest to those of FRONT:UPPER b. The width/thickness index value of 217 is lower than in any unit of Level 5. In the latter, this index decreases through time to lows of 230–240 in FRONT:UPPER and REAR as pieces become increasingly narrow for their thickness. This trend in Level 5 is obviously associated with and partly explained by increasing heaviness of backing through time. But heavy backing is not as common in Level 4 as in the later units of Level 5, so that there is in the former a different relationship of width to thickness. The Level 4 length/width index of 651 is higher than in any unit of Level 5, the Level 4 pieces being more "spiky." Compared with Level 3, the Level 4 Gravettes are slightly longer and certainly wider and thicker; in this respect, their di-

mensions are intermediate between those of the Périgordian IV and VI.

The Level 4a Gravettes are larger than those of Level 4. The width, thickness, and width/thickness index are all exactly within the range of the Level 5: REAR values. They are not in these characteristics transitional between the Périgordian IV and VI.

The numbers of complete and almost complete Gravette points in the two series are so small that statements about gross morphology cannot be very firm. In Level 4, parallel/subparallel-sided forms are dominant, and the Châtelperronoid form is absent. In Level 4a, parallel/subparallel-sided and expanding-center forms occur in nearly equal frequencies in the very small sample. The presence here of one very clearly bellied piece suggests a closer similarity to Level 5; bellied forms are absent in both Level 4 and Level 3.

Having summarized the data on the Level 4 Gravette points obtained by attribute analysis, we may restate the interpretative problem that they present. Either they are: (a) for the most part introduced into Level 4 from Level 5: REAR by the pit-digging operations discussed above; (b) in large part the products of Noaillian workmanship; or (c) indicative of some form of culture contact or acculturation between Périgordians and Noaillians.

The first of these possibilities would be exemplified by the overall similarity of the Level 4 Gravette point sample to those of later Level 5. Although such similarity might exist were the second hypothesis correct, there might also be significant differences. If the third is the true interpretation, then the Gravette points of Level 4, located stratigraphically between the Périgordian IV and VI levels at the site, might show some transitional characters between those of the latter levels, which, as already discussed, do have a major element of continuity.[2]

In cross-section, extent of retouch on the edge opposite the backing, proportion of inversely worked butts, and frequency of Vachons-style butts, the Level 4 Gravette points resemble those of Level 5. In butt:segment ratio, the relative frequency of retouch on the edge opposite the backing, and in the proportion of unretouched butts, they are unlike. They are intermediate in backing side, overall dimensions, and gross morphology. In contrast, the Gravette points of Level 4a show in their attributes either similarities to those of later Level 5, or they are intermediate between Level 5 and Level 3.

Any attempt to interpret this confused picture founders on the problem of sample size. Thus, whereas the relative frequency of bidirectional backing in Level 4 is unlike that of later Level 5, it is not significantly different when tested by Chi-square from the proportion found in Level 4a, which in this respect is very similar to later Level 5. This same absence of significant difference is found for other attributes. In short, the evidence does not permit us to decide among the three hypotheses suggested above, far less to give approximate weightings to the contribution each possible source may have made to the Level 4 Gravette point series. It can only be said that while there is no reason to deny that backed tools were on occasion manufactured by the Level 4 knappers, these artifacts are quantitatively an insignificant component of the assemblage.

The Level 4a Gravette points, like those of Level 4, are located stratigraphically between the Périgordian IV and VI levels at the Abri Pataud, and they are contemporary with characteristically Noaillian tools. But the Level 4a Gravette attributes show many and strong resemblances to those of the Gravettes of later Level 5—in butt:segment ratio, triangular cross-section, bidirectional backing, all the details of the edge opposite the backing, and the dimensions of the piece. In other attributes—heavy backing and butt typology—they are intermediate between Level 5 and Level 3. In no way (except perhaps in the frequency of Vachons

butts, to be discussed below) do they exhibit important differences from both Level 5 and Level 3.

Whereas in Level 4, Gravette points represent a very small proportion of the total assemblage, in Level 4a they make up some 15%. Their presence in the latter level is to be explained by one of the following situations:

> Manufacture by the same artificers who made the Noaillian tools. Accepting as fact that the Gravette point is the typological hallmark of the Upper Périgordian cultural tradition, production of these tools by Noaillians might have resulted from some degree of acculturation.

> Very temporary occupation of the shelter by Upper Périgordians, either in the company of or in the absence of Noaillians, a difference that would be indistinguishable in the stratigraphic record.

The evidence from the Abri Pataud does not permit either of these scenarios to be satisfactorily demonstrated. (Another possibility, that the Gravette points were trade goods, can be discounted in view of the presence in both Level 4 and 4a of examples that are unfinished or were broken in manufacture.)

As stated above, a Gravette point series intermediate in time between the Périgordian IV and the Périgordian VI would be welcome as providing information on the continuing development of this tool class. But the data from Levels 4 and 4a furnish two quite different answers. In one case, Level 4, they are in some ways off the line of typological development. In the other, they are just as firmly on that line. This contrast strongly suggests that the Level 4 series does in fact include a substantial proportion of backed tools made by Noaillians in addition to an increment derived through Noaillian digging in Level 5. The Level 4a series, on the other hand, and in spite of its association with typically and diagnostically Noaillian burin types, is more probably the work of Upper Périgordians, since it would appear difficult for Noaillians to have borrowed *en bloc* the whole Upper Périgordian functional-stylistic complex associated with their manufacture.

The occurrence of Vachons butt retouch in the various Abri Pataud series merits special attention. Frequencies of this attribute, very feeble in early and middle Level 5 times, increase in later Level 5, continue to rise in Level 4, reach a maximum in Level 4a, and decrease in Level 3. Have we to do here with a stylistic feature, the frequency occurrence of which behaves like a horizon marker regardless of broader cultural context? Our Pataud data suggest that the answer is yes. If the frequency of Vachons butt retouch behaves in this manner, then an important conclusion gleaned from the Gravettes of Level 4a is that Vachons maximum frequency occurs in Terminal Noaillian times and before the Périgordian VI.

---

2. An overall developmental trend in the Périgordian Gravette point series need not, on the other hand, be reflected in regular unidirectional trends in single attributes.

IV

Attribute Analysis of Burins from Level 4

The proportion of burins in Level 4 is very high, exceeding even that of Level 3. The Level 4 burin series poses problems which require modification of the approach developed for the study of the Level 5 and Level 3 burins. One aspect of the study, comparison with Levels 5 and 3, is unexpectedly simple. The differences between the Périgordian IV and VI burins and those of the Noaillian are of such magnitude and importance, involving both the use of different techniques in the manufacture of burins and the production of specialized types, that an attribute-by-attribute comparison of the artifacts is rendered superfluous. The technical innovations which characterize the Level 4 series include the use of a notch, perhaps combined with the removal of burin spalls by pressure, termed the Noailles technique, and the modification and reduction in width of the burin edge following the removal of the burin spall by the striking of small removals from the burin facet onto the dorsal surface of the piece. Such modification is termed "tertiary" (Movius and David 1970), because it is subsequent to the two basic processes of burin manufacture: the creation or choice of a spall removal surface (SRS) and the removal of burin spalls. Another characteristic of Level 4 burins is that morphologically similar pieces that we must assign to a single well-characterized type are occasionally manufactured by different techniques. The most striking characteristic of the burins is the ingenuity employed in their manufacture and resharpening. Typological innovations include: (a) the Noailles burin; (b) the burin-point; and (c) the Raysse burin.

The specialization, particularly of the truncation and retouched edge techno-types (SRS types), combined with the rapid internal development of the burins within the Noaillian horizon, makes seriation an efficient and practicable method for tracing cultural change. After a definition of burin types, a seriation of the samples is presented which serves as a basis for the analysis and comparison of other assemblages. Descriptive analysis of the types is largely relegated to tables.

The quantity of burins in Level 4 permits a more detailed breakdown of the assemblage than is useful for other tool classes. The units studied are those distinguished above (p. 5).

DEFINITION OF BURIN TYPES

Noailles Burins (figs. 12–15; 16:1–12; 20:12–38)

The Noailles burin, long known in the literature, is the type fossil of the "Périgordian Vc" (Noaillian) horizon. It was first signalled and illustrated by L. Bardon, J. Bouyssonie, and A. Bouyssonie (1903) from the Grotte de Noailles, south of Brive in the Corrèze. The pieces they illustrated are indeed Noailles burins, but the "new type" of burin defined by the article was the truncation burin, *not* specifically or exclusively the Noailles burin. It was not until 1908 that these authors began to refer, in their report on the site of Font-Robert (L. Bardon, A. Bouyssonie, and J. Bouyssonie 1908, p. 319), to a characteristic type, "fin et délicat, si abondant à Noailles," distinct from other truncation burins. Noailles burins have been the subject of a detailed study by Tixier (1958) to which we are indebted. De Sonneville-Bordes and Perrot (1956a, p. 412) defined the Noailles burin as:

> . . . sur troncature retouchée, souvent multiple, sur éclat ou lame mince, de petite ou très petite dimension, les enlèvements de coup-de-burin étant le plus souvent arrêtés par une petite encoche.

Delporte (1959, p. 27) gave a similar definition, emphasizing particularly the concavity of the truncation. De Sonneville-Bordes regards the Noailles burin as a type independent of the "normal" truncation burin and does not include it in her Index of Truncation Burins. Laplace (1964a, p. 13), on the other hand, considers it only as a variety of truncation burin. Before proceeding to the examination of the evidence for the typological independence of the Noailles burin, it should be said that for many characteristics of these burins we have little to add to the observations of Tixier (1958). The difference between Tixier's approach and that employed here lies in the definition of Noailles burins. Tixier begins his study by stating that 99 Noailles burins were discovered at the Abri André Ragout (Commune de Vilhonneur, Charente) and then proceeds to study them. Here we ask if there

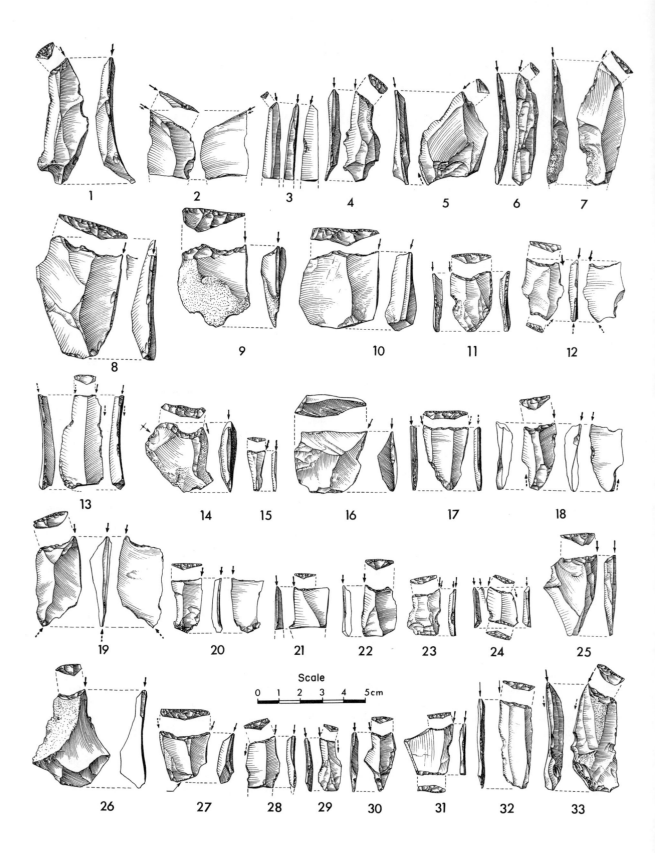

Scale
0 1 2 3 4 5cm

Figure 12.   NOAILLES BURINS FROM LEVEL 4: LOWER

SRS TYPE, ANGLE, AND CLASS

Retouched Truncation

1	(13,692): LOWER-1: 80°; Class 2c		17	(13,938): LOWER-2: 60°; Class 4
2	(14,823): LOWER-2: 50°; Class 2c		18	(7019): LOWER-2a: 80°; Class 4
3	(7020): LOWER-2: 60°; Class 2c		19	(13,381): LOWER-1: 70°; Class 4
4	(14,597): LOWER-2: 60°; Class 2c		20	(13,341): LOWER-1: 50°; Class 2c
5	(14,810): LOWER-2: 60°; Class 2c		21	(13,003): LOWER-1: 80°; Class 4
6	(7827): LOWER-2: 70°; Class 2c		22	(13,577): LOWER-1: 70°; Class 5
7	(14,310): LOWER-1: 80°; Class 2c		23	(13,717): LOWER-2: 60°; Class 5
8	(12,769): LOWER-1: 70°; Class 3		24	(14,023): LOWER-2: 80°; Class 5
9	(13,044): LOWER-1: 60°; Class 3		25	(14,069): LOWER-2: 60°; Class 5
10	(13,299): LOWER-1: 70°; Class 3		26	(14,013): LOWER-1: 70°; Class 5
11	(14,352): LOWER-1: 70°; Class 3		27	(13,413): LOWER-1: 60°; Class 5
12	(14,792): LOWER-2: 90°; Class 3		28	(13,972): LOWER-1: 80°; Class 5
13	(14,416): LOWER-2: 80°; Class 3		29	(8672): LOWER-2: 60°; Class 5
14	(13,705): LOWER-1: 80°; Class 3		30	(6997): LOWER-2: 60°; Class 5
15	(7840): LOWER-2a: 70°; Class 3		31	(7825): LOWER-2: 60°; Class 5
16	(13,664): LOWER-1: 60°; Class 3		32	(10,515): LOWER-2: 70°; Class 5
			33	(13,274): LOWER-1: 80°; Class 6

BURIN EDGE SHAPE AND WIDTH

Straight

1	(13,692): 2 mm		17	(13,938): 1 mm
2	(14,823): <1 mm		18	(7019): 1 mm
3	(7020): 1 mm		19	(13,381): 1 mm
4	(14,597): 1 mm		20	(13,341): <1 mm
5	(14,810): 1 mm		21	(13,003): <1 mm
6	(7827): <1 mm		22	(13,577): 1 mm
7	(14,310): 1 mm		23	(13,717): 1 mm
8	(12,769): 1 mm		24	(14,023): 1 mm
9	(13,044): 1 mm		25	(14,069): 1 mm
10	(13,299): 1 mm		26	(14,013): 2 mm
11	(14,352): 1 mm		27	(13,413): 1 mm
12	(14,792): 1 mm		28	(13,972): 1 mm
13	(14,416): 2 mm		29	(8672): 1 mm
14	(13,705): 1 mm		30	(6997): 1 mm
15	(7840): 1 mm		31	(7825): 1 mm
16	(13,664): 1 mm		32	(10,515): 1 mm
			33	(13,274): 1 mm

Figure 12 (continued).

OBLIQUITY

Lateral		Oblique		High Oblique	
1	(13,692)	3	(7020)	2	(14,823)
7	(14,310)	4	(14,597)	14	(13,705)
8	(12,769)	5	(14,810)	17	(13,938)
9	(13,044)	6	(7827)	22	(13,577)
12	(14,792)	10	(13,299)		
13	(14,416)	11	(14,352)		
15	(7840)	19	(13,381)		
16	(13,664)	24	(14,023)		
18	(7019)	25	(14,069)		
20	(13,341)	27	(13,413)		
21	(13,003)	28	(13,972)		
23	(13,717)	30	(6997)		
26	(14,013)	31	(7825)		
29	(8672)				
32	(10,515)				
33	(13,274)				

SRS SHAPE

Concave		Pronounced Concave		Straight	
13	(14,416)	8	(12,769)	1	(13,692)
16	(13,664)	9	(13,044)	2	(14,823)
17	(13,938)	10	(13,299)	3	(7020)
18	(7019)	11	(14,352)	4	(14,597)
20	(13,341)	12	(14,792)	5	(14,810)
21	(13,003)	14	(13,705)	6	(7827)
24	(14,023)	15	(7840)	7	(14,310)
25	(14,069)	19	(13,381)		
27	(13,413)	22	(13,577)		
28	(13,972)	23	(13,717)		
29	(8672)	26	(14,013)		
32	(10,515)	30	(6997)		
33	(13,274)	31	(7825)		

Figure 12 (continued).

LATERAL POSITION

Left Lateral		Left Asymmetrical		Median		Right Asymmetrical		Right Lateral	
2	(14,823)	6	(7827)	5	(14,810)	1	(13,692)	8	(12,769)
4	(14,597)	7	(14,310)			3	(7020)	9	(13,044)
11	(14,352)							10	(13,299)
17	(13,938)							12	(14,792)
21	(13,003)							13	(14,416)
22	(13,577)							14	(13,705)
24	(14,023)							15	(7840)
29	(8672)							16	(13,664)
30	(6997)							18	(7019)
32	(10,515)							19	(13,381)
33	(13,274)							20	(13,341)
								23	(13,717)
								25	(14,069)
								26	(14,013)
								27	(13,413)
								28	(13,972)
								31	(7825)
								33	(13,274)

NOTCHES

  1 (13,692): Right
  2 (14,823): Left
  3 (7020): Right
  4 (14,597): Left
  9 (13,044): Right
 11 (14,352): Left
 12 (14,792): Right
 13 (14,416): Right
 15 (7840): Right
 17 (13,938): Left
 18 (7019): Right
 19 (13,381): Right
 22 (13,577): Left
 23 (13,717): Right
 24 (14,023): Left
 28 (13,972): Right
 29 (8672): Left
 30 (6997): Left
 31 (7825): Right
 32 (10,515): Left

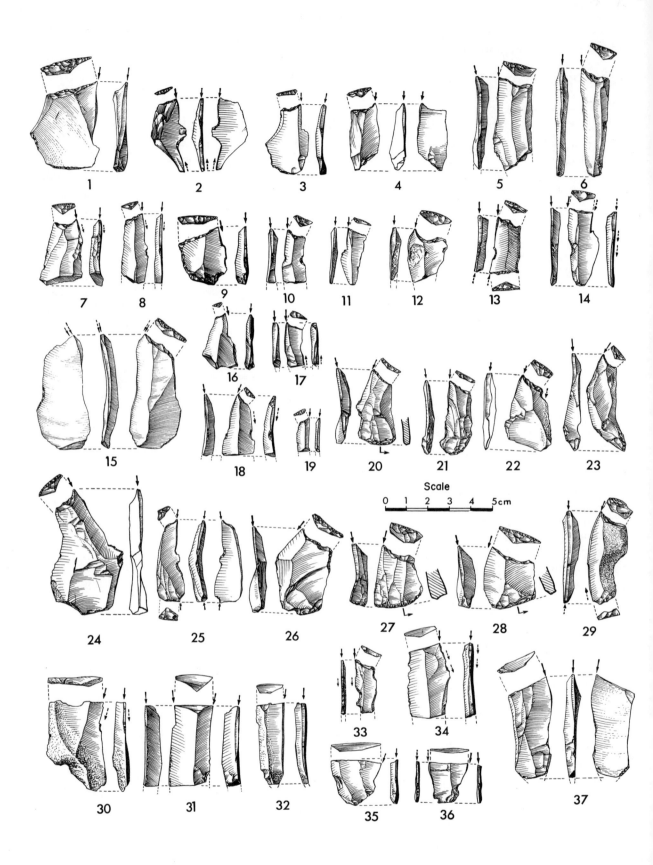

Scale

0 1 2 3 4 5cm

Figure 13. NOAILLES BURINS FROM LEVEL 4: LOWER

SRS TYPE, ANGLE, AND CLASS

Retouched Truncation

1	(10,845):	LOWER-2: 50°; Class 6
2	(14,100):	LOWER-2: 80°; Class 6
3	(13,803):	LOWER-2: 70°; Class 6
4	(13,294):	LOWER-1: 60°; Class 6
5	(13,934):	LOWER-2: 70°; Class 6
6	(7473):	LOWER-1: 70°; Class 6
7	(14,449):	LOWER-2: 70°; Class 6
8	(14,379):	LOWER-2: 70°; Class 6
9	(13,672):	LOWER-2: 70°; Class 6
10	(10,699):	LOWER-2: 60°; Class 6
11	(14,209):	LOWER-2: 70°; Class 6
12	(13,396):	LOWER-1: 60°; Class 6
13	(11,041):	LOWER-2: 70°; Class 6
14	(13,200):	LOWER-1: 70°; Class 5
15	(7328):	LOWER-2: 80°; Class 7
16	(14,596):	LOWER-2: 70°; Class 7
17	(12,548):	LOWER-2: 40°; Class 7
18	(13,309):	LOWER-1: 60°; Class 7
19	(13,315):	LOWER-1: 40°; Class 7
20	(6624):	LOWER-1: 60°; Class 7
21	(13,365):	LOWER-1: 50°; Class 7
22	(14,837):	LOWER-2: 70°; Class 7
23	(12,364):	LOWER-1: 60°; Class 7
24	(6842):	LOWER-1: 60°; Class 7
25	(13,937):	LOWER-2: 40°; Class 7
26	(10,433):	LOWER-2: 60°; Class 7
27	(6529):	LOWER-1: 60°; Class 7
28	(6679):	LOWER-1: 70°; Class 7
29	(13,395):	LOWER-1: 60°; Class 7

Break

30	(13,756):	LOWER-1: 70°; Class 8
31	(12,962):	LOWER-1: 90°; Class 8
32	(14,498):	LOWER-2: 80°; Class 8
33	(14,598):	LOWER-2: 60°; Class 8
34	(14,574):	LOWER-2: 80°; Class 8
35	(14,230):	LOWER-2: 80°; Class 8
36	(12,842):	LOWER-1: 80°; Class 8
37	(7469):	LOWER-2: 70°; Class 8

Figure 13 (continued).

BURIN EDGE SHAPE AND WIDTH

Straight

1	(10,845):	1 mm	19	(13,315):	1 mm
2	(14,100):	1 mm	20	(6624):	1 mm
3	(13,803):	1 mm	21	(13,365):	1 mm
4	(13,294):	1 mm	22	(14,837):	2 mm
5	(13,934):	1 mm	23	(12,364):	2 mm
6	(7473):	1 mm	24	(6842):	1 mm
7	(14,449):	1 mm	25	(13,937):	1 mm
8	(14,379):	1 mm	26	(10,433):	1 mm
9	(13,672):	1 mm	27	(6529):	2 mm
10	(10,699):	1 mm	28	(6679):	1 mm
11	(14,209):	1 mm	29	(13,395):	2 mm
12	(13,396):	1 mm	30	(13,756):	1 mm
13	(11,041):	1 mm	31	(12,962):	1 mm
14	(13,200):	1 mm	32	(14,498):	1 mm
15	(7328):	2 mm	33	(14,598):	1 mm
16	(14,596):	1 mm	34	(14,574):	1 mm
17	(12,548):	2 mm	35	(14,230):	<1 mm
18	(13,309):	1 mm	36	(12,842):	<1 mm
			37	(7469):	<1 mm

OBLIQUITY

Dorsal Oblique	Lateral	Oblique	High Oblique
32 (14,498)	2 (14,100)	1 (10,845)	4 (13,294)
	3 (13,803)	11 (14,209)	10 (10,699)
	5 (13,934)	12 (13,396)	
	6 (7473)	14 (13,200)	
	7 (14,449)	17 (12,548)	
	8 (14,379)	19 (13,315)	
	9 (13,672)	20 (6624)	
	13 (11,041)	21 (13,365)	
	15 (7328)	24 (6842)	
	16 (14,596)	25 (13,937)	
	18 (13,309)	26 (10,433)	
	22 (14,837)	29 (13,395)	
	23 (12,364)	33 (14,598)	
	27 (6529)	34 (14,574)	
	28 (6679)	35 (14,230)	
	30 (13,756)		
	31 (12,962)		
	36 (12,842)		
	37 (7469)		

Figure 13 (continued).

SRS SHAPE

Concave		Pronounced Concave		Straight	
1	(10,845)	3	(13,803)	30	(13,756)
2	(14,100)	4	(13,294)	31	(12,962)
5	(13,934)	6	(7473)	32	(14,498)
8	(14,379)	7	(14,449)	34	(14,574)
9	(13,672)	10	(10,699)	35	(14,230)
11	(14,209)	12	(13,396)	36	(12,842)
14	(13,200)	13	(11,041)		
16	(14,596)	15	(7328)		
17	(12,548)	23	(12,364)		
18	(13,309)	24	(6842)		
19	(13,315)	26	(10,433)		
20	(6624)	27	(6529)		
21	(13,365)	28	(6679)		
22	(14,837)	29	(13,395)		
25	(13,937)				
33	(14,598)				
37	(7469)				

LATERAL POSITION

Left Lateral		Left Asymmetrical		Median		Right Asymmetrical		Right Lateral	
5	(13,934)	11	(14,209)	20	(6624)	2	(14,100)	1	(10,845)
6	(7473)	12	(13,396)	23	(12,364)	7	(14,449)	3	(13,803)
10	(10,699)	15	(7328)	26	(10,433)	16	(14,596)	4	(13,294)
13	(11,041)	18	(13,309)	29	(13,395)	37	(7469)	8	(14,379)
14	(13,200)	22	(14,837)					9	(13,672)
17	(12,548)	27	(6529)					19	(13,315)
21	(13,365)	28	(6679)					25	(13,937)
31	(12,962)							30	(13,756)
33	(14,598)							32	(14,498)
35	(14,230)							34	(14,574)
								36	(12,842)

NOTCHES

2	(14,100):	Right	14	(13,200):	Left	25	(13,937):	Right
3	(13,803):	Right	16	(14,596):	Right	26	(10,433):	Left
7	(14,449):	Right	18	(13,309):	Left	27	(6529):	Left
8	(14,379):	Right	19	(13,315):	Right	30	(13,756):	Right
9	(13,672):	Right	20	(6624):	Left	33	(14,598):	Left
10	(10,699):	Left	21	(13,365):	Left	34	(14,574):	Right
11	(14,209):	Left	23	(12,364):	Left	36	(12,842):	Right
13	(11,041):	Left	24	(6842):	Right			

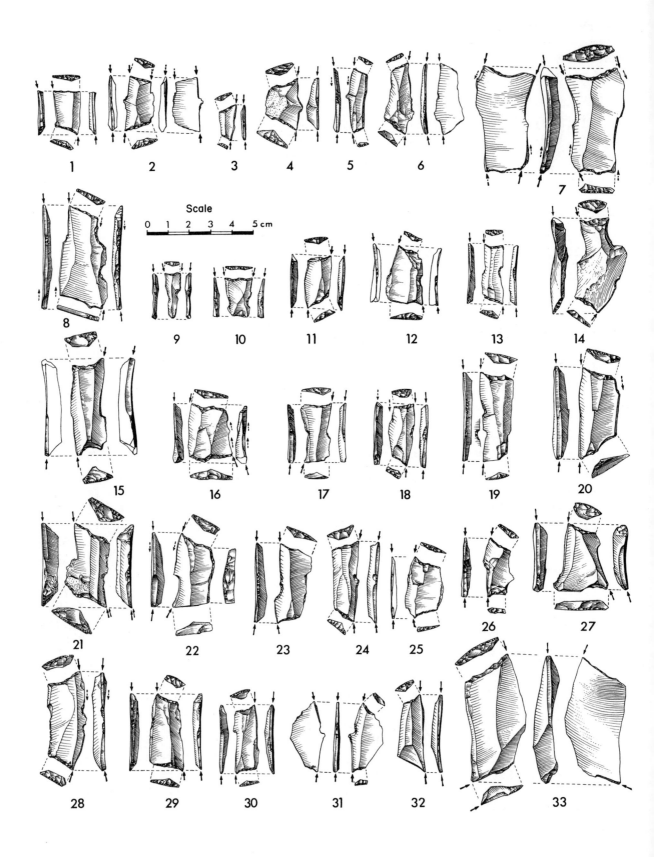

Scale
0 1 2 3 4 5 cm

1   2   3   4   5   6   7

8   9   10   11   12   13   14

15   16   17   18   19   20

21   22   23   24   25   26   27

28   29   30   31   32   33

Figure 14. NOAILLES BURINS FROM LEVEL 4: LOWER

SRS TYPE, ANGLE, AND CLASS

Retouched Truncation

1 (12,900): LOWER-1: A: 70°;
   Class 1; D: 60°; Class 5
2 (12,761): LOWER-1: A: 70°;
   Class 2a; C: 70°; Class 2b
3 (14,111): LOWER-2: B: 60°;
   Class 2b; D: 70°; Class 6
4 (14,555): LOWER-2: B: 60°;
   Class 7; D: 70°; Class 2b
5 (14,790): LOWER-2: A: 70°;
   Class 2b; C: 70°; Class 6
6 (14,175): LOWER-1: B: 70°;
   Class 2b; D: 60°; Class 2c
7 (10,873): LOWER-2: A: 70°;
   Class 1; B: 80°; Class 2c; C:
   90°; Class 3
8 (14,248): LOWER-2: A: 70°;
   Class 2b; D: 70°; Class 2a
9 (13,920): LOWER-2: A: 70°;
   Class 3; B: 90°; Class 1
10 (13,352): LOWER-2: A: 70°;
   Class 3; B: 70°; Class 3
11 (13,805): LOWER-2: B: 70°;
   Class 4; C: 70°; Class 7
12 (14,347): LOWER-2: A: 70°;
   Class 4; D: 60°; Class 6
13 (13,623): LOWER-2: A: 70°;
   Class 3; D: 60°; Class 6
14 (13,445): LOWER-1: A: 60°;
   Class 4; D: 80°; Class 4
15 (12,824): LOWER-1: B: 70°;
   Class 5; C: 60°; Class 5
16 (13,306): LOWER-1: A: 70°;
   Class 5; D: 90°; Class 1
17 (13,682): LOWER-2: B: 80°;
   Class 5

18 (14,051): LOWER-2: B: 70°;
   Class 5; D: 60°; Class 7
19 (14,668): LOWER-2: A: 90°;
   Class 5
20 (13,893): LOWER-1: A: 80°;
   Class 5
21 (12,103): LOWER-2: A: 60°;
   Class 6; D: 60°; Class 6
22 (14,627): LOWER-2: A: 60°;
   Class 6
23 (12,912): LOWER-1: A: 70°;
   Class 6; C: 70°; Class 6
24 (13,295): LOWER-1: B: 70°;
   Class 7; D: 60°; Class 6
25 (13,317): LOWER-1: A: 60°;
   Class 6; C: 70°; Class 6
26 (14,121): LOWER-2: A: 60°;
   Class 6; C: 70°; Class 7
27 (13,108): LOWER-1: A: 70°;
   Class 6; D: 50°; Class 3
28 (11,033): LOWER-2: B: 80°;
   Class 6; D: 50°; Class 6
29 (13,153): LOWER-1: A: 80°;
   Class 6; D: 70°; Class 5
30 (13,167): LOWER-2: B: 70°;
   Class 4; C: 60°; Class 6
31 (13,941): LOWER-2: A: 60°;
   Class 7; C: 70°; Class 6
32 (13,066): LOWER-1: B: 50°;
   Class 7
33 (13,508): LOWER-1: B: 80°;
   Class 7

Figure 14 (continued).

Break

17 (13,682): LOWER-2: C: 60°;
    Class 8
19 (14,668): LOWER-2: C: 80°;
    Class 8
20 (13,893): LOWER-2: C: 60°;
    Class 8
22 (14,627): LOWER-2: C: 50°;
    Class 8
32 (13,066): LOWER-1: D: 40°;
    Class 8

Retouched Edge

33 (13,508): LOWER-1: C: 70°;
    Class 7

BURIN EDGE SHAPE AND WIDTH

Straight

 1 (12,900): A: 1 mm; D: 1 mm
 2 (12,761): A: <1 mm; C: <1 mm
 3 (1411): A: 1 mm; C: 1 mm
 4 (14,555): A: 1 mm; C: 1 mm
 5 (14,790): A: <1 mm; C: 1 mm
 6 (14,175): B: 1 mm; D: 1 mm
 7 (10,873): A: 1 mm; B: 1 mm;
    C: 2 mm
 8 (14,248): A: 1 mm; D: 1 mm
 9 (13,920): A: 1 mm; B: 1 mm
10 (13,352): A: 1 mm; B: 1 mm
11 (13,805): B: 1 mm; C: 1 mm
12 (14,347): A: 1 mm; D: 1 mm
13 (13,623): A: 1 mm; D: 1 mm
14 (13,445): A: 1 mm; D: <1 mm
15 (12,824): B: 2 mm; C: 2 mm
16 (13,306): A: 1 mm; D: 1 mm

17 (13,682): B: 1 mm; C: 2 mm
18 (14,051): B: 1 mm; D: 1 mm
19 (14,668): A: 1 mm; C: <1 mm
20 (13,893): A: 1 mm; C: 3 mm
21 (12,103): A: 2 mm; D: 2 mm
22 (14,627): A: 1 mm; C: 2 mm
23 (12,912): A: 1 mm; C: 1 mm
24 (13,295): B: 1 mm; D: 1 mm
25 (13,317): A: <1 mm; C: 1 mm
26 (14,121): A: 1 mm; C: 1 mm
27 (13,108): A: 2 mm; D: 1 mm
28 (11,033): B: 1 mm; D: 2 mm
29 (13,153): A: 2 mm; D: 1 mm
30 (13,167): B: 1 mm; C: 1 mm
31 (13,941): A: 1 mm; C: 1 mm
32 (13,066): B: 1 mm; D: 2 mm
33 (13,508): B: 2 mm; C: 1 mm

Figure 14 (continued).

OBLIQUITY

Lateral			Oblique			High Oblique		
1	(12,900):	A	1	(12,900):	D	10	(13,352):	A
2	(12,761):	A	2	(12,761):	C	17	(13,682):	C
3	(14,111):	B	3	(14,111):	D	27	(13,108):	D
4	(14,555):	D	4	(14,555):	B			
6	(14,175):	D	5	(14,790):	A			
7	(10,783):	C		and C				
8	(14,248):	D	6	(14,175):	B			
9	(13,920):	A	7	(10,783):	A			
11	(13,805):	B		and B				
	and C		8	(14,248):	A			
12	(14,347):	A	9	(13,920):	B			
	and D		10	(13,352):	B			
14	(13,445):	A	13	(13,623):	A			
	and D			and D				
15	(12,824):	B	15	(12,824):	C			
16	(13,306):	D	16	(13,306):	A			
17	(13,682):	B	18	(14,051):	D			
18	(14,051):	B	20	(13,893):	A			
19	(14,668):	A	21	(12,103):	A			
	and C			and D				
20	(13,893):	C	23	(12,912):	C			
22	(14,627):	A	24	(13,295):	D			
	and C		26	(14,121):	A			
23	(12,912):	A		and C				
24	(13,295):	B	28	(11,033):	D			
25	(13,317):	A	30	(13,167):	B			
	and C		31	(13,941):	A			
27	(13,108):	A	33	(13,508):	C			
28	(11,033):	B						
29	(13,153):	A						
	and D							
30	(13,167):	C						
31	(13,941):	C						
32	(13,066):	B						
	and D							
33	(13,508):	B						

Figure 14 (continued).

SRS SHAPE

Concave			Pronounced Concave			Straight		
1	(12,900):	D	13	(13,623):	A	1	(12,900):	A
3	(14,111):	D	15	(12,824):	B	2	(12,761):	A
4	(14,555):	B		and C			and C	
5	(14,790):	C	16	(13,306):	A	3	(14,111):	B
7	(10,873):	C	17	(13,682):	B	4	(14,555):	D
9	(13,920):	A	19	(14,668):	A	5	(14,790):	A
10	(13,352):	A	20	(13,893):	C	6	(14,175):	B
	and B		23	(12,912):	A		and D	
11	(13,805):	B	25	(13,317):	A	7	(10,873):	A
	and C		27	(13,108):	D		and B	
12	(14,347):	A	28	(11,033):	B	8	(14,248):	A
	and D			and D			and D	
13	(13,623):	A	31	(13,941):	A	9	(13,920):	B
	and D		32	(13,066):	B	16	(13,306):	D
14	(13,445):	A				17	(13,682):	C
	and D					19	(14,668):	C
18	(14,051):	B				21	(12,103):	D
	and D					22	(14,627):	C
20	(13,893):	A				33	(13,508):	C
21	(12,103):	A						
22	(14,627):	A						
23	(12,912):	C						
24	(13,295):	B						
	and D							
25	(13,317):	C						
26	(14,121):	A						
	and C							
27	(13,108):	A						
29	(13,153):	A						
	and D							
30	(13,167):	B						
	and C							
31	(13,941):	C						
32	(13,066):	D						
33	(13,508):	B						

LATERAL POSITION

Left Lateral			Left Asymmetrical			Right Asymmetrical			Right Lateral		
1	(12,900):	A and D	6	(14,175):	D	32	(13,066):	B	2	(12,761):	C
2	(12,761):	A	27	(13,108):	A				3	(14,111):	D
3	(14,111):	B	28	(11,033):	D				4	(14,555):	D
4	(14,555):	B							5	(14,790):	C
5	(14,790):	A							6	(14,175):	B
7	(10,873):	A							7	(10,873):	B and C
8	(14,248):	A and D							9	(13,920):	B
9	(13,920):	A							10	(13,352):	B
10	(13,352):	A							11	(13,805):	B and C
12	(14,347):	A and D							15	(12,824):	B and C
13	(13,623):	A and D							17	(13,682):	B and C
14	(13,445):	A and D							18	(14,051):	B
16	(13,306):	A and D							19	(14,668):	C
18	(14,051):	D							20	(13,893):	C
19	(14,668):	A							22	(14,627):	C
20	(13,893):	A							24	(13,295):	B
21	(12,103):	A and D							25	(13,317):	C
22	(14,627):	A							26	(14,121):	C
23	(12,912):	A and C							28	(11,033):	B
24	(13,201):	D							30	(13,167):	B and C
25	(13,317):	A							31	(13,941):	C
26	(14,121):	A							33	(13,508):	B and C
27	(13,108):	D									
29	(13,153):	A and D									
31	(13,941):	A									
32	(13,066):	D									

NOTCHES

2	(12,761):	Right and left	17	(13,682):	Right and left
3	(14,111):	Right	18	(14,051):	Right
4	(14,555):	Right (2)	19	(14,668):	Left (2)
5	(14,790):	Left (2)	21	(12,103):	Left
6	(14,175):	Right (2)	23	(12,912):	Left
8	(14,248):	Right and left	24	(13,295):	Right (2)
9	(13,920):	Right and left	26	(14,121):	Left
10	(13,352):	Right and left	27	(13,108):	Left
11	(13,805):	Left	28	(11,033):	Right
12	(14,347):	Right and left	29	(13,153):	Left
13	(13,623):	Right and left	30	(13,167):	Right
14	(13,445):	Right and left	31	(13,941):	Left
15	(12,824):	Right	32	(13,066):	Right

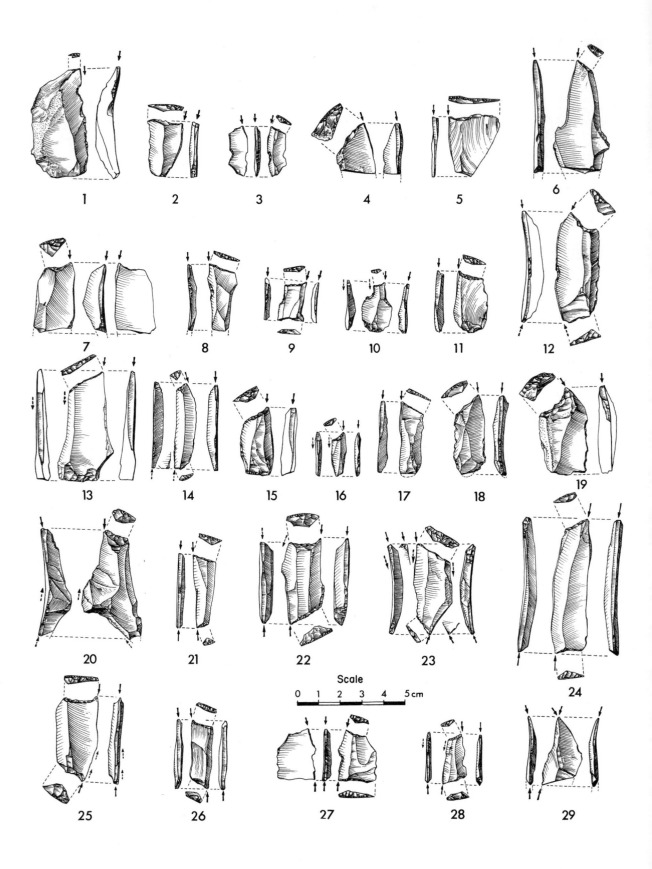

Scale
0 1 2 3 4 5 cm

1   2   3   4   5   6

7   8   9   10   11   12

13   14   15   16   17   18   19

20   21   22   23   24

25   26   27   28   29

Figure 15.   NOAILLES BURINS FROM LEVEL 4: MIDDLE

SRS TYPE, ANGLE, AND CLASS

Retouched Truncation

1 (6376): MIDDLE-2: 70°; Class 2b
2 (6576): MIDDLE-2: 80°; Class 2a
3 (11,566): MIDDLE-2: 70°;
   Class 2b
4 (9776): MIDDLE-1: 70°; Class 2c
5 (7269): MIDDLE-1: 80°; Class 3
6 (9861): MIDDLE-1: 70°; Class 2c
7 (7424a): MIDDLE-2: 70°; Class 5
8 (7882): MIDDLE-2: 60°; Class 5
9 (10,491): MIDDLE-1: 70°; Class 5
10 (7202): MIDDLE-1: 60°; Class 6
11 (7886): MIDDLE-1: 60°; Class 6
12 (10,264): MIDDLE-1: 80°; Class 5
13 (7400): MIDDLE-1: 50°; Class 7
14 (7880): MIDDLE-2: 80°; Class 5
15 (7361): MIDDLE-2: 60°; Class 7
16 (11,501): MIDDLE-2: 60°; Class 7
17 (7362): MIDDLE-2: 60°; Class 7
18 (9370): MIDDLE-1: 70°; Class 6
19 (10,449): MIDDLE-1: 50°; Class 7
20 (9656): MIDDLE-1: 60°; Class 7
21 (6374): MIDDLE-2: A: 70°; Class
   2a; C: 70°; Class 2b
22 (7132): MIDDLE-1: B: 50°;
   Class 4; C: 70°; Class 2c
23 (7250): MIDDLE-1: A: 60°;
   Class 6; D: 60°; Class 7
24 (9516): MIDDLE-1: B: 80°;
   Class 5; C: 70°; Class 2c
25 (10,544): MIDDLE-2: B: 70°;
   Class 6; D: 50°; Class 7
26 (9535): MIDDLE-1: A: 60°;
   Class 6; D: 60°; Class 6
27 (6365): MIDDLE-2: A: 80°;
   Class 5; C: 70°; Class 3
28 (10,230): MIDDLE-2: B: 60°;
   Class 6; C: 50°; Class 2c

Break

29 (8276): MIDDLE-1: Proximal
   extremity; 60°; Class 8

Dihedral

29 (8276): MIDDLE-1: Distal
   extremity; 50°

Figure 15 (continued).

BURIN EDGE SHAPE AND WIDTH

Straight   Beveled

 1 (6376): 1 mm   11   (7886):   2 mm
 2 (6576): 1 mm
 3 (11,566): 1 mm
 4 (9776):   2 mm
 5 (7269): 1 mm
 6 (9861): 1 mm
 7 (7424a): 1 mm
 8 (7882): 1 mm
 9 (10,491): 1 mm
10 (7202): 1 mm
12 (10,264): 2 mm
13 (7400): 2 mm
14 (7880): 1 mm
15 (7361): 2 mm
16 (11,501): <1 mm
17 (7362): 1 mm
18 (9370): 1 mm
19 (10,449): 3 mm
20 (9656): A: 2 mm
21 (6374): A: 2 mm; C: 1 mm
22 (7132): B: 1 mm; C: 1 mm
23 (7250): A: 2 mm; D: 1 mm
24 (9516): B: 1 mm; C: 2 mm
25 (10,544): B: 1 mm; D: 3 mm
26 (9535): A: 2 mm; D: 1 mm
27 (6365): A: 1 mm; C: 1 mm
28 (10,230): B: 1 mm; C: 1 mm
29 (8276): Both extremities: <1 mm

Figure 15 (continued).

OBLIQUITY

Dorsal Oblique	Lateral	Oblique	High Oblique
11 (7886)	1 (6376)	6 (9861)	9 (10,491)
	2 (6576)	7 (7424a)	20 (9656)
	3 (11,566)	10 (7202)	23 (7250): A
	4 (9776)	13 (7400)	
	5 (7269)	17 (7362)	
	8 (7882)	19 (10,449)	
	12 (10,264)	21 (6374): C	
	14 (7880)	22 (7132): C	
	15 (7361)	24 (9516): C	
	16 (11,501)	25 (10,544): B	
	18 (9370)	27 (6365): C	
	21 (6374): A	28 (10,230): C	
	22 (7132): B		
	23 (7250): D		
	24 (9516): B		
	25 (10,544): D		
	26 (9535): A and D		
	27 (6365): A		
	28 (10,230): B		
	29 (8276): Both extremities		

SRS SHAPE

Concave	Pronounced Concave	Straight
5 (7269)	12 (10,264)	1 (6376)
7 (7424a)	19 (10,449)	2 (6576)
8 (7882)	22 (7132): B	3 (11,566)
9 (10,491)	25 (10,544): B and D	4 (9776)
10 (7202)	26 (9535): A and C	6 (9861)
11 (7886)	27 (6365): A	21 (6374): A and C
13 (7400)		22 (7132): C
14 (7880)		24 (9516): C
15 (7361)		28 (10,230): C
16 (11,501)		29 (8276) Both extremities
17 (7362)		
18 (9370)		
20 (9656)		
23 (7250): A and D		
24 (9516): B		
27 (6365): C		
28 (10,230): B		

Figure 15 (continued).

LATERAL POSITION

Left Lateral	Left Asymmetrical	Median	Right Asymmetrical
3 (11,566)	8 (7882)	6 (9861)	14 (7880)
5 (7269)	11 (7886)	23 (7250): D	19 (10,449)
17 (7362)	12 (10,264)	29 (8276):	24 (9516): C
20 (9656)	25 (10,544): D	Distal	
21 (6374): A	28 (10,230): C	extremity	
23 (7250): A			
26 (9535): A			
and C			
27 (6365): A			

Right
Lateral

1 (6376)		18 (9370)	
2 (6576)		21 (6374): C	
4 (9776)		22 (7132): B	
7 (7424a)		and C	
9 (10,491)		24 (9516): B	
10 (7202)		25 (10,544): B	
13 (7400)		27 (6365): C	
15 (7361)		28 (10,230): B	
16 (11,501)		29 (8276): C	

NOTCHES

1 (6376): Right
2 (6576): Right
3 (11,566): Left
5 (7269): Left
6 (9861): Left
7 (7424a): Right
8 (7882): Left
9 (10,491): Right
10 (7202): Right
12 (10,264): Left
17 (7362): Left
18 (9370): Right
19 (10,449): Right
20 (9656): Left
21 (6374): Left
27 (6365): Left
28 (10,230): Right and left
29 (8276): Right and left

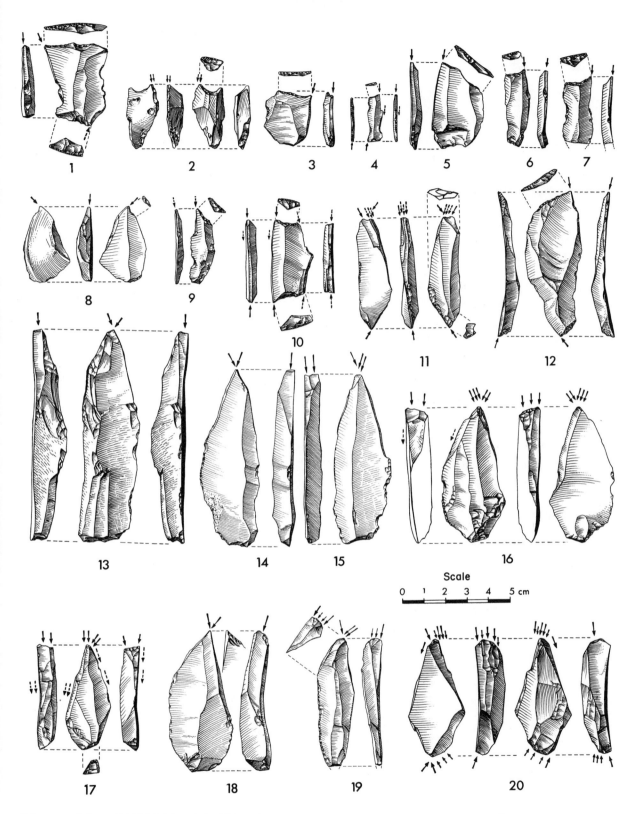

Figure 16.   NOAILLES, RAYSSE, AND DIHEDRAL BURINS FROM LEVEL 4: UPPER

Figure 16.   NOAILLES, RAYSSE, AND DIHEDRAL BURINS FROM LEVEL 4: UPPER

NOAILLES BURINS

SRS TYPE, ANGLE, AND CLASS

Retouched Truncation   Unretouched End

 1 (6206): UPPER-2: 70°; Class 5   12 (6138): UPPER-1: Proximal
 2 (11,584): UPPER-1: 70°; Class 3   extremity: 80°; Class 8
 3 (5947): UPPER-1: 70°; Class 4
 4 (4747): UPPER-2: 70°; Class 5
 5 (6657): UPPER-2: 80°; Class 5
 6 (6308): UPPER-2: 60°; Class 5
 7 (6286): UPPER-2: 50°; Class 6
 8 (9171): UPPER-1a: 60°; Class 7
 9 (6323): UPPER-2: 60°; Class 7
10 (9176): UPPER-2: A: 70°; Class 5;
   C: 70°; Class 6
11 (9315): UPPER-1: Proximal
   extremity: 60°; Class 2c
12 (6138): UPPER-1: Distal extremity:
   80°; Class 2b

BURIN EDGE SHAPE AND WIDTH

Straight

 1 (6206): 1 mm
 2 (11,584): 2 mm
 3 (5947): 1 mm
 4 (4747): 1 mm
 5 (6657): 1 mm
 6 (6308): 2 mm
 7 (6286): 1 mm
 8 (9171): 2 mm
 9 (6323): 1 mm
10 (9176): A: 1 mm; C: 2 mm
11 (9315): Proximal extremity: 1 mm
12 (6138): Both extremities: 1 mm

OBLIQUITY

Lateral   Oblique   High Oblique

 1 (6206)   6 (6308)   9 (6323)
 2 (11,584)   7 (6286)
 3 (5947)   8 (9171)
 4 (4747)   11 (9315):
 5 (6657)   Proximal
10 (9176): A   extremity
   and C
12 (6138): Both
   extremities

Figure 16 (continued).

SRS SHAPE

Concave	Pronounced Concave	Straight
1 (6206)	2 (11,584)	11 (9315):
3 (5947)	6 (6308)	Proximal
4 (4747)	7 (6286)	extremity
5 (6657)	8 (9171)	12 (6138): Both
9 (6323)	10 (9176): C	extremities
10 (9176): A		

LATERAL POSITION

Left Lateral	Left Asymmetrical	Median	Right Asymmetrical
1 (6206)	5 (6657)	8 (9171)	6 (6308)
2 (11,584)		11 (9315):	12 (6138): Both
9 (6323)		Proximal	extremities
10 (9176): A		extremity	
and C			

Right
Lateral

3 (5947)
4 (4747)
7 (6286)

NOTCHES

1 (6206): Left
4 (4747): Right
5 (6657): Inverse left
6 (6308): Right
7 (6286): Right
8 (9171): Left
9 (6323): Left

Figure 16 (continued).

RAYSSE BURIN

SRS TYPE

11 (9315): UPPER-1: Distal
    extremity on dihedral

NUMBER OF REMOVALS

11 (9315): 1+3

FIRST REMOVAL

Lateral (80-100°)

11 (9315): 80°

LAST REMOVAL

High Oblique (140-150°)

11 (9315): 150°

SRS SHAPE

Straight

11 (9315)

LATERAL POSITION

Median

11 (9315)

DIHEDRAL BURINS

SRS TYPE AND ANGLE

Dihedral

13 (9310): UPPER-1:   60°
14 (8039): UPPER-1:   50°
15 (8060): UPPER-1:   60°
16 (8742): UPPER-1:   70°
17 (6962): UPPER-1:   50°
18 (6613): UPPER-2:   50°
19 (8388): UPPER-1a: 80°
20 (5690): UPPER-1: Both extremities:
    60°

BURIN EDGE SHAPE AND WIDTH

Straight   Rounded   Angulated

13 (9310): 4 mm   19 (8388): 7 mm   16 (8742): 12 mm
14 (8039): 4 mm   20 (5690): Distal
15 (8060): 7 mm   extremity:
17 (6962): 7 mm   11 mm
18 (6613): 6 mm
20 (5690):
    Proximal
    extremity: 5 mm

Figure 16 (continued).

OBLIQUITY

Lateral	Oblique
13 (9310)	18 (6613)
14 (8039)	
15 (8060)	
17 (6962)	
20 (5690):	
Proximal	
extremity	

SRS SHAPE

Straight

13 (9310)
14 (8039)
15 (8060)
16 (8742)
17 (6962)
18 (6613)
19 (8388)
20 (5690): Both
    extremities

LATERAL POSITION

Left Asymmetrical	Median	Right Asymmetrical
20 (5690):	13 (9310)	18 (6613)
Proximal	14 (8039)	19 (8388)
extremity	15 (8060)	
	16 (8742)	
	17 (6962)	
	20 (5690): Distal	
	extremity	

ASSOCIATIONS

11 (9315): Mixed burin: A: Raysse burin on dihedral; C: Noailles burin
on retouched truncation

Table 15

CROSS-TABULATION, SHOWING OBSERVED AND EXPECTED FREQUENCIES,
OF BURIN EDGE WIDTH AND PRESENCE OF STOP-NOTCH ON TRUNCATION BURINS
IN LEVEL 4: REAR:LOWER

Edge Width		Stop-Notch +	−	n
0.5–3 mm	Observed	54	58	112
	Expected	42.48	69.52	
4–16 mm	Observed	1	32	33
	Expected	12.52	20.48	
n		55	90	145

Note: Chi-square (with Yates's correction) = 20.23; Degrees of freedom = 1; $P < 0.001$.

are any characteristics or combinations of characteristics of truncation burins in our samples which justify the distinction of a Noailles burin type. Are there, for example, bimodal distributions of attributes suggesting that two or more types are subsumed under the general rubric of truncation burins?

In the REAR:LOWER sample, there are 145 truncation burins (plus one burin-point made by the truncation technique that is not counted here). The mean burin edge width is 2.49 mm, the modal class is 1 mm, and the range runs from 0.5 mm (i.e., 0.26–0.75 mm) to 11 mm. The characteristic stop-notch, long considered a feature of Noailles burins, is associated with small burin edges (table 15). This distribution shows a nonrandom ($P < 0.001$) association of notches with burin edges of 3 mm or less and allows burins with edges of 3 mm or less and stop-notches to be differentiated from burins with larger burin edges and without stop-notches. The attributes "small burin edge" plus "stop-notch" thus allow preliminary characterization of the Noailles type (e.g., fig. 12:1–4). In both these characteristics the truncation burins of Level 4: REAR:LOWER are differentiated from those of Levels 5 and 3. There remain 58 burins with small burin edges but without stop-notches (e.g., fig. 13:4–6). Tixier (1958, p. 630) remarks that the stop-notch is often partially effaced by the removal of the burin spall. It is therefore very possible that in some cases it was entirely removed; consequently, many of the 58 problem pieces may be Noailles burins that have lost their notches.

There are at least two suggestions as to the significance of the stop-notch of Noailles burins, neither of which is adequate. Siret (1933, p. 126) suggests that the purpose of the notch was to encourage the burin spall to continue down the side of the piece and prevent it from breaking out too soon. As Tixier points out, the artificers were capable of striking burin spalls successfully without the use of a notch. His suggestion is that the stop-notch was intended to prevent the burin spall from running too far down the edge of the piece, thus making the manufacture of a burin on the other end of the piece impossible. This explanation conforms with the fact that multiplicity is a frequent characteristic of Noailles burins, but it fails to explain why the stop-notch is so closely associated with burins that have very small burin edges. Nor does it explain why in the same level the burins with large edges do *not* have the notch. Furthermore, in Level 4, as in Level 3, larger truncation burins are frequently multiple but lack stop-notches in almost every case. A satisfactory explanation of the notch must account for not only its presence on Noailles burins, but also its absence on other burins.

The stop-notch is associated with burin edges of 3 mm or less, the modal class for REAR:LOWER being 1 mm. Such a burin is fragile and, as our own experiments have shown, is liable to be crushed in the process of spall removal. The application of the notch, rarely more than 20 mm from the burin edge, has an important structural effect (fig. 17) in that it materially reduces the distance through which the force of the burin blow must pass to remove the burin spall. It thus allows the burin blow—or perhaps pressure, which Tixier suggests may have been used to remove the burin spall—to be applied more lightly. In this way, the combination of the desire for a small burin edge together with the inherent fragility of such an edge requires or at least encourages the use of the notch technique for the regular production of successful burins. Burins with larger burin edges are less fragile; even though a heavier blow must be struck, the edge is less likely to be damaged in manufacture. There is therefore no necessity to facilitate spall removal by the application of a notch to the side of the piece.

Not all burins with edges of 3 mm or less were originally notched; in fact, one of the conclusions of this study is that the notch technique became less frequently employed through time. Some burins, in every other respect identical with notched Noailles burins, were never notched. These pieces

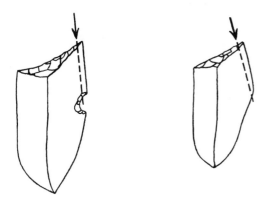

Figure 17. UNSTRUCK NOAILLES BURINS SHOWING THE FUNCTION OF THE NOTCH.

are sometimes those which did not require a notch because the form of the margin of the piece lent itself to easy spall removal. A piece reasonably interpreted as an unstruck notchless Noailles burin is illustrated in figure 17.

The notch is not therefore a stylistic whim of the artificers, but an important, if not always essential, part of the manufacture of burins with very small burin edges. It is a technical innovation peculiar to the Noaillian. Because it is a special technique of burin manufacture, Noailles burins may justifiably be distinguished from other forms of truncation burins and can be normatively defined as *truncation burins with a burin edge of 3 mm or less, manufactured by a technique that includes the notching of the side of the piece prior to the removal of the burin spall.*

If this hypothesis to explain the significance of the notch is accepted, it follows that the problem of definition gives way to the problem of the detection of other, notchless Noailles burins. It is fairly certain that the 32 burins of table 15 with burin edges of 4 mm or more and without notches are not Noailles burins, but the status of the 58 notchless burins with small burin edges remains to be determined. Some of these pieces probably lost their notches in the process of spall removal, while others are associated on the same blank with notched examples (e.g., fig. 14:21, 27). When these notched and unnotched pieces are grouped together and considered as one sample, the sample distributions by other attributes show no abnormalities; neither do the distributions of the notched pieces by other attributes differ significantly from those of the notched pieces. As is recognized by the de Sonneville-Bordes and Perrot definition, the notch is an optional character. To exclude unnotched burins from the Noailles type when they are indistinguishable in other respects is to do violence to cultural reality, but on the other hand it is necessary to make the separation between burins which *either have a notch or are liable to have a notch* and burins in which the notch did not play an actual or potential part in the technique of manufacture.

An estimator is required that will serve to differentiate Noailles burins from other truncation burins. The choice is not easy since the types are not absolutely distinguished. There is a gradient from pieces with very small burin edges, which most often have notches, to pieces with slightly larger burin edges, on which the notch is less commonly found, to pieces which were always manufactured without the use of the notch technique. Comparison of the distribution of the notched and notchless burins of all sizes by maximum width of the blank and burin edge width acts as an imperfect but useful estimator. It is hypothesized that the distribution of notchless Noailles burins will parallel that of notched Noailles burins. The parallelism will be modified by the fact that Noailles burins on which the notch has been removed are likely to have slightly larger burin edges than notched Noailles burins, since such burin edges will tend to have been worked (or reworked) closer to the thicker central portion of the blank.

A circular graph was used to investigate the notched and unnotched truncation burins. Graphs for the FRONT:LOWER-2 (fig. 18) and MIDDLE (fig. 19) subdivisions are shown by way of examples. Notched pieces are plotted in the right semicircle. Distance from the center increases with burin edge width, from 0.5 mm at the center to 9 mm and above in the outer rings. Maximum width of the blank increases from the bottom to the top of the page, the radii of the circle enclosing 4 mm classes. Only complete pieces are plotted.

In the three LOWER subdivisions, notched pieces are clustered with maximum widths from 8–24 mm and burin edge widths from 0.5–1 mm. Pieces with burin edge widths of 2 mm are less common, and at 3 mm and above there are only isolated examples (e.g., fig. 20:4, 7, 8, 10, 11). Notched pieces with edge widths of 4 mm or over, absent in FRONT:LOWER-2, are either reworked (and may have passed through a Noailles stage, an especially deep notch remaining visible), or they are pieces with a notch further away from the burin edge than on the remainder of the series. The notch may be fortuitous and not necessarily associated with the burin. These pieces are excluded from the Noailles type. Pieces above 24 mm in maximum width are absent in FRONT:LOWER-2 but are proportionately more common in the other LOWER samples.

On the left (notchless) side of the plots, the distributions are less clustered. In each sample, pieces with burin edges of 2 mm and less closely mirror the distribution of notched Noailles burins on the opposite side. Almost all these pieces are considered to be notchless Noailles burins (e.g., fig. 22:28). Burins with 3 mm edges are slightly more frequent than on the notched side. Since it is expected that burins which have lost their notch should tend to have burin edges fractionally larger than notched examples, such pieces *may* be attributed to the Noailles type (in fact, the three examples from FRONT:LOWER-2 (fig. 18) are not regarded as Noailles burins). Only in REAR:LOWER is there a quantitatively important increment of notchless burins with burin edges of 4 mm and above and with widths generally greater than Noailles burins.

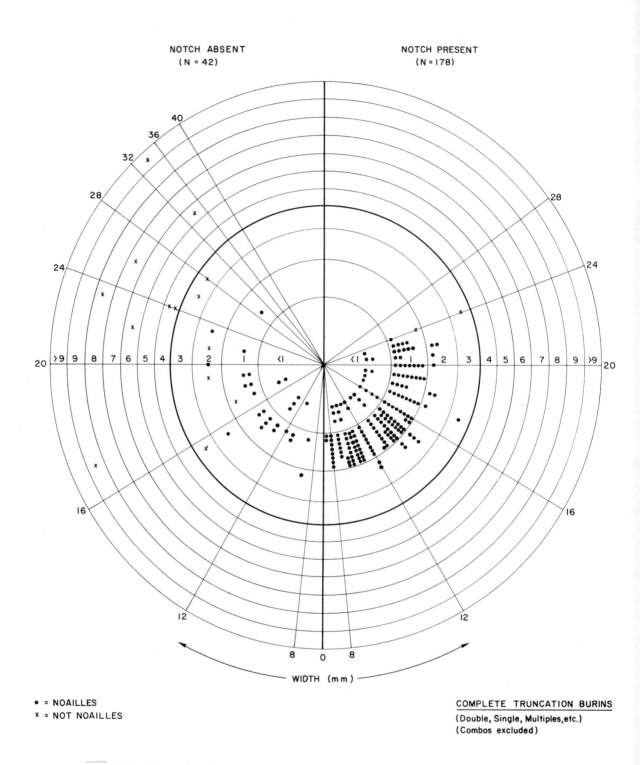

Figure 18.   CIRCULAR GRAPH SHOWING THE DISTRIBUTION OF COMPLETE NOAILLES
AND OTHER TRUNCATION BURINS BY WIDTH, SIZE OF BURIN EDGE, AND PRESENCE/
ABSENCE OF NOTCH IN FRONT:LOWER-2.

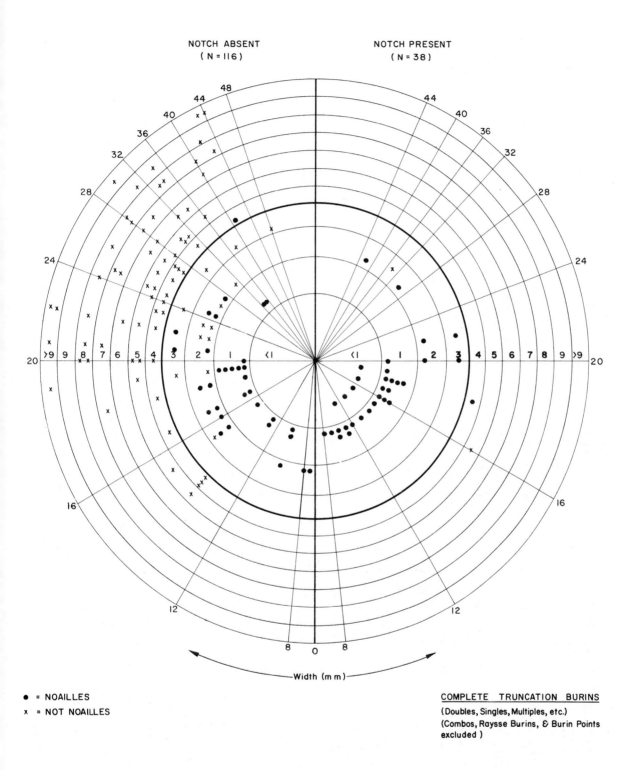

Figure 19. CIRCULAR GRAPH SHOWING THE DISTRIBUTION OF COMPLETE NOAILLES AND OTHER TRUNCATION BURINS BY WIDTH, SIZE OF BURIN EDGE, AND PRESENCE/ ABSENCE OF NOTCH IN MIDDLE.

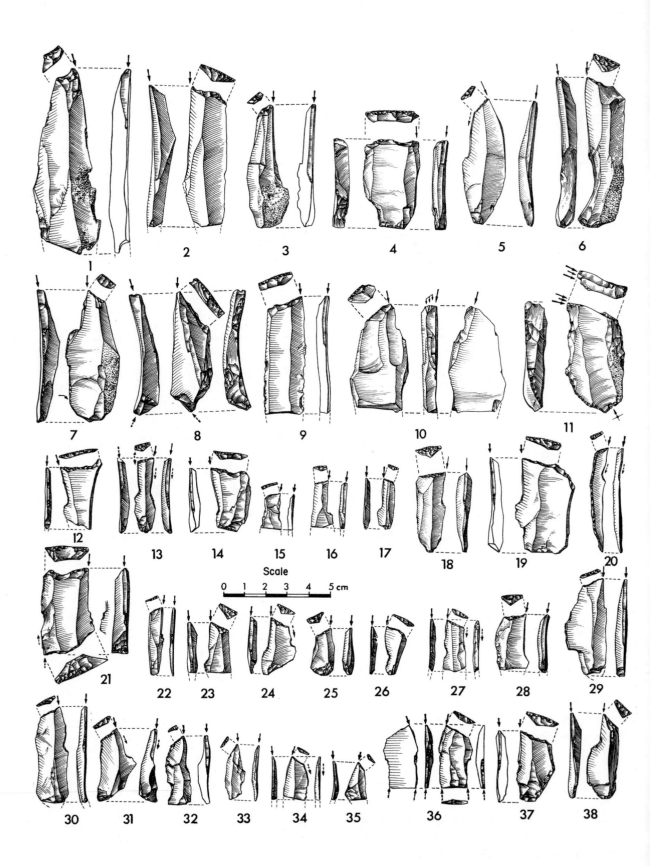

Scale

0 1 2 3 4 5 cm

Figure 20.   TRUNCATION AND NOAILLES BURINS FROM LEVEL 4: LOWER

TRUNCATION BURINS

SRS TYPE AND ANGLE

Retouched Truncation

1 (14,423): LOWER-2: 60°
2 (13,472): LOWER-2: 50°
3 (14,500): LOWER-2: 60°
4 (7410): LOWER-2a: 70°
5 (10,853): LOWER-2: 60°
6 (13,442): LOWER-1: 80°
7 (13,204): LOWER-1: 60°
8 (13,282): LOWER-1: 50°
9 (13,074a+b): LOWER-1: 70°
10 (7482): LOWER-1: 60°

Retouched Edge

11 (9904): LOWER-2: 80°

BURIN EDGE SHAPE AND WIDTH

Straight

1 (14,423): 2 mm
3 (14,500): 2 mm
4 (7410): 3 mm
5 (10,853): 2 mm
6 (13,442): 2 mm
7 (13,204): 3 mm
8 (13,282): 5 mm
9 (13,074a+b): 2 mm
10 (7482): 7 mm
11 (9904): 3 mm

Beveled

2 (13,472): 2 mm

OBLIQUITY

Lateral   Oblique

1 (14,423)   3 (14,500)
2 (13,472)   4 (7410)
6 (13,442)   5 (10,853)
7 (13,204)
8 (13,282)
9 (13,074a+b)

SRS SHAPE

	Pronounced		
Concave	Concave	Convex	Straight
6 (13,442)	1 (14,423)	3 (14,500)	5 (10,853)
9 (13,074a+b)	2 (13,472)		7 (13,204)
	4 (7410)		8 (13,282)
	11 (9904)		10 (7482)

Figure 20 (continued).

LATERAL POSITION

Left Lateral	Median	Right Asymmetrical	Right Lateral
2 (13,472)	7 (13,204)	5 (10,853)	1 (14,423)
6 (13,442)	8 (13,282)		3 (14,500)
	10 (7482)		4 (7410)
			9 (13,074a+b)
			11 (9904)

NOAILLES BURINS

SRS TYPE, ANGLE, AND CLASS

Retouched Truncation

12 (10,206): LOWER-2:   90°; Class 1
13 (13,084): LOWER-1:   80°; Class 2a
14 (13,541): LOWER-1:   80°; Class 2a
15 (13,207): LOWER-1:   70°; Class 2b
16 (10,885): LOWER-2:   80°; Class 2a
17 (8275): LOWER-2: 80°; Class 2a
18 (7831): LOWER-2a: 80°; Class 2a
19 (13,119): LOWER-1:   70°; Class 2b
20 (14,057): LOWER-2:   60°; Class 2c
21 (12,784): LOWER-1:   90°; Class 1
22 (13,988): LOWER-2:   80°; Class 2a
23 (12,743): LOWER-1:   80°; Class 2a
24 (11,020): LOWER-2:   70°; Class 2b
25 (13,059): LOWER-1:   60°; Class 2c
26 (8677): LOWER-2: 80°; Class 2a
27 (13,465): LOWER-1:   70°; Class 2b
28 (13,091): LOWER-1:   60°; Class 2c
29 (12,938): LOWER-1:   70°; Class 2b
30 (13,359): LOWER-1:   70°; Class 2b
31 (7667): LOWER-2: 70°; Class 2b
32 (12,290): LOWER-1:   60°; Class 2c
33 (14,570): LOWER-2:   50°; Class 2c
34 (13,711): LOWER-1:   70°; Class 2b
35 (13,166): LOWER-1:   60°; Class 2c
36 (14,187): LOWER-2:   70°; Class 2b
37 (13,709): LOWER-1:   60°; Class 2c
38 (14,114): LOWER-2:   50°; Class 2c

Figure 20 (continued).

BURIN EDGE SHAPE AND WIDTH

Straight

12	(10,206):	1 mm	25	(13,059):	1 mm
13	(13,084):	1 mm	26	(8677):	>1 mm
14	(13,541):	1 mm	27	(13,465):	1 mm
15	(13,207):	>1 mm	28	(13,091):	1 mm
16	(10,885):	1 mm	29	(12,938):	1 mm
17	(8375):	1 mm	30	(13,259):	1 mm
18	(7831):	1 mm	31	(7667):	1 mm
19	(13,119):	1 mm	32	(12,290):	1 mm
20	(14,057):	1 mm	33	(14,570):	1 mm
21	(12,784):	2 mm	34	(13,711):	1 mm
22	(13,988):	1 mm	35	(13,166):	1 mm
23	(12,743):	1 mm	36	(14,187):	1 mm
24	(11,020):	1 mm	37	(13,709):	1 mm
			38	(14,114):	1 mm

OBLIQUITY

Lateral		Oblique		High Oblique	
13	(13,084)	15	(13,207)	12	(10,206)
14	(13,541)	16	(10,885)	29	(12,938)
17	(8275)	20	(14,057)		
18	(7831)	21	(12,784)		
19	(13,119)	25	(13,059)		
22	(13,988)	28	(13,091)		
23	(12,743)	31	(7667)		
24	(11,020)	33	(14,570)		
26	(8677)	36	(14,187)		
27	(13,465)	37	(13,709)		
30	(13,359)				
32	(12,290)				
34	(13,711)				
35	(13,166)				
38	(14,114)				

SRS SHAPE

Straight

12	(10,206)	21	(12,784)	30	(13,359)
13	(13,084)	22	(13,988)	31	(7667)
14	(13,541)	23	(12,743)	32	(12,290)
15	(13,207)	24	(11,020)	33	(14,570)
16	(10,885)	25	(13,059)	34	(13,711)
17	(8275)	26	(8677)	35	(13,166)
18	(7831)	27	(13,465)	36	(14,187)
19	(13,119)	28	(13,091)	37	(13,709)
20	(14,057)	29	(12,938)	38	(14,114)

Figure 20 (continued).

LATERAL POSITION

Left Lateral	Left Asymmetrical	Median	Right Asymmetrical	Right Lateral
12 (10,206)	34 (13,711)	31 (7667)	33 (14,570)	13 (13,084)
14 (13,541)		35 (13,166)		15 (13,207)
17 (8275)				16 (10,885)
19 (13,119)				18 (7831)
23 (12,743)				20 (14,057)
24 (11,020)				21 (12,784)
26 (8677)				22 (13,988)
27 (13,465)				25 (13,059)
36 (14,187)				28 (13,091)
37 (13,709)				29 (12,938)
38 (14,114)				30 (13,359)
				32 (12,290)

NOTCHES

12 (10,206): Left		23 (12,743): Left	
13 (13,084): Right		24 (11,020): Left	
14 (13,541): Left		26 (8677): Left	
15 (13,207): Right		27 (13,465): Left	
16 (10,885): Right		30 (13,359): Right	
17 (8275): Left		31 (7667): Right	
18 (7831): Right		32 (12,290): Right	
19 (13,119): Left		35 (13,166): Left	
20 (14,057): Right		36 (14,187): Left	
21 (12,784): Right		37 (13,709): Left	
22 (13,988): Right		38 (14,114): Left	

It is clear from the above, and from figures 18 and 19, that *most* truncation burins with an edge of 3 mm or less are included in the Noailles category, but it is also clear that there are exceptions. A few pieces plotted in figure 18 with edges of 3 mm or less are *not* Noailles burins, and some few examples in figure 19 with larger edges *are* Noailles burins. In the first group, the disqualification rests on stylistic criteria (or rather, it must be admitted, on our intuition of style); even though the burin edge is small and the blank sufficiently narrow, the overall character of the blank is unlike that of the undoubted Noailles burins. In the second group a few pieces are admitted on stylistic criteria and others because they form parts of double burins. Whereas the burin at one end is an undoubted Noailles burin, with a small burin edge and often a notch, the burin at the other end happens to have a wider edge, perhaps as a result of resharpening. In such circumstances, the whole piece is considered to belong in the Noailles category. It is perhaps unfortunate that such exceptions must be recognized, but it was stated above that the combination of maximum blank width and burin edge width provide an estimator, and an imperfect one at that. If the dimensions of variation which combine to make up the undeniably distinctive morphology of the Noailles burin blank, truncation shape, and various geometric relationships were to be more rigorously codified, it might then be possible to define attribute combinations that would provide better discrimination between Noailles and other truncation burins. But regardless of the theoretical possibility of developing such a discriminator, it is certain that it cannot be done in terms of the methods used here. The estimator employed in this study is generally useful, accounting for all but a small fraction of cases, and it distinguishes what we believe to be the most important characteristics of Noailles burins.

The low frequency of ordinary truncation burins in the LOWER subdivisions raises the question whether there are any burins in these samples manufactured by the truncation technique that are not in some way related to the Noailles type. With the exception of the pieces already mentioned from REAR:LOWER and isolated examples from

FRONT:LOWER having both blank width and edge width larger than among the Noailles burins, all the truncation burins in LOWER are either Noailles burins or could once have been Noailles burins, later reworked to a burin edge width that did not require the use of the notch technique. In the LOWER subdivision, the Noailles burin is the truncation burin norm.

In the MIDDLE (fig. 19) and UPPER subdivisions, the number of notched Noailles burins decreases and burins with wider edges and wider blanks are more frequent. Comparison of notched and unnotched sides of the graph still allows most pieces with burin edges of 2 mm and less to be classified as Noailles burins, but there is difficulty, particularly in the 3 mm class, in deciding whether particular burins are Noailles or other forms of truncation burin (e.g., fig. 21:3 is not a Noailles burin). The presence of tertiary modification (reduction of the size of the burin edge by striking off small chips from the burin facet onto the dorsal surface of the tool) accounts for the small width of burin edge of many of these pieces and may be taken to exclude them from the Noailles category (e.g., fig. 22:11, 15). Others are excluded on the grounds of blank thickness greater than that found on notched Noailles burins or because in other attributes they are more closely similar to the larger notchless truncation burins. There remain a very few pieces which must be classified on general stylistic grounds.

As a type, Noailles burins are not absolutely distinct from other truncation burins, partly because in manufacture they may lose their most characteristic feature and partly because this feature is optional. The fact that all truncation burins are classified in or out of the Noailles type does not imply that the types were emically separate in the minds of the makers, although it is justifiable and useful to create a Noailles type and to attribute burins to it.[3] It is the makers' structuring of the burin and other tool classes as revealed indirectly by typological analysis that gives qualitative information concerning cultural change, differentiation, and development.

Up to this point Noailles burins have been considered as if they were manufactured only on spall removal surfaces prepared by the truncation technique. This is not the case. Since it is the technique for the removal of the burin spall that is most characteristic of the type, there is no reason to limit the term ''Noailles'' to those burins made on a retouched truncation. In order to find out whether burins were made on spall removal surfaces other than truncations, the attributes of other techno-types must be taken into consideration, including:

The width of the burin edge. Break burin edges, for example, tend to be narrower than those of other SRS types and more similar in size to Noailles burins. Normal variations from the mean might therefore include pieces of Noailles size.

The presence of specifically Noailles features, including a notch associated with a small burin edge, or the association of the burin in question with a Noailles truncation burin.

In distinguishing Noailles burins made by other than the truncation technique, the most important criterion is similarity with Noailles truncation burins in other attributes. If the burin in question closely resembles a Noailles burin in all respects *save* the techno-type, it is considered to be a Noailles burin. Break burins made on small blanks but with wide burin edges and break burins with small edges made on large blanks unsuitable for the production of Noailles truncation burins are excluded from the series by this criterion. Both ends of mixed burins having a Noailles truncation burin at one end and a break burin at the other are considered to be Noailles burins. All break burins associated with demonstrably non-Noailles burins are excluded. Most break burins classed as Noailles burins have burin edges of 1 mm or less (e.g., fig. 13:30–37).

A similar approach was used to find Noailles burins made on retouched and unretouched edges and dihedral spall removal surfaces. (The distribution of Noailles burins made by other techniques is shown in table 16.) Breaks are the most common (e.g., fig. 14:17, 19, 20, 22, 23), followed by pieces on retouched edges (e.g., fig. 14:33). There is one Noailles dihedral burin (fig. 15:29) and one made on an unretouched end (fig. 16:12).

The nature of the phenomenon of Noailles burins is such that it is impossible to provide a clear-cut definition of the type. The special technique of manufacture that most clearly distinguishes the type is not applied to all blanks and cannot be shown to apply to all burins that on the evidence of other attributes were functionally identical. The normative defi-

---

3. The range of the Noailles burin type is treated here as more restricted than in David (1966), thus excluding marginal pieces from the type (e.g., fig. 20:1–7, 9). Direct comparison of frequencies is difficult because of slightly different samples, but the ratios between Noailles burins made on truncations and retouched edges and unmodified truncation and retouched edge burins have changed as follows:

		Noailles:Unmodified TB
UPPER	1966	1 : 2.59
	this volume	1 : 4.91
MIDDLE	1966	1 : 1.11
	this volume	1 : 1.37
LOWER	1966	1 : 0.11
	this volume	1 : 0.20

Since the reassignment of pieces was carried out by H. L. Movius, Jr., and H. M. Bricker, the variation between the statistics is a good indication of the variability in different archaeologists' assessments of the Noailles burin type range. My personal view is that the statistics on burin type frequencies given in this volume underestimate the number of Noailles burins and that the reassignment of pieces, unduly influenced by a Noailles stereotype, paid insufficient attention to the nature of variability within the various series. However, since putting pieces into labelled boxes is only, or should be only, a by-product of understanding of the nature of the underlying variability, the differences in the 1966 and present statistics are unimportant.

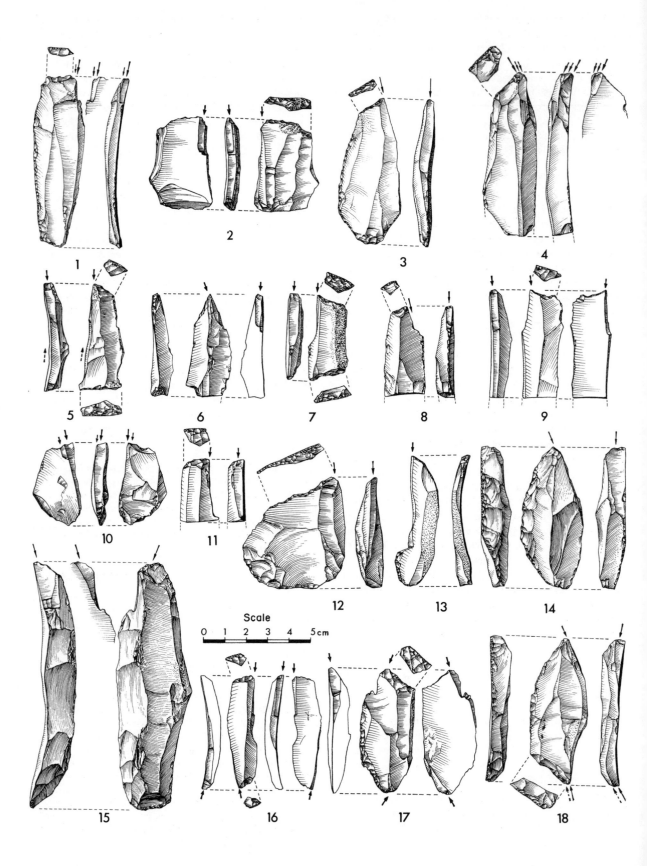

Scale

0 1 2 3 4 5 cm

Figure 21.   TRUNCATION AND OTHER BURINS FROM LEVEL 4: MIDDLE

TRUNCATION BURINS

SRS TYPE AND ANGLE

Retouched Truncation

```
 1  (9381):  MIDDLE-1:  80°
 2  (10,458):  MIDDLE-1:  60°
 3  (10,350):  MIDDLE-1:  70°
 4  (9573):  MIDDLE-1:  60°
 5  (7388):  MIDDLE-1:  60°
 6  (7085):  MIDLLE-1:  50°
 7  (9503):  MIDDLE-1:  60°
 8  (9488):  MIDDLE-1:  60°
 9  (10,156):  MIDDLE-1:  60°
10  (10,390):  MIDDLE-1:  50°
11  (9621):  MIDDLE-1:  80°
12  (9484):  MIDDLE-1:  70°
13  (7326):  MIDDLE-1:  60°
16  (9994):  MIDDLE-1:  B:  70°; C:  80°
17  (9809):  MIDDLE-1:  A:  70°; D:  60°
```

Retouched Edge

```
14  (10,121):  MIDDLE-2:  70°
18  (9468):  MIDDLE-1:  Distal
    extremity:  60°
```

BURIN EDGE SHAPE AND WIDTH

Straight

```
 1  (9381):  3 mm
 3  (10,350):  3 mm
 4  (9573):  4 mm
 5  (7388):  5 mm
 6  (7085):  3 mm
 7  (9503):  4 mm
 8  (9488):  4 mm
 9  (10,156):  4 mm
10  (10,390):  7 mm
16  (9994):  B and C:  4 mm
17  (9809):  A and D:  2 mm
18  (9468):  Distal extremity: 5 mm
```

Beveled

```
 2  (10,458):  6 mm
11  (9621):  6 mm
12  (9484):  3 mm
13  (7326):  4 mm
14  (10,121):  10 mm
```

OBLIQUITY

Lateral	Oblique	High Oblique
3 (10,350)	1 (9381)	10 (10,390)
4 (9573)	2 (10,458)	17 (9809):
7 (9503)	5 (7388)	Proximal
8 (9488)	6 (7085)	extremity
9 (10,156)	11 (9621)	
13 (7326)	12 (9484)	
14 (10,121)	16 (9994): B and C	
	17 (9809): Distal extremity	
	18 (9468): Distal extremity	

Figure 21 (continued).

SRS SHAPE

	Pronounced		
Concave	Concave	Convex	Straight
7 (9503)	10 (10,390)	11 (9621)	1 (9381)
8 (9488)		13 (7326)	2 (10,458)
9 (10,156)		14 (10,121)	3 (10,350)
12 (9484)		17 (9809):	4 (9573)
17 (9809):		Proximal	5 (7388)
Distal		extremity	6 (7085)
extremity			16 (9994): B
			and C
			18 (9468):
			Distal
			extremity

LATERAL POSITION

Left	Left		Right
Lateral	Asymmetrical	Median	Lateral
2 (10,458)	13 (7326)	3 (10,350)	1 (9381)
5 (7388)		4 (9573)	11 (9621)
7 (9503)		6 (7085)	12 (9484)
9 (10,156)		8 (9488)	16 (9994): B
		10 (10,390)	and C
		14 (10,121)	
		17 (9809): Both	
		extremities	
		18 (9468):	
		Distal	
		extremity	

BURIN-POINT

SRS TYPE

15 (10,104): MIDDLE-1: On
    retouched edge; Class 1

OBLIQUITY

Oblique

15 (10,104)

SRS SHAPE

Straight

15 (10,104)

LATERAL POSITION

Median

15 (10,104)

POINT ANGLE

15 (10,104): 65°

RIDGE ANGLE

15 (10,104): 55°

RIDGE LENGTH

15 (10,104):
    14 mm

Figure 21 (continued).

RAYSSE BURIN

SRS TYPE

18 (9468): MIDDLE-1: Proximal
    extremity: On retouched
    truncation

NUMBER OF REMOVALS

18 (9468): Proximal extremity: 1+1

FIRST REMOVAL

Lateral

18 (9468): Proximal extremity: 90°

LAST REMOVAL

High Oblique (140-150°)

18 (9468): Proximal extremity: 140°

SRS SHAPE

Concave

18 (9468): Proximal extremity

LATERAL POSITION

Left Lateral

18 (9468): Proximal extremity

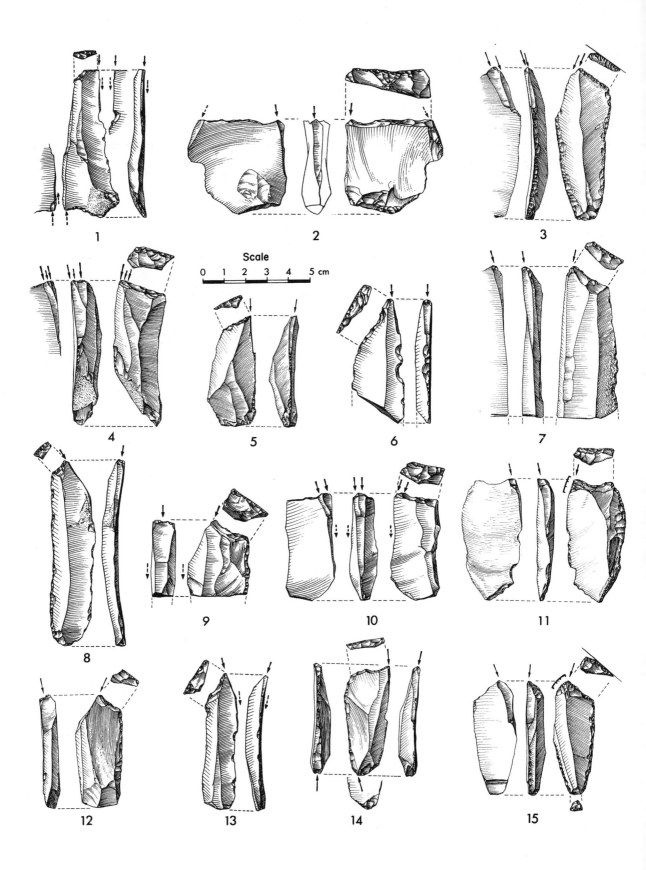

Scale

0 1 2 3 4 5 cm

1

2

3

4

5

6

7

8

9

10

11

12

13

14

15

Figure 22.   TRUNCATION BURINS FROM LEVEL 4: UPPER

SRS TYPE AND ANGLE

Retouched Truncation

```
 1  (6010):   UPPER-1a:   80°
 2  (7124):   UPPER-1:    60°
 3  (9009):   UPPER-1:    50°
 4  (9249):   UPPER-1:    80°
 5  (6741):   UPPER-2:    60°
 6  (7956):   UPPER-1a:   60°
 7  (8743):   UPPER-1:    70°
 8  (8314):   UPPER-1a:   70°
 9  (5661):   UPPER-1:    60°
10  (6098):   UPPER-1a:   70°
11  (8493):   UPPER-1:    80°
12  (7932):   UPPER-1a:   70°
13  (9084):   UPPER-2:    50°
14  (8444):   UPPER-1:    B:   70°;
    Proximal extremity:   80°
15  (9154):   UPPER-2:    60°
```

BURIN EDGE SHAPE AND WIDTH

Straight		Beveled	
1 (6010):	1 mm	12 (7932):	6 mm
2 (7124):	1 mm		
3 (9009):	5 mm		
4 (9249):	7 mm		
5 (6741):	2 mm		
6 (7956):	5 mm		
7 (8743):	3 mm		
8 (8314):	3 mm		
9 (5661):	11 mm		
10 (6098):	8 mm		
11 (8493):	4 mm		
13 (9084):	2 mm		
14 (8444):	B: 3 mm;		
Proximal extremity:	7 mm		
15 (9154):	2 mm		

Figure 22 (continued).

OBLIQUITY

Lateral	Oblique	High Oblique
5 (6741)	1 (6010)	3 (9009)
8 (8314)	2 (7124)	15 (9154)
9 (5661)	4 (9249)	
13 (9084)	6 (7956)	
	7 (8743)	
	10 (6098)	
	11 (8493)	
	12 (7932)	
	14 (8444): B	

SRS SHAPE

Concave	Pronounced Concave	Straight
6 (7956)	2 (7124)	1 (6010)
7 (8743)	8 (8314)	3 (9009)
10 (6098)	9 (5661)	4 (9249)
12 (7932)	11 (8493)	5 (6741)
13 (9084)	14 (8444): B	14 (8444): C
15 (9154)		

LATERAL POSITION

Left Lateral	Left Asymmetrical	Median	Right Asymmetrical	Right Lateral
2 (7124)	7 (8743)	3 (9009)	13 (9084)	1 (6010)
4 (9249)	9 (5661)	6 (7956)	14 (8444): C	5 (6741)
10 (6098)	11 (8493)	8 (8314)		14 (8444): B
		12 (7932)		
		15 (9154)		

ASSOCIATIONS

14 (8444): Double truncation burin

nition of Noailles burins given by de Sonneville-Bordes and Perrot (1956a, p. 412) is the best characterization of these tools and can be reduced to the form "burins which, on account of the small size of burin edge desired, were made, or were liable to be made, by a technique which included the use of a notch." The application of this definition must be in terms of the tools present in a particular sample.

Modified Truncation Burins (e.g., figs. 21:14, 17; 22:7, 11, 15; 23:6)
Burin-Points (figs. 24–26)
Raysse Burins (figs. 27; 28:1, 9, 10, 14; 29; 30; 39:11–17)

The distinctive burin types of the Noaillian manufactured with the use of tertiary modification have been defined and illustrated in a separate publication (Movius and David 1970). Only the briefest summary of their main characteristics is required here.

Tertiary modification ("tertiary" because it follows sequentially the two major processes of burin manufacture) consists of small removals struck from the burin spall scar onto the dorsal surface of the piece. It is sometimes used simply to thin the burin edge, usually on truncation burins. Such pieces are known as modified truncation burins. Tertiary modification of this sort is found also on retouched edge/end burins and infrequently on dihedral burins.

Tertiary modification is used also in the creation of two specialized forms of burin: (a) the burin-point; and (b) the Raysse burin. On burin-points, the tertiary retouch removals destroy the original chisel-like burin edge and create a point formed by the intersection of the ventral surface of the tool and a line of tertiary retouch that slopes down from the dorsal surface. Burin-points are most commonly either truncation or dihedral burins, but they are made also on retouched or unretouched edges or ends.

The Raysse burin is the most complex of all Noaillian forms. As in the case of burin-points, an original chisel-like edge is destroyed by the tertiary modification retouch. A complex resharpening process then creates a series of burin spall removals canted progressively onto the ventral surface, the last removal being usually high oblique or flat-faced. Raysse burins are usually made on truncations or retouched edges or ends, although some are dihedral or unretouched edge/end burins.

INTERRELATIONSHIPS OF BURIN TYPES IN THE NOAILLIAN

Raysse burins, even in their simplest form, are manufactured over a previous, usually lateral, burin, the edge of which has been obliterated by tertiary retouch. It is not necessary to suppose that the original burin was made only in preparation for a Raysse burin. Let us assume that the whole process of Raysse burin manufacture is evidence not of the

creation of a specialized and functionally different burin type, but *only* of a resharpening technique employed in order to make the most out of a single piece of flint. Three things are implied by this suggestion. First, the normal truncation burin is the primary form, both as a constructional idea and as a functional tool. Second, when the blank was too thick for the manufacture of a burin with a narrow edge or when by normal resharpening the burin was worked in toward the thickest part of the blank, compensating tertiary modification was applied to reduce the edge to the required width. Third, when it was no longer possible by simple resharpening blows to make a new burin on the same piece, the burin edge was obliterated and the piece was refashioned as a Raysse burin.

This hypothesis may be tested in several ways: in the study of the burins from the MIDDLE-1 and UPPER subdivisions, unmodified and modified truncation burins are compared in terms of their burin edges and other attributes. Raysse burins, the edges of which are impossible to delimit in a standardized and reproducible manner, cannot be compared directly in terms of the burin edge. A sample of Raysse burins with fresh, undamaged edges was measured, and the results give some support to this interpretation (see p. 141).

There is one further complexity that may serve to support the hypothesis. There exist among the truncation and retouched edge burins of the UPPER and MIDDLE subdivisions a small number of pieces which have passed through a Raysse burin stage and then have been remodeled as unmodified or even modified truncation burins. On these pieces, the process of Raysse burin reworking has continued to the point where the last removal was almost parallel to the ventral surface of the tool, rendering it impossible to recreate an angled intersection from which to strike another blow but at the same time thinning this part of the blank. The artificers reacted with typical ingenuity, and obliterating the flat-faced burin edge with tertiary retouch indistinguishable *in orientation* from that of the original truncation, returned to the edge of the piece and struck a lateral burin blow. Such "full circle" burins are naturally rare, since the Raysse burin process normally removes much of the side of the piece and precludes the striking of a later lateral blow (fig. 28:14, distal extremity).

Burin-points are technically similar to modified truncation and Raysse burins in that tertiary working is employed in their manufacture. Typologically, burin-points are divergent in that the tertiary retouch is applied to produce a pointed tool that is no longer a burin as the term is generally used. On the other hand, a burin-point is analogous to a Raysse burin at that stage in manufacture when the original burin edge has been removed but before the removal of the canted blows. Raysse burins exist which probably are burin-points converted by a burin blow struck at the point.

Noailles burins stand in a special relationship to the other truncation burin types. In the LOWER subdivision they make up 86% of all pieces manufactured by the truncation technique and must cover all or virtually all the functional range served by truncation burins. In the UPPER subdivision

Figure 23.   TRUNCATION BURINS FROM LEVEL 4: UPPER

SRS TYPE AND ANGLE

Retouched Truncation				Retouched Edge			
1	(6267):	UPPER-1:	70°	6	(11,743):	UPPER-2:	40°
2	(9311):	UPPER-1:	60°	8	(8746):	UPPER-1:	70°
3	(5827):	UPPER-1a:	60°				
4	(8662):	UPPER-1:	70°				
5	(6698):	UPPER-2:	60°				
7	(6001):	UPPER-1a:	70°				

BURIN EDGE SHAPE AND WIDTH

Straight			Beveled			Irregular	
2	(9311):	7 mm	3	(5827):	5 mm	1	(6267)
4	(8662):	4 mm	5	(6698):	5 mm		
6	(11,743):	3 mm	8	(8746):	5 mm		
7	(6001):	2 mm					

OBLIQUITY

Lateral		Oblique		High Oblique	
4	(8662)	2	(9311)	1	(6267)
8	(8746)	6	(11,743)	3	(5827)
		7	(6001)	5	(6698)

SRS SHAPE

Concave		Pronounced Concave		Convex		Straight	
1	(6267)	5	(6698)	2	(9311)	3	(5827)
				4	(8662)	6	(11,743)
						7	(6001)
						8	(8746)

LATERAL POSITION

Left Lateral		Left Asymmetrical		Median		Right Asymmetrical		Right Lateral	
5	(6698)	1	(6267)	4	(8662)	3	(5827)	2	(9311)
		8	(8746)			6	(11,743)	7	(6001)

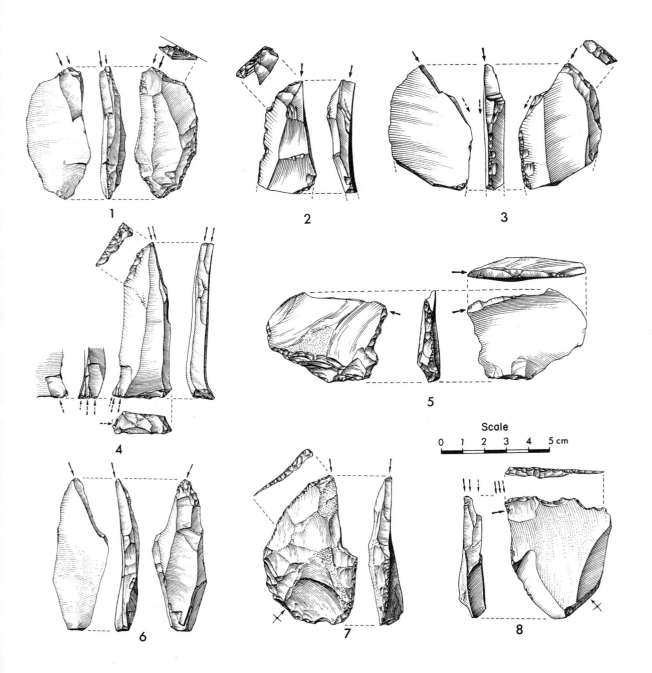

Scale

0　1　2　3　4　5 cm

1

2

3

4

5

6

7

8

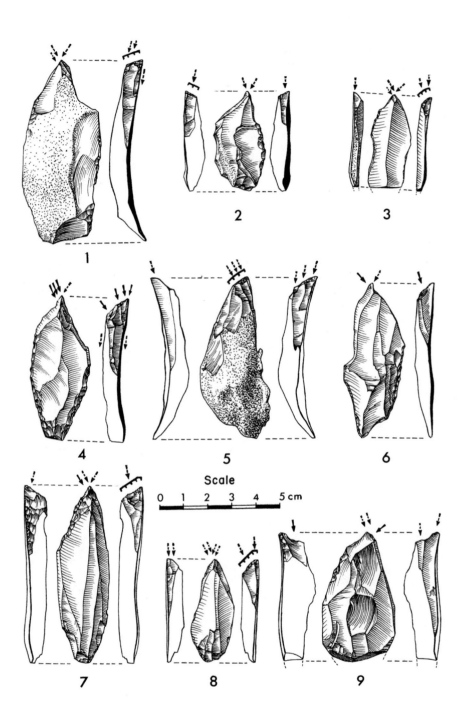

Scale

0 1 2 3 4 5 cm

Figure 24.   BURIN-POINTS FROM LEVEL 4: LOWER

SRS TYPE

1   (7504): LOWER-2: On dihedral; Class 1
2   (12,851): LOWER-1: On dihedral; Class 1
3   (14,696): LOWER-2: On dihedral; Class 2
4   (12,857): LOWER-1: On dihedral; Class 2
5   (10,798): LOWER-1: On dihedral; Class 3
6   (15,228): LOWER-1: On dihedral; Class 3
7   (14,269): LOWER-2: On dihedral; Class 4
8   (6858): LOWER-2a: On dihedral; Class 4
9   (13,631): LOWER-1: On retouched edge; Class 4

OBLIQUITY		SRS SHAPE	
Lateral	Oblique	Concave	Straight
2 (12,851)	1 (7504)	4 (12,857)	1 (7509)
3 (14,696)	9 (13,631)	9 (13,631)	2 (12,851)
4 (12,857)			3 (14,696)
5 (10,798)			5 (10,798)
6 (15,228)			6 (15,228)
7 (14,269)			7 (14,269)
8 (6858)			8 (6858)

LATERAL POSITION

Left Asymmetrical	Median	Right Asymmetrical	Right Lateral
6 (15,228)	1 (7504)	9 (13,631)	2 (12,851)
	3 (14,696)		5 (10,798)
	4 (12,857)		
	7 (14,264)		
	8 (6858)		

POINT ANGLE	RIDGE ANGLE	RIDGE LENGTH
1 (7504): 60°	1 (7504): 60°	1 (7504): 6 mm
2 (12,851): 35°	2 (12,851): 60°	2 (12,851): 5 mm
3 (14,696): 80°	3 (14,696): 65°	3 (13,696): 5 mm
4 (12,857): 55°	4 (12,857): 55°	4 (12,857): 10 mm
5 (10,798): 60°	5 (10,798): 65°	5 (10,798): 11 mm
6 (15,228): 50°	6 (15,228): 80°	6 (15,228): 7 mm
7 (14,269): 55°	7 (14,269): 90°	7 (14,269): 11 mm
8 (6858): 90°	8 (6858): 85°	8 (6858): 9 mm
9 (13,631): 70°	9 (13,631): 90°	9 (13,631): 12 mm

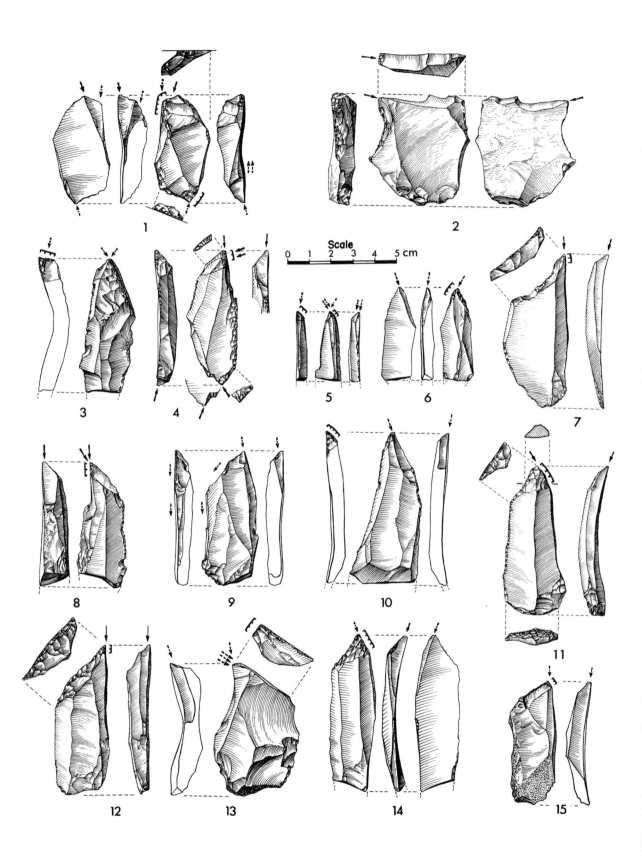

Scale
0 1 2 3 4 5 cm

1

2

3

4

5

6

7

8

9

10

11

12

13

14

15

Figure 25. BURIN-POINTS FROM LEVEL 4: MIDDLE

SRS TYPE

```
 1  (10,281):  MIDDLE-1:  Proximal extremity on retouched end; Class 4
 3  (10,447):  MIDDLE-1:  On unretouched edge; Class 1
 4  (9823):    MIDDLE-1:  Distal extremity on retouched truncation; Class 1
 5  (6580):    MIDDLE-2:  On dihedral; Class 1
 6  (7283):    MIDDLE-1:  On retouched truncation; Class 2
 7  (9789):    MIDDLE-1:  On retouched truncation; Class 2
 8  (9727):    MIDDLE-1:  On dihedral; Class 1
 9  (9848):    MIDDLE-1:  Retruncation technique; Class 3
10  (9846):    MIDDLE-1:  On retouched edge; Class 2
11  (7263):    MIDDLE-1:  On retouched truncation; Class 3
12  (10,394):  MIDDLE-1:  On retouched truncation; Class 3
13  (10,602):  MIDDLE-2:  On retouched end; Class 3
14  (9845):    MIDDLE-1:  On retouched truncation; Class 4
15  (10,187):  MIDDLE-1:  On dihedral; Class 4
```

OBLIQUITY

Lateral	Oblique	High Oblique
3 (10,447)	1 (10,281): D	6 (7283)
4 (9823): Distal extremity	8 (9727)	
5 (6580)	11 (7263)	
7 (9789)	13 (10,602)	
9 (9848)	15 (10,187)	
10 (9846)		
12 (10,394)		
14 (9845)		

SRS SHAPE

Concave	Pronounced Concave	Straight
1 (10,281): D	7 (9789)	3 (10,447)
11 (7263)		4 (9823): Distal extremity
12 (10,394)		5 (6580)
		6 (7283)
		8 (9727)
		10 (9846)
		13 (10,602)
		14 (9845)
		15 (10,187)

Figure 25 (continued).

LATERAL POSITION

Left Lateral	Left Asymmetrical	Median	Right Asymmetrical	Right Lateral
8 (9727)	1 (10,281):	3 (10,447)	4 (9823):	7 (9789)
13 (10,602)	D	5 (6580)	Distal	12 (10,394)
	10 (9846)	6 (7283)	extremity	14 (9845)
			9 (9848)	15 (10,187)
			11 (7263)	

POINT ANGLE	RIDGE ANGLE	RIDGE LENGTH
3 (10,447): 80°	3 (10,447): 70°	3 (10,447): 7 mm
4 (9823): Distal extremity: 75°	4 (9823): Distal extremity: 40°	4 (9823): Distal extremity: 10 mm
5 (6580): 60°	5 (6580): 60°	5 (6580): 5 mm
6 (7283): 40°	6 (7283): 60°	6 (7283): 6 mm
7 (9789): 50°	7 (9789): 70°	7 (9789): 5 mm
8 (9727): 50°	8 (9727): 90°	8 (9727): 11 mm
9 (9848): 70°	9 (9848): 90°	9 (9848): 5 mm
10 (9846): 50°	10 (9846): 55°	10 (9846): 6 mm
11 (7263): 85°	11 (7263): 85°	11 (7263): 12 mm
12 (10,394): 55°	12 (10,394): 60°	12 (10,394): 5 mm
13 (10,602): 65°	13 (10,602): 70°	13 (10,602): 6 mm
14 (9845): 65°	14 (9845): 90°	14 (9845): 11 mm
15 (10,187): 70°	15 (10,187): 90°	15 (10,187): 8 mm

RAYSEE BURIN

SRS TYPE

1 (10,281): MIDDLE-1: Distal extremity on retouched end

NUMBER OF REMOVALS

1 (10,281): 1+1

FIRST REMOVAL

Lateral

1 (10,281): 80°

LAST REMOVAL

Oblique

1 (10,281): 120°

SRS SHAPE

Convex

1 (10,281)

LATERAL POSITION

Left Asymmetrical

1 (10,281)

Figure 25 (continued).

BURINS

SRS TYPE AND ANGLE

Retouched Truncation

2 (10,434): MIDDLE-1: Distal
  extremity: 70°
4 (9823): Proximal extremity: 60°

OBLIQUITY

Lateral

2 (10,434)
4 (9823)

LATERAL POSITION

Left Asymmetrical

4 (9823)

BURIN EDGE SHAPE AND WIDTH

Straight   Beveled

2 (10,434):   4 (9823):
  5 mm   4 mm

SRS SHAPE

Pronounced
Concave   Straight

2 (10,434)   4 (9823)

Right Lateral

2 (10,434)

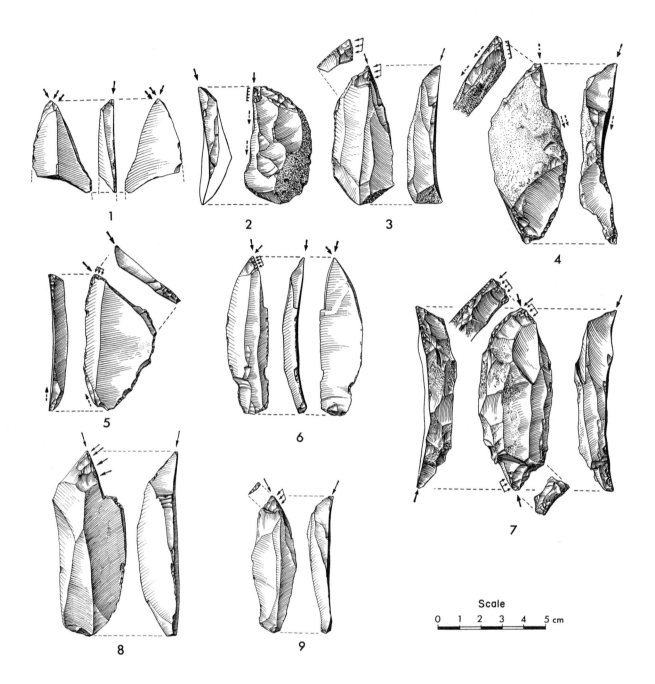

1

2

3

4

5

6

7

8

9

Scale

0 1 2 3 4 5 cm

Figure 26. BURIN-POINTS FROM LEVEL 4: UPPER

SRS TYPE

1 (5641): UPPER-1: On dihedral;
   Class 1
2 (4369): UPPER-1a: On retouched
   truncation; Class 1
3 (8948): UPPER-1: On retouched
   edge; Class 2
4 (8371): UPPER-1a: Retruncation
   technique; Class 2
5 (6810): UPPER-1: On retouched
   edge; Class 2
6 (6079): UPPER-2: On dihedral;
   Class 3
7 (11,748): UPPER-2: Distal
   extremity: On retouched edge;
   Class 1; Proximal extremity: On
   retouched truncation; Class 5
8 (6686): UPPER-2: On unretouched
   end; Class 4
9 (6000): UPPER-1a: On retouched
   truncation; Class 4

OBLIQUITY

Lateral		Oblique	
2	(4369)	1	(5641)
3	(8948)	5	(6810)
4	(8371)	6	(6079)
7	(11,748):	7	(11,748):
	Proximal		Distal
	extremity		extremity
8	(6686)		
9	(6000)		

SRS SHAPE

Concave		Straight	
3	(8948)	1	(5641)
7	(11,748): Proximal extremity	2	(4369)
		4	(8371)
		5	(6810)
		6	(6079)
		7	(11,748): Distal extremity
		8	(6686)
		9	(6000)

LATERAL POSITION

Left Lateral		Left Asymmetrical		Median	
5	(6810)	1	(5641)	2	(4369)
				3	(8948)
				4	(8371)
				6	(6079)
				7	(11,748): Both extremities
				8	(6686)
				9	(6000)

Figure 26 (continued).

POINT ANGLE	RIDGE ANGLE	RIDGE LENGTH
1 (5641): 80°	1 (5641): 50°	1 (5641): 8 mm
2 (4369): 90°	2 (4369): 55°	2 (4369): 11 mm
3 (8948): 55°	3 (8948): 50°	3 (8948): 13 mm
4 (8371): 55°	4 (8371): 70°	4 (8371): 11 mm
5 (6810): 75°	5 (6810): 50°	5 (6810): 9 mm
6 (6079): 65°	6 (6079): 55°	6 (6079): 11 mm
7 (11,748): Distal extremity: 85°; Proximal extremity: 90°	7 (11,748): B: 55°; C: 65°	7 (11,748): Distal extremity: 16 mm; Proximal extremity: 12 mm
8 (6686): 65°	8 (6686): 90°	8 (6686): 20 mm
9 (6000): 85°	9 (6000): 90°	9 (6000): 15 mm

Figure 27.   RAYSSE BURINS FROM LEVEL 4: MIDDLE

SRS TYPE

1 (9708): MIDDLE-1: On retouched edge
2 (7176): MIDDLE-1: On retouched edge
3 (9788): MIDDLE-1: On retouched truncation
4 (10,191): MIDDLE-1: On retouched edge
5 (9764): MIDDLE-1: On retouched truncation
6 (7237): MIDDLE-1: Both extremities on retouched truncations
7 (10,148): MIDDLE-1: Both extremities on retouched truncations
8 (9611): MIDDLE-1: Both extremities on retouched truncations
9 (9892): MIDDLE-1: Both extremities on retouched ends
10 (9471): MIDDLE-1: Both extremities on retouched truncations
11 (9912): MIDDLE-1: Upper extremity on retouched end; lower extremity on dihedral removal

NUMBER OF REMOVALS

1 (9708): 1+2
2 (7176): 1+2
3 (9788): 1+1
4 (10,191): 1+1
5 (9764): 1+3
6 (7237): Distal extremity: 1+1; Proximal extremity: 1+1
7 (10,148): Distal extremity: worked out; Proximal extremity: 1+3
8 (9611): Distal extremity: 1+2; Proximal extremity: 1+1
9 (9892): Distal extremity: 2+1; Proximal extremity: 2+2
10 (9471): Distal extremity: 1+3; Proximal extremity: 1+?
11 (9912): Distal extremity: 1+2; Proximal extremity: 1+3

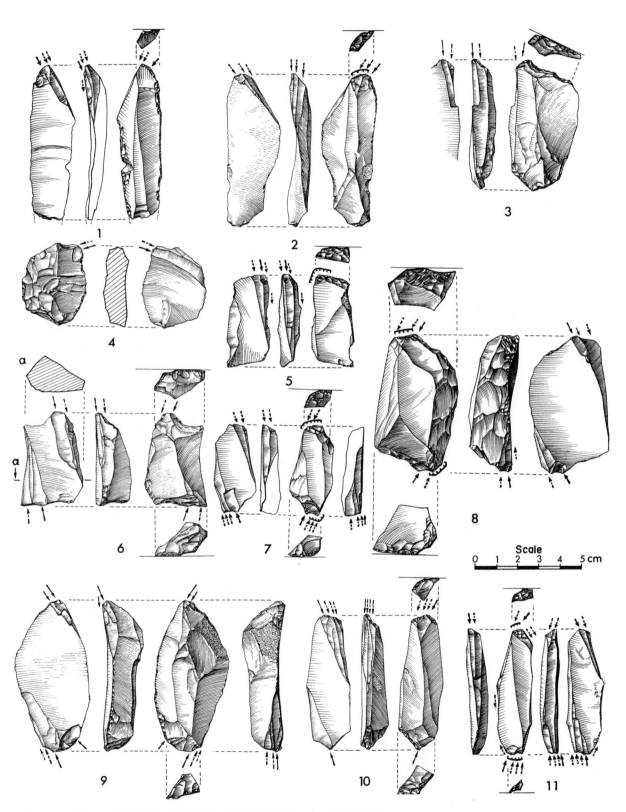

Figure 27.   RAYSSE BURINS FROM LEVEL 4: MIDDLE

Figure 27 (continued).

FIRST REMOVAL

Dorsal Oblique
(<80°)

 9 (9892): Proximal
     extremity: 70°
11 (9912): Distal
     extremity: 60°

Lateral
(80–100°)

 1 (9708): 90°
 2 (7176): 90°
 3 (9788): 90°
 6 (7237): Proximal
     extremity: 90°
 7 (10,148): Both
     extremities: 90°
 8 (9611): Both
     extremities: 90°
10 (9471): Distal
     extremity: 100°
11 (9912): Proximal
     extremity: 90°

Oblique
(110–130°)

4 (10,191): 110°
5 (9764): 110°
6 (7237): Distal
   extremity: 110°
9 (9892): Distal
   extremity: 120°

LAST REMOVAL

Oblique
(110–130°)

 9 (9892): Proximal
     extremity: 130°
11 (9912): Proximal
     extremity: 120°

High Oblique
(140–150°)

 6 (7237): Distal
     extremity: 150°
 7 (10,148): Proximal
     extremity: 140°
 8 (9611): Distal
     extremity: 150°;
     Proximal extremity:
     140°
 9 (9892): Distal
     extremity: 150°
11 (9912): Distal
     extremity: 150°

Flat-Faced
(160–180°)

 1 (9708): 160°
 2 (7176): 160°
 3 (9788): 160°
 4 (10,191): 170°
 5 (9764): 170°
 6 (7237): Proximal
     extremity: 160°
 7 (10,148): Distal
     extremity: 170°
10 (9471): Distal
     extremity: 170°

Figure 27 (continued).

SRS SHAPE

Pronounced Concave   Concave   Straight

6 (7237): Distal   3   (9788)   1   (9708)
   extremity   4   (10,191)   2   (7176)
                           6   (7237): Proximal   5   (9764)
                               extremity   9   (9892): Distal
                           7   (10,148): Both   extremity
                               extremities   10   (9471): Proximal
                           8   (9611): Both   extremity
                               extremities   11   (9912): Both
                                                          extremities

Convex

 9 (9892): Proximal
     extremity
10 (9471): Distal
     extremity

LATERAL POSITION

Left Lateral   Left Asymmetrical   Median

5   (9764)   7   (10,148): Both   1   (9708)
6   (7237): Both   extremities   3   (9788)
    extremities   8   (9611): Both   9   (9892): Both
                              extremities   extremities
                                                     10   (9471): Both
                                                          extremities

Right Asymmetrical   Right Lateral

 2 (7176)   4   (10,191)
11 (9912): Both
    extremities

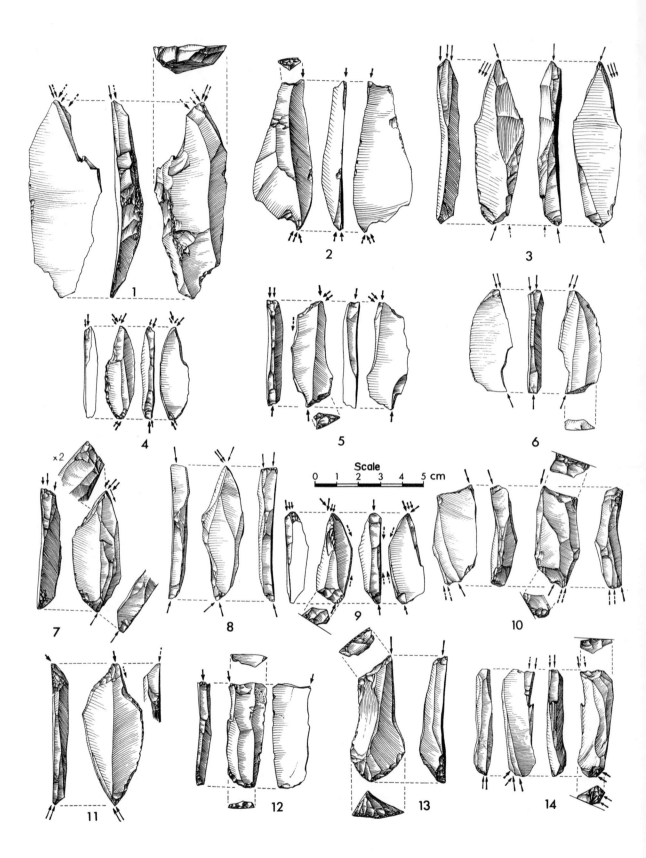

Scale
0 1 2 3 4 5 cm

1

2

3

4

5

6

7

8

9

10

11

12

13

14

×2

Figure 28.   BURINS FROM LEVEL 4: MIDDLE

RAYSSE BURINS

SRS TYPE   NUMBER OF REMOVALS

 1 (7183): MIDDLE-1: On dihedral   1 (7183): 1+4
 9 (9367): MIDDLE-1: Proximal extremity on   9 (9367): 1+4
    retouched truncation   10 (10,205): 1+2
10 (10,205): MIDDLE-1: Proximal extremity   14 (10,090): 1+1
    on retouched truncation
14 (10,090): MIDDLE-1: Proximal extremity
    on dihedral with truncation modification

FIRST REMOVAL

Dorsal Oblique (<80°)   Lateral (80-100°)

10 (10,205): Proximal   1 (7183): 100°
    extremity: 50°   9 (9367): Proximal
                        extremity: 90°
                  14 (10,090): Proximal
                        extremity: 80°

LAST REMOVAL

Oblique (110-130°)   High Oblique (140-150°)

 9 (9367): Proximal   1 (7183): 140°
    extremity: 130°   10 (10,205): Proximal
                        extremity: 140°
                  14 (10,090): Proximal
                        extremity: 140°

SRS SHAPE

Concave   Convex   Straight

 9 (9367): Proximal   14 (10,090): Proximal   1 (7183)
    extremity   extremity
10 (10,205): Proximal
    extremity

LATERAL POSITION

Left Lateral   Median   Right Asymmetrical

 9 (9367): Proximal   10 (10,205): Proximal   1 (7183)
    extremity   extremity
                  14 (10,090): Proximal
                        extremity

Figure 28 (continued).

BURINS

SRS TYPE AND ANGLE

Dihedral

2 (11,163): MIDDLE-1:
   Proximal extremity:
   60°
3 (10,087): MIDDLE-1:
   Distal extremity:
   70°
4 (9827): MIDDLE-1:
   Distal extremity:
   80°
5 (9392): MIDDLE-1:
   Distal extremity:
   80°
6 (9742): MIDDLE-1:
   Distal extremity:
   70°
7 (9558): MIDDLE-1:
   Distal extremity:
   70°
8 (7067): MIDDLE-1:
   Distal extremity:
   60°
9 (9367): MIDDLE-1:
   Distal extremity
   70°

Retouched
Truncation

5 (9392): MIDDLE-1:
   Proximal extremity:
   80°
7 (9558): MIDDLE-1:
   Proximal extremity:
   70°
10 (10,205): MIDDLE-1:
   Distal extremity:
   60°
13 (7059): MIDDLE-1:
   Distal extremity:
   60°
14 (10,090): MIDDLE-1:
   Distal extremity:
   70°

Break

6 (9742): MIDDLE-1:
   Proximal extremity:
   60°
12 (9668): MIDDLE-1:
   Distal extremity:
   60°

Retouched Edge

11 (7131): MIDDLE-1:
   Proximal extremity:
   70°

Retouched End

3 (10,087): MIDDLE-1:
   Proximal extremity:
   70°
4 (9827): MIDDLE-1:
   Proximal extremity:
   90°

Figure 28 (continued).

BURIN EDGE SHAPE AND WIDTH

Straight

3 (10,087): Distal
   extremity: 6 mm;
   Proximal extremity:
   3 mm
4 (9827): Distal
   extremity: 4 mm
5 (9392): Distal
   extremity: 5 mm;
   Proximal extremity:
   5 mm
6 (9742): Proximal
   extremity: 3 mm
7 (9558): Distal
   extremity: 6 mm
8 (7067): Distal
   extremity: 8 mm
12 (9668): Distal
   extremity: 4 mm
13 (7059): Distal
   extremity: 4 mm
14 (10,090): Distal
   extremity: 4 mm

Beveled

7 (9558): Proximal
   extremity: 4 mm
10 (10,205): Distal
   extremity: 8 mm
11 (7131): Proximal
   extremity: 2 mm

Angulated

2 (11,163): Proximal
   extremity: 5 mm
9 (9367): Distal
   extremity: 6 mm

Curved

6 (9742): Proximal
   extremity: 7 mm

Irregular

4 (9827): Proximal
   extremity: 4 mm

OBLIQUITY

Dorsal Oblique

12 (9668): Distal
   extremity

Lateral

3 (10,087): Distal
   extremity
4 (9827): Distal
   extremity
5 (9392): Proximal
   extremity
6 (9742): Proximal
   extremity
7 (9558): Both
   extremities
8 (7067): Distal
   extremity
10 (10,205): Distal
   extremity
11 (7131): Proximal
   extremity
13 (7059): Distal
   extremity
14 (10,090): Distal
   extremity

Oblique

3 (10,087): Proximal
   extremity
5 (9392): Distal
   extremity

Figure 28 (continued).

SRS SHAPE

Concave

 3 (10,087): Distal
   extremity
10 (10,205): Distal
   extremity
12 (9668): Distal
   extremity
13 (7059): Distal
   extremity
14 (10,090): Distal
   extremity

Straight

 2 (11,163): Proximal
   extremity
 3 (10,087): Proximal
   extremity
 4 (9827): Both
   extremities
 5 (9392): Both
   extremities
 6 (9742): Both
   extremities
 7 (9558): Both
   extremities
 8 (7067): Distal
   extremity
 9 (9367): Distal
   extremity
11 (7131): Proximal
   extremity

LATERAL POSITION

Left Lateral

10 (10,205): Distal
   extremity
12 (9668): Distal
   extremity
14 (10,090): Distal
   extremity

Left Asymmetrical

 2 (11,163): Proximal
   extremity
 6 (9742): Distal
   extremity
 9 (9367): Distal
   extremity

Median

 3 (10,087): Both
   extremities
 4 (9827): Both
   extremities
 7 (9558): Proximal
   extremity
 8 (7067): Distal
   extremity
11 (7131): Proximal
   extremity

Right Asymmetrical

 5 (9392): Both
   extremities
 6 (9742): Proximal
   extremity
 7 (9558): Distal
   extremity
13 (7059): Distal
   extremity

Figure 28 (continued).

NOAILLES BURIN

SRS TYPE AND ANGLE	BURIN EDGE SHAPE AND WIDTH	

Retouched Truncation

2 (11,163): MIDDLE-1:
Distal extremity:
70°

Straight

2 (11,163): Distal
extremity: 2 mm

OBLIQUITY   LATERAL POSITION   SRS SHAPE

Oblique   Right Lateral   Pronounced Concave

2 (11,163)   2 (11,163)   2 (11,163)

BURIN-POINTS

SRS TYPE   OBLIQUITY

8 (7067): MIDDLE-1:   Oblique
Proximal extremity
on dihedral; Class 2   8 (7067): Proximal
11 (7131): Distal   extremity
extremity: tip
broken (not studied)

SRS SHAPE   LATERAL POSITION

Straight   Median

8 (7067)   8 (7067)

POINT ANGLE   RIDGE ANGLE   RIDGE LENGTH

8 (7067): Proximal   8 (7067): Proximal   8 (7067): Proximal
extremity: 60°   extremity: 90°   extremity: 7 mm

ASSOCIATION (COMBINATION TOOL)

13 (7059): Proximal extremity: blunt point end-scraper; medium;
semi-convergent

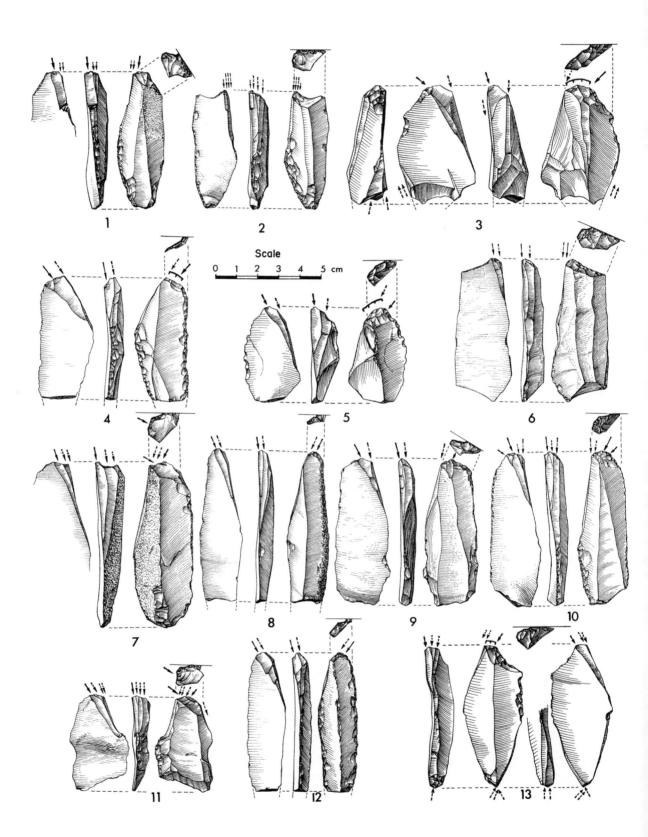

Scale

0 1 2 3 4 5 cm

Figure 29. RAYSSE BURINS FROM LEVEL 4: UPPER

SRS TYPE	NUMBER OF REMOVALS

SRS TYPE

1 (6355): UPPER-2: On retouched
   truncation
2 (6594): UPPER-2: On retouched
   truncation
3 (8921): UPPER-1: On retouched
   truncation
4 (8121): UPPER-1a: On retouched
   truncation
5 (8390): UPPER-1: On retouched
   truncation
6 (8907): UPPER-1: On retouched
   truncation
7 (7219): UPPER-2: On retouched edge
8 (8833): UPPER-2: On retouched end
9 (8047): UPPER-1a: On retouched
   truncation
10 (6329): UPPER-2: On retouched
    truncation
11 (4419): UPPER-1a: On dihedral with
    truncation modification
12 (5755): UPPER-2: On retouched edge
13 (8525): UPPER-1a: On retouched
    truncation

NUMBER OF REMOVALS

1   (6355): 1+2
2   (6594): 1+3
3   (8921): 1+1
4   (8121): 1+1
5   (8390): 1+1
6   (8907): 1+1
7   (7219): 1+2
8   (8833): 1+1
9   (8047): 1+1
10 (6329): 2+2
11 (4419): 1+3
12 (5755): 1+1
13 (8528): 1+2

FIRST REMOVAL

Dorsal Obliquity (<80°)

1   (6355): 70°
8   (8833): 50°
13 (8525): 60°

Lateral (80-100°)

2   (6594): 80°
3   (8921): 80°
4   (8121): 90°
5   (8390): 100°
6   (8907): 90°
7   (7219): 80°
9   (8047): 80°
10 (6329): 100°
11 (4419): 80°
12 (5755): 100°

LAST REMOVAL

Oblique (110-130°)

1 (6355): 130°
2 (6594): 130°
3 (8921): 130°
4 (8121): 130°
5 (8390): 130°

High Oblique (140-150°)

6   (8907): 140°
7   (7219): 140°
8   (8833): 140°
9   (8047): 150°
10 (6329): 150°
11 (4419): 150°
12 (5755): 150°
13 (8525): 150°

Figure 29 (continued).

SRS SHAPE

Pronounced Concave	Concave	Straight	Convex
2 (6594)	1 (6355)	4 (8121)	11 (4419)
13 (8525)	3 (8921)	7 (7219)	
	5 (8390)	8 (8833)	
	6 (8907)	9 (8047)	
		10 (6329)	
		12 (5755)	

LATERAL POSITION

Left Lateral	Left Asymmetrical	Median
7 (7219)	2 (6594)	1 (6355)
	6 (8907)	3 (8921)
	10 (6329)	4 (8121)
	11 (4419)	5 (8390)
	13 (8525)	8 (8833)
		9 (8047)
		12 (5755)

MISCELLANEOUS

13 (8525): UPPER-1a: Mixed burin: Distal extremity: Raysse burin;
      Proximal extremity: Dihedral burin; tip broken, not studied.

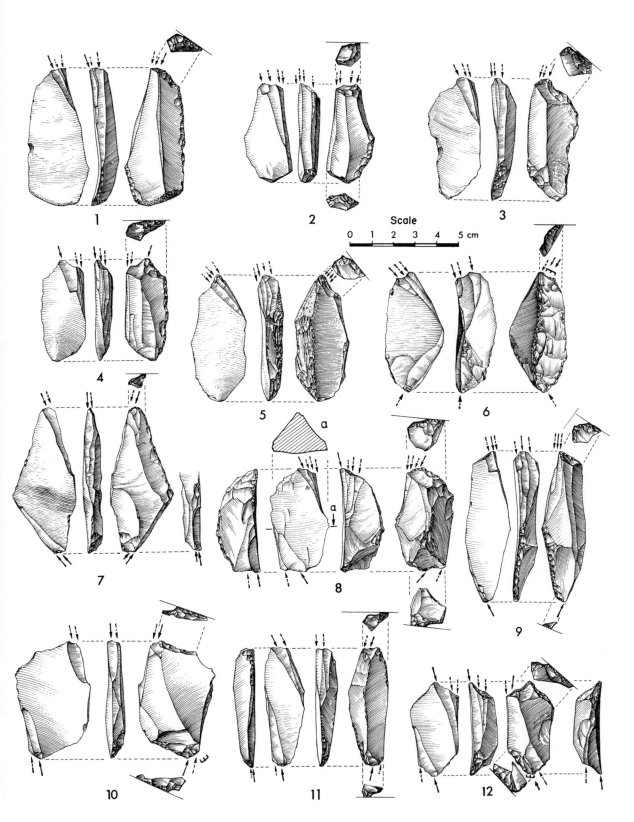

Scale

0 1 2 3 4 5 cm

Figure 30.   RAYSSE BURINS FROM LEVEL 4: UPPER

Figure 30.   RAYSSE BURINS FROM LEVEL 4: UPPER

SRS TYPE   NUMBER OF REMOVALS

1 (3814): UPPER-1a: On retouched   1   (3814): 1+2
   truncation   2   (5715): 1+3
2 (5715): UPPER-2: On retouched   3   (5612): 1+2
   truncation   4   (6913): 1+2
3 (5612): UPPER-1: On retouched   5   (6204): 1+3
   truncation   6   (8287): 1+2
4 (6913): UPPER-2: On retouched   7   (6540): Both extremities: 1+1
   truncation   8   (8852): Distal extremity: 1+3;
5 (6204): UPPER-1: On retouched   Proximal extremity: 1+1
   truncation   9   (4854): Distal extremity: 1+2
6 (8287): UPPER-1: On retouched   10   (8512): Both extremities: 1+1
   end   11   (8038): Both extremities: 1+1
7 (6540): UPPER-2: Double. Both   12   (8552): B: 1+2; C: 1+1
   extremities: Retouched end
8 (8852): UPPER-1: Double. Both
   extremities: Retouched truncation
9 (4854): UPPER-1: Distal
   extremity; on retouched truncation
10 (8512): UPPER-1a: Double. Both
   extremities: Retouched truncation
11 (8038): UPPER-1: Double. Both
   extremities: Retouched end
12 (8552): UPPER-1a: Double. Both
   extremities: Retouched truncation

FIRST REMOVAL

Dorsal Oblique (<80°)   Lateral (80-100°)

2 (5715): 50°   3   (5612): 100°
7 (5640): Distal extremity: 60°   5   (6204): 80°
8 (8852): Proximal extremity: 60°   6   (8287): 100°
                                          7   (6540): Proximal extremity: 90°
                                          8   (8852): Distal extremity: 90°
                                          9   (4854): Distal extremity: 80°
                                         10   (8512): A: 80°; D: 90°
                                         11   (8038): Distal extremity: 90°
                                         12   (8552): Distal extremity: 100°

Oblique (110-130°)

1 (3814): 110°
4 (6913): 110°
11 (8038): Proximal extremity: 110°
12 (8552): Proximal extremity: 110°

Figure 30 (continued).

LAST REMOVAL

Oblique (110-130°)   High Oblique (140-150°)

  7 (6540): Distal extremity: 120°   6 (8287): 150°
10 (8512): A and D: 130°   7 (6540): Proximal extremity: 140°
                                             8 (8852): Distal extremity: 140°
                                             9 (4854): Distal extremity: 150°
                                           11 (8038): A and D: 140°
                                           12 (8552): A and D: 150°

Flat-Faced (160-180°)

  1 (3814): 160°
  2 (5715): 160°
  3 (5612): 160°
  4 (6913): 160°
  5 (6204): 160°
  8 (8852): Proximal extremity: 160°
12 (8552): Proximal extremity: 160°

SRS SHAPE

Pronounced
Concave   Concave   Convex   Straight

  3 (5612)   4 (4913)   8 (8852): Both   1 (3814)
  5 (6204)   6 (8287)   extremities   2 (5715)
                 10 (8512): Distal   7 (6540): Both
                   extremity   extremities
                 12 (8552): Distal   9 (4854): Distal
                   extremity   extremity
                                                                    10 (8512): Proximal
                                                                      extremity
                                                                    11 (8038): Both
                                                                      extremities
                                                                    12 (8552): Proximal
                                                                      extremity

LATERAL POSITION

Left Lateral   Left Asymmetrical

  2 (5715)   3 (5612)
12 (8552): Distal extremity   4 (6913)
                                             8 (8852): Both extremities

Median   Right Asymmetrical

  1 (3814)   5 (6204)
  6 (8287)   7 (6540): Proximal extremity
  9 (4854): Distal extremity
10 (8512): Both extremities   Right Lateral
11 (8038): Both extremities
12 (8552): Proximal extremity   7 (6540): Distal extremity

Figure 30 (continued).

SRS TYPE, MODIFICATION, AND ANGLE   BURIN EDGE SHAPE AND WIDTH

Retouched Truncation   Straight

  9 (4854): UPPER-1: Proximal   9 (4854): Proximal extremity: 4 mm
    extremity: 70°

OBLIQUITY   SRS SHAPE

Oblique   Straight

  9 (4854): Proximal extremity   9 (4854): Proximal extremity

LATERAL POSITION

Median

  9 (4854): Proximal extremity

MISCELLANEOUS

  6 (8287): Attempt to manufacture Raysse burin at proximal extremity

---

they are much less important (8% of all truncation burins), and their place is taken by modified and unmodified truncation burins and by Raysse burins. The changes in frequency indicate a difference in the use of burins reflected in the width of the burin edge. Noailles burins survive into the later stages of the Noaillian in a subsidiary and complementary role as an alternative to burins with small burin edges produced by modification of other truncation forms.

With the exception of the Noailles burin, which stands apart, the varieties of truncation burins in the Noaillian are closely interrelated, so much so that it becomes useful to think in terms of individual burins passing through a cycle of manufacture. This progression is diagrammed in figure 31. It is not suggested that all burins passed through these stages or that it was necessary to pass through simpler forms to achieve a more specialized and developed stage. This certainly occurred, but it is not demanded by the model, which is a formula for the comprehension of the burins in terms of each other and an attempt at reconstructing the way in which the artificers themselves conceived of their truncation burins.

THE SERIATION OF LEVEL 4 BURINS

Types of burins peculiar to Level 4 have been defined without consideration of their stratigraphic provenience within the level. The vertical distribution of burins within the level is characterized by a development amounting almost to a replacement of certain types during the period of occupation. Study of the horizontal distribution of the artifacts does not constitute part of this study, but the changes in frequency in the LOWER subdivision between FRONT and REAR samples give some indication of the kind and extent of the

variation which may occur within a large occupation area.

The distribution of burins by type and techno-type is shown in table 16; the same data are presented in the form of a bar graph in figure 32. The main trends may be summarized as follows:

Noailles burins. These comprise almost two-thirds of the total burin series in the LOWER subdivision. In the MIDDLE-2 subdivision, they fall to 43%, and to 10% in MIDDLE-1. In the UPPER subdivision, the decrease continues, the proportions falling from 7% to 3%.

Unmodified and modified truncation burins and Raysse burins. Unmodified truncation (and retouched edge/end) burins are infrequent (11%) in the LOWER subdivision and are composed of miscellaneous pieces (probably including some redeposited from Level 5) and of burins which in the process of reworking have lost their Noailles characteristics. Their importance increases to 13% in the MIDDLE-2 subdivision and to 22% in MIDDLE-1, from which point their proportion remains fairly constant. In the MIDDLE-2 subdivision, modified truncation burins appear for the first time in significant proportions (5%). Raysse burins are present in insignificant numbers in LOWER and MIDDLE-2. In the MIDDLE-1 subdivision there is an increase of over 20% in the proportion of Raysse burins, much larger than the corresponding increase in the percentage of modified truncation burins. In the UPPER subdivision, the latter increase together with Raysse burins. The UPPER proportions by subdivision remain very constant, with 11–13% modified truncation burins and 28–32% Raysse burins.

Burin-points. In contrast to Noailles and Raysse burins,

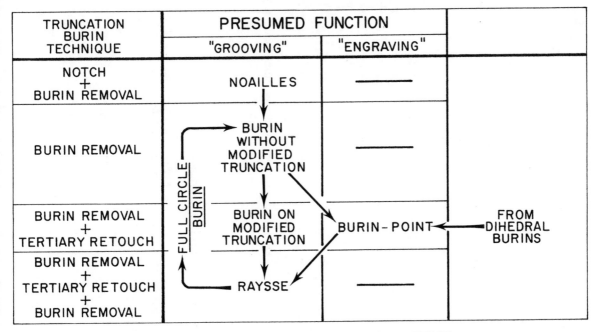

Figure 31.   INTERRELATIONS OF SOME NOAILLIAN BURIN TYPES.

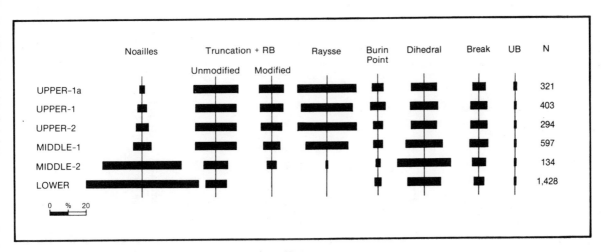

Figure 32.   SERIATION OF LEVEL 4 BURINS.

these form a more constant element in Level 4, appearing in every subdivision in proportions which vary only from 2% to 8%. It is the change from dihedral to truncation and retouched edge/end technique in MIDDLE-1 and later subdivisions that is of temporal significance.

Dihedral, break, and unretouched edge/end burins. Dihedral and break burins display a limited variation through time but show no major trends or sudden changes in frequency. In a later section we subject them to descriptive analysis. Unretouched edge/end burins are rarely employed in Level 4 and never form a significant proportion of the burins.

EARLY AND LATE NOAILLIAN

In the study of the end-scrapers from Level 4, it was seen that the MIDDLE and UPPER subdivisions of the level were distinct from the LOWER subdivision. This difference is of a similar order of magnitude as that between later Level 5 and Level 3. The burins confirm and refine this differentiation, allowing the point at which the differentiation occurs to be determined more accurately. The major change in proportions is between Noailles burins, on the one hand, and unmodified and modified truncation burins and Raysse burins on the other. The latter group is quantitatively small

Table 16

DISTRIBUTION BY SUBDIVISION OF VARIOUS KINDS OF BURIN IN LEVEL 4

		Noailles					Unmodified		Modified		Raysse				Burin-Points				Dihedral Burin		Break Burin	Unretouched Edge/End Burin	N
		TB	RB	BB	DB	UB	TB	RB	TB	RB	TB	RB	DB	UB	TB	RB	DB	UB	Modified	Unmodified			
UPPER-1a	n	9	-	-	-	-	57	14	31	8	60	31	5	2	10	3	5	-	3	38	21	5	302
	%			(9) 2.98			(71) 23.51		(39) 12.91		(98) 32.45				(18) 5.96				(41) 13.58		6.95	1.66	100.00
UPPER-1	n	18	1	-	-	1	64	25	40	10	86	23	2	-	9	15	7	-	5	56	36	2	400
	%			(20) 5.00			(89) 22.25		(50) 12.50		(111) 27.75				(31) 7.75				(61) 15.25		9.00	0.50	100.00
UPPER-2	n	18	-	2	-	-	46	20	23	10	68	25	2	-	6	3	5	2	3	38	26	3	300
	%			(20) 6.66			(66) 22.00		(33) 11.00		(95) 31.67				(16) 5.33				(41) 13.67		8.67	1.00	100.00
MIDDLE-1	n	54	2	3	1	-	100	29	38	14	99	34	7	-	13	6	7	1	7	114	61	9	599
	%			(60) 10.02			(129) 21.54		(52) 8.68		(140) 23.37				(27) 4.51				(121) 20.20		10.18	1.50	100.00
MIDDLE-2	n	50	-	4	-	-	10	6	6	-	-	-	-	1	1	1	1	-	2	34	9	1	126
	%			(54) 42.86			(16) 12.70		(6) 4.76		(1) 0.79				(3) 2.38				(36) 28.57		7.14	0.79	99.99
LOWER	n	821	12	59	-	-	128	37	-	1	1	2	2	-	1	4	39	1	2	265	75	16	1466
	%			(892) 60.84			(165) 11.25		(1) 0.07		(5) 0.34				(45) 3.07				(267) 18.21		5.12	1.09	99.99
Total																							3193

Note: Unlike most Palaeolithic archaeologists, the Noaillians were prepared to cross techno-type boundaries as blanks and tasks dictated, even though similar functions could normally best be performed by burins manufactured in the same way.

Abbreviations: TB = truncation burin; RB = burin on retouched edge; BB = break burin; DB = dihedral burin; UB = burin on unretouched edge.

Table 17

DISTRIBUTION BY SUBDIVISION OF VARIOUS KINDS OF BURIN IN LEVEL 4: LOWER

		Noailles			Unmodified		Modified		Raysse				Burin-Points				Dihedral Burin		Break Burin	Unretouched Edge/End Burin	N
		TB	RB	BB	TB	RB	TB	RB	TB	RB	DB	UB	TB	RB	DB	UB	Modified	Unmodified			
FRONT:LOWER-1	n	409	9	22	46	14	-	-	1	1	1	-	-	3	18	-	-	68	17	4	613
	%		(440) 71.78		(60) 9.79		-		(3) 0.49				(21) 3.43				(68) 11.09		2.77	0.65	100.00
FRONT:LOWER-2	n	311	1	27	38	7	-	-	-	1	1	-	-	-	14	1	1	101	34	8	545
	%		(399) 62.20		(45) 8.26		-		(2) 0.37				(15) 2.75				(102) 18.72		6.24	1.47	100.01
REAR	n	101	2	10	44	16	-	1	-	-	-	-	1	1	7	-	1	96	24	4	308
	%		(113) 36.69		(60) 9.48		(1) 0.32		-				(9) 2.92				(97) 31.49		7.79	1.30	99.99
Total																					1466

in the LOWER subdivision but somewhat larger in MIDDLE-2, where the Noailles burin is still dominant. In MIDDLE-1, by far the larger series, the changeover has taken place, and the industry has taken on a quite different complexion. It is at this point also that burin-points begin to be manufactured mainly on truncations and retouched edges.

On the basis of this evidence, the Noaillian might be subdivided into two or even three phases. In view of the small size of the MIDDLE-2 sample and the possibility of contamination, inevitable when two levels lie in direct contact, we consider it the safer course to restrict the breakdown into two phases: Early Noaillian, in which Noailles burins are dominant over other forms of truncation and retouched edge burins, and Late Noaillian, in which unmodified truncation burins and, in particular, Raysse burins dominate the burin assemblage, the Noailles burins remaining present but as a diminishing element. With evidence from other sites, it may be possible to subdivide the Early phase into Early and Middle phases, the Early characterized by the absence or near absence of Raysse and intermediate forms, and the Middle phase (represented at the Abri Pataud by the MIDDLE-2 subdivision) characterized by the presence of these forms in significant but not yet dominant quantities.

THE HORIZONTAL DISTRIBUTION OF BURINS AND ITS SIGNIFICANCE

It is not our intention to consider in detail the horizontal distribution of burins within the site, but only to show that in the LOWER subdivision there is a major difference in the proportions of burin types between the front and rear of the site. In table 17 the LOWER series is subdivided into FRONT:LOWER-1 and FRONT:LOWER-2 samples and a REAR sample that includes all the material attributable to the LOWER subdivision from the rear of the site. The REAR sample is distinguished from both FRONT samples by a lower proportion of Noailles burins and a higher percentage of dihedral burins. This tendency is visible also in the MIDDLE-2 subdivision, which, although it is mainly localized in the rear of the shelter, is the only other subdivision of the level to reach Square B. Mrs. H. L. Movius, Jr., has suggested that the anomaly may be simply explained by the fact that work with such delicate and minute tools required light. This suggestion is supported by the virtual absence of Noailles burins in Lens O-2, enclosed by the stone ring that may represent a hut. On the other hand, Noailles burins, admittedly for the most part somewhat larger, were used in the depths of the Grotte d'Isturitz (Basses-Pyrénées). The contrast in horizontal distribution of burins carries the implication that there was a tendency to discard these tools at their location of use and that they represent primary refuse.

The absence of MIDDLE-1 and UPPER deposits in the front of the site raises the possibility that the proportional decrease in Noailles burins in these levels may be simply attributed to this factor. While it is possible that there may be some exaggeration of the proportional shift, the propor-

tions of burins in Lens M-1a, which includes material slumped or washed down from on top of the Éboulis 4-5 rockfall, where we should expect Noailles burins to have been used, show no indication of this whatsoever. It is unlikely that there is any major distortion of the percentages on this account.

DESCRIPTIVE ANALYSIS OF LEVEL 4 BURINS

The description of the Level 4 burins is presented in tabular form and accompanied by a brief text. Where samples are very small, it has been necessary to group subdivisions. (Refer to Movius, David, Bricker, and Clay 1968, pp. 23–37, for definitions.)

A. Total studied burins

B. Attributes of studied burins

1. Nature of blank: Double burins (counted once) and mixed burins tabulated separately; combination tools excluded

Blade
Irregular blade   ⊢ Blade component
Trimming blade

Flake or blade
Flake   ⊢ Flake component
Trimming flake

2. Dimensions: Complete burins only. Double burins (counted once) and mixed burins tabulated separately; combination tools excluded

Length (mm): Mean ± standard error of mean
              Range
              Standard deviation

Width (mm): Mean ± standard error of mean
             Range
             Standard deviation

3. Burin edge

Shape: Straight
        Beveled
        Angulated
        Curved and rounded ⊢ Variously grouped in different tables
        Irregular

Width (mm): Mean ± standard error of mean
             Range
             Standard deviation

Angle: Mean ± standard error of mean
        Range
        Standard deviation

Obliquity: Dorsal oblique and lateral
            Oblique
            High oblique and flat-faced
            Complex

4. Lateral position

Left $\left\{\begin{array}{l}\text{Lateral}\\\text{Asymmetrical}\end{array}\right.$

Median

Right $\left\{\begin{array}{l}\text{Asymmetrical}\\\text{Lateral}\end{array}\right.$

5. Spall removal surface

Angle: Mean ± standard error of mean
      Range
      Standard deviation

Shape: Convex
       Straight
       Concave
       Pronounced concave

6. Burin association

Association pattern: On double burin

On mixed burin (differing techno-types)

On triple burin (may include differing techno-types)

On quadruple burin (may include differing techno-types)

Modal pattern of association (of live burin edges):
AB: Two burin edges at same end of blank
AC (=BD): Two burin edges on same side but opposite ends of blank
BC (=AD): Two burin edges on opposite sides and opposite ends of blank

Index of association:
I = Number of burins associated × 100/Number of pieces bearing burins

7. Marginal retouch: Double burins counted once; mixed burins and combination tools excluded

Index of marginal retouch:
I = Number of pieces with marginal retouch × 100/Number of pieces

Modal retouch type

8. Other attributes where applicable

Noailles Burins (figs. 12–15; 16:1–12; 20:12–38; 28:2; 33:13–15)

Noailles burins on truncations (table 18) are separated from Noailles burins made by other techniques. The Noailles burins on retouched edges and ends and on breaks from the LOWER subdivision are also presented in table 19 for comparison.

The smallest Noailles burins are from the FRONT:LOWER-2 subdivision; there are appreciable differences between the mean length of this sample and those of REAR:LOWER and FRONT:LOWER-1. It cannot be said how much the FRONT:LOWER-2/REAR:LOWER difference is the product of horizontal variation and how much it indicates that

the REAR:LOWER subdivision is chronologically later than FRONT:LOWER-2. The stratigraphic connection between the front and rear of the site is tenuous, and although REAR:LOWER should include material of the same age as FRONT:LOWER-2, it is quite possible that during the LOWER occupation material deposited early was thrown out slightly later toward the front of the site. If so, the FRONT:LOWER-2 series would represent the earliest Noaillian material at the Abri Pataud. A trend toward increasing size is clearly marked for Noailles burins forming part of double or mixed burins, as Noailles burins approximate more and more to small truncation burins and lose their distinctive character. Single Noailles burins, however, do not show such a regular trend of change through time even though mean length and width vary greatly from subdivision to subdivision. Blanks on which two or more burins appear are usually longer and sometimes wider than blanks bearing a single burin.

The burin edge shape is almost always straight, except in the UPPER subdivision where there is an increase in beveled edges. The width of the burin edge increases regularly through time. There is little change in burin angle from a mean of about 67°. Noailles burin edges may be lateral or oblique, with few high oblique specimens except in MIDDLE-1, where they reach 13%. In the MIDDLE and UPPER subdivisions, there is an increase in the proportion of median pieces paralleling a similar increase in other truncation types. In the UPPER subdivision, there also may be some preference for pieces with burin edge on the right, but this is of doubtful significance. The mean SRS angle shows a slight but regular decrease through time, from 72° in FRONT:LOWER-1 to 67° in UPPER. The SRS shape is always predominantly concave.

Noailles burins are frequently associated (indices in the 30s) but are rarely found on pieces with other burin types. They may, however, be associated with Noailles burins made by other techniques. There is one case of a Noailles burin associated with a Raysse burin (from the UPPER subdivision). Marginal retouch is rare but increases through time following the general trend. The proportion of Noailles burins with notches decreases irregularly through time. In LOWER, a majority of Noailles burins have a stop-notch, whereas in MIDDLE and UPPER the majority lack this feature. In spite of the possibility of differential loss of notch in the various subdivisions, this is a real phenomenon, fitting in with other data and suggesting that through time Noailles burins become not only less important quantitatively, but also less typologically distinct.

The sample of Noailles burins which are not truncation burins from the LOWER subdivision does not differ from the truncation Noailles series except in those characteristics which reflect technique of manufacture and SRS angle and shape.

For purposes of convenience in illustrating Noailles burins, they were divided into several classes based on the shape and angle of the SRS. Such a typological breakdown of Noailles burins was proposed by Tixier (1958), but the scheme used here differs somewhat from his. There are ten classes, as follows:

Class	SRS Angle (degrees)	SRS Shape
1	90	Straight
2a	80	Straight
2b	70	Straight
2c	60 or less	Straight
3	90	Concave
4	80 or 90	Concave, with small, abruptly upcurved projection ("horn") at corner of truncation adjacent to burin edge
5	80	Concave
6	70	Concave
7	60 or less	Concave
8	(any Noailles break burin)	

The distribution of Noailles burins by classes is shown for various subdivisions in table 20. Classes are so grouped as to control variation of SRS angle and SRS shape with maximum clarity. The slight differences in frequencies which exist between FRONT:LOWER and REAR:LOWER are not significant when tested by Chi-square ($0.5 > P > 0.25$). Certain frequency shifts through time visible in the table are also reflected in the fact that the mean SRS angle decreases slightly (i.e., becomes more oblique to the working axis) from LOWER to UPPER. The distribution by classes suggests that this change is most marked for burins with a concave SRS. Chi-square tests and analysis of variance have shown that in a given unit and in the level as a whole, Noailles burins with the lowest SRS angles tend to be made on longer blanks than pieces with the highest SRS angles. There are no significant differences among classes in width of the blank.

Figure 33. BURINS FROM LEVEL 4: LOWER

SRS TYPE AND ANGLE

Dihedral

6 (10,950): LOWER-2: Distal extremity: 80°
7 (13,822): LOWER-1: Distal extremity: 80°; Proximal extremity: 60°
8 (6864): LOWER-2a: Distal extremity: 60°; Proximal extremity: 70°
10 (6846): LOWER-1: Distal extremity: 60°; Proximal extremity: 70°
11 (10,831): LOWER-1: Proximal extremity: 80°
15 (13,483): LOWER-1: Proximal extremity: 70°
16 (6974): LOWER-2a: Distal extremity: 70°
17 (13,380): LOWER-1: Distal extremity: 50°
19 (8724): LOWER-2: Distal extremity: 60°

Retouched Truncation

5 (12,941): LOWER-1: A: 70°; C: 60°; D: 80°
6 (10,950): LOWER-2: D: 70°
9 (7471): LOWER-1: A: 60°
11 (10,831): LOWER-1: A: 70°
12 (12,894): LOWER-1: C: 70°
13 (13,377): LOWER-1: D (with dihedral modification): 80°
16 (6974): LOWER-2a: C: 80°

Break

1 (10,857): LOWER-2: 90°
2 (13,039): LOWER-2: 80°
3 (13,841b): LOWER-2: 60°
9 (7471): LOWER-1: C: 80°
12 (12,894): LOWER-1: A: 80°; B: 80°

Retouched Edge

18 (10,862): LOWER-2: A: 60°

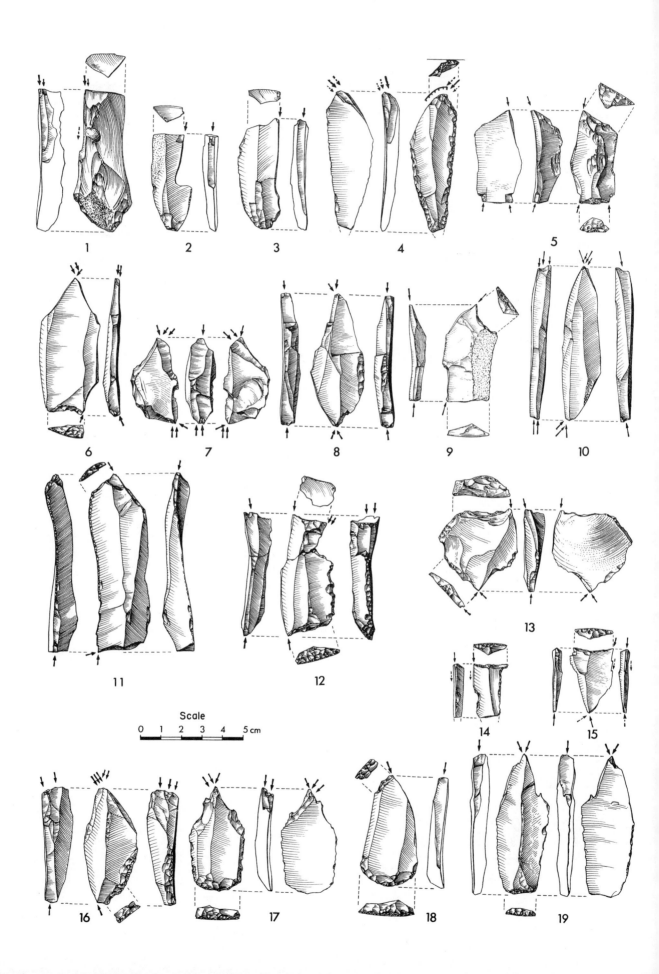

Scale

0   1   2   3   4   5 cm

Figure 33 (continued).

BURIN EDGE SHAPE AND WIDTH

Straight   Beveled

 1 (10,857): 5 mm   16 (6974): C: 7 mm
 2 (13,039): 3 mm
 3 (13,841b): 4 mm
 5 (12,941): A: 1 mm; C: 4 mm;
   D: 2 mm
 6 (10,950): Distal extremity: 2 mm
 8 (6864): A: 5 mm; C: 7 mm
 9 (7471): A: 1 mm; C: 1 mm
10 (6846): A: 5 mm; C: 6 mm
11 (10,831): A: 1 mm; C: 2 mm
12 (12,894): A: 6 mm; B: 7 mm;
   C: 2 mm
13 (13,377): D: 3 mm
15 (13,483): C: 2 mm
16 (6974): A: 13 mm
17 (13,380): A: 7 mm
18 (10,862): A: 5 mm

Angulated   Irregular

 7 (13,822): Distal extremity: 6 mm;   6 (10,950): D: 5 mm
   D: 5 mm
19 (8724): A: 7 mm

OBLIQUITY

Dorsal   Lateral   Oblique   Flat-Faced

9 (7471): C   2 (13,039)   1 (10,857)   5 (12,941): C
                    3 (13,841b)   5 (12,941): A
                    6 (10,950):   and D
                      Distal   10 (6846): C
                      extremity   13 (13,377): D
                    8 (6864): A   16 (6974): C
                      and C   17 (13,380): A
                    9 (7471): A   18 (10,862): A
                   10 (6846): A
                   11 (10,831): A
                      and C
                   12 (12,894): A,
                      B, and C
                   15 (13,483):
                      Proximal
                      extremity
                   16 (6974): A

Figure 33 (continued).

SRS SHAPE

Pronounced Concave	Concave	Straight	Convex
6 (10,950): D	3 (13,841b)	1 (10,857)	8 (6864): A
9 (7471): A	11 (10,831): A	2 (13,039)	
12 (12,894): C	12 (12,894): A and B	5 (12,941): A, C, and D	
	16 (6974): C	6 (10,950): Distal extremity	
		7 (13,822): Distal extremity: D	
		8 (6864): C	
		9 (7471): C	
		10 (6846): A and C	
		11 (10,831): C	
		13 (13,377): D	
		15 (13,483): B	
		16 (6974): A	
		17 (13,380): A	
		18 (10,862): A	
		19 (8724): A	

LATERAL POSITION

Left Lateral	Left Asymmetrical	Median	Right Asymmetrical
1 (10,857)	13 (13,377): D	6 (10,950): Distal extremity	7 (13,822)
5 (12,491): A and D	16 (6974): A	8 (6864): A and C	16 (6974): C
6 (10,950): D	18 (10,862): A	9 (7471): A	
7 (13,822): D		10 (6846): A	
12 (12,894): A		11 (10,831): A	
		13 (13,483): C	
		17 (13,380): A	
		19 (8724): A	

Right Lateral

2 (13,039)
3 (13,841b)
5 (12,941): C
9 (7471): C
10 (6846): C
11 (10,831): C
12 (12,894): B and C

Figure 33 (continued).

NOAILLES BURINS

SRS TYPE, ANGLE, AND CLASS   BURIN EDGE SHAPE AND WIDTH

Retouched Truncation   Straight

13 (13,377): LOWER-1: B: 60°;   13 (13,377): B: 3 mm
    Class 7   14 (12,748): A: 1 mm
14 (12,748): LOWER-1: A: 80°;   15 (13,483): B: 1 mm
    Class 3
15 (13,483): LOWER-1: B: 70°;
    Class 5

OBLIQUITY   SRS SHAPE

Oblique   High Oblique   Concave   Straight

14 (12,748): A 13 (13,377): B 14 (12,748): A 13 (13,377): B
                  15 (13,483): B 15 (13,483): B

LATERAL POSITION

Left   Right   Right
Lateral   Asymmetrical   Lateral

14 (12,748): A 13 (13,377): B 15 (13,483): B

NOTCHES

13 (13,377): Right
14 (12,748): Left

RAYSSE BURIN

SRS TYPE   NUMBER OF REMOVALS

 4 (12,291): LOWER-1: On retouched   4 (12,291): 1+2
    truncation

FIRST REMOVAL   LAST REMOVAL

Lateral   High Oblique

 4 (12,291): 90°   4 (12,291): 150°

SRS SHAPE   LATERAL POSITION

Pronounced Concave   Right Asymmetrical

 4 (12,291)   4 (12,291)

Figure 33 (continued).

MIXED TOOLS AND COMBINATION TOOLS

14 (12,748): LOWER-1: Noailles burin at A; *Bec* at B
15 (13,483): LOWER-1: Distal extremity: Noailles burin; Proximal
    extremity: Dihedral burin
17 (13,380): LOWER-1: Distal extremity: Dihedral burin; Proximal
    extremity: Arc-of-circle end-scraper; 80°; 1.75 cm; medium; non-
    convergent
18 (10,862): LOWER-2: Distal extremity: Burin on retouched edge;
    Proximal extremity: Arc-of-circle end-scraper; 120°; 1.50 cm; medium;
    non-convergent
19 (8724): LOWER-2: Distal extremity: Dihedral burin; Proximal extremity:
    Irregular end-scraper; steep; non-convergent

What this means is that Noailles burin users tended, when they had a suitable blank, to work it to the maximum unless the task was completed first. The high frequency of multiple Noailles burins is an obvious example of this; variation in SRS angle and concavity is another, more subtle, expression. On longer pieces, that is to say on blanks that in many cases might have been reburinated several times, a sharp burin edge is most easily achieved by creating a low-angle SRS. As the blank gets shorter with reworking, higher—that is to say more nearly perpendicular—SRS angles conserve flint and when combined with concavity of the truncation still permit sharp burin edges to be produced. The effects of such microeconomizing behavior can easily be read as stylistic in origin.

Unmodified and Modified Truncation and Retouched Edge/End Burins (figs. 16:1–12; 20:1–11; 21:1–14, 16–18; 22; 23; 28:3–5, 7, 10, 11, 14; 33:5, 6, 9, 11–13, 16; 34:3, 5)

Truncation and retouched edge/end techno-types, which can be readily distinguished in Levels 5 and 3, grade into each other in Level 4 and cannot be consistently and meaningfully separated. This gradation reflects both lower SRS angles and less steep retouch of the SRS (e.g., fig. 23:6). A common technique of SRS preparation is to block out the end with a few medium-angle blows and then to strike a series of very small, steep removals as finishing retouch (e.g., fig. 22:7). In the LOWER subdivision (which probably contains a few pieces from Level 5), the truncation/retouched edge distinction is clearer than in the later Level 4 subdivisions. They are considered together in all subdivisions (table 21) and are usually referred to in the text as simply modified or unmodified truncation burins. The MIDDLE-2 sample is too small for analysis.

Modified and unmodified truncation burins are generally manufactured on blades (always more than 70%), rarely on flakes. The proportion of modified truncation burins made on flakes is always greater than that of unmodified truncation burins. As in the case of end-scrapers, blades tend to be less parallel-sided and to have less regular dorsal ridge patterns than in later Level 5 or in Level 3, although there is a definite improvement in technique of production from Early to Late Noaillian. There is no patterned variation in mean blank size through time, but modified truncation burins tend to be slightly longer and wider than unmodified truncation burins. Largely as a result of less steep working of truncations, there is a higher proportion of beveled edges on unmodified truncation burins in Level 4 than in Level 3. Beveled edge frequencies for unmodified truncation burins are about the same as or slightly lower than those for truncation burins in later Level 5. The proportion of beveled edges on unmodified truncation burins shows a general but uneven increase through time. Within the same subdivision, modified truncation burins almost always have a much higher frequency of beveled edges than the unmodified truncation burins. This is an expected difference, because frequently the tertiary or previous tertiary modification removals create a beveled edge.

A major difference between modified and unmodified truncation burins appears in the width of the burin edge. The unmodified burins are rather consistently about 1 mm wider in mean width than the modified burins, with average readings of about 5 mm and 4 mm respectively. The mean edge widths of the unmodified truncation burins are approximately comparable to those of later Level 5 and Level 3, with all values (except the slightly lower one in Level 4: LOWER) falling between 4.72 and 5.64 mm. In burin angle, both forms are somewhat sharper than the truncation burins of later Level 5 and Level 3. There is very little change through time in Level 4, but modified truncation burins always have a somewhat duller mean angle than unmodified truncation burins. The modal obliquity class is usually oblique, with lateral (plus dorsal oblique) the next most frequent class. There are no regular trends of change through time, but there are frequency differences between the modified and unmodified forms. Modified truncation

Table 18

ATTRIBUTE SUMMARY BY SUBDIVISION FOR NOAILLES TRUNCATION BURINS IN LEVEL 4

	REAR:LOWER				FRONT:LOWER-2			
TOTAL BURINS STUDIED	101				311			
	Single		Double, Mixed		Single		Double, Mixed	
	n	%	n	%	n	%	n	%
NATURE OF BLANK								
Blade	64	88.89	16	(100.00)	179	89.95	60	96.77
Flake/Blade	7	9.72	–	–	13	6.53	1	1.61
Flake	1	1.39	–	–	7	3.52	1	1.61
n	72	100.00	16	(100.00)	199	100.00	62	99.99
LENGTH (mm)								
$\bar{X} \pm s_{\bar{X}}$	31.06 ± 0.59		37.38 ± 2.85		27.33 ± 0.77		27.34 ± 1.07	
Range	16–67		21–64		13–60		12–50	
s	3.56		11.40		7.73		8.45	
WIDTH (mm)								
$\bar{X} \pm s_{\bar{X}}$	16.03 ± 1.22		18.12 ± 1.41		14.99 ± 0.47		14.61 ± 0.48	
Range	6–33		7–28		4–29		8–23	
s	7.34		5.65		4.68		3.79	
n	36		16		101		62	

	All Burins		All Burins	
	n	%	n	%
EDGE SHAPE				
Straight and Beveled	100	99.01	309	99.36
Other	1	0.99	2	0.64
EDGE WIDTH (mm)				
$\bar{X} \pm s_{\bar{X}}$	1.41 ± 0.07		1.04 ± 0.02	
Range	0.5–4		0.5–3	
s	0.74		0.39	
BURIN ANGLE				
$\bar{X} \pm s_{\bar{X}}$	68.32 ± 1.01		67.62 ± 0.59	
Range	50–90		30–90	
s	10.11		10.36	
OBLIQUITY				
Dorsal Oblique and Lateral	51	50.50	148	47.59
Oblique	44	43.56	134	43.09
High Oblique and Flat-Faced	5	4.95	27	8.68
Complex	1	0.99	2	0.64

Table 18 (continued)

	REAR:LOWER		FRONT:LOWER-2	
	n	%	n	%
LATERAL POSITION				
Left	42	41.58	145	46.62
Median	6	5.94	18	5.79
Right	53	52.48	148	47.59
SRS ANGLE				
$\bar{X} \pm s_{\bar{x}}$	70.99 ± 1.16		71.99 ± 0.83	
Range	40-90		0-90	
s	11.62		14.57	
SRS SHAPE				
Convex	1	0.99	2	0.64
Straight	34	33.66	91	29.26
Concave	40	39.60	141	45.34
Pronounced Concave	26	25.74	77	24.76
ASSOCIATIONS				
On Double	20		92	
On Mixed	4		8	
On Triple	5		–	
On Quadruple	–		–	
Modal Pattern	AC		AC	
Index	32.95		38.31	
Index of Marginal Retouch	1.22		0.40	
NOTCH				
Single Notch	50	49.51	231	74.28
Sharing Notch	4	3.96	22	7.07
No Notch	47	46.53	58	18.65
Transverse	–	–	5	1.61

	FRONT:LOWER-1				MIDDLE-2			
TOTAL BURINS STUDIED	409				50			
	Single		Double, Mixed		Single		Double, Mixed	
	n	%	n	%	n	%	n	%
NATURE OF BLANK								
Blade	254	85.23	55	90.16	33	97.06	9	100.00
Flake/Blade	21	7.05	4	6.56	–	–	–	–
Flake	23	7.72	2	3.28	1	2.94	–	–
n	298	100.00	61	100.00	34	100.00	9	100.00

Table 18 (continued)

	FRONT:LOWER-1		MIDDLE-2	
	Single	Double, Mixed	Single	Double, Mixed
LENGTH (mm)				
$\bar{X} \pm s_{\bar{X}}$	34.08 ± 1.02	33.76 ± 1.39	28.85 ± 1.37	39.00 ± 5.39
Range	20-71	16-60	17-41	20-75
s	10.46	10.61	6.13	16.18
WIDTH (mm)				
$\bar{X} \pm s_{\bar{X}}$	19.58 ± 0.69	19.40 ± 0.81	14.90 ± 0.81	18.44 ± 3.14
Range	8-40	10-36	8-21	10-41
s	7.07	6.16	3.61	9.42
n	106	58	20	9

	All Burins		All Burins	
	n	%	n	%
EDGE SHAPE				
Straight and Beveled	408	99.76	50	100.00
Other	1	0.24	-	-

EDGE WIDTH (mm)		
$\bar{X} \pm s_{\bar{X}}$	1.23 ± 0.03	1.24 ± 0.11
Range	0.5-3	0.5-4
s	0.53	0.76

BURIN ANGLE		
$\bar{X} \pm s_{\bar{X}}$	67.38 ± 0.54	66.40 ± 1.42
Range	40-90	40-80
s	10.97	10.05

OBLIQUITY	n	%	n	%
Dorsal Oblique and Lateral	198	48.41	30	60.00
Oblique	176	43.03	16	32.00
High Oblique and Flat-Faced	34	8.31	4	8.00
Complex	1	0.27	-	-

LATERAL POSITION	n	%	n	%
Left	191	46.70	20	40.00
Median	22	5.38	4	8.00
Right	196	47.92	26	52.00

SRS ANGLE		
$\bar{X} \pm s_{\bar{X}}$	70.42 ± 0.69	68.40 ± 1.58
Range	0-90	30-90
s	13.90	11.15

Table 18 (continued)

	FRONT:LOWER-1		MIDDLE-2	
	n	%	n	%
SRS SHAPE				
Convex	1	0.24	–	–
Straight	123	30.07	15	30.00
Concave	169	41.32	23	46.00
Pronounced Concave	116	28.36	12	24.00
ASSOCIATIONS				
On Double	89		14	
On Mixed	11		2	
On Triple	3		–	
On Quadruple	–		–	
Modal Pattern	AC		AC and BC	
Index	28.69		37.21	
Index of Marginal Retouch	0.29		2.44	
NOTCH				
Single Notch	208	50.86	25	50.00
Sharing Notch	6	1.47	6	12.00
No Notch	195	47.68	19	38.00
Transverse	8	1.96	–	–

	MIDDLE-1				UPPER			
TOTAL BURINS STUDIED	54				45			
	Single		Double, Mixed		Single		Double, Mixed	
	n	%	n	%	n	%	n	%
NATURE OF BLANK								
Blade	33	(86.84)	10	(100.00)	25	(83.33)	10	(100.00)
Flake/Blade	1	(2.63)	–	–	3	(10.00)	–	–
Flake	4	(10.53)	–	–	2	(6.67)	–	–
n	38	(100.00)	10	(100.00)	30	(100.00)	10	(100.00)
LENGTH (mm)								
$\bar{X} \pm s_{\bar{X}}$	34.68 ± 2.72		41.90 ± 4.42		32.19 ± 1.88		41.80 ± 3.36	
Range	17–63		20–67		20–45		28–64	
s	11.88		13.97		7.53		10.63	
WIDTH (mm)								
$\bar{X} \pm s_{\bar{X}}$	18.95 ± 1.69		18.00 ± 2.21		18.69 ± 1.24		21.10 ± 1.79	
Range	5–34		6–30		11–30		11–30	
s	7.38		6.99		4.96		5.65	
n	19		10		16		10	

Table 18 (continued)

	MIDDLE-1 All Burins		UPPER All Burins	
	n	%	n	%
EDGE SHAPE				
Straight and Beveled	53	98.15	45	(100.00)
Other	1	1.85	–	–
EDGE WIDTH (mm)				
$\bar{X} \pm s_{\bar{X}}$	1.55 ± 0.11		1.68 ± 0.10	
Range	0.5–5		0.5–3	
s	0.80		0.64	
BURIN ANGLE				
$\bar{X} \pm s_{\bar{X}}$	66.11 ± 1.67		66.89 ± 1.14	
Range	30–90		50–80	
s	12.24		7.63	
OBLIQUITY				
Dorsal Oblique and Lateral	20	37.04	28	(62.22)
Oblique	26	48.15	14	(31.11)
High Oblique and Flat-Faced	7	12.96	3	(6.67)
Complex	1	1.85	–	–
LATERAL POSITION				
Left	27	50.00	14	(31.11)
Median	4	7.41	8	(17.78)
Right	23	42.59	23	(51.11)
SRS ANGLE				
$\bar{X} \pm s_{\bar{X}}$	68.33 ± 1.51		67.11 ± 2.03	
Range	40–90		30–90	
s	11.12		13.59	
SRS SHAPE				
Convex	–	–	–	–
Straight	8	14.81	12	(26.67)
Concave	27	50.00	21	(46.67)
Pronounced Concave	19	35.19	12	(26.67)
ASSOCIATIONS				
On Double	13		10	
On Mixed	3		4	
On Triple	–		–	
On Quadruple	–		–	
Modal Pattern	AD		AC and BC	
Index	33.33		35.00	
Index of Marginal Retouch	4.44		0.00	

Table 18 (continued)

	MIDDLE-1		UPPER	
	n	%	n	%
NOTCH				
Single Notch	21	38.89	19	(42.22)
Sharing Notch	-	-	-	-
No Notch	33	61.11	26	(57.78)
Transverse	2	3.70	1	2.22

Table 19

ATTRIBUTE SUMMARY FOR NOAILLES BREAK AND RETOUCHED EDGE/END BURINS
IN LEVEL 4: LOWER

LOWER

TOTAL BURINS STUDIED 71

	Single		Double, Mixed	
	n	%	n	%
NATURE OF BLANK				
Blade	34	(80.95)	23	(88.46)
Flake/Blade	4	(9.52)	2	(7.69)
Flake	4	(9.52)	1	(3.85)
n	42	(99.99)	26	(100.00)
LENGTH (mm)				
$\bar{X} \pm s_{\bar{X}}$		25.97 ± 1.56		30.44 ± 1.84
Range		19-41		16-58
s		6.41		9.22
WIDTH (mm)				
$\bar{X} \pm s_{\bar{X}}$		16.94 ± 0.92		16.32 ± 1.07
Range		11-22		7-28
s		3.78		5.34
n		17		25

	All Burins	
	n	%
EDGE SHAPE		
Straight and Beveled	71	100.00
Other	-	-
EDGE WIDTH (mm)		
$\bar{X} \pm s_{\bar{X}}$		1.13 ± 0.07
Range		0.5-3
s		0.59

Table 19 (continued)

	n	%
BURIN ANGLE		
$\bar{X} \pm s_{\bar{X}}$	70.56 ± 1.44	
Range	40–90	
s	12.18	
OBLIQUITY		
Dorsal Oblique and Lateral	41	57.75
Oblique	23	32.39
High Oblique and Flat-Faced	7	9.86
Complex	–	–
LATERAL POSITION		
Left	23	32.39
Median	10	14.08
Right	38	53.52
SRS ANGLE		
$\bar{X} \pm s_{\bar{X}}$	70.42 ± 2.64	
Range	10–90	
s	22.26	
SRS SHAPE		
Convex	1	1.41
Straight	52	73.24
Concave	15	21.13
Pronounced Concave	3	4.23
ASSOCIATIONS		
On Double	4	
On Mixed	23	
On Triple	2	
On Quadruple	–	
Modal Pattern	–	
Index	41.43	
Index of Marginal Retouch	2.22	
NOTCH		
Single Notch	41	57.75
Sharing Notch	2	2.82
No Notch	28	39.44
Transverse	3	4.23

Table 20
DISTRIBUTION OF NOAILLES BURIN CLASSES IN LEVEL 4

	REAR:LOWER		FRONT:LOWER		LOWER		MIDDLE		UPPER	
	n	%	n	%	n	%	n	%	n	%
1 + 2a	13	11.50	69	8.86	82	9.19	8	7.02	3	(6.12)
2b	13	11.50	57	7.32	70	7.85	5	4.39	4	(8.16)
2c	11	9.73	94	12.07	105	11.77	11	9.65	5	(10.20)
3 + 4 + 5	29	25.66	252	32.35	281	31.50	24	21.05	11	(22.45)
6	18	15.93	142	18.23	160	17.94	31	27.19	11	(22.45)
7	20	17.70	116	14.89	136	15.25	27	23.68	12	(24.49)
8	9	7.96	49	6.29	58	6.50	8[a]	7.02	3	(6.12)
	113	99.98	779	100.01	892	100.00	114	100.00	49	(99.99)

a. Includes one Noailles dihedral burin.

burins have fewer oblique edges and more high oblique and flat-faced edges than unmodified truncation burins. The dominance of oblique over lateral found in Level 4 is characteristic also of the truncation burins of later Level 5 and Level 3.

Median burin edges are much more common in Level 4 than in later Level 5 or Level 3, and there is an overall tendency among the unmodified truncation burins for the frequency of median pieces to increase through time (e.g., fig. 23:4). Unmodified truncation burins with burin edges on the right are always more common that those with burin edges on the left, with differences of almost 20% in some cases. Preference for right orientation is not, however, a consistent feature of modified truncation burins. The right orientation of unmodified truncation burins may reflect preference, but it is more likely to result from the absence from the unmodified series of many pieces with left orientation that were converted into Raysse burins (which in almost every case have the burin edge on the left). A left orientation is largely dominant among the truncation burins in later Level 5, but in Level 3 left and right orientation occur in approximately equal frequencies.

The SRS angle in Level 4 is much more oblique than in later Level 5 or Level 3, averaging usually between 50° and 55°. There are no consistent changes through time or differences between the modified and unmodified samples. The most common SRS shape is always straight; this is true also for the truncation burins of later Level 5 and Level 3, but the Level 4 frequencies of straight shape are usually greater than in the latter two. Simple concavity in Level 4 is usually about twice as frequent as pronounced concavity; in the other two levels, the frequencies of simple and pronounced concavity are more nearly balanced. The index of association is variable, but unmodified truncation burins have in all cases a higher index value than modified truncation burins. For the former, there is a marked increase in the index

value between the LOWER and the later subdivisions. The distinction between Early and Late Noaillian is seen also in the marginal retouch index: 8.89 in LOWER, increasing to 20.69 in UPPER-2 (unmodified sample). The index value for modified truncation burins is usually somewhat higher than that for the unmodified form. Throughout the level, scaled retouch is the dominant variety.

Although truncation burins in the LOWER subdivision differ in some attributes from the MIDDLE and UPPER series, the latter differ very little among themselves, and, with few exceptions, there is no clear evidence of directional change in burin attributes through time. There are some patterned and consistent differences between modified and unmodified truncation burins, the most important of which is surely the narrower burin edge of the modified examples. The distributions of modified and unmodified truncation burins overlap, and, although the technique of tertiary modification is used in some cases to make a particularly small burin edge comparable to that of a Noailles burin, its main function is simply to reduce the burin edge in order to render usable a burin edge that by the normal processes of resharpening would have become too large. The typological distinction of the two forms is important because the technique is almost entirely restricted to the Noaillian, but it need not signify functional differentiation.

Raysse Burins (figs. 16:11; 28:1, 9, 10, 14; 29; 30; 33:4; 34:1, 2, 8, 9; 39:11–17)

Raysse burins (table 22), like modified and unmodified truncation burins, are most often made on blades, but other kinds of blanks are also represented. Single Raysse burins are generally shorter and slightly narrower than other single truncation burins. Double and mixed Raysse burins have essentially the same dimensions as their modified and unmodified truncation burin counterparts. The burin angle and

Table 21
ATTRIBUTE SUMMARY BY SUBDIVISION
FOR TRUNCATION, RETOUCHED EDGE, AND RETOUCHED END BURINS IN LEVEL 4,
WITH MODIFIED AND UNMODIFIED BURINS TABULATED SEPARATELY
IN THE MIDDLE AND UPPER SUBDIVISIONS

	LOWER				MIDDLE-1: Modified			
TOTAL BURINS STUDIED	166				52			
	Single		Double, Mixed		Single		Double, Mixed	
	n	%	n	%	n	%	n	%
NATURE OF BLANK								
Blade	99	76.74	18	(75.00)	29	(79.38)	10	(83.33)
Flake/Blade	16	12.40	3	(12.50)	3	(8.11)	1	(8.33)
Flake	14	10.85	3	(12.50)	5	(13.51)	1	(8.33)
n	129	99.99	24	(100.00)	37	(100.00)	12	(99.99)
LENGTH (mm)								
$\bar{X} \pm s_{\bar{x}}$	56.49 ± 2.35		48.00 ± 2.64		59.75 ± 4.52		48.25 ± 0.73	
Range	32-111		28-83		33-105		39-61	
s	17.41		12.92		18.09		2.51	
WIDTH (mm)								
$\bar{X} \pm s_{\bar{x}}$	27.82 ± 1.11		24.87 ± 1.21		28.00 ± 2.34		21.83 ± 1.55	
Range	12-49		12-35		16-51		14-31	
s	8.24		5.92		9.36		5.38	
n	55		24		16		12	

	All Burins		All Burins	
	n	%	n	%
EDGE SHAPE				
Straight	127	74.70	29	55.77
Beveled	19	11.45	16	30.77
Other	23	13.86	7	13.46
EDGE WIDTH (mm)				
$\bar{X} \pm s_{\bar{x}}$	4.37 ± 0.22		4.56 ± 0.32	
Range	1-16		2-13	
s	2.88		2.32	
BURIN ANGLE				
$\bar{X} \pm s_{\bar{x}}$	68.37 ± 0.97		69.42 ± 1.56	
Range	40-90		40-90	
s	12.52		11.27	

Table 21 (continued)

	LOWER		MIDDLE-1: Modified	
	n	%	n	%
OBLIQUITY				
Dorsal Oblique and				
Lateral	64	38.55	16	30.77
Oblique	68	40.96	22	42.31
High Oblique	12	7.23	6	11.54
Flat-Faced	1	0.60	1	1.92
Complex	21	12.65	7	13.46
LATERAL POSITION				
Left	44	26.51	15	28.85
Median	54	32.53	20	38.46
Right	68	40.96	17	32.69
SRS ANGLE				
$\bar{X} \pm s_{\bar{X}}$	56.14 $\pm$ 1.61		50.58 $\pm$ 2.73	
Range	0–90		10–90	
s	20.76		19.75	
SRS SHAPE				
Convex	6	3.61	6	11.54
Straight	85	51.20	29	55.77
Concave	49	29.52	11	21.15
Pronounced Concave	26	15.66	6	11.54
ASSOCIATIONS				
On Double	8		8	
On Mixed	18		6	
On Triple	4		–	
On Quadruple	–		–	
Modal Pattern	AD and AC		AD	
Index	19.61		28.57	
MARGINAL RETOUCH				
Index	8.89		25.58	
Modal Style	Scaled		Scaled	
Transverse	3	1.81	1	1.92

Table 21 (continued)

	MIDDLE-1: Unmodified				UPPER-2: Modified			
TOTAL BURINS STUDIED	129				33			
	Single		Double, Mixed		Single		Double, Mixed	
	n	%	n	%	n	%	n	%
NATURE OF BLANK								
Blade	70	85.37	28	(75.68)	17	(70.83)	6	(85.71)
Flake/Blade	4	4.88	4	(10.81)	2	(8.33)	–	–
Flake	8	9.76	5	(13.51)	5	(20.83)	1	(14.29)
n	82	100.00	37	(100.00)	24	(99.99)	7	(100.00)

LENGTH (mm)

$\bar{X} \pm s_{\bar{X}}$	56.76 ± 3.03	51.57 ± 1.64	62.12 ± 5.98	a
Range	32–123	33–73	40–132
s	18.40	9.98	24.63

WIDTH (mm)

$\bar{X} \pm s_{\bar{X}}$	27.30 ± 1.33	25.00 ± 1.05	29.59 ± 1.84	a
Range	10–48	14–43	20–51
s	8.10	6.39	7.58
n	37	37	17	7

	All Burins		All Burins	
	n	%	n	%
EDGE SHAPE				
Straight	89	68.99	23	(69.70)
Beveled	28	21.71	7	(21.21)
Other	12	9.30	3	(9.09)

EDGE WIDTH (mm)

$\bar{X} \pm s_{\bar{X}}$	5.64 ± 0.22	4.21 ± 0.38
Range	1–14	1–12
s	2.47	2.18

BURIN ANGLE

$\bar{X} \pm s_{\bar{X}}$	66.59 ± 0.91	66.36 ± 2.26
Range	40–90	40–90
s	10.34	12.95

OBLIQUITY

Dorsal Oblique and				
Lateral	48	37.21	5	(15.15)
Oblique	58	44.96	17	(51.52)
High Oblique	12	9.30	8	(24.24)
Flat-Faced	–	–	1	(3.03)
Complex	11	8.53	2	(6.06)

a. No calculations made, as sample was too small.

Table 21 (continued)

	MIDDLE-1: Unmodified		UPPER-2: Modified	
	n	%	n	%
LATERAL POSITION				
Left	35	27.13	12	(36.36)
Median	36	27.91	12	(36.36)
Right	58	44.96	9	(27.27)
SRS ANGLE				
$\bar{X} \pm s_{\bar{x}}$	54.96 ± 1.87		52.12 ± 3.01	
Range	0–90		20–80	
s	21.29		12.95	
SRS SHAPE				
Convex	9	6.98	2	(6.06)
Straight	68	52.71	16	(48.48)
Concave	35	27.13	11	(33.33)
Pronounced Concave	17	13.18	4	(12.12)
ASSOCIATIONS				
On Double	20		5	
On Mixed	21		3	
On Triple	–		–	
On Quadruple	–		–	
Modal Pattern	–		–	
Index	34.45		25.81	
MARGINAL RETOUCH				
Index	18.37		17.86	
Modal Style	Scaled		Scaled	
Transverse	3	2.33	1	(3.03)

	UPPER-2: Unmodified				UPPER-1: Modified			
TOTAL BURINS STUDIED	66				50			
	Single		Double, Mixed		Single		Double, Mixed	
	n	%	n	%	n	%	n	%
NATURE OF BLANK								
Blade	38	(88.37)	15	(88.24)	34	(87.18)	9	(100.00)
Flake/Blade	1	(2.33)	1	(5.88)	1	(2.56)	–	–
Flake	4	(9.30)	1	(5.88)	4	(10.26)	–	–
n	43	(100.00)	17	(100.00)	39	(100.00)	9	(100.00)

Table 21 (continued)

	UPPER-2: Unmodified		UPPER-1: Modified	
	Single	Double, Mixed	Single	Double, Mixed
	n %	n %	n %	n %
LENGTH (mm)				
$\bar{X} \pm s_{\bar{X}}$	53.10 ± 3.01	51.88 ± 2.99	50.44 ± 1.86	a
Range	28–81	35–78	38–62	
s	13.46	12.43	7.45	
WIDTH (mm)				
$\bar{X} \pm s_{\bar{X}}$	27.85 ± 1.92	25.24 ± 1.52	31.00 ± 2.32	a
Range	17–47	16–40	23–50	
s	8.58	6.25	9.28	
n	20	17	16	9

	All Burins		All Burins	
	n %		n %	
EDGE SHAPE				
Straight	46 69.70		32 64.00	
Beveled	15 22.73		13 26.00	
Other	5 7.58		5 10.00	
EDGE WIDTH (mm)				
$\bar{X} \pm s_{\bar{X}}$	5.42 ± 0.37		4.32 ± 0.32	
Range	2–18		2–10	
s	3.03		2.25	
BURIN ANGLE				
$\bar{X} \pm s_{\bar{X}}$	64.24 ± 1.70		69.60 ± 1.74	
Range	30–90		40–90	
s	13.82		12.28	
OBLIQUITY				
Dorsal Oblique and Lateral	26 39.39		6 12.00	
Oblique	23 34.85		33 66.00	
High Oblique	9 13.64		6 12.00	
Flat-Faced	4 6.06		2 4.00	
Complex	4 6.06		3 6.00	
LATERAL POSITION				
Left	19 28.79		22 44.00	
Median	23 34.85		19 38.00	
Right	24 36.36		9 18.00	
SRS ANGLE				
$\bar{X} \pm s_{\bar{X}}$	52.12 ± 2.83		55.00 ± 2.97	
Range	0–90		0–90	
s	22.97		21.02	

Table 21 (continued)

	UPPER-2: Unmodified		UPPER-1: Modified	
	n	%	n	%
SRS SHAPE				
Convex	1	1.52	3	6.00
Straight	36	54.55	18	36.00
Concave	17	25.76	16	32.00
Pronounced Concave	12	18.18	13	26.00
ASSOCIATIONS				
On Double	8		4	
On Mixed	11		6	
On Triple	–		–	
On Quadruple	–		–	
Modal Pattern	–		–	
Index	31.67		20.83	
MARGINAL RETOUCH				
Index	20.41		30.95	
Modal Style	Scaled and Heavy		Scaled	
Transverse	5	7.58	1	2.00

	UPPER-1: Unmodified				UPPER-1a: Modified			
TOTAL BURINS STUDIED	89				39			
	Single		Double, Mixed		Single		Double, Mixed	
	n	%	n	%	n	%	n	%
NATURE OF BLANK								
Blade	53	92.98	24	(96.00)	19	(70.37)	7	(87.50)
Flake/Blade	3	5.26	–	–	2	(7.41)	1	(12.50)
Flake	1	1.75	1	(4.00)	6	(22.22)	–	–
n	57	99.99	25	(100.00)	27	(100.00)	8	(100.00)
LENGTH (mm)					a			
$\bar{X} \pm s_{\bar{X}}$	54.15 ± 2.74		51.20 ± 2.70					
Range	37–87		27–74					
s	12.26		13.49					
WIDTH (mm)					a			
$\bar{X} \pm s_{\bar{X}}$	26.70 ± 1.65		25.20 ± 1.22					
Range	19–45		15–39					
s	7.38		6.10					
n	20		25		9		8	

Table 21 (continued)

	UPPER-1: Unmodified All Burins		UPPER-1a: Modified All Burins	
	n	%	n	%
EDGE SHAPE				
Straight	65	73.03	20	(51.28)
Beveled	13	14.61	16	(41.03)
Other	11	12.36	3	(7.69)
EDGE WIDTH (mm)				
$\bar{X} \pm s_{\bar{x}}$	5.31 ± 0.27		5.15 ± 0.39	
Range	2–13		2–14	
s	2.53		2.43	
BURIN ANGLE				
$\bar{X} \pm s_{\bar{x}}$	67.87 ± 1.22		68.46 ± 1.86	
Range	40–90		40–90	
s	11.53		11.59	
OBLIQUITY				
Dorsal Oblique and Lateral	35	39.33	7	(17.95)
Oblique	35	39.33	21	(53.85)
High Oblique	7	7.87	8	(20.51)
Flat-Faced	5	5.62	–	–
Complex	7	7.87	3	(7.69)
LATERAL POSITION				
Left	18	20.22	7	(17.95)
Median	36	40.45	23	(58.97)
Right	35	39.33	9	(23.08)
SRS ANGLE				
$\bar{X} \pm s_{\bar{x}}$	51.69 ± 2.22		47.44 ± 2.64	
Range	0–90		0–80	
s	20.90		16.50	
SRS SHAPE				
Convex	7	7.87	1	(2.56)
Straight	46	51.69	22	(56.41)
Concave	25	28.09	13	(33.33)
Pronounced Concave	11	12.36	3	(7.69)
ASSOCIATIONS				
On Double	11		5	
On Mixed	17		4	
On Triple	–		–	
On Quadruple	–		–	
Modal Pattern	BC		–	
Index	34.15		25.71	

Table 21 (continued)

	UPPER-1: Unmodified	UPPER-1a: Modified
MARGINAL RETOUCH		
Index	16.92	25.81
Modal Style	Scaled	Scaled
Transverse	2 2.25	– –

UPPER-1a: Unmodified

TOTAL BURINS STUDIED   71

	Single		Double, Mixed	
	n	%	n	%
NATURE OF BLANK				
Blade	42	(87.50)	17	(94.44)
Flake/Blade	1	(2.08)	–	–
Flake	5	(10.42)	1	(5.56)
n	48	(100.00)	18	(100.00)

LENGTH (mm)		
$\bar{X} \pm s_{\bar{X}}$	57.90 ± 2.87	50.44 ± 2.55
Range	41–83	35–69
s	13.16	10.81

WIDTH (mm)		
$\bar{X} \pm s_{\bar{X}}$	28.62 ± 1.93	24.94 ± 1.65
Range	16–48	16–36
s	8.83	7.01
n	21	18

	All Burins	
	n	%
EDGE SHAPE		
Straight	45	63.38
Beveled	20	28.17
Other	6	8.45

EDGE WIDTH (mm)	
$\bar{X} \pm s_{\bar{X}}$	4.72 ± 0.26
Range	1–11
s	2.15

BURIN ANGLE	
$\bar{X} \pm s_{\bar{X}}$	66.90 ± 1.37
Range	40–90
s	11.54

Table 21 (continued)

	UPPER-1a: Unmodified	
	n	%
OBLIQUITY		
Dorsal Oblique and		
Lateral	19	26.76
Oblique	40	56.34
High Oblique	8	11.27
Flat-Faced	1	1.41
Complex	3	4.23
LATERAL POSITION		
Left	17	23.94
Median	31	43.66
Right	23	32.39
SRS ANGLE		
$\bar{X} \pm s_{\bar{X}}$	54.23 ± 2.45	
Range	0-90	
s	20.68	
SRS SHAPE		
Convex	7	9.86
Straight	28	39.44
Concave	27	38.03
Pronounced Concave	9	12.68
ASSOCIATIONS		
On Double	14	
On Mixed	8	
On Triple	—	
On Quadruple	—	
Modal Pattern	AC	
Index	33.33	
MARGINAL RETOUCH		
Index	20.69	
Modal Style	Scaled	
Transverse	—	—

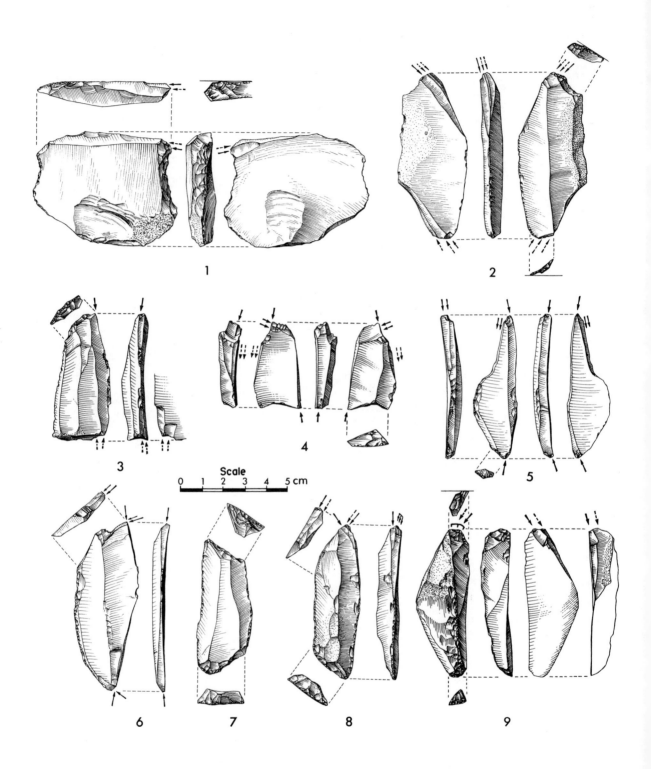

Scale
0 1 2 3 4 5 cm

Figure 34.   BURINS FROM LEVEL 4: UPPER

SRS TYPE AND ANGLE

Dihedral

  4 (7580): UPPER-1a: Distal
     extremity: 80°
  5 (8150): UPPER-2: Distal
     extremity: 60°

Break

  4 (7580): UPPER-1a: Proximal
     extremity: C: 60°

Retouched Truncation

  3 (9148): UPPER-2: Proximal
     extremity: B: 70°

Retouched Edge

  5 (8150): UPPER-2: Proximal
     extremity: D: 70°

BURIN EDGE SHAPE AND WIDTH

Straight

  3 (9148): B: 3 mm
  4 (7580): Both extremities: A:
  7 mm; D: 3 mm
  5 (8150): Proximal extremity: 3 mm

Angulated

  5 (8150): Distal extremity: 7 mm

OBLIQUITY

Lateral

  3 (9148)
  4 (7580): Distal extremity

Oblique

  4 (7580): Proximal extremity
  5 (8150): Both extremities

SRS SHAPE

Pronounced Concave

  4 (7580): Proximal extremity

Straight

  4 (7580): Distal extremity
  5 (8150): Both extremities

Convex

  3 (9148)

LATERAL POSITION

Left Asymmetrical

  5 (8150): Proximal extremity

Median

  4 (7580): Distal extremity
  5 (8150): Distal extremity

Right Lateral

  3 (9148)
  4 (7580): Proximal extremity

Figure 34 (continued).

RAYSSE BURINS

SRS TYPE

1 (8849): UPPER-1: On retouched
   truncation
2 (6489): UPPER-1a: Distal
   extremity: On retouched edge;
   Proximal extremity: On retouched
   truncation
8 (6634): UPPER-1a: Distal
   extremity: On dihedral
9 (8069): UPPER-2: Distal
   extremity: On retouched edge

NUMBER OF REMOVALS

1 (8849): 1+1
2 (6489): A: 1+2; D: 1+2
8 (6634): 1+1
9 (8069): 1+1

FIRST REMOVAL

Lateral (80-100°)

9 (8069): 100°

Oblique (110-130°)

1 (8849): 110°
2 (6489): Both extremities: 110°
8 (6634): 110°

LAST REMOVAL

Oblique
(110-130°)

8 (6634): 130°

High Oblique
(140-150°)

2 (6489): Distal extremity: 140°;
   Proximal extremity: 150°
9 (8069): B: 140°

Flat-Faced
(160-180°)

1 (8849): 160°

SRS SHAPE

Pronounced Concave

1 (8849)
2 (6489): Proximal extremity

Straight

2 (6489): Distal extremity
8 (6634)
9 (8069)

LATERAL POSITION

Left Lateral

1 (8849)

Median

2 (6489): Proximal extremity
8 (6634)
9 (8069)

Left Asymmetrical

2 (6489): Distal extremity

Figure 34 (continued).

MIXED BURINS AND COMBINATION TOOLS

6 (6742): UPPER-2: Distal extremity: Burin point on dihedral removal;
   Class 4; point: 80°; ridge: 90°; ridge length: 5 mm; oblique; lateral
   position: median. Proximal extremity: Dihedral burin; 80°; lateral
   position: median; SRS shape: straight; edge shape: curved; 4 mm.

7 (8847): UPPER-1: Distal extremity: Slightly concave/oblique
   truncation; 60°; right. Proximal extremity: Blunt point end-scraper;
   retouch angle: medium; non-convergent.

8 (6634): UPPER-1a: Distal extremity: Raysse burin on angle of dihedral
   removal. Proximal extremity: Retouched truncation; 50°; oblique;
   right.

9 (8069): UPPER-2: Distal extremity: Raysse burin on angle of retouched
   edge. Proximal extremity: Arc-of-circle end-scraper; 140°; 0.5 cm;
   medium; semi-convergent.

the shape and width of the burin edge[4] cannot be measured accurately, the burin edge often being difficult to define since crushing and damage received in use is not distinguishable in every case from modifying retouch. A sample of 50 pieces was measured on which the edges were fresh and undamaged; this gave:

Burin angle	Mean 57°; mode 60°
Burin edge width	Mean 2.5 mm; mode 2 mm; range 1–5 mm

But by taking only fresh specimens on which burin angle and edge width can be measured, the angle appears sharper and the edge narrower than on other burins. In both attributes Raysse burins are more similar to modified truncation burins than is apparent from these statistics. The shape of the fresh edge varies from the straight to a slightly convex form. Two pieces in the measured sample exhibited burin edges worked almost to a point by retouch following the burin blow; the angulated variant is also found.

The distribution of Raysse burins by the obliquity of the most ventrally canted spall scar distinguishes them from all other burin types. Between 50% and 60% are high oblique, and there are between 15% and 20% flat-faced pieces. Lateral pieces are lacking entirely. Earlier removals on the piece may be oblique, lateral, or even dorsal oblique, whence the term "burin d'angle et double plan" (Pradel 1965). The classes of Raysse burins refer to the degree of obliquity of the most ventral removal. For this purpose, the most frequent class is divided into "high oblique" (obliquity angle of ca. 140°) and "very high oblique" (obliquity angle of ca. 150°).

For an unknown reason, but with rare exceptions, the SRS of Raysse burins is on the right. The burin edge is therefore most often left or median, but there are some pieces in each sample (20% or less) on which the burin edge has been worked completely across the working axis of the tool to the right side (fig. 30:2). The SRS in these cases has been almost worked away. A count of the frequency of reworking on a sample of 150 pieces from the UPPER subdivision showed that after first manufacture as a Raysse burin:

46 pieces were not reworked

72 pieces were reworked once

26 pieces were reworked twice

6 pieces were reworked three or more times

The mean SRS angle of Raysse burins (between 45° and 51°) is generally more oblique than that of other truncation burins, but the SRS shape, most frequently straight, is similar.

Evaluation of the nature of typological variation among Raysse burins is difficult since their burin edges cannot be measured accurately. Most of the characteristics which distinguish them from other truncation and retouched edge/end burins, including the orientation and position of the burin edge, are determined by the process of manufacture. This is not the case, however, for the somewhat smaller dimensions of the blank. The left-sided burin edge, for which there is no good technological explanation, can be used to support the argument for functional specialization, but the characteristics of the burin edge itself, so far as can be seen, are not very different from those of other truncation burins. With some reserve, we suggest that Raysse burins are the products of a specialized resharpening technique peculiar to the Noaillian, but that their typological distinction, as in the

---

4. The burin edge refers to the live edge formed at the intersection of the latest burin spall scar and the SRS, and *not* to the obliterated edges of the old spall scars.

Table 22

ATTRIBUTE SUMMARY BY SUBDIVISION FOR RAYSSE BURINS IN LEVEL 4

	MIDDLE-1				UPPER-2			
TOTAL BURINS STUDIED	140				95			
	Single		Double, Mixed		Single		Double, Mixed	
	n	%	n	%	n	%	n	%
NATURE OF BLANK								
Blade	56	74.67	37	(88.10)	46	86.79	21	(87.50)
Flake/Blade	11	14.67	4	(9.52)	1	1.89	1	(4.17)
Flake	8	10.67	1	(2.38)	6	11.32	2	(8.33)
n	75	100.01	42	(100.00)	53	100.00	24	(100.00)

LENGTH (mm)

	MIDDLE-1 Single	MIDDLE-1 Double, Mixed	UPPER-2 Single	UPPER-2 Double, Mixed
$\bar{X} \pm s_{\bar{X}}$	47.90 ± 1.78	49.55 ± 1.33	58.35 ± 2.76	47.29 ± 2.16
Range	32–88	37–70	37–88	27–63
s	11.10	8.64	15.38	10.58

WIDTH (mm)

	MIDDLE-1 Single	MIDDLE-1 Double, Mixed	UPPER-2 Single	UPPER-2 Double, Mixed
$\bar{X} \pm s_{\bar{X}}$	26.33 ± 1.29	24.55 ± 0.78	26.29 ± 1.18	25.04 ± 1.02
Range	13–54	15–37	13–38	17–37
s	8.02	5.07	6.56	5.02
n	39	42	31	24

	MIDDLE-1 All Burins		UPPER-2 All Burins	
	n	%	n	%
OBLIQUITY				
Simple ("Full Circle")[a]	13	9.29	2	2.11
Complex (Last Removal)				
Oblique	32	22.86	21	22.11
High Oblique	69	49.29	52	54.74
Flat-Faced	26	18.57	20	21.05
LATERAL POSITION				
Left	56	40.00	25	26.32
Median	68	48.57	51	53.68
Right	16	11.43	19	20.00
SRS ANGLE				
$\bar{X} \pm s_{\bar{X}}$	51.14 ± 0.82		44.53 ± 2.09	
Range	10–90		0–90	
s	9.68		20.41	
SRS SHAPE				
Convex	19	13.57	2	2.11
Straight	68	48.57	48	50.53
Concave	32	22.86	32	33.69
Pronounced Concave	21	15.00	13	13.68

a. Cf. Movius and David 1970, p. 454.

Table 22 (continued)

	MIDDLE-1		UPPER-2	
	n	%	n	%
ASSOCIATIONS				
On Double	34		19	
On Mixed	27		15	
On Triple	–		–	
On Quadruple	–		–	
Modal Pattern	AD		AD	
Index	52.14		44.16	
MARGINAL RETOUCH				
Index	18.56		34.38	
Modal Style	Scaled		Scaled	
Transverse	1	0.71	–	–

	UPPER-1				UPPER-1a			
TOTAL BURINS STUDIED	111				98			
	Single		Double, Mixed		Single		Double, Mixed	
	n	%	n	%	n	%	n	%
NATURE OF BLANK								
Blade	54	80.60	21	(75.00)	56	88.89	19	(90.48)
Flake/Blade	8	11.94	5	(17.86)	2	3.17	1	(4.76)
Flake	5	7.46	2	(7.14)	5	7.94	1	(4.76)
n	67	100.00	28	(100.00)	63	100.00	21	(100.00)

LENGTH (mm)	Single	Double, Mixed	Single	Double, Mixed
$\bar{X} \pm s_{\bar{X}}$	53.03 ± 1.85	46.75 ± 1.87	54.26 ± 2.44	52.86 ± 2.47
Range	21–76	32–68	38–90	35–74
s	10.13	9.90	13.59	11.32

WIDTH (mm)	Single	Double, Mixed	Single	Double, Mixed
$\bar{X} \pm s_{\bar{X}}$	28.50 ± 1.45	24.43 ± 1.32	28.81 ± 1.28	26.57 ± 1.54
Range	17–50	15–50	18–49	18–49
s	7.96	7.00	7.16	7.07
n	30	28	31	21

	All Burins		All Burins	
	n	%	n	%
OBLIQUITY				
Simple ("Full Circle")	8	7.21	4	4.08
Complex (Last Removal)				
Oblique	25	22.52	23	23.47
High Oblique	61	54.95	56	57.14
Flat-Faced	17	15.32	15	15.31

Table 22 (continued)

	UPPER-1		UPPER-1a	
	n	%	n	%
LATERAL POSITION				
Left	34	30.63	22	22.45
Median	69	62.16	63	64.29
Right	8	7.21	13	13.27
SRS ANGLE				
$\bar{X} \pm s_{\bar{X}}$	46.94 ± 1.64		45.41 ± 1.82	
Range	10–90		0–90	
s	17.26		18.00	
SRS SHAPE				
Convex	5	4.50	8	8.16
Straight	61	54.95	45	45.92
Concave	35	31.53	26	26.53
Pronounced Concave	10	9.01	19	19.39
ASSOCIATIONS				
On Double	27		11	
On Mixed	12		19	
On Triple	–		–	
On Quadruple	–		–	
Modal Pattern	AD		AD	
Index	41.05		35.71	
MARGINAL RETOUCH				
Index	21.43		24.29	
Modal Style	Scaled		Scaled	
Transverse	1	0.90	–	–

case of modified truncation and retouched edge/end burins, does not necessarily signify functional differentiation.

Burin-Points (figs. 21:15; 24; 25; 26; 28:8, 11)

Burin-points are grouped for analysis into two samples, LOWER plus MIDDLE-2 and MIDDLE-1 plus UPPER (table 23). This grouping corresponds to the division within the level between burin-points made predominantly by the dihedral and the truncation techniques.

Over 90% of burin-points are made on blades. They are markedly longer and wider in the UPPER sample, where they are the largest burins, than in the LOWER, where they are of average size. The major burin spall facet is usually lateral (57–83%), with more variation from this norm in the UPPER sample. Forty-eight percent to 54% are median, and there is some preference for a right rather than a left orientation. The mean SRS angle is low in both samples, lower (29°) in the LOWER sample, with a high proportion of

dihedral burins, than in the UPPER sample (36°), with a high proportion of truncation burins. The SRS shape is predominantly straight, although again the UPPER sample is more variable in this attribute. Even in the UPPER sample, where the truncation technique is predominant, burin-points retain a dihedral-like morphology. Burin-points are less frequently associated with each other or other burins than are other types of burins, with the single exception of dihedral burins in some subdivisions. In the LOWER subdivision, the percentage of pieces with marginal retouch is similar to that of regular dihedral burins; in the UPPER subdivision, burin-points are somewhat less frequently retouched. In both samples, the modal retouch type is heavy.

Because of the functional distinctiveness of burin-points, several special attributes which replace those normally used for burins are necessary for their study. These attributes concern the functional, pointed part of the tool. Measurement to the nearest 5° is made of the point angle, i.e., the angle formed at the ventral edge between the burin spall

Table 23
ATTRIBUTE SUMMARY BY GROUPED SUBDIVISIONS FOR BURIN-POINTS IN LEVEL 4

	LOWER + MIDDLE-2		MIDDLE-1 + UPPER	
TOTAL BURINS STUDIED	48		92	

	Single		Double, Mixed		Single		Double, Mixed	
	n	%	n	%	n	%	n	%
NATURE OF BLANK								
Blade	42	(95.46)	3	(75.00)	64	91.43	18	(100.00)
Flake/Blade	1	(2.27)	1	(25.00)	2	2.86	–	–
Flake	1	(2.27)	–	–	4	5.71	–	–
n	44	(100.00)	4	(100.00)	70	100.00	18	(100.00)

LENGTH (mm)

$\bar{X} \pm s_{\bar{X}}$	56.17 ± 2.78 ᵃ	63.94 ± 2.37 59.72 ± 3.00
Range	24–82	41–110 41–82
s	13.32	13.40 12.74

WIDTH (mm)

$\bar{X} \pm s_{\bar{X}}$	25.96 ± 1.26 ᵃ	29.09 ± 1.14 24.33 ± 1.48
Range	17–39	20–43 15–37
s	6.07	6.47 6.29
n	23 4	32 18

	n	%	n	%
OBLIQUITY				
Dorsal Oblique and Lateral	40	(83.33)	52	56.52
Oblique	6	(12.50)	36	39.13
High Oblique	–	–	4	4.35
Flat-Faced	–	–	–	–
Complex	2	(4.17)	–	–
LATERAL POSITION				
Left	8	(16.67)	15	16.30
Median	23	(47.92)	50	54.35
Right	17	(35.42)	27	29.35

SRS ANGLE

$\bar{X} \pm s_{\bar{X}}$	28.75 ± 2.32	35.76 ± 1.86
Range	0–70	0–90
s	16.06	17.87

SRS SHAPE	n	%	n	%
Convex	3	(6.25)	4	4.35
Straight	42	(87.50)	69	75.00
Concave	2	(4.17)	14	15.22
Pronounced Concave	1	(2.08)	5	5.43

a. No calculations made, as sample was too small.

Table 23 (continued)

	LOWER + MIDDLE-2		MIDDLE-1 + UPPER	
	n	%	n	%
ASSOCIATION				
On Double	3		6	
On Mixed	1		13	
On Triple	–		–	
On Quadruple	–		–	
Index		8.33		21.59
MARGINAL RETOUCH				
Index		27.66		22.37
Modal Style		Heavy		Heavy
CLASS				
1	12	(25.00)	24	26.09
2	10	(20.83)	22	23.91
3	12	(25.00)	21	22.83
4	14	(29.17)	25	27.17
POINT ANGLE				
$\bar{X} \pm s_{\bar{x}}$	64.38 ± 2.11		71.90 ± 1.41	
Range	35–90		35–90	
s	14.61		13.56	
RIDGE ANGLE				
$\bar{X} \pm s_{\bar{x}}$	71.67 ± 2.22		72.99 ± 1.65	
Range	35–90		40–90	
s	15.36		15.81	
RIDGE LENGTH (mm)				
$\bar{X} \pm s_{\bar{x}}$	7.60 ± 0.38		8.43 ± 0.32	
Range	3–14		2–20	
s	2.61		3.10	
Transverse	–	–	–	–

scar and the SRS. Burin-points are divided for purposes of convenience into four classes based on the shape of the ridge viewed in profile (see fig. 35). The ridge angle, i.e., the angle formed by the intersection of the ridge and the ventral edge of the burin spall scar and the ridge length, i.e., the straight-line distance between the tip of the point and the most posterior extension of the ridge, are also measured.

The proportions of ridge profile class are almost equally divided (ca. 25% of each class) in both samples. Class 4 pieces, on which a minute part of the original burin edge is preserved, are perhaps slightly more numerous. The mean point angle increases through time (from 64° to 72°) coincident with the increase in mean SRS angle and the increas-

ing predominance of the truncation technique. Mean ridge angle remains constant through time, which is understandable in view of the stability of ridge profile class proportions. Mean ridge length increases slightly from the LOWER to the UPPER sample; this may well reflect a slight increase through time of blank thickness.

In spite of the change in technique of manufacture between Early and Late Noaillian, burin-points retain their "dihedroid" morphological characteristics little altered. The evidence of wear and the obliteration of the burin edge by tertiary retouch to form a point demonstrate the functional differentiation, if not independence, of the type. But the attribution of individual pieces to the type is not always easy. Particularly in the later Level 4 subdivisions, where

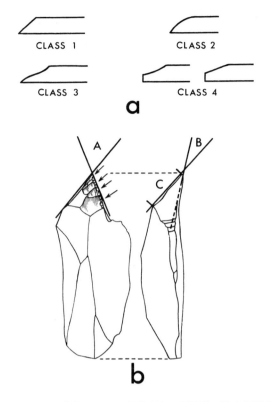

Figure 35. a, BURIN-POINT CLASSES;
b, BURIN-POINT ANGLE (A), RIDGE
ANGLE (B), AND RIDGE LENGTH (C).

tertiary retouch is frequent, there is what amounts to a morphological continuum between modified truncation burins and burin-points. Use and damage help to blur the minor morphological distinctions, themselves less well marked than the functional differentiation indicated by the treatment of the point and the overall morphology of the tools, which suggests that they were manipulated more like dihedral than truncation burins. In spite of their consistently small numerical importance, burin-points are a characteristic Noaillian tool type, and change in the technique of their manufacture is of value as a phase marker.

Burin-points are occasionally made without the application of tertiary retouch (figs. 25:9; 26:4). In this variation, the typical burin-point morphology is created by the retruncation of an old burin, the retruncation retouch forming a sharp point at its intersection with an old burin facet. The morphology and evidence of utilization of the tool is the same as on pieces manufactured directly by a true burin technique. These burins, which are not included in tables 16, 17, or 23, number:

UPPER subdivision	8
MIDDLE subdivision	3
LOWER subdivision	2
Total	13

Dihedral Burins (figs. 16:13–20; 28:2–9; 33:6–8, 10, 11, 15–17, 19; 34:1, 5; 36; 37:1–4)

On inspection, Level 4 dihedral burins appear to be a miscellaneous and unstandardized class much affected by reworking. Within each sample (table 24) there are a small number of pieces with burin edges of 13 mm or greater which fall outside the range of the greater part of the sample. These, often nucleiform or on flakes, show no internal grouping (fig. 37:13).

In most subdivisions, over 80% of single dihedral burins are made on blades, a considerably higher proportion than in later Level 5 and somewhat higher than in Level 3. Mean length of single specimens varies between 50 and 60 mm, with mean width falling between 23 and 29 mm. Double and mixed burins are often somewhat shorter and narrower. There are no regular changes in dihedral burin dimensions through time, but those from REAR:LOWER are distinctly larger than those from FRONT:LOWER. The Level 4 dihedral burins are usually somewhat shorter and narrower than those of later Level 5; in comparison with those of Level 3, they are much shorter and slightly narrower. There is much variation from a straight burin edge, with angulated edges accounting for about one-quarter of the sample in all subdivisions except UPPER-1a. The variation in angulated pieces is wide, and there is no justification for the creation of a separate type. Compared with the dihedral burins of later Level 5 and Level 3, those of Level 4 have somewhat higher frequencies of straight edges and lower frequencies of irregular edges. In neither edge shape nor burin edge width is there any patterned change within Level 4. When straight-edged dihedral burins are considered apart from the remainder, variation in edge width decreases, with mean values (ca. 5 mm) almost always lower than those for the complete samples. Dihedral burin edges are smaller than in Level 3 and slightly smaller or the same as those in later Level 5.

Mean burin angle for dihedral burins varies between 66° and 70°, well within the range of modified and unmodified truncation burins and Noailles burins. These values are quite comparable to that for dihedral burins in later Level 5. The high proportion of dihedral burins with nonstraight edges raises the frequency of complex obliquity to a high level. For burins with straight edges, lateral obliquity is most frequent, with high oblique and flat-faced of little quantitative importance. This is true as well of dihedral burins in Levels 5 and 3. The most common orientation is median, with some preference for deviation to the right rather than to the left. There is neither the normal variation from median found in later Level 5 nor the median/lateral distinction typical of Level 3, but only an unpatterned variation with lateral specimens sometimes exceeding and sometimes fewer in number than asymmetrical ones.

The association index for dihedral burins is irregular, but in general does not differ from other burin types (excluding Noailles burins). The LOWER and MIDDLE-2 subdivisions are characterized by a predominance of heavy marginal re-

Figure 36. DIHEDRAL BURINS FROM LEVEL 4: LOWER

SRS TYPE AND ANGLE

Dihedral

```
 1  (14,353):  LOWER-1:  60°        9  (10,623):  LOWER-1:  70°
 2  (7424b):   LOWER-2:  80°       10  (10,669):  LOWER-2:  Distal
 3  (10,844):  LOWER-1:  60°            extremity:  80°
 4  (7512):    LOWER-2:  70°       11  (10,776):  LOWER-2:  80°
 5  (12,953):  LOWER-1:  80°       12  (10,741):  LOWER-2:  70°
 6  (6620):    LOWER-1:  60°       13  (10,984):  LOWER-2:  90°
 7  (12,828):  LOWER-1:  60°       14  (10,739):  LOWER-2:  50°
 8  (7082):    LOWER-2:  60°       15  (7479):   LOWER-1:  80°
```

BURIN EDGE SHAPE AND WIDTH

Straight   Curved

```
 1  (14,353):  4 mm                 6  (6620):  5 mm
 2  (7424b):   2 mm                 9  (10,623):  10 mm
 3  (10,844):  10 mm
 4  (7512):  9 mm
 5  (12,953):  4 mm
 7  (12,828):  8 mm
 8  (7082):  7 mm
10  (10,669):  Distal extremity:  5 mm
12  (10,741):  4 mm
13  (10,984):  10 mm
15  (7479):  5 mm
```

Angulated   Irregular

```
14  (10,739):  15 mm               11  (10,776):  5 mm
```

OBLIQUITY   SRS SHAPE

Lateral   Oblique   Straight

```
 1  (14,353)        5  (12,953)       1  (14,353)
 2  (7424b)         6  (6620)         2  (7424b)
 3  (10,844)                          3  (10,844)
 7  (12,828)                          4  (7512)
 8  (7082)                            5  (12,953)
10  (10,669):                         6  (6620)
    Distal                            7  (12,828)
    extremity                         8  (7082)
12  (10,741)                          9  (10,623)
13  (10,984)                         10  (10,669)
15  (7479)                           11  (10,776)
                                     12  (10,741)
                                     13  (10,984)
                                     14  (10,739)
                                     15  (7479)
```

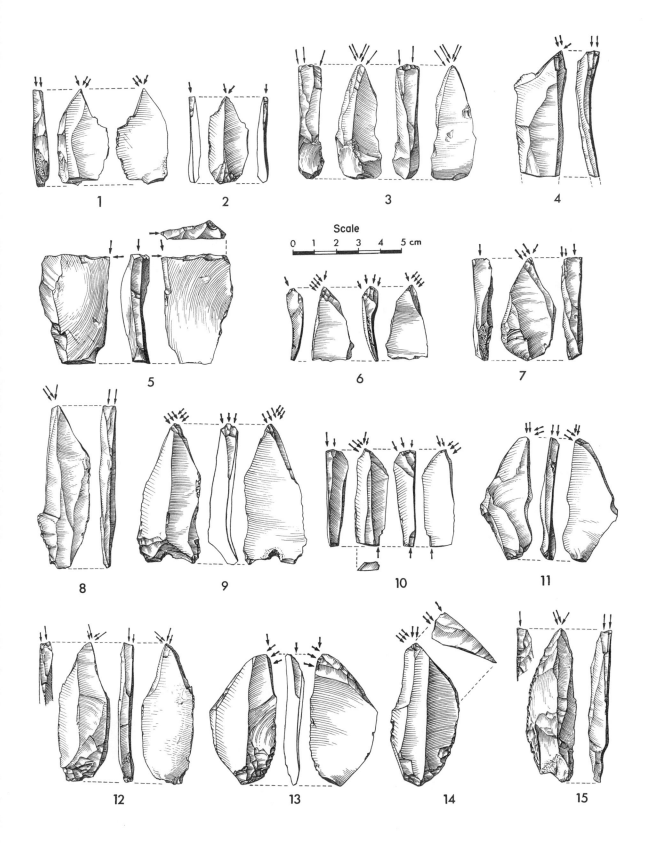

Scale
0 1 2 3 4 5 cm

1   2   3   4

5   6   7

8   9   10   11

12   13   14   15

Figure 36 (continued).

LATERAL POSITION

Left Lateral	Left Asymmetrical	Median	Right Asymmetrical
5 (12,953)	8 (7082)	1 (14,353)	4 (7512)
6 (6620)	10 (10,669):	2 (7424b)	7 (12,828)
13 (10,984)	Distal extremity	3 (10,844)	12 (10,741)
		9 (10,623)	
		15 (7479)	

Right
Lateral

11 (10,776)
12 (10,741)

MISCELLANEOUS

10 (10,669): Proximal extremity: D: Noailles burin; Class 6; break;
    edge shape: straight; 2 mm; lateral

Table 24

ATTRIBUTE SUMMARY BY SUBDIVISION FOR DIHEDRAL BURINS IN LEVEL 4

	REAR:LOWER				FRONT:LOWER-2			
TOTAL BURINS STUDIED	97				102			
	Single		Double, Mixed		Single		Double, Mixed	
	n	%	n	%	n	%	n	%
NATURE OF BLANK								
Blade	59	80.82	16	(94.12)	60	84.51	15	(78.95)
Flake/Blade	7	9.59	–	–	4	5.63	2	(10.53)
Flake	7	9.59	1	(5.88)	7	9.86	2	(10.53)
n	73	100.00	17	(100.00)	71	100.00	19	(100.01)

LENGTH (mm)

	REAR:LOWER Single	Double, Mixed	FRONT:LOWER-2 Single	Double, Mixed
$\bar{X} \pm s_{\bar{X}}$	58.80 ± 2.51	49.56 ± 3.87	51.00 ± 2.33	53.21 ± 3.07
Range	32–100	24–83	30–73	33–78
s	16.05	15.48	11.66	13.39

WIDTH (mm)

	Single	Double, Mixed	Single	Double, Mixed
$\bar{X} \pm s_{\bar{X}}$	28.37 ± 0.79	24.62 ± 1.28	25.16 ± 1.58	23.42 ± 1.30
Range	15–39	14–33	15–44	16–40
s	5.04	5.10	7.91	5.68
n	41	16	25	19

	n	%	n	%
EDGE SHAPE				
Straight	54	55.67	70	68.63
Angulated	25	25.77	18	17.65
Curved and Rounded	10	10.31	9	8.82
Irregular	8	8.25	5	4.90

EDGE WIDTH (mm)

	REAR:LOWER	FRONT:LOWER-2
$\bar{X} \pm s_{\bar{X}}$	6.69 ± 0.32	6.12 ± 0.35
Range	1–15	1–23
s	3.18	3.54
(Straight $\bar{W}$)	(5.67)	(4.94)

BURIN ANGLE

	REAR:LOWER	FRONT:LOWER-2
$\bar{X} \pm s_{\bar{X}}$	70.41 ± 1.17	67.94 ± 1.06
Range	40–90	40–90
s	11.57	10.75

OBLIQUITY

	n	%	n	%
Dorsal Oblique and Lateral	37	38.14	53	51.96
Oblique	14	14.43	16	15.69
High Oblique and Flat-Faced	3	3.09	2	1.96
Complex	43	44.33	31	30.39

Table 24 (continued)

	REAR:LOWER		FRONT:LOWER-2	
	n	%	n	%
LATERAL POSITION				
Left Lateral	10	10.31	15	14.71
Left Asymmetrical	13	13.40	17	16.67
Median	41	42.27	37	36.27
Right Asymmetrical	20	20.62	16	15.69
Right Lateral	13	13.40	17	16.67
SRS OR NON-SRS ANGLE				
$\bar{X} \pm s_{\bar{X}}$	45.57 ± 1.25		43.04 ± 2.00	
Range	0-90		10-90	
s	12.29		20.19	
SRS SHAPE				
Convex	1	1.03	2	1.96
Straight	94	96.91	97	95.10
Concave	2	2.06	3	2.94
ASSOCIATIONS				
On Double	6		23	
On Mixed	13		6	
On Triple	-		-	
On Quadruple	-		-	
Index	21.11		32.22	
MARGINAL RETOUCH				
Index	28.57		11.90	
Modal Style	Heavy		Heavy and Scaled	
Transverse	3	3.09	4	3.92

	FRONT:LOWER-1				MIDDLE-2			
TOTAL BURINS STUDIED	68				36			
	Single		Double, Mixed		Single		Double, Mixed	
	n	%	n	%	n	%	n	%
NATURE OF BLANK								
Blade	43	(89.58)	9	(81.82)	16	(72.73)	6	(85.71)
Flake/Blade	1	(2.08)	1	(9.09)	3	(13.64)	-	-
Flake	4	(8.33)	1	(9.09)	3	(13.64)	1	(14.29)
n	48	(99.99)	11	(100.00)	22	(100.01)	7	(100.00)
LENGTH (mm)								
$\bar{X} \pm s_{\bar{X}}$	51.53 ± 3.39		a		55.15 ± 3.75		a	
Range	30-75				40-92			
s	13.97				13.54			

a. No calculations made, as sample was too small.

Table 24 (continued)

	FRONT:LOWER-1		MIDDLE-2	
	Single	Double, Mixed	Single	Double, Mixed
WIDTH (mm)		a		a
$\bar{X} \pm s_{\bar{X}}$	22.76 ± 1.02		28.00 ± 1.72	
Range	13-31		17-36	
s	4.19		6.22	
n	17		13	

	n	%	n	%
EDGE SHAPE				
Straight	49	72.06	19	(52.78)
Angulated	15	22.06	8	(22.22)
Curved and Rounded	2	2.94	4	(11.11)
Irregular	2	2.94	5	(13.89)
EDGE WIDTH (mm)				
$\bar{X} \pm s_{\bar{X}}$	4.65 ± 0.30		7.11 ± 0.62	
Range	1-15		1-15	
s	2.45		3.70	
(Straight $\bar{W}$)	(4.18)		(4.63)	
BURIN ANGLE				
$\bar{X} \pm s_{\bar{X}}$	65.59 ± 1.31		69.17 ± 1.84	
Range	40-90		50-90	
s	10.84		11.05	
OBLIQUITY				
Dorsal Oblique and Lateral	36	52.94	17	(47.22)
Oblique	13	19.12	2	(5.56)
High Oblique and Flat-Faced	-	-	1	(2.78)
Complex	19	27.94	16	(44.44)
LATERAL POSITION				
Left Lateral	9	13.24	5	(13.89)
Left Asymmetrical	9	13.24	2	(5.56)
Median	29	42.65	19	(52.78)
Right Asymmetrical	15	22.06	5	(13.89)
Right Lateral	6	8.82	5	(13.89)
SRS OR NON-SRS ANGLE				
$\bar{X} \pm s_{\bar{X}}$	36.91 ± 2.14		41.67 ± 3.58	
Range	10-90		10-90	
s	17.64		21.45	

Table 24 (continued)

	FRONT:LOWER-1		MIDDLE-2	
	n	%	n	%
SRS SHAPE				
Convex	–	–	2	(5.56)
Straight	66	97.06	33	(91.67)
Concave	2	2.94	1	(2.78)
ASSOCIATIONS				
On Double	12		6	
On Mixed	3		4	
On Triple	–		–	
On Quadruple	–		–	
Index	25.42		34.48	
MARGINAL RETOUCH				
Index	25.00		36.00	
Modal Style	Heavy		Heavy	
Transverse	4	5.88	1	(2.78)

	MIDDLE-1				UPPER-2			
TOTAL BURINS STUDIED	121				41			
	Single		Double, Mixed		Single		Double, Mixed	
	n	%	n	%	n	%	n	%
NATURE OF BLANK								
Blade	74	88.10	23	(76.67)	31	(96.87)	4	(57.14)
Flake/Blade	2	2.38	1	(3.33)	–	–	–	–
Flake	8	9.52	6	(20.00)	1	(3.13)	3	(42.86)
n	84	100.00	30	(100.00)	32	(100.00)	7	(100.00)
LENGTH (mm)								
$\bar{X} \pm s_{\bar{X}}$	57.03 ± 2.11		47.70 ± 2.00		49.33 ± 3.99		[a]	
Range	38–86		29–73		21–79			
s	12.68		10.97		15.43			
WIDTH (mm)								
$\bar{X} \pm s_{\bar{X}}$	29.94 ± 1.28		23.87 ± 1.30		23.33 ± 2.11		[a]	
Range	18–51		14–46		9–42			
s	7.69		7.11		8.18			
n	36		30		15			

Table 24 (continued)

	MIDDLE-1		UPPER-2	
	n	%	n	%
EDGE SHAPE				
Straight	73	60.33	23	(56.10)
Angulated	34	28.10	11	(26.83)
Curved and Rounded	9	7.44	5	(12.20)
Irregular	5	4.13	2	(4.88)
EDGE WIDTH (mm)				
$\bar{X} \pm s_{\bar{X}}$	5.91 ± 0.28		5.41 ± 0.38	
Range	2–17		2–12	
s	3.05		2.41	
(Straight $\bar{W}$)	(5.01)		(4.52)	
BURIN ANGLE				
$\bar{X} \pm s_{\bar{X}}$	68.43 ± 0.88		68.05 ± 1.79	
Range	50–90		40–90	
s	9.66		11.45	
OBLIQUITY				
Dorsal Oblique and Lateral	52	42.98	13	(31.71)
Oblique	19	15.70	8	(19.51)
High Oblique and Flat-Faced	2	1.65	2	(4.88)
Complex	48	39.67	18	(43.90)
LATERAL POSITION				
Left Lateral	11	9.09	5	(12.20)
Left Asymmetrical	20	16.53	4	(9.76)
Median	53	43.80	18	(43.90)
Right Asymmetrical	15	12.40	5	(12.20)
Right Lateral	22	18.18	9	(21.95)
SRS OR NON-SRS ANGLE				
$\bar{X} \pm s_{\bar{X}}$	42.40 ± 2.51		41.95 ± 2.99	
Range	10–90		10–80	
s	27.63		19.13	
SRS SHAPE				
Convex	–	–	1	(2.44)
Straight	119	98.35	40	(97.56)
Concave	2	1.65	–	–

Table 24 (continued)

	MIDDLE-1		UPPER-2	
	n	%	n	%
ASSOCIATIONS				
On Double	10		2	
On Mixed	24		5	
On Triple	–		–	
On Quadruple	–		–	
Index		29.82		17.95
MARGINAL RETOUCH				
Index		18.89		20.59
Modal Style		Scaled		Scaled
Transverse	4	3.31	–	–

	UPPER-1				UPPER-1a			
TOTAL BURINS STUDIED		61				41		
	Single		Double, Mixed		Single		Double, Mixed	
	n	%	n	%	n	%	n	%
NATURE OF BLANK								
Blade	36	(83.72)	13	(92.86)	23	(95.83)	11	(100.00)
Flake/Blade	4	(9.30)	1	(7.14)	–	–	–	–
Flake	3	(6.98)	–	–	1	(4.17)	–	–
n	43	(100.00)	14	(100.00)	24	(100.00)	11	(100.00)

LENGTH (mm)

	UPPER-1			UPPER-1a	
	Single	Double, Mixed	Single		
$\overline{X} \pm s_{\overline{X}}$	57.13 ± 4.05	49.21 ± 3.78	60.46 ± 2.60		[a]
Range	21–112	29–72	48–77		
s	19.45	14.12	9.41		

WIDTH (mm)

	Single	Double, Mixed	Single		
$\overline{X} \pm s_{\overline{X}}$	26.83 ± 1.34	24.21 ± 1.57	26.62 ± 1.58		[a]
Range	16–41	15–39	17–37		
s	6.44	5.88	5.72		
n	23	14	13		

	n	%	n	%
EDGE SHAPE				
Straight	31	50.82	32	(78.05)
Angulated	15	24.59	2	(4.88)
Curved and Rounded	9	14.75	6	(14.63)
Irregular	6	9.84	1	(2.44)

Table 24 (continued)

	UPPER-1		UPPER-1a	
	n	%	n	%
EDGE WIDTH (mm)				
$\bar{X} \pm s_{\bar{X}}$	6.74 ± 0.39		5.02 ± 0.33	
Range	1–15		2–10	
s	3.17		2.10	
(Straight $\bar{W}$)	(6.13)		(4.56)	
BURIN ANGLE				
$\bar{X} \pm s_{\bar{X}}$	67.38 ± 1.46		70.00 ± 1.68	
Range	40–90		50–90	
s	11.39		10.72	
OBLIQUITY				
Dorsal Oblique and				
Lateral	20	32.79	21	(51.22)
Oblique	11	18.03	8	(19.51)
High Oblique and				
Flat-Faced	–	–	3	(7.32)
Complex	30	49.18	9	(21.95)
LATERAL POSITION				
Left Lateral	4	6.56	2	(4.88)
Left Asymmetrical	3	4.92	4	(9.76)
Median	40	65.57	21	(51.22)
Right Asymmetrical	5	8.20	6	(14.63)
Right Lateral	9	14.75	8	(19.51)
SRS OR NON-SRS ANGLE				
$\bar{X} \pm s_{\bar{X}}$	40.82 ± 2.84		41.71 ± 2.94	
Range	10–90		10–90	
s	22.16		18.83	
SRS SHAPE				
Convex	1	1.64	1	(2.44)
Straight	58	95.08	37	(90.24)
Concave	2	3.28	3	(7.32)
ASSOCIATIONS				
On Double	5		6	
On Mixed	11		7	
On Triple	–		–	
On Quadruple	–		–	
Index	28.07		37.14	
MARGINAL RETOUCH				
Index	19.57		39.29	
Modal Style	Scaled		Scaled	
Transverse	2	3.28	1	(2.44)

Figure 37.   DIHEDRAL BURINS FROM LEVEL 4: MIDDLE

SRS TYPE AND ANGLE

Dihedral

1 (7359): MIDDLE-2: 50°
2 (9467): MIDDLE-1: 70°
3 (9670): MIDDLE-1: 80°
4 (10,307): MIDDLE-1: 60°
5 (9932): MIDDLE-1: 80°
6 (10,609): MIDDLE-2: 60°
7 (10,514): MIDDLE-2: 80°
8 (9920): MIDDLE-1: 60°
9 (9952): MIDDLE-1: 70°

10 (10,481): MIDDLE-1: Distal
    extremity: 80°; Proximal
    extremity: 80°
11 (9335): MIDDLE-1: 70°
12 (9223): MIDDLE-1: 70°
13 (7145): MIDDLE-1: 80°
14 (9459): MIDDLE-1: 70°
15 (7305): MIDDLE-1: A: 60°;
    B: 70°

BURIN EDGE SHAPE AND WIDTH

Straight

1 (7359): 4 mm
2 (9467): 7 mm
5 (9932): 3 mm
8 (9920): 5 mm
9 (9952): 4 mm
10 (10,481):
    Proximal
    extremity: 4 mm
11 (9335): 6 mm
12 (9223): 5 mm
14 (9459): 3 mm
15 (7305): A:
    5 mm; B: 3 mm

Curved

6 (10,609):
   12 mm

Rounded

10 (10,481):
    Distal
    extremity:
    5 mm
13 (7145): 17 mm

Angulated

3 (9670): 6 mm
4 (10,307):
   8 mm

Irregular

7 (10,514):
   14 mm

OBLIQUITY

Dorsal
Oblique

2 (9467)

Lateral

1 (7359)
5 (9932)
8 (9920)
9 (9952)
10 (10,481):
    Proximal
    extremity
11 (9335)
14 (9459)

Oblique

12 (9223)
15 (7305): A
    and B

Lateral/
Flat-Faced

3 (9670)

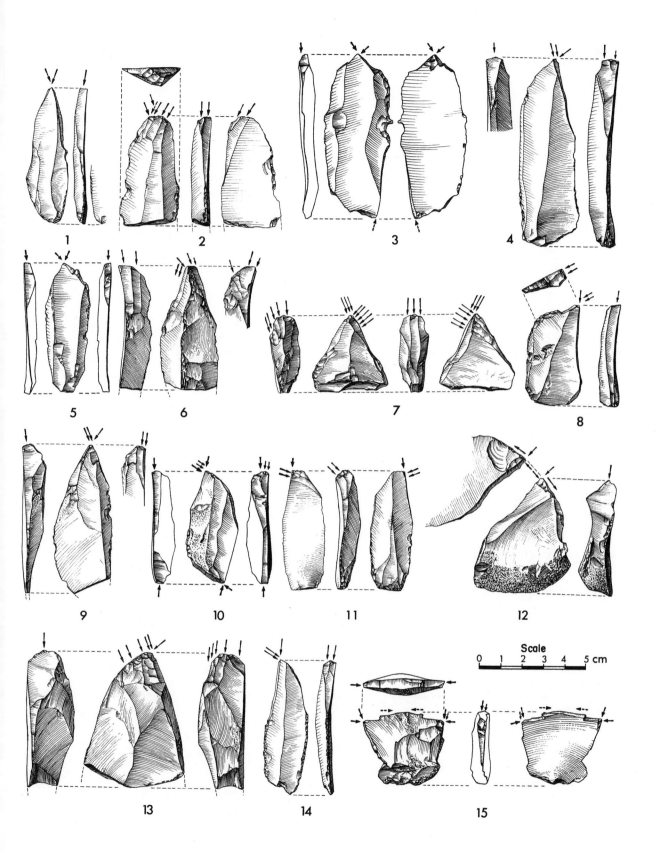

Figure 37 (continued).

SRS SHAPE

Straight

1 (7359)	5 (9932)	9 (9952)	12 (9223)
2 (9467)	6 (10,609)	10 (10,481):	13 (7145)
3 (9670)	7 (10,514)	Both	14 (9459)
4 (10,307)	8 (9920)	extremities	15 (7305): A
		11 (9335)	and B

LATERAL POSITION

Left Lateral	Left Asymmetrical	Median	Right Asymmetrical
10 (10,481): Distal extremity	10 (10,481): Proximal extremity	1 (7359)	13 (7145)
12 (9223)		2 (9467)	
14 (9459)		3 (9670)	
15 (7305): A		4 (10,307)	
		5 (9932)	
		6 (10,609)	
		7 (10,514)	
		9 (9952)	

Right Lateral

8 (9920)
11 (9335)
15 (7305): B

MISCELLANEOUS

15 (7305): Transverse

touch. In the MIDDLE-1 and UPPER subdivisions, scaled retouch is the modal style.

Differentiated in many attributes from those of later Level 5 and Level 3, dihedral burins in Level 4 constitute an unstandardized grouping, less highly structured than burins made by the truncation technique. Tertiary modification, applied to burin-points made by the dihedral technique and to other burins in the Late Noaillian series, is also found on regular dihedral burins in all subdivisions (see table 16 and fig. 37:9). The fact that this technique occurs already in the LOWER subdivision on dihedral burins suggests that the idea of modifying a burin edge subsequent to the removal of the burin spall was first developed for application to dihedral burins and later transferred to truncation and retouched edge/end burins.

Break Burins (figs. 28:6, 12; 33:1–3, 9, 12; 34:4; 38:5–10; 39:1–10)

The proportion of break burins—single, double, or mixed—which are made on blades is always close to 90% (table 25). This percentage is comparable to that of Level 3 but much higher than that of later Level 5. Length and width increase between the LOWER and MIDDLE-1 subdivisions, the dimensions of UPPER being like those of MIDDLE-1. In all subdivisions, break burins are smaller than other burins (excluding Noailles). They are shorter than break burins in later Level 5 and Level 3; all Level 4 width means are lower than that of later Level 5, but except for LOWER, which is smaller, they are greater than that of Level 3. The predominant burin edge shape is straight, present on 82–85%

Table 25

ATTRIBUTE SUMMARY BY SUBDIVISION FOR BREAK BURINS IN LEVEL 4

	LOWER				MIDDLE-1			
TOTAL BURINS STUDIED	75				61			
	Single		Double, Mixed		Single		Double, Mixed	
	n	%	n	%	n	%	n	%
NATURE OF BLANK								
Blade	41	(87.23)	19	(86.36)	32	(91.43)	17	(94.44)
Flake/Blade	1	(2.13)	2	(9.09)	–	–	1	(5.56)
Flake	5	(10.64)	1	(4.55)	3	(8.57)	–	–
n	47	(100.00)	22	(100.00)	35	(100.00)	18	(100.00)

LENGTH (mm)				
$\bar{X} \pm s_{\bar{X}}$	43.68 ± 2.30	41.76 ± 2.19	50.61 ± 2.63	45.88 ± 2.29
Range	19–64	26–68	33–75	29–63
s	12.15	10.05	11.15	9.42

WIDTH (mm)				
$\bar{X} \pm s_{\bar{X}}$	22.71 ± 1.79	23.19 ± 1.29	26.83 ± 1.47	24.53 ± 1.34
Range	12–59	12–35	17–40	16–37
s	9.48	5.93	6.25	5.53
n	28	21	18	17

	n	%	n	%
EDGE SHAPE				
Straight	63	84.00	50	81.97
Beveled	3	4.00	1	1.64
Other	9	12.00	10	16.39

EDGE WIDTH (mm)		
$\bar{X} \pm s_{\bar{X}}$	3.03 ± 0.22	3.44 ± 0.25
Range	1–9	1–14
s	1.89	1.96

BURIN ANGLE		
$\bar{X} \pm s_{\bar{X}}$	75.47 ± 1.19	72.95 ± 1.43
Range	50–90	50–90
s	10.31	11.16

	n	%	n	%
OBLIQUITY				
Dorsal Oblique and				
Lateral	45	60.00	36	59.02
Oblique	16	21.33	10	16.39
High Oblique	6	8.00	4	6.56
Flat-Faced	–	–	1	1.64
Complex	8	10.67	10	16.39

Table 25 (continued)

	LOWER			MIDDLE-1	
	n	%		n	%
LATERAL POSITION					
Left	31	41.33		29	47.54
Median	5	6.67		3	4.92
Right	39	52.00		29	47.54

SRS ANGLE

	LOWER	MIDDLE-1
$\bar{X} \pm s_{\bar{x}}$	77.47 ± 1.61	79.18 ± 1.79
Range	30–90	20–90
s	13.96	13.98

	LOWER			MIDDLE-1	
SRS SHAPE					
Convex	–	–		1	1.64
Straight	60	80.00		44	72.13
Concave	15	20.00		16	26.23

	LOWER	MIDDLE-1
ASSOCIATIONS		
On Double	6	9
On Mixed	19	13
On Triple	–	–
On Quadruple	–	–
Index	36.23	41.51

	LOWER	MIDDLE-1
MARGINAL RETOUCH		
Index	14.00	30.00
Modal Style	Heavy	Scaled and Fine

	LOWER		MIDDLE-1	
Transverse	–	–	–	–

UPPER

TOTAL BURINS STUDIED   83

	Single		Double, Mixed	
	n	%	n	%
NATURE OF BLANK				
Blade	51	89.47	20	(100.00)
Flake/Blade	2	3.51	–	–
Flake	4	7.02	–	–
n	57	100.00	20	(100.00)

LENGTH (mm)

	Single	Double, Mixed
$\bar{X} \pm s_{\bar{x}}$	47.86 ± 2.56	48.05 ± 2.93
Range	24–92	27–82
s	15.58	12.78

Table 25 (continued)

UPPER

	Single	Double, Mixed
WIDTH (mm)		
$\bar{X} \pm s_{\bar{X}}$	26.00 ± 1.31	24.63 ± 1.21
Range	13-42	15-35
s	7.96	5.28
n	37	19

	n	%
EDGE SHAPE		
Straight	71	85.54
Beveled	1	1.20
Other	11	13.25
EDGE WIDTH (mm)		
$\bar{X} \pm s_{\bar{X}}$	3.60 ± 0.20	
Range	1-10	
s	1.87	
BURIN ANGLE		
$\bar{X} \pm s_{\bar{X}}$	74.22 ± 1.23	
Range	50-90	
s	11.17	
OBLIQUITY		
Dorsal Oblique and Lateral	46	55.42
Oblique	20	24.10
High Oblique	5	6.02
Flat-Faced	–	–
Complex	12	14.46
LATERAL POSITION		
Left	36	43.37
Median	4	4.82
Right	43	51.81
SRS ANGLE		
$\bar{X} \pm s_{\bar{X}}$	79.88 ± 1.40	
Range	30-90	
s	12.75	
SRS SHAPE		
Convex	1	1.20
Straight	67	80.72
Concave	15	18.07

Table 25 (continued)

	UPPER	
	n	%
ASSOCIATIONS		
On Double	5	
On Mixed	17	
On Triple	–	
On Quadruple	–	
Index		28.57
MARGINAL RETOUCH		
Index		16.67
Modal Style	Scaled and Heavy	
Transverse	–	–

Figure 38. BURINS FROM LEVEL 4: UPPER

SRS TYPE AND ANGLE

Dihedral

1	(6468):	UPPER-1a:	80°
2	(8728):	UPPER-1:	80°
3	(9100):	UPPER-2:	80°
4	(9032):	UPPER-1:	50°

Break

5	(6273):	UPPER-1:	80°
6	(8485):	UPPER-1a:	70°
7	(6025):	UPPER-2:	80°
8	(6642):	UPPER-1a:	60°
9	(9103):	UPPER-1a:	50°
10	(8770):	UPPER-1:	60°

BURIN EDGE SHAPE AND WIDTH

Straight

1	(6468):	3 mm
5	(6273):	2 mm
6	(8485):	3 mm
7	(6025):	2 mm
8	(6642):	3 mm
9	(9103):	3 mm

Curved

4	(9032):	8 mm

Angulated

2	(8728):	9 mm

Irregular

3	(9100):	10 mm
10	(8770):	4 mm

OBLIQUITY

Dorsal

9. (9103)

Lateral

1	(6468)
6	(8485)
7	(6025)

Oblique

8 (6642)

High Oblique

5 (6273)

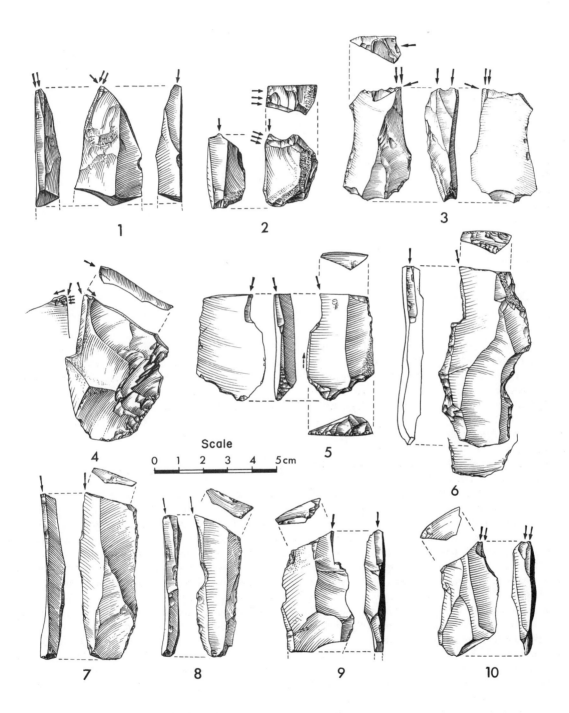

Scale

0 1 2 3 4 5cm

1

2

3

4

5

6

7

8

9

10

Figure 38 (continued).

SRS SHAPE

Concave   Straight

10   (8770)   1   (6468)   5   (6273)
                                       2   (8728)   6   (8485)
                                       3   (9100)   7   (6025)
                                       4   (9032)   8   (6642)
                                                         9   (9103)

LATERAL POSITION

Left   Left   Right
Lateral   Asymmetrical   Lateral

4   (9032)   1   (6468)   2   (8728)
5   (6273)   3   (9100)
6   (8485)   9   (9103)
7   (6025)   10   (8770)
8   (6642)

MISCELLANEOUS

2   (8728):   Transverse
3   (9100):   Transverse

of pieces; these frequencies are about midway between those of later Level 5 and Level 3. The mean width of the burin edge is small (3.03–3.60 mm), falling in general between the mean values for modified truncation burins and Noailles burins. In this attribute also, the Level 4 break burins are smaller than their later Level 5 and Level 3 counterparts. Between 75% and 81% of the burin edges are either lateral or oblique, which is also the case in the other two levels. Median orientation is rare; right orientation is usually slightly more frequent than left orientation, but there is no clear or constant preference. This situation differs from that of both later Level 5, where left orientation is dominant, and Level 3, where right orientation is dominant.

The mean SRS angle increases slightly between the LOWER and MIDDLE-1 subdivisions; at just under 80°, this angle for break burins is closer to a right angle than for any other burins in the level. The mean SRS angles are exactly comparable with those of break burins in later Level 5 but considerably greater than the Level 3 value. As in the other two levels, the SRS shape is predominantly straight. Break burins are frequently associated, usually on mixed burins. The marginal retouch style is variable, with heavy and scaled most frequently represented.

Level 4 break burins are, except for increases through time in burin edge width and SRS angle, as internally consistent as other burin types within the level. They stand in the same relationship to truncation (excluding Noailles) and

dihedral burins in dimensions and burin edge width as they do in later Level 5 and Level 3. These characteristics are linked with the technique of manufacture. As in the case of dihedral burins, nothing can be learned of the internal development of the Noaillian from the break burins that is not more clearly and easily extracted from the various forms of the truncation techno-type.

The Association of Level 4 Burins

The indices of association of Level 4 burins are varied and do not generally show regular changes through time, a decrease in the index for Raysse burins from 52.14 in MIDDLE-1 to 35.71 in UPPER-1a being an exception. The associations of burins are considered here in two ways. Table 26 shows the association of burins as double or mixed burins and as combination tools. Both grouped samples show significant departures from randomness. In the LOWER + MIDDLE-2 sample, the tendencies for Noailles burins to appear as double (and not as mixed) burins (fig. 14), for truncation burins to be single, and for dihedral burins to form part of combination tools are noticeable, as is the low frequency of association of burin-points. In the MIDDLE-1 + UPPER sample, Raysse burins are seen to appear as double or mixed burins much more often than expected (figs. 27; 28; 30). Most of the tendencies noted can probably be explained in terms of practicalities; the nature of the blank

Figure 39.   BREAK AND RAYSSE BURINS FROM LEVEL 4: MIDDLE

BREAK BURINS

SRS TYPE AND ANGLE

 1 (9537):   MIDDLE-1:   80°
 2 (10,357): MIDDLE-1:   With dihedral modification; 60°
 3 (9913):   MIDDLE-1:   With truncation modification; 60°
 4 (6584):   MIDDLE-2:   B: 90°; D: 80°
 5 (10,253): MIDDLE-1:   80°
 6 (8178):   MIDDLE-1:   70°
 7 (9734):   MIDDLE-1:   80°
 8 (9562):   MIDDLE-1:   60°
 9 (9780):   MIDDLE-1:   70°
10 (7063):   MIDDLE-1:   90°

BURIN EDGE SHAPE AND WIDTH

Straight	Beveled	Angulated
1 (9537): 4 mm	5 (10,253): 5 mm	2 (10,357): 3 mm
3 (9913): 2 mm		7 (9734): 3 mm
4 (6584): B: 1 mm;		
D: 1 mm		
6 (8178): 5 mm		
8 (9562): 3 mm		
9 (9780): 1 mm		
10 (7063): 3 mm		

OBLIQUITY

Dorsal Oblique	Lateral	Oblique
10 (7063)	1 (9537)	2 (10,357)
	3 (9913)	4 (6584): B
	4 (6584): D	6 (8178)
	5 (10,253)	9 (9780)
	8 (9562)	

SRS SHAPE

Concave	Straight
1 (9537)	2 (10,357)
5 (10,253)	3 (9913)
9 (9780)	4 (6584): B and D
	6 (8178)
	7 (9734)
	8 (9562)
	10 (7063)

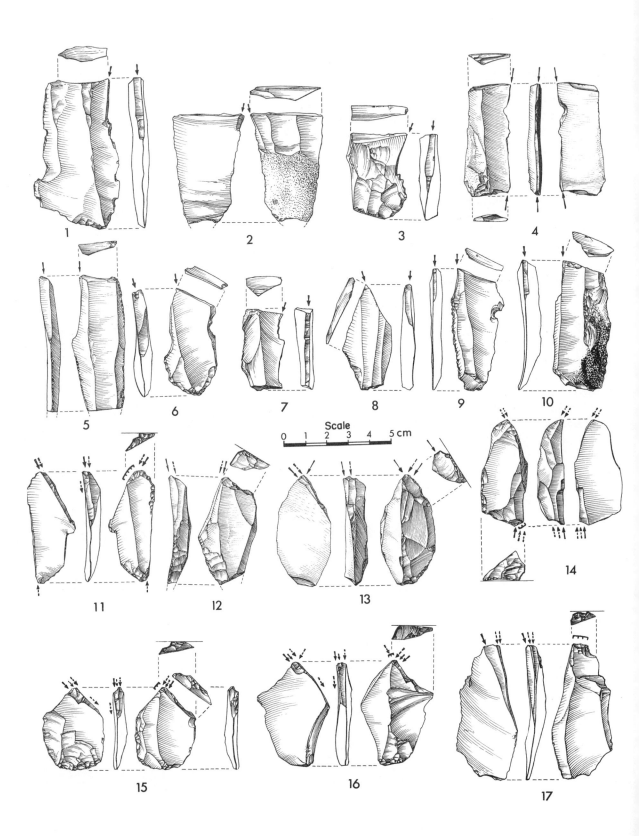

Scale
0 1 2 3 4 5 cm

Figure 39 (continued).

LATERAL POSITION

Left Lateral	Median	Right Lateral
2 (10,357)	6 (8178)	1 (9537)
4 (6584): D	8 (9562)	3 (9913)
5 (10,253)		4 (6584): B
9 (9780)		7 (9734)
10 (7063)		

RAYSSE BURINS

SRS TYPE

11 (9477): MIDDLE-1: On retouched edge
12 (10,250): MIDDLE-1: On retouched truncation
13 (9767): MIDDLE-1: On retouched truncation with
    dihedral modification
14 (10,026): MIDDLE-1: On retouched truncation
15 (9757): MIDDLE-1: On retouched truncation
16 (9591): MIDDLE-1: On retouched truncation
17 (10,035): MIDDLE-1: On retouched truncation

NUMBER OF REMOVALS

11 (9477): 1+1
12 (10,250): 1+1
13 (9767): 1+2
14 (10,026): 1+2
15 (9757): 1+3
16 (9591): 2+2
17 (10,035): 1+2

FIRST REMOVAL

Dorsal Oblique (<80°)	Lateral (80–100°)	Oblique (110–130°)
13 (9767): 50°	11 (9477): 80°	15 (9757): 110°
	12 (10,250): 90°	
	14 (10,026): 90°	
	16 (9591): 90°	
	17 (10,035): 90°	

LAST REMOVAL

Oblique (110–130°)	High Oblique (140–150°)
11 (9471): 110°	15 (9757): 140°
12 (10,250): 130°	16 (9591): 150°
13 (9767): 130°	17 (10,035): 150°
14 (10,026): 130°	

SRS SHAPE

Concave	Pronounced Concave	Straight
15 (9757)	12 (10,250)	11 (9477)
	16 (9591)	13 (9767)
		14 (10,026)
		17 (10,035)

Figure 39 (continued).

LATERAL POSITION

Left Lateral   Median

14 (10,026)   11 (9477)
                                12 (10,250)
                                13 (9767)
                                15 (9757)
                                16 (9591)
                                17 (10,035)

MISCELLANEOUS

14 (10,026): Distal extremity: Broken burin; not studied

and the technique of burination employed to create the first burin edge exercise a strong influence on the subsequent history of the piece.

Details of the association patterns are further considered in table 27. In the LOWER subdivision it is obvious by inspection that the table shows a significant departure from randomness, but that all burins associate with all other kinds except for Noailles burins, which appear, when in association, almost always as part of double burins. This tendency is another characteristic of the type. If Noailles burins are removed from the table, the remaining associations appear random. In the UPPER subdivision, there is a tendency for all burin types except burin-points to assort preferentially with themselves, particularly in the cases of truncation and Raysse burins. This need not be taken to indicate that double burins were to these Noaillians more than the sum of their parts. It is more economical to suppose that many of the individual burin associations are narrowly task-specific, and that if in the process of performing a task, a burin became worn or damaged, the workman would tend to continue the job with a similar tool, made on the same blank if it was still suitable.

The association details of burins forming part of combination tools are presented in table 28 (figs. 28:13; 33:14, 15–19; 34:7–9; 40). There is no reason to consider combination tools as more than pieces on which two types of tool happen to be associated on the same blank. The incidence of combination tools is no more than an indication of flint economizing behavior.

Marginal Retouch

The frequencies of different kinds of marginal retouch, expressed as percentages of all burins bearing marginal retouch, and the total frequency of marginal retouch per subdivision, expressed as a percentage of all burins, are shown in table 29. The frequency of marginal retouch on

different types, expressed as the marginal retouch index, has already been listed in the preceding tables. The percentage is low (7%) in the LOWER subdivision but increases in the MIDDLE and UPPER subdivisions to about 20%. The MIDDLE-2 sample appears similar in frequency to the Late Noaillian samples, a reversal of the usual pattern, but the sample, which is qualitatively similar to the LOWER subdivision, is small. From Early to Late Noaillian, there is a change in the modal retouch type from heavy to scaled and a progressive decrease in the proportion of fine retouch.

Throughout the level, marginal retouch is rarely applied to Noailles burins, though it becomes more common on these tools as retouch itself becomes more common. Variation in the frequency of retouch applied to different burin types in the UPPER and MIDDLE-1 subdivisions suggests that marginal retouch is applied randomly to suitable pieces over a certain size and is not associated with particular burin types.

Functional Interrelations of Level 4 Burin Types

The percentage frequency of burin types by burin edge angle (fig. 41) shows a different situation from that of later Level 5 and Level 3. Dihedral burins are not sharper than other forms and, with the exception of break burins, which are as usual the bluntest, there is little differentiation among the burin types. In burin edge width (fig. 42), the specialization of Noailles burins covering the narrow end of the range is very clear. Dihedral burins increase their proportions toward the wide end of the scale, as in later Level 5 and Level 3, though their importance steadily decreases as truncation burins become more and more frequent. As in the other levels, break burins have smaller burin edges than truncation burins. The similarity of the pattern of relationship among dihedral, truncation (excluding Noailles), and break burin edges in Levels 5, 4, and 3 indicates that burin edge widths are strongly affected by the technique of man-

Table 26

CROSS–TABULATION, SHOWING OBSERVED AND EXPECTED VALUES,
OF KINDS OF BURINS AND THEIR MODES OF OCCURRENCE IN LEVEL 4

LOWER + MIDDLE-2[a]		As Double or Mixed	Combination Tool	Single	Total
Noailles	Observed	287	12	647	946
	Expected	255.04	22.91	688.05	
Truncation and Retouched Edge/End	Observed	31	7	150	188
	Expected	50.68	4.55	132.77	
Burin–Point	Observed	4	0	44	48
	Expected	12.94	1.16	33.90	
Dihedral	Observed	73	16	214	303
	Expected	81.69	7.34	213.97	
Break	Observed	28	3	53	84
	Expected	22.65	2.03	59.32	
		423	38	1108	1569

MIDDLE-1 + UPPER[b]		As Double or Mixed	As Combination Tool	Single	Total
Noailles	Observed	37	1	71	109
	Expected	33.42	4.55	71.03	
Truncation and Retouched Edge/End	Observed	151	21	357	529
	Expected	162.18	22.07	344.75	
Raysse	Observed	164	22	258	444
	Expected	136.12	18.52	289.36	
Burin–Point	Observed	19	3	70	92
	Expected	28.20	3.84	59.96	
Dihedral	Observed	70	11	183	264
	Expected	80.94	11.01	172.05	
Break	Observed	44	8	92	144
	Expected	41.15	6.01	93.84	
		485	66	1031	1582

Note: $X^2 = 45.06$, d.f. = 8, $P < 0.001$ for LOWER + MIDDLE-2; $X^2 = 22.06$, d.f. = 10, $P < 0.025$ for MIDDLE-1 + UPPER.

a. Unretouched edge/end burins and Raysse burins are excluded.
b. Unretouched edge/end burins are excluded.

Table 27

MATRICES OF OBSERVED AND EXPECTED VALUES OF BURIN ASSOCIATION PATTERNS
IN LEVEL 4

		Number	Truncation Burin and Retouched Burin	Dihedral Burin	Break Burin
Level 4: LOWER[a]					
Noailles	Observed	137			
	Expected	97.37			
Truncation and Retouched Edge/End	Observed	1	4		
	Expected	18.98	0.93		
Dihedral	Observed	2	10	23	
	Expected	47.10	4.59	5.70	
Break	Observed	0	8	9	3
	Expected	16.17	1.58	3.91	0.67

Total: 197 pieces, 394 burins

		Truncation Burin and Retouched Burin	Burin-Point	Raysse Burin	Dihedral Burin	Break Burin
Level 4: UPPER[b]						
Truncation and Retouched Edge/End	Observed	27				
	Expected	18.68				
Burin-Point	Observed	5	1			
	Expected	5.80	0.45			
Raysse	Observed	25	4	30		
	Expected	36.63	5.69	17.96		
Dihedral	Observed	11	4	8	7	
	Expected	14.87	2.31	14.63	2.96	
Break	Observed	8	1	4	4	3
	Expected	8.34	1.30	8.18	3.32	0.93

Total: 142 pieces, 284 burins

a. Burin-points, Raysse, and unretouched edge/end burins excluded.
b. Noailles and unretouched edge/end burins excluded.

Table 28

ASSOCIATION PATTERNS OF BURINS FORMING PART OF COMBINATION TOOLS IN LEVEL 4

UPPER

Combined with

Burin Type	End-Scraper	Truncated Piece	Perforator or Bec	Point
Noailles	–	1	–	–
Truncation and Retouched Edge/End	13	–	–	1
Burin-Point	3	–	–	–
Raysse	13	4	–	1
Dihedral	6	1	–	1
Break	3	1	–	–

MIDDLE-1

Combined with

Burin Type	End-Scraper	Truncated Piece	Perforator or Bec	Point
Truncation and Retouched Edge/End	3	2	1	1
Raysse	3	1	–	–
Dihedral	1	2	–	–
Break	2	–	–	2

MIDDLE-2:   3 Dihedral Burin + End-Scraper; 1 Dihedral Burin + Side-Scraper

LOWER

Combined with

Burin Type	End-Scraper	Truncated Piece	Perforator or Bec	Point	Side-Scraper
Noailles	4	7	1	–	–
Truncation and Retouched Edge/End	5	–	–	1	1
Dihedral	12	–	–	–	–
Break	2	–	–	1	–
Unretouched Edge/End	1	–	–	–	–

Figure 40. COMBINATION TOOLS (BURIN + END SCRAPER) FROM LEVEL 4: UPPER

SRS TYPE AND ANGLE

Dihedral

2 (8889): UPPER-1: Distal extremity: 60°

3 (7960): UPPER-1a: Distal extremity: 70°

Break

4 (9063): UPPER-1: 80°

Retouched Truncation

1 (8582): UPPER-1a: 60°; Raysse burin

7 (9187): UPPER-2: 70°

Retouched Edge

5 (8284): UPPER-1a: 80°

BURIN EDGE SHAPE AND WIDTH

Straight

1 (8582): 4 mm
2 (8889): 4 mm
4 (9063): 3 mm

Curved

3 (7960): 8 mm

Beveled

5 (8284): 4 mm
7 (9187): 4 mm

OBLIQUITY

Lateral

2 (8889)

Oblique

1 (8582)
4 (9063)
5 (8284)
7 (9187)

Dorsal Oblique/ High Oblique

6 (8406): UPPER-1a: Raysse burin

Lateral/ Flat-Faced

9 (5666): UPPER-1: Raysse burin

Lateral/ High Oblique

8 (8690): UPPER-1: Raysse burin

SRS SHAPE

Concave

1 (8582)
9 (5666)

Straight

2 (8889)
3 (7960)
4 (9063)
5 (8284)

6 (8406)
7 (9187)
8 (8690)
9 (5666)

LATERAL POSITION

Median

2 (8889)
3 (7960)
7 (9187)

Right Asymmetrical

5 (8284)

Right Lateral

1 (8582)
4 (9063)

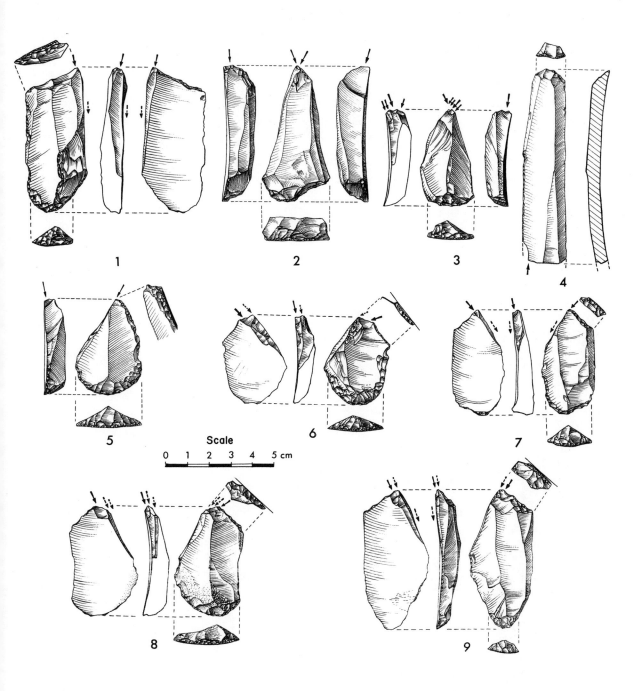

RAYSSE BURINS

SRS TYPE

6 (8406): UPPER-1a: On retouched
   truncation

8 (8690): UPPER-1: On retouched
   truncation

9 (5666): UPPER-1: On retouched
   truncation

NUMBER OF REMOVALS

6 (8406): 1+1
8 (8690): 1+2
9 (5666): 1+1

Figure 40 (continued).

FIRST REMOVAL

Dorsal Oblique   Lateral Oblique
(<80°)   (80–100°)

6 (8406): 70°   8 (8690):   90°
                    9 (5666):   90°

LAST REMOVAL

High Oblique   Flat-Faced
(140–150°)   (160–180°)

6 (8406): 140°   9 (5666): 160°
8 (8690): 150°

LATERAL POSITION

Median

6 (8406)
8 (8690)
9 (5666)

END SCRAPERS

SHAPE OF END

Arc of Circle   Asymmetrical

3 (7960): Proximal extremity: 80°;   1 (8582): Proximal extremity
   1.75 cm   8 (8690): Proximal extremity
4 (9063): Distal extremity: 130°;
   0.75 cm
5 (8284): Proximal extremity: 130°;
   1.75 cm
6 (8406): Proximal extremity: 160°;
   1.25 cm

Blunt Point   Irregular

9 (5666): Proximal extremity   2 (8889): Proximal extremity
                                         7 (9187): Proximal extremity

RETOUCH ANGLE

Acute   Medium

4 (9063): Distal extremity   2 (8889): Proximal extremity
6 (8406): Proximal extremity   5 (8284): Proximal extremity
9 (5666): Proximal extremity   8 (8690): Proximal extremity

Steep   Perpendicular

3 (7960): Proximal extremity   1 (8582): Proximal extremity
7 (9187): Proximal extremity

Figure 40 (continued).

RETOUCH PATTERN

Convergent

6 (8406): Proximal extremity
9 (5666): Proximal extremity

Semi-Convergent

1 (8582): Proximal extremity
3 (7960): Proximal extremity
5 (8284): Proximal extremity
7 (9187): Proximal extremity
8 (8690): Proximal extremity

Non-Convergent

2 (8889): Proximal extremity
4 (9063): Distal extremity

COMBINATION TOOLS (Recapitulation)

1 (8582): Distal extremity: Truncation burin; Proximal extremity: Asymmetrical end-scraper
2 (8889): Distal extremity: Dihedral burin; Proximal extremity: Irregular end-scraper
3 (7960): Distal extremity: Dihedral burin; Proximal extremity: Arc-of-circle end-scraper
4 (9063): Proximal extremity: Break burin; Distal extremity: Arc-of-circle end-scraper
5 (8284): Distal extremity: Burin on retouched edge; Proximal extremity: Arc-of-circle end-scraper
6 (8406): Distal extremity: Raysse burin; Proximal extremity: Arc-of-circle end-scraper
7 (9187): Distal extremity: Truncation burin; Proximal extremity: Irregular end-scraper
8 (8690): Distal extremity: Raysse burin; Proximal extremity: Asymmetrical end-scraper
9 (5666): Distal extremity: Raysse burin; Proximal extremity: Blunt point end-scraper

Table 29

DISTRIBUTION OF MARGINAL RETOUCH ON BURINS IN LEVEL 4

	Fine		Heavy		Scaled		Other		Total	% of All Pieces
	n	%	n	%	n	%	n	%		
UPPER	24	13.64	52	29.55	86	48.86	14	7.95	176	21.49
MIDDLE-1	20	21.74	22	23.91	45	48.91	5	5.43	92	18.89
MIDDLE-2	7	35.00	7	35.00	4	20.00	2	10.00	20	18.87
LOWER	27	26.37	33	36.26	24	26.37	10	10.99	91	7.29

ufacture. Break burins have smaller burin edges than truncation burins, we suggest, because the SRS angle—closer to the perpendicular on break burins—normally allows only one or two burin edges to be manufactured sequentially from the same SRS. At this point, the angle becomes too great for another burin blow to be struck. On truncation burins, the obliquity of the SRS permits several resharpening removals to be made, and the burin edge is thus generally closer to the center of the piece and therefore larger. If this is so, then the rank order of the three types is mainly determined not by cultural factors but by the technique of manufacture. However this may be, the use of the truncation technique to manufacture burins with very small edges and the application of other modifying techniques to obtain small burin edges in level 4 differentiates the level unequivocally from both Level 5 and Level 3.

DISCUSSION AND CONCLUSIONS

It is unnecessary to insist on the distinctiveness of the burins of the Noaillian. In blanks, in dimensions, in technique, and in numerous other ways they differ fundamentally from the series of both the Périgordian IV and VI. The Noailles burin appears in the sequence suddenly, without forerunners; the Raysse burin disappears finally before the start of the Périgordian VI occupation. Even the less specialized tool types, truncation burins, break burins, and dihedral burins are typologically distinct from their Périgordian IV and VI counterparts in ways that imply both functional and stylistic differentiation (Clay 1976). Seen against the background of the total range of variation of burins in the time period concerned, the Périgordian IV and VI assort together in sharp contrast to the exotic and stratigraphically intervening Noaillian. It is true that in the ratio of dihedral burins to burins made on truncations, the Périgordian VI resembles the Noaillian more closely than the Périgordian IV. It is perfectly possible, even likely, that the increasing frequency of burins in the former level, the specialization for truncation burins, and the decrease in the width of truncation burin

edges are evidence of some kind of contact with, or influence from, the Noaillians. If so, then demonstration of this relationship must come from sites other than the Abri Pataud. The evidence of the Pataud series is clear: the Noaillian burin samples are the expression of a tradition radically different from that which produced the burins of the Périgordian IV and VI.

The dramatic replacement of the Noailles burin by truncation burins and Raysse burins is the criterion for the establishment and distinction of the Early and Late Noaillian phases. In the LOWER subdivision, the chronological development of the industry is obscured by the absence of refined stratigraphic connections between the front and rear of the site and by typological and quantitative differences between these two areas. The evidence of the Noailles burins suggests that the FRONT:LOWER-2 subdivision is the oldest deposit attributable to the Noaillian and that the REAR:LOWER is more closely contemporary with the FRONT:LOWER-1 subdivision. On the other hand, the dihedral burins in the front are more similar to each other than either are to the REAR sample. The suddenness of the change from Early to Late Noaillian is seen in the ratio of Noailles to Raysse and modified truncation burins in the two MIDDLE subdivisions:

	Noailles	*Raysse*	*Modified TB*
MIDDLE-1	60	140	52
MIDDLE-2	54	1	6

But once this change has occurred, there follows a period of conservatism lasting until the end of the occupation, in which there is little change in the nature or proportions of tool types. It seems as if, having once made the technological shift, there was no further incentive to change. The contrast between the inventiveness of the MIDDLE subdivisions and the conservatism of the UPPER is striking, too much so to be accepted at face value, but to understand it other kinds of evidence and the evidence of other sites is required.

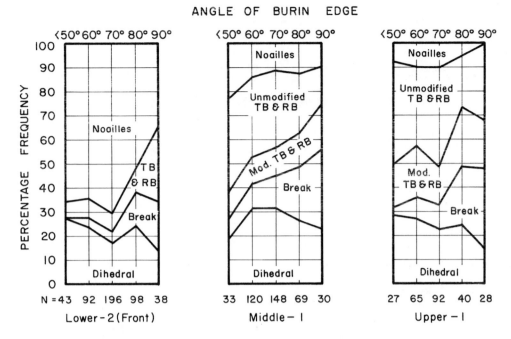

Figure 41. PERCENTAGE FREQUENCIES OF BURIN TYPES BY BURIN EDGE ANGLE IN LEVEL 4 (selected subdivisions).

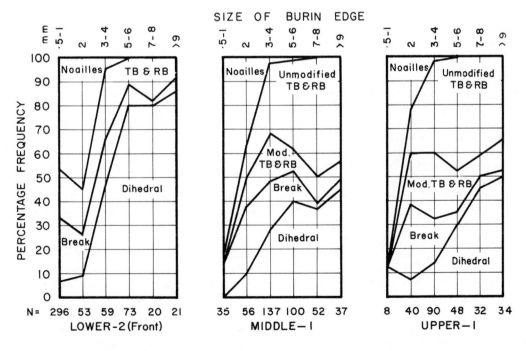

Figure 42. PERCENTAGE FREQUENCIES OF BURIN TYPES BY BURIN EDGE SIZE IN LEVEL 4 (selected subdivisions).

V

Truncated and Marginally Retouched Pieces and Nuclei from Level 4

TRUNCATED PIECES FROM LEVEL 4

The majority of truncated pieces in Level 4, as in Levels 5 and 3, are related to the burins. There are no tool types independent of the burins, but the truncation technique is used in the manufacture of "retruncation burin-points," which, as a tool type, appear functionally identical to burin-points made by the burin technique followed by tertiary retouch. The remaining truncated pieces are described under the headings of "retruncated burins" and "undifferentiated truncated pieces." All of the former and most of the latter are considered by-products of burin manufacture.

Retruncated Burins

Retruncated burins are the most closely and obviously related to the burins of all tools classified as truncated pieces. They are retruncations of old burins, identified by the fact that the retouch of the truncation cuts across the burin facet. No trace of the original burin edge or negative bulb of percussion remains on the spall facet, and its intersection with the truncation retouch tends to be tilted slightly backward onto the dorsal surface of the piece (fig. 43).

It is possible that the retruncation technique was used occasionally to create burin-like tools differentiated from true burins by the reversal of the normal sequence of processes. Detailed studies of wear need to be made on these pieces before this hypothesis can be substantiated. It is often difficult to distinguish retruncated burins from truncation burins whose burin edge has been removed by pressure from the ventral surface; only clear examples are included here. Retruncated burins are sometimes found on pieces which have a live burin at the other end or, occasionally, on combination tools. Such pieces are not included in the totals below:

UPPER	19
MIDDLE	11
LOWER	21

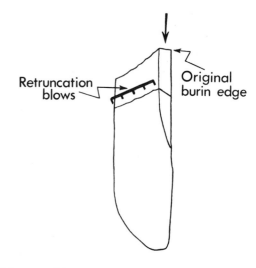

Figure 43. RETRUNCATION OF A BURIN.

Retruncation Burin-Points

The technique of retruncation is sometimes used to create pieces morphologically and functionally identical to burin-points (figs. 25:9; 26:4). The normal process of manufacture of these tools is for a burin edge to be modified by a series of small tertiary removals in such a way as to tilt the burin edge back onto the dorsal surface of the piece, forming a point at the intersection of the burin edge and the ventral surface of the tool. The retruncation technique forms this point directly, the angle of the retruncation retouch being sufficient to create the inclination required. While few in number, these pieces show the same utilization and tip damage common to burin-points made by the normal process. They occur in all subdivisions in small numbers:

UPPER	8
MIDDLE	3
LOWER	2

Table 30
DISTRIBUTION OF TRUNCATION SHAPE AND TRUNCATION ANGLE OF TRUNCATED PIECES IN LEVEL 4

Truncation Shape	LOWER n	LOWER %	MIDDLE n	MIDDLE %	UPPER n	UPPER %
Convex	11	17.74	6	(16.67)	13	(31.71)
Straight	12	19.35	14	(38.89)	12	(29.27)
Concave	21	33.87	7	(19.44)	6	(14.63)
Pronounced Concave	13	20.97	1	(2.78)	5	(12.20)
Concave/Convex	5	8.06	8	(22.22)	5	(12.20)
	62	99.99	36	(100.00)	41	(100.00)

Truncation Angle	LOWER	MIDDLE	UPPER
$\bar{X} \pm s_{\bar{X}}$	70.00 ± 1.98	73.61 ± 2.68	72.44 ± 2.31
Range	30–90	40–90	40–90
s	15.58	16.06	14.80
n	62	36	41

Undifferentiated Truncated Pieces (fig. 5:6–8)

The distribution of undifferentiated truncated pieces by shape and angle of truncation is shown in table 30. The shape of the truncation varies greatly through time, being dominantly concave in LOWER, straight in MIDDLE, and convex in UPPER. Concavo-convex truncations are less frequent in LOWER than in the later subdivisions. The truncation angle is very constant through time, with means between 70° and 75° in all subdivisions. It is interesting to compare these attributes of truncated pieces with those of the truncation burins (see table 31), specifically the Noailles truncation burins of FRONT:LOWER-2 and all the truncation burins of MIDDLE-1 and UPPER-1. In LOWER, the truncated pieces and burins are closely similar in terms of mean angle of truncation and in the distribution of truncation shape (dominantly concave). In the later subdivisions, the mean angle for truncated pieces is much higher than that for burins. Many truncated pieces with very high truncation angles thus may have been rejected as unsuitable for burin manufacture. The MIDDLE-1 truncation burins are like the truncated pieces from that subdivision, in that the dominant truncation shape is straight. In UPPER-1, however, the truncated pieces have a high proportion of convex truncations, a feature which is not present on truncation burins, where the dominant shapes are straight and slightly concave.

The size of the truncated pieces in each subdivision parallels the size of the truncation burins. In the LOWER subdivision they are mostly small, of Noailles burin dimensions. Several, in fact, are equipped with a notch in preparation for a burin blow which was never struck. In UPPER and MIDDLE, truncated pieces are larger. In all subdivisions, pieces are found with minor marginal retouch along the edge adjacent to the truncation, which, had a burin blow been struck, would have produced a retouched burin spall. Truncated pieces are also combined with burins. The relationship of these tools to the truncation burins cannot reasonably be doubted.

Study of the wear on truncated pieces has not enabled us to establish the presence of types. One pattern of utilization recognized is limited to pieces with a concave truncation, the inside of which shows rounding by wear (four in UPPER and nine each in MIDDLE and LOWER). These pieces vary in truncation angle from 90° to 60°, contributing to the over-representation of the 90° class. The shape of the truncation is, in some cases, very deeply concave. Morphologically they are quite variable, in some cases approximating Noailles burins, on which similar wear is sometimes visible. They are not classed as a separate type.

Conclusions

Truncated pieces, in both the Noaillian and the Upper Périgordian, constitute a heterogeneous category that includes within it very different kinds of tools. To the limited extent to which one can speak of the class as a whole, truncated pieces are most closely related to truncation burins. The *technique* of truncation, however, is employed to make other kinds of tools. In Levels 5 and 3, it is used for the manufacture of truncation borers, characterized by a pattern of wear on the truncation and adjacent margin and a morphological range different from that of the truncation burins. In Level 4, the truncation technique is employed in the manufacture of a special kind of burin-point. Retruncated burins exist in all the series. There is no other indication of the presence of distinguishable types, although individual pieces appear to have been used as scrapers or as spokeshaves. The proportional frequency of truncated pieces within assemblages is of dubious value for inferences concerning culture.

PIECES WITH MARGINAL RETOUCH

Description

Marginal retouch is considerably more frequent in Level 4 than in either Level 5 or Level 3. This increase lies mainly in its application to other tools. The number of retouched pieces not associated with other tools (complete specimens and distal fragments with at least one side continuously retouched) remains very low.

Retouch styles (described by David 1966, table 67) are exemplified in figure 6. The internal proportions of the various styles (table 32) change decisively between the LOWER and MIDDLE subdivisions, fine retouch declining from 49% to 23% and scaled retouch increasing from 21% to 51%. This trend continues in the UPPER subdivision, where scaled retouch reaches 54%. Heavy retouch falls from 28% in LOWER to 20% in UPPER. The break between the LOWER and MIDDLE subdivisions corresponds with that seen in other tool types.

In the LOWER subdivision, the majority of the retouch is nondescript; both fine and heavy tend to be less steep than in Levels 5 and 3. Scaled retouch is not well developed, although good examples exist. In UPPER and MIDDLE, scaled retouch is the norm, and most pieces with heavy and fine retouch may be considered as variations. Both the latter are less steep than in Levels 5 and 3. There is a clear preference for retouch on the left side in UPPER and MIDDLE but not in LOWER. Right to left ratios are 1:1.2 in the LOWER subdivision and 1:3.5 and 1:2.8 in the MIDDLE and UPPER subdivisions respectively. Scaled retouch is virtually restricted to blades, the majority of which are retouched on one margin only.

Study of the complete specimens does not suggest the presence of specific, independent types of retouched blades. Some regularly formed "knives" do exist, but they are rare, reflecting only the primary blank morphology.

Marginal retouch is rarely applied to blades less than 50 mm long. The length of retouched blades in the UPPER and MIDDLE subdivisions is most frequently 70–90 mm, and the width is 20–35 mm. The form of the distal extremity is usually rather bluntly and irregularly pointed, varying to rounded forms with no detectable patterned morphology. The shape of the edge affected by marginal retouch varies from straight to slightly convex. From the localization of retouch on the pieces, especially on partially retouched examples, it can be seen that retouch is applied to regularize a preexisting edge and that for the majority of scaled pieces it has the effect of creating a strong "cutting" edge with

minimal modification of that edge, in terms of the amount of flint removed and the decrease in sharpness of the edge.

Discussion and Conclusions

The low frequency of pieces that can be demonstrated not to have been associated with other tool types in their original, unbroken state shows that while marginal retouch is applied with varying frequency to blades and flakes in the several subdivisions of Level 4 (and in Levels 5 and 3), marginally retouched pieces are *not* in themselves an independent tool type. They are merely artifacts, suitable on account of their size and conformation, to which marginal retouch was applied that did not happen also to be made into end-scrapers, burins, or other tools. *The retouched edge is the significant unit and not the retouched piece.* Detailed study of retouched flakes and blades is not likely to be of as much interest as the study of the application of marginal retouch to other tools. Retouched pieces can be used for the qualitative study of retouch and, although their proportional frequency is not of the same positive significance as that of, for instance, end-scrapers, it is still of value as a crude index of marginal retouch in an assemblage.

In Levels 5 and 3, marginal retouch is infrequent, both on retouched pieces and on the margins of recognized tool classes. In Level 4, marginal retouch is more frequent, especially in the MIDDLE and UPPER subdivisions. Retouch on end-scrapers is throughout more common than on burins. Much of the discrepancy in LOWER is explained by the high frequency of Noailles burins, to which, on account of their small size, marginal retouch was applied only exceptionally. But in MIDDLE and UPPER, the difference is clear and real, though both tool classes have a high incidence of marginal retouch. With the exception of Noailles burins, there are no consistent differences in the percentage frequency of marginal retouch on different burin types. In spite of some slightly greater degree of association of the use of retouched edges with end-scrapers than with burins, marginal retouch is very generally applied to pieces larger than those employed for the manufacture of Noailles burins.

Marginal retouch of the Périgordian IV and VI differs from that of the Noaillian both in its lower frequency and in details of the retouch styles. Although scaled retouch is present in Level 5 and of quantitative importance on certain tool classes, the norm lies somewhere near the borderline between fine and heavy retouch. In Level 3 there is better characterization of the fine retouch style. In Level 4, scaled retouch produces sharp, strong, acute-angle edges. Such retouch increases in quantity and quality from the LOWER to the MIDDLE and UPPER subdivisions. The distribution of scaled retouch expresses the same break between Early and Late Noaillian that is characteristic of all other tool types.

Table 31

DISTRIBUTION OF SRS ANGLE AND SRS SHAPE OF CERTAIN BURINS IN LEVEL 4

	Noailles Truncation Burins		Truncation Burins		Truncation Burins	
SRS Angle	FRONT: LOWER-2		MIDDLE-1		UPPER-1	
$\bar{X} \pm s_{\bar{X}}$	71.99 ± 0.83		59.35 ± 1.49		57.60 ± 1.89	
Range	0-90		0-90		0-90	
s	14.57		17.48		19.28	
n	311		138		104	
SRS Shape	n	%	n	%	n	%
Convex	2	0.64	12	8.70	5	4.81
Straight	91	29.26	63	45.65	37	35.58
Concave	141	45.34	40	28.99	38	36.54
Pronounced Concave	77	24.76	23	16.67	24	23.08
Total	311	100.00	138	100.01	104	100.01

Table 32

DISTRIBUTION OF RETOUCH STYLE ON PIECES WITH MARGINAL RETOUCH IN LEVEL 4

		LOWER		MIDDLE		UPPER	
		n	%	n	%	n	%
Fine	Fragments	40		23		46	
	Complete	4		2		7	
		44	49.44	25	23.15	53	19.92
Heavy	Fragments	20		20		50	
	Complete	5		3		3	
		25	28.09	23	21.30	53	19.92
Scaled	Fragments	18		44		142	
	Complete	1		11		2	
		19	21.35	55	50.93	144	54.14
Other		-	-	1	0.93	4	1.50
Mixed		1	1.12	4	3.70	12	4.51
Totals	Blades	79		91		240	
	Flakes	10		17		26	
		89	100.00	108	100.01	266	99.99

NUCLEI

Disgracefully, by the standards of modern research—which quite rightly emphasize the critical importance of reduction techniques both in themselves and as determinant of many aspects of the retouched tool component—I never studied the nuclei from Level 4. Neither were examples selected for illustration. Harvey M. Bricker has very kindly contributed the following section, and the reader is referred to Bricker (1973, chap. 24) and to Bricker and David (1984) for full explanation of the terms employed. Basic shapes may be described briefly as follows:

Prismatic: The stereotypic, prism-shaped Upper Palaeolithic blade core. Face of nucleus shows a series of (sub-) parallel removals that tend to wrap around the piece; may have a platform at one or both ends.

Pyramidal: Normally has only one platform from which blades are removed around all or most of the circumference, producing a grossly pyramidal/conic shape.

Tabular: Imagine the core as a book you are about to open, the binding (the back of the core) held away from you. Removals have been taken down the face of the core that is toward you and do not extend far onto the sides (the book covers). One or both sides is often covered in cortex.

Flat: Similar to tabular, but with removals in the plane of the greatest dimension.

Irregular: Residual category, often largely cortical or with multiple striking platforms at irregular and divergent angles to one another.

Shape

The distribution of nuclei by shape is shown in table 33. Prismatic and flat forms account for ca. 40–60% in all three subdivisions, being most frequent in LOWER. Tabular nuclei are always rare, and pyramidal nuclei are absent. Irregular nuclei are quantitatively important, especially in MIDDLE, where they form a majority of the series. None of the forms shows a regular trend of frequency change through time. Nor is there an Early versus Late Noaillian pattern visible if MIDDLE-1 and MIDDLE-2 are tabulated separately, because the small MIDDLE-2 sample (n = 27) gives undoubtedly distorted percentages. One feature not shown in the table is the distinctiveness of FRONT:LOWER-2, which has a high frequency (55.00%) of prismatic nuclei and a low frequency (26.67%) of irregular nuclei. Among the 33 prismatic nuclei of this subdivision is a series of five small, delicate, and very regular micro-blade cores, the last removals from which would have provided excellent blanks for small backed tools. All of these come from Trench V(North), one from Lens O-3 and four from Lens O-4. They have no close parallels from other areas of the FRONT:LOWER-2 subdivision or from other subdivisions

of Level 4. A possible explanation for their distinctiveness is suggested by the fact that two of them were found in a light-colored sand inclusion in Lens O-4 that is believed to represent backdirt from the large pit dug into and through Level 5 (Périgordian IV). While their intrusiveness is by no means demonstrated, they suggest that the apparently high proportion of prismatic nuclei of any size in FRONT:LOWER-2, hence in all of LOWER, should be viewed with caution.

Approximately half the prismatic nuclei in each subdivision have only one striking platform. On those with two striking platforms, the opposed pattern (with platforms on the same side but opposite ends) is always heavily dominant over the alternate pattern (with platforms on opposite sides and opposite ends of the piece). Although less regular, the distributions for flat nuclei are approximately the same, but the occurrence of crossed platforms is more frequent.

The shape distribution of nuclei in Level 4 is clearly different from those of Level 3 and the later units of Level 5. Prismatic forms are far less frequent in Level 4 (except in FRONT:LOWER-2, where, as noted above, some contamination from Level 5 is a distinct possibility). Flattened forms are slightly more numerous than in later Level 5, but they are in the same frequency range as Level 3. Except in LOWER, the Level 4 frequencies of prismatic plus flat forms are distinctly lower than those of Level 5 and particularly of Level 3. Irregular nuclei, on the other hand, are more common in Level 4 (with, again, the exception of the LOWER subdivision) than in the other two levels. All these shape differences would seem to suggest the lesser importance of the blade blank in Level 4 than in Levels 5 and 3, but reference to the tool samples shows that this is not the case. Blade blanks are of overwhelming importance in the Noaillian, but as has been noted in the tool analysis chapters, the Noaillian blades differ qualitatively from those of the Périgordian IV and VI. This observation, combined with the nucleus data, indicates basic differences in blank production technique. The present study has not been oriented toward the examination of such differences, but the few facts which are reported here leave no doubt that a fuller analysis of the technique of *débitage*, based on a detailed study of the nuclei and waste flakes as well as on the tool sample, would be able to document important and culturally very significant differences between the Noaillian and the Périgordian IV–VI.

Flint Variety

The distribution of the flint variety of the nucleus sample is shown in table 34. Almost all the flint—mostly black, but sometimes gray, tan, or blond—represents one or another variety of the Campanian or Coniacian (Upper Cretaceous) flint which occurs in the limestone of the Les Eyzies vicinity. Maestrichtian (Upper Cretaceous) flint, from outcrops in the Bergerac vicinity or the Couze River Valley, is extremely rare in LOWER and MIDDLE and entirely absent in UPPER. All of the examples of Maestrichtian flint

Table 33
DISTRIBUTION OF SHAPE OF NUCLEI IN LEVEL 4

	UPPER		MIDDLE		LOWER	
	n	%	n	%	n	%
Prismatic						
With One Striking Platform	15		12		26	
With Two Alternate Striking Platforms	2		6		11	
With Two Opposed Striking Platforms	8		11		21	
With Two Crossed Striking Platforms	1		–		1	
Total prismatic	26	31.33	29	28.43	59	45.38
Flat						
With One Striking Platform	11		4		8	
With Two Alternate Striking Platforms	2		2		2	
With Two Opposed Striking Platforms	2		4		7	
With Two Crossed Striking Platforms	1		2		2	
Total flat	16	19.28	12	11.76	19	14.62
Irregular	38	45.78	55	53.92	46	35.38
Tabular	3	3.61	6	5.88	6	4.62
Pyramidal	–	–	–	–	–	–
Subtotal	83	100.00	102	99.99	130	100.00
Fragments	3		7		11	
Chunks (ébauches)	9		6		15	
Attempts	5		12		17	
Subtotal	17		25		43	
Total	100		127		173	

Table 34
DISTRIBUTION OF FLINT VARIETY OF NUCLEI IN LEVEL 4

	UPPER		MIDDLE		LOWER	
	n	%	n	%	n	%
Campanian and Coniacian	96	96.00	124	97.64	168	97.11
Maestrichtian	–	–	1	0.79	4	2.31
With Lustrous White Patination[a]	4	4.00	2	1.57	1	0.58
Total	100	100.00	127	100.00	173	100.00

a. See text for discussion of flint with lustrous white patination.

in LOWER (three pieces of banded "Bergerac" flint and one piece of *jaspe moucheté*) come from FRONT:LOWER-2, and three of them were found in deposits which could include backdirt from the pit dug into and through Level 5 (Périgordian IV).

The provenience of the flint with the so-called lustrous white patination cannot be determined without breaking the piece to examine the unpatinated interior. The lustrous, porcelain-like patination, which may be up to 2–3 mm thick, effectively masks the original properties of the material. Several *débitage* flakes which we intentionally broke revealed an unaltered core of either gray or blond flint of the Campanian/Coniacian series. It is reasonable to suppose from this evidence and from the general distribution that most or all of the seven nuclei bearing this particular patination are also the local flint of the Les Eyzies vicinity.

Even allowing for the uncertainties about the Maestrichtian nuclei in FRONT:LOWER-2 and the provenience of the white patinated flint, it is perfectly clear from table 34 that evidence of use at the Abri Pataud of flint other than that available in the Les Eyzies vicinity is, for all practical purposes, absent. Although several nuclei of Maestrichtian flint were found in Level 4, use of this material formed no important part of flint tool production at the Abri Pataud. This situation is quite different from that in the later units of Level 5, where the frequencies of Maestrichtian flint vary between about 14% and 20%. It is, however, quite like Level 3, where the representation of Maestrichtian flint in the nucleus sample is also very small (about 4%).

Summary

About half of the Level 4 nuclei are prismatic or flat, and almost all the rest are irregular. The flint sources represented by the nuclei are almost without exception those of the Campanian and Coniacian formations of the Les Eyzies vicinity. FRONT:LOWER-2 is somewhat anomalous with respect to both attributes, but the possibility exists that some mixture of Level 5 (Périgordian IV) artifacts is present. Otherwise, the Level 4 nuclei form a consistent series and one that is clearly different from the nuclei of later Level 5 and Level 3, themselves quite similar. Although this study does not provide the needed documentation, it seems likely that there were basic and fundamental differences between the core reduction techniques of the Noaillian and the Périgordian IV–VI.

VI

The Nonflint Industry of Level 4

OBJECTS OF STONE OTHER THAN FLINT (table 35)

Flaking Tools or Anvil Stones

There are several different forms of stone-flaking tools in Level 4. Two are small, regular-shaped, but unpolished pebbles bearing at one or both ends the cuts, scratches, and abrasions showing use as a flaking tool. One larger, ovoid pebble has been so used on both faces, and at one end there is a rounded facet worn smooth by rubbing. Two of the flaking tools are long, cylindrical pebbles used at the pointed end and along both margins. Two objects may be described as anvil stones: a flat, tabular fragment of sandstone and a large irregular pebble of cemented gritstone. These tools are very similar to those in Level 5; there are none of the dolomite flaking tools found in Level 3.

Hammerstones

All but one of the eleven hammerstones in Level 4 are medium or large, water-rolled, quartz pebbles. The exception is an ovoid, well-rounded pebble of some hard, fine-grained rock. It has been used at both ends as a hammerstone and on both surfaces as a flaking tool. One side of the pebble bears three pronounced, striated facets of unknown origin or purpose.

Rolled and/or Polished Pebbles

A large series of water-rolled and sometimes polished pebbles was found in Level 4. They range from the size of a small pea to pieces 20–25 mm in maximum dimension. They were sorted according to shape (regular or irregular) and degree of polishing (highly polished, polished, not polished), as shown in table 36.

All the highly polished, polished, and regular unpolished examples are various kinds of hard resistant rocks, including several examples of quartz crystal. They have been rounded by water action into spheroid or ovoid shapes. The polished and unpolished pieces are like those that can be found today in the gravels of the Dordogne River. It seems unlikely,

however, that the pebbles described as highly polished could have received such a glistening surface finish by purely natural means. One is led to suppose that these pieces received their high polish from being carried around, handled, and manipulated over a period of time.

Pebbles of the highly polished, polished, and regular unpolished varieties are virtually absent except in MIDDLE and UPPER. Furthermore, only five of the total of 52 such pebbles in MIDDLE are from MIDDLE-2. This sharp break in frequencies is another example of a difference between the two MIDDLE subdivisions seen in various attributes of the flint tools. The quantitatively important occurrence of small rolled and sometimes polished river pebbles is a distinctive feature of the Late Noaillian of Level 4. Such pieces are absent from both Level 5 and Level 3.

The irregular unpolished pieces are about equally divided between hard rocks of various kinds and limestone or dolomite examples. They are present throughout the level, and there is no great difference in frequencies between MIDDLE-2 and MIDDLE-1. Pebbles of this sort, irregular and unpolished, are common throughout Level 5 but are virtually absent in Level 3.

The lateral distribution of rolled and/or polished pebbles in Lens N-1 of MIDDLE-1 was investigated. The pebbles were not associated in localized clusters, but the sample as a whole was definitely concentrated toward the rear of the site, in Squares E and F, between the eastern edge of the N-1 hearth and the back wall.

Coloring Matter

Coloring matter, whether hematite or manganese dioxide, is not particularly abundant in Level 4. Quantities given in table 35 refer to find spots, not individual fragments, but in most cases only one small or very small fragment was found in any one spot. The majority of the series comes from the MIDDLE subdivision, especially from Lens N-1 and the N-1 hearth area. Two pieces from LOWER have slightly rounded corners and smoothed surfaces, as if the piece had been rubbed, but there are no faceted hematite crayons of the kind found in Level 3. In this way, the Level 4 hematite sample is like that of Level 5 but is far smaller.

Table 35
DISTRIBUTION OF OBJECTS MADE OF STONE OTHER THAN FLINT IN LEVEL 4

	LOWER	MIDDLE	UPPER
Flaking Tools or Anvil Stones	2	3	2
Hammerstones	3	4	4
Rolled and/or Polished Pebbles	23	84	75
Coloring Matter: Hematite	11	32	8
Coloring Matter: Manganese Dioxide	7	25	9
Coloring Matter: Limonite	–	–	1
Miscellaneous Fossils	2	9	–
Miscellaneous Stone Objects	2	–	5

Table 36
DISTRIBUTION OF ROLLED AND/OR POLISHED PEBBLES IN LEVEL 4,
CLASSIFIED BY SHAPE AND DEGREE OF POLISHING

	LOWER	MIDDLE	UPPER	ALL LEVEL 4
Highly Polished; Regular Shape	–	14	3	
Polished; Regular Shape	1	5	5	
Polished; Irregular Shape	–	7	11	
Rounded, Not Polished; Regular Shape	4	26	16	
Rounded, Not Polished; Irregular Shape	18	32	40	
Total	23	84	75	182

Table 37
DISTRIBUTION OF MARINE MOLLUSC SHELLS
PERFORATED FOR USE AS ORNAMENTS IN LEVEL 4

	LOWER	MIDDLE	UPPER
Littorina littoralis	–	14	20
Littorina littorea	–	1	2
Nucella lapillus	–	1	2
Neverita josephinia	–	–	1
Phalium saburon	–	–	1
Nassarius reticulatus	–	–	1
Callista chione	–	–	2
Total	–	16	29

The use of hematite in the living area was evidently of considerably less importance in the Noaillian than in the Périgordian IV and VI.

In relation to the amount of hematite, the amount of manganese dioxide in Level 4 is rather large. Like hematite, manganese is concentrated in MIDDLE, especially in Lens N-1. Although faceted crayons are not present, several of the manganese chunks are somewhat rounded or rubbed. The importance of this black coloring matter in Level 4 is in clear contrast to both Level 5 and Level 3. One piece of limonite (yellow ochre) was found in UPPER.

One use of the hematite and manganese was for the decoration of the then-existing roof of the shelter. Fallen roof slabs bearing traces of red and black paintings were found immediately overlying Level 4.

Miscellaneous Fossils

Several kinds of fossils were brought to the site by the Level 4 inhabitants. These include three fossil shark teeth, two from MIDDLE and one from LOWER, and one indeterminate fossil from LOWER, probably also a tooth. There are seven small ammonites (*Lissoceratoides* sp.) from MIDDLE (fig. 44:17, 18), all of which have a hole in the center. According to Dance (1975, p. 156), the hole may result from natural causes, and it is not clear that any of the specimens have been artificially perforated. Two casts of brachyopods (*Cyclothyris difformis*), which occur in the limestone bedrock of the shelter itself, were found in MIDDLE.

Miscellaneous Stone Objects

Included here in the residual category of miscellaneous stone objects are four fragments of calcite crystal, one fragment of galena, and two calcareous concretions.

PERFORATED MOLLUSC SHELLS

Level 4 is rich in marine mollusc shells brought to the site presumably for use as ornaments. The origin of these shells and their environmental implications are fully discussed elsewhere (Dance 1975, pp. 154–159), but those that have been artificially perforated are considered here (table 37). Many are poorly preserved and fragmentary; the totals of perforated examples given in the table should be regarded as minimum figures, since it is impossible to determine whether or not badly broken examples were originally perforated.

The technique of perforation is usually indeterminate; the hole is often irregular and, except for one specimen from UPPER, the wall of the hole shows no certain traces of drilling or cutting. A special technique of perforation was used on both examples of *Callista chione* and the single example of *Phalium saburon* from UPPER. On these shells, thicker than the other species that were perforated, a short, deep groove was sawn or incised on the convex outer part of the shell just beyond the valve hinge. When this groove penetrated into the concave inner surface, it created in the center of the grooved line an elongate hole, much shorter than the groove, without drilling. This perforation technique is not found on any other species in Level 4.

The vertical distribution of the perforated shells shows the same clear difference between Early and Late Noaillian that has been noted for other artifacts. Of the 16 examples from MIDDLE, all but one come from MIDDLE-1, most from Lens N-1. Although perforated shells are not uncommon in MIDDLE-1 and UPPER, the species distributions are different. A broader range is present in UPPER, including four species not found elsewhere in the level. With one exception, however, the species differences do not indicate different source areas for the molluscs. *Neverita josephinia*, found only in UPPER, occurs exclusively in the Mediterranean.[5] All other species occur today on the Atlantic coast of France. The great majority of perforated shells in MIDDLE-1 are *Littorina littoralis*, and they occur in localized clusters. In Trench IV, Square F, of Lens N-1, 20 *Littorina littoralis* shells, not all of them perforated, were found associated with five fossil ammonites (see above) in an area ca. 20 by 40 cm. A small number of marine shells were found in LOWER, but none of them is definitely perforated. All the species in LOWER are found today on the Atlantic coast of France. The perforated mollusc shells of the Late Noaillian assemblages of Level 4 are far more numerous and more varied than those of Levels 5 and 3.

ARTIFACTS MADE OF TOOTH, BONE, ANTLER, AND IVORY

Because artifacts of tooth, bone, antler, and ivory are less well preserved and far rarer than artifacts of stone, they are not amenable to the kind of attribute analysis that has been developed for the study of flint tools and used in the foregoing chapters (table 38). But the greater malleability of these materials permits the artisan to express himself more directly and personally on the tools he manufactures and gives them a special value as "type-fossils," or horizon markers, that has been well understood since the earliest days of Palaeolithic archaeology. The English terminology for bone and antler tools is not yet standardized. The common classes descriptively defined and discussed below are identified by names which are for the most part literal translations from the French.

Perforated and Grooved Teeth

There are seven such teeth in Level 4. One is probably a badger canine (fig. 44:12); the other canines are definitely

---

5. Fragmentary examples of two other Mediterranean species, *Cypraea pyrum* and *Cypraea ivrida*, were found in UPPER, but the extant portions of these shells are not perforated.

Table 38

DISTRIBUTION OF OBJECTS MADE OF TOOTH, BONE, ANTLER, AND IVORY IN LEVEL 4

	LOWER	MIDDLE	UPPER
Perforated (or Grooved) Teeth	1	2	4
Sagaies d'Isturitz	5	9	13
Other Sagaies	8	10	19
Bone Awls	2	12	10
Antler Awls	–	1	1
Bone Smoothers	2	1	1
Antler Smoothers	1	1	2
Antler Polishers	2	1	4
Bone Polishers	1	–	1
Bone Pins or Needles	1	1	1
Bone Gorges	–	1	3
Bone Flaking Tools or Anvils	1	–	–
Antler Punches	–	2	–
Tubular Bone Beads	–	–	14
Bone Whistle	1	–	–
Antler Cut by Groove-and-Splinter Technique	18	18	16
Bones with Incised Decoration	–	4	–
Bones with Miscellaneous Transverse Incisions	6	3	1
Bones with Miscellaneous Longitudinal Incisions	1	6	1
Bones with Traces of Decarnization	4	1	2
Miscellaneous Worked Bone	1	4	7
Miscellaneous Worked Antler	3	6	3
Spherical Ivory Object	–	–	1

or probably from red fox (fig. 44:13, 14, 16). There are, in addition, a perforated bear incisor (fig. 44:15) and another bear incisor grooved for suspension (fig. 44:11). The perforation technique is similar to that employed in Level 5. All but one example have a flattened facet and lead-in groove on one or both surfaces of the root. The method of making the hole is indeterminate in many cases, but one piece is biconically drilled. Another seems to have been drilled, but the walls of the hole are straight and parallel. Although it is not certain, some of the holes probably were not drilled, but rather were cut or punched through the thin layer of material separating the bottoms of the lead-in grooves. The crown of four of the teeth is beveled; two examples (fig. 44:16) are deliberately cut, but the other two may have been damaged accidentally.

The perforated teeth of Level 4 resemble the much larger series of Level 5, particularly in what can be ascertained of the perforation technique. On the same basis, there are differences from the small Level 3 series. Level 4 differs from both other series in its concentration on canine teeth and in the deliberate beveling of the crown. Also, there are no *os de crache*[6] examples in Level 4. The validity of all com-

parative statements is hampered, of course, by the scarcity of perforated teeth in Levels 4 and 3.

Sagaies d'Isturitz (table 39)

The most characteristic artifact in the Level 4 bone and antler industry is the antler armature named by R. de Saint-Périer (1965) the "sagaie d'Isturitz" after the Pyrenean site of Isturitz, at which it is most abundant. The weapon is generally large and is distinguished especially by its pointed, conical-shaped, and striated base, which may be treated in various ways (figs. 45; 46; 47:2, 3, 5, 6, 8–11). The shaft, of plano-convex or suboval cross-section, is made of an antler shaft split by the groove-and-splinter technique, and tends to follow quite closely the natural rounding on the exterior of the antler on one surface. The inner surface is flatter where the spongy interior of the antler has been worked down and smoothed, but on well-preserved examples it is still slightly convex, yielding a suboval shape for the total cross-section of the shaft. Sometimes this softer portion of the antler is decayed, leaving the piece with a shallow U-shaped cross-section. No absolutely complete examples of these sagaies are present in the Level 4 assemblage.

Sagaies d'Isturitz are represented in the LOWER sample

6. The upper canine tooth of a male *Cervus elaphus* (red deer).

Table 39

DISTRIBUTION OF SAGAIES AND SAGAIE FRAGMENTS IN LEVEL 4

		LOWER	MIDDLE	UPPER
Sagaies d'Isturitz: Bases	Antler	4	6	6
	Bone	–	–	–
Sagaies d'Isturitz: Segments and Points	Antler	1	3	7
	Bone	–	–	–
Medium Size, Plano-Convex Section	Antler	1	1	3
	Bone	–	–	–
Small, Broad, Oval Section, Constricted Base	Antler	1	1	–
	Bone	–	–	–
Small, Slender, Subcircular or Oval Section: Extremities	Antler	–	2	2
	Bone	–	3	6
Small, Slender, Subcircular or Oval Section: Segments	Antler	1	1	2
	Bone	1	2	1
Small, Slender, Grooved	Antler	–	–	2
	Bone	–	–	–
Small, Broad, Single Side-Beveled Base	Antler	1	–	1
	Bone	1	–	–
Various	Antler	2	–	2
	Bone	–	–	–

by four base fragments and one possible segment. One of the bases (fig. 47:8) is sharply pointed, with deep, transverse, parallel incisions on the upper surface and shallower, diagonal incisions on the lower surface. Another, from an originally larger piece (fig. 47:10), has a series of deeply and regularly cut notches on the right side and a series of short transverse incisions on the left. Notching of the base is a special treatment which is present also on a piece from the UPPER subdivision of the southern test trench, Trench II(North) (fig. 47:9); it occurs also at Isturitz and elsewhere. A large antler segment, finished in the same way as a sagaie d'Isturitz shaft, may have been subsequently employed as a wedge at one end (fig. 48:4).

The MIDDLE series includes six bases, two possible segments, and one possible distal extremity. The bases may be symmetrically or asymmetrically pointed, with parallel transverse and less regular diagonal incisions. A smaller sagaie, represented by most of the shaft and part of the base, has faint transverse incisions on both surfaces of the base and a cut notch on the right side (fig. 47:5); it is the smallest sagaie d'Isturitz in Level 4. A long shaft segment (fig. 47:4) is probably a fragment of an only slightly larger example.

The sample from UPPER contains six bases, six possible segments, and one possible distal extremity. The bases in UPPER tend to be more bluntly pointed than in the earlier subdivisions (figs. 45:3; 46:4). The largest sagaie d'Isturitz in Level 4 (fig. 45:1) comes from the UPPER-1 subdivision. It is 3 cm wide and 2 cm thick just above the base and must have been over 40 cm long in its unbroken state. It has deeply incised, parallel diagonal incisions on both surfaces

of the base. A different kind of base treatment, a distinct beveling of the base, is seen in UPPER (fig. 46:1); perhaps this is a development from the slightly asymmetrical bases of the MIDDLE subdivision.

The sagaie with the beveled base referred to above is almost complete, lacking only the distal tip. On the basis of this example, it seems likely that at least one kind of distal extremity was flat and bluntly pointed. The spongy interior tissue of the antler has not been flattened and worked down to the level of the burin-cut grooves on either side of the lower surface. This would seem to distinguish a sagaie d'Isturitz tip from the tip of an antler smoother (lissoir), which otherwise has a very similar morphology. Working from this analogy, two pieces in the Level 4 assemblage have been identified as possibly being broken distal extremities of sagaies d'Isturitz—one in UPPER and one (fig. 47:6) in MIDDLE. The latter, on which the tip is missing, has widely spaced diagonal incisions on the lower surface. If these pieces are not parts of sagaies d'Isturitz, they should be considered as antler smoothers.

There are six possible sagaies d'Isturitz segments in UPPER, one from near the distal extremity and five from the midsection of the shaft. The upper surface of one of the latter is decorated by fine diagonal incisions occurring in regularly spaced pairs. Another of the segments has a series of very short, fine, transverse incisions along one edge, a treatment found also on a large example from the UPPER subdivision of Trench V(North), not in the studied series (fig. 46:2).

In spite of its wide dimensional range and the variety of

Figure 44. OBJECTS OF BONE, ANTLER, TOOTH, SHELL, AND IVORY

1 (7053+7054): UPPER-1: Small antler sagaie with longitudinal groove; segment.
2 (8632): LOWER-2: Small antler sagaie with beveled base; segment.
3 (7151): MIDDLE-1: Small antler sagaie with constricted base; distal portion.
4 (8313): UPPER-1a: Small antler sagaie; segment.
5 (6650): UPPER-2: Small antler sagaie with single-beveled base; proximal portion.
6 (10,832): LOWER-1: Small antler sagaie; tip broken.
7 (14,258): LOWER-2: Small bone sagaie with single-beveled base; proximal portion.
8 and 9 (7128a+b): UPPER-2: Tubular bone beads made of sawn rabbit long bone.
10 (2281): UPPER: Decorated segment of bird bone.
11 (4954): UPPER-1a: Bear incisor with root grooved for suspension.
12 (9214): UPPER-2: Perforated badger canine.
13 (3448): UPPER-1: Perforated fox canine.
14 (11,046): LOWER-2: Perforated fox canine.
15 (4634): LOWER: Perforated bear incisor.
16 (9749): MIDDLE-1: Perforated fox canine.
17 (10,181): MIDDLE-1: Perforated fossil shell (ammonite).
18 (10,216): MIDDLE-1: Perforated fossil shell (ammonite).
19 (6145): UPPER-1: Spherical ivory object.

butt treatments, the sagaie d'Isturitz is a well-defined form of armature very characteristic of the Noaillian[7] and is of value as a horizon marker. It is doubtful whether its varieties, such as the form with the side-beveled base, can be used as horizon markers for smaller chronological units, if only because the sample is so small.

Other Sagaies of Bone and Antler (table 39)

The sagaie d'Isturitz is not the only kind of sagaie in Level 4. The other kinds, of both bone and antler, are morphologically diverse and do not form a very consistent series.

Antler sagaies of medium size (about as big as the smallest sagaies d'Isturitz) with plano-convex cross-section are represented by three pieces. A piece from MIDDLE with an asymmetrically pointed and transversely incised base (fig. 47:3) is obviously related typologically to the sagaies d'Isturitz. Another sagaie, from the UPPER subdivision of the southern test trench, has a subconical, incised base and is intermediate in character between the sagaie d'Isturitz and

other, less distinctive forms (fig. 47:2). A sagaie from the same subdivision, broken at the tip and without diagnostic base treatment, has a groove along most of the left edge (fig. 47:1), but this may be a by-product of manufacture rather than an intentional feature of the finished piece. There are, finally, four antler segments—three from UPPER and one from LOWER—which may have been parts of similar sagaies.

Two small, broad antler sagaies, one from MIDDLE (fig. 44:3) and one from LOWER (fig. 49:19) have an oval section and a roughly cut, constricted base. Although both pieces are complete in their present state, they may be broken and reworked examples of originally larger objects.

The largest and most consistent series of other sagaies in Level 4 are small and slender, with subcircular or oval cross-section. They are made of bone (fig. 49:2) and of antler. Although none of the specimens is complete, it seems likely that this type was pointed at both ends. A series of small bone and antler segments are probably parts of such pieces. The one piece from MIDDLE, a bone segment, comes from MIDDLE-2. The virtual absence of this variety from the Early Noaillian (LOWER and MIDDLE-2) is probably significant. A few similar antler pieces—long, slender, straight, and with subcircular section—occur in Level 3, but the extreme simplicity of form militates against the drawing of inferences regarding cultural relationships.

---

7. One conical sagaie base with transverse incisions occurs in the Périgordian VI of Level 3, but it differs, particularly in cross-section, from the sagaies d'Isturitz of Level 4.

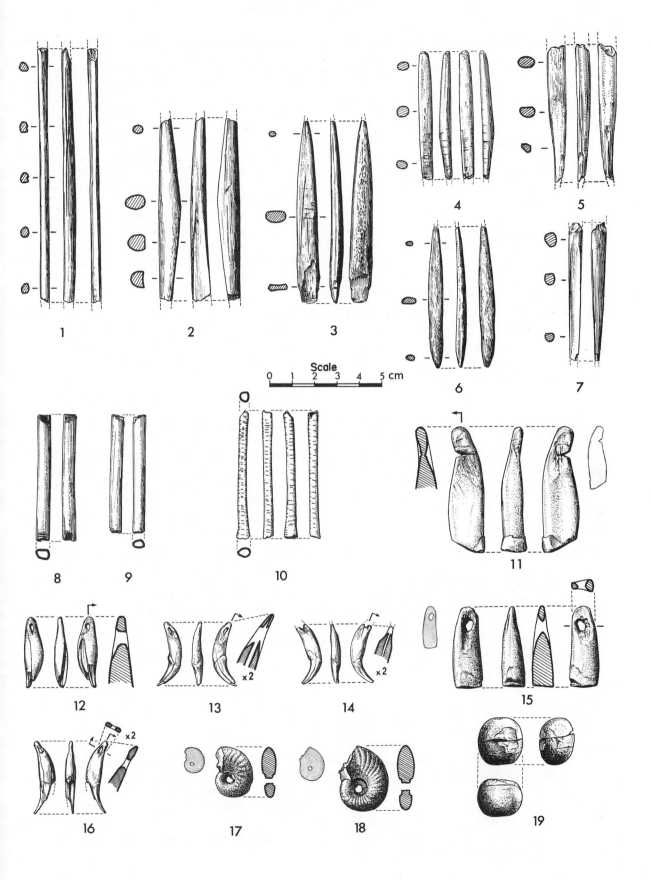

Scale
0 1 2 3 4 5 cm

1 2 3 4 5 6 7 8 9 10 11 12 13 14 15 16 17 18 19

Similar small, slender sagaies also occur with an artificial groove (*cannelure*) near the distal end. There are two such pieces made of antler, both from UPPER (fig. 44:1). A bone piece which may be either similar but unfinished, or from a different kind of sagaie, was found in the UPPER-1 subdivision of Trench V(North).

There are three small sagaies with a single side-bevel on the base. Two are made of antler, one from UPPER (fig. 44:5) and one from LOWER (fig. 44:2). Another sample from LOWER (fig. 44:7) is made of bone.

Finally, there are various unique examples of sagaies or possible sagaies:

A bluntly pointed antler piece from UPPER which may be a sagaie base. The cross-section is almost square, and the top surface has a groove (*cannelure*).

Two short, flat, losangic pieces from LOWER that may be small sagaies (fig. 44:6, 14).

A small, broken, and possibly reused piece with a flattened base from UPPER (fig. 44:4).

A crude but complete bone sagaie from the UPPER subdivision of Trench II(South). The lower surface bears a groove that is at least partly artificial (fig. 49:1).

The wide range of sizes and forms of sagaies in Level 4 and, with the exception of the sagaies d'Isturitz, the lack of standardization, restrict possibilities for interassemblage comparisons. The small, slender sagaies with subcircular or oval cross-section seem to be almost completely limited in Level 4 to the Late Noaillian, but this is not a form that one can easily use as a horizon marker.

Awls (*poinçons* or *alènes*)

Bone Awls. There is a large series of bone awls from Level 4, of several very different kinds. Two are large and fairly robust; one is from UPPER (fig. 49:4), and one from the LOWER subdivision of the southern test trench. Most of the awls are of medium (fig. 49:9) or small size. Among the medium awls are five made on hollow bones—three on the radius of hare (*Lepus* sp.) (fig. 49:6), one on the tibia

of red fox (*Vulpes vulpes*), and one on a small, hollow bird bone. An awl from the UPPER subdivision of the southern test trench is made on a hare (*Lepus* sp.) tibia (fig. 49:5). Five small awls are made on naturally grooved fragments of bone (fig. 49:7, 8). Finally, two of the awls are minimally modified bone splinters (*poinçons frustes*).

With a bone awl sample of reasonable size, it is again possible to see a distributional difference between the Late Noaillian and the Early Noaillian. Only two of the awls in MIDDLE are from MIDDLE-2; the total for the Late Noaillian subdivisions is 20, whereas that for the Early Noaillian subdivisions is only four.

Although bone awls are common in both Levels 5 and 3, the Level 4 series is rather different from both. It does not have the large, well-worked, and sometimes decorated awls of Level 5. The emphasis on small, very delicate tools and on tools made of hollow bone is not found in either of the other levels.

Antler Awls. Only two awls in Level 4 are made of antler, and one is a very crude example (*poinçon fruste*). The other is very carefully worked; the proximal end has been formed into a slightly bulbous head (fig. 49:10).

Smoothers (*lissoirs*) and Polishers (*polissoirs*)

Bone Smoothers. Bone smoothers are spatulate tools made on split herbivore ribs. They are thin in cross-section, and at least one end terminates in a blunt, flattened point. They are likely to have been used as beamers in dressing skins, or conceivably as snow knives. Bone smoothers in Level 4 are represented by four fragmentary examples only (fig. 48:1, 2). Such tools are barely present in Level 5, but Level 3 has a good series, including some very large examples.

Antler Smoothers. The antler smoothers are thin pieces of antler shaft with plano-convex section and rounded, spatulate distal ends. The outer surface of the antler is essentially unmodified, but the split inner surface has been completely smoothed and flattened (fig. 48:3). The fact that the entire inner surface is smoothed and polished distinguishes these objects from otherwise very similar pieces which are described as possible distal extremities of sagaies d'Isturitz. Two of the four examples in the studied series are very

Figure 45.   SAGAIES D'ISTURITZ FROM LEVEL 4

1 (8953): UPPER-1: Very large sagaie d'Isturitz with parallel diagonal incisions on base and series of fine incisions along right side; distal portion; base missing; estimated original length = c. 50 cm.
2 (7322): MIDDLE-1: Large sagaie d'Isturitz with parallel transverse incisions on base; proximal portion.
3 (7126): UPPER-2: Sagaie d'Isturitz with deep diagonal incisions on base; proximal portion.

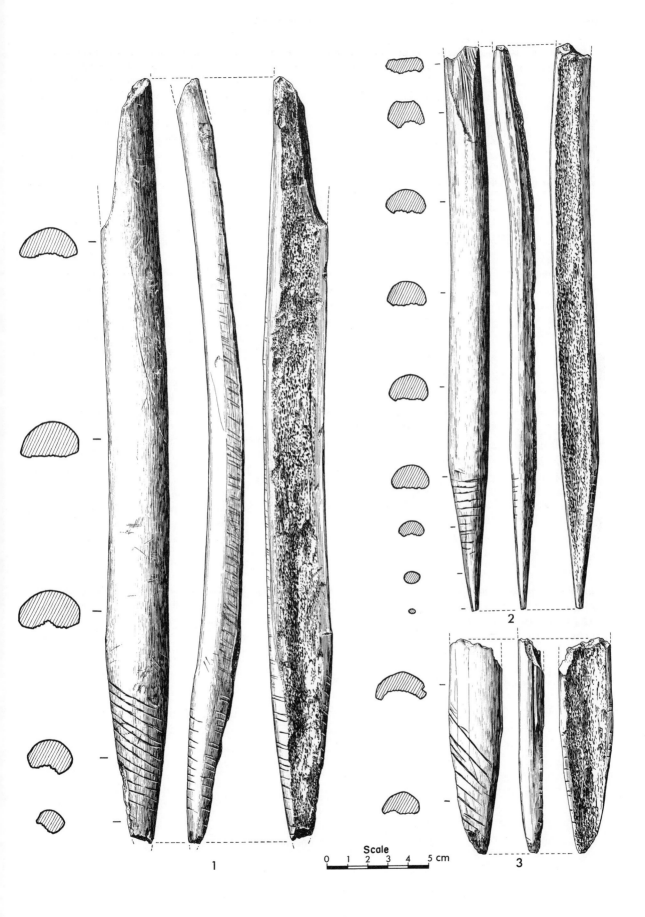

Scale

0 1 2 3 4 5 cm

1

2

3

crudely finished (*lissoirs frustes*). Smoothers made of antler are not present in Level 5, but the Level 4 examples are similar to ones in Level 3.

Antler Polishers. Morphologically similar to smoothers, polishers are thicker and usually have a plano-convex cross-section; they end in a blunt, often spatulate point. The largest antler polisher in Level 4 (fig. 50:1) is broad and thick, but flat in profile; it is a variety not present in Levels 5 and 3. The typical plano-convex variety of polisher is represented by one large fragment and five distal tips from the studied series and one fragmentary piece (fig. 50:3) from Trench V(North). These tools, cut from the antler shaft by the groove-and-splinter technique, are like those of Level 3 but much less numerous.

Bone Polishers. Two thick, bluntly pointed implements made on large ribs can also be called polishers. The larger fragment (fig. 50:2) has cuts, scratches, and pitting on both surfaces, showing use as a flaking tool or anvil. Polishers made of bone are not present in Levels 5 or 3.

Other Bone and Antler Artifacts

Bone Pins or Needles. Three very small, delicate, pointed fragments of bone could be either pins or eyeless needles (fig. 49:16).

Bone Gorges. There are four good examples of bone gorges in Level 4. These small, bipointed bone objects are thought to be fishing tackle (there are several fish vertebrae in the Level 4 fauna). Two of the gorges have a slightly expanded central region (fig. 49:12, 13), and one is slightly constricted at the center. Bone gorges may be present in Levels 5 and 3, but examples are doubtful.

Bone Flaking Tools or Anvils (*compresseurs*). Only one convincing example of this category of tool was found in Level 4, a thick long bone fragment from LOWER, extensively used as an anvil.

Antler Punches (*chasse-lames*). A punch is understood to be a sturdy piece of antler shaft, bluntly pointed at one end, which is used as the intermediate tool for punching blades from a specially prepared blade nucleus. One or possibly two pieces in Level 4 may be such tools. The first (fig. 47:7) is a thick shaft fragment with a circular section worked at one end to a blunt, conical point. The tip of this point has been crushed, deformed, and slightly splayed. The object is broken some 6–8 cm behind the point, and the other end, which might be expected to show traces of smashing from the hammer, cannot be examined. The piece is unlike any sagaies in Level 4. The other object is the base of an antler shaft, over 21 cm long. The shaft has been cut in such a way as to form a thick, beveled distal end. As on the other piece, this end is splayed and deformed, and the proximal end is somewhat smashed. No punches or possible punches are present in Levels 5 or 3.

Tubular Bone Beads. Tubular bone beads were found at two places in Level 4, both in the UPPER subdivision. One is a single hollow (bird?) bone segment 20 mm long, cut at both ends. All the other beads, made of hollow long bones of *Lepus* sp., were found together in one place in Lens M-2. There are two complete examples, both between 50 and 55 mm long, cut at both ends (fig. 44:8, 9). The other associated beads are fragmentary, and some are badly smashed. The number of originally complete beads cannot be determined, but there are at least 11 pieces cut at one end and broken at the other. None of the beads is decorated. There are three tubular bone beads in Level 5 and none in Level 3.

Bone Whistle (*sifflet*). A reindeer phalange from LOWER with a regular round perforation is regarded as a whistle (fig. 49:11). There is a similar piece in Level 5, but there the hole is very irregular and may represent a bite wound or accidental damage.

Antler Cut by the Groove-and-Splinter Technique. Level 4 produced a series of 52 antler fragments cut by the groove-and-splinter technique. The majority of them are shaft

Figure 46.   SAGAIES D'ISTURITZ FROM LEVEL 4

1   (8080): UPPER-2: Sagaie d'Isturitz with diagonal incisions on base made of reindeer antler; proximal portion; base missing; note bevel on left side of base.
2   (11,842): UPPER-1: Sagaie d'Isturitz with diagonal incisions on base made of reindeer antler; proximal portion.
3   (9542): MIDDLE-1: Sagaie d'Isturitz with subparallel transverse incisions on base of reindeer antler; proximal portion.
4   (7127): UPPER-2: Sagaie d'Isturitz with short transverse incisions on base made of reindeer antler; proximal portion.

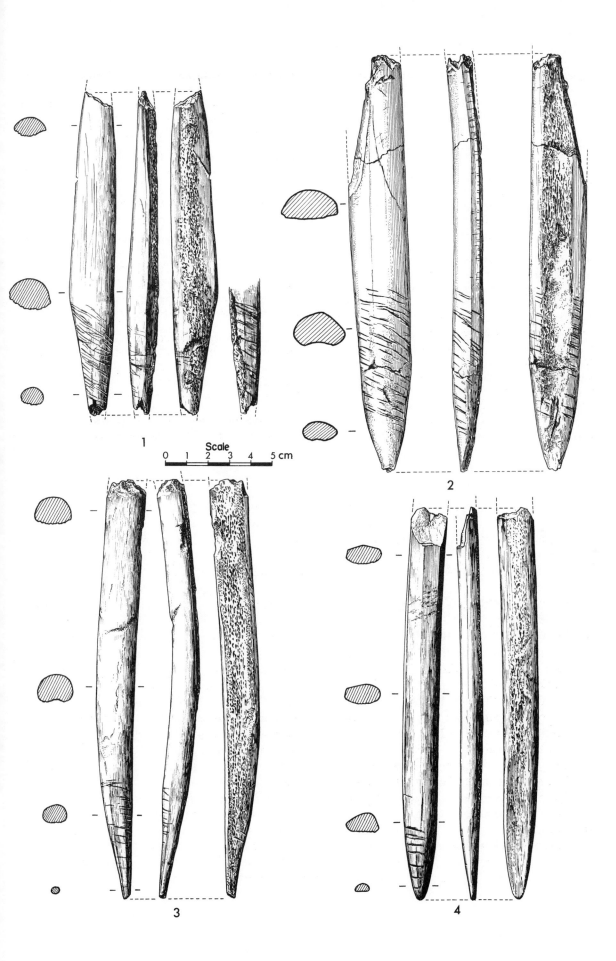

Scale

0 1 2 3 4 5 cm

1

2

3

4

fragments of all sizes, from small splinters to very long fragments (longest = ca. 27 cm). All of these have been detached from the body of the shaft by burin-cut grooves on one or both sides. Several bear shallow, roughed-out grooves that were not completed on the outer surface. This series of antler *débitage* products gives the impression, from the general size and shape of the pieces, that most were related to the manufacture of sagaies d'Isturitz. Three of the antler fragments have deep transverse diagonal grooves that seem to record the detachment of the end of the splinter. There are, finally, five small tines detached from the shaft by parallel grooves at the tine/shaft junction.

Bone with Incised Decoration. Four fragments of bone in the studied series bear incisions which are regular enough to be described as decoration. One is a fragment of reindeer metatarsal with two lines of transverse incisions of varying length (fig. 48:6). A rib fragment has been fashioned into a point, and both surfaces are decorated with parallel bands (fig. 49:18). The two other pieces are fragments of a rib and a long bone. There is, finally, a hollow long bone segment of a bird from the UPPER subdivision of the southern test trench which has short transverse incisions on all surfaces (fig. 44:10); both ends of the piece are broken. It may be a tubular bead, but all the clear examples of tubular beads from Level 4 are undecorated.

Bone with Miscellaneous Transverse Incisions. This small series of pieces is composed of rib and long bone fragments that have some transverse incisions. They are too regular to be seen as resulting from use as a flaking tool, but not regular or extensive enough to be described as decoration.

Bone with Miscellaneous Longitudinal Incisions. Five small fragments bear shallow longitudinal incisions of unknown purpose. Four long bone fragments have deeper, burin-cut grooves (fig. 48:5), but none is a clear example of the groove-and-splinter technique.

Bone with Traces of Decarnization. One rib and six long bone fragments have several short, shallow cut marks oriented variously. The cuts are regarded as traces of decarnization, places where the knife scored the bone in the butchering process. If this interpretation is correct, the pieces are unintentionally modified and are not tools.

Miscellaneous Worked Bone. This is a residual category containing pieces that cannot be included elsewhere. All are fragmentary, and we can determine only that the bone has been deliberately cut, smoothed, or pointed in some way. Several of the fragments are partially charred.

Miscellaneous Worked Antler. This is a residual category containing pieces, often fragmentary, that cannot be as-

```
Figure 47.   SAGAIES D'ISTURITZ AND OTHER TOOLS FROM LEVEL 4

  1  (3844):   UPPER:  Sagaie made of reindeer antler with groove on left
     side; proximal portion.
  2  (3882):   MIDDLE-1:  Sagaie d'Isturitz made of reindeer antler; proximal
     portion.
  3  (9500):   MIDDLE-1:  Sagaie d'Isturitz made of reindeer antler; proximal
     portion.
  4  (9548+9549):  UPPER:  Medium-sized sagaie made of reindeer antler,
     possibly a sagaie d'Isturitz; segment.
  5  (10,364):  MIDDLE-1:  Medium-sized sagaie d'Isturitz made of reindeer
     antler; base slightly broken and distal portion missing.
  6  (7964):   MIDDLE-1:  Medium-sized sagaie d'Isturitz(?) made of
     reindeer antler; note diagonal incisions on lower surface; segment.
  7  (8007):   MIDDLE-2:  Roughly pointed object (sagaie?) made of reindeer
     antler; punch(?) (chasse-lame); distal portion; tip missing.
  8  (10,687):  LOWER-1:  Sagaie d'Isturitz with transverse incisions on
     base made of reindeer antler; proximal portion.
  9  (3833):   UPPER:  Sagaie d'Isturitz with notched and transversely
     incised base made of reindeer antler; proximal portion; tip missing.
 10  (6823+7140):  LOWER-2a:  Sagaie d'Isturitz with notched and transversely
     incised base made of reindeer antler; proximal portion; tip missing.
 11  (9415):   MIDDLE-1:  Sagaie d'Isturitz with transverse incisions on
     base made of reindeer antler; proximal portion.
```

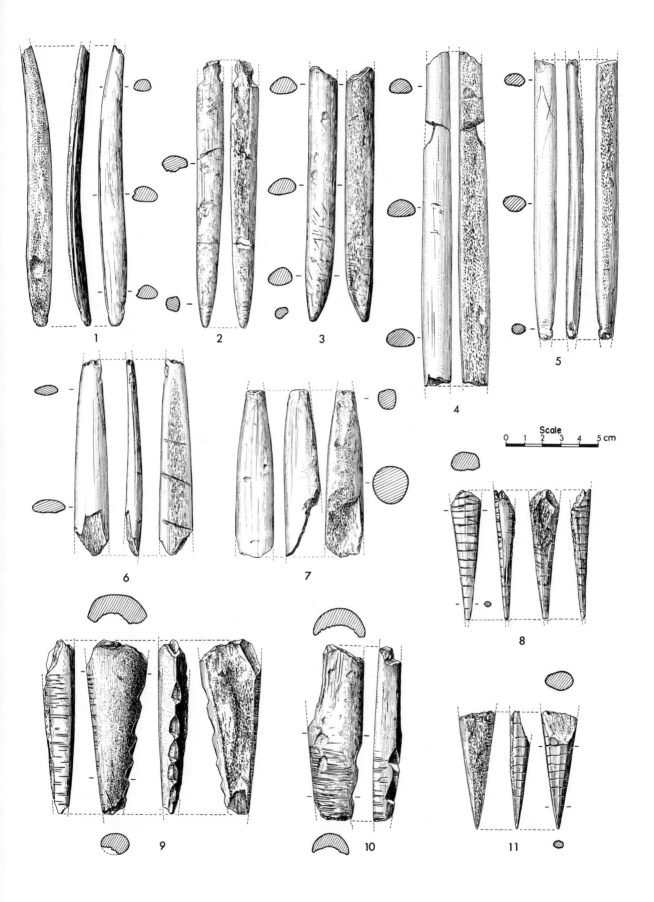

Scale
0 1 2 3 4 5 cm

signed to a more formal category for objects made of bone. Two pieces merit special mention. A small fusiform object from LOWER as a long, single-beveled point at one end and a shorter point at the other (fig. 49:15). Another pointed piece, from the LOWER subdivision of Trench II(North), may be the point of a sagaie (fig. 49:17); the right side of the upper surface has a shallow groove that is decorated with short diagonal incisions.

Spherical Ivory Object. Only one ivory object was found in Level 4; this is a small ball of subspherical shape from the UPPER subdivision (fig. 44:19).

SUMMARY AND CONCLUSIONS

The nonflint industry of Level 4 is both rich and distinctive. This statement applies particularly to the subdivisions of the Late Noaillian: MIDDLE-1 and UPPER. The Level 4 series contrasts markedly with those of Levels 3 and 5, even though the latter differ between themselves. It is true that Levels 4 and 3 resemble each other in the relative frequency of bone and antler tools, but this similarity need not necessarily be of more cultural significance than is that of the proportion of burins in the two assemblages. Indeed, the two phenomena are related.

The most striking characteristic of the Level 4 series is the presence throughout the level of the sagaie d'Isturitz. The typology of sagaies has traditionally been used as an index of cultural similarity and difference, and on this basis alone the Noaillian of Level 4 is very different from either the Périgordian IV or VI. The high frequency in Level 4 of antler shafts cut by the groove-and-splinter technique is a likely concomitant of this form of sagaie. Another variety of sagaie—small, slender, and with subcircular or suboval section—is also present in Level 4, but it seems almost to be restricted to the Late Noaillian subdivisions.

The importation into the site for unknown purposes of regular and sometimes polished water-rolled pebbles is a special characteristic of Level 4, particularly of the Late Noaillian subdivisions. These very distinctive objects are absent from both Level 5 and Level 3. Although manganese dioxide is minimally present in Level 3, its use during certain periods of the Level 4 occupation far surpasses the situation in the Périgordian VI, and consequently it must be seen as a characteristic feature of the Noaillian assemblage at the Abri Pataud. Similarly, the importation of marine and other exotic mollusc shells for use as objects of personal adornment was practiced during the occupations of both Levels 3 and 5. But the quantity of such shells found in the Late Noaillian subdivisions and the concentration on *Littorina littoralis* (Dance 1975, p. 158) in Lens N-1 are true differences.

The distinctive character of the sagaie series and its importance in interassemblage comparison have already been mentioned. Bone gorges, occurring only dubiously in Levels 5 and 3, are rare but definitely present in Level 4. Bone awls are numerous, and there are differences from those of Levels 5 and 3 that transcend the generic similarity of all bone awls. These may be characterized as an emphasis upon small, delicate tools and the use of hollow bird or hare bones. The rest of the bone and antler industry is neither very numerous nor very distinctive. Polishers and smoothers are present, but they are infrequent and unstandardized. The presence of tubular bone beads is a point of comparison with Level 5, but one of doubtful significance. As in the other two levels, decoration occurs on bone and antler objects, but figurative art objects of engraved bone are absent.

The general conclusion resulting from comparative examination of the nonflint industry of Levels 5, 4, and 3 is that whereas the continuity between the Périgordian IV and VI shown by the flint tools is not shown by the other materials, the strong dissimilarity between either the Périgordian IV or VI and the Noaillian is demonstrated by the whole assemblage, flint and nonflint alike. Whatever cultural development may have occurred between the intervals designated Périgordian IV and Périgordian VI, the nonflint industry of the Noaillian of Level 4 offers no evidence for its derivation from the Périgordian IV or for development into the Périgordian VI.

Figure 48.   OBJECTS OF BONE AND ANTLER FROM LEVEL 4

1 (10,637): LOWER-1: Smoother, or *lissoir*, made of reindeer rib.
2 (7165): MIDDLE-1: Smoother made of fragment of rib of large ungulate.
3 (4013): UPPER: Smoother made of fragment of reindeer antler.
4 (4930): LOWER-2: Wedge made of segment of reindeer antler cut by groove-and-splinter technique; possible a broken portion of a large sagaie d'Isturitz, subsequently used at one end as a wedge.
5 (9973): MIDDLE-1: Splinter of reindeer metatarsal cut longitudinally by groove-and-splinter technique.
6 (9693+9694): MIDDLE-1: Fragment of reindeer metatarsal decorated with a series of incisions.

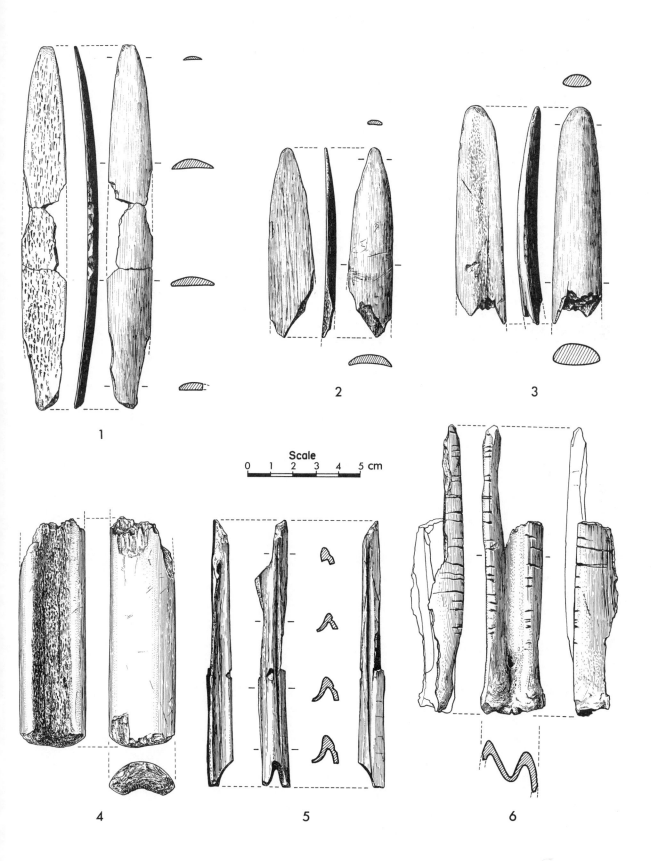

1

2

3

Scale

0 1 2 3 4 5 cm

4

5

6

Figure 49.   OBJECTS OF BONE AND ANTLER FROM LEVEL 4

 1 (4074):   UPPER: Elongated bone sagaie; irregular.
 2 (7280):   MIDDLE-1: Elongated bone sagaie.
 3 (4579):   LOWER: Bone awl, or *poinçon*.
 4 (8192):   UPPER-1a: Bone awl.
 5 (4452):   UPPER: Bone awl (hare tibia).
 6 (10,937): LOWER-2: Bone awl.
 7 (8745):   UPPER-1: Bone awl.
 8 (10,393): MIDDLE-1: Bone awl.
 9 (10,385): MIDDLE-1: Bone awl.
10 (9087):   UPPER-2: Antler awl with head.
11 (14,312): LOWER-2: Perforated reindeer phalange whistle (*sifflet*).
12 (9031):   UPPER-1: Bone gorge.
13 (6324):   UPPER-2: Bone gorge.
14 (13,428): UPPER-1: Small fusiform-shaped antler sagaie.
15 (13,016): LOWER-2: Small fusiform-shaped antler object.
16 (8282):   UPPER-1a: Bone pin, or needle(?); distal portion.
17 (9013):   UPPER: Decorated antler point; distal portion.
18 (10,172): MIDDLE-2: Incised bone point; distal portion.
19 (7526):   LOWER-2: Small, slightly incised antler sagaie.

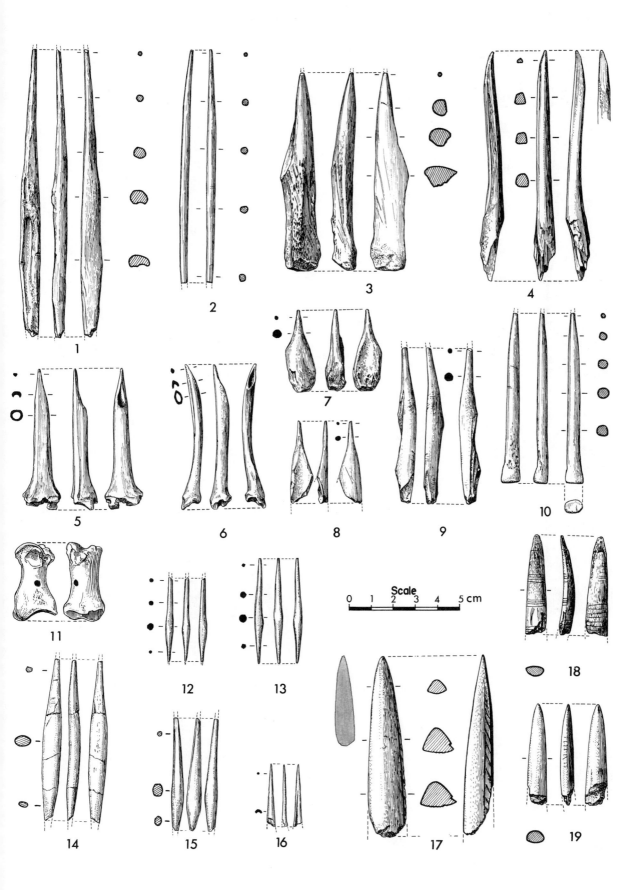

1   2   3   4

5   6   7   8   9   10

11   12   13   Scale
                                                       0   1   2   3   4   5 cm   18

14   15   16   17   19

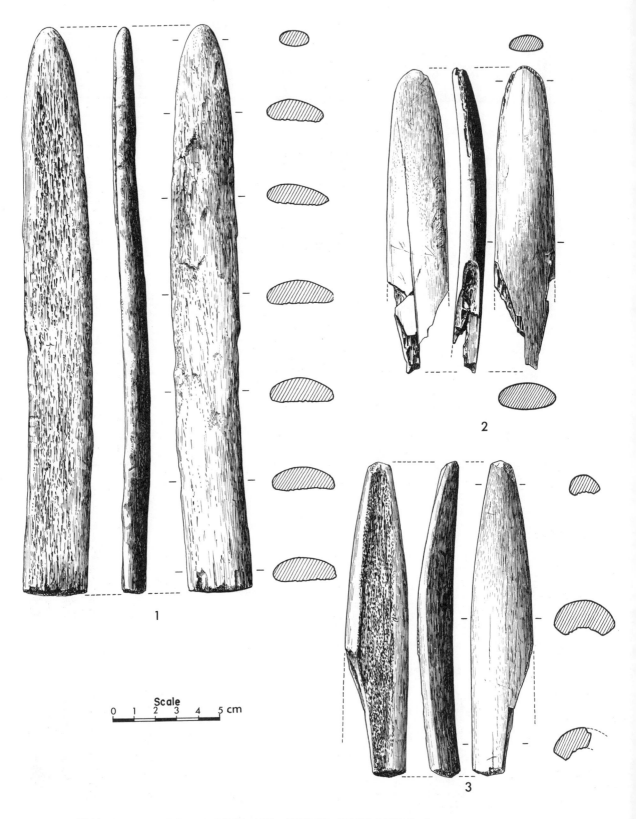

Figure 50. POLISHERS OF BONE AND ANTLER FROM LEVEL 4

1 (8720): LOWER-2: Polisher, or *polissoir*, made of reindeer antler.
2 (5940): UPPER-1a: Polisher made of large rib of *Equus* or *Bos*.
3 (6922): LOWER: Polisher made of reindeer antler.

VII

The Assemblages of Éboulis 3-4 and Level 4a

Below the Éboulis 3-4: Yellow, the Éboulis 3-4 is subdivisible into Éboulis 3-4: Red, Level 4a, and a lower unit that includes Éboulis 3-4: Tan and Pebbly Red. Level 4a was a thin and discontinuous archaeological horizon situated stratigraphically between the overlying Éboulis 3-4: Red and the underlying Éboulis 3-4: Tan. The horizontal discontinuity of the level and the absence of hearths or other structural features testify to a very brief occupation, or, perhaps, several intermittent occupations over a short time span.[8] Where the LOWER (Tan and Pebbly Red) and MIDDLE (Red) subdivisions of Éboulis 3-4 were not separated stratigraphically by Level 4a, the contact between the two was often not sufficiently sharp to permit consistent separation of the archaeological materials. The artifacts discussed below as coming from Éboulis 3-4: MIDDLE + LOWER include pieces older than Level 4a, pieces at approximately the same stratigraphic level as 4a but from parts of the site where this horizon could not be recognized by modification of the sediment, and again a few pieces younger than Level 4a. This situation is unsatisfactory, but the majority of the MIDDLE + LOWER series is from immediately above Level 4 and must, therefore, represent pre-Level 4a materials.

ÉBOULIS 3-4

The Éboulis 3-4: MIDDLE + LOWER Series

An inventory of the flint tools is given in terms of the de Sonneville-Bordes/Perrot list in table 40, and the cumulative graph is shown in figure 51.

The flint tool series from Éboulis 3-4: MIDDLE + LOWER is similar to Level 4: UPPER and can be assigned to the Late Noaillian. Examination of the typological indices shows that tool class proportions in Éboulis 3-4 are closer to those of Level 4: UPPER than to those of Level 4a (see below). The proportion of backed tools (5.79% of all graphed tools) is higher than in any subdivision of Level 4, but it is still much lower than in Level 4a. Marginally retouched pieces are significantly less frequent in Éboulis 3-4: MIDDLE + LOWER (12.67%) than in Level 4: UPPER (19.74%).

The detailed typology of the flint tool series is also very similar to Level 4: UPPER. The distribution of special Noaillian kinds of burins (with double burins counted twice) is as follows:[9]

	n	%
Noailles burins	21	35.59
Raysse burins	34	57.63
Burin-points	4	6.78
Total	59	100.00

The nonflint industry includes one complete and several possible fragments of small, slender antler sagaies with subcircular or suboval cross-section. Such pieces were mentioned above as characteristic of the Late Noaillian subdivisions of Level 4. There are also two basal portions and one distal portion of antler sagaies with almost square cross-section and a groove on the upper surface. One basal fragment of this kind of sagaie was found in Level 4: UPPER. A number of very well made bone smoothers are represented by ten fragments. Bone smoothers are very rare in Level 4, and there is only one example from the UPPER subdivision.

LEVEL 4a

The Flint Series

The Level 4a assemblage is very small (n = 181), and, cultural formation processes apart, interpretation is consequently difficult. It can nevertheless provide information on the interesting span of time between the main Noaillian

---

8. Much of the Éboulis 3-4: Red and Tan, including the ill-defined scatters of archaeological material between them, was excavated before the Lens system of excavation had been developed at the Abri Pataud. Furthermore, a large part of the digging was done by inexperienced excavators. Although checks on artifact provenience by vertical and horizontal plotting have indicated that the general stratigraphic information obtained is essentially correct, obvious excavation errors and cases of artifact mixtures were found. Thus, while we refer to a Level 4a "assemblage," this series may not be a true assemblage in the sense of artifactual materials produced by members of a single cultural group over a delimited period of time.

---

9. Most of the Noailles burins come from the front of the site, where the Éboulis 3-4 rested directly on the LOWER subdivision of Level 4. Their high relative frequency, anomalous in a Late Noaillian series, is most probably to be explained by mechanical derivation from this source.

Table 40

DISTRIBUTION OF TOOL TYPES AND INDICES OF TOOL GROUPS
FROM ÉBOULIS 3-4: MIDDLE + LOWER AND LEVEL 4a SHOWN IN THE CUMULATIVE GRAPH

Type No.	Type	Level 4a		Éboulis 3-4: MIDDLE + LOWER	
		n	%	n	%
1	End-Scraper	7	4.73	14	3.69
2	Atypical End-Scraper	5	3.38	11	2.90
3	Double End-Scraper	-	-	2	0.53
4	Ogival End-Scraper	3	2.03	5	1.32
5	End-Scraper on Retouched Blade or Flake	8	5.41	6	1.58
6	End-Scraper on Aurignacian Blade	-	-	-	-
7	Fan-Shaped End-Scraper	-	-	-	-
8	Discoidal Scraper	-	-	-	-
9	Circular Scraper	-	-	-	-
10	Thumbnail Scraper	-	-	-	-
11	Carinate Scraper	-	-	-	-
12	Atypical Carinate Scraper	1	0.68	2	0.53
13	Thick Nose-Shaped Scraper	-	-	-	-
14	Flat Nose-Shaped or Shouldered End-Scraper	-	-	-	-
15	Nucleiform Scraper	-	-	-	-
16	Rabot or Plane	-	-	-	-
17	End-Scraper + Burin	4	2.70	7	1.85
18	End-Scraper + Truncated Piece	-	-	2	0.53
19	Burin + Truncated Piece	1	0.68	1	0.26
20	Perforator + Truncated Piece	-	-	-	-
21	Perforator + End-Scraper	-	-	-	-
22	Perforator + Burin	-	-	2	0.53
23	Perforator	5	3.38	1	0.26
24	Bec or Atypical Perforator	2	1.35	3	0.79
25	Multiple Perforator or Bec	-	-	-	-
26	Microperforator	4	2.70	-	-
27	Symmetrical Dihedral Burin	1	0.68	6	1.58
28	Asymmetrical Dihedral Burin	3	2.03	13	3.43
29	Transverse or Transverse/Oblique Dihedral Burin	1	0.68	-	-
30a	Burin on Broken Surface	-	-	18	4.75
30b	Burin on Unretouched Edge or End of Flake or Blade	1	0.68	1	0.26
31	Multiple Burin Associating Types 27-30	-	-	6	1.58
32	Busked Burin	-	-	-	-
33	Parrot Break Burin	-	-	-	-
34	Burin on Straight, Right-Angle Truncation	1	0.68	4	1.06
35	Burin on Straight, Oblique Truncation	4	2.70	16	4.22

Table 40 (continued)

Type No.	Type	Level 4a		Éboulis 3-4: MIDDLE + LOWER	
		n	%	n	%
36	Burin on Concave Truncation	3	2.03	20	5.28
37	Burin on Convex Truncation	–	–	6	1.58
38	Transverse Burin on Straight or Convex Lateral Truncation	–	–	2	0.53
39	Transverse Burin on Concave Lateral Truncation	–	–	1	0.26
40	Multiple Burin Associating Types 34-39	2	1.35	19	5.01
41	Mixed Multiple Burin, Types 27-30 + Types 34-39	3	2.03	5	1.32
42	Noailles Burin	4	2.70	17	4.49
43	Nucleiform Burin	–	–	–	–
44	Flat-Faced Burin	13	8.78	42	11.08
45	Abri Audi Knife	–	–	–	–
46	Chatelperron Point	–	–	–	–
47	Atypical Chatelperron Point	–	–	–	–
48	Gravette Point	15	10.14	6	1.58
49	Atypical Gravette Point	–	–	–	–
50	Les Vachons Point	–	–	–	–
51	Micro-Gravette Point	5	3.38	11	2.90
52	Font-Yves Point	–	–	–	–
53	Gibbous Backed Piece	2	1.35	1	0.26
54	Fléchette	–	–	–	–
55	Tanged Point	–	–	–	–
56	Périgordian Shouldered Point	–	–	–	–
57	Shouldered Piece	–	–	–	–
58	Completely Backed Blade	2	1.35	–	–
59	Partially Backed Blade	–	–	3	0.79
60	Piece with Straight, Right-Angle Truncation	–	–	1	0.26
61	Piece with Straight, Oblique Truncation	1	0.68	5	1.32
62	Piece with Concave Truncation	3	2.03	12	3.17
63	Piece with Convex Truncation	1	0.68	3	0.79
64	Bitruncated Piece	–	–	–	–
65	Piece with Continuous Retouch on One Edge	8	5.41	30	7.92
66	Piece with Continuous Retouch on Both Edges	7	4.73	17	4.49
67	Aurignacian Blade	1	0.68	1	0.26
68	Strangled Blade	–	–	–	–
69-72	Solutrean Tools	–	–	–	–
73	Pick	1	0.68	2	0.53
74	Notched Piece	18	12.16	41	10.82
75	Denticulate Piece	–	–	4	1.06

Table 40 (continued)

		Level 4a		Éboulis 3-4: MIDDLE + LOWER	
Type No.	Type	n	%	n	%
76	Splintered Piece	–	–	6	1.58
77	Side-Scraper	–	–	1	0.26
78	<u>Raclette</u>	–	–	–	–
79-83	Geometric Pieces	–	–	–	–
84	Truncated Bladelet	–	–	1	0.26
85	Backed Bladelet	6	4.05	1	0.26
86	Truncated Backed Bladelet	–	–	–	–
87	Denticulate Backed Bladelet	–	–	–	–
88	Denticulate Bladelet	–	–	–	–
89	Notched Bladelet	1	0.68	–	–
90	Dufour Bladelet	–	–	–	–
91	Azilian Point	–	–	–	–
92	Other Tools, Not Included in Types 1-91	1	0.68	1	0.26
Total		148	100.06	379	99.97

Indices:		Level 4a	Éboulis 3-4: MIDDLE + LOWER
IG	(Scraper Index)	16.21	10.55
IB	(Burin Index)	24.32	46.44
IBd	(Dihedral Burin Index)	4.05	11.61
IBt	(Truncation Burin Index)	9.46	21.64
IP	(Perforator Index)	4.73	1.06
GP	(Périgordian Characteristic Group Index)	23.65	11.61

Table 41

DISTRIBUTION OF THE TABULATED ASSEMBLAGE FROM LEVEL 4a

Assemblage	n
Flint Tools Shown on Cumulative Graph (fig. 51)	148
Miscellaneous Slightly Retouched and/or Utilized Flakes and Blades	8
Nuclei	7
Perforated Shell	1
Perforated Teeth	9
Bone Artifacts	6
Antler Artifacts	2
Total	181

occupation (Level 4)—to which we can assimilate, with
reservations, the Éboulis 3-4: MIDDLE and LOWER series—and the first traces of Périgordian VI occupation in
the Éboulis 3-4: Yellow. Although in many ways the Level
4a assemblage raises more questions thah it answers, it is
nonetheless worthwhile to extract from it as much information as possible.

The total tabulated assemblage from Level 4a is shown
in table 41. River-stones and *débitage* flakes are not tabulated. The major part of the flint industry is classified according to the de Sonneville-Bordes/Perrot 92-type list in
table 40 and shown graphically in figure 51.

The typology of the flint tools of Level 4a demonstrates
many clearly Late Noaillian affinities, but there are substantial differences in tool frequencies between Level 4a and
Level 4: UPPER. The burin index (IB = 24.32) still dominates the scraper index (IG = 16.21) in Level 4a, but the
values are very close compared to Level 4: UPPER (IB =
55.65; IG = 8.67). The relative proportions are much more
similar to those in the overlying Level 3 assemblage (IB =
31.39; IG = 13.76). Among the end-scrapers, however, an
irregular, shouldered end-scraper (fig. 11:4) and ogival end-
scrapers (fig. 11:3) are characteristically Noaillian, as is the
relative abundance of end-scrapers on marginally retouched,

including fan-shaped, blades (5.41%) (fig. 11:2, 3). The
marginal retouch is predominantly of the scaled variety so
important in the Late Noaillian subdivisions of Level 4. The
absence of discoidal scrapers is another way in which the
Level 4a assemblage differs from that of Level 3. The one
atypical carinate scraper shows no characteristically Aurignacian features.

Perforating tools are more frequent in Level 4a (IP =
4.73) than in Level 4: UPPER (IP = 1.86). The series is
quite varied, including long, well-degaged perforators (fig.
11:5), shorter *becs*, and very small microperforators; the
latter are not found in either Level 4: UPPER or in Level 3.

The truncation burin index (IBt = 9.46) is extraordinarily
low for a Noaillian series, but slightly over twice as high
as the dihedral burin index (IBd = 4.05). It should be
remembered that the dihedral burin index includes break
and unretouched edge/end burins, as well as true dihedral
burins. All three special burin types of the Noaillian are
present. Noailles burins (fig. 11:14, 15) are quite infrequent
(2.70% of the graphed tools) and are represented by single
examples only. This frequency is almost identical with that
of Level 4: UPPER (2.44%). The relatively high frequency
of flat-faced burins is caused for the most part by the presence of Raysse burins. These are very typical examples (fig.

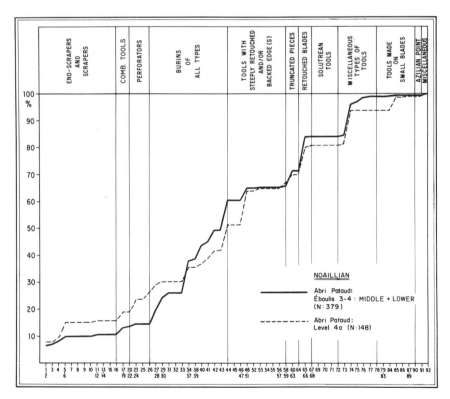

Figure 51.   CUMULATIVE GRAPHS OF THE ÉBOULIS 3-4: MIDDLE + LOWER AND LEVEL
4a SERIES.

Table 42

DISTRIBUTION OF NOAILLES BURINS, RAYSSE BURINS, AND BURIN-POINTS
IN LEVELS 4a AND 4: UPPER-1a

	Level 4a		Level 4: UPPER-1a	
	n	%	n	%
Noailles Burins	4	(16.00)	9	7.20
Raysse Burins	17	(68.00)	98	78.40
Burin-Points	4	(16.00)	18	14.40
Total	25	(100.00)	125	100.00

11:17), including some double Raysse burins (fig. 11:16). Burin-points (made by the truncation, dihedral, and retruncation (fig. 11:12) techniques), which cannot be identified from the cumulative graph, are also present in small numbers. The rest of the burin series includes unmodified (fig. 11:11) and modified truncation burins, with a straight oblique truncation slightly dominant over a concave shape. Regular dihedral burins are rare; the majority are asymmetrical (fig. 11:13).

The distribution of specifically Noaillian kinds of burins is shown in table 42 and compared with the same data for Level 4: UPPER-1a. Each burin edge is tabulated, so that double burins appear twice. Allowing for the very small sample from Level 4a, the relative frequencies are quite close, those of Noailles and Raysse burins permitting no doubt about Late Noaillian assignment.

The backed tools from Level 4a were discussed in some detail in Chapter III on the basis of attribute analysis; the most important characteristics of the series are summarized here. The frequency of backed tools reaches the very high figure of 20.27% of all graphed tools. This is completely different from any subdivision of Level 4 and approaches more closely values for Level 5 (Périgordian IV) or Level 3 (Périgordian VI). Most of the backed tools are Gravette (fig. 11:9) or Micro-Gravette points (14.86% of all graphed tools), and, *unlike* the Gravettes of Level 4, they are either similar to those of later Level 5 or typologically intermediate between the Level 5 and Level 3 series. The presence of the bellied morphology (fig. 11:7) is a specific characteristic of Level 5. The frequency of Vachons retouch at the butt (fig. 11:6, 10) is higher than at any other level at the Abri Pataud. The rest of the backed tool series is made up of backed blades and bladelets, some with partial backing. One backed bladelet (fig. 11:8) has a microburin fracture.

Truncated pieces are infrequent and miscellaneous. Marginally retouched pieces, on the other hand, account for 10.82% of the graphed tools, less than in Level 4: UPPER, but much more than in Level 3. Over half the pieces bear the scaled retouch typical of the Late Noaillian (fig. 11:1). The one tool assigned to Type 92 is the distal extremity of a very carefully retouched point.

The Nonflint Industry

There is one marine shell from Level 4a; it is perforated for suspension. Nine of the nonflint artifacts are perforated teeth. Two are incisors, one of *Bos* (fig. 11:19) and one of deer. The other seven are canine teeth, four of fox and three of badger. Perforation techniques vary, but the majority has some combination of flattening, lead-in grooves, and biconical drilling. Eight of the nine perforated teeth were found in close proximity in Trench IV, Square F, and very probably formed part of a single string. The two incisors and two fox canines from this group are identically decorated with short transverse incisions on the front and back surfaces of the root. One decorated and one undecorated fox canine have beveled crowns like those found on similar teeth in Level 3.

Bone artifacts from Level 4a are limited to one fragmentary awl and probable distal tips of two others, a fragment of a pin or needle, a miscellaneously worked rib segment with plano-convex section, and a short (length = 60 mm) fusiform object (fig. 11:18). One end of the latter is a conical point; the other end terminates in a tapering, doubly beveled base. Perhaps the object is a small sagaie. There are only two pieces of worked antler; both are small and miscellaneous. Sagaies d'Isturitz are absent.

DISCUSSION AND CONCLUSIONS

In the admittedly somewhat heterogeneous Éboulis 3-4: MIDDLE + LOWER series, the frequency of backed tools reaches 5.79%. In Level 4a the proportion more than triples. The question arises whether this increase is best attributed to mixture, natural or artificial, or whether it must be explained in terms of cultural factors.

Were it not for the frequency anomalies, in particular the quantity of backed tools present in Level 4a, and for their typological characteristics, the assemblage would undoubtedly be designated as Late Noaillian. The typological characteristics of certain scrapers, marginally retouched pieces, and most particularly the burins relate Level 4a to the Late Noaillian of Level 4: UPPER. Nor is there any question that the Gravette points and other backed tools were physically in association with the other tools in the assemblage. They were not localized laterally, nor were they found on a slightly different stratigraphic level. They occurred beneath, on the same level with, and above such tools as Noailles burins and Raysse burins within the thickness of Level 4a. Either the backed tools form an integral part of a Level 4a Noaillian assemblage or else they represent a temporary non-Noaillian (i.e., Périgordian) occupation of the shelter that was so nearly contemporaneous with the Noaillian occupation that they were not separated stratigraphically.

In spite of its intermediate stratigraphic position between Levels 4 and 3, the Level 4a assemblage shows no evidence of typological development from Noaillian to Périgordian VI. The detailed typology of the tools does not appear intermediate between the Noaillian and Périgordian VI. Some features of the Gravette points seem to record a development into the Périgordian VI, but this is from the late Périgordian IV and *not* from Level 4.

In view of: (a) the frequency anomalies, which are such as might arise from an admixture of Late Noaillian and Périgordian IV–VI assemblages; (b) the presence in significant numbers of tool types characteristic of one or other of the two traditions in these sectors of the assemblage—burins and backed blades—that are most obviously differentiated; and (c) the relative lack of excavation controls, it is clearly more parsimonious to interpret the Level 4a series as a mixture of Late Noaillian and Périgordian tool scatters than to invoke some form of acculturation between the two traditions. If this view is provisionally accepted, it follows that Late Noaillian and Périgordian were both exploiting the Les Eyzies locality, if only casually, at approximately the same time. Whether or not the Level 4a series is itself evidence of diffusion between or acculturation of the two cultures, it must minimally imply that they occupied overlapping territories at this time and that contact between Noaillians and Upper Périgordians was inevitable.

VIII

Noaillian or Périgordian Vc at the Abri Pataud?

The analysis set forth in the preceding chapters has proved the Noaillian assemblages to be differentiated from both the Périgordian IV, on the one hand, and the Périgordian VI, on the other. The two latter series resemble each other. With the possible exception of backed tools, types which occur in all three industries are in every case qualitatively distinguishable in Noaillian versus Périgordian assemblages. Other forms, common in one or more levels, are absent elsewhere. Backed tools, "type fossils" of the Périgordian tradition, make a minimal contribution to the Level 4 series and are only of quantitative importance in Level 4a. Unlike other tool types, the backed tools present in the Level 4 assemblage show some relationship to similar tools from the Périgordian IV and VI horizons, especially to the former. Evidence of Noaillian digging in the rear of the site suggests a mechanism by which some Périgordian IV backed tools could have found their way into the Noaillian occupation horizon. A Gravette point fragment found in the Level 4: LOWER subdivision and fitting a piece found *in situ* in Level 5 provides confirmation of this process. In the MIDDLE and UPPER parts of Level 4, backed tools comprise a minute proportion of the series and cannot be considered as an important part of the Noaillian tool kit, although examples were occasionally manufactured. Alternatively, it is possible to account for these pieces and for those in the Éboulis 3-4: MIDDLE + LOWER and Level 4a series by suggesting culture contact or visits to the site by Upper Périgordian groups manufacturing backed tools. Noailles, modified truncation, and Raysse burins, on the other hand, are found only in Noaillian horizons and in Level 4a. The techniques which produced them appear almost never to have been used by the makers of the Périgordian IV and VI assemblages. The remaining tool types all show qualitative differences in their various attributes; the comparative homogeneity of the Périgordian IV and VI and the anomalous position of the Noaillian are expressed even in the morphology of end-scrapers, the most common and seemingly least differentiated tool of the entire Upper Palaeolithic.

Quantitative analysis by tool classes of the assemblages supports the differentiation of the Noaillian. In table 43 and figure 52 the proportions of the major classes of tools are compared. By "major classes" we mean end-scrapers and other scrapers, dihedral burins, truncation burins, truncated pieces, marginally retouched pieces, and backed tools, and we refer to them as comprising the *core industry*.[10] The proportions of Noailles and Raysse burins are indicated in figure 52 by unfilled areas at the left and right, respectively, of the truncation burin bar. The most marked breaks in the percentage frequencies of tool types between the Périgordian IV, Noaillian, and Périgordian VI are in the truncation burin and backed tool categories. End-scrapers are consistently less common in the Noaillian, but increase to Upper Périgordian frequencies in Level 4a. Dihedral burins are generally more common in the Noaillian assemblages than in the Upper Périgordian, but show a marked decrease in the UPPER subdivision of Level 4, continuing into the overlying Éboulis 3-4. Their frequency relative to truncation burins is of significance. The earlier subdivisions of the Périgordian IV show very low frequencies of truncation burins, and throughout, dihedral burins are the dominant form. In the Noaillian, truncation burins are not only far more frequent, but are three or more times as common as

---

10. Percentages of types in the core industries are calculated in such a way as to preserve comparability with those series studied by Mme de Sonneville-Bordes. *End-scrapers* and other scrapers include her types 1–15, double end-scrapers being counted twice. *Dihedral burins* include types 27–29 and 31–32, doubles again being counted twice. Unretouched edge burins are included with dihedral burins. *Truncation*, with which are included retouched edge/end *burins*, include types 33–40, 42, and 44. Type 40, double truncation burins, are counted twice, together with triple burins, which Mme Bordes does not differentiate. Type 42 is defined here to include all *Noailles burins* made on truncations; again following Mme Bordes, double Noailles burins are counted as single burins. Burin-points are assimilated either to dihedral or truncation burins according to their techno-type. Combination tools are excluded. *Break burins* are also excluded from these statistics, on the ground they are likely to be underrepresented in samples from early excavations and would distort comparisons between the Abri Pataud and other assemblages. Although the preservation of comparability with Mme Bordes's data entails some loss of information about burins, separate statistics for the burin increment take into consideration all the recognized typological distinctions. *Truncated pieces* include types 60–64 and Type 84. *Marginally retouched pieces* include types 65–68, partially retouched pieces being excluded. *Backed tools and related forms* include types 45–59, 85–87, and Type 90.

Table 43

THE CORE INDUSTRIES OF LEVELS 3, 4a, Éboulis 3-4, 4, AND 5
PERCENTAGES BY MAJOR TOOL CLASSES CALCULATED FROM 92-TYPE COUNTS

Level	End-Scrapers and Other Scrapers	Dihedral and Unretouched Edge/End Burins	Truncation and Retouched Edge/End Burins	Truncated Pieces	Marginally Retouched Pieces	Backed Tools	N	Noailles Truncation Burins	Raysse Truncation Burins
Level 3	19.78	6.10	31.10	6.30	3.15	33.56	1016	–	–
Level 4a	21.82	5.45	26.36	4.55	14.55	27.27	110	3.63	13.64
Éboulis 3-4: MIDDLE + LOWER	13.64	9.09	47.40	7.14	15.59	7.14	308	6.81	11.04
Level 4: UPPER	10.11	12.16	50.29	4.49	22.40	0.53	1513	2.51	18.24
Level 4: MIDDLE	15.55	20.10	47.30	4.17	12.23	0.66	1055	9.86	14.69
Level 4: LOWER	11.12	19.74	52.53	4.07	9.71	2.82	1915	41.25	0.16
Level 5: REAR + FRONT:UPPER[a]	29.18	14.93	10.39	4.00	4.49	37.00	2251	–	–
Level 5: FRONT:MIDDLE	19.95	12.56	3.29	3.52	5.40	55.28	852	–	–
Level 5: FRONT:LOWER	20.17	11.99	2.54	3.67	6.91	54.72	709	–	–

a. Later Level 5.

dihedral burins. This pattern continues into the Périgordian VI, where the percentage frequency of truncation burins is well below that of the main Noaillian level, though at least three times that of the Périgordian IV. Level 4a is again anomalous in its lower frequency of truncation burins. Noailles and Raysse burins occur only in the Noaillian horizons and Level 4a. Truncated pieces are infrequent throughout. In the Périgordian VI, and probably also in the Périgordian IV, they include the truncation borers.

Marginally retouched pieces, which act in these statistics as crude indices of the frequency of retouch within assemblages, are throughout more common in the Noaillian than in the Périgordian, reaching their maximum frequency in Level 4: UPPER. Backed tools, absolutely dominant in the earlier subdivisions of Level 5 and comprising approximately one-third of later Level 5 and Level 3 core industries, are virtually absent except in the LOWER subdivision of the Noaillian and in the series from the Éboulis 3-4. In summary, analysis of tool-class frequencies supports the

findings of attribute analyses of the tool types studied.[11] It is not without interest that the changes in type frequencies between the Périgordian IV and the Périgordian VI are such as might indicate Noaillian influence to have acted on the Périgordian VI or its immediate forebears, stimulating elaboration of the bone and antler component of the tool kit and the production of stone tools used in its manufacture.

The degree of differentiation of the Noaillian of Level 4 is such as to imply that its makers were expressing a set of manufacturing norms that produced a radically divergent tool kit. The transformation does not affect one group of tools alone, but the entire assemblage. The same is true for the Éboulis 3-4: MIDDLE + LOWER series, though admixture of Upper Périgordian tools is not improbable. The Level 4a series shows both qualitatively and quantitatively mixed characteristics. In terms of the Abri Pataud sequence,

---

11. The places of the Périgordian IV and VI within the general Périgordian development are discussed elsewhere in this volume.

the Périgordian VI assemblage marks a return to norms that are still recognizably similar to those of the Périgordian IV. The interpretation of this tripartite sequence must take into account both economic and social factors.

In all three main levels, hearths, food debris and by-products of flint manufacture are found, and reindeer remain the staple source of meat throughout. The same basic economic activities continued to be practiced during the entire Upper Périgordian-Noaillian succession. The inconstancies of the material culture do not reflect these underlying similarities in the use of the site. Seasonal variation in the tool kit can also be rejected as a causative factor (Bouchud 1975; Spiess 1979, pp. 186–196). It is, in any case, extremely unlikely that, during the lengthy occupations of Levels 5, 4, and 3, seasonal nomadism with seasonally specific tool kits should have been so standardized as to produce the typological continuities and discontinuities found in the Abri Pataud sequence. It is equally unlikely that the qualitative variability in, for example, end-scrapers is attributable to seasonality. Although the environment changed during the ca. seven-thousand-year period represented by the occupations of Levels 5 through 3, there are no simple relationships between environmental change and variation in artifact frequency and typology. The possibility that the Noaillian industry reflects temporarily different demands made by a changing environment can be unequivocally denied. Even if the environments of Levels 5 and 3 could be shown to be more similar to each other than either is to that of Level 4, which is not the case, the cultural norms materialized in the Périgordian IV assemblage could not have shifted into a Level 4 mode and then back into one recalling the first in so many and detailed ways.

Variations in trade or exchange patterns, if these existed, cannot have affected the whole assemblage, nor is there any reason to believe that the shelter was occupied by different classes or other subgroups of the same society. If specialists are to be invoked, then the problem does not change in kind, it is only writ small.

Such hypotheses and variations on them find no support in the data. In spite of the stratigraphic interdigitation of the Noaillian strata, we provisionally accept the hypothesis that the Noaillian industry of Level 4 stems from a cultural tradition separate from that of the Périgordian IV and VI.

The indicated position of the Level 4a Gravette points in a Périgordian IV to Périgordian VI typological continuity raises important questions about cultural relationships in the Les Eyzies region. If our interpretation of this "assemblage" and the positioning of these tools on a Périgordian IV/Périgordian VI typological continuum are correct, then it is possible to imagine that the separateness and distinctiveness of the two cultural blocs (Noaillian and Upper Périgordian) that had previously obtained may have diminished, or have been liable to diminish, at this time. For the Abri Pataud, Level 4a provides the only hint of this possibility; with the exception of the increased quantitative importance of truncation burins and of nonflint armatures in the assemblage, such evidence is emphatically not present in the overlying Level 3. This raises general questions about the final stages of the Upper Périgordian in the Greater Périgord area, and information from other sites will have to be taken into account. The possible situation being considered here has already been suggested by Bordes (1968, p. 69) in his comments on the possible "polymorphism" of the Upper Périgordian on the Périgordian VI time level. It is obvious,

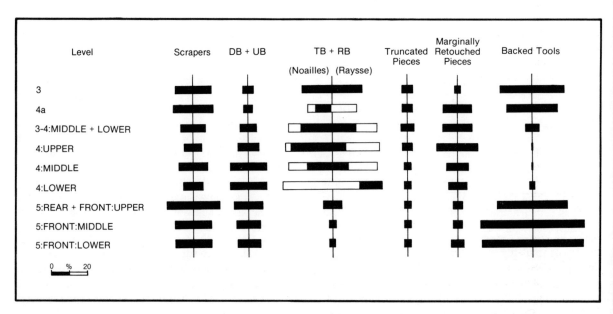

Figure 52.   BAR GRAPH REPRESENTATION OF THE CORE INDUSTRIES OF LEVELS 3 THROUGH 5.

however, that the possibilities and implications discussed in this paragraph run far beyond the data provided by the Abri Pataud.

The Upper Palaeolithic of Western Europe is not "monolithic," and occupation of neighboring or overlapping territories by culturally varied peoples must at times have occurred. There is no need to point to ethnographic parallels, such as the extraordinary linguistic and cultural diversity of California, or, and more to the point, the proximity of Inuit to Athapaskan and Algonkin groups in northern North America. Comparable stratigraphic interdigitation is paralleled elsewhere in the Upper Palaeolithic of southwestern France (Bordes and Labrot 1967; Bordes 1968; Champagne and Éspitalie 1967; Pradel 1959b). The Abri Pataud succession is by no means unique.

The arguments against the attribution of the Level 4 Noaillian assemblage to an independent cultural tradition that might be founded upon the evidence of other sites will be considered at length in later chapters. At this juncture, it is sufficient to state that the Upper Périgordian-Noaillian sequence of the Abri Pataud is the longest and the stratigraphically best controlled yet known, and has produced some of the richest assemblages. Whether or not the Noaillian industry is found in association with Périgordian IV or VI materials at other sites, and whatever their relations may have been elsewhere, at the Abri Pataud it would appear that two radically differing cultural traditions are present.

The differentiation of the Noaillian from the Périgordian IV and Périgordian VI (or "Périgordian III," as it was called then), has already found expression in Denis Peyrony's (1946) distinction of two "groups" within the Périgordian tradition, to the second of which he attributed his "Périgordian Vc" on the grounds of the presence of Aurignacian forms (carinate scrapers, blades with heavy marginal retouch, and notched blades are particularly mentioned). Diagnostic Aurignacian forms are, however, absent from the Noaillian of the Abri Pataud. Mme de Sonneville-Bordes's demonstration (1955a; 1955b; 1955c; 1955d; 1960) that the two earliest stages of the Périgordian of the second group are in fact Aurignacian in character seriously weakened Peyrony's argument. Bricker (1973) has demonstrated that the Upper Périgordian Level with *fléchettes* develops without stratigraphic or typological break into Peyrony's Périgordian IV, thus removing the last stratigraphic support. Nevertheless, Peyrony's achievement in recognizing the peculiarity of the Noaillian on the basis of insufficient and unreliable data is remarkable. He never made clear to what extent he believed the two Périgordian groups were differentiated, nor did he define his use of "group" or "facies" in cultural terms; their basic similarity was not in doubt. In the light of Mme de Sonneville-Bordes's realignment of the assemblages postulated as representing the earliest phases of the Périgordian of the second group, and of the new evidence from the Abri Pataud, his position can no longer be defended, any more than can Mme Bordes's argument (1960, p. 492) for a return to Peyrony's first theory of the Périgordian as the devel-

opment of a single cultural tradition. A variation on the above is Laville and Rigaud's (1973) suggestion that the various "Périgordian V" industries of the Périgord are indicative of a "trifurcation" within the Upper Périgordian tradition. This underplays the differentiation of the Noaillian at the Abri Pataud, where the assemblages can in no way be assimilated to the Upper Périgordian. Laville and Rigaud's reasoning and the later development of their arguments (Laville et al. 1980) will be extensively discussed in later chapters in the light of evidence from other sites.

For these reasons, we consider the term "*Noaillian*"— after the site in the Corrèze at which its most characteristic artifact was first recognized—the most suitable name for the culture which produced the Abri Pataud Level 4 assemblage. Noaillian has implicit precedence over other possible terms on grounds of priority, and it is moderately euphonious and short. These positive qualities outweigh the disadvantage that the assemblage excavated from the Grotte de Noailles by the Abbé Bardon and the Abbés Bouyssonie (1904; 1905) is inextricably mixed and does not cover the span of "Noaillian" culture (inf., p. 247).

Further inquiry into the social correlates of the Noaillian-Périgordian distinction would, at this stage and without the evidence of other sites, be inappropriate, but the *internal* typological development of the Noaillian can usefully be considered in more detail, strictly in terms of the Abri Pataud: Level 4 sequence. The developmental pattern characterizing the Upper Périgordian is one of slow morphological shifts accompanied by minor stylistic changes. New types— the backed and truncated bladelet, the truncation borer, and a variant form of dihedral burin—may be produced, but always by the same techniques. The absence of technological innovation is perhaps the single feature which contrasts most sharply with the Noaillian development.

The Late Noaillian phase, succeeding directly upon the Early Noaillian, is defined by an improvement in the technique of blank—especially blade—production, and by technological developments that revolutionize the burin component of the assemblage. The change is reflected in other tool types, including end-scrapers and truncated pieces, and can be discerned also in a refinement in the quality and an increase in the incidence of marginal retouch. In its order of magnitude, this change is little less than that which distinguishes the Périgordian IV from the Périgordian VI. Subsequent to the establishment of the Late phase, there are no further technological innovations, and, at least in the UPPER subdivision, scarcely any morphological shifts. The stratigraphic juxtaposition of inventiveness and stagnation appears dramatically displayed. If the reality of a Noaillian developmental leap can be proved, then it constitutes an important contribution to our knowledge of the modes of Upper Palaeolithic culture change. Is it possible that it is the artifact, not of the Noaillians, but of the archaeologist?

The development from Early to Late Noaillian takes place between the MIDDLE-2 and MIDDLE-1 units and not between two of the major natural subdivisions of the level.

Minor naturally and culturally caused movements and exchanges of pieces between the units—not excluding those due to small errors in excavation—would tend to blur rather than emphasize the differences between the Early and Late Noaillian phase industries, which, in their pristine form, must have been more rather than less distinct. Although the hearth and ash scatter of MIDDLE-1 covers most of the rear of the site, over the excavated area as a whole the MIDDLE deposits are less discolored and less rich in flint and bone than are either the UPPER or the LOWER subdivisions, in places differing only slightly in color from uncontaminated pale yellow éboulis. At the time of excavation there was no sterile interval separating the MIDDLE-1 and MIDDLE-2 archaeological horizons, but it is not impossible that the lesser discoloration of the deposits and the lower density of archaeological finds represent not merely decreased intensity of occupation but an actual abandonment of the site for an appreciable length of time. If this is so, then we might reconstruct the history of the site over this period.

The reconstructed sequence of events would start with the deposition of the MIDDLE-2 subdivision as a direct continuation of the LOWER and be followed by abandonment of the site, during which interval sterile éboulis would have accumulated. Elsewhere, away from the Abri Pataud, the development from Early to Late Noaillian was taking place, perhaps quite slowly. With the reoccupation of the site by Late Noaillians, a shallow "drainage" ditch was excavated in the rear of the site parallel to the cliff wall, and the series of large "bonfire" hearths typical of the Late Noaillian began to be accumulated. At the same time, the sterile deposits, already disturbed by ditch digging, would have been further trampled and displaced, with the final result that they lost their identity and became incorporated into the MIDDLE-1, and, to a lesser extent, the MIDDLE-2 subdivision.

This interpretation, with its quite different implications for the rate of culture change within the Noaillian, cannot be affirmed or denied on the basis of the stratigraphic evidence, but it receives some support from the change in the pattern of occupation of the shelter that occurred simultaneously with the Early to Late Noaillian development. In the absence of change in the shape of the shelter or the collapse of a part of the vault, the Late Noaillian withdrawal into the rear of the site and the absence of contemporary deposits in the front seem to reflect a restructuring of the habitat. These conflicting interpretations of Noaillian development can be resolved only by the study of other localities.

PART 2. THE NOAILLIAN IN AQUITAINE AND OTHER AREAS

IX

Introduction

TYPOLOGY

The peculiar features of the Noaillian assemblages at the Abri Pataud indicate that the Noaillian tradition is culturally independent of that represented by the Périgordian IV and VI. Confirmation is required from other sites. Since it cannot be assumed that the whole course of Noaillian evolution is represented at the Abri Pataud, earlier phases and later developments must be sought in other assemblages. Through them, the problem of Noaillian origins in Aquitaine must be considered. With the help of the chronological, environmental, and distributional evidence available, the limits of Noaillian territory and influence must be located in space and time, regional facies of the culture defined, and, lastly, some understanding sought of the social and behavioral correlates of the flint-working tradition and of the relationships, if any, between the bearers of what appear to be separate but contemporary Noaillian and Périgordian cultures.

In the following pages the analysis of the Abri Pataud series is extended to all assemblages that, to my knowledge, have given Noailles burins, with the exception of those in Cantabrian Spain.[12] These assemblages are subjected to a form of quantitative analysis based upon a descriptive typology arranged in such a way as to bring out the typological features which the Abri Pataud study has shown to be most relevant for Upper Périgordian and Noaillian assemblages.[13] Our statistics are calculated in terms of the core industry,[14] i.e., all end-scrapers, dihedral burins, truncation burins, truncated pieces, retouched blades, and backed tools. The type list is presented below.

Scrapers
Ordinary end-scrapers: end-scrapers with arc, asymmetrical, or flattened contours
End-scrapers with irregular contours and miscellaneous end-scrapers
Ordinary or irregular end-scrapers with marginal retouch down one or both sides
Double end-scrapers
End-scrapers with a tendency toward the ogival form of contour. The type includes all well-developed blunt point end-scrapers.
Ogival or blunt point end-scrapers with one or both sides retouched
Fan-shaped end-scrapers
Fan-shaped end-scrapers with one or both sides retouched
End-scrapers on flakes
Circular scrapers
Subcircular scrapers
Thumbnail scrapers
Carinate scrapers
Atypical carinate scrapers
Nose-ended scrapers
Atypical nose-ended scrapers
Nose-ended scrapers on blades
Nucleiform end-scrapers
Rabots: nuclei showing signs of modification for use as scrapers and, in particular, regularization of the striking platform by retouch.[15]
Side-scrapers, the term being limited to pieces made on flakes or blades where the edge defined by retouch is definitely convex.[15]
Raclettes[15]

---

12. In 1965, I was unable to provide definite evidence of Noaillian assemblages in Spain. McCollough's (1971) findings support and supplement my interpretation of the Noaillian in the French Pyrénées. I thank him for making available to me a comment summarizing this aspect of his work (inf., p. 305).

13. It will be apparent that there is considerable overlap between the special-purpose type list used here and the standard Upper Palaeolithic typology of de Sonneville-Bordes and Perrot (1954–1956). Although the latter provides much of the basic framework for my list, it seemed better to refrain from using the de Sonneville-Bordes/Perrot type numbers, which could imply a closer identity of type definition than actually exists.

14. Where it has been necessary to rely upon de Sonneville-Bordes's inventories, the statistics for the core industry are calculated as described in footnote 10 (p. 212).

15. Excluded from core industry statistics.

Perforators
  Perforators and *becs*
  Double perforators
  Microperforators
Dihedral Burins
  Median (or symmetrical) dihedral burins
  Asymmetrical dihedral burins
  Lateral dihedral burins
  Busked burins
  Large nucleiform burins, generally made by the dihedral technique[15]
Truncation Burins
  Truncation burins with and without tertiary modification are kept separate. The form of the truncation is adjusted to the characteristics of the spall removal surface (SRS) in the table that follows. Note that burins on retouched edges and ends are not distinguished from truncation burins in the typology.

	SRS Shape		
SRS Angle	*Concave*	*Straight*	*Convex*
0			
10			
20			
30	Concave	Straight	Convex
40	oblique	oblique	
50			
60			
70			
80	Concave	Straight	
90			

Transverse truncation burins
Other Burins
  Single Noailles burins on truncations and retouched edges/ends
  Single Noailles burins made by other SRS techniques[15]
  Single Raysse burins on truncations and retouched edges/ends[16]
  Single Raysse burins made by other SRS techniques[16]
  Burin-points made by the truncation technique[16]
  Burin-points made by the dihedral technique[17]
  Break burins[15]
  Unretouched edge/end burins[17]
Double and Mixed Burins: Combinations of burins are tabulated separately. All double Noailles[18] and Raysse[19] burins, made by whatever technique, are included in the tabulation. Triple burins[20] are listed individually.
Backed Tools and Related Forms: The Gravette/Micro-

Gravette, blade/bladelet limit is arbitrarily set at width 7.5 mm. Since so few pieces are found complete, length is not considered, it being preferable to use a single criterion applicable to all pieces.
  Abri Audi points or knives
  Châtelperron points or knives
  Atypical Châtelperron points, including those described as "Châtelperronoid" Gravette points (Movius et al., 1968, fig. 22)
  Gravette points
  Atypical Gravette points
  Micro-Gravette points
  Atypical Micro-Gravette points
  Font-Yves points
  Fléchettes
  Font-Robert points
  Completely backed blades
  Completely backed bladelets
  Denticulate backed bladelets
  Dufour bladelets
  Backed and truncated blades
  Backed and truncated bladelets
  Gibbous backed pieces
  Shouldered pieces
  Partially or irregularly backed blades and bladelets
Truncated Pieces[21]
  Truncated pieces
  Bitruncated pieces
  Truncated bladelets, in the Noailles burin size range
Marginally Retouched Blades
  Blades with continuous marginal retouch down both sides
  Blades with continuous marginal retouch down one side only
  Blades with partial marginal retouch only[15]
  Blades with "Aurignacian" marginal retouch
Combination Tools: Combination tools are tabulated separately.

---

16. Included with truncation burins in core industry statistics.

17. Included with dihedral burins in core industry statistics.

18. Counted as single burins in core industry statistics.

19. Counted as double in core industry statistics.

20. Triple Noailles burins are counted as single burins in core industry statistics. Other combinations are counted as double unless they are mixed by techno-type (in which case they are excluded).

21. Retruncated burins are included with truncated pieces.

Points (formed by retouch)[22]
　Symmetrical points
　Asymmetrical points
　Mousterioid points
Solutrean Tools
　Pointes à face plane
　Laurel-leaf points
　Willow-leaf points
　Solutrean shouldered points
Miscellaneous
　Geometric forms
　Picks
　Notched pieces
　Notched bladelets
　Denticulate pieces
　Denticulate bladelets
　Splintered pieces
　Other (listed individually)

In the separate tabulations of double and mixed burins and combination tools, the following abbreviations are used:

TBu	Unmodified Truncation Burin
TBm	Modified Truncation Burin
DB	Dihedral Burin
BB	Break Burin
UB	Unretouched Edge/End Burin
No.	Noailles Burin
Ray.	Raysse Burin
Br.-Pt.	Burin-Point

In addition to quantitative studies of assemblages in terms of the foregoing type list, certain series of artifacts from other sites were subjected to attribute analysis (David 1966, app.). The results of those studies are incorporated in the present text.

THE WÜRM III SEQUENCE

Since completion of the dissertation cited above, quantities of new data have become available on the climatic sequence and environments of the Last Glacial. These, including several of the papers in Movius (ed.), 1975, will be drawn upon in a subsequent discussion of the Noaillian biome (inf., chap. XVII). It is necessary at this stage only to choose a working terminology to apply to the climatic phases of the relevant part of the Würm III stadial within which the Aurignacian and "Upper Périgordian" developments took place.

22. Included with marginally retouched blades in core industry statistics.

For the Abri Pataud we have of course Farrand's (1975) sequence (summarized above in fig. 1). The single most important contribution to cultural-stratigraphic studies is Laville, Rigaud, and Sackett's (1980) *Rock Shelters of the Périgord*, which describes the theory and praxis of the sedimentological work that has been carried out, primarily by Laville, for well over a decade. This study includes a lengthy account of the Aurignacian and "Upper Périgordian" sequence (ibid., pp. 217–288) in which several site sequences are correlated (ibid., p. 228, fig. 8.2) within a framework of nine climatic phases that are for the most part subdivided into three subphases. A third competing terminology is that of Arlette Leroi-Gourhan and Renault-Miskovsky (1977), which differs in that it is based primarily upon the results of their and others' palynological studies.

The differences and disagreements between these sources *as they refer to the Abri Pataud sequence* are set out in figure 53. It should be recognized that the differences are not merely terminological, and that for correlation with other sites a standard terminology is essential in order to avoid confusion. Since the Abri Pataud gave an extremely thick succession of deposits, excellently studied by Farrand, I have chosen to use his terminology and to apply it to other sites.

A contention of the present study is that the correlations between sites proposed by Laville, Rigaud, and Sackett (1980) are in some cases seriously in error, with the result that inferences derived regarding cultural development are thoroughly misleading. A brief general discussion of why this might be so and of where my cultural inferences differ from those of Rigaud—the author primarily responsible for interpretation of the "Upper Périgordian"—follows.

The prime difference between Rigaud and myself concerns the nature of the cultural variation within the "Périgordian V" *sensu lato*. Our disagreements center on two points: (1) the degree of differentiation of the Noaillian and its significance, and (2) the respective abilities of typology, on the one hand, and sedimentology, on the other, to provide fine chronological resolution. Whereas I, on the basis of the Pataud sequence, see the Périgordian IV–VI continuum as separate from the Noaillian, Rigaud (1976, p. 59) regards assemblage variability within the "Périgordian V" as an expression of activity differences:

Nous préférons voir dans les fluctuations quantitatives des burins de Noailles, des pointes et micropointes de la Gravette et des burins plans de type Raysse ou Bassaler, le résultat d'activités différentes ayant entrainé la prolifération de certains types d'outils.

The "Périgordian V" is seen as oscillating between three poles characterized by the abundance of these three groups of tools. In addition, Font-Robert points and *éléments tronqués*, which Peyrony proposed as diagnostic of his Périgordian Va and Vb phases, are no longer accepted as phase

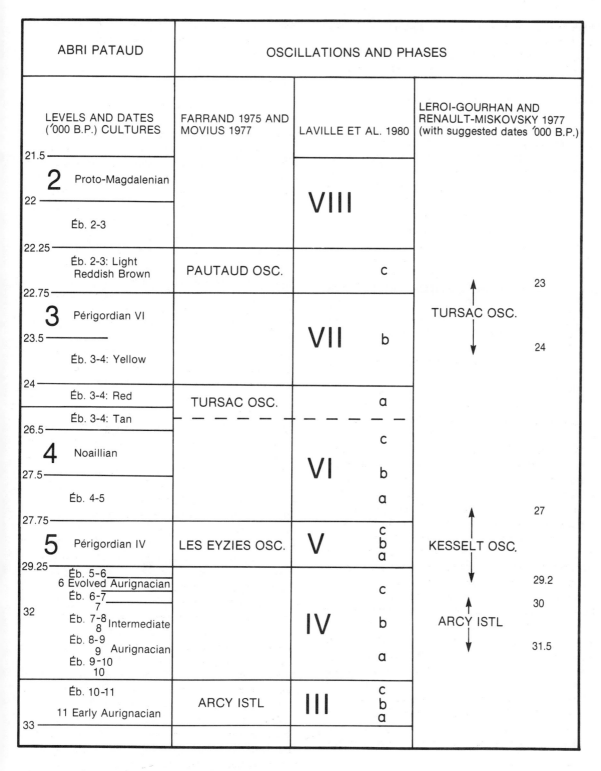

Figure 53.   A COMPARISON OF THREE TERMINOLOGIES APPLIED TO THE ABRI PATAUD
EARLY AURIGNACIAN THROUGH UPPER PÉRIGORDIAN SEQUENCE.

markers but as types that may assort with any of the three supposed activity variants.

To the best of my knowledge no evidence has been put forward to support the activity variant hypothesis, which in the previous chapter was found inadequate to account for variability at the Abri Pataud. However, support for Rigaud's view is provided by Laville's sedimentologically-based stratigraphic correlations, which for example place the typologically Early Noaillian of the Abri du Facteur (inf., p. 225) later than the Pataud Late Noaillian. I shall argue: (a) that because Rigaud is unfortunately unfamiliar with the massive Noaillian series of the Pataud and of the result of the attribute analyses described in Part 1 of this monograph, he grossly underestimates the stylistic differentiation of Late and Early Noaillian materials; (b) that both Laville and Rigaud have paid insufficient attention to the natural and cultural formation processes that have resulted in the accumulation of "assemblages" in various levels; and (c) that for this and other reasons inherent in the difficult nature of sedimentological evidence, the relative chronology derived from it and from related disciplines is, for the moment at least, simply too imprecise to serve as the yardstick for calibration of culture change in the "Périgordian V" period; while (d) undesirable though it is, artifact classification based upon the findings of attribute analysis and interpreted in the light of the precepts of "behavioral archaeology" (Schiffer 1976) is presently capable, in combination with intrasite succession, of finer chronological discrimination.

My hypothesis then is that, in addition to the independence of the Périgordian and Noaillian, the complexes of stylistic traits represented by the Early and Late Noaillian are sufficiently distinct from each other to render it extremely improbable that they either persisted as entities for long periods or recurred at different times. This hypothesis can be provisionally accepted, I propose, and that of Laville and Rigaud rejected, if it can be shown that an ordering of levels based upon typology and intrasite stratigraphy results also in a sorting by climatic conditions (as these are inferred by Laville), and by extension an inferred climatic sequence that does not conflict with that derived from typology. For example, if, after paying due attention to formation processes responsible for the accumulation of artifact assemblages, it appears that Early Noaillian assemblages appear both in very cold and dry conditions that precede a brief warmer episode and in cool moist conditions that succeed a warmer phase, my hypothesis should be rejected. Similarly, if Late Noaillian precedes a typologically Early Noaillian in any one stratigraphic succession, my hypothesis falls.

Only after establishing a sound time/space systematic

framework can much more interesting questions regarding lifeways and culture changes be entertained.

GEOGRAPHY

The study is organized geographically by a slight modification of the spatio-cultural divisions of Willey and Phillips' *Method and Theory in American Archaeology* (1958). As these divisions were developed primarily for application to sedentary societies, they are modified here in order to adapt them to the particularities of the settlement patterns characteristic of many hunter-gatherers. For this purpose we have borrowed the terminology applied by June Helm (1968, p. 118) to Dogrib socio-territorial groups. Sites are grouped by *vicinities*,[23] defined as "varying in size from a single site to a district of uncertain dimensions; it is generally not larger than the space that might be occupied by a single community or social group" (Willey and Phillips 1958, p. 18). The group in question would, in Helm's terminology, most closely approximate the "local band." The vicinity generally implies a stretch of river valley, not more than 25 km long, and the plateau or hilly country on either side. Where sites are few and far between, it is sometimes more economical to group them by larger river valley units, but the concept of "vicinity" is an essential part of the following study. Variations in the cultural contents of assemblages within vicinities can and must be assessed in terms of the finest local stratigraphy. Assemblages with mixed characteristics in a vicinity that has given unmixed assemblages are most likely to be the product of natural or artificial mixture of deposits, possibly of acculturation.

The *regions* into which vicinities are combined are described by Willey and Phillips (1958, pp. 19–20) as being "likely to coincide with minor physiographic subdivisions . . . and are . . . roughly equivalent to the space that might be occupied by a social unit larger than the community, a unit to which we may with extreme trepidation apply the term 'tribe' or 'society'." A more appropriate term for Upper Palaeolithic hunters would be the "regional band." As provisional analytic units of this magnitude, we may take the five physiographic regions defined below, testing their cultural reality against the data. Aquitaine itself is the archaeological *area*, corresponding not "to the culture area of the ethnographer" (ibid., p. 20), which might well include all of Western and Central Europe, but to a smaller spatio-cultural unit, the ethnographic correlate of which will be investigated in the following chapters.

Aquitaine[24] is a lowland area of some 91,400 square kilometers, bounded to the west by the Atlantic Ocean, to the east by the Primary rocks of the Massif Central, and to the south by the Pyrenean mountain chain. It communicates via the Poitou with the plains of Northern France, while to

---

23. The term used by Willey and Phillips is "locality," but in the Old World the word "locality" has traditionally had a different and more restricted meaning, referring always to a single site. In order to avoid any possible confusion, we here used the term "vicinity" to mean exactly what Willey and Phillips refer to as "locality."

---

24. Few provinces have changed their boundaries more often or more profoundly than Aquitaine. The term is used here as a synonym for southwestern France (*le Sud-Ouest*).

the southeast the Carcassonne gap allows easy passage to the Mediterranean. The northwest-southeast axis of the Garonne-Gironde river system gives the province a certain cohesion, but Aquitaine is not a geological or climatic unity. If we exclude the Pyrenées as a separate province, Aquitaine may be divided into five physiographic regions (Barrère, Heisch, and Lerat 1959) (fig. 54).

Coastal Lowlands and Landes Plateau

Homogeneous low-lying plains and gently rolling plateaus extend from the Gironde estuary south to the Basque country. The region forms a broad triangle with the Atlantic coast as its hypotenuse and the Garonne as its northern side, extending inland as far as the confluence of the Garonne and the Gelise. The Midouze and Adour rivers mark its southern boundary. Over most of this area recent sand and dunes, covering impermeable clayey and pebbly deposits,

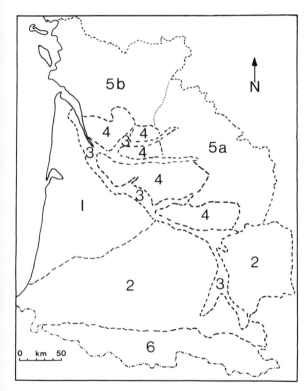

Figure 54. THE REGIONS OF AQUITAINE (after Barrère, Heisch, and Larat 1959).
Key: 1, Coastal lowlands and Landes Plateau; 2, South Aquitanian hills and piedmont; 3, Terraced alluvial valleys; 4, Low riverine plateaus; 5, Mesozoic limestone plateau (a) and plain (b); 6, Pyrenean mountains (above 1,000 m).

allow poor drainage and encourage pond formation behind the coastal dunes. The region appears to have been virtually unoccupied during the "Upper Périgordian" period.

South Aquitanian Hills and Piedmont

From the Pyrenees northward to the Garonne, and in the east to the Aveyron, the countryside shows more marked relief. Limestone is locally exposed in the south, but the hills of the *molasse*, calcareous sand with clay and quartz, are the dominant features of the landscape. They are dissected by the fan of rivers, the Garonne and its tributaries, which flow north from the mountains through steep-sided dysymmetric valleys. In the west, the Adour and its tributaries enclose the piedmont area of the Basque country and the Béarn, which receive a rainfall of over 1200 mm a year. To the north and east, rainfall decreases, reaching a low of 600 mm around Toulouse where Mediterranean influence is dominant, and increasing again toward the Massif Central. The Pyrenean foothills were extensively occupied during the latter part of the Upper Palaeolithic; in earlier periods and in other parts of the region there is much less evidence of occupation.

Terraced Alluvial Valleys

The valleys of the Garonne, lower Dordogne, and lower Isle, cut over most of their length into soft limestone, were graded and enlarged by their Quaternary rivers, producing, in combination with the glacial cycle, a topography of alluvial plains bordered by fluvial and glacio-fluvial terraces. Neither this nor the next region to be described has as yet produced more than sporadic evidence of Upper Palaeolithic occupation.

Low Riverine Plateaus

On the right banks of the Dordogne and Garonne, low, often tabular, limestone plateaus are capped with gravelly clay and some aeolian deposits, with a wide variety of soil types; to the south, the more dissected Pays des Serres of the Agenais is transitional to the higher limestone plateau.

Mesozoic Limestone Plateau and Plain

Abutting the Massif Central, the dissected plateaus and plains of northeast Aquitaine follow the great band of Cretaceous and Jurassic limestone that outcrops from the Aveyron in the south and runs northwestward to the ocean. The plateau is highest, relief and dissection greatest, and soil cover thinnest in the south; from the Causses de Quercy the plateaus slope gradually down to the northwest to grade into the plains of the Charentes.

During the Middle and Upper Palaeolithic, this region of Aquitaine was occupied more intensively than any other.

Within it, the maximum concentration of sites is found in the central section, the "classic" area of the Périgord, an old administrative entity largely corresponding to the modern department of the Dordogne.[25] To the north and south the density of known sites rapidly diminishes, and few sites are known from the northern plains. By Denis Peyrony's count, no less than 173 Upper Palaeolithic sites were known

from the Périgord in 1949 (Peyrony 1949, quoted by de Sonneville-Bordes 1960, p. 1); the number must now exceed two hundred. The Middle and Upper Palaeolithic sequences of France are founded mainly upon their evidence.

The study of Noaillian assemblages and asemblages that have given Noailles burins commences with those in the Les Eyzies vicinity and the eastern portion of the Mesozoic limestone plateau and plain; it is then extended to Southern Aquitaine and other regions, and eventually outside the Aquitanian area.

25. For a fuller description of the Périgord see de Sonneville-Bordes (1960, pp. 7–9).

X

Noaillian Sites in the Mesozoic Plateau and Plain

THE LES EYZIES VICINITY (DORDOGNE)

The greatest concentration of Upper Périgordian and Noaillian sites is in the Les Eyzies vicinity, here defined as the stretch of the Vézère River valley and adjacent plateau extending from Sergeac to Le Bugue, a distance of 17 km (fig. 55). The river and its floodplain are bordered along much of this stretch by steep cliffs. The many streams and rivulets that run down into the Vézère have produced a broken topography of minor but marked relief. Just as the stratigraphic sequence of Les Eyzies and the neighboring vicinities is standard throughout Aquitaine, so other vicinities, even in other regions, tend to recreate, often on a minor scale, the Les Eyzies topography. Although such similarities have themselves encouraged archaeological investigation and so distorted real site distribution patterns, it is clear that this kind of broken country, with its many caves and rock shelters, was especially congenial to Upper Palaeolithic peoples.

The Noaillian sites of the Les Eyzies vicinity are discussed below, first three sites of major importance, then other sites of lesser bearing on our understanding of the Noaillian culture.

Abri du Facteur (or de la Forêt) (Commune de Tursac)

The Abri du Facteur is situated on the left bank of the Vézère, 20 m above the river. It opens into the small valley of Fonpeyrine beside the Les Eyzies-Montignac road (N. 706) between the Lespinasse bridge and the Maison Forte de Reignac. In 1933, Elie Peyrony (1934a, 1934b) undertook the first serious work at this much-plundered site, sieving backdirt and excavating in the Noailles level. Delporte carried out his extensive and refined excavations from 1955 until 1960.

The small rock shelter, about 17 m in length, faces northwest. At the time of the Noaillian occupation, little overhang remained. The archaeological horizons tend to be concentrated near the cliff. In front of a platform about 6 m wide, the talus slope drops steeply to the river. Although Delporte investigated the talus slope, this proved virtually sterile. His excavations were therefore concentrated in the area directly below the cliff face. The stratigraphic summary given below

represents a compilation from several of Delporte's papers (1956, 1957, 1958, 1959, 1961b, 1962, 1968).

Level	Description
1–7	Virtually sterile. The finest stratigraphy comes from an éboulis cone peripheral to the main part of the site, originating from a chimney-like cleft in the cliff. Beneath a lightly humified surface deposit are alternating levels of stony and platy éboulis with lenses of *éboulis secs*. Within the complex are three lenses, localized close to the cleft, either cemented or containing concretions. The deposit is here 60 cm thick. Elsewhere the superficial deposits are thinner (10–40 cm); humus and backdirt from earlier excavations cover fallen roof blocks, enclosed in the rear of the site in a clayey matrix and in *éboulis secs* toward the front.
8 (8 cm)	Brown stony éboulis (angles of stones rounded). Localized in éboulis cone and in fine sandy matrix. Noaillian (derived from Levels 10 and 11).
9 (17 cm)	Strongly cemented platy éboulis localized in the éboulis cone at the mouth of the cleft. Sterile.
10 (5–10 cm)	Pale yellow platy éboulis with concretions toward the base. Noaillian Venus figurine found in back éboulis believed to be equivalent to Level 10 or 11 (Delporte 1968, pp. 97–99).

COMPLEX B

⌊11

Fine clayey matrix with few stones, but with localized deposits of platy éboulis. This is the main Noaillian level, subdivided into three lenses: 11a (5–10 cm), red; 11b (1–25 cm), light yellow; 11c (3–8 cm), gray-black to dark brown.

12–14 (30–60 cm)

Platy éboulis and *éboulis secs* with large blocks. Virtually sterile.

15

Thin occupation level with problematical industry.

16 (25–30 cm)

Platy, slabby éboulis with large blocks in front of the site. Virtually sterile.

17–21

Aurignacian II and I levels separated by light-colored éboulis. Major rockfalls contemporary with Levels 16–18.

–

Vertically or diagonally inclined "back éboulis" grading into the Cretaceous limestone bedrock.

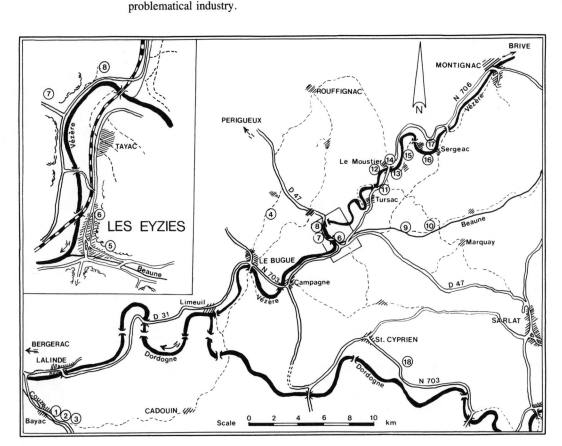

Figure 55. MAP SHOWING NOAILLIAN AND UPPER PÉRIGORDIAN SITES IN THE LES EYZIES VICINITY AND PARTS OF THE DORDOGNE AND COUZE VALLEYS. Key: 1, Abri de la Gravette; 2, Termo-Pialat; 3, Abri du Roc de Combe-Capelle; 4, Abri and Grotte de la Ferrassie; 5, Abri Audi Inférieur; 6, Abris Pataud and Vignaud; 7, Grotte d'Oreille d'Enfer and Abri du Poisson; 8, Abri de Laugerie-Haute; 9, Abri du Masnaigre; 10, Grand Abri de Laussel; 11, Abri du Facteur; 12, Abri du Ruth and Cellier; 13, Abri de la Roque-Saint-Christophe; 14, Abri Sous-le-Roc; 15, Abri de Fongal; 16, Castelmerle sites: Rochers de l'Acier, Second Abri Blanchard, Abri Labattut, and Abri des Merveilles; 17, La Rochette; 18, Gisement de Flageolet 1.

Table 44
CORE INDUSTRIES OF THE ABRI DU FACTEUR: LEVELS 10–11 AND 15
COMPARED WITH THAT FROM ABRI PATAUD: LEVEL 4: LOWER

| | Abri du Facteur | | | | Abri Pataud |
| | Levels 10–11 | | Level 15 | | Level 4: LOWER |
Type	n	%	n	%	%
End–Scrapers	89	8.9	30	25.9	11.12
Dihedral Burins	185	18.6	36	31.0	19.7
Truncation Burins	633	63.6	24	20.7	52.5
Truncated Pieces	53	5.3	3	2.6	4.1
Retouched Blades	13	1.3	3	2.6	9.7
Backed Tools	22	2.2	20	17.2	2.8
N	995	99.9	116	100.1	99.9
Noailles Burins	439	44.1	2	1.7	41.2
Raysse Burins (author's count)	4	0.4	0	0.0	0.1

Source: Delporte 1968.

Two carbon-14 dates for the Abri du Facteur have been determined by the Saclay laboratory. They give Gsy-69: 23,180 ± 1500 B.P. for Level 11 and Gsy-67: 27,890 ± 2000 B.P. for Level 21 (Coursaget and Le Run 1966, p. 131). Both dates appear much too young in comparison with GrN dates for the Aurignacian, Périgordian, and Noaillian levels at the Abri Pataud (Vogel and Waterbolk 1967; Waterbolk 1971).

The sediment analysis of Laville (1968) indicates the presence of two climatic oscillations during the time period of interest to this study. The earlier reached its climax after the deposition of Level 15. The later began to make its effects felt in Level 11 and reached its climax, a slight halt in sedimentation, after the deposition of Level 8. The palynological analysis of Arlette Leroi-Gourhan (1968) also led to the recognition of two temperate oscillations in this time period. However, she places the maximum of the former in Level 15, while the maximum of the latter may not be represented among her samples (ibid., p. 130 and fig. 4). The faunal study by Bouchud (1968) confirms in a general way the climatic sequence. The overall similarity of these data, especially the information about the oscillation associated with the Noaillian industries, to those from the Abri Pataud (Farrand 1975, pp. 63–64) is clear. The Noaillian occupations at both sites are certainly to be assigned to the same climatic phase.

The few pieces found in Level 8 are believed (Delporte 1968, p. 93) to derive from Levels 10 and 11, which are locally in direct contact; they will not be further considered. The statistics of the core industry of Levels 10 and 11 (table 44) are taken from the final site report (Delporte 1968, p.

71). The core industry consists of 995 tools.[26] The end-scrapers (8.9%)[27] tend to be larger than those of the Abri Pataud Early Noaillian, but are similar in other respects. They include a high proportion of blunt point forms (Delporte 1959, p. 237, fig. 3:4) but few arc types (ibid., p. 237, fig. 3:2); also irregularly contoured pieces (ibid., p. 237, fig. 3:3), and ones with irregularly or little-developed shoulders (ibid., p. 237, fig. 3:10). A carinate scraper, patinated differently from the remainder of the assemblage, is almost certainly intrusive or was brought into the shelter by the Noaillians. Backed tools (2.2%) are rare, as at the Abri Pataud. Typical Gravette points are present (ibid., p. 240, fig. 6:2), as are several smaller pieces.

Burins are the most numerous class of tools, with Noailles burins the most common single form (44.1%) (ibid., p. 239, fig. 5:5–9, 14–16, 21–22, 25). Modified truncation burins are rare, and Raysse burins virtually absent (0.4%). The dihedral burins (18.6%) include a majority of small, ill-worked examples (ibid., p. 238, fig. 4:1), some with tertiary modification. Of a total of forty-six burin-points (ibid., p. 239, fig. 5:18), thirty-eight are manufactured by the dihedral technique. The truncated blades (5.3%) include several pieces within the Noailles burin size range. Retouched blades (1.3%) are almost absent from the series.

Among the nonflint industry are two atypical (reworked?)

---

26. The reader is referred to David (1966, app.) for the attribute analysis of the burins from the 1955–1957 excavations in Levels 10 and 11, as well as all the Complex B end-scrapers.

27. Percentages are always of the core industry unless otherwise noted.

fragments of sagaies d'Isturitz, one with a side bevel (ibid., p. 240, fig. 7). This is a specifically Noaillian form.

Levels 12–14 contain very few pieces; some are of typically Upper Périgordian morphology. The site appears to have been scarcely visited during the period of deposition of these levels.

Level 15, the surface of which is greatly modified by gullying (Laville et al. 1980, p. 246), shows a concentration of materials in the northwest part of the site and is much less well developed in the area to the southeast that was subsequently occupied intensively by Noaillians. The materials and core industry statistics show an apparent admixture of Aurignacian and Upper Périgordian components, and there are two Noailles burins. Despite Delporte's (1968, pp. 48–50) arguments in favor of the series representing a true Aurignaco-Périgordian culture, the evidence, significant by inspection, of differential distribution of backed blades and bladelets versus nosed and carinated scrapers and busked and carinated burins argues very potently for mixture:

	Backed Blades and Bladelets	Nosed and Carinate Scrapers; Busked and Carinated Burins
Squares E–H (near back wall of shelter)	2	21
Squares I–L	12	9

The aforementioned gullying of the deposits is likely to be the main agent responsible, and the two Noailles burins are also best regarded as strays (as is a single example from Level 21 (ibid., p. 17)).

The correlation proposed here between the Facteur and Pataud sequences (fig. 56) differs from that of Laville and his colleagues (1980, pp. 246–249) only in the upper part of the sequence. They regard Levels 13 through 8 as equivalent to the entire Éboulis 4-5 through Level 3 complex at the Pataud, Level 8 equating with the alteration at the top of Level 3. I propose a much shorter span with Levels 13 and 12 equivalent to Éboulis 4-5; Levels 10 and 11 to Level 4: LOWER; and Levels 9 and 8 to Level 4: MIDDLE and UPPER and part, at least, of the Éboulis 3-4: TAN and RED sequence. This reading follows that of Farrand (1975, pp. 63–64), who notes the lesser expression of periods of temperate climates at Facteur, a difference that may be influenced not only by the microtopography of the site but also by its northwest-facing aspect. This factor apart, Farrand's and Laville's inferences regarding climate fit at least as well in this correlation as in Laville's, and there is typological synchrony.

In summary, the Facteur Noaillian assemblage of Levels 10 and 11 supports the hypothesis of independence of the Noaillian cultural tradition in the Les Eyzies vicinity. Both in relative tool frequencies and in typology, it is very similar to the Abri Pataud Early Noaillian series. An early dating within this phase is suggested by attribute analysis of the

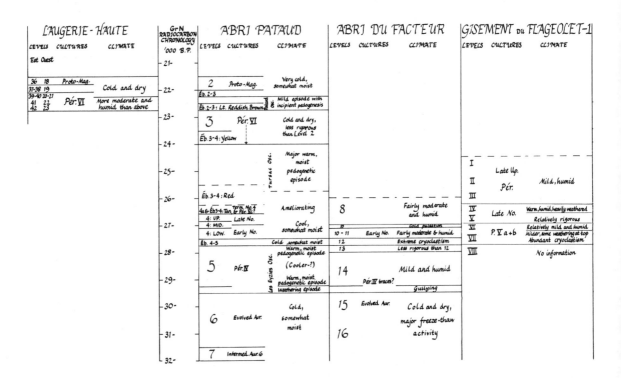

Figure 56. SITE CORRELATION CHART (data on climate for Abri Pataud from Farrand 1975; for other sites from Laville et al. 1980).

Noailles burins. The component differs in its somewhat higher proportion of truncation burins. The rarity of backed tools of all types parallels the Abri Pataud, demonstrating their lack of importance in the Early Noaillian phase. It is interesting that the Early Noaillian artifact inventory from this small, and thus presumably functionally different, site should so closely parallel that of the Abri Pataud.

Abri de Masnaigre (or Du Masnègre or Pont du Roulier) (Commune de Marquay)

The Abri de Masnaigre is situated beneath a cliff on the right bank of the Beune River where this is crossed by the Les Eyzies–Saint Geniès road (D. 48). The site was first excavated in 1909 by Bourlon and was published by him (1913) in an article which must rank as one of the best excavation reports of its day. Two years previously he had published some drawings of the burins, including a Raysse burin (Bourlon 1911, p. 269, fig. 2:20) in his important "Essai de classification des burins." In the early 1950s, the site was re-excavated by Séverin Blanc and René Sordes.

The site extends for about 20 m along the foot of the small cliff, facing toward the south. The overhang, which never seems to have extended more than 5 m forward, collapsed immediately after the Level D occupation. Bourlon's published section (1913) and the sequence described to me by Blanc differ in one crucial respect (fig. 57).

Level	Description
A (10–15 cm)	Humus, stated by Blanc to contain *raclettes*. Early Magdalenian?
B (40 cm)	Bourlon: tightly packed "tuff," within which are superposed lenses and hearths. "Upper Périgordian" (Noaillian).
	Blanc: Red occupation layer, dipping into pocket behind block "C" and resting on rock shelf "S." Thickness at this point of 60 cm. "Upper Périgordian" (Noaillian).
C (80 cm)	Huge fallen limestone roof block extending the length of the shelter.
D (30 cm)	Black occupation horizon. Périgordian IV–Va. Bourlon (1913, p. 244) states that block "C" fell directly onto this underlying level, its collapse being stopped only by the rock shelf "S." The material beneath the rock was compressed to the depth "h" on the section, but the material behind it on the shelf was not affected and remained in its original position. Blanc agrees with the compression of the underlying level but considers that a gap was left between the block and the back wall of the shelter. The gap was later filled with occupation material from Level B. He further states that the Font-Robert points of his Level B were found resting directly on the rock shelf.
E (60 cm)	Large blocks of éboulis in sandy matrix. Sterile.
F (15 cm)	Black level, localized near the back wall. Aurignacian.
G (30 cm)	Sterile. As E, continuing down to water table.
H	Water table.

Little evidence about chronology and environment is available. Bone was very badly preserved. Teeth of reindeer and horse were found in Levels B and D.

Blanc's collection from Level B is considered below (tables 45 and 46). The smaller Sordes collection (at Suresnes, near Paris) is not included. Reference is made to the series published by Bourlon (1913).

The problem of the mixture of levels apart, the Blanc collection cannot be considered reliable. In the first place, it has suffered mixture since its removal from the ground. Secondly, a part of the collection was away for exhibition at the time of my study in 1964. Thirdly, almost all the backed tools were missing from the Level D series, although

ROC DE COMBE

LEVELS	CULTURES	CLIMATE
1a 1b		Moderate freeze-thaw activity
1c		Notable cryoclastism
		Gullying of deposits and partial removal of Levels 2-5
2	Early No.	Humid, particularly fine-textured and heavily with.
3	Pér. Va+b	Cold, dry, rigorous cryoclastism
4	Pér. IV	Mild, humid
5	Evolved Aur.	Cold and dry

GISEMENT DE LA CHEVRE

LEVELS	CULTURES	CLIMATE
2 3 4 5	Term. No. & Up. Pér.? Late No.	Mild and humid, heavily weathered
6		Colder and drier than 2-5
7	Pér. IV	Mild, humid
8		Cold and dry

(depth scale: 21, 22, 23, 24, 25, 26, 27, 28, 29, 30, 31, 32)

Table 45
TYPE FREQUENCIES AND PERCENTAGES
OF THE ABRI DE MASNAIGRE: LEVEL B ASSEMBLAGE (Blanc collection)

Type	TBu	TBm	n	%
Ordinary End-Scraper			30	4.5
Irregular End-Scraper			7	1.0
End-Scraper with Marginal Retouch			2	0.3
Blunt Point End-Scraper			4	0.6
Blunt Point End-Scraper with Marginal Retouch			3	0.4
Fan-Shaped End-Scraper			2	0.3
Fan-Shaped End-Scraper with Marginal Retouch			2	0.3
End-Scraper on Flake			3	0.4
Circular or Subcircular Scraper			1	0.1
Nose-Ended Scraper			1	0.1
Side-Scraper			2	0.3
Perforator or Bec			3	0.4
Median Dihedral Burin			32	4.8
Asymmetrical Dihedral Burin			17	2.5
Lateral Dihedral Burin			8	1.2
Truncation Burin: Straight, 80-90°	1	2		0.4
Truncation Burin: Straight, Oblique	16	9		3.7
Truncation Burin: Concave, Oblique	10	3		1.9
Truncation Burin: Concave, 80-90°	6	0		0.9
Truncation Burin: Convex	4	1		0.7
Transverse Truncation Burin	1	0		0.1
Single Noailles Burin on Truncation or Retouched Edge/End			141	21.0
Single Noailles Burin Made by Other Technique			16	2.4
Single Raysse Burin on Truncation or Retouched Edge/End			17	2.5
Single Raysse Burin Made by Other Technique			2	0.3
Burin-Point by Truncation Technique			2	0.3
Burin-Point by Dihedral Technique			5	0.7
Break Burin			16	2.4
Unretouched Edge/End Burin			5	0.7
Gravette Point			68	10.1
Atypical Gravette Point			1	0.1
Micro-Gravette Point			13	1.9
Fléchette(?)			2	0.3
Font-Robert Point			3	0.4
Completely Backed Blade			13	1.9
Dufour Bladelet			1	0.1
Completely Backed Bladelet			6	0.9
Backed and Truncated Blade			2	0.3
Backed and Truncated Bladelet			1	0.1
Shouldered Piece			4	0.6
Partially or Irregularly Backed Blade or Bladelet			12	1.8
Truncated Piece			15	2.2
Truncated Bladelet			7	1.0
Retouched Blade: Continuous Both Sides			8	1.2

Table 45 (continued)

Type	n	%
Retouched Blade: Continuous One Side	4	0.6
Retouched Blade: Partial	13	1.9
Symmetrical Point	1	0.1
Notched Piece	24	3.6
Denticulate Piece	10	1.5
Splintered Piece	4	0.6
Other: Blade Fragment with Partial Inverse Retouch, Possibly a Font-Robert Point Broken in Manufacture	1	0.1
Combination Tools	9	1.3

	End-Scraper	Truncation
DB	3	-
TBu	2	1
TBm	2	-
BB	1	-

Double and Mixed Burins									75	11.1
	DB	TBu	TBm	No.	Ray.	Br.-Pt.	BB	UB		
DB	2	1	-	-	-	3	-	2		
TBu		4	1	-	-	-	4	1		
TBm				-	1	-	-	-		
No.				53	-	-	-	-		
Ray.					-	-	-	1		
BB							1	1		

Triple Burins	2	0.3
Triple Noailles Burin 1		
TBu + Ray. + Ray. 1		
Total	673	99.2

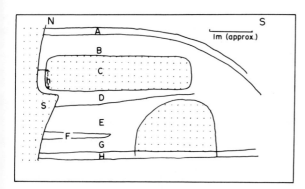

Figure 57. ABRI DU MASNAIGRE:
SECTION (redrawn from Bourlon 1913).

Table 46
TYPE FREQUENCIES AND PERCENTAGES
OF BURINS OF THE ABRI DE MASNAIGRE:
LEVEL B ASSEMBLAGE (Blanc collection)

Burin Type	n	%
No.	266	55.6
TBu	56	11.7
TBm	19	4.0
Ray.	23	4.8
Br.-Pt.	10	2.1
BB	24	5.0
UB	10	2.1
DB	70	14.6
N	478	99.9

they were there when I first saw the collection in 1961. Although no firm conclusions can be based upon the Blanc collection in its present state, it is possible to attempt to sort out the elements present in it on the evidence of the well-controlled series from the Abri Pataud and the Abri du Facteur.[28]

The end-scraper series is closely similar to that of the Abri Pataud Noaillian, although individual pieces might be attributed to the Périgordian on grounds of their size and morphology (fig. 58:1, 2). A large flake scraper illustrated by Bourlon (1913, p. 257, fig. 1:7) is of Périgordian style. The bulk of the series is stylistically Noaillian and includes fan-shaped pieces (fig. 36:11) with or without marginal retouch, pieces with a slight tendency toward a shoulder (fig. 58:4, 6), and blunt point forms (Bourlon 1911, p. 269, fig. 2:20, combined with a Raysse burin). One example resembles a carinate scraper. The proportion of end-scrapers is low (9.6% of the core industry) for either Noaillian or Périgordian series; that of backed tools (22.0%) is much higher than in Noaillian components and lower than in the late Périgordian IV of the Abri Pataud. The Gravettes are atypical in their sample parameters but show no special characteristics linking them to Gravettes found in the Noaillian series. They include many specifically Périgordian IV forms (fig. 58:9, 10, 12, 17, 18) and large pieces (fig. 58:11) similar to those of the Périgordian IV, together with smaller pieces (fig. 58:13, 14) more likely to occur in later Périgordian contexts. One very lightly backed piece (fig. 58:19) would, in an Aurignacian context, be classified as a variant of a Dufour bladelet without inverse retouch. Partially backed blades (unfinished Gravettes?) are also present. Besides Gravettes, the backed tools include large and small backed and truncated pieces (fig. 58:7, 8), Font-Robert points, and two possible *fléchettes* (fig. 58:15, 16). This combination of forms would seem to place the backed tool series later than the Abri Pataud Périgordian IV and roughly contemporary with La Ferrassie: J–K and Les Vachons: 3 (see below).

---

28. The reader is referred to David (1966, app.) for the attribute analysis of end-scrapers, Gravette points, and dihedral and truncation burins. Conclusions are incorporated into the text of the present study.

In view of the likelihood of mixture of assemblages at Masnaigre, the association of Noailles burins with these Périgordian forms cannot be used to ascertain the moment of Noaillian development or arrival in the region. The Noaillian character of much of the Masnaigre B series is most clearly expressed by the burins, which form 62.5% of the core industry. The typology of the burins and their frequencies (table 46) may be taken to suggest a Noaillian-Périgordian mixture. The Noailles burins (33.9%) are accompanied by a larger number of non-Noailles truncation burins than in Early Noaillian levels. Typologically the Noailles burins are most similar to those of the Abri Pataud: FRONT:LOWER-2 sample, with many minute pieces (fig. 58:24-26), besides medium-sized (fig. 58:20) and large examples (fig. 58:22). One piece (fig. 58:23) shows evidence of tertiary working and modification of the burin edge. A series of 23 Raysse burins (fig. 58:29–32, 35) of varied but well-developed form (3.3% of the core industry) suggests the possibility that a minor lens of Late Noaillian date could have been present at the site, excavated together with the richer Early Noaillian part of the level. The remaining truncation burins (12.2% of the core industry) include both unmodified pieces of Noaillian style, modified truncation burins (fig. 58:33, 37), and burin points (fig. 58:36) made by the truncation technique. Most burin points, however, are made by the dihedral technique, and there is one on an unretouched edge. Typical of the truncation burins unaffected by tertiary modification is a corner-struck piece (fig. 58:34). Among the dihedral burins (13.1%), some large and well-made pieces should be referred stylistically to the Périgordian rather than to the Noaillian, while the majority are less regular (fig. 58:28) with, in some cases, tertiary working (fig. 58:38).

One-third of the truncated pieces (3.8%) are within the Noailles burin size range; the retouched blades (2.1%) show equal proportions of scaled and heavy retouch.

The Bourlon series from Level B is very different. Not only did Bourlon recover many fewer Noailles burins and backed tools, but an Aurignacian increment seems to be included in the sample, represented by carinate scrapers (some of which may be utilized nuclei or *rabots*) and busked burins. Dihedral burins are more frequent than truncation burins, a reversal of the proportions of the Blanc sample.

Figure 58. ARTIFACTS FROM THE ABRI DU MASNAIGRE: LEVEL B (Blanc collection)

1: Combination tool (end-scraper + truncation burin). 2-6: End-scrapers. 7: Backed and truncated bladelet. 8: Backed and truncated blade. 9-14, 17, 18: Gravette and Micro-Gravette points. 15, 16: Fléchettes (?). 19: Backed bladelet (*lamelle à dos*). 20-27: Noailles burins (23 is with tertiary modification). 28, 38: Dihedral burins. 29, 31, 32, 35: Raysse burins (35 is double). 30: Mixed burin (double Raysse burin + unmodified truncation burin). 33: Modified truncation burin. 34: Double unmodified truncation burin. 36: Burin-point. 37: Combination tool (modified truncation burin + end-scraper).

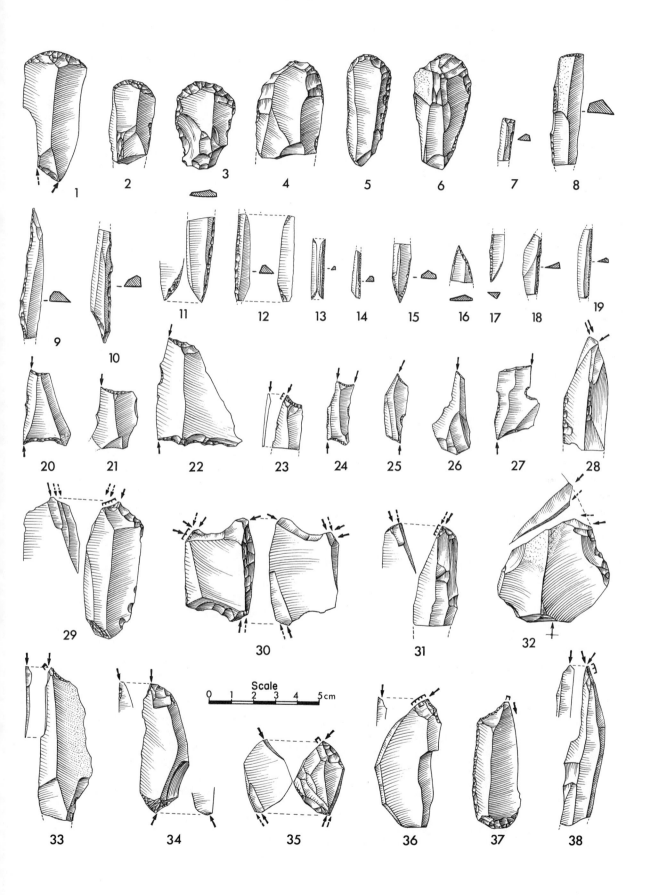

Scale
0 1 2 3 4 5 cm

End-scrapers are also much more common. Bourlon also found Font-Robert points in Level B and, at the top of the level, two unfinished Solutrean laurel-leaf points. These major disagreements in the artifact content of the level perhaps can be explained partly by selective collection of pieces by workmen excavators. Bourlon's accurate situation of these levels in his section does not necessarily imply that they were recognized, and the materials from them separated, during the excavation (cf. de Sonneville-Bordes 1960, pp. 124–125).

The presence of Font-Robert points on the rock shelf jutting out from the cliff would indicate, if Bourlon's interpretation of the stratigraphy is correct, that Level D is attributable to the Périgordian "Va" phase. The series from Blanc's excavations in this level is similar to the Abri Pataud Late Périgordian IV samples. According to Bourlon's report, Font-Robert points were also found above the rockfall "C," presumably at the base of Level B.

The evidence in favor of the independence of the Noaillian tradition from stratigraphically more reliable sites in the Les Eyzies vicinity supports the interpretation of Level B as a mixture of Noaillian and Périgordian elements. Level B may or may not have included a minor Périgordian "Va" lens at its base, but the bulk of the series seems clearly to be Early Noaillian.

Abri de la Roque-Saint-Christophe (Commune de Peyzac-le-Moustier)

The Abri de la Roque-Saint-Christophe takes its name from a huge cliff, 80–100 m in height, which flanks the left bank of the Vézère River opposite the village of Le Moustier. The Le Moustier-Saint Léon road (D. 66) runs in front of the northward-facing shelter. The cliff was fortified in the Middle Ages, and the fortification was later burnt.

Denis Peyrony excavated or, more exactly, supervised the excavations by workmen of the Roque-Saint-Christophe in 1912–1913, publishing his report in 1939. He was preceded by various collectors whose work has left no scientific trace. In the 1930s, Dr. G. Durville and P. Fitte undertook the excavation of three more trenches but did not publish. The samples considered below come from the Peyrony excavations (Musée de Préhistoire des Eyzies) and one small part of the Durville-Fitte excavation (Paul Fitte collection).

Both excavations were made in the largest of a series of rock shelters formed at the base of the cliff. It is 70 m long and 15 m deep. The old vault has collapsed and part of the occupation horizons are still covered by a gigantic block. The site is subject to frequent flooding. It is not clear from Peyrony's publication exactly where his trenches were situated. The sections given are of two trenches, 3 m apart, perpendicular to the cliff wall (Peyrony 1939, fig. 2).

Level	Description
G–C	Section 1: 315 cm; Section 2: 100 cm. Neolithic, Bronze Age, and Iron Age deposits

overlain by éboulis, backdirt, and modern deposits.

B	Section 1: 10 cm; Section 2: 70 cm. Éboulis. In Section 1 it has been largely removed by Neolithic digging and is localized 850 cm away from the back wall. In Section 2, where the Neolithic horizon is missing, it contains large blocks. Sterile.
A	Section 1: ca. 10 cm. Pale yellow, sandy level. Section 2: 60 cm. Subdivided clearly into two brown levels separated, according to the figure, by a lighter horizon: upper subdivision: 25 cm; middle subdivision: 20 cm; lower subdivision: 15 cm. "Périgordian IV."

Level A rests on a reddish-yellow, silty sediment described by Peyrony as "un sol de sable terreux d'inondation."

In spite of the 1939 publication date, it should be remembered that the site was excavated in 1912–1913. It is unfortunate that the two (or three?) subdivisions of Level A were not rigorously segregated even though, in Peyrony's words, their industries were "sensiblement les mêmes," a comment to be seen in the context of its time. Although the flint tools were not marked, the provenience of the bone artifacts is given. In the area from which the Fitte collection comes, there is no suggestion of two archaeological horizons. Fitte says (personal communication) that the artifacts came from a thin occupation level that did not appear to have been disturbed by flooding or by any other agency. The artifacts show no signs of rolling or luster.

The Peyrony collection[29] (core industry = 859 tools, by my count) is considered first (tables 47 and 48). As demonstrated by the measurements of tool types studied by attribute analysis, the Peyrony collection has been selected and cannot be considered a reliable sample. Long, unbroken "belles pièces" are greatly overrepresented, and there are too few smaller tools, particularly Noailles burins and small Gravette points. Morphological characters and their sample parameters are not seriously affected.

The end-scrapers (22.1%) are stylistically quite close to the Late Noaillian norm and include blunt point (fig. 59:1, 2) and rounded forms (fig. 59:3, 4). There are no large, shallow arc-contour pieces typical of the Abri Pataud Périgordian IV or VI assemblages. The most distinctive form of Gravette point is the Vachons variety with flat inverse retouch at the base. There is one possible fragment of a Font-Robert point (fig.59:5), although this is more likely to be a variant of the Vachons-style Gravette point.

Burins dominate the core industry (59.3%). Noailles burins are very rare but include typical small forms (fig. 59:6), besides much larger pieces (fig. 59:7). Raysse burins (15.8% of all burins) and modified truncation burins (15.6% of all burins) are together more frequent than unmodified trun-

---

29. See David (1966, app.) for an attribute analysis of end-scrapers, Gravette points, dihedral, Raysse, and other truncation burins from the Peyrony collection.

Table 47
TYPE FREQUENCIES AND PERCENTAGES OF BURINS
OF THE ABRI DE LA ROQUE-SAINT-CHRISTOPHE: LEVEL A

Burin Type	Peyrony Collection		Fitte Collection	
	n	%	n	%
No.	11	1.6	10	8.2
TBu	166	23.4	30	24.6
TBm	111	15.6	16	13.1
Ray.	112	15.8	8	6.6
Br.-Pt.	56	7.9	5	4.1
BB	35	4.9	9	7.4
DB	206	29.0	39	31.9
UB	13	1.8	5	4.1
N	710	100.0	122	100.0

Table 48
THE CORE INDUSTRIES OF THE ABRI DE LA ROQUE-SAINT-CHRISTOPHE: LEVEL A

Type	Peyrony Series		Fitte Series	
	n	%	n	%
End-Scrapers	190	22.1	71	35.9
Dihedral Burins	164	19.1	38	19.2
Truncation Burins	345	40.2	61	30.8
Truncated Pieces	29	3.4	4	2.0
Retouched Blades	51	5.9	8	4.0
Backed Tools	80	9.3	16	8.1
N	859	100.0	198	100.0
Noailles Burins	7	0.8	8	4.0
Raysse Burins	92	10.7	8	4.0

cation burins (23.4% of all burins). The Raysse burins cover a wide range of forms, from pieces on narrow blades to short, chunky double burins on broad blades or flake/blades (fig. 59:8–12). The modified truncation burins include examples with very narrow burin edges as well as larger examples (fig. 59:13). Some unmodified truncation burins may once have been Noailles burins; others are thicker, yet still of Noaillian style (fig. 59:14, 15). Forms more typical of the Périgordian are also present. A series of burin-points is made principally by the truncation technique (fig. 59:17, 20), though there are some examples made by the dihedral technique (fig. 59:22). The dihedral burins (22.1%), like other tools, are longer than in other Noaillian or Périgordian series. In width, they are close to the Noaillian or Périgordian VI means and are well distinguished from the Périgordian IV. Even on very large pieces, Noaillian traits are

present; for example, tertiary retouch (fig. 59:19) or flat-faced removals (fig. 59:18). One piece resembles an atypical flat-faced example from La Rochette (fig. 59:16). Scaled retouch is present on some pieces (fig. 59:21, 23). Other dihedral burins could, morphologically, be Périgordian. There is a small series of truncated pieces (3.4%) and a larger number of retouched blades (5.9%) on which scaled retouch is the dominant variety.

The Fitte collection (tables 47–49) is a small sample (core industry = 198 pieces) coming from one part of the Fitte-Durville excavations. It includes more broken and small tools, indicating better collection. On the other hand, there is no way of knowing whether the sample is qualitatively or quantitatively representative of the whole, unstudied Fitte-Durville collection. Among the end-scrapers (35.9%), which are more frequent than in the Peyrony series, fan-shaped

Table 49

TYPE FREQUENCIES AND PERCENTAGES

OF THE ABRI DE LA ROQUE-SAINT-CHRISTOPHE ASSEMBLAGE (FITTE COLLECTION)

Type	TBu	TBm	n	%
Ordinary End-Scraper			28	13.4
Irregular End-Scraper			2	1.0
End-Scraper with Marginal Retouch			5	2.4
Double End-Scraper			8	3.8
Blunt Point End-Scraper			2	1.0
Blunt Point End-Scraper with Marginal Retouch			3	1.4
Fan-Shaped End-Scraper			4	1.9
Fan-Shaped End-Scraper with Marginal Retouch			1	0.5
End-Scraper on Flake			1	0.5
Subcircular Scraper			1	0.5
Carinate Scraper			2	1.0
Atypical Carinate Scraper			3	1.4
Nose-Ended Scraper			1	0.5
Nucleiform End-Scraper			2	1.0
Side-Scraper			1	0.5
Median Dihedral Burin			16	7.7
Asymmetrical Dihedral Burin			8	3.8
Lateral Dihedral Burin			2	1.0
Busked Burin (Atypical)			2	1.0
Nucleiform Burin			1	0.5
Truncation Burin: Straight, 80-90°	2	–		1.0
Truncation Burin: Straight, Oblique	9	5		6.7
Truncation Burin: Concave, Oblique	5	2		3.3
Truncation Burin: Concave, 80-90°	3	1		1.9
Truncation Burin: Convex	2	–		1.0
Single Noailles Burin on Truncation or Retouched Edge/End			6	2.9
Single Raysse Burin on Truncation or Retouched Edge/End			5	2.4
Burin-Point by Truncation Technique			5	2.4
Break Burin			7	3.3
Unretouched Edge/End Burin			4	1.9
Gravette Point			9	4.3
Micro-Gravette Point			6	2.9
Fléchette			1	0.5
Truncated Piece			4	1.9
Retouched Blade: Continuous Both Sides			1	0.5
Retouched Blade: Continuous One Side			7	3.3
Retouched Blade: Partial			3	1.4
Notched Piece			3	1.4
Denticulated Piece			3	1.4
Other: Very Large Backed "Dagger" Fragment			1	0.5

Table 49 (continued)

Type						n	%
Combination Tools						6	2.9

	End-Scraper	Truncation
TBu	1	–
TBm	–	1
BB	2	–
UB	1	–
Trunc.	1	–

Double and Mixed Burins							15	7.2

	DB	TBu	TBm	No.	Ray.	BB
DB	3	1	2	–	–	1
TBu		2	–	–	–	–
TBm			1	–	3	–
No.				2	–	–

Triple Burin		1	0.5
TBu + TBu + TBu			
Total		209	100.3

and blunt point pieces are present but rare. There are very few well-developed arc contours. There is one possibly Périgordian subcircular scraper. Six carinate and nose-ended scrapers suggest the presence of an Aurignacian increment.

Backed tools (8.1%) are again much less frequent than in the Abri Pataud Périgordian assemblages. The Vachons style of Gravette point is present also in this collection. A piece described by de Sonneville-Bordes (1960, p. 187, fig. 113:9) as a triangle is probably a Gravette point, broken and then partially retouched across the break. There is one *fléchette*, but, with the exception of the "triangle" mentioned above, no backed and truncated pieces.

Burins form 50% of the core industry. Unmodified truncation burins are twice as common as modified examples. Noailles and Raysse burins are rare. One in five of the dihedral burins (19.2%) shows some modification of the burin edge, but there are several well-struck median pieces morphologically more characteristic of the Upper Périgordian. Both truncated pieces and retouched blades are rare.

According to Peyrony, his series belonged to the Périgordian IV. De Sonneville-Bordes also referred to the Roque-Saint-Christophe materials as Périgordian IV (1960, p. 218), with the qualification that they were not really like the industry of La Gravette, but may approach more closely the Périgordian (VI) of Laugerie-Haute (ibid., p. 189). These interpretations are at variance with the artifact typology. The Peyrony collection, which it will be remembered came in Section 2 from either two or three subdivisions of a level 60 cm thick, can only be a mixture of Noaillian and Upper Périgordian types. The Fitte collection appears to include

in addition an Aurignacian element. Whereas the Noaillian increment in the Peyrony collection is Late, as shown by the high frequency of modified truncation and Raysse burins, that in the Fitte sample cannot be definitely assigned and may include tools of both Noaillian phases.

Although further excavation would be required for any certainty, it may be suggested that, at least in parts of the site, there were originally separate Noaillian and Upper Périgordian horizons. According to Peyrony, the upper subdivision of Level A was richer than the lower. Bone and antler tools *were* separated by subdivision. While those from the lower are few and undiagnostic, the upper contains at least seven fragments of sagaies d'Isturitz and several gorges. Given that the Noaillian increment in the flint series appears dominant, it is not unreasonable to suppose that the upper subdivision may have been Late Noaillian, the lower Périgordian.

The typology of the Gravette points also invites speculation. In both collections these are similar in style to samples from Les Vachons: 4 and Laraux: 3. At the former site, the assemblage is stratified over a horizon containing Font-Robert points; in the latter, over one containing *éléments tronqués*. The large, shallow arc end-scrapers especially typical of the Périgordian IV at the Pataud are also absent from the Roque-Saint-Christophe samples. This suggests that the Périgordian increment may be later than the Périgordian IV and may represent a Late Périgordian phase characterized by an emphasis on Vachons-style Gravette points.

Abri du Ruth (or Abri Pagès au Ruth) (Commune de Tursac)

This small site on the right bank of the Vézère between Lespinasse and Le Moustier was excavated in 1908 by its proprietor, Robert Pagès, with the advice and help of Denis Peyrony (Peyrony 1908, 1909). The standard of excavation can be assessed by the mixture of Aurignacian and Upper Périgordian types in Level B. Further excavation at the site was done in 1925 by Prorock (unpublished; see de Sonneville-Bordes 1960, p. 83), and there is a small series from his excavation in the Musée de Préhistoire des Eyzies. Level D of the Pagès excavation (Peyrony 1909), with three stratigraphic subdivisions, has an "Upper Aurignacian" (= "Upper Périgordian") industry containing Gravette points, backed and truncated pieces, and Noailles burins. The small Prorock series contains Noailles burins, mainly of large size, and burin-points manufactured by the dihedral technique. The presence of an Early Noaillian occupation at the site appears certain, and mixture with an Upper Périgordian (Vb?) level is highly likely.

Grotte d'Oreille d'Enfer (or Des Chênes-Verts) (Commune des Eyzies)

The Grotte d'Oreille d'Enfer is a small cave on the northern side of the Gorge d'Enfer, a small side valley leading down to the right bank of the Vézère, 1.5 km upstream of Les Eyzies. The cave was excavated in the nineteenth century by Rivière (1906). In later years the remaining deposits were plundered by clandestine excavators, until in 1941 Dr. L. Pradel was authorized to salvage the small portion which remained (Pradel 1959). The site originally contained Solutrean and "Upper Périgordian" levels, but at the time of Pradel's excavation only a tiny fragment of the level with Noailles burins remained.

The total assemblage, which Dr. Pradel kindly permitted me to study, amounts to 137 pieces, the core industry to 111 (table 50). The end-scrapers (14.4%) are mainly of Noaillian form, and two fan-shaped examples are present. Backed tools (5.4%) are more common than at the Abri Pataud: Level 4 or at the Abri du Facteur. They include one backed and truncated piece (ibid., fig. 3:11) and two Gravette point fragments (ibid., fig. 3:10). There are also two *fléchettes* (ibid., fig. 3:13).

The burins are the most numerous class of tools, and Noailles burins (44.1%) are the most common category.

They are mostly of small size. Modified truncation burins and burin-points are absent from the sample, but there are two Raysse burins. The dihedral burins (21.8%) include several irregular pieces, one buskoid example, and other better-made tools. The truncated pieces (3.6%) are mostly within the Noailles burin size range. There are only two retouched blades.

This small series of artifacts from the remains of a Noaillian level can be attributed to the Early Noaillian phase. Qualitatively and quantitatively, the sample is very close to the Early Noaillian of the Abri Pataud. The presence of *fléchettes* would suggest some admixture.

Abri du Poisson (Commune des Eyzies)

This site is a small shelter on the north side of the Gorge d'Enfer. It was excavated by Girod and Massenat in 1892 (Girod 1906) and later by Galou and Marsan. In 1917, Denis Peyrony (1932b) salvaged the remaining deposits. Peyrony's Level D ("Upper Aurignacian") yielded only 57 pieces (de Sonneville-Bordes 1960, p. 203) including 12 backed tools plus a *fléchette*, and 29 Noailles burins. Late Noaillian forms are absent. The series can be attributed in part to the Early Noaillian, while the presence of a *fléchette* among 23% of backed tools argues strongly for Périgordian admixture.

Grand Abri de Laussel (Commune de Marquay)

This huge shelter, 115 m long and 15–25 m deep, is situated 7.5 km east and slightly north of Les Eyzies, on the right bank of the Beune River 500 m upstream from the Château de Laussel. It was excavated between 1908 and 1914 by the workmen of Dr. Lalanne. After Lalanne's death, the site was published by J. Bouyssonie (Lalanne and J. Bouyssonie 1941–1946), who makes quite clear how little the series is to be trusted. The industry of Level 3 ("Upper Aurignacian" of Bouyssonie) contains a mixture of Périgordian and Noaillian tools. There are *fléchettes*, Gravette and Micro-Gravette points (including some with Vachons butt retouch), large and small backed and truncated pieces, and Font-Robert points. The Noaillian increment is best seen in the burins, unfortunately little studied by Bouyssonie. A series at the Institut de Paléontologie Humaine in Paris includes both Noailles and Raysse burins. From Bouyssonie's tabulation of the burins from this level, it would seem that the latter were the more common form. Noailles burins are not given a special place in the tabulation, although they

Figure 59. ARTIFACTS FROM THE ABRI DE LA ROQUE-SAINT-CHRISTOPHE: LEVEL A (Peyrony collection)

1-4: End-scrapers. 5: Vachons-style Gravette point (or Font-Robert (?) point fragment). 6, 7: Noailles burins. 8-12: Raysse burins (8 and 12 are double). 13: Modified truncation burin. 14, 15: Unmodified truncation burins (both are double). 16: Double dihedral burin, distal end flat-faced. 17, 20, 22: Burin-points (17, 21 = TB; 22 = DB). 18, 19, 21, 23: Dihedral burins.

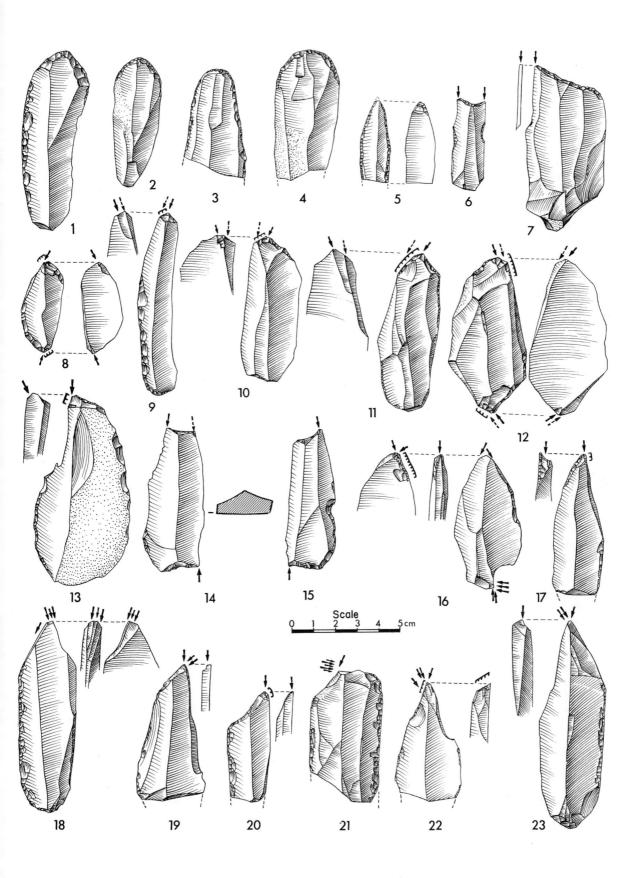

Scale
0 1 2 3 4 5 cm

Table 50
TYPE FREQUENCIES AND PERCENTAGES
OF THE OREILLE D'ENFER ASSEMBLAGE (PRADEL COLLECTION)

Type	n	%
Ordinary End-Scraper	7	5.1
Irregular End-Scraper	3	2.2
Double End-Scraper	2	1.5
Blunt Point End-Scraper	1	0.7
Fan-Shaped End-Scraper	2	1.5
Nose-Ended Scraper	1	0.7
Rabot	1	0.7
Side-Scraper	1	0.7
Perforator or Bec	2	1.5
Median Dihedral Burin	11	8.0
Asymmetrical Dihedral Burin	6	4.4
Lateral Dihedral Burin	2	1.5
Nucleiform Burin	3	2.2
	TBu	
Truncation Burin: Straight, 80-90°	2	1.5
	3	2.2
Truncation Burin: Concave, 80-90°	1	0.7
Single Noailles Burin on Truncation or Retouched Edge/End	41	29.9
Single Noailles Burin Made by Other Technique	8	5.8
Single Raysse Burin on Truncation or Retouched Edge/End	1	0.7
Break Burin	5	3.7
Unretouched Edge/End Burin	1	0.7
Gravette Point	2	1.5
Fléchette	2	1.5
Backed and Truncated Piece	1	0.7
Partially or Irregularly Backed Blade or Bladelet	1	0.7
Truncated Piece	1	0.7
Bitruncated Piece	1	0.7
Truncated Bladelet	2	1.4
Retouched Blade: Continuous One Side	1	0.7
Retouched Blade: Partial	1	0.7
Notched Piece	1	0.7
Other: Nucleus or Chopping Tool, and Microburin	2	1.5
Combination Tools	5	3.7

	End-Scraper
No.	1
TBu	1
BB	1
DB	1
Trunc.	1

Double and Mixed Burins	13	9.5

	DB	TBu	No.	Ray.
DB	2	1	–	–
TBu		1	–	1
No.			8	–

Total	137	100.0

are stated to exist, and the high frequency of flat-faced burins must include many of the Raysse type. It is likely, then, that the Noaillian element at Laussel is Late rather than Early.

Station de la Rochette (Commune de Saint-Léon-sur-Vézère)

The site of La Rochette, including a small cave, a collapsed shelter, and a large talus, is located on the right bank of the Vézère near the village of Sergeac. The major early digs were those of Hauser (1911) and Coutier and Emetaz (Coutier 1925; Coutier and Emetaz 1926). The two series considered here are from test excavations in the talus, the first by Daniel in 1928 (Schmider 1969), the second by Delporte in 1961 (Delporte 1961a). According to Schmider (1969, p. 260) their soundings were made in close proximity.

Level 1 was better defined in the six to eight square meters of Daniel's excavation, and it is likely that the small series from Delporte's test, where the unit is up to 90 cm thick, covers a wider chronological range. The core industries are set out separately and in combined form in table 51.

End-scrapers constitute 15.2% of the combined core industries and include a few, probably Aurignacian, carinate scrapers. Vachons-style Gravette points are not present among the rare backed tools (2.7%), though a piece illustrated by Schmider (ibid., p. 266, fig. 5:3) appears to be a backed and truncated bladelet. The lower frequency of backed tools in the Daniel series might imply either greater cultural homogeneity in a deposit only 30 cm thick, or less efficient collection. Burins (77.2%) are overwhelmingly dominant as a class. There are 11 Noailles to nine Raysse burins in the Delporte series, but in addition to the latter type there are, by my count, no less than 11 modified truncation burins,

Level	Description Delporte	Daniel
0 (1.5 m)	Modern humus and backdirt of earlier excavations.	
?	Not represented	Slope deposits with derived Aurignacian and Mousterian artifacts.
1	(30–90 cm) Complex of red sandy lenses with lenses of éboulis and more-or-less brecciated "cailloutis." Upper Périgordian (Noaillian).	(25–30 cm) Very compact red sandy level. Upper Périgordian (Noaillian).
2	Light yellow "cailloutis" with Aurignacian, Châtelperronian, and Mousterian tools.	Sterile deposits overlying Mousterian at a depth of 4 m.

suggesting a significant Late Noaillian increment. This is confirmed by the much larger number of typical Raysse burins in the Daniel sample. Their frequency is underestimated by the number of "burins plan sur troncature." Among the dihedral burins in the Delporte collection there is an atypical flat-faced example (Delporte 1961a, p. 42, no. 7) similar to pieces from Level 4 at the Abri Pataud and others from Facteur. Although it is possible that Daniel did not keep all he found, the low frequency of retouched blades

Table 51
THE CORE INDUSTRIES OF STATION DE LA ROCHETTE

Type	Delporte Series n	%	Daniel Series n	%	Combined Series n	%
End-Scrapers	21	19.8	40	13.5	61	15.2
Dihedral Burins	17	16.0	50	16.9	67	16.7
Truncation Burins	49	46.2	194	65.5	243	60.5
Truncated Pieces	6	5.7	5	1.7	11	2.7
Retouched Blades	7	6.6	2	0.7	9	2.2
Backed Tools	6	5.7	5	1.7	11	2.7
N	106	100.0	296	100.0	402	100.0
Noailles Burins	11	10.4	4	1.4	15	3.7
Raysse Burins	9	8.5	71[a]	24.0	80	19.9

Source: Author's count of the Delporte Series, and Schmider 1969.
a. "Burins plans sur troncature," of which 25 are double.

(2.2%) and the rarity of scaled marginal retouch suggest a relatively early dating in the Late Noaillian.

Abri Labattut (or Labutut) (Commune de Sergeac)

This site is one of the shelters in the Castelmerle Valley, overlooking the Vézère River near Sergeac. It was excavated by Didon, but the only information about it comes from two articles by the Abbé Breuil (1927, 1929). The industry of the two "Upper Périgordian" levels has been studied by de Sonneville-Bordes (1960, pp. 200–202). Noailles burins and Raysse burins are present in a small collection at the Institut de Paléontologie Humaine in Paris. Three sagaie d'Isturitz fragments, two with side-notches, and a grooved bone armature are on display at the Musée de l'Homme, where part of Didon's collection is stored. The collections have become hopelessly mixed, and beyond the fact that a Noaillian occupation was present, nothing useful can be said about this once magnificent site.[30]

Abri des Merveilles (Commune de Sergeac)

This is another of the rock shelters in the Castelmerle Valley and is best known for its Mousterian industries. Both MacCurdy's excavations in the 1920s (MacCurdy 1931) and those of Delage in 1933 (Delage 1937) record a thin "Upper Périgordian" level containing Noailles burins and Gravette points.

La Ferrassie (Grotte and Grand Abri) (Commune de Savignac-du-Bugue)

La Ferrassie lies some 6 km WNW of Les Eyzies at the junction of a side valley and a slightly larger valley that leads down to the Vézère River. The site has three areas: (a) the collapsed Grand Abri, facing south; (b) the Petit Abri, immediately to the east and containing Mousterian levels; and (c) the Grotte, a small cave directly above the Grand Abri. In the Grand Abri, Peyrony (1934) distinguished three "Upper Périgordian" levels—J, K, and L—which he was able to separate only locally in part of the rear of the site. Peyrony's collections from these levels have been previously studied by de Sonneville-Bordes (1960, pp. 190–197). They are divided into four series, one from each level in the area where they could be separated, plus one "série globale" from the rest of the area. Unfortunately, Peyrony extracted the "type fossils" from his série globale and placed them with the series to which he thought they were related, thus irretrievably biasing the percentages of tool types (ibid., p. 192).

The assemblage from Level J (Périgordian Va) contains no definitely Noaillian tools. That of Level K (Périgordian

Vb) contains three Noailles burins out of a total of 192 tools. The Level L assemblage ("Périgordian Vc") is numerically insignificant, containing 13 tools, of which two are Noailles burins. The absence of Late Noaillian forms in the série globale and in that part of the Capitan collection on display at the Musée des Antiquités Nationales at Saint-Germain-en-Laye (which includes a sagaie d'Isturitz and a grooved bone point) allow the series to be attributed to the Early Noaillian phase.

In the Grotte de la Ferrassie, Capitan and Peyrony (1912) found an "Upper Périgordian" level which contained all the special types present in Levels J, K, and L of the Grand Abri. Large numbers of Noailles burins were also recovered by sieving the backdirt of previous excavations.

Delporte's excavations at La Ferrassie were intended to check and refine Peyrony's very gross stratigraphy (Delporte and Tuffreau 1972–1973; Delporte and Mazière 1977). To do this he cut back two of the existing sections, a north-south "sagittal" section running from the rear to the front of the shelter, and an east-west "frontal" section located in the rear of the site, close to the back wall. The eastern end of the latter abutted the north end of the sagittal section, but it was extremely difficult to follow certain of the Upper Périgordian horizons from one to the other. This necessitated the distinction of the artifactual materials as frontal or sagittal series. Further, in the Upper Périgordian levels, major differences in the stratigraphy between the northern (rear) and southern part of the sagittal section required that the D2–D3 levels with Font-Robert points be treated separately, the North series being considered equivalent to both E1 frontal (in which Font-Robert points make their first appearance) and to D2–D3 frontal. The only section published to date is the upper part of the sagittal (Delporte and Tuffreau 1972–1973, fig. 1) and does not show the base of the D series of deposits nor the E1 frontal level.

D3 (including lens D2ζ) is an up to 1½-meter-thick horizon of blocky éboulis, which in the rear of the site appears to have been largely removed, perhaps by water action or, it might be suggested, by the Upper Périgordians themselves. Thus in the rear of the site there is a series of D2 lenses, D2α through D2ε, in a "poche," or depression, up to 75 cm deep, the base of which truncates D2ζ and much of D3. The section also shows an absence of direct connection between the D2 levels in the rear and those toward the front (D2a through D2e), some of which contain blocks up to about 75 cm in maximum (visible) dimension.[31]

The artifact series from E1 through D2 are clearly Upper Périgordian and contain significant quantities of Font-Robert points (table 52). It may be noted that a typical Noailles burin with stop-notch and another possible Noailles (ibid., fig. 5:19) were found in D2 sagittal (north). Bricker's seriation of Gravette point attributes of the Peyrony series from Level J, which may reasonably be considered the equivalent of these horizons, indicates that they are later than Abri

---

30. See David (1966, app.) for further details.

31. There is also a lens D2g even further toward the front of the site that appears to lie within the body of D3.

Table 52

INDICES AND PERCENTAGES OF SELECTED TOOL GROUPS AND TYPES BY LEVEL (with actual frequencies for B4-B3)
FOR THE ABRI DE LA FERRASSIE (Delporte excavations)

	El Frontal	D3-D2 Frontal	D2 Sagittal North	D2 Sagittal South	D1-C4	B4-B3
IG	25.55	37.19	28.34	26.58	35.38	1
IB	4.38	7.85	5.88	10.13	13.85	
IBd	1.46	3.31	2.14	7.60	7.70	2
IBt	2.19	1.24	2.67	2.53	3.08	10
Gravettes	27.73	22.31	33.69	11.39	10.77	0
Micro-Gravettes	3.65	4.13	5.35	7.59	1.54	0
Font-Robert Points	13.87	4.13[a]	5.88	13.92	1.54-3.08	0
Backed Blades	7.30	Present	"Quelques"	Present	Present	0
Éléments tronqués	-	-	-	-	?1.54	0
N	137	?	?	79	65	15
Noailles Burins	0	0	1 or 2	0	0	6+

Source: Delporte and Tuffreau 1973-1974.

a. Excluding some possible fragments with flat inverse retouch at the point.

Pataud: Level 5 (Périgordian IV), and should be approximately contemporary with Pataud: 4, Laraux: 5, and Vachons II: 3 (Bricker 1973, p. 1709).

Above the D2 complex, a thin sandy lens (D1; ca. 10 cm) is confined to the rear of the site and is itself overlain by a complex of C lenses. D1 and C4, the lowest unit of the C complex, contained a small series of 65 tools that may be the equivalent of Peyrony's Level K, Périgordian "Vb." This is highly questionable; there is one lightly and partially backed piece with a truncation at one end, hardly a typical *élément tronqué*. Two probable Font-Robert fragments are also present (table 52).

Levels C3-B5, totalling approximately 125 cm in thickness and virtually sterile, separate the last-mentioned assemblage from a series of only 15 tools, of which at least six are, however, Noailles burins, found in B4 and B3.

A series of dates (Gif-2696, 2698, 2699) run on samples from D2 sagittal and one (Gif-2700) from E1 frontal ranges from 24,650 ± 550 B.P. to 22,520 ± 550 B.P. and appears much too young in terms of the Pataud radiocarbon chronology, a view supported by a single date of 23,580 ± 550 B.P. (Gif-2701) for the latest Aurignacian of E1 sagittal (Delporte 1976, pp. 18-19).

It is clear from the above that the information published to date leaves many important questions concerning interpretation of the stratigraphy unanswered—indeed, since Delporte's excavation consisted of little more than a *rafraichissement* of Peyrony's old sections, some may well be unanswerable:

Does level E1 frontal really predate the D3 sagittal éboulis as its designation suggests?

Is the D2 *poche* in the rear of the shelter natural or artificial?

If the latter, does some of the D2 deposit in the front represent backdirt thrown forward by Font-Robert

Périgordians in a manner similar to the refurbishing of the rear of the Abri Pataud during its Périgordian IV occupation?

How do we explain the extraordinary conflict between the Peyrony section, in which his Level L (with Noailles burins) directly overlies K (with *éléments tronqués*), and the Delporte section, where the latest Upper Périgordian of D1-C4 is separated from B4 by 1.25 m of deposit?

Are the Noailles and Noailles-like burins from D2 sagittal (north) evidence of a Noaillian presence or influence at that time horizon?

Could the tiny but clearly Early Noaillian series from B4 and B3 perhaps be accounted for not as resulting from a minor occupation but as the product of erosion and redeposition of materials from the Grotte de la Ferrassie, where the Noaillian appears to have been quite strongly represented?

Interpretation of the La Ferrassie sequence in terms of the cultural and climatic phases represented is of great significance to students of Upper Périgordian systematics and basic to any attempt at correlation of the Ferrassie with other sequences. Unfortunately, although Laville's work at the site has to date resulted in only "preliminary findings based largely upon observations in the field rather than upon completed laboratory analyses" (Laville, Rigaud, and Sackett 1980, p. 232), he and his colleagues have taken this complex and apparently highly sensitive sequence—in which, however, neither the "Périgordian Vb" nor the Noaillian can be satisfactorily pinned down—as the effective standard for the period in which we are interested (see ibid., fig. 8.2). I submit that until the questions I have raised are definitively answered, the correlations they propose must be regarded as premature at least as regards the Périgordian V *sensu lato*.

Palynology is of no help. Paquereau's (1976) findings have not been published *in extenso*. There are disagreements (1) between Leroi-Gourhan and Renault-Miskovsky's (1977, fig. 6) diagram (on which sample attributions to levels are not given and the cultural sequence is grossly and inaccurately represented) and data provided by Delporte and Tuffreau (1973–1974, p. 96) on the "taux de boisement" (? = frequency of arboreal pollen); and (2) between the Leroi-Gourhan/Renault-Miskovsky (ibid., p. 44 and fig. 6) and Paquereau assignations of the more temperate periods to their sequence of oscillations.

The data from La Ferrassie cannot be used to test the hypothesis of Noaillian independence nor to study Upper Périgordian-Noaillian relationships. Laville and his colleagues have, on the other hand, made a strong case on sedimentological grounds for correlating the generally mild and humid period represented by Levels F1 through G4 with Pataud: 5. This implies the contemporaneity of the Ferrassie Aurignacian IV with the Pataud Périgordian IV. Bricker's interpretation of the Gravettes from the Peyrony excavations referred to above places the J series later than that from Pataud: 5 and thus supports Laville's correlation. The Upper Périgordian V of La Ferrassie is likely therefore to be at least partially contemporary with the Early Noaillian of the Abri Pataud, and in this connection it may be remembered that not only are there possible traces of the Noaillian in Delporte's D2 sagittal north unit, but Peyrony claimed three Noailles burins from his Level K.

Abri de Fongal (Commune de Peyzac-le-Moustier)

This site is located in a small side valley leading down to the left bank of the Vézère between Peyzac and Saint-Léon. It was excavated by Hauser (1911), whose collections in the Musée de Préhistoire des Eyzies were later studied by Denis Peyrony (1941). It includes Aurignacian, Périgordian, and Noaillian elements (de Sonneville-Bordes 1960, p. 97). Noailles burins and Raysse burins are present.

Abri Sous-le-Roc (Commune de Saint-Léon-sur-Vézère)

The Abri Sous-le-Roc is located 1 km from Le Moustier, near the road from Le Moustier to Montignac. In the Peyrony collection from this site in the Musée de Préhistoire des Eyzies there are three Gravette points and one Noailles burin mixed in with a generally Aurignacian series (de Sonneville-Bordes 1960, p. 207).

The Noaillian in the Les Eyzies Vicinity

The Abri Pataud sequence is characterized by great typological differences between the Périgordian and Noaillian assemblages, indicative of a basic cultural differentiation. Only three other assemblages in the vicinity—Facteur, Rochette, and Oreille d'Enfer—show as clear a picture of the Noaillian, but they are the most recently and reliably excavated. No assemblage combining or fusing Noaillian and Périgordian characteristics of comparable reliability exists on which a contrary argument might be based. At Masnaigre, for example, not only is the stratigraphy disputed, but the collections have been mixed subsequent to their excavation. Nor have we found any evidence of structured variation in activities. In the Les Eyzies vicinity, therefore, the Noaillian may reasonably be interpreted as stemming from an independent cultural tradition.

The sample from La Rochette and conceivably the Fitte collection from the Roque-Saint-Christophe are suggestive of a phase of Noaillian development, unrepresented at the Abri Pataud, which might cover the possible gap between the MIDDLE-1 and MIDDLE-2 occupations. If such were the case, our tentative interpretation of a significant technological and typological break between the Early and Late Noaillian phases would require revision. The evidence is very weak.

The evidence for the diffusion of types from one culture to the other, or for acculturation, is scarcely more convincing. The presence of backed tools in the well-excavated sites may be taken to exemplify this point. In Early Noaillian series, backed tools represent 2.2% of the core industry of the Facteur 10–11 and 5.4% at Oreille d'Enfer, where some degree of mixture is suggested by the presence of *fléchettes*. Neither assemblage includes Vachons-style Gravette points. At the Roque-Saint-Christophe this type, perhaps a horizon marker, is present among the backed tools which make up 9.3% and 8.1% of the Peyrony and Fitte series respectively. Only the Roque-Saint-Christophe materials could be used to argue for diffusion in the Late phase. At none of the sites for which we have statistics—except the obviously mixed Masnaigre: B assemblage—does the proportion of backed tools reach that of Level 4a at the Abri Pataud, a finding that may be taken to indicate either that the latter series includes pieces representing two or more brief occupations, or that significant diffusion and/or acculturation occurred only at the very end of the Noaillian occupation of the Les Eyzies vicinity.

To date, no Noaillian assemblage in the Les Eyzies vicinity can be firmly assigned to a period preceding or postdating the Abri Pataud Noaillian occupation. The culture appears already differentiated and specialized, and intrusive into the local Upper Périgordian sequence. Noaillian origins and later development (if any) must be sought elsewhere.

THE DORDOGNE RIVER DRAINAGE (DORDOGNE AND LOT)

The "Dordogne River drainage" is not a "vicinity," merely a convenient heading under which are grouped several sites falling into two distinct categories: (a) sites which have suffered from early and poor excavation and which can no longer make a substantive contribution to our understanding of the Noaillian; and (b) sites about which only preliminary information is available.

Roc de Combe Capelle (Commune de Saint-Avit Sénieur)

The Roc de Combe Capelle is located in the valley of the Couze River, a small left-bank tributary flowing into the Dordogne 15 km below the latter's confluence with the Vézère (fig. 55). The site was excavated by Hauser (Klaatsch and Hauser 1910), but Breuil (1907) and J. Bouyssonie and D. Peyrony (in D. Peyrony 1943) also made small control excavations and published sections disagreeing with that drawn for Hauser by Bächler (Klaatsch and Hauser 1910, Tafel XXV). Peyrony recognized three "Upper Périgordian" horizons with a combined thickness of about 40 cm. De Sonneville-Bordes states (1960, p. 116) "Il n'en existe aucune série représentative pour aucun niveau." Gravette and Font-Robert points and Noailles burins are present in the collections in the Musée de Préhistoire des Eyzies. There are also Proto-Solutrean points from the uppermost level.

Termo-Pialat (Commune de Saint-Avit-Sénieur)

This site, a few hundred meters downstream from the Roc de Combe Capelle, is best known for its Aurignacian materials. But Bordes and Fitte found some Noailles burins on the surface that had been brought up by burrowing animals (de Sonneville-Bordes 1960, p. 211).

Gisement du Flageolet 1 (Commune de Bézenac)

The Gisement du Flageolet is composed of two contiguous rock shelters lying 50 m above the right bank of the Dordogne River near the hamlet of Quatre, between Saint-Cyprien and Beynac. Excavations begun in 1967 by Rigaud (1969) have shown the existence of a succession of "Périgordian" industries in the east-facing shelter, Flageolet 1. The "Périgordian" materials occur behind and overlying huge blocks from a major roof fall, some of which remained above the surface in the front of the site, sloping steeply toward the back wall of the shelter, throughout the period of deposition of Levels I through VII, which total about 130 cm in thickness. Rigaud has published a special study of the Level VII occupation (7–15 cm thick), which occurs at the top of the geological stratum (Rigaud 1976, p. 94fn.). The ground surface was artificially truncated in historic times.

Full details of the assemblages appear in Rigaud's thesis, which is not available to me; however, Harvey M. Bricker (personal communication) has extracted the following information from that source:

	Levels				
	I–III	IV	V	VI	VII
Total retouched tools	174	174	506	619	914
Noailles burins	1	1	14	10	10
Raysse burins	1	6	33	3	0
Gravettes (+ Micro-Gravettes and Châtelperron points)	4	4	2	28	101
Lamelles à dos	14	0	2	10	93
Lamelles à dos tronqueés	4	0	0	4	7
Éléments tronqués	0	0	2	27	7
Font-Robert points	0	0	0	3	7
% end-scrapers	11.5	8.6	8.1	14.1	22.1
% burins	31.6	53.5	54.6	18.9	14.6
% dihedral burins	13.8	20.1	20.8	10.2	7.1
% truncation burins	16.1	32.8	30.4	7.8	5.8
% backed pieces (blades)	5.2	3.5	1.8	13.9	15.2
% backed pieces (bladelets)	10.4	3.5	7.5	14.2	13.7
Diagnosis	Late Upper Périgordian		Late Noaillian	Périgordian Va+b	

I agree with Rigaud (1969, p. 75) that Levels I–III contain a Late Upper Périgordian. Burin typology indicates that Levels IV and V are Late Noaillian, and there are very low frequencies of backed pieces. In Levels VI and VII it would appear that a small Noaillian element is Early rather than Late, but the assemblages are Upper Périgordian and characterized by éléments tronqués and Font-Robert points. In this connection it should be noted that, on the evidence of this and other sites, Bricker (1973, pp. 1755–1769) has shown that there is little justification for Peyrony's subdivision of the Périgordian with Font-Robert points (Va) and éléments tronqués (Vb) into successive phases, and I shall henceforth refer to them as "Périgordian Va+b."

Assuming that the Noaillian types in Levels VI and VII are genuinely associated and not strays from above, the Flageolet sequence would suggest that (1) during the Noaillian period, there was a greater Upper Périgordian influence or presence in this part of the Dordogne valley than in the Les Eyzies vicinity, except perhaps at La Ferrassie; and (2) Périgordian V assemblages with Font-Robert points and éléments tronqués are locally at least in part contemporary with the Noaillian.

The sediments of Flageolet 1 have been studied by Laville (Laville, Rigaud, and Sackett 1980, pp. 255–259); however, my reading of the correlation between this site and the Abri Pataud is different. The correlation suggested in figure 56, while making the whole sequence rather older, results in a good climatic fit with the Abri Pataud.

Abri de Cantelouve (Commune de Carsac)

This site, excavated in the nineteenth century by de Gerard (1883), is reported by Tixier (1958, p. 639) to have produced Noailles burins.

Grotte de Péchialet (or du Chien) (Commune de Grolejac, Department of Lot)

The southwest-facing cave is situated on the eastern slope of the Germaine River valley. The Germaine is a small left-bank tributary that flows into the Dordogne near Grolejac, 3 km to the north. The cave is entered by a narrow passage that leads into a chamber with radiating galleries. Early excavations by the Abbés Arlié and Fajol discovered the art objects for which the site is chiefly known. Breuil (1927) found a small side chamber with undisturbed deposits containing a single occupation horizon. Among about 100 miscellaneous blades and flakes, he found a few Noailles burins, an end-scraper, and a backed blade (Institut de Paléontologie Humaine).

Gisement de Roc de Combe (Commune de Nadaillac, Department of Lot)

The Roc de Combe site, some 5 km northwest of Gourdan and near the hamlet of Roq de Val, is located in a rocky outcrop on the south side of a dry valley that leads down to the Germaine River valley. It is a small cave with a rock shelter extension and was discovered in 1950 by J. Labrot, who made a test excavation in 1959. This removed a large proportion of the "Upper Périgordian" deposits, including all those from the front of the site. In 1966 Bordes and Labrot carried out a second excavation. A preliminary report (Bordes and Labrot 1967) has been published, and this, together with the results of a study by Laville (Laville et al. 1980, pp. 235–241), provided the stratigraphic information summarized below.

During the 1966 excavation, Bordes made a determined effort to understand site formation processes. Bordes and Labrot (1967) noted the presence of rodent burrows, which perhaps may account for the presence of a single typical Noailles burin in Level 8, and interpreted the truncation of Levels 2–4 and the upper part of Level 5 in the rear of the site as due to prehistoric digging. Laville regards it rather as the result of natural gullying of the deposits during a wetter period (Laville et al. 1980, p. 238). This reading is to be preferred, but in either case some mixture of deposits must have occurred both from this cause and from the activities of burrowing rodents, whose bones are locally abun-

Level	Description
1a–c (30–50 cm)	Gravelly; three subdivisions with much cryoclastic éboulis in 1c. Poor in artifacts at top, rich at base. Evolved Upper Périgordian.
–	Gullying (according to Laville) of deposits with partial removal of Levels 2–5 in the back of the shelter.
2 (ca. 10–20 cm)	Fine-textured and heavily leached. Upper Périgordian with Noailles burins.
3 (ca. 10 cm)	Heterogeneous bed of calcareous granules of variable thickness, locally with pockets and mixed with brown earth. Upper Périgordian with Noailles burins.
4 (ca. 10–20 cm)	Fine-textured and heavily leached; locally very rich in microfauna. Upper Périgordian with Gravette points.
5 (ca. 10–30 cm)	Stony éboulis with carbonates redeposited from above. Evolved Aurignacian.
6–10	Aurignacian, Lower Périgordian, and Mousterian horizons.

dant in Level 4 and between Levels 6 and 7. The greatest care would therefore have to be exercised in interpreting the succession of industries even if full qualitative and quantitative data were available, which they are not.

With the exception of Level 1, which produced 1039 pieces (of which 80% are from 1c), the numbers of tools in the "Upper Périgordian" assemblages are not given in Bordes and Labrot's (1967) preliminary report, nor is it absolutely clear whether, as I believe is the case, they include only materials from the second excavation. The Level 4 series is described as Upper Périgordian although it contains only 2.15% Gravette points and a similar percentage of Micro-Gravettes. There is one atypical Noailles burin. Further information is lacking. Level 3 gave Gravettes, Micro-Gravettes, and backed bladelets, totalling 20.1%, and 13.8% Noailles burins. Level 2 has 10.2% of the foregoing Périgordian types and 1.1% éléments tronqués, besides 10.8% Noailles burins. According to Laville et al. (1980, p. 238) there are also a "few" Font-Robert points; this may be an error since they are not mentioned by Bordes and Labrot. Level 1 has 13.8% Gravette points, 15.3% Micro-Gravettes, 4.9% backed bladelets, 0.8% éléments tronqués, and two (0.2%) Font-Robert points, of which one is in questionable stratigraphic position. Thirty-four Noailles burins represent 3.3% of the assemblage.

According to Laville et al. (1980, pp. 235–241), who note that the presence of two bedrock facies that have contributed to the formation of the deposits renders comparative analysis of the sediments particularly difficult, Levels 1 and 2 were laid down in periods characterized by only moderate frost-thaw activity, although Level 1c corresponds to a colder and less humid episode. Level 2 is "particularly fine-textured and heavily leached" and was succeeded by a period of greater humidity that resulted in the gullying noted above. Level 3 was also altered subsequent to its deposition, making "it difficult to define with precision the original nature of the sediments . . .''; however, rigorous cryoclasticism is inferred. The Level 4 deposits are indicative of mildness and humidity, whereas the climate of the underlying Level 5 (Evolved Aurignacian) was cold and dry.

This sequence correlates well with that from the Abri Pataud (fig. 56) in terms of climate and agrees in almost every respect with Laville's reading. There are, on the other hand, significant differences in the cultural sequence. The "evolved Upper Périgordian" designation of the Level 1 series fits the limited information on the typology of the backed pieces. The series might be designated "Early Périgordian VI" were it not for the 34 Noailles burins present. (Neither Raysse nor flat-faced burins are either mentioned or illustrated.) However, Bordes considers it possible that the Noailles burins are derived from Level 2 or perhaps 3— whether, in his view, by prehistoric diggings (Bordes and Labrot 1967, p. 18), or as a result of gullying. The presence of at least one Font-Robert point indisputably *in situ* could nonetheless be the result of admixture, but this type may well be time-transgressive. Levels 2 and 3 obviously contain both Upper Périgordian and Noaillian types, the former including Gravette points with Vachons-style butt treatment. They are thus generally similar to Flageolet 1, Levels IV to VII, though there is here no trace of Late Noaillian presence or influence.

It is, I think, evident from the Flageolet 1 and Roc de Combe sequences why Rigaud views the Early and Late Noaillian as specializations within the Périgordian V. From a Dordogne Valley perspective this is a reasonable interpretation. However, since the Les Eyzies vicinity, as little as 10 km away, has produced convincing proof of the independence of the two traditions from several sites, and since it appears that developments in the Dordogne Valley were effectively contemporary with those around Les Eyzies, and since no evidence of activity-controlled variation in typology has been adduced, Rigaud's hypothesis must be rejected. Upper Périgordian-Noaillian relationships in the Dordogne Valley could still take many forms. Attribute analysis of the series might be able to demonstrate diffusion or acculturation, but not a separate typological development. The Dordogne Valley materials must imply at the very least a continuing interaction with Noaillians elsewhere. Although we cannot propose a definitive interpretation of the materials from this subregion, it is at least equally possible that, during the period of Noaillian dominance in the Les Eyzies vicinity, the Dordogne Valley was used, seasonally or otherwise, by members of both groups. The nature of their interaction and of technological and stylistic transfers will hopefully one day be investigated through attribute analysis.

THE BRIVE VICINITY (CORRÈZE)

The city of Brive-la-Gaillarde lies on the border between Mesozoic Aquitaine and the Massif Central. Upper Palaeolithic habitation sites are limited to the Mesozoic formations and are particularly concentrated in and near the valley of the Planchetorte, 3 km south of Brive, a small stream which runs north to join the Corrèze River just above its confluence with the Vézère. The Planchetorte Valley, often little more than 200 m wide, is a Vézère Valley in miniature, lined with caves and shelters eroded into the local Triassic sandstone.

The majority of the sites were excavated by the Abbé Bardon and the Abbés A. and J. Bouyssonie, aided often by their pupils at the École Bossuet, in the early years of this century. Little natural stratigraphy is visible in the sandy cave deposits, through which artifacts are liable to migrate, and sequences are based almost entirely upon the succession of lenses of hearth debris (*foyers*) that discolor the deposits. Archaeological materials from intervening deposits were lumped together with the series from the *foyers*.

Soil acidity has caused the destruction of almost all faunal remains, including bone and antler tools.

Grotte de Noailles (or Chez Serre)

The Grotte de Noailles is eroded into a sandstone spur lying on the left bank of the (Haute-)Couze River close to the hamlet of Champdron. It is 2 km southeast of the Noailles railroad station and a little over 1 km north of the small road (D. 73) which leads from the N. 20 to join the D. 38 at Nazareth. The cave opens to the northeast; it is 16 m deep by a maximum of 10 m wide and 7 m high (Andrieu and Dubois 1966, p. CLXVIII, fig. 1). The front part of the vault has collapsed. Gay and Soulingeas discovered the site in 1879 and excavated in the rear part of the cave, finding *two* occupation levels separated by about 20 cm of sterile deposit (Gay 1880). The Bardon and Bouyssonie excavations took place between 1900 and 1903, lasting a little over a week in all. They were aided by their pupils and, on at least one occasion, by the Abbé Breuil. According to Bardon and the Bouyssonies (Bardon, J. Bouyssonie, and A. Bouyssonie 1904, 1905), there was only *one* archaeological level. This contained an industry ("Solutreo-Magdalenian") now seen to include tools characteristic of the Noaillian, the Upper Périgordian, and the Aurignacian. The deposit is described as sandy, hard, and gray when dry, greasy and black when damp. Within it were four large hearths (Bardon, J. Bouyssonie, and A. Bouyssonie 1905, p. 67, fig. 1). Hearths 1 and 2 lay in front of hearths 3 and 4, below a step in the bedrock. The hearths were thought to be in the same stratigraphic position (same age), although on two different topographical levels.

In 1961, Mme Andrieu and Maître Dubois (1966) began further excavations. These consisted of a transverse trench across the entire front of the cave and longitudinal trenches in the front of the western half of the cave. The following stratigraphy was recorded in the latter area (Andrieu and Dubois 1966, p. CLXIX, fig. 2):

Level	Description
6 (15 cm)	Black humus layer.
5 (30 cm)	Friable gray sand with modern debris.
C–4 (40 cm)	Compact ochreous sand containing river-stones. At its base are fallen roof blocks. Contains within it part of *Foyer* III, the rest having been removed by previous excavators. "Level with Noailles burins" (Noaillian).
3 (40 cm)	Compact reddish-gray sand, containing at its base fallen roof blocks. Sterile.
B–3 *bis* (35 cm)	Very hard red sand, containing the lenticular *Foyer* II. "Level with Gravette points" (Périgordian IV?).
A–2 (60 cm max.)	Compact yellowish sand, thickening toward exterior of cave, containing *Foyer* I at its base. "Evolved Aurignacian."
–	Triassic sandstone bedrock.

When the plans and sections of the Bardon and Bouyssonies' (1905, figs. 1 and 2) and Andrieu and Dubois's (1966, figs. 1 and 2) excavations are compared, it would appear that some of the same areas were excavated twice! The two western hearths (1 and 4) shown on the plan of the 1904 excavations correspond to Andrieu and Dubois's *Foyers* II and III. Both plans would be more accurately described as reconstructions than as precise excavation records. The two sections, drawn 60 years apart, represent the same body of deposit and must have been taken only a few centimeters from each other. The marked difference in the thickness of the deposits represented is largely attributable to the presence of sandy Level 5, absent from Bardon and the Bouyssonies' section, which Andrieu and Dubois describe (1966, p. CLXXVII) as having spread toward the opening of the cave, covering the underlying levels. The deposit is better interpreted as backdirt of earlier excavations. On a visit to the site in June 1964, made at Mme Andrieu's kind invitation, I saw a buried soil line separating Levels 3 and 5 in the north (exterior) wall of her transverse trench. This most probably represents the 1904 ground surface.

In Andrieu and Dubois's description of the assemblage of Level 4 (or C), the numerous artifacts recovered from the backdirt are included with materials claimed as *in situ*. In the BCD: 2–4 meter squares (Andrieu and Dubois 1966, fig. 1) the buried soil was not present. Here the 1904 excavations had removed Levels 3 *bis*, 3, 4, and the upper part of Level 2, whence the Aurignacian pieces in the Bardon and Bouyssonie collections; the material found by Andrieu and Dubois above the remnants of Level 2 is all redeposited.

It is unfortunate that these complications are not discussed in detail in the 1966 article.

The Andrieu Collection. The comments on the assemblages given below are based on a brief examination of the Andrieu collection, kindly made available to me in 1964 before the excavations were finished, and on the published site report.

Level 3 *bis*, containing *Foyer* II, has yielded 145 tools. It is Périgordian and includes no Noaillian forms. End-scrapers (ibid., p. CLXXV, fig. 6:2–4) are not abundant (ca. 10% of the total assemblage). There are forty-six Gravette points or Gravette point fragments (32% of the total industry), only a very few of which are bidirectionally backed (ibid., p. CLXXV, fig. 6:6,7; p. CLXXVIII, fig. 8:4–7). They are described as generally short and thick. The presence of *fléchettes* is noted, but their frequency is not given. Burins are more numerous than end-scrapers, and dihedral burins clearly outnumber truncation burins. This *Foyer* II assemblage would seem to correspond typologically to a Périgordian IV phase earlier than that represented by later Level 5 at the Abri Pataud.

Of the 188 tools studied by Andrieu and Dubois as the Level 4 (or C) assemblage, only 44 are claimed as having been found strictly *in situ* (Andrieu, letter to the author, 14 April 1969). Noailles burins and backed tools constitute an extraordinary 92% of the series. (The relative proportions of these types in the *in situ* and disturbed series are consistent with a hypothesis of homogeneity of the two series—or of the deposits.) Noailles burins are stated to have been concentrated in the immediate area of *Foyer* III. There are 136 (72%) Noailles burins in the combined series, and they are very similar upon inspection to those of the Abri Pataud Early Noaillian. The 37 (20%) Gravette points include several pieces with bidirectional backing that would seem typologically later than the Gravettes of Level 3 *bis* (*Foyer* II). *Fléchettes*, Font-Robert points, and backed and truncated pieces are absent; no Late Noaillian burin forms are represented.

The Bardon and Bouyssonie Collection. The material from the excavations of 1900–1903 has been dispersed (de Sonneville-Bordes 1960, p. 189); only a small series remains in the Musée Érnest Rupin at Brive. Mme Andrieu's sieving of the backdirt has shown that the frequencies of types given by Bardon and the Bouyssonies (1905, p. 83) must be quite unreliable. The assemblage is a mixture of Aurignacian,

Périgordian, and Noaillian forms. The first is represented by carinate and nose-ended scrapers, and the second by large arc end-scrapers, by well-made dihedral burins, and by certain forms of Gravette point, stylistically similar to those of the Abri Pataud Périgordian IV series. They include large Châtelperronoid pieces (Bardon, J. Bouyssonie, and A. Bouyssonie 1904, p. 287, fig. 75:3), small narrow lanceolate pieces (ibid., p. 286, fig. 74:2), straight parallel-sided pieces with heavy obverse retouch on the edge opposite backing (ibid., p. 287, fig. 75:2), and bellied forms. They are accompanied by at least one *fléchette* (ibid., p. 286, fig. 74:6). The Noaillian increment is characterized by quantities of Noailles burins, from very small to medium and large pieces (ibid., p. 293, fig. 78). The collection in Brive includes one modified truncation burin but no Raysse burins. A fragment of a bifacially worked Solutrean point was also found.

Discussion. The excavations of Andrieu and Dubois have demonstrated the presence of separate Aurignacian and (probably early) Périgordian IV levels at the Grotte de Noailles. In addition there are the backdirt and *in situ* series containing Gravette points and Noailles burins. The former tools are comparable to those of later Level 5 at the Abri Pataud, while the Noailles burins are similar to those of Level 4: LOWER.

The type site of the Noaillian cultural tradition is a type site in name only. Its Noaillian assemblage is irretrievably dispersed and inextricably mixed with Aurignacian and Périgordian series. "Noaillian" may be a *nomen quasi nudum*, but it is nevertheless the term which is most likely to be accepted by prehistorians. For this reason it is preferable to any other, even though it is the Abri Pataud assemblage which most clearly shows the differentiation of this industry from the Périgordian and which covers a longer period of occupation than any other Noaillian site north of the Pyrénées.

Abri du Raysse (or Grotte Fouillade) (Commune de Brive-la-Gaillarde)

The Abri du Raysse is situated in the Planchetorte Valley, 3 km south of the center of Brive. It is 550 m upstream (ESE) of the railway viaduct that crosses the valley close to the main Brive-Souillac road (N. 20) and about 100 m from the right bank of the Planchetorte stream.

According to J. Bouyssonie and Pérol (1960), who published the Solutrean level, the site has been known since the days of Philibert Lalande, who explored a large cave nearby around 1866. Lalande and Massénet also collected pieces from the talus in front of the site. Lalande's small collection (Musée Érnest Rupin, Brive) enabled Bardon and the Bouyssonies to recognize the presence of "Upper Aurignacian" and Solutrean increments (Bardon, A. Bouyssonie, and J. Bouyssonie 1924b). About 1930, Pérol began to find tools in the entrances of badger sets in front of the site, and in 1952 he undertook the excavation of the Solutrean level, while Dr. L. Pradel and J. H. Pradel were

left responsible for the underlying Noaillian and Aurignacian horizons. Dr. Pradel kindly allowed me to study the Noaillian assemblage before the final publication of the site (Pradel and Pradel 1966) had appeared.

The shelter is 10 m long and 5 m deep and faces SSW. The stratigraphy is as follows (Pradel and Pradel 1966, pp. 226, 227, fig. 1):

Level	Description
8 (25–30 cm)	Humus. Sterile.
7 (20 cm)	Small éboulis. Sterile.
6 (2–5 cm)	Solutrean.
5 (125–150 cm)	Virtually sterile (contains infiltrated material). Éboulis with large blocks from collapse of vault.
4 (20–25 cm)	The major archaeological horizon at the site. "Upper Périgordian" (Noaillian).
3 (50–100 cm)	Blocky éboulis. Sterile.
2 (15–20 cm)	Aurignacian.
1 (100 cm)	Sterile. Disintegrated sandstone overlying Triassic sandstone bedrock.
–	Triassic sandstone bedrock.

Almost no bone is preserved, but teeth of reindeer, bovid, cervid, and horse were found in Level 4.

Level 4 contains 1069 pieces (table 53); the core industry numbers 920.[32] Qualitatively and quantitatively it resembles the Late Noaillian of the Abri Pataud: Level 4: UPPER. There is a good representation of blunt point forms (Pradel and Pradel 1966, p. 244, fig. 8:2, 3, 7) among the end-scrapers (11.5%) and a high proportion of pieces with (mainly scaled) marginal retouch (ibid., p. 244, fig. 8:12). Fan-shaped end-scrapers are present but rare (ibid., p. 244, fig. 8:9, 19), and there are a few flake scrapers and side-scrapers. Aurignacian forms are absent. Among the backed tools (1.6%) are one complete Gravette point with obverse butt treatment and a Micro-Gravette made on a burin spall. The Vachons style is present on one piece (ibid., p. 245, fig. 9:1). As in the Abri Pataud: Level 4 series, the backed tool is not a quantitatively significant part of the Noaillian tool kit.

Burins (80.0%) are by far the most frequent class of tools (table 54). The Noaillian character of the dihedral burins (16.7%) is evident in the tertiary modification that affects a quarter of the pieces. Nonstraight, mainly angulated edges are common, and on some pieces the burin edge projects dorsally. Modified and unmodified truncation burins are present in almost equal frequencies. There is a high pro-

---

32. My counts differ very slightly from those appearing in the final report. These differences are minimal, e.g., Pradel and Pradel (1966, pp. 236–237, table II) have 1072 rather than my 1069 pieces.

Table 53
TYPE FREQUENCIES AND PERCENTAGES
OF THE ABRI DU RAYSSE: LEVEL 4 ASSEMBLAGE (PRADEL COLLECTION)

Type	TBu	TBm	n	%
Ordinary End-Scraper			47	4.4
Irregular End-Scraper			8	0.7
End-Scraper with Marginal Retouch			32	3.0
Blunt Point End-Scraper			11	1.0
Fan-Shaped End-Scraper			4	0.4
End-Scraper on Flake			4	0.4
Side-Scraper			1	0.1
Perforator or Bec			2	0.2
Median Dihedral Burin			60	5.6
Asymmetrical Dihedral Burin			45	4.2
Lateral Dihedral Burin			20	1.9
Busked Burin (Atypical)			1	0.1
Nucleiform Burin			7	0.7
Truncation Burin: Straight, 80–90°	6	10		1.5
	83	59		13.2
Truncation Burin: Concave, 80–90°	12	11		2.1
Truncation Burin: Convex	4	4		0.7
Transverse Truncation Burin	4	2		0.6
Single Noailles Burin on Truncation or Retouched Edge/End			61	5.7
Single Noailles Burin Made by Other Technique			10	0.9
Single Raysse Burin on Truncation or Retouched Edge/End			84	7.8
Single Raysse Burin Made by Other Technique			6	0.6
Burin-Point by Truncation Technique			15	1.4
Burin-Point by Dihedral Technique			2	0.2
Gravette Point			5	0.5
Micro-Gravette Point			3	0.3
Completely Backed Bladelet			3	0.3
Dufour Bladelet			1	0.1
Partially or Irregularly Backed Blade or Bladelet			3	0.3
Truncated Piece			27	2.6
Bitruncated Piece			1	0.1
Truncated Bladelet			8	0.7
Retouched Blade: Continuous Both Sides			7	0.7
Retouched Blade: Continuous One Side			20	1.9
Retouched Blade: Partial			15	1.4
Asymmetrical Point (Atypical)			1	0.1
Mousterioid Point			1	0.1
Pick			1	0.1
Notched Piece			6	0.6
Denticulate Piece			7	0.7
Splintered Piece			38	3.5
Break Burin			44	4.1
Unretouched Edge/End Burin			13	1.2

Table 53 (continued)

Type			n	%
Combination Tools			54	5.0

	End-Scraper	Truncation
DB	12	1
TBu	3	1
TBm	11	2
No.	–	1
Ray.	7	–
Br.-Pt.	2	1
BB	9	–
Trunc.	4	–

Double and Mixed Burins								n	%
								193	18.0

	DB	TBu	TBm	No.	Ray.	Br.-Pt.	BB	UB
DB	12	10	7	–	7	1	11	1
TBu		7	20	1	10	–	6	2
TBm			5	1	23	1	6	1
No.				18	–	1	–	–
Ray.					25	5	3	2
Br.-Pt.						1	–	–
BB							6	–

Triple Burins		n	%
		2	0.2

No. + No. + No. 1
TBu + BB + BB 1

Quadruple Burins	n	%
	1	0.1

TBu + TBm + TBm + Ray. 1

Total	n	%
	1069	100.0

portion of median pieces on concave oblique truncations. Less common than other forms of truncation burin, the Noailles burins (ibid., p. 239, fig. 5:1–18) are distributed:

Noailles Burins	Single	Double	Triple
Small	35	10	1
Large	26	6	–
On break	10	2	–

The high incidence of large pieces is characteristic of Late Noaillian samples.

The large series of Raysse burins (n = 198)—single, double, or combined with other burins or other tools—provides an excellent type series (Pradel 1966, and references therein) in which all varieties of form, technique of manufacture, and extent of reworking are represented (fig. 60:1–7). They cannot be differentiated by inspection from the samples of the Abri Pataud Late Noaillian phase. Five

Table 54

TYPE FREQUENCIES AND PERCENTAGES OF BURINS FROM THE ABRI DU RAYSSE: LEVEL 4 (PRADEL COLLECTION)

Burin Type	n	%
No.	114	11.3
TBu	178	17.6
TBm	170	16.8
Ray.	198	19.6
Br.-Pt.	30	3.0
BB	93	9.2
DB	207	20.5
UB	19	1.9
N	1009	

pieces are made by the dihedral technique, and one is on an unretouched edge. The truncation form of measurable single Raysse burins is distributed:

Truncation Form	n
Convex	5
Straight	5
Concave oblique or oblique	59
Concave	11

They may be manufactured on well-struck, narrow blades, on broader blades, or on flakes. There are five transverse examples. Double Raysse burins are common, and the very characteristic chunky form is represented. The degree of working varies from pieces with the minimum of one blow following the tertiary preparation to pieces on which the burin edge has been worked and reworked across the piece until it is on the same side as the SRS.

In spite of their rarity, the burin-points, with only two examples made by the dihedral technique as against twenty-five on truncations and three retruncated pieces, help to confirm the Late Noaillian dating of the level. The break burins include a number of pieces with very small (3 mm) burin edges. As at the Abri Pataud, unretouched edge burins are extremely rare.

In general, the truncated pieces (3.9%) parallel the burins. There are eight pieces in the Noailles size range and nine retruncated burins. Among the retouched blades (2.9%), scaled retouch, tending toward heavy retouch, is the modal style (Pradel and Pradel 1966, p. 245, fig. 9:13,15).

The Abri du Raysse: Level 4 assemblage differs from the Abri Pataud Late Noaillian samples in its higher proportion of truncation burins of all types and in the lower frequency of retouched blades. Since the proportion of the latter is largely dependent upon breakage of other tools, and moreover end-scrapers are in many cases marginally retouched, this second difference may be more apparent than real. Nevertheless, it suggests an early dating within the Late Noaillian phase that is also indicated by a proportion of Noailles burins intermediate between those of the Abri Pataud: Level 4: MIDDLE-1 and UPPER-2 subdivisions. There is no evidence from the Abri du Raysse to suggest that the Noaillian of the Brive vicinity differs from that of the Les Eyzies vicinity, although the data are inadequate for other than typological correlation of the sequences.

Grotte de Bassaler-Nord (Commune de Brive-la-Gaillarde)

The Grotte de Bassaler-Nord looks out over the city of Brive from the northern edge of the Bassaler plateau, on the left bank of the Corrèze River. It is situated 2.7 km southwest of the city's center and lies immediately below the Château de Bassaler. The archaeological horizons were discovered in 1954 by the owner of the château, who entrusted Jean Couchard with the excavation.

The cave is 11 m deep and 10 m wide at the entrance, broadening to 17 m at its widest point. It faces almost due north. Much of the upper archaeological horizon (Noaillian) had been destroyed before excavation began. The following stratigraphy was recorded near the entrance (Couchard and de Sonneville-Bordes 1960, p. 418, fig. 2):

Level	Description
1 (20 cm)	Humus and material disintegrated from the roof.
2 (60 cm)	Coarse sand disintegrated from the parent sandstone. Sterile.
3 (5 cm)	Yellow-white clayey sand. Sterile.
4 (10–15 cm)	"Périgordian Vc" (Noaillian).
5 (40 cm)	Sand. Sterile.
6 (5 cm)	White clay. Sterile.
7 (20 cm)	Aurignacian (with Dufour bladelets).
7a (10 cm)	Clay locally impregnated with red ochre. Sterile?
8 (30 cm)	Loosely packed white sand and rockfall. Two large sandstone blocks which were still partially exposed at the time of the Level 4 occupation. Sterile.
9 (25 cm)	Yellow, loosely packed sand. Sterile.
10 (10 cm)	Sterile. White, tightly packed clay overlying Triassic sandstone bedrock.
–	Triassic sandstone bedrock.

At the time of my study, the assemblage in the Couchard collection from Level 4 contained 125 pieces, the core industry 134 tools (table 55). The series closely resembles that of Le Raysse. The end-scrapers (12.7%) are too few to permit statistical analysis; they include one blunt point piece and several with marginal retouch. There are three very rounded pieces, besides shallower arc forms (Couchard and de Sonneville-Bordes 1960, fig. 9:6, 11). One end-scraper is combined with a modified truncation burin (ibid., p. 431, fig. 9:4) and one with a Raysse burin. Backed tools (three pieces: 2.2%) are very few. Truncation burins of all types (70.1%) dominate the assemblage almost to the exclusion of dihedral burins (3.7%) (table 56). Raysse burins (ibid., p. 430, fig. 8:15, 17, 18, 20) are more frequent than either modified or unmodified truncation burins. The proportion of Noailles burins (10.5% of all burins) is similar to that in the assemblage from Le Raysse. The eight burin-points (ibid., p. 430, fig. 8:7, 10) are all manufactured by the truncation technique. There are six truncated pieces (4.5%) and nine retouched blades (6.7%), besides five with partial retouch (ibid., p. 431, fig. 9:12–16). Scaled retouch is the most common kind.

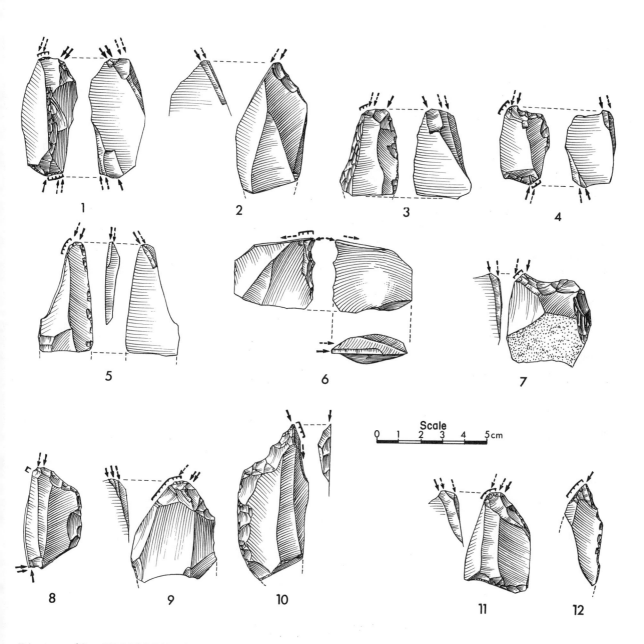

Figure 60. NOAILLIAN ARTIFACTS

ABRI DU RAYSSE (Pradel collection): 1-7: Raysse burins (1 and 4 are double; 6 is transverse).
GROTTE DE PRÉ-AUBERT: *FOYERS* I-III (Institut de Paléontologie Humaine collection): 8: Mixed burin (modified truncation + dihedral). 9: Raysse burin. 10: Burin-point (TB).
GROTTE DE LA CHÈVRE: LEVEL 5 (Arambourou and Jude collection): 11: Raysse burin. 12: Burin-point.

Table 55
TYPE FREQUENCIES AND PERCENTAGES
FROM THE GROTTE DE BASSALER-NORD: LEVEL 4 ASSEMBLAGE (COUCHARD COLLECTION)

Type		n	%
Ordinary End-Scraper		7	5.6
End-Scraper with Marginal Retouch		1	0.8
Double End-Scraper		4	3.2
Blunt Point End-Scraper		1	0.8
Median Dihedral Burin		1	0.8
Asymmetrical Dihedral Burin		3	2.4
Lateral Dihedral Burin		1	0.8

	TBu	TBm	%
Truncation Burin: Straight, 80–90°	2	2	3.2
Truncation Burin: Straight, Oblique	4	3	5.6
Truncation Burin: Concave, Oblique	7	6	10.4
Truncation Burin: Concave, 80–90°	–	1	0.8

Type	n	%
Single Noailles Burin on Truncation or Retouched Edge/End	8	6.4
Single Raysse Burin on Truncation or Retouched Edge/End	12	9.6
Burin-Point by Truncation Technique	6	4.8
Break Burin	2	1.6
Micro-Gravette Point	2	1.6
Completely Backed Blade	1	0.8
Truncated Piece	6	4.8
Retouched Blade: Continuous One Side	9	7.2
Retouched Blade: Partial	5	4.0
Combination Tools	6	4.8

	End-Scraper	Truncation	Point
TBu	–	1	1
TBm	1	–	–
Ray.	1	2	–

		n	%
Double and Mixed Burins		25	20.0

	TBu	TBm	No.	Ray.	Br.-Pt.	BB
DB	–	2	–	–	–	–
TBu	1	3	–	2	–	1
TBm		2	–	3	1	–
No.			2	–	–	–
Ray.				7	1	–

	n	%
Total	125	100.0

The tools of the Bassaler-Nord assemblage appear to be generally smaller than those of Le Raysse. They are certainly smaller than the Abri Pataud: Level 4 series from which they differ only in such attributes as are affected by lack of raw materials: in absolute dimensions, and in some morphological—as opposed to technological—features. The same style is being expressed under different circumstances. Apart from this, Bassaler-Nord and Le Raysse resemble each other very closely, Bassaler-Nord having many fewer dihedral burins and rather more retouched blades, and a higher proportion of modified truncation and Raysse burins. On the evidence of the frequencies of Noailles burins and of retouched blades, it may be assigned, with Le Raysse, to an early part of the Late Noaillian phase.

Grotte de Pré-Aubert (Commune de Brive-la-Gaillarde)

The Grotte de Pré-Aubert is situated on the right bank of the Planchetorte stream, immediately downstream from the Grotte Lacoste and about 40 m from the railroad viaduct. The site was excavated by Bardon and the Bouyssonies, aided by their pupils, between the years 1907 and 1909 (Bardon, J. Bouyssonie, and A. Bouyssonie 1920; Bardon, A. Bouyssonie, and J. Bouyssonie 1924a). More a shelter than a cave, the site is some 15 m long and 6 m deep; it faces SSW. A series of four occupation horizons was recognized (Bardon, A. Bouyssonie, and J. Bouyssonie 1924a, p. 142, fig. 1):

Level	Description
1 (40 cm)	Humus and rockfall.
2 (70 cm)	Stratified (waterlaid?) sands and sandstone blocks. Sterile.
3 (10 cm)	*Foyer* IV. Solutrean.
4 (30 cm)	Traces of an occupation containing *pointes à face plane*. Solutrean.
5 (15 cm)	*Foyer* III. Late Noaillian.
6 (20 cm)	Sand and sandstone blocks. Sterile.
7 (20 cm)	*Foyer* II. Late Noaillian.
8 (45 cm)	Sand and sandstone blocks. Sterile.
9 (35 cm)	*Foyer* I, localized behind a rockfall. Late Noaillian.
–	Triassic sandstone bedrock.

The occupation horizons and their associated hearth concentrations move through time steadily back toward the present cliff. *Foyers* II, III and IV are localized in the eastern part of the site; the richer *Foyer* I is more extensive.

The collection of Bardon and the Bouyssonies has been dispersed. A small collection at the Institut de Paléontologie Humaine in Paris is probably a mixture of the artifacts from *Foyers* I–III (table 57). Collections from *Foyers* I–III in the Musée Érnest Rupin at Brive are mixed with pieces from the Solutrean *Foyer* IV. Bardon and the Bouyssonies describe the typology of *Foyers* I–III globally, and only the quantitative data are presented by *foyers* (1924a, p. 158). As in the case of the Grotte de Noailles, the percentages cannot be considered reliable.

In the percentages of the core industries of the three levels (table 58), compiled from the data of Bardon, A. Bouyssonie, and J. Bouyssonie (1924a), no account is taken of double tools; the proportion of end-scrapers is exaggerated by the presence of some truncated pieces, and the total proportion of the latter cannot be assessed, since they are divided between end-scrapers and perforators. The Institut de Paléontologie Humaine collection (author's count) is certainly also quantitatively unreliable; there is a noticeable

Table 56
TYPE FREQUENCIES AND PERCENTAGES OF BURINS FROM THE GROTTE DE BASSALER-NORD: LEVEL 4 ASSEMBLAGE (COUCHARD COLLECTION)

Burin Type	n	%
No.	12	10.5
TBu	23	20.2
TBm	26	22.8
Ray.	35	30.7
Br.-Pt.	8	7.0
BB	3	2.6
DB	7	6.2
UB	–	–
N	114	100.0

deficiency of small tools. The Noaillian character of the series is nevertheless apparent.

No Aurignacian types are represented among the end-scrapers, which include blunt point and shouldered forms. Marginal retouch, mainly scaled, is common on these and other tools. Burins are the most frequent class of tools, Raysse burins (fig. 60:9) being the most common form. Unmodified, modified truncation (fig. 60:8) and Noailles burins (Bardon, A. Bouyssonie, and J. Bouyssonie, 1924a, p. 146, nos. 3, 7, 8) are represented in decreasing order of frequency. Burin-points (fig. 60:10) are also present. The dihedral burins are said to be mostly "*mal venus*" (ibid., p. 148). Backed tools are very rare; one small backed and truncated piece was found in *Foyer* I.

The three Late Noaillian horizons of Pré-Aubert, had they been excavated by modern techniques, would almost certainly have provided a developmental sequence of the Late Noaillian in the Brive vicinity comparable to that of the Abri Pataud for Les Eyzies. From the evidence available, their attribution to the Late Noaillian is clear, but further refinement of this interpretation is not possible.

Grotte Lacoste (Commune de Brive-la-Gaillarde)

The Grotte Lacoste, another of the Planchetorte sites, is situated between the Grotte de Pré-Aubert and the railroad viaduct. It was excavated in 1906 by Bardon and the Bouyssonies (Bardon, A. Bouyssonie, and J. Bouyssonie 1910; A. Bouyssonie, J. Bouyssonie, and Bardon 1910) following some preliminary investigation in 1899, their first in the Planchetorte Valley. The cave is 14 m wide and has a maximum depth of 8 m. Like Pré-Aubert, it is rather a shelter than a cave. The stratigraphy of the site is composed

Table 57
TYPE FREQUENCIES AND PERCENTAGES
FROM THE GROTTE DE PRÉ-AUBERT: *FOYERS* I, II, AND III COMBINED SERIES
(Institut de Paleontologie Humaine)

Type		n	%
Ordinary End-Scraper		1	1.3
Irregular End-Scraper		1	1.3
End-Scraper with Marginal Retouch		6	7.6
Blunt Point End-Scraper with Marginal Retouch		1	1.3
End-Scraper on Flake		1	1.3
Carinate Scraper		1	1.3
Atypical Nose-Ended Scraper		1	1.3
Perforator or <u>Bec</u>		2	2.5
Median Dihedral Burin		2	2.5
Asymmetrical Dihedral Burin		2	2.5
Nucleiform Burin		1	1.3
	TBu	TBm	
Truncation Burin: Straight, 80-90°	2	–	2.5
Truncation Burin: Straight, Oblique	3	2	6.3
Truncation Burin: Concave, Oblique	2	1	3.8
Truncation Burin: Convex	–	1	1.3
Single Noailles Burin on Truncation or Retouched Edge/End	5		6.3
Single Raysse Burin on Truncation or Retouched Edge/End	9		11.4
Burin-Point by Truncation Technique	1		1.3
Burin-Point by Dihedral Technique	1		1.3
Gravette Point	2		2.5
Micro-Gravette Point	2		2.5
Truncated Piece	1		1.3
Truncated Bladelet	1		1.3
Retouched Blade: Continuous Both Sides	1		1.3
Retouched Blade: Continuous One Side	2		2.5
Retouched Blade: Partial	2		2.5
Notched Piece	2		2.5
Denticulate Piece	1		1.3
Splintered Piece	2		2.5
Combination Tools	5		6.3

	End-Scraper	Truncation
TBm	1	1
Ray.	1	1
Br.-Pt.	1	–

		n	%
Double and Mixed Burins		12	15.2

	DB	TBu	TBm	No.	Ray.	UB
DB	1	–	–	–	–	–
TBu		–	2	1	4	–
TBm			–	–	1	1
No.				2	–	–

		n	%
Total		79	100.1

Table 58
CORE INDUSTRY PERCENTAGES BY TYPE
FROM THE GROTTE DE PRÉ-AUBERT: *FOYERS* I, II, AND III

Tool Type	Bardon and Bouyssonie			I.P.H.
	Foyer I	*Foyer* II	*Foyer* III	*Foyers* I–III
	%	%	%	%
End-Scrapers	12.5	9.6	14.6	16.7
Dihedral Burins	19.0	23.3	18.3	9.7
Truncation Burins	49.8	52.6	42.9	61.1
Truncated Pieces	not determinable			2.8
Retouched Blades	16.1	12.4	22.9	4.2
Backed Tools	2.6	2.1	2.3	5.5
N	1201	532	824	72
Noailles Burins	4.3	5.8	4.4	9.7
Burins plans	21.3	20.9	16.6	% Ray. Br. 12.5

Source: Bardon, A. Bouyssonie, and J. Bouyssonie 1924a; core industry of combined series from Institut de Paleontologie Humaine (author's count).

Table 59
CORE INDUSTRY PERCENTAGES BY TYPE
FROM THE GROTTE LACOSTE: *FOYERS* 1, 2, AND 3

Tool Type	*Foyer* 1		*Foyer* 2		*Foyer* 3	
	n	%	n	%	n	%
End-Scrapers	142	23.5	56	20.4	16	11.2
Dihedral Burins	132	21.9	46	16.7	22	15.4
Truncation Burins	161	26.7	81	29.5	42	29.4
Truncated Pieces	?		?		?	
Retouched Blades	138	22.9	56	20.4	56	39.2
Backed Tools	30	5.0	36	13.1	7	4.9
N	603		275		143	
Noailles Burins	43	7.1	4	1.5	5	3.5

Source: Bardon, A. Bouyssonie, and J. Bouyssonie 1910; J. Bouyssonie and Cheynier 1969, p. 132.

of five successive hearth levels (A. Bouyssonie, J. Bouyssonie, and Bardon 1910, p. 220, fig. 5), of which the two lowest (*Foyers* 1 and 2) appear virtually contemporaneous in the published section. The upper, and poorer, hearth levels are separated from this and from each other by sterile levels of sand and rockfall.

The collections are dispersed, but a small mixed series remains in the Musée Érnest Rupin at Brive. The description is taken from the literature, including later observations on the industries by J. Bouyssonie and Cheynier (1961). The quantitative data, assembled from the 1910 and 1961 publications, are certainly not reliable (table 59).

Foyer 1. The end-scrapers include a number of Aurignacian forms in addition to Noaillian fan-shaped pieces with marginal retouch (Bardon, A. Bouyssonie, and J. Bouyssonie 1910, p. 36, fig. 10:30). Backed tools are rare but include small backed and truncated pieces and Gravette points, perhaps including ones with Vachons retouch. The assemblage is dominated by burins, though truncation burins are less frequent than in other Noaillian levels. Both Noailles burins (ibid., p. 34, fig. 9:15, 16) and Raysse burins (ibid., p. 34, fig. 9:19, 20) are represented, but their relative frequencies cannot be determined. The dihedral burins include pieces described as "busked," but these are not typical Aurignacian specimens (J. Bouyssonie and Cheynier 1961, p. 131).

Foyer 2. This assemblage is stated to be very similar to that of *Foyer* 1, differing in the absence of Aurignacian forms, in lower frequencies of Noailles burins and dihedral burins, and in a higher proportion of backed tools. The *Foyer* 3 assemblage is smaller, with proportionately fewer end-scrapers, many more retouched blades, and rare backed pieces.

Foyers 4, 5, and 6. These are small series in which dihedral burins dominate the burins, and backed tools are virtually absent. There are two Noailles burins in *Foyer* 4 and none in *Foyers* 5 and 6. It is not clear to what cultural unit they should be assigned.

It is no longer possible to assess the significance of the Lacoste sequence. *Foyers* 1 and 2 may or may not be the same level. The Bardon-Bouyssonie excavations are thoroughly unreliable, both on account of their excavation techniques and because of the sandy nature of the deposits through which artifacts are liable to migrate. All that can be said is that two or three Noaillian series were represented, unequally mixed with artifacts of one or more other traditions. Although detailed information on the burins (specifically Raysse burins, modified truncation burins, and burin-points) is absent, the very low frequency of Noailles burins permits a tentative assignment to the Late Noaillian phase. If our information were better, the assemblages of the Grotte Lacoste would presumably be found to be similar to the better excavated and documented Late Noaillian manifestations at the Abri du Raysse and the Grotte de Bassaler-Nord.

Grotte des Morts (Commune de Brive-la-Gaillarde)

The Grotte des Morts lies 700 m upstream from the Grotte Lacoste and the Grotte de Pré-Aubert in the Planchetorte Valley. Its cultural sequence closely resembles that of the former site and of the lower levels of the latter (A. Bouyssonie, J. Bouyssonie, and Bardon 1939). The site is atypical in that its sediments are of clay, allowing the preservation of bone and antler. It was pillaged from 1866 on by various *chercheurs* and was tested in 1900 by Bardon and the Bouyssonies, who at that time found only disturbed deposits. In 1923, they were successful in locating an area that had escaped disturbance or at least was disturbed only superficially. It measured 10 meters square and lay close to the entrance under a small overhang. The deposit was some 50 cm thick, with three superposed hearth levels (*foyers*). The assemblages, each numbering over 500 retouched tools, were segregated by level and tabulated separately in the site report (ibid., p. 133); the series were subsequently integrated and partially dispersed. Some pieces remain in the Musée Érnest Rupin at Brive.

All three series may be described as Late Noaillian with varying amounts of Aurignacian (and Upper Périgordian?) admixture. Burins are throughout the most common tool class; flat-faced burins, many of them Raysse burins, are the single most common tool type. Noailles burins are present but very rare. Busked burins, some with notches, appear in low frequencies in all three levels. End-scrapers are about one-quarter as common as burins. They include a small proportion of Aurignacian scrapers (carinate and nose-ended), which are present in every level.

Backed tools are virtually absent, accounting for less than 2% of the tools in any level. Since large numbers of burin spalls were collected, their near absence cannot be attributed to inefficient collection. A Font-Robert point, worked by flat retouch over its ventral surface, and a more finely worked tanged point, are attributed to the upper hearth level. Retouched blades are common, especially in the lowest level.

The bone and antler tools include several smoothers or polishers, a polisher fragment with short incised notches down both sides (lower level), a short, grooved fragment of bone rod (middle), and a pointed bone (upper). In the disturbed deposits inside the cave, the excavators found a piece of bone with rows of short incisions and a bone fragment on which is engraved the head of an ibex. An indecipherable engraving on slate was also found *in situ* in the upper occupation horizon.

As at Lacoste and Pré-Aubert, there is no apparent internal typological development from level to level, but it is clear that the larger part of all three series should be attributed to the Late Noaillian phase. The apparent association of some Aurignacian forms and of a few Upper Périgordian pieces need not be accepted as significant at a site that had suffered almost fifty years of pillaging before its first controlled excavation.

Grotte de Champ (Commune de Brive-la-Gaillarde)

The Grotte de Champ lies 200 m upstream from the railroad viaduct, on the left side of the Planchetorte Valley. According to Bardon, A. Bouyssonie, and J. Bouyssonie (1924b), artifacts found here can be assigned to the Mousterian, the "Aurignacian," and the Solutrean. Some part at least of the "Aurignacian" was Noaillian, for both Noailles and Raysse burins are present in the collections of the Musée Érnest Rupin at Brive.

Grotte de la Font-Robert (Commune de Brive-la-Gaillarde)

The Grotte de la Font-Robert, on the right bank of the Planchetorte, is 1.4 km downstream from the railroad viaduct on the south slope of the Bassaler plateau. The site was excavated about 1905 by Pierre, "*vieux domestique*" of the Thévenard family, at that time proprietors of the Château de Bassaler. His work was directed by Mme Thévenard, "sous le contrôle occasionel de l'abbé J. Bouyssonie" (Bardon, A. Bouyssonie, and J. Bouyssonie 1906, 1908; de Sonneville-Bordes 1960, p. 189). The archaeological horizon, 20 cm thick, was sandwiched between bedrock and humus. Given this kind of excavation, it is not surprising that the series, while mainly Périgordian V and Early Noaillian, should also contain Aurignacian tools. A few Late Noaillian forms are also represented.

Grotte Thévenard (Commune de Brive-la-Gaillarde)

The Grotte Thévenard is located less than 100 m to the northeast of the Grotte de la Font-Robert, on the western side of a small side valley that separates the plateaus of Bassaler and Ressaulier (Bardon, A. Bouyssonie, and J. Bouyssonie 1924b). According to the authors, the site produced Mousterian and Solutrean tools, as well as some Noailles burins. Raysse burins are present in a small collection in the Musée Érnest Rupin at Brive.

Grotte du Bos-del-Ser (Commune de Brive-la-Gaillarde)

The Grotte du Bos-del-Ser is 4.6 km southwest of the center of Brive and 0.7 km NNE of the hamlet of Labrousse. It lies on the right bank of the Courolle, above the D. 154 road. The site was excavated by J. Bouyssonie in 1912 (J. Bouyssonie 1923). A single archaeological level was found, some 40–50 cm thick and containing numerous hearth scatters. No clear superpositions were recognized. Bouyssonie considered the series homogeneous, as indeed it was in terms of the cultural units then distinguished. Since that date, the association of Aurignacian and Châtelperronian (Périgordian I) tool types has given rise to much discussion. The Musée Érnest Rupin collection—2651 pieces, according to Laplace (1958–1961)—contains a few typical Noailles burins. A Raysse burin is present in a small series at the Institut de Paléontologie Humaine. Like the majority of the Planchetorte sites, Bos-del-Ser should be considered quite unreliable.

The Noaillian in the Brive Vicinity

Thanks to the work of Bardon and the Bouyssonie brothers, of Couchard and de Sonneville-Bordes at Bassaler-Nord, and of Pradel at Le Raysse, the presence of the Noaillian is firmly established in the Brive vicinity. The quality of the data from the majority of sites is so poor, however, that it is often futile even to attempt to reconstruct their cultural-stratigraphic sequences.

The Early Noaillian is only certainly represented by materials from the Grotte de Noailles itself. Even here only 44 pieces are claimed to come from undisturbed deposits, and 20% of the two series studied as the Level 4 (or C) "assemblage" is made up of Gravette points, differentiated from those of the underlying Level 3 *bis* in such a way as to suggest that they are chronologically later. Under these circumstances and in view of the very low frequencies of backed tools in the better-excavated Late Noaillian assemblages of the vicinity, it would be foolish to hypothesize radically differing Early Noaillian manifestations in Brive and Les Eyzies.

At a later date the Brive vicinity was occupied more often and for longer periods. The typological and quantitative evidence suggests that Le Raysse and Bassaler-Nord should be dated early in the Late Noaillian phase, and it may be that the Planchetorte Valley was at this time the home base of a regional band and that several caves were simultaneously occupied on several occasions.

The time of arrival of the Noaillian in the Brive vicinity cannot be precisely determined, but is likely to have been the same as at Les Eyzies. The Brive Noaillian is not demonstrably different culturally from that of the latter vicinity, and there is no necessity to postulate more than one socio-cultural grouping moving up and down the Vézère Valley between the two vicinities.

THE PÉRIGUEUX VICINITY (DORDOGNE)

Les Jambes (Commune de Périgueux)

The open-air site of Les Jambes is located on the south slope of the plateau of Cap-Blanc, on the right bank of the Isle River. It is in the suburb of Toulon, 2 km from the center of Périgueux and 400 m east of the Périgueux-Angoulême road (N. 139). The site was discovered by Louis Peyrille. Guy Célérier's investigations began with a sounding in 1963, and fuller excavations were carried out in following years. The results of the 1964 and 1965 seasons have been published (Célérier 1967), as has an analysis of the sediments (Célérier, Laville, and Thibault 1967).

The stratigraphy of the site is as follows (Célérier 1967, pp. 54–55):

Level	Description
– (20 cm)	Humus.
1 (120 cm)	Modern colluvium formed of rounded thermoclastic éboulis with a matrix of sandy clay. Contains modern objects (bricks, tiles, etc.).

2 (110 cm)   Well-developed, calcareous, brown soil. At the base is the *upper archaeological horizon*. "Upper Périgordian with Noailles burins" (Noaillian).

3 (400 cm)   Thick sequence of thermoclastic éboulis in a matrix of brown sandy-silty clay. Only the top 35–40 cm of this level has been excavated. The top of the level, composed of limestone blocks heavily rounded on their upper surfaces and underlying small éboulis and *plaquettes de gel*, is sterile. Directly beneath is the *lower archaeological horizon*. "Upper Périgordian" (Noaillian).

A few rare fragments of identifiable fauna, all from Level 3, include horse and reindeer. A preliminary analysis of the pollen in the upper archaeological horizon (Level 2) shows a very high component of arboreal pollen (53.8%). This is interpreted to indicate a temperate climate corresponding to a mild and humid oscillation within the Würm III stadial.

The study of the sediments (Célérier, Laville, and Thibault 1967) indicates that the lower archaeological horizon and the overlying sediments of Level 3 were deposited during a cold, dry climate. After the deposition of Level 3, the onset of a more humid interval resulted in the rounding of the tops of the limestone blocks, in gully erosion, and in the concretion of the top of Level 3. During the continuation of the milder, more humid climate, a new cycle of sedimentation began with the deposits enclosing the upper archaeological horizon (base of Level 2). This humid interval is taken by Laville and Thibault (1967, p. 2365) as another example of the climatic oscillation contemporary with Noailles burin-bearing levels—e.g., Gisement de la Chèvre, Roc de Gavaudun, and Isturitz. The formation of the soil in the Level 2 deposits is presumed to date from the Würm III/IV interstadial.

M. Célérier kindly permitted me to examine a small series of artifacts during an early stage of his excavation, but the comments on the assemblage given below are based principally on his published report (Célérier 1967).

The assemblages from both Level 2 (173 tools) and Level 3 (202 tools) are very similar; the principal differences, discussed below, occur in the burin series (table 60). End-scrapers are not common, and most do not exhibit marginal retouch. Both blunt point and shouldered (ibid., p. 57, fig. 1:1) forms are present. Backed tools form relatively high proportions of the core industries, 14.2% in Level 2 and 9.7% in Level 3. The majority of the backed tools are Gravette points; bidirectional backing occurs on somewhat less than half the examples. At least one Gravette butt (ibid., p. 62, fig. 3:5) bears the Vachons retouch style.

Over half the tools in both levels are burins. In both, dihedral, break, and unretouched burins together make up only about 12% of the total assemblage. Truncation burins of various types are dominant. Although some of the illus-

Table 60

CORE INDUSTRY PERCENTAGES BY TYPE FROM LES JAMBES: LEVELS 3 AND 2

Tool Type	Level 3 %	Level 2 %
End-Scrapers	6.8	4.7
Dihedral Burins	9.7	14.2
Truncation Burins	54.5	48.7
Truncated Pieces	10.8	12.8
Marginally Retouched Pieces	8.5	5.4
Backed Tools	9.7	14.2
N	176	148
Noailles Burins	0.0	3.4
Raysse Burins (estimated)	18.2	12.2

Source: Célérier 1967.

trations allow one to suspect the presence of burin-points (ibid., p. 57, fig. 1:8) and modified truncation or retouched edge burins (ibid., fig. 1:12), no firm information is available on these forms. Five Noailles burins, one of them double, were found in Level 2 (3.4% of the core industry); there are no Noailles burins from Level 3. In spite of the feeble presence of Noailles burins in one level and their absence in another, this difference cannot be regarded as important in view of the otherwise overwhelming similarity of the assemblages. Raysse burins are definitely present and apparently numerous in both (ibid., p. 59, fig. 2:6). Because Raysse burins were not counted separately from other flat-faced burins, no exact totals can be given, but the data for all such burins (10.4% and 15.8% of the total assemblage in Levels 2 and 3 respectively) provide a rough approximation. Within the burin series, flat-faced burins make up 9% of the dihedral/break/unretouched burins, 20% of the single truncation burins, and 12% of the double truncation burins in Level 2. The corresponding figures for Level 3, where flat-faced burins are more abundant, are 17% (dihedral/break/unretouched), 34% (single truncation), and 30% (double truncation).

Truncated pieces, mostly blades, generally reflect the distribution of truncation shapes of the truncation burins. Three small truncated pieces bearing marginal notches from Level 2 are identified as unstruck Noailles burins (ibid., p. 62, fig. 3:2, 3). Retouched blades, more common in Level 3 (9.4% of the assemblage) than in Level 2 (4.6%), most commonly bear scaled retouch.

Many questions about the Les Jambes assemblages remain unanswered, and, as Célérier has emphasized, the published data must be regarded as provisional awaiting results of further excavation. It seems already clear, how-

ever, that both assemblages must be referred to the Noaillian. The data available on the burins strongly suggest
that the series are representative of the Late and Terminal
Noaillian phases, with Level 3 comparable to Abri Pataud
Level 4: UPPER, and Level 2, on the sedimentological and
palynological evidence, perhaps contemporary with the Abri
Pataud Éboulis 3-4 and Level 4a materials.

It is tempting to accept the high frequency of backed tools
in the two Les Jambes assemblages as indicating diffusion
or Noaillian-Périgordian acculturation toward and after the
end of the Late Noaillian phase. Certainly it is the best
evidence yet available; even so it must be treated with caution. The assemblages come from slope deposits. With reference to pieces found somewhat isolated from the main
concentration of artifacts in Level 2, the excavator (Célérier
1967, p. 55) writes

. . . leur position est vraisemblablement liée au mode de
formation du sol où le ruissellement a été l'élément dé-
terminant.

If this is so, then the association of Noaillian and Périgordian
increments *might* be the product of natural, rather than cultural, factors. Attribute analysis might be able to demonstrate acculturation. Use of the vicinity by both Périgordians
and Noaillians is another possibility.

Abri du Petit Puyrousseau (Commune de Périgueux)

This site, close to Les Jambes, was excavated by Féaux
(1878, 1905, 1912) in the 1870s and by others around the
turn of the century. The "Upper Aurignacian" assemblage
includes backed and truncated pieces, Vachons-style Gravette
points, and Noailles burins (de Sonneville-Bordes 1960, p.
211). According to Célérier (personal communication), Raysse
burins are also present in small numbers. The Delugin collection in the Musée du Périgord at Périgueux contains one
large fragment of a characteristically Noaillian sagaie d'Isturitz plus a smaller portion of a second example.

THE SAINT-LOUIS-EN-L'ISLE VICINITY (DORDOGNE)

Solvieux (Commune de Saint-Louis-en-l'Isle)

Solvieux, some 20 km downstream and WSW of Périgueux,
is the name of an area of the Isle River terrace, over two
hectares in extent, that has given evidence of numerous
Palaeolithic occupations. While best known as yet for its
Early Magdalenian structural remains (Gaussen and Sackett
1976), the cultural sequence ranges from Mousterian to
Magdalenian VI. The materials are unpublished, and I am
indebted to James R. Sackett of the University of California,
Los Angeles (personal communication), for information regarding the Noaillian horizons.

Trench A, 185 m long, extends along the terrace and
parallel to a low cliff that marks the site's northern boundary. Excavations adjacent to Trench A are dominated by
rich Raysse-bearing levels (Locality 2:IIIb in Solvieux-Ouest;
Locality 4:III in Centre; and Locality 6:Main in Est). The
assemblages "differ considerably from each other in general
aspect and debitage; 2:IIIb for example is made mainly on
flakes and has only a small Gravettian, i.e., backed blade,
element, whereas 6:Main is totally on blades and has a
significant number of backed pieces. Nevertheless all three
are very similar in burin frequencies and have a very strong
classic Raysse burin component" (Sackett, personal communication). Frequencies of burins by techno-type are given
below and make it clear that these are Late Noaillian
assemblages.

Burins	Locality 2 Level IIIb		Locality 6 Main level	
	n	%	n	%
Dihedral	75	17.9	39	17.8
Truncation	325	77.8	170	77.6
Break	18	4.3	10	4.6
N	418		219	
Noailles	6 + 3 possible	2.2	1 possible	0.5
Raysse	168	40.2	80	36.6

Early Noaillian assemblages seem also to have been present. In Locality 2 in northern Solvieux-Ouest the stratigraphy "lends itself to the interpretation that middle and
lower Level IIIb actually incorporated material from an older,
largely destroyed, horizon, remnants of which are visible
below upper IIIb. The situation in Solvieux-Centre (Locality
3-4) is less equivocal. Beneath a Raysse-bearing level that
contains Noailles burins only south of Trench A, there is a
distinct sedimentological level, lying flat and being truncated by Level III. In the truncated unit were found several
Noailles but no Raysse burins, and it is hard not to think
of this as being a distinct Noailles level, partially cut off
and incorporated into the deposits of a subsequent Raysse
occupation" (Sackett, personal communication).

Thus while Flageolet 1 strictly can be said only to exhibit
the same stratigraphic relationships of the two classic Noaillian burin types as the Abri Pataud, Solvieux can be taken
provisionally as confirming the sequence of Early and Late
Noaillian phases. The new data also testify to a substantial
increase in the known area of Late Noaillian distribution.

THE BRANTÔME VICINITY (DORDOGNE)

The Brantôme vicinity covers a stretch of the Dronne River
and its tributaries between the town of Brantôme and the
village of Bourdeilles, a distance of 7 km. The river, tending
toward the southwest, follows a winding course flanked by
limestone cliffs at the foot of which are many caves and
rock shelters. The locality resembles Les Eyzies, 55 km to
the southeast.

Gisement (Grotte, Trou) de la Chèvre (Commune de Bourdeilles)

The Gisement de la Chèvre lies beneath a low limestone cliff on the right bank of the Dronne River, 600 m north of the village of Bourdeilles. The D. 106E road runs directly in front of the shelter. A portion of the deposits, which had been exploited for road metal, remained when Arambourou and Jude began the first controlled excavations at the site in 1948.

The shelter faces southeast; it consists of three parts: (1) a main shelter, 80 m in length, for the most part destroyed before 1948; (2) a terrace 10 m in length, which is the southern continuation of the main shelter but which lies in front of the present overhang; and (3) the *grotte* or *trou*, contiguous to the terrace and formed by huge slabs fallen from the shelter roof. The terrace was also partly quarried away, while the dolmen-like cave remained intact.

The site was excavated in sectors (Arambourou and Jude 1964, p. 14, fig. 1); Sector S corresponds with the main shelter, Sectors A, B, K, L, and M with the terrace, and Sectors F and G with the cave. Two test pits put down to the south of the cave were designated R and T. The most detailed stratigraphy comes from Sector B, close to the cliff (ibid., p. 16, fig. 2:1; p. 18):

Level	Description
1 (15 cm)	Humus.
2 (10–25 cm)	Light-colored sandy matrix and limestone fragments. Virtually sterile.
3 (3 cm)	"Archaeological level 5-III." Red occupation horizon. "Upper Périgordian."
4 (8 cm)	As Level 2 above. Virtually sterile.
5 (10 cm)	"Archaeological level 5-II." Dark red-black occupation horizon. "Upper Périgordian."
6 (5–10 cm)	Light-colored zone with small-sized gravelly matrix near base resting on a bed of stony éboulis. Virtually sterile, but contained material infiltrated from Levels 5 and 7.
7 (5 cm)	"Archaeological level 5-I." Reddish-brown occupation horizon with fragments of burnt bone and ash. Périgordian IV.
8 (12–15 cm)	Gravelly éboulis with clay and medium sand-sized matrix. Virtually sterile.
9–23	Long thick succession of archaeological and sterile levels resting on limestone bedrock. Aurignacian, Lower Périgordian (Châtelperronian), and Mousterian.

In other sectors, the stratigraphy is compressed or partial, the "Upper Périgordian" levels being sometimes in contact with each other or represented by a single thin lens. Blanc's statement (1948, p. 395) that in Sector G a Périgordian IV level was overlain by one containing Noailles burins and foliate points is not sustained by Arambourou and Jude. Only 19 tools were found in the "Upper Périgordian" deposits of this sector.

The "Upper Périgordian" assemblages were studied at the Musée de Brantôme. In all sectors except B and part of A, separation of the "Upper Périgordian" levels was impossible, the thin lenses having been crushed together by the collapsed overhang. They therefore were excavated as one unit. In Sector B, excavated by Arambourou, the detailed stratigraphy permits the distinction of Périgordian and Noaillian occupations.

The levels of the "Upper Périgordian" complex are grouped by Arambourou and Jude into three units. The lower unit comprises Levels 7 and 8 and some material from Sector A that forms a continuation of these horizons. The middle unit is made up of the occupation horizon of Level 5 and of the material from the underlying Level 6. The upper unit is made up of Levels 2, 3, and 4.

The series from Sector A (lower unit) is essentially Périgordian. Besides typical arc forms of end-scrapers (Arambourou and Jude 1964, pl. 19:11), twenty-nine of a total of forty-nine tools are backed tools. Two Noailles burins are also present. According to Arambourou (letter to the author, 23 September 1964), "Les pièces [marquées] 'A. sup.' et 'A. moy.' ont été rencontrées immédiatement sous l'herbe dans le secteur A. C'est ce qui restait après l'utilisation du gisement en carrière, sans doute pour arranger le chemin! D'où le tri que j'ai fait pour la publication parmi les pièces receuillies à ce moment là . . . L'utilisation du gisement en carrière a parfaitement pu amener un peu de mélange dans ce secteur." The presence of a few Noaillian tools in this series is not therefore significant.

Levels 7 and 8 of Sector B are qualitatively and quantitatively similar to the material from Sector A. The same large arc end-scrapers are present; dihedral burins (Arambourou and Jude 1964, p. 87, pl. 20:13) are almost as common as truncation burins, and there is a high proportion of backed tools (ibid., p. 89, pl. 21:16, 30), almost all Gravette points. Two Noailles burins (which could not be found at the time of my study) are noted (ibid., p. 112), but their presence does not negate the overwhelmingly Périgordian character of the assemblage.

The middle unit consists of an occupation horizon (Level 5) and the underlying Level 6. Of Level 6, Arambourou and Jude write (ibid., p. 91), "Comme dans sa partie supérieure, on trouve quelques pièces qui proviennent manifestement par infiltration de l'habitat dont témoigne le foyer susjacent (Level 5), on a groupé ces deux strates . . ." But Level 6 also contains pieces which may originate from Level 7, including a Gravette point fragment which the present writer was able to fit to another from Level 7. The assem-

Table 61

DETAILED TYPOLOGY OF BURINS FROM THE GISEMENT DE LA CHÈVRE: SECTOR B

Burin Type	Level 8, 7	Level 6	Level 5	Level 4, 3, 2
No.	(2)[a]	–	2	–
TBu	1	4	1	–
TBm	–	1	4	–
Ray.	–	–	3	1
Br.-Pt.	–	–	1	–
BB	1	–	1	1
DB	2	10	4	1
UB	–	–	1	–

Note: Includes pieces with precise indications of level only.

a. Pieces stated to be present by Arambourou and Jude but not seen by author.

Table 62

TYPE FREQUENCIES AND PERCENTAGES OF THE CORE INDUSTRIES
FROM THE GISEMENT DE LA CHÈVRE "UPPER PÉRIGORDIAN" COMPLEX

	Stratigraphic Unit[a]					
	Lower (7 and 8)		Middle (5 and 6)		Upper (4–2)	
Tool Type	n	%	n	%	n	%
End-Scrapers	37	17.6	17	17.2	11	15.7
Dihedral Burins	24	11.4	22	22.2	11	15.7
Truncation Burins	29	13.8	21	21.2	24	34.3
Truncated Pieces	1	0.5	10	10.1	6	8.4
Retouched Blades	7	3.3	5	5.1	8	11.4
Backed Tools	112	53.4	24	24.2	10	14.3
N	210		99		70	

Source: Arambourou and Jude 1964.

a. The Lower unit includes material from Sector A, the Middle and Upper units from Sector B only.

blage shows mixed Périgordian and Noaillian characteristics, but these tend to disappear when the Level 5 and 6 series are considered apart. This can be done only in cases where the pieces are exactly marked. In spite of the small number of such pieces, comparison of the burins (table 61) shows that dihedral burins are dominant in Level 6, and there is only one modified truncation burin. The moment of Noaillian influx comes in Level 5, where Raysse burins and a burin-point appear for the first time (fig. 60:11,12). As is shown by these figures and by the percentages of the

core industry (table 62), Levels 5, and probably 4, 3, and 2, are wholly or at least largely Noaillian. Backed tools are more common in Level 6 than in Level 5 but still constitute 14.3% of the core industry in the upper unit.

Noailles burins are dubiously present from the start of the "Upper Périgordian" sequence, but in Level 5, and in the upper unit, they are less frequent than Raysse and modified truncation burins. This suggests that Levels 5 and above correspond with the Late and perhaps Terminal Noaillian phases of the Abri Pataud. In the total "Upper Périgordian" assemblage, the majority of the Gravette points are between 6 mm and 8 mm in width, very large and very small pieces also being represented. Morphologically they resemble the late Périgordian IV sample from the Abri Pataud. The bellied form (Arambourou and Jude 1964, p. 89, pl. 21:24) and parallel-sided spiky pieces, sometimes retouched along the opposite edge (ibid., p. 89, pl. 21:23), are all characteristic of this phase, together with larger examples (ibid., p. 89, pl. 21:17). The butt treatments are also congruent with a later Périgordian IV chronological position (ibid., p. 89, pl. 21:13, 29). One piece shows a kind of Vachons-style butt treatment (ibid., p. 89, pl. 21:20), but there are no clear examples of backed and truncated pieces nor of Font-Robert points. The most characteristically Périgordian IV pieces come from Levels 7 and 8. In the upper unit there are fewer backed tools in all, fewer well-developed Gravette points, and more miscellaneous pieces and backed bladelets.

We suggest that the "Upper Périgordian" complex of La Chèvre corresponds broadly with the Abri Pataud sequence, Level 8 being contemporary with Éboulis 5-6, Level 7 with Level 5 (Périgordian IV) occupation, the *deposits* of Level 6 with Éboulis 4-5 and the Early Noaillian phase at the Abri Pataud, and Levels 5, 4, 3, and 2 with the Late and Terminal Noaillian of Level 4, Level 4a, Éboulis 3-4: Tan, and including perhaps all or part of Éboulis 3-4: Red. Once again this correlation differs from that of Laville while offering a good climatic fit (fig. 56).

The presence of a comparatively high proportion of backed tools in the upper unit at La Chèvre finds its closest parallels at Les Jambes and at the Abri Pataud in Level 4a. The typology of the backed tools, however, differs in the last two cases, Vachons-style Gravette points being common at the Abri Pataud and rare here. The possibility of mixture of Périgordian and Noaillian materials in the upper unit cannot be entirely discounted.

Fourneau du Diable (Commune de Bourdeilles)

The Fourneau du Diable is located 1 km upstream from the Gisement de la Chèvre, also on the right bank of the Dronne River. The site, excavated in the 1920s by D. Peyrony, aided by Belvès and E. Peyrony (D. Peyrony 1932a), is a rock shelter within which the archaeological horizons are disposed on two platforms. On the lower platform, which may always have been partially exposed, Peyrony found an "Upper Périgordian" level, followed by a Solutrean level, a roof fall, and finally by Hallstatt Iron Age remains.

As de Sonneville-Bordes has demonstrated (1960, p. 212), the "Upper Périgordian" assemblage is essentially Périgordian but contains rare Noaillian elements. The backed tools include Vachons-style Gravette points and backed and truncated pieces, suggesting that the assemblage must be attributed to a Périgordian V phase, though the thickness of the deposit would allow more than one phase to be represented. In addition to Noailles burins, very rare Raysse burins are present in the Peyrony collection in the Musée de Préhistoire des Eyzies.

There are several reasons to think that a Noaillian level exists in another part of the site. A small collection, made by J. Delfaud (Musée de Brantôme) from the backdirt of collectors (who in 1964 were plundering what remained of the unprotected deposits), contains Solutrean and Périgordian tools and eight Noailles burins, more than de Sonneville-Bordes records in the whole of the Peyrony collection. But the principal evidence of a major Noaillian occupation comes from the talus below the platform where Peyrony dug. Daniel (1969), partly from his own excavations in undisturbed deposits and partly from the backdirt of previous clandestine excavators, found a series of 165 Noailles burins, besides end-scrapers, burins, and backed tools. The yellowish-brown level yielding this industry is 30–40 cm thick. The illustrations (ibid., p. 17, figs. 1, 2) make it clear that these Noailles burins—small, often notched, often multiple—are essentially identical with those of the Early Noaillian assemblages of the Abri Pataud.

Abri du Bonhomme and Abri Durand-Ruel (or Rebières II) (Commune de Brantôme)

These sites, 2.2 km SSE of Brantôme, are situated high up on the northern slope of the Rebières Valley, which runs eastward from the Perigueux-Brantôme road (N. 139) to join the valley of the Dronne. Both sites were excavated by Pittard, who began his work in the valley in 1906 (Pittard 1912a, 1912b, 1912c; Sauter 1946). In both sites the assemblages of several levels, now recognizable as Aurignacian, Périgordian, and Noaillian, were collected together under the general designation of "Aurignacian." Because of the failure to separate material from different levels, the sites are virtually useless to an understanding of Upper Palaeolithic development in the region. The Noaillian increment in the series includes quantities of Noailles burins, but apparently no Raysse burins. Whatever the sequence may have been, the presence of an Early Noaillian level appears certain.

In 1919 Daniel made a small excavation at Abri Durand-Ruel of part of a witness block that had escaped the attention of "*les clandestins*." His work went unpublished until recently, when it was briefly described by Daniel and Schmider (1972). In this paper the following stratigraphy is reported:

Level	Description
1 (15 cm)	Yellow. Suggested to be equivalent to the upper part of Pittard's Level 3 (frontal section) and 1 and 2 of his sagittal (i.e., front to back) section. "Upper Périgordian."
2 (10 cm)	Reddish. May correspond with Pittard's Level 3 (frontal) and 2 (sagittal). "Upper Périgordian."
3 (30 cm)	Gray. Apparently sterile.
4 (20 cm)	Aurignacian.

Level 1 gave 98 tools and Level 2 only 39. Core industry frequencies can be calculated as follows:

	Level 2	Level 1
End-scrapers	13	22
Dihedral burins	7	15
Truncation burins	4	30
Truncated pieces	4	2
Marginally retouched blades	–	6
Backed tools	2	21
N	30	96
Noailles burins	–	6
Raysse burins	–	3 at least (ibid., fig. 2:1, 2, 13)

While Level 1 might be read as evidence of a Noaillian occupation heavily influenced by Périgordians, it would be extremely dangerous to base such an interpretation on data that lay so long (and under what circumstances?) unpublished. They are cited here for the record and because they document the presence of Raysse burins at Durand-Ruel.

The Noaillian in the Brantôme Vicinity

The independence of the Noaillian tradition cannot be demonstrated as clearly in this vicinity as at Les Eyzies or Brive. The existence of an unmixed Early Noaillian occupation to the north (see below) and proximity to Les Eyzies make it unlikely that the early part of the cultural sequence for the period should be markedly divergent. There are indications that the Dronne Valley was occupied during the Périgordian IV and at least part of the V phases, though with the exception of an atypical piece from Durand-Ruel, there is no evidence of Font-Robert points. Early Noaillian occupations of some importance are suggested by the mixed series of Bonhomme and Durand-Ruel and by the talus series from the Fourneau du Diable. During the Late and Terminal Noaillian phases, evidence of Noaillian occupation is effectively limited to La Chèvre, whence we have evidence suggestive of Noaillian interaction with Périgordians. It might well be hypothesized, though the evidence available is not adequate for testing, that during the latter part of the Noaillian occupation the cultures were indeed becoming less distinct, as perhaps was also the case around Périgueux.

THE VILHONNEUR VICINITY (CHARENTE)

The Vilhonneur vicinity, on the edge of the plains of the Angoumois, resembles Brantôme and Les Eyzies, the latter lying 95 km to the southeast. The limestone plateau is dissected by the Tardoire River, flowing in a northeasterly direction, but here its left bank is bordered not by cliffs but by rocky spurs jutting out from the plateau. Balout (1957) has described four groups of sites within a radius of 2 km

from Vilhonneur, three in the sides of the spurs and a fourth in a rocky outcrop detached from the plateau. This is the "Bois du Roc," some 600 m NNE of the Vilhonneur church, situated in a bend in the river by the side of the D. 109 road. Two of its fourteen caves and shelters have produced evidence of Noaillian occupation.

Abri André Ragout (Commune de Vilhonneur)

The Abri André Ragout is situated on the south side of the Bois du Roc and faces east. A test excavation shortly after World War II demonstrated the presence of Upper Palaeolithic levels. Much of the front part of the site was destroyed by vandals in 1956, and a year later Balout began his excavations. The work is not fully published, but preliminary reports have appeared (Balout 1957, 1958, 1965). Professor Balout kindly allowed me to inspect the collections in 1964.

At the time of the Upper Palaeolithic occupations, the shelter was about 16 m long and 11 m deep. The following stratigraphy was recorded in the rear of the site (Balout, 1958):

Level	Description
N	Humus and surface deposits, containing Bronze Age and derived Upper Palaeolithic material around and between large limestone blocks fallen from the collapsed overhang.
A (30–40 cm)	Blocky éboulis with brown matrix. Early Magdalenian.
B (25–30 cm)	Slabby éboulis (*dallage*) with hearth and reddish zones. Early Magdalenian.
C (60–80 cm)	Gray ashy level, cemented near the back wall of the shelter. Upper Solutrean.
D (10 cm)	Yellow *limoneuse* matrix. Virtually sterile, containing material derived from C and E.
E (50 cm)	Blocky éboulis and occupation materials. "Périgordian V" (Noaillian).
F (50 cm)	Large limestone blocks at the surface, underlain by an "Upper Périgordian" horizon in yellow clayey matrix (*argile de décalcification*).
–	Bajocian (Middle Jurassic) limestone bedrock.

The exact relation of Levels E and F outside the area where they are separated by large blocks is not yet clear.

In the 1957 excavations it was found that Level E contained an industry characterized by the presence of Noailles burins and the absence of backed tools. In Level F, both types are present, and a few backed tools have since been found in Level E. The assemblage of Level E closely resembles that of the Abri Pataud: Level 4: LOWER subdivision. Noailles burins are the most common tool type. They are mainly of small size and show the same range of forms, sizes, and blanks as at the Abri Pataud (Tixier 1958). A direct comparison of the sample studied by Tixier from the backdirt of the pillagers is not possible, since his definition covers only part of the range of pieces attributable to the type. Large forms of Noailles burin are present at the site, and the series is not distinguishable by inspection from that of the Abri Pataud Early Noaillian. Accompanying the Noailles burins and the much less common truncation burins are extremely rare Raysse burins. The end-scrapers are few in number but include no large arc forms typical of the Périgordian. Marginal retouch is rare. Among the few backed tools are Gravette points and several small backed and truncated pieces. The assemblage may confidently be attributed to the Early Noaillian phase.

In Level F, the same forms are present, accompanied by a higher proportion of backed tools (Balout 1958, p. 625, fig. 12:11, 12). The fauna of this level is stated to consist mainly of reindeer, also present in Level E (for which no further data are given). A bovid and horse are also present.

The final report on the Abri André Ragout will no doubt clarify the relationship between Levels E and F and provide additional information about the industry of the latter. It is already clear that the occupation of Level E is to be assigned to the Early Noaillian.

Abri du Chasseur (Commune de Vilhonneur)

The Abri du Chasseur is situated on the west side of the Bois du Roc, away from the river, facing south. Following a test excavation by Hervé in 1932, the site was excavated by Ragout (1935, 1939–1940) from 1933 to 1938, and by Balout (1956, 1959) from 1946 to 1951. Beneath a level containing Bronze Age and derived Upper Palaeolithic materials is a Level A containing, in three subdivisions, a mixture of Aurignacian, "Upper Périgordian," and Solutrean artifacts. Périgordian I and Aurignacian I artifacts were found together in Level B below. It is not clear to what extent Levels A and B are in primary position; Balout (1956, pp. 202–203) writes of them as

. . . fortement inclinés vers le fond de l'abri et ils résultent vraisemblablement d'un comblement par une entrée naturelle encore visible. . . . L'épaisseur des differents niveaux est fort variable; ceci est en rapport avec leur emboîtement, leur pendage, la fréquence des éboulis, les nombreuses poches; . . .

Although the agency which produced the mixture of artifacts cannot be identified, the typology leaves no room for doubt of the fact of mixture.

"Upper Périgordian" forms first appear in the lowest unit of Level A. Font-Robert points, Noailles burins, and a sa-

gaie d'Isturitz (Ragout 1939–1940, p. 698, figs. 1, 2) were recovered from this subdivision, together with forms typical of the Aurignacian (busked burins and nose-ended scrapers). The Aurignacian tools continue to be found in the overlying subdivisions, together with rare Solutrean pieces. In the middle subdivision, Font-Robert points disappear and Noailles burins, accompanied by large and small Gravette points, are at their most frequent. The assemblage of the upper subdivision is characterized by Gravette points and a few Noailles burins, along with the ubiquitous Aurignacian and Solutrean tool types.

The degree of mixture present throughout the Upper Palaeolithic series is too high to permit conclusions of any sort to be drawn from the Abri du Chasseur. Given the isolation of levels at the neighboring Abri André Ragout, there is no justification for considering that the Vilhonneur sequence of industries differs from others to the south.

THE VOULGÉZAC VICINITY (CHARENTE)

The Voulgézac vicinity differs from those previously described in being out on the plains of the Angoumois instead of in the dissected Mesozoic plateau. Even here, occupation was limited to a small, narrow, cliff-lined valley.

Les Vachons (Abri 1, Abri 2, and Grotte) (Commune de Voulgézac)

The Vachons sites are located in a valley running west from the Angoulême-Libourne road (N. 674), 15 km due south of Angoulême. The first excavations in the valley were conducted by de Rochebrune in 1867, followed by Chauvet in 1896. Coiffard (1914, 1922, 1937) excavated here before 1914 and again later, at the same time as J. Bouyssonie. Pierre David (1930) made an extensive test excavation in the Grotte des Vachons (known to him as the Grotte de l'Oeuil de Boeuf) in the 1920s. The last major excavation (1929–1933) was undertaken by J. Bouyssonie on behalf of the Institut de Paléontologie Humaine (J. Bouyssonie 1948; J. Bouyssonie and de Sonneville-Bordes 1957).

The sites considered are three of nine caves and shelters on the northern side of the valley. They are contiguous; westernmost is Abri 2, with Abri 1 in the center and the Grotte des Vachons to the east. Although Noailles burins and other specifically Noaillian burin types occur sporadically in three levels, the Vachons Valley never seems to have been occupied for any length of time by Noaillians. The sites are considered here on account of their importance for establishing the Périgordian sequence before, during, and perhaps subsequent to the major Noaillian manifestation to the south.

Bouyssonie excavated in Abri 1, on the platform beneath it, and in the Grotte. Coiffard worked on both Abris, but not in the Grotte. The stratigraphies they recorded for the Abris are almost identical.

Level			Description
	Abri 1	Abri 2	
	(1 m)	(2.5 m)	Humus and éboulis with some clayey matrix and lenses of *éboulis secs*. Sterile.
5	(5 cm)	(5 cm)	*Éboulis secs* and little matrix. Final Périgordian?
4–5	(20 cm)	(50 cm)	Yellow clayey deposit with limestone fragments. Sterile.
4	(15 cm)	(10 cm)	Red-gray-black level containing hearths. Périgordian (Level with Vachons-style Gravette points).
3–4	(45 cm)	absent	Large limestone blocks and éboulis.
3	(20 cm)	(10 cm)	Gray-black deposit with hearths. Périgordian Va–Vb (Levels with Font-Robert points and backed and truncated pieces).
2–3	(20 cm)	absent	Sandy level. Sterile.
2	(10 cm)	(10 cm)	Light brown level, friable in the rear of the shelter, more compact toward the front, where it lay beneath fallen blocks. Aurignacian (Evolved).
1	(20 cm)	(25 cm)	Red ochreous deposits of stony éboulis with clayey, earthy matrix. Aurignacian (Typical) localized in the rear.
–			Limestone bedrock.

At the edge of the platform of Abri 1, the bedrock dips sharply down to form a second platform 3.5 m lower. Bouyssonie gives the following stratigraphy for the deposits directly beneath the Abri:

Level	Description
– (1.5 m)	Humus and sterile materials.
3 bis (35 cm)	A series of thin occupation horizons separated by sandy lenses. Périgordian Va–Vb.
–	Limestone bedrock.

Six meters to the east, nearer the Grotte, he gives a more detailed stratigraphy. The lenses, dislocated by a fault, are essentially the same as those in the center of the platform:

Level	Description
–	Large limestone blocks.
3 bis	Complex of thin occupation lenses with sterile intervals. J. Bouyssonie (1948, p. 9) describes these as follows: "The lowest of these disarranged (*bousculés*) hearth levels contained several carinate scrapers or *rabots* . . . ; they could be contemporary with Level 2 of Abri No. 1. At approximately the same level I noticed nice specimens of *fléchettes* of the type of La Gravette; the other hearth levels, more or less superposed, always furnished tanged points . . ."
–	Limestone bedrock.

Little data are given on chronology and environment. It might be suggested that the Éboulis 4-5 (yellow clayey deposit with limestone fragments) to Level 5 (*éboulis secs*) sequence resembles the Éboulis 3-4: Red to Éboulis 3-4: Yellow sequence at the Abri Pataud, but if so the weathering would seem to be less marked at Les Vachons. The fauna of Level 5 is very poor and entirely made up of horse. In Level 4, horse and a bovid (stated to be *Bos*) are dominant. Reindeer is rare in Abri 1, more frequent in Abri 2. In Level 3, horse is more frequent than *Bos* (?), and reindeer is rare. The dominance of horse in these levels is perhaps to be explained by the location of Les Vachons on the plain.

The Bouyssonie series from each level contain far fewer backed tools than the Coiffard series, probably the result of inefficient collection. If this is taken into consideration, the level-by-level quantitative similarity of the Bouyssonie and Coiffard series is as apparent as is their qualitative similarity (table 63).

Level 3. The bulk of the series is Périgordian, with an Aurignacian increment of carinate and nose-ended scrapers and busked burins, presumably derived from Level 2 below. Burins are less common than end-scrapers and backed tools. Dihedral burins are dominant over truncation burins except in Abri 2, where the latter are slightly more frequent. The backed tools and related forms include Font-Robert points in quantity (especially in the Coiffard series) and Gravette points with butt styles similar to those of the Abri Pataud later Level 5 (Périgordian IV) series; *fléchettes* are also present, and, in the upper part of the level, backed and truncated pieces similar to those from La Ferrassie: K and Laraux: 5 (inf., p. 271). Noaillian elements are very rare. Bouyssonie illustrates two Noailles burins (J. Bouyssonie 1948, fig. 7:18, 20) and, from my own count (table 64) of the Coiffard series at the Musée de Préhistoire des Eyzies, there is one Noailles burin from Abri 1 and ten from Abri 2, which sample also includes one burin-point made by the retruncation technique (fig. 61:7).

It is difficult to interpret the significance of these few Noaillian forms. Bricker (1973, fig. 40-1) places the Abri 2 Gravette series in the same group as Ferrassie: K, Laraux:

Table 63
TYPE FREQUENCIES AND PERCENTAGES
OF THE CORE INDUSTRIES FROM LES VACHONS, ABRIS 1 AND 2

| | Abri 1 | | | | Abri 2 | |
| | J. Bouyssonie Collection | | Coiffard Collection | | Coiffard Collection | |
Tool Type	n	%	n	%	n	%
LEVEL 5 (the latest)						
End-Scrapers	12	16.4	18	21.2	4	19.4
Dihedral Burins	32	43.9	21	24.7	39	31.5
Truncation Burins	16	21.9	21	24.7	20	16.1
Truncated Pieces	4	5.5	13	15.3	18	14.5
Retouched Blades	3	4.1	4	4.7	6	4.8
Backed Tools	6	8.2	8	9.4	17	13.7
N	73		85		124	
Noailles Burins	–	–	1	1.2	–	–
LEVEL 4						
End-Scrapers	61	20.8	18	13.7	52	23.4
Dihedral Burins	56	19.0	12	9.2	25	11.3
Truncation Burins	68	23.1	21	16.0	33	14.9
Truncated Pieces	17	5.8	3	2.3	4	1.8
Retouched Blades	9	3.1	2	1.5	6	2.7
Backed Tools	83	28.2	75	57.3	102	45.9
N	294		131		222	
Noailles Burins	1	0.3	7	5.3	8	3.6
Raysse Burins	?		1	0.8	1	0.5
LEVEL 3						
End-Scrapers	39	37.7	33	24.7	50	17.9
Dihedral Burins	76	20.6	13	9.8	14	5.0
Truncation Burins	44	11.9	9	6.8	23	8.2
Truncated Pieces	6	1.6	3	2.3	30	10.8
Retouched Blades	14	3.8	–	–	2	0.7
Backed Tools	90	24.4	75	56.4	160	57.4
N	369		133		279	
Noailles Burins	2	0.5	1	0.8	10	3.6
Font-Robert Points	18	4.9	38	28.6	70	25.0

Source: J. Bouyssonie and de Sonneville-Bordes 1956; Noailles and Raysse burin count of Coiffard series by author.

Table 64
SPECIFICALLY NOAILLIAN BURIN TYPES
FROM LES VACHONS, ABRIS 1 AND 2 (COIFFARD SERIES)

	Level 3		Level 4		Level 5
Burin Type	Abri 1	Abri 2	Abri 1	Abri 2	Abri 1
Noailles					
Small	0	5	6	5	1
Large	1	5	1	3	0
TBm	0	0	2	4	0
Raysse	0	0	1	1	0
Burin-Point	0	1	0	0	0

5, and Pataud: 4, the latter being possibly the latest in the sequence. If, as is argued below, the Noaillians entered Aquitaine from the south, their presence in the Voulgézac vicinity is likely to have begun rather later than around Les Eyzies. This is quite possible. Noaillian burin types are absent on the lower platform in Level 3 *bis* and are represented only by isolated pieces in Abri 1:3, where Levels 3 and 4 are separated by 45 cm of éboulis and limestone blocks (within which some artifacts were found). In Abri 2:3 they are rather more common, but there is here no separation between Levels 3 and 4. It is not unreasonable therefore to suppose that the moment of Noaillian contact was either late in the period of deposition of Level 3 or subsequent to it, in which case the pieces would have been derived from above.

Level 4. Very similar in its general characteristics, Level 4 lacks the (presumably derived) Aurignacian increment of Level 3. Font-Robert points have virtually, and *fléchettes* completely, disappeared. The characteristic artifact is the Gravette point with Vachons-style butt treatment, which is sometimes accompanied by flat inverse retouch at the point. Bricker's (1973, pp. 1710–1711) analysis of the Gravette points demonstrates that their closest relationships are to the Pataud: 4a, Roque-Saint-Christophe, and Laraux: 3 series. Noaillian forms are still rare though more common than in Level 3. Their presence is responsible for a change in dominance among the burins, truncation burins being here more frequent than dihedrals. There are two Raysse burins in the Coiffard series (fig. 61:6, 8), six modified truncation burins (fig. 61:5), and fifteen Noailles burins (fig. 61:2–4). This minor influx of probably late Early Noaillian types suggests, as do other sequences, that all but the earliest Noaillian is broadly contemporary with a Périgordian phase characterized by the presence in some numbers of Vachons-style Gravette points. This phase is shown, both here and at Laraux, to postdate the Périgordian Va+b phase with Font-Robert points and/or *éléments tronqués*. It therefore might

be termed the "Périgordian Vc" proper, taking over the designation formerly applied to the Noaillian.

Level 5. The small series from Level 5 cannot be firmly attributed. Bouyssonie considered it Final Périgordian, while de Sonneville-Bordes, on the evidence of the subcircular scrapers, large burins—including transverse dihedral burins on chunky flakes—and well-made perforators, suggested Magdalenian affinities (J. Bouyssonie and de Sonneville-Bordes 1956, p. 301). Later Mme Bordes came to favor a tentative Périgordian attribution (de Sonneville-Bordes 1960, p. 191). All the tool types mentioned are present in the Pataud and Laugerie-Haute Périgordian VI assemblages. The quantities of Micro-Gravette points found at these latter sites are absent at Les Vachons, but the truncation borer or *coutelas* is present. There is also one Noailles burin in the Coiffard collection from Abri 1, though this piece may be a stray (fig. 61:1). The assemblage may be tentatively attributed to (perhaps an early form of) the Périgordian VI. The thick clayey deposit, separating the *éboulis secs* of Level 5 from Level 4 would then be equivalent to the Éboulis 3-4: Red at the Abri Pataud.

La Grotte des Vachons. Beneath a disturbed Solutrean level, the sequence recapitulates the "Upper Périgordian" sequence of the Abris. The series are typologically similar and include a very small percentage of Noailles burins.

In summary, the Noaillian tools from Les Vachons are more characteristic of the Early than of the Late Noaillian, although the presence of Raysse burins militates against an early dating within that phase. Their low frequency in assemblages that are of the greatest importance in unravelling the Upper Périgordian sequence proper (Bricker 1973) is definitely not evidence of the development of the Noaillian from the Périgordian. The Noaillian types need indicate no more than brief visits by Noaillians to a vicinity within Périgordian territory. Or they could be taken as evidence of diffusion. However this may be, they do establish the

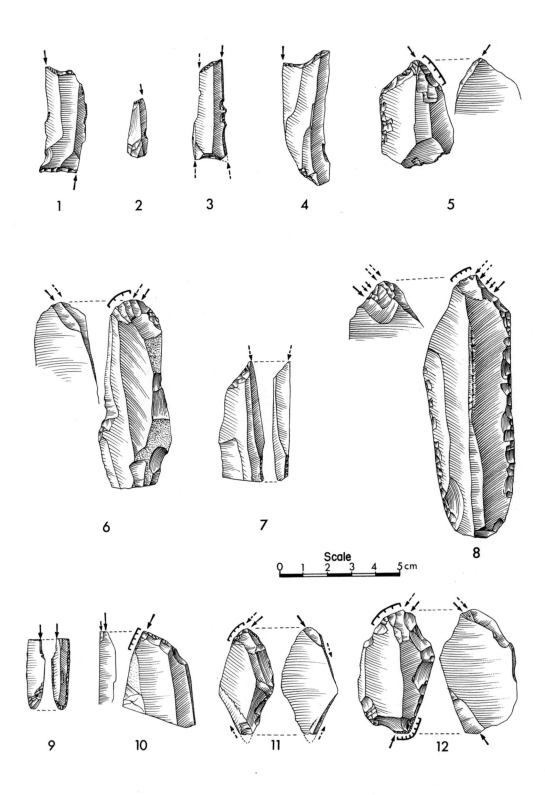

1   2   3   4   5

6   7   8

Scale
0   1   2   3   4   5 cm

9   10   11   12

contemporaneity of the Noaillian with parts, at least, of the Périgordian Va+b and "Vc" phases, the latter characterized by Vachons-style Gravette points in some numbers.

THE LUSSAC-LES-CHÂTEAUX VICINITY (VIENNE)

Lussac-les-Châteaux, 165 km NNW of Les Eyzies, lies outside the Southwest proper, but is still in (Jurassic) limestone country, the northwestern foothills of the Massif Central. It is situated similarly to Voulgézac, a little farther from the 200 m contour than most Noaillian localities and on the edge of the Plain of Touraine. The main channel of communication with the Southwest in Upper Palaeolithic times was probably along the valley of the Vienne, a tributary of the Loire, which flows northward past Lussac. Near Exideuil (Charente), it is only 30 km distant from Vilhonneur, with an easy route between the valleys following the path of the modern N. 141 road. It is the northernmost vicinity to have given an Early Noaillian series.

Abri de Laraux (Commune de Laraux)[33]

The Abri de Laraux is situated 3.5 km due north of Lussac in the village of Laraux, which is grouped around the intersection of the D. 11 and D. 16 roads (from Chauvigny and Saint Savin). The shelter lies on the right bank of the Petit Moulin stream, which flows into the Vienne 3.75 km to the east. Various prehistorians had made test excavations at the site before Dr. L. Pradel and A. Chollet began work in 1947.

The shelter faces south. It is 11.50 m long and was originally some 9 m deep. The lower archaeological level is subject to flooding from the Petit Moulin stream, 22 m away. The stratigraphy is described as follows (Pradel and Chollet 1950):

---

33. See David (1966, app.) for the attribute analysis of the Gravette points from Level 5 and the end-scrapers, Gravette points, dihedral and truncation burins from Level 3.

Level	Description
1 (20 cm)	Humus with Medieval pottery.
2 (40 cm)	Brownish sand with scattered, medium-sized limestone fragments. Sterile.
3 (15 cm)	Upper part: lenses of reddish (hematitic) sand, about 5 cm thick, sometimes in superposition. "Upper Périgordian Vc." Middle part: discontinuous sandy level (sterile). Lower part: fine gray sandy lenses (sterile).
4 (50 cm)	Blocky éboulis with sandy matrix. Sterile.
5 (15 cm)	Dark sandy level localized in the eastern part of the rear of the site. In front, a red sandy lenticule (X) contains two Font-Robert points. Périgordian Va+b.
6 (30 cm)	Stony éboulis with sandy matrix. Sterile.
–	Bedrock: Middle Jurassic limestone.

For typological reasons, Pradel considers lenticule X to be earlier than the body of Level 5. It is in an identical stratigraphic position, and there is no reason to doubt its contemporaneity.

There are two radiocarbon dates, both on bone (Evin et al. 1979, p. 447): Level 3: 21,530 ± 910 B.P. (Ly-1739); and Level 5: 23,510 ± 640 B.P. (Ly-1740). Both are unacceptably late in terms of the chronological framework based on the GrN series from the Abri Pataud and Laugerie-Haute. Few data are given on the environment. The fauna, not distinguished by level, consists mostly of reindeer and horse. Bison, red deer, chamois, wild boar, and wolf are also represented. This assemblage would indicate a steppe-forest environment without permafrost.

Level 5 (Pradel collection). Level 5 is characteristically Périgordian. The series (core industry = 187 tools) includes broad arc end-scrapers on flakes and a high proportion of backed tools, consisting largely of Gravette points and large and small backed and truncated pieces. The Gravette points are shown by Bricker's (1973, fig. 40-1) seriation to be most closely similar to those from Ferrassie: J and Vachons

Figure 61. NOAILLIAN ARTIFACTS

LES VACHONS: ABRI 2 (Coiffard collection): 1-4: Noailles burins (1 from Level 5; 2-4 from Level 4). 5: Modified truncation burin (Level 4). 6, 8: Raysse burins (Level 4). 7: Burin-point (TB; Level 3). ABRI DE LARAUX: LEVEL 3 (Pradel collection): 9: Vachons-style Gravette point (butt with burin removal at distal break). 10: Modified truncation burin. 11, 12: Raysse burins (12 is double).

Table 65

CORE INDUSTRY PERCENTAGES BY TYPE

FOR THE ABRI DE LARAUX: LEVELS 3 AND 5

Tool Type	Level 5 %	Level 3 %
End-Scrapers	14.4	12.4
Dihedral Burins	13.4	22.2
Truncation Burins	4.3	39.7
Truncated Pieces	1.6	3.6
Retouched Blades	1.6	1.3
Backed Tools	64.7	20.8
N	187	476
Noailles Burins	–	21.8
Raysse Burins	–	0.6

Source: Level 5: Pradel and Chollet 1950; de Sonneville-Bordes 1960. Level 3: author's count.

2:3. Burins are relatively unimportant, and truncation burins much less common than dihedral burins.

The frequencies and percentages of types are unreliable (table 65). Only the backed tools were counted by the present writer, not realizing that major discrepancies existed between the Pradel-Chollet and the de Sonneville-Bordes counts. The number of end-scrapers, proportionately infrequent for a Périgordian component in the Pradel-Chollet count, decreased incomprehensibly between 1950 and 1960. The number of backed tools has also decreased with every count. It is possible that tools, which are not individually marked, may have been lost or transferred from their correct drawers to other series. These inconsistencies do not put the Périgordian Va+b nature of the assemblage in doubt.

Level 3 (Pradel and Chollet collections) (table 66). Noaillian and Périgordian types are both present in the assemblage (545 pieces). The frequencies of tools in the core industry are intermediate between those of "pure" Noaillian and Périgordian components. While this may be evidence of mixture, it should be remembered that the assemblage is stratigraphically well controlled and that in this area, to the north of the main Noaillian concentration, the sequence and interrelationships of industries may be different.

While showing some relationship to the Masnaigre series, the end-scrapers are most similar in contour to those of the Périgordian VI. Statistically significant bimodalities in their length and width distributions are unparalleled in any other Noaillian (or, as far as I know, Périgordian) series. The backed tools, studied also by Bricker (1973, fig. 40-1), are most similar to those from Roque-Saint-Christophe: A and Vachons: 4. Vachons-style Gravette points are a character-

istic form (fig. 61:1; Pradel and Chollet 1950, fig. 4:21–23).

Noailles burins (table 67) are less common than in Early Noaillian assemblages to the south, but there is no corresponding increase in modified truncation or Raysse burins, represented by only fifteen and three examples respectively (fig. 61:10–12). The frequency of unmodified truncation burins is correspondingly high. The Noailles burins are closely similar to the Abri Pataud REAR:LOWER and FRONT:LOWER-1 samples. Modified and unmodified truncation burins again show an unprecedented bimodality in length, though not in width. They have a very high proportion of beveled burin edges, but in other respects cannot be clearly differentiated from Early Noaillian series to the south. The dihedral burins are intermediate in size between series from Noaillian and Périgordian levels and show a high frequency of angulated burin edges. Several of the truncated pieces are in the Noailles burin size range. Marginally retouched pieces are very rare.

The bone and antler industry is poorly represented and includes no specifically Noaillian types. A decorated awl and a bone, ornamented with short parallel incisions (*marques de chasse*), might perhaps be attributed to either culture; there is also a limestone plaque engraved with the head and forequarters of a horse.

In 1966, I argued that the series from Laraux Level 3 could best be interpreted as a mixture of two virtually contemporaneous increments of which the larger was Early Noaillian and the smaller Périgordian. Such a mixture could, I believed, account for the atypically high frequencies of backed tools and of dihedral burins and for certain variations away from Early Noaillian norms (as established for the Périgord vicinities) in the attribute distributions of end-scrapers and other types. I further suggested stream action as a possible agent of mixture, citing as evidence Pradel and Chollet's (1950, p. 215) description of the deposits and occasional flooding of the site at the present time. The argument was weakened by the necessity to use series from the Dordogne for comparative purposes. I had no attribute data on the assemblages from Les Vachons, which, on grounds of their position both in time and space, might have been expected to approximate most closely the culture from which the Périgordian elements in the Laraux: 3 series were drawn. H. M. Bricker (1973) subsequently studied much of the Vachons materials in detail and restudied parts of the Laraux assemblages. His findings may be summarized briefly as showing that, whereas the backed tools in the Laraux series are indeed typically Périgordian, variations away from the Early Noaillian norm among tool types common to both traditions are *not* such as might easily be explained by the admixture of Périgordian types similar to those from Les Vachons. He therefore suggests that some, at least, of the peculiar characters of the Level 3 series can be explained best by positing the diffusion of parts of the Périgordian hunting technology to Noaillians. Further, differences which cannot be accounted for in terms of limited diffusion may

Table 66
TYPE FREQUENCIES AND PERCENTAGES
OF THE ABRI DE LARAUX: LEVEL 3 ASSEMBLAGE (Pradel and Chollet collections)

Type	n	%
Ordinary End-Scraper	32	5.9
Irregular End-Scraper	4	0.7
End-Scraper with Marginal Retouch	9	1.6
Double End-Scraper	4	0.7
Blunt Point End-Scraper	5	0.9
Fan-Shaped End-Scraper	1	0.2
Rabot	1	0.2
Perforator or Bec	2	0.4
Median Dihedral Burin	47	8.6
Asymmetrical Dihedral Burin	17	3.1
Lateral Dihedral Burin	11	2.0
Nucleiform Burin	8	1.5

	TBu	TBm	%
Truncation Burin: Straight, 80-90°	2	1	0.6
Truncation Burin: Straight, Oblique	22	4	4.8
Truncation Burin: Concave, Oblique	13	3	2.9
Truncation Burin: Convex	6	–	1.1
Transverse Truncation Burin	1	–	0.2
Single Noailles Burin on Truncation or Retouched Edge/End	75		13.8
Single Noailles Burin Made by Other Technique	7		1.3
Single Raysse Burin on Truncation or Retouched Edge/End	2		0.4
Single Raysse Burin Made by Other Technique	1		0.2
Burin-Point by Truncation Technique	3		0.6
Burin-Point by Dihedral Technique	3		0.6
Break Burin	24		4.4
Unretouched Edge/End Burin	10		1.8
Gravette Point	39		7.1
Micro-Gravette Point	25		4.6
Completely Backed Blade	3		0.6
Backed and Truncated Blade	7		1.3
Backed and Truncated Bladelet	8		1.5
Partially or Irregularly Backed Blade or Bladelet	17		3.1
Truncated Piece	10		1.8
Truncated Bladelet	7		1.3
Retouched Blade: Continuous Both Sides	2		0.4
Retouched Blade: Continuous One Side	4		0.7
Retouched Blade: Partial	2		0.4
Notched Piece	5		0.9
Denticulate Piece	1		0.2
Combination Tools	9		1.6

	End-Scraper	Truncation
DB	3	–
TBu	2	–
No.	–	2
UB	1	–
Trunc.	1	

Table 66 (continued)

Type									n	%
Double and Mixed Burins									81	14.9

	DB	TBu	TBm	No.	Ray.	Br.-Pt.	BB	UB
DB	9	15	2	1	-	-	4	-
TBu		7	2	1	-	2	2	1
TBm		1	-	-	-	1	-
No.			29	-	-	-	-
BB						3	1

	n	%
Triple Burins	5	0.9

Triple Noailles TB   3
Triple Noailles BB   1
BB + BB + TBu   1

	n	%
Total	545	100.0

indicate that the Laraux vicinity lies beyond the limits of the Noaillian facies characteristic of the Mesozoic plateau and plain.

His seriation of the Level 3 Gravette points can, however, be read as favoring mixture. As mentioned above, the series assorts most closely with those from the Roque-Saint-Christophe and Vachons 1 and 2:4. At the former site the association, apparent or real, is with a Late Noaillian increment, at Les Vachons with a probably late Early Noaillian. At Laraux: 3, on the other hand, the Noaillian burin increment is typologically very early. The Gravette point and Noailles burins series thus appear out of phase and may well not be contemporary. We have no evidence to suggest that the typological development of the Noaillian in the north was retarded and/or that of the Périgordian precocious.

None of these hypotheses—mixture of series, regional factors, diffusion, or acculturation—whether taken singly or in combination have at present the virtue of testability. Although the stratigraphy is well controlled as French Upper Palaeolithic sites go, we have neither the micro-geomorphological data nor the three-dimensional artifact plots necessary to prove or disprove mixture of assemblages. There are no other sites in or near the Lussac-les-Châteaux vicinity that might serve, with Laraux, as the basis for the establishment of a regional facies. Limited diffusion of hunting technology accounts neither for the high frequency of dihedral burins nor for atypical characters of the end-scrapers, truncation or dihedral burins. If acculturation were taking place, it is surprising that the backed tools should be so typically Périgordian and the Noailles burins so nearly identical to series from Early Noaillian assemblages in the Périgord.

It is worth emphasizing that only where the highest standards of excavation and subsequent processing of finds and samples prevail, will the archaeologist ever be in a position to resolve such puzzles.

In this connection we should mention the site of Les Roches de Pouligny, a rock shelter some 35 km NNE of Laraux in the Commune de Pouligny-Saint-Pierre (Department of Indre), that has given faint indications of the Noaillian. There were several early excavations (Charbonnier 1962) and one in the early 1960s by Pradel (1965). Bricker (1973, pp. 1475–1505) has reported on the "Périgordian Vb" materials recovered by Pradel from his Level 3. This unit, reddish in color and only 5 cm thick, overlies a sterile clayey level 70 cm thick and is overlain by 60 cm of loose yellow éboulis. Its stratigraphic placement would seem therefore very grossly comparable with the Pataud: Éboulis 4-5, Level 4 through Éboulis 3-4: Red sequence.

As with the Laraux series, there are problems in reconciling the inventory of retouched tools given by Pradel (1965) with the materials present at the time of Bricker's study. Bricker counted 15 scrapers (IG ≃ 5.7), 151 burins, excluding those on combination tools (IB ≃ 57.6), and 70 backed pieces and truncations (IGP ≃ 26.7). The series is definitely Périgordian and, like Laraux, has a high proportion of burins. Bricker found approximately equal numbers of backed and truncated pieces and Gravette points, the latter characterized by a low frequency of Vachons-style butt treatments. Truncation burins dominate the burin component; however, dihedrals constitute about one-third of this class. Of special interest are three single truncation burins with tertiary modification of the burin edge, one Noailles burin lacking a stop-notch, and one atypical Noailles. There were also three Raysse burins in the series studied by Bricker, but it is not certain that they were originally present, and they may have been misfiled.

The high frequency of burins in this and the Laraux Level 5 series may, Bricker (1973, p. 1758) suggests, be a regional characteristic of the "Périgordian Va+b." Even if the Raysse burins are discounted, other characteristically Noaillian forms

Table 67

TYPE FREQUENCIES AND PERCENTAGES
OF BURINS FROM THE ABRI DE LARAUX:
LEVEL 3

Burin Type	n	%
No.	156	34.9
TBu	86	19.2
TBm	15	3.4
Ray.	3	0.7
Br.-Pt.	8	1.8
BB	40	8.9
DB	126	28.2
UB	13	2.9
N	447	

Level	Description
4 (10–20 cm)	Humus.
3 (40–150 cm)	Éboulis containing large lime-stone blocks in whitish earthy matrix, strongly cemented at a period subsequent to its deposition. Sterile.
2 (50 cm average)	Light medium-brown clayey deposit with a high proportion of limestone fragments. 30% of the total sediment is made up of concretions. The whiter upper part is often strongly cemented by infiltration from Level 3. "Upper Périgordian" (Noaillian).
1 (0–several meters)	Yellow-brown clayey earth (*limoneuse*) matrix with a high proportion of limestone frag-ments increasing in frequency toward the base. Sterile.
–	Cretaceous limestone bedrock.

are present and constitute evidence of either contact or an actual visit to the site by Noaillians.

From the north, we turn now to vicinities in the southern part of the Mesozoic plateau and plain.

THE GAVAUDUN VICINITY (LOT-ET-GARONNE)

The Gavaudun vicinity, 43 km SSW of Les Eyzies, resembles the latter very closely. The Lède River, a south-flowing tributary of the Lot River, is enclosed between high limestone cliffs containing several caves and shelters, in two of which the Noaillian is represented. Open-air sites have been found on the plateau to the north and east of Gavaudun.

Abri du Roc de Gavaudun (or Bas du Roc) (Commune de Gavaudun)

The Abri du Roc de Gavaudun is situated very near the village of Gavaudun on the right bank of the Lède River and above the road (*route vicinale*) from Gavaudun to Bonnenouvelle, 35 m from its junction with the D. 150. The site was discovered in 1925 by Monméjean, and excavation began in 1931. In 1933 and 1936 Monméjean was assisted by F. Bordes.

The site consists of a talus and a platform; the latter is part of the old shelter, the roof of which has collapsed. The back wall was quarried away at some undetermined time in the past. The talus slope descends steeply to the river terrace. Excavation began near the base of the talus, and a trench was later driven up toward the platform, excavated in 1937. The stratigraphy of the talus is described by Monméjean et al. (1964, pp. 259–261; 258, fig. 4) and summarized here:

The deposits on the platform lie parallel to the back wall and are separated from the talus by a row of large blocks. Level 1 is lacking, but otherwise the stratigraphy is similar to that on the talus. The occupation horizon, largely limited to an area 7 m long and 75 cm wide between the blocks and the back wall, consisted of a hearth scatter surrounded by hard whitish deposits. Flints occur throughout but are especially frequent near the top. Little artifactual material was found between the blocks and the top of the talus slope. According to Monméjean (personal communication), the detailed stratigraphic connection between terrace and talus has not been determined exactly, since because the edge of the platform was so much poorer in artifacts, he refrained from digging it extensively. As will appear below, the absence of detailed connection between the two units, talus and platform, permits an interesting question to be posed.

According to Monméjean et al. (sedimentological analysis by Claude Thibault), the sequence of deposits on the talus indicates a cold and dry climate (Level 1) followed by a still cold but wetter period (Level 2). Level 3 was formed under very cold conditions and was subsequently cemented during a humid phase. The period of humidity recorded in Level 2 is regarded by Laville and Thibault (1967) as the climatic oscillation associated with Noaillian assemblages at several sites in the Southwest of France. The climax of this oscillation at the Abri Pataud is found at the top of the Éboulis 3-4: Red. The sparse faunal sample is dominated by reindeer (46.8%), horse (32.3%), and bovid (16.5%); the high proportion of horse is taken to indicate that the cold was not extremely rigorous.

With the publication of the complete series (Monméjean

Table 68

COMPARISON OF THE CORE INDUSTRIES OF THE ABRI DU ROC DE GAVAUDUN: LEVEL 2
AND THE ABRI PATAUD: LEVEL 4: LOWER SUBDIVISION

| | Gavaudun: Level 2 | | Pataud: Level 4: LOWER |
Tool Type	n	%	%
End-Scrapers	697	14.3	11.1
Dihedral Burins	1003	20.6	19.7
Truncation Burins	2465	50.5	52.5
Truncated Pieces	413	8.5	4.1
Retouched Blades	96	1.9	9.7
Backed Tools	204	4.2	2.8
N	4878		1915
Noailles Burins	1459	29.9	41.2
Flat-Faced Truncation Burins	182	3.7	0.2 (Raysse)

Source: Gavaudun data from Monméjean et al. 1964.

et al. 1964), the earlier study of the F. Bordes collection is seen to be quantitatively misleading and to include too high a proportion of backed tools (de Sonneville-Bordes 1960, p. 200). M. Monméjean informed me in 1966 that the assemblages from the talus and the platform appeared to differ in their typology and proportions of artifacts by types. At that time, however, the materials recovered by Monméjean's excavations of 1964 and 1965 were still being separated and sorted. Although M. Monméjean very kindly permitted me to examine the then unpublished materials, it was not possible for me to form any conclusions about lateral facies differences. The quantitative description of the assemblage given in table 68 summarizes that of the 1964 site report and includes my own observations on the more recently excavated materials. The Bordes and Monméjean collections (5614 pieces) are not differentiated. The assemblage is largely Early Noaillian.

The end-scrapers (14.3%), mainly single and rarely marginally retouched, are said to be mostly of arc form. Typically Noaillian forms are all represented: fan-shaped end-scrapers, with and without marginal retouch, blunt point end-scrapers, and pieces with a slight shoulder or tendency toward a flat, nose-ended form. Flake scrapers are rare. There is a small increment of Aurignacian forms: five carinate scrapers, only two of which are typical, and six nose-ended scrapers, also mostly atypical. In spite of a low representation of blunt point end-scrapers, the sample is comparable to that of the Abri Pataud Early Noaillian in the kind of blanks employed, in the range of forms present, and in the rarity of marginally retouched pieces. Large, well-made arc types are conspicuously absent.

Most of the backed tools (4.2%) are Gravette and Micro-

Gravette points, the former being more numerous. Frequencies of heavy backing, bidirectional backing, and retouch on the edge opposite backing, based on information given by the authors (Monméjean et al. 1964, p. 291, table III), are almost identical with those for the Level 4 series at the Abri Pataud. There is at least one Gravette with Vachons butt retouch (ibid., p. 295, fig. 24:17) and one with inverse retouch at the point (ibid., p. 295, fig. 24:16). There are several backed and truncated pieces, essentially identical to the one from Level 4: LOWER at the Abri Pataud. Also present are twelve *fléchettes* (ibid., p. 297, fig. 25:1–7), including very typical foliate examples. The presence of *fléchettes* strongly suggests that the talus levels contained some material from a Périgordian IV occupation and that some of the Gravette points (and doubtless some of the end-scrapers, burins, etc.) should also be referred to such a pre-Noaillian occupation. However, the important observation about the backed tool series is that it is, except for the *fléchettes*, very similar to the backed tool series from Level 4 at the Abri Pataud.

Burins (71.1%) are the dominant tool class. The truncation burins (50.5%) are dominated by the Noailles[34] form (29.9% by the author's count) (ibid., p. 288, fig. 18; p. 289, fig. 19). Some of the other truncation burins should be classed as large Noailles burins (e.g., ibid., p. 277, fig. 13:12). The distinction made between "small" and "large" Noailles burins includes as "large" those pieces which,

---

34. Monméjean et al. include with the Noailles burins a series of 125 "proto-Noailles," i.e., truncated pieces in the Noailles burin size range (Monméjean et al., 1964, p. 290, fig. 21). In table 68 these are counted as truncated pieces.

although "plus grands que la dimension courante seront classés parmi les burins de Noailles par tout typologiste experimenté" (ibid., p. 284), but size limits are not stated.

Noailles Burins	Single	Double	Triple	Quadruple
Small	839	202	16	1
Large	215	41	3	
On break	46	2		

The breakdown demonstrates the overwhelming dominance of smaller pieces, typical of Early Noaillian horizons. Upon inspection, no points of difference can be seen to exist between this sample and that of the Early Noaillian at the Abri Pataud. The range of forms is the same, the AC pattern of association is the most common, and there are detailed resemblances, such as the association of a Noailles burin with a small perforator at the end of the truncation opposite the burin edge or elsewhere on the blank (ibid., p. 290, fig. 20:5–8), which appear in both assemblages.

Modified truncation burins are present in small numbers, and there is a series of 182 flat-faced truncation burins, many of which are Raysse burins (ibid., p. 281, fig. 15:4, 7, 10; p. 283, fig. 16:1, 3, 4, 6, 7). Although their frequency is low (3.7%), they are significant in that they are distributed within the site differently from Noailles burins (Monméjean, personal communication). They are more frequent on the platform than on the talus and may even outnumber Noailles burins in this part of the site. The possibility that a small Late Noaillian occupation followed the major Early Noaillian occupation and was situated similarly to that of the Abri Pataud in the rear of the site, not extending onto the talus, can be seen to exist.

Among the dihedral burins (20.6%), the authors note the presence of pieces with rounded and angular burin edges, also of burin-points (*gouge-becs*), most of which are made by the dihedral technique (ibid., p. 273, fig. 10:2–5; p. 276, fig. 12:4, 6), though some truncation burin-points are also present. Flat-faced dihedral burins are rare. A small number of buskoid types (some made by the truncation technique) are not out of place in a Noaillian assemblage, where few dihedral burins are of the well-made, sturdy forms characteristic of the Périgordian IV and VI.

As at the Abri Pataud and other sites, the truncated pieces (8.5%) are similar in form to the truncation burins. Of these, 125 are "proto-Noailles" in the Noailles burin size range. Retouched blades are very rare (1.9%). Scaled retouch is scarcely represented.

Bone and antler tools were very infrequently preserved and then only from the general area of the platform. They include a sagaie d'Isturitz, atypical in that it is made on a rib (ibid., p. 312, fig. 32:1), an armature fragment with a single-bevel base, and a semicircular cross-sectioned fragment.

The Abri du Roc de Gavaudun assemblage is overwhelmingly Early Noaillian. Typologically and quantitatively it very closely resembles the Abri Pataud series, from which it differs in the much lower proportion of Noailles burins. This difference is one of definition; it may be noted that a *preliminary* count of the Pataud series from the LOWER subdivision of Level 4, made before the definition of the type had been considered in conjunction with attribute analysis, gave the percentage of Noailles burins as 29.5%, identical to the Gavaudun figure. In addition to the Early Noaillian occupation materials, there is the possibility of a minor Late Noaillian assemblage limited to the platform. A full attribute analysis of the assemblage might refine, but is unlikely to modify, this interpretation in any important respect.

Abri Peyrony (Commune de Gavaudun)

The Abri Peyrony is located 65 m downstream from the Abri du Roc de Gavaudun in the same line of cliffs. The site was discovered by Denis Peyrony and Alban Vergne in 1926 and was subsequently excavated by Vergne and his workman (Vergne 1929). A single archaeological level was recognized, made up of a dozen hearth scatters, some of which were in superposition and separated by sterile intervals. The artifacts, considered globally to be Upper Aurignacian, were not kept separate. The publication illustrates carinate scrapers, strangled blades, Gravette points, backed and truncated pieces, Font-Robert points, and Noailles burins.

The site was re-excavated by Le Tensorer (1981) in 1969. He found seven *in situ* cultural levels:

B2	Noaillian
B1	Noaillian
C2	Upper Périgordian
C1	Upper Périgordian
D	Aurignacian
E	Aurignacian
G	Indeterminate

From levels B1 and B2 combined, which were sampled in a one-square-meter test pit, he obtained 502 artifacts, of which 90 were retouched tools. The series is almost certainly Early Noaillian:

IG	12.2
IB	46.5
IBd	16.7
IBt	28.9 (including 13 Noailles burins: 14.4%)

The only backed piece is a large Gravette point with Vachons butt treatment. The Périgordian series of C1 and C2 are too small for analysis but are described as "Périgordien à pointes de la Gravette."

Le Tensorer's sedimentological study places B2 in phase VIIb and c, and B1 in VIIa. Level B is separated from C1 and C2, which are attributed to the generally mild and humid phase V, by a level (C3) of large, sharp-angled congelifracts. It might be suggested that the latter is equivalent to Pataud Éboulis 4-5. However, this does not explain why the Early Noaillian should appear in a deposit indicative of a mild humid climate.[35]

Plateau Baillart (or Baillard) (Commune de Gavaudun)

The open-air site of Plateau Baillart is located on a gently rolling plateau beside the *route vicinale* from Gavaudun to Biron, 0.75 km northwest of Gavaudun. The site is first mentioned in the literature in 1874 by the Abbé Landesque (cited by Vergne 1929, pp. 129–130). The sample discussed here was collected by F. Bordes over many visits. The Upper Palaeolithic series (198 pieces), which has been studied by de Sonneville-Bordes (1953), was separated from material of earlier periods on typological grounds aided by differences in patination. Aurignacian and Noaillian increments are represented (table 69).

The end-scrapers include five carinate and four nose-ended scrapers as well as rounded arc, irregularly contoured, and fan-shaped forms. Backed tools are entirely absent. Burins form 59.2% of the core industry, truncation burins being more frequent than dihedral burins. De Sonneville-Bordes divides the truncation burins into Noailles burins (less than 3 cm in length), the dominant form, and other truncation burins. The dihedral burins, described as being mostly "peu soignés," include five busked burins and three similar transverse pieces. There are a number of truncated pieces, 37 retouched blades (plus 25 pieces with partial or atypical retouch not counted in the percentages), one blade-let with heavy marginal retouch, and eleven "Aurignacian blades."

Neither the qualitative nor the quantitative information is at variance with an interpretation of the series as a mixture of Aurignacian and Early Noaillian components, the Aurignacian increment accounting for inflation of the end-scraper, dihedral burin, and retouched blade categories.

M. Monméjean has informed me that he knows of at least three other open-air sites on the plateau near Gavaudun that have yielded Noailles burins. One of these is probably the "Station du Métayer," adjacent to and immediately south of Baillart. Le Tensorer (1981) has studied a sample of 1173 tools from this site, and the series appears very similar to that from Plateau Baillart, though with a smaller Aurignacian increment. There are 407 truncation burins, including 60 Noailles and 12 Bassaler (Raysse) burins, as against only 18 backed pieces.

The Noaillian in the Gavaudun Vicinity

During the "Upper Périgordian" period, the Gavaudun vicinity was occupied by Périgordians of the IV/V phases and

---

35. Le Tensorer (ibid.) also tested a third rock shelter in the Gavaudun vicinity, the Abri de Roquecave, where he found an *in situ* level (D2) overlying an Upper Périgordian with Gravette points (E2). The assemblages are very small, but D2, assigned to phase VIIa, includes Noailles burins.

Table 69

TYPE FREQUENCIES AND PERCENTAGES OF THE CORE INDUSTRY OF THE PLATEAU BAILLART UPPER PALAEOLITHIC COMPONENT

Tool Type	n	%
End-Scrapers	40	24.4
Dihedral Burins	35	21.4
Truncation Burins	62	37.8
Truncated Pieces	15	9.1
Retouched Blades	12	7.3
Backed Tools	–	–
N	164	
Noailles Burins	32	19.5

Source: de Sonneville-Bordes 1953.

more intensively by Early Noaillians. It may also have been visited on occasion by Late Noaillians. The sedimentological evidence presented by Le Tensorer does not fit at all well with the Pataud sequence, the earliest Early Noaillian seeming to appear during a mild-humid phase. However, since the relations of the archaeological materials to the sedimentary units at the Roc de Gavaudun are uncertain, and since only very small areas were exposed at the other sites from which we have data, the conflict may be more apparent than real. Given the close typological similarity of the Early Noaillian at the Roc de Gavaudun to that of the Abri Pataud, it is, in our view, quite unlikely that there is any significant difference in time. On the basis of present evidence there is no good reason to differentiate the Noaillian of this and the Les Eyzies vicinities.

It is also of interest that, at the open sites, once allowance is made for the presence of Aurignacian materials, the Early Noaillian series appear very like those from caves and rock shelters.

THE MONTCABRIER VICINITY (LOT-ET-GARONNE)

Montcabrier is situated 15 km east and slightly south of Gavaudun, on the Thèze River, a tributary of the Lot. Its topography resembles that of Gavaudun, with limestone cliffs bordering the river.

Abri du Roc de Cavart (Commune de Montcabrier)

The shelter is in the cliffs on the northern side of the Thèze, on the other side of which runs the Fumels-Cazals road (N. 673). Following early diggings prior to World War I (Daniel

1968), which did not attain the "Upper Périgordian" level, Maître Coulonges (1949) undertook an excavation in 1927. He reported the presence of two archaeological levels, Solutrean and "Upper Périgordian," separated by a very thin layer of éboulis.

There are major differences between my interpretation of the assemblage shown to me by Maître Coulonges in 1964 and that of Le Tensorer (1981) as relayed to me by Bricker. Separated by twenty years from the material, I cannot resolve this disagreement, but merely reproduce my former statement, appending to it the alternative view as formulated by Bricker. David (1966) described the series as follows.

Stratigraphically and typologically (table 70), the small assemblage (core industry = 113 tools) from the "Upper Périgordian" level poses problems that are at present insoluble. These problems concern principally the burins and the backed tools. Dihedral burins are very rare (3.5% of the core industry). The truncation burins (23.9%) are, with one exception, unmodified and include a small series of 10 Noailles burins (8.8%). Raysse burins and burin-points are absent.

The backed tools (51.3%) consist largely of Micro-Gravette points, three of which are of the very small variety commonly found in the Périgordian VI (Coulonges 1949, p. 559, fig. 1:18). There are five larger Gravette points, one Châtelperronoid piece 4.5 cm in length, and a small point (ibid., p. 559, fig. 1:13) on which the flattish obverse retouch continues from the backing to form a rounded base. The most characteristic but unusual objects among the backed tool series are 15 backed and truncated pieces, mostly from 2 cm to 4 cm in length (ibid., p. 559, fig. 1:3, 4, 12). With two exceptions these are points; the backing is sometimes slightly incurved, and the truncation is either perpendicular to or forms an obtuse angle with the backing. Although somewhat similar pieces are present at Laraux (though even here the parallel is not close), these artifacts appear much more Mesolithic than Périgordian, resembling pieces from the site of La Borie del Rey (Blanquefort-sur-Briolance, Lot-et-Garonne) also excavated by Coulonges (1963).

While the Noaillian elements can without question be attributed to the Early Noaillian phase, the backed tools, forming over half the core industry, do not find their place in any part of either the Noaillian or Périgordian sequences. Their mean size would suggest relations with the Périgordian VI rather than the Périgordian IV or V, but the absence of Périgordian VI affinities in other tool classes (burins, scrapers, truncated pieces) does not support this interpretation. Confirmation from another site, excavated by modern methods and giving a larger sample, is required before the series can be accepted as other than a mixture of two or more cultural increments.

Harvey M. Bricker (letter to the author, 25 February 1984) writes:

Le Tensorer has studied the same Coulonges collection, and I find his conclusions more plausible than yours. He says that, "l'industrie périgordienne de Cavart est un Périgordien évolué intermédiaire entre le Périgordien VI

de Laugerie et celui de Corbiac." I think his diagnosis is right on target. He gives four pages of artifact illustrations, and I am struck by the strong resemblances to both the Périgordian VI and to Corbiac. Some of the things that puzzled you about the backed tools are quite at home in the late (or final) Upper Périgordian. The only thing that puzzles me is the discrepancy between your study and Le Tensorer's over the burins. Your inventory gives four dihedral burin *pieces* (including 1 DB + BB) as against 24 truncation burins (including 7 single and 3 double Noailles). Le Tensorer, using de Sonneville-Bordes indices, gives IBd as 11.5 and IBt as 15.6, much nearer parity. Stranger yet, he records only two Noailles burins, in contrast to your ten. Two Noailles burins out of a total of 77 burins (by Le Tensorer's count) is unexceptional for a final Upper Périgordian (including the Périgordian VI of Pataud). Could you have been over-zealous in your search for another Noaillian site? My own conclusion on Cavart is that it has nothing to do with the Early Noaillian. . . .

Overzealous I certainly was, but if after attribute analysis of the Pataud Périgordian IV (Upper), Noaillian, and Périgordian VI assemblages, my typological eye was so poorly trained as to make gross errors of this sort, this monograph is worthless. The reader must judge. I prefer to believe, and the marked quantitative discrepancy bears me out, that through some misunderstanding Le Tensorer and I studied rather different series—a situation not unlike that affecting the several successive investigations of the Laraux materials.

THE BRUNIQUEL VICINITY (TARN AND TARN-ET-GARONNE)

The Bruniquel vicinity, best known for its many Magdalenian sites, is situated at the southern limit of the Mesozoic plateau region at the confluence of the Aveyron and the Vère rivers. Just before the village of Bruniquel, the Aveyron, flowing in a narrow valley between cliffs or steep hillsides, makes a sudden bend to the south before continuing on its easterly course. The topography is similar to that of Les Eyzies, 115 km to the NNW, though more dissected and with greater relief.

Abri des Battuts (or des Batuts) (Commune de Penne)

The Abri des Battuts is situated about 500 m north of Bruniquel, high above the right bank of the Aveyron, in the Department of Tarn. This site is to be distinguished from a second site, the Grotte des Battuts, which is located about 25 m to the left of and 3 m below the shelter. The site was excavated as early as 1863 by Victor Brun (1865), who recorded two thick archaeological levels between almost sterile roof-fall debris and the bedrock. Brun's collection was not, however, segregated by levels; his results were

Table 70

TYPE FREQUENCIES AND PERCENTAGES

OF THE ABRI DU ROC DE CAVART: LEVEL 4 SERIES (Coulonges collection)

Type	n	%
Ordinary End-Scraper	2	1.5
Irregular End-Scraper	3	2.2
Blunt Point End-Scraper	1	0.7
End-Scraper on Flake	2	1.5
Thumbnail Scraper	1	0.7
Atypical Nose-Ended Scraper	1	0.7
Nucleiform End-Scraper	1	0.7
Perforator or Bec	3	2.2
Median Dihedral Burin	1	0.7
Asymmetrical Dihedral Burin	1	0.7
Truncation Burin: Straight, 80-90°	2	1.5
Truncation Burin: Straight, Oblique	4	3.0
Truncation Burin: Concave, Oblique	5	3.7
Single Noailles Burin on Truncation or Retouched Edge/End	7	5.2
Châtelperron Point or Knife	1	0.7
Atypical Châtelperron Point	1	0.7
Gravette Point	5	3.7
Micro-Gravette Point	29	21.6
Dufour Bladelet	1	0.7
Backed and Truncated Blade	1	0.7
Backed and Truncated Bladelet	14	10.4
Partially or Irregularly Backed Blade or Bladelet	6	4.5
Truncated Piece	4	3.0
Bitruncated Piece (atypical)	1	0.7
Truncated Bladelet	2	1.5
Retouched Blade: Continuous Both Sides	1	0.7
Retouched Blade: Continuous One Side	1	0.7
Symmetrical Point	3	2.2
Asymmetrical Point	1	0.7
Notched Piece	9	6.7
Denticulate Piece	3	2.2
Combination Tools	6	4.5

	End-Scraper	Truncation
TBu	4	—
No.	—	1
Trunc.	1	—

	n	%
Double and Mixed Burins	11	8.2

	DB	TBu	TBm	No.	BB
DB	1	1	—	1	1
TBu		2	1	—	—
No.				3	—
BB					1

	n	%
Total	134	99.1

summarized by Cartailhac (1903). Daniel (1935, p. 512n) found several Gravette points and Noailles burins in disturbed deposits at the site.

Recent work at the site has been undertaken by J. F. Alaux, who in 1961 began sieving the backdirt of the previous excavations (Alaux 1963). Fortunately, Alaux (1969) also found small areas of *in situ* deposits against the back wall; his section, agreeing reasonably well with the description given by Brun, is given below:

Level	Description
1 (10 cm)	Stalagmite capping the deposits.
2 (75–80 cm)	Thick limestone debris separated into at least four layers by thin stalagmite bands.
3 (10 cm)	Stalagmite.
4 (90–95 cm)	Yellow level, subdivided into two units: (a) 60–70 cm. With large limestone blocks and an indeterminate industry; and (b) 30–35 cm. Compact yellowish level containing isolated ''Périgordian'' tools.
5 (20–40 cm)	Black level. ''Périgordian Vc'' (Noaillian).

Alaux (1973) reports a much extended stratigraphy from his 1970 excavations nearer the front of the site. Thicknesses are not given.

Couche	Description
13	Iron Age–Mediaeval.
12	Yellow. ''Périgordien supérieur tardif, avec quelques burins de Noailles.''
10–11	Light yellow. Sterile.
9	Light yellow, compact, with fairly large blocks at the base. Poor series with a few Noailles burins. ''Périgordien supérieur tardif.''
8	Rockfall.
6–7	''Périgordien Vc à nombreux burins de Noailles.''
5	''Périgordien V à nombreux pointes de la Gravette et à éléments tronqués typiques.''
4	Sterile.
2–3	Aurignacian.
1	Sterile.

I studied two collections, the original Victor Brun collection (Musée d'Histoire Naturelle, Montauban) and that part of the Alaux collection coming from the sieving of the backdirt as of 1965. These are designated B and A, respectively. They contain Upper Périgordian, Noaillian, Solutrean, and perhaps Magdalenian elements. In addition, reference is made to the *in situ* material coming from Level 5 (Alaux 1969) and from Couches 6–7 (Alaux 1973), for

which some percentage frequencies based on the total retouched count are given.

End-scrapers are comparatively few and small (14.9% in Level 5; 4% in Couches 6–7). End-scrapers and other scrapers made on flakes are more common in A than are end-scrapers on blades. The great majority of the latter lack marginal retouch. There are three fan-shaped pieces in B, one with marginal retouch, and a large piece with an arc contour. Backed tools are quite common:

	Level 5 (1969) (%)	Couches 6–7 (1973) (%)
Gravette points	11.4	6
Gravette points with Vachons retouch	2.6	(? included in the above)
Micro-Gravettes	1.8	6
Backed bladelets	3.5	3
Éléments tronqués	?	1.2

Backing is very often bidirectional. The A series contains six backed bladelets and the B series, one typical Font-Robert point. Level 5 contained a fragment of another, ''malheureusement très détérioré,'' and there are two from the upper part of Couches 6–7. Alaux (1969, p. 11, pl. I:15) also figures a large *élément tronqué* from the A series.

Burins are the most common tool class:

	Level 5 (1969) (%)	Couches 6–7 (1973) (%)
Burins	57.9	61
Noailles burins	28.9	37.5
Dihedral burins	9.7	?

The Noailles burins show the same ranges of size and form as those of the Abri Pataud: Level 4: LOWER series. Typical Raysse burins are also present, those from the backdirt having been the subject of a special study by Alaux (1965–1966, 1967). The frequency of specifically Raysse burins is not given (flat-faced burins in Level 5 total 8.8%), but they are certainly far less numerous than Noailles burins. Truncation burins other than these are very rare (0.9% in Level 5). The dihedral burins include large, well-made median pieces and small crude examples, some double. There is one burin-point made by the dihedral technique in B and another in A. No information is available for the *in situ* series.

Retouched blades (3.5% in Level 5) and truncated pieces are both rare.

The bone and antler artifacts include a fragment of a sagaie d'Isturitz (A) and other miscellaneous armatures, fragments of smoothers and pointed bones, two fragments of elongated awls (B), and a gorge (A). A pierced reindeer phalange is present in B together with an antler wedge. The A series includes a piece of dentalium shell.

The Brun and backdirt (A) series are hopelessly mixed. The Level 5 series, from directly above bedrock, may also include some materials that are earlier than the Noaillian. The Couches 6–7 assemblage, on which we have the least evidence, is presumably uncontaminated. Both *in situ* series are clearly Early or possibly Early to Middle Noaillian. More exact placement within the Noaillian cannot be made in the absence of further information on the position in the sequence of Raysse burins and burin-points. At least some of the former may derive from the later Couches 9 and 12. Besides the relatively high frequencies of backed tools in the Couches 6–7 assemblage, the presence of Font-Robert points and *éléments tronqués* is suggestive of trait diffusion between Noaillians and Périgordians. Although we lack evidence on chronology, the Battuts sequence would seem to be essentially similar to that of Les Eyzies.

Grotte de Rouset (or Rouzet or Roset) (Commune de Larroque)

The Grotte de Rouset is located high above the right bank of the Vère River, opposite the village of Puycelci in the Department of Tarn. Information about a Noaillian occupation comes from the work of Alaux (1964–1965), who obtained a series of tools from disturbed deposits at the cave. Included are 21 Noailles burins, some Gravette points, and one small backed and truncated piece.

XI

The Noaillian of the Mesozoic Plateau and Plain: Cultural Differentiation and Typological Development

In chapter IX above, I suggested a number of tests of the hypothesis of Noaillian-Périgordian cultural differentiation. These now have been applied, and, before proceeding to the study of the Noaillian in other regions and areas, it will be useful to summarize.

Although Noaillian and Périgordian artifacts appear to be associated in the majority of series from the eastern region of Aquitaine, the evidence adduced confirms the view that the Noaillian and Périgordian derive from different cultural stocks. Most of the more recently and better-excavated assemblages—Facteur: 10–11, Rochette, Raysse, Bassaler-Nord, Solvieux (according to the information available), and Gavaudun—resemble ones from the Abri Pataud: Level 4 very closely, both in the typology of the assemblages and in their low frequencies of backed tools and diagnostic Périgordian artifact types. Oreille d'Enfer has also given a series that, while recovered from a very small portion of the original site and perhaps including a small Périgordian increment, shows similar features. At the only published Early Noaillian open sites Aurignacian components are present, but backed tools and Périgordian types are lacking. Together these sites cover a wide spatial and temporal range. It is unfortunate that more of them do not demonstrate Early to Late Noaillian successions, but the Solvieux sequence appears to parallel that of the Abri Pataud, while at the Roc de Gavaudun there is a strong suggestion of a minor Late Noaillian occupation located on the platform, as opposed to the talus from which the majority of the Early Noaillian materials were recovered. At no site does a typologically Late assemblage *precede* an Early Noaillian. Thus intrasite evidence constitutes a partial rejection of the "cultural trifurcation" hypothesis of Laville and Rigaud (1973).

Taken as a group these sites also represent a broad range of sizes and situations in which evidence of activity variation might be expected. Excavations were, however, rarely carried out with a view to isolating this potential source of assemblage variability. Nevertheless, on presently available evidence we are unable to attribute any part of the variability expressed to this cause. Furthermore, there appears to be no pattern of activity differences characterizing Noaillian as against Périgordian assemblages. This constitutes a second, if weak, partial rebuttal of "cultural trifurcation."

Among the above-mentioned sites, sedimentological analyses are available only for the Pataud, Facteur, and the Roc de Gavaudun. I have attempted to show that the Facteur sequence can be correlated with Pataud without violence to either typology or inferences regarding climate. The Abri Pataud Noaillian date for Level 4 of $27,060 \pm 370$ B.P. is consistent in terms of the GrN series, and we reject the much later Gsy dates from Facteur (as we do also the Lyons dates from Laraux). The Gavaudun sequence, now amplified by Le Tensorer's work, is still somewhat ambiguous, possibly indeed conflicting with the Pataud. Nevertheless, we consider that the weight of the evidence favors our position and that our findings again constitute a partial rebuttal of the views of cultural development implicit in Laville, Rigaud, and Sackett's (1980, fig. 8.2) rendering of the chronostratigraphic sequence.

We may therefore claim on the basis of the sites so far discussed that, minimally, some Noaillian assemblages represent a culture distinct from the Périgordian, and that some Noaillian groups were able to maintain their industrial traditions for a considerable period of time—expressed typologically as the Early and Late phases—in the Mesozoic plateau and plain with little detectable interaction with Périgordians.

A second group of sites comprises those recently and, for the most part, well-excavated that have given series that seemingly combine characteristics of both cultures and that might result from: (a) the borrowing of traits (diffusion); or from (b) acculturation, using Kroeber's (1948, p. 387) definition of "increasing contact of culture wholes, with attrition, penetration, and adjustments of these" at whatever scale, from occasional exchange of individuals to fusion of cultures in whatever proportions. Apparent diffusion or acculturation can of course result from poor excavation and a failure to look for, understand, or recognize the formation processes responsible for the accumulation of artifacts in a layer. Because this is so, it behooves the archaeologist to take a hard line and, before inferring complex cultural interactions, to exclude from consideration those sites and samples that fail to meet these specifications. Such series are only too numerous. Among the more important are Masnaigre: B and Roque-Saint-Christophe. Both must be dismissed on the grounds of stratigraphic ambiguities or conflicts and/or on the typological evidence. Neither they nor many others, including the Grotte de Noailles itself, are worth further discussion in this context.[36]

Those that remain include sites that have given evidence of Early and/or Late Noaillian materials apparently in association with Périgordian increments. In considering the record of such sites it should be borne in mind that the presence of Noaillian and Périgordian tools in the same stratum does not, given the often lengthy duration of deposition of these strata and the possibly brief periods of occupation within them, necessarily imply contemporaneity of the two cultures in the vicinity. However, a repeating pattern of association at different sites must surely indicate that there was, in that region and period, interaction between the two cultures.

Among the sites with apparent Early Noaillian and Périgordian associations are Flageolet 1, Roc de Combe, and the outlying Les Battuts, Les Vachons, and Laraux. At the first of these, the small series from Level VI may well be evidence of interrelations between the Périgordian Va+b and the Early Noaillian. This would have occurred in a period that immediately follows one characterized by abundant cryoclasticism and that may reasonably be equated with

the Éboulis 4-5 at the Abri Pataud. While both here and at the Roc de Combe, where in Levels 3 and 2 there are similar associations, final interpretation must await further information on formation processes and attribute analysis of the series, it would be foolish to dismiss the possibility of a sequence of events in the Dordogne drainage different from that taking place across the plateau in the Les Eyzies vicinity. It is doubly unfortunate that the Ferrassie sequence for this period should be so problematic.

As noted above, Les Battuts, Les Vachons, and Laraux are all marginal in terms of the known distribution of Early Noaillian sites in this region (fig. 62). As such they are the most liable to have seen Noaillian-Périgordian interaction. While questions can be raised about the reality of the association in Laraux: 3, those of (minimally) Les Battuts: Couches 6–7 and Vachons 1 and 2:4 do not seem disputable. All in all there can be little doubt that Noaillians and Périgordians did come into contact, though the evidence from these sites does not allow us to specify its nature.

Among the sites of the second group that have given Late Noaillian with Périgordian elements are the Abri Pataud: Éboulis 3-4: Lower and Level 4a, Flageolet 1:V and IV, Les Jambes, and probably the upper unit at La Chèvre. While queries may again be raised in individual cases, what is most striking about these sites is their overall distribution, much closer than in the previous phase to the Noaillian "heartland" in the Vézère Valley. The suggestion of a marked reduction in Noaillian territory and of increased interaction with Périgordians, especially in the culture's latest phase, is very strong.

Taken as a whole and in conjunction with our inferences

36. I cannot, however, forbear from noting that if my suggestion that two levels were present in that part of the Roque-Saint-Christophe excavated by Peyrony is correct, and if the lower was indeed Périgordian and the upper Late Noaillian, then this might well imply a Périgordian incursion into the Les Eyzies vicinity at about the time of the break between the Early and Late Noaillian phases.

Figure 62. MAP OF NOAILLIAN VICINITIES IN THE MESOZOIC LIMESTONE PLATEAU AND PLAIN (size of symbol is an indication of the importance of the Noaillian occupation in each phase)

Listing of vicinities and sites by Late/Terminal (L) and Early (E) phases:
LES EYZIES: Pataud (E + L); Facteur (E); Ruth (E); Oreille d'Enfer (E); Poisson (E?); Masnaigre (E + L?); Laussel (E? + L); Roque-Saint-Christophe (L); Fongal (E? + L); Rochette (L); Labattut (E?); Merveilles (E?); Ferrassie (E); Sous-le-Roc (E?).
DORDOGNE VALLEY: 1, Roc de Combe-Capelle (E?); 2, Termo-Pialat (E?); 3, Flageolet 1 (E + L); 4, Cantelouve (E?); 5, Pechialet (E?); 6, Roc de Combe (E).
BRIVE: Noailles (E); Raysse (1); Pré-Aubert (L); Lacoste (L); Bassaler-Nord (L); Champ (?); Font-Robert (E?); Thévenard (E?); Bos-del-Ser (E?); Morts (L).
PÉRIGUEUX: Les Jambes (L); Petit Puy-Rousseau (E?).
SAINT-LOUIS-EN-L'ISLE: Solvieux (E + L).
BRANTÔME: La Chèvre (L); Fourneau du Diable (E); Bonhomme (E); Durand-Ruel (E).
GAVAUDUN: Roc de Gavaudun (E + L?); Baillart (E); Peyrony (E); Métayer (E); Roquecave (E).
MONTCABRIER: Roc de Cavart (E?).
BRUNIQUEL: Battuts (E + L?); Rouset (E?).

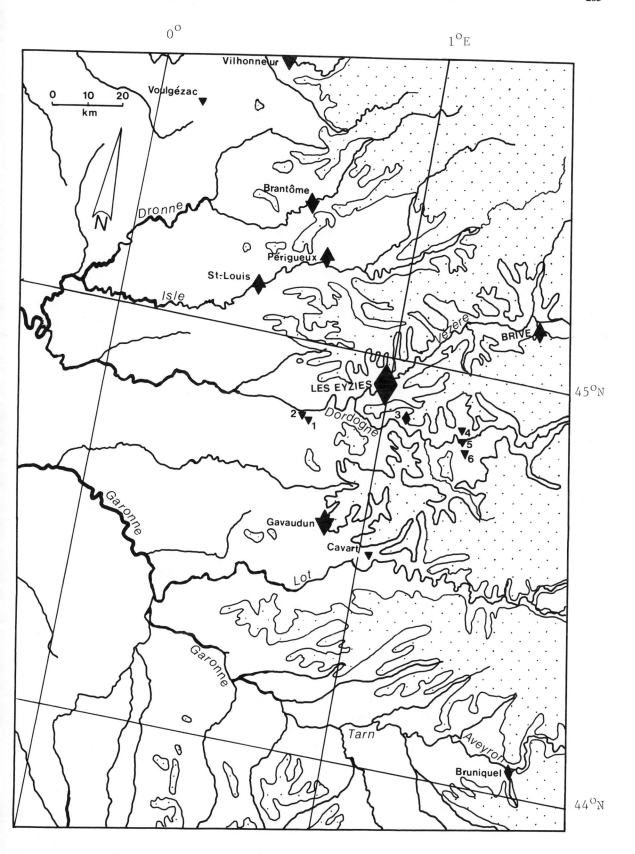

Early Noaillian ▼   Late/Terminal Noaillian ▲

regarding intersite correlations, these findings constitute a powerful rebuttal of Laville and Rigaud's "cultural trifurcation" hypothesis.

Study of the assemblages from the region has not produced evidence of Noaillian materials demonstrably older than those of the Abri Pataud, Level 4: LOWER subdivision. The culture arrives suddenly and in characteristic form. This must be interpreted as evidence of intrusion, occurring after the start of the Périgordian Va+b phase. If our interpretation is accepted, the latter part of the Early, and the Late and Terminal phases are grossly contemporary with the Périgordian "Vc" phase characterized by the presence in some numbers of Vachons-style Gravette points.

The distribution of sites by phase (fig. 62) shows that the Early Noaillian was the widest spread, extending from the extreme south of the region beyond the plateau to the northern plains, with Laraux: 3 an outlier in the Poitou. The Late Noaillian is more restricted—especially the larger assemblages—to the Vézère Valley (Les Eyzies and Brive vicinities) and to the Isle Valley (Périgueux and Saint-Louis vicinities), with some evidence of minor occupations as far north as Brantôme and south to Bruniquel. The distribution of contemporary Périgordian assemblages will be contrasted with that of the Noaillian in a later chapter (p. 338), but we may note here that the reduction in Noaillian territory in the later phases may well be connected with Périgordian pressure.

Noaillian series unaffected by any significant Périgordian admixture reveal a unified development within the region that is reflected in typology and, less clearly, in the percentage frequencies of types. Quantitative seriation of these series, however, does nothing to refine the sequence (fig. 63). Patterns of quantitative change are distorted by the incomparability of series, some of which probably represent intermittent occupation over more than one phase, while others may cover only part of one. Other factors, including differential collection and perhaps also economic and seasonal effects that we are unable to recognize, also contribute to our inability to achieve finer than phase discrimination. Given these factors and also the reciprocal contamination and/or small scale diffusion of types that unequally affect even the best-excavated series, similar seriation of assemblages is of little or no value in our investigation beyond bringing out overall quantitative similarities and the Early versus Late phase difference, best expressed by changes in the truncation burin class. End-scrapers, varying irregularly within a limited range, are generally less frequent than in Périgordian assemblages. Dihedral burins show some tendency to decrease in frequency through time. Their rarity at Bassaler-Nord and Pré-Aubert may perhaps reflect a shortage of flint; if so, this effect is not in evidence at the Abri du Raysse. Truncation burins remain in high, though variable, frequency, the Noailles type being replaced by the Raysse burin. Truncated pieces show little change or de-

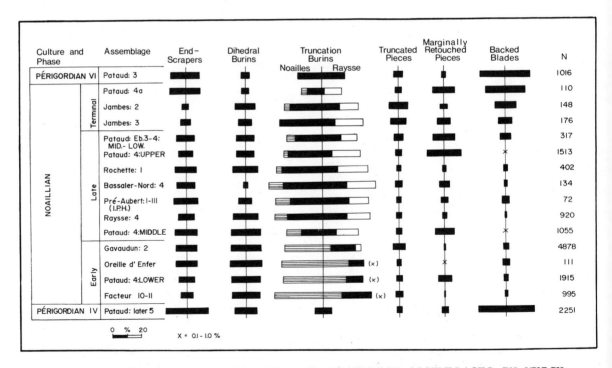

Figure 63. SERIATION OF EARLY AND LATE NOAILLIAN ASSEMBLAGES IN WHICH SIGNIFICANT ADMIXTURE OF PÉRIGORDIAN MATERIALS IS NOT SUSPECTED, OF TERMINAL NOAILLIAN SERIES INCLUDING PATAUD: 4a, AND FOR COMPARISON, OF PATAUD: 3 (Périgordian VI) AND LATER 5 (Périgordian IV).

velopment, while marginally retouched pieces become rather more common through time. Their especially high frequencies at the Abri Pataud in both Early and Late Noaillian may be misleading, reflecting differences in field and laboratory procedures. Backed tools maintain minimal to low frequencies until the Terminal phase.

When burins in series inventoried by the present writer are considered apart, finer seriation based upon detailed changes within the truncation burin subclass becomes possible (fig. 64). However, the precise placing of assemblages that are not in stratigraphic relationship to each other is again, and for the same reasons, very doubtful. The well-expressed decrease in the frequency of Noailles burins and the increase first in other truncation and then in Raysse burins depends to a great extent upon the Roque-Saint-Christophe, Rochette (Delporte series), and Masnaigre components, the reliability of which, for various reasons, cannot be trusted. The combined Rochette series would include a much higher percentage of Raysse and significantly lowered proportions of Noailles burins. The reality of the break between the Early and Late phases is clearly seen in figure 65, where Noailles burins, modified truncation burins together with Raysse burins, and other burins are plotted against each other.

In summary, the Early versus Late Noaillian phase division is the finest that can as yet be made; unstratified assemblages cannot be ordered within phases with any confidence, though both quantitative and qualitative analyses suggest similar orderings. In mixed series the Noaillian and Périgordian increments can also normally be attributed to phases with a good degree of confidence, even though seriation is obviously not applicable to them.

Neither the brusque Early to Late phase transition nor the end of the Noaillian in this region is easily explicable. I would suggest that the former may have resulted from the sort of ecological catastrophe that I invoked—too generally—as an alternative to an overreliance on migration as an explanation of Upper Palaeolithic culture change (David 1973). But evidence is lacking either for or against. Besides the Pataud: Éboulis 3-4: MIDDLE and LOWER and 4a series, only those from Les Jambes: 2 and 3 and perhaps those from La Chèvre: 4–2 appear to be later than Pataud: Level 4. The Les Jambes series have uncharacteristically, for Noaillian series, low frequencies of end-scrapers and an abnormally high representation of truncated pieces. While the Pataud: Éboulis series can be interpreted reasonably as a very Late series that includes a number of derived Noailles burins, the 4a series sits most uneasily with other Noaillian assemblages—and not only because of its high frequency of backed tools. While abnormal qualitative and quantitative features, varying from one site to another, might not be unexpected in assemblages representing the last gasps of a

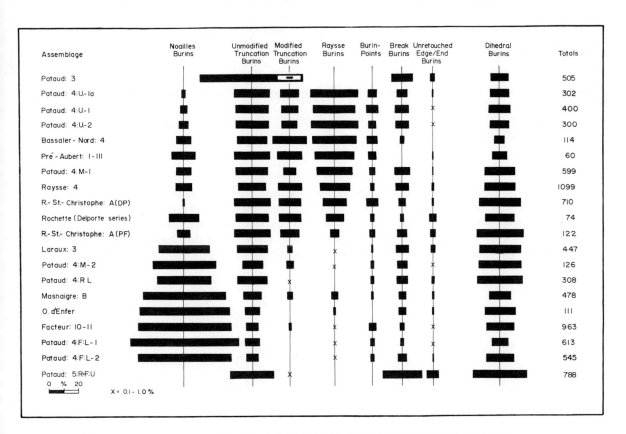

Figure 64.   SERIATION OF BURIN COMPONENTS IN INVENTORIED SERIES.

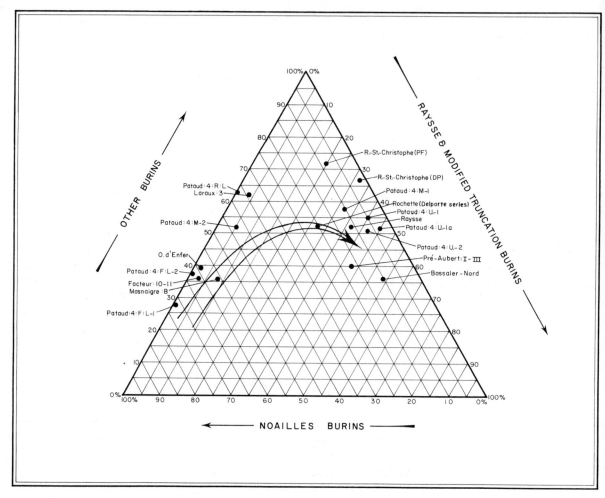

Figure 65. PLOT OF BURIN COMPONENTS SHOWING THE BREAK BETWEEN THE EARLY AND LATE NOAILLIAN.

culture, in this case mixture of Périgordian and Noaillian increments is the preferred interpretation. The Les Jambes materials are, on the other hand, suggestive of an acculturative process that may have ended with the submergence of the Noaillian within the Périgordian, its heritage recognizable only in the massive increase in truncation burins, in the numbers of bone and antler tools, and also in the presence of the Venus motif in the Périgordian VI of the Abri Pataud and Laugerie-Haute. Why this should have occurred will be discussed in chapter XVIII.

XII

The Noaillian in the South Aquitanian Hills, the Pyrenean Piedmont, and Cantabrian Spain

THE ISTURITZ VICINITY (BASSES-PYRÉNÉES)

Isturitz, approximately 250 km southwest of Les Eyzies and 40 km SSE of the Atlantic at Biarritz, lies in the Cretaceous limestone foothills of the western Pyrénées, well outside the area of maximum extension of the Würm moraines. The country shows marked relief, but averages only 100 to 300 m above sea level. The isolation of the vicinity is not simply a matter of distance, but also of accessibility. With the sea to the west and the Pyrénées to the south and southwest, it is ringed to the east and north by the many rivers that, flowing northward from the Pyrénées, swing west to join the Adour, entering the sea below Bayonne. Movement to or from Isturitz thus must be across, not along, the river valleys.

Grotte d'Isturitz (Communes d'Isturitz et de Saint-Martin-d'Arberoue)

The Grotte d'Isturitz is situated in an isolated limestone outcrop known by the name of Castellou (or Gastellou), 8.5 km southeast of Hasparren and 1 km SSW of the village of Isturitz. The site first appears in the literature in 1896 when Boule, recognizing its importance, protested against the exploitation of the deposits for fertilizer (Boule 1896). A significant part of the site had already been destroyed in this manner when Passemard began excavation in 1912. He continued, with interruptions, until 1922 (Passemard 1924, 1944). The site was subsequently leased by the Comte and Comtesse de Saint-Périer, whose work there extended from 1928 to 1948.

The cave was formed by the Arberoue River, a subtributary of the Adour, which today flows 77 m below the cave. There are two entrances (R. de Saint-Périer and S. de Saint-Périer 1952, p. 5, fig. 2), one to the north, opening into the Commune of Isturitz, and the other, blocked for long periods during the Upper Palaeolithic, opening south into the Commune of Saint-Martin-d'Arberoue. The cave is oriented approximately north-south and is divided into an east and a west chamber, separated by huge pillars of uneroded rock. To the west is the Salle d'Isturitz or Grande

Salle, ca. 100 m long by 15–20 m wide; to the east is the Salle Saint-Martin, low-roofed, ca. 80 m long by 20 m wide. The entrance to the Salle Saint-Martin was blocked at about the time of the end of its Aurignacian occupation. In the analyses of the assemblages which follow, the small quantity of "Upper Périgordian" material found in this part of the site is ignored. It is largely mixed with the underlying Aurignacian materials.

The entrance to the Salle d'Isturitz is estimated to have been about 5.50 m wide and 5 m high in Magdalenian times. The deposits slope down from the entrance to an engraved rock pillar 35 m inside the cave, in the vicinity of which the deposits become more nearly level before rising again toward the south, where they mix with a cone of debris that entered the cave through a chimney. The occupation levels are concentrated around and in the general area of the rock pillar, although they extend toward the entrance and back some 15 m behind the pillar, fading out near the first and most easily negotiable passage to the Salle Saint-Martin.

The generalized stratigraphy summarized below is that of the de Saint-Périers (de Saint-Périer 1936; de Saint-Périer and de Saint-Périer 1952). It differs in certain respects from the stratigraphy given by Passemard (1924, p. 113, fig. 62; 1944, p. 12, fig. 2); insofar as the differences are important to the present study, they are summarized below in the text.

Level	Description
–	Cone of dejection at mouth of cave, behind which are roof blocks and surface rubble. Iron Age, Bronze Age, and Neolithic objects.
St. (0–1 m)	Stalagmite of variable thickness.
Ia (0–20 cm)	Discontinuous black lens. Final Magdalenian-Azilian.
I (50–60 cm)	Black compact stony level. Magdalenian V–VI.
II (10 cm–1 m)	Gravelly, stony éboulis, either grayish with little matrix or enclosed in red clay. Magdalenian IV above; traces of Magdalenian III below.

– (10 cm)	Discontinuous level of limestone slabs and brownish *limon* and clay. Scattered Solutrean pieces on and between the slabs.
IIIa (30–40 cm) and III (40 cm)	Compact, greenish-gray, sandy clay. The separation of Levels IIIa and III was arbitrary, the result of a decision to excavate the thick clay deposit in two spits. Level IIIa contains localized concentrations of Solutrean materials. Somewhere, presumably in the lower part of the excavation unit, was another concentration of Solutrean materials; this was designated Level IIIb but does not appear on the sections. Level III, considerably richer in archaeological remains, is "Final Aurignacian" (Noaillian).
IV (50–60 cm)	Black level with more ashes, cinders, and archaeological material than matrix, which is described as dusty (*pulvérulent*) and cemented at base. "Upper Aurignacian or Gravettian" (Noaillian).
V (60–80 cm)	Light yellow sandy clay with large blocks, partly cemented. Upper 15–20 cm are sterile. Middle and lower zones contain Middle Aurignacian.
– (ca. 2 m)	Various sterile levels including a stalagmite floor.
–	Lower Cretaceous (Aptian) limestone bedrock.

The samples considered in tables 71–73 are taken from the de Saint-Périer collections and derive from their excavations in Levels IV, III, and IIIa in the Salle d'Isturitz. The flint assemblages[37] are considered first, followed by a brief discussion of the bone and antler tools.

Level IV. The description of the assemblage given by de Saint-Périer and de Saint-Périer (1952) does not do justice to its overwhelmingly Noaillian character. The designation "Aurignacian supérieur (Gravettien)" rests upon a series of about 470[38] backed tools of all types, which are, in view of the gigantic size of the series, of only minor quantitative importance.

The raw material is almost entirely flint, with a very small proportion of quartzite pieces, mostly of large dimensions. The production technique is more standardized and is capable of producing more regular blades than that characteristic of Early Noaillian series from the Périgord. Blades are better struck, with fewer and more regular dorsal ridges, but they are less similar to the large, well-formed, sturdy pieces of the Périgordian than to Late Noaillian series. Greater

mastery of core reduction techniques is not expressed in the manufacture of large tools. Pieces longer than 7.5 cm are uncommon.

End-scrapers (36.7%) are usually small or of medium length, many pieces being only 30 mm long. The modal length lies around 50 mm. They differ in several respects from Noaillian series of the Dordogne. Arc forms are not well developed. The blunt point contour is comparatively rare; the majority of pieces have slightly irregular, rounded contours. The sample is distinguished by a high proportion of pieces with marginal retouch (de Saint-Périer 1952, p. 94, fig. 44:1) and by the presence of many fan-shaped end-scrapers. These are sometimes made on a blank which determines the fan form but are more usually shaped by marginal retouch on one or both sides, reducing the width of the proximal end of the tool. Fan-shaped end-scrapers are usually short (ibid., p. 96, fig. 45:3), but there are some longer, narrower forms (ibid., p. 94, fig. 44:3). Three pieces in the counted series approach the pedunculate form (ibid., p. 94, fig. 44:6), though this tendency should be considered as an extreme variant of long, fan-shaped pieces rather than as a distinct variety. As in the Périgord, there are very few flake or carinate scrapers or side-scrapers.

Backed tools make up 4.4% of the core industry. The majority are Gravette points (ibid., p. 90, fig. 42; p. 91, fig. 43), usually of medium or large dimensions. Micro-Gravette points (width less than 7.5 mm) are rare. The most frequent butt treatment, often accompanied by flat working at the point, is the Vachons style, often the classic obverse-inverse Vachons variety. Obverse butt styles and specifically Périgordian IV morphologies are virtually absent. The backs of Gravette points tend to be slightly curved and are made more frequently on the right side than on the left. Backed and truncated pieces are present though extremely rare, all with square truncations. Backed blades and bladelets that

---

37. It was necessary to sample the huge Isturitz collections. The tools are stored in boxes, most of which contain between 50 and 80 pieces. To sample the collection from Level IV, the pieces in each box were turned out, stirred, and divided by a straightedge into four lots judged equal by eye. One lot was then selected at random to be counted. One-half of the Level III assemblage was selected in a similar manner. The whole of the Level IIIa series was studied.

The de Saint-Périers (1952, p. 227) give a total of 11,010 pieces for Level IV, whereas my estimate is: 4 × 2984 pieces studied = 11,936. Their total for Level III is 1834, while my estimate is: 2 × 845 = 1690 pieces. The high estimate for Level IV might be explained by the omission from their counts of partially or irregularly backed or retouched blades, and of other minor categories of tools, for example, splintered pieces. I am at a loss to explain the difference between the de Saint-Périer total and my low estimate for Level III.

The separation of tools from waste flakes and blades is that of the de Saint-Périers.

38. The total given by the de Saint-Périers is 378, or 3.4% of their total of 11,010 pieces. They may have excluded partially or irregularly backed pieces.

Table 71
TYPE FREQUENCIES AND PERCENTAGES
OF THE GROTTE D'ISTURITZ (Salle d'Isturitz) SAMPLES FROM LEVELS IV AND III
(de Saint-Périer collection)

Type	Level IV n	Level IV %	Level III n	Level III %
Ordinary End-Scraper	368	12.3	63	7.5
Irregular End-Scraper	9	0.3	12	1.4
Double End-Scraper	56	1.9	1	0.1
End-Scraper with Marginal Retouch	240	8.0	55	6.5
Blunt Point End-Scraper	27	0.9	13	1.5
Blunt Point End-Scraper with Marginal Retouch	30	1.0	15	1.7
Fan-Shaped End-Scraper	48	1.6	11	1.3
Fan-Shaped End-Scraper with Marginal Retouch	141	4.7	47	5.6
End-Scraper on Flake	8	0.3	8	0.9
Circular Scraper	2	0.1	1	0.1
Subcircular Scraper	1	0.03	–	–
Thumbnail Scraper	2	0.1	–	–
Carinate Scraper	–	–	2	0.2
Atypical Carinate Scraper	3	0.1	2	0.2
Nose-Ended Scraper	1	0.03	2	0.2
Atypical Nose-Ended Scraper	–	–	2	0.2
Nucleiform End-Scraper	1	0.03	2	0.2
Rabot	2	0.1	2	0.2
Side-Scraper	8	0.3	7	0.8
Perforator or Bec	7	0.2	8	0.9
Median Dihedral Burin	169	5.7	56	6.6
Asymmetrical Dihedral Burin	89	3.0	33	3.9
Lateral Dihedral Burin	34	1.1	14	1.7
Nucleiform Burin	8	0.3	5	0.6

Type	Level IV TBu	Level IV TBm	Level IV %	Level III TBu	Level III TBm	Level III %
Truncation Burin: Straight, 80–90°	4	2	0.2	2	–	0.2
Truncation Burin: Straight, Oblique	33	25	1.9	11	12	2.7
Truncation Burin: Concave, Oblique	16	10	0.9	6	5	1.3
Truncation Burin: Concave, 80–90°	7	1	0.3	1	2	0.4
Truncation Burin: Convex	4	3	0.2	4	1	0.6
Transverse Truncation Burin	–	–	–	1	–	0.1

Type	Level IV n	Level IV %	Level III n	Level III %
Single Noailles Burin on Truncation or Retouched Edge/End	427	14.3	104	12.3
Single Noailles Burin Made by Other Technique	36	1.2	10	1.2
Burin-Point by Truncation Technique	7	0.2	1	0.1
Burin-Point by Dihedral Technique	23	0.8	7	0.8
Break Burin	15	0.5	9	1.1
Unretouched Edge/End Burin	9	0.3	6	0.7
Atypical Chatelperron Point	2	0.1	–	–
Gravette Point	89	3.0	16	1.9
Micro-Gravette Point	7	0.2	4	0.5
Completely Backed Blade	3	0.1	2	0.2
Completely Backed Bladelet	3	0.1	–	–

Table 71 (continued)

Type	Level IV n	Level IV %	Level III n	Level III %
Backed and Truncated Blade	5	0.2	1	0.1
Backed and Truncated Bladelet	3	0.1	–	–
Gibbous Backed Piece	2	0.1	1	0.1
Shouldered Piece	1	0.03	–	–
Partially or Irregularly Backed Blade or Bladelet	3	0.1	3	0.4
Truncated Piece	14	0.5	9	1.1
Bitruncated Piece	–	–	2	0.2
Truncated Bladelet	8	0.3	6	0.7
Retouched Blade: Continuous Both Sides	88	2.9	30	3.6
Retouched Blade: Continuous One Side	130	4.4	34	4.0
Retouched Blade: Partial	74	2.5	16	1.9
Symmetrical Point	38	1.3	14	1.7
Asymmetrical Point	23	0.8	11	1.3
Mousterioid Point	5	0.2	3	0.4
Notched Piece	5	0.2	7	0.8
Denticulate Piece	5	0.2	7	0.8
Splintered Piece	3	0.1	1	0.1
Other: Burin on Gravette Point Fragment;	1	0.03	–	–
Point-Borers;	–	–	4	0.5
Discs	2	0.1	–	–
Combination Tools	141	4.7	48	5.7

	Level IV End-Scraper	Level IV Truncation	Level IV Other	Level III End-Scraper	Level III Truncation	Level III Other
DB	48	3	1	17	–	–
TBu	21	2	–	10	2	–
TBm	8	2	–	7	–	–
No.	21	13	–	3	1	–
Br.-Pt.	5	1	–	1	1	–
BB	10	–	–	1	–	–
UB	1	–	–	2	–	–
Trunc.	4	–	–	–	–	–
Other	1	–	–	3	–	–

Double and Mixed Burins

Level IV   438   14.7

	DB	TBu	TBm	No.	Ray.	Br.-Pt.	BB	UB
DB	30	14	15	15	3	3	17	4
TBu		7	3	2	1	–	5	1
TBm			3	2	1	–	2	1
No.				301	–	–	–	–
Br.-Pt.						2	1	–
BB							3	2

Table 71 (continued)

	Level IV		Level III	
Type	n	%	n	%
Triple Burins	15	0.5		

  Triple Noailles 12
  BB + BB + TBu 2
  BB + BB + TBm 1

Level III									82	9.7
	DB	TBu	TBm	No.	Ray.	Br.-Pt.	BB	UB		
DB	10	12	4	2	1	1	3	–		
TBu		2	1	1	–	1	–	1		
No.				45	–	1	–	–		

Triple Burins									1	0.1

  Triple Noailles 1

Total	2984	100.2	845	99.6

Table 72
TYPE FREQUENCIES AND PERCENTAGES
OF THE CORE INDUSTRIES OF LEVELS IV, III, AND IIIA OF THE GROTTE D'ISTURITZ

Tool Type	Level IV		Level III		Level IIIa	
	n	%	n	%	n	%
End-Scrapers	993	36.7	237	33.0	173	47.0
Dihedral Burins	392	14.5	136	19.0	12	3.3
Truncation Burins	894	33.1	208	29.0	85	23.1
Truncated Pieces	22	0.8	17	2.4	9	2.4
Retouched Blades[a]	284	10.5	92	12.8	64	17.4
Backed Tools	118	4.4	27	3.8	2	0.5
Solutrean Types	–		–		23	6.3
N	2703		717		368	
Noailles Burins	728	26.9	149	20.8	72	19.6
Retouched Points	66	2.4	28	3.9	18	4.9

Note: Samples taken as for assemblage count.

a. Includes retouched points.

Table 73
TYPE FREQUENCIES AND PERCENTAGES
OF BURINS FROM THE GROTTE D'ISTURITZ: LEVELS IV, III, AND IIIA

Burin Type	Level IV		Level III		Level IIIa	
	n	%	n	%	n	%
No.	1154	58.6	215	42.7	115	78.6
TBu	129	6.6	57	11.3	12	8.0
TBm	82	4.2	32	6.4	4	2.7
Ray.	5	0.3	1	0.2	–	–
Br.–Pt.	44	2.2	13	2.6	1	0.7
BB	62	3.1	13	2.6	3	2.0
DB	475	24.1	163	32.4	13	8.7
UB	18	0.9	9	1.8	2	1.3
N	1969		503		150	

cannot be attributed to the Gravette type are present in very low frequency.

Burins (table 73) are the most abundant class of tools, but because of the high proportion of end-scrapers, they are not absolutely dominant in the core industry. Dihedral burins (14.5%) (ibid., p. 102, fig. 49:4) are frequently ill-made or much reworked, with a high proportion of nonstraight burin edges. About one-fifth have burin edges reduced by tertiary or comparable modification. A few rare specimens tend toward the busked form (ibid., p. 102, fig. 49:5).

The vast majority of burins made by the truncation technique (33.1%) are Noailles burins (26.9%). The remainder includes many pieces on blanks large enough to have passed through a Noailles stage and to have been further reworked, losing their Noailles characteristics. Another form of truncation, or more exactly retouched edge, burin is described by the de Saint-Périers as on pointed blade. These pieces form about half of the non-Noailles truncation burins, are usually median, and may be modified. They appear as a special form characteristic of this industry. Almost one-third of the non-Noailles truncation burins are modified by tertiary retouch. There are 1101 Noailles burins in the sample studied (ibid., p. 98, fig. 46; p. 99, fig. 47), excluding those that form part of mixed burins or combination tools. They are distributed on 776 pieces in the following manner:

Noailles Burins	Single	Double	Triple
Small	307	208	8
Large (length > 4.5 cm)	120	81	4
On break	26	12	–
On dihedral	10	–	–

The proportion of large Noailles burins would be high for an Early Noaillian series in the Dordogne. Perhaps the poor light within the cave encouraged the use of less delicate tools, or it may be that some of the smaller pieces were missed by the excavators. The second explanation would also help to explain the rarity of smaller backed tools. The proportion of Noailles burins made on breaks is low, as is the proportion of break burins in the series as a whole. As is to be expected in a series characterized by quite high frequencies of marginal retouch, many of the large Noailles burins are made on retouched blades. Pieces made on broad, thin flakes are virtually absent. The AC pattern of association is the most common.

Burin-points are rare, the dihedral form being the most common. One piece is made by the retruncation technique. Burins on breaks, on retouched edges and ends, and large nucleiform burins are rare. Raysse burins are represented in the series by only five examples, all associated with other burin types.

Truncated pieces (ibid., p. 86, fig. 39:1, 6) are exceptionally rare; retruncated burins are represented by only one example. Isturitz is markedly deficient in these artifacts compared with other Noaillian assemblages.

Retouched blades are described in some detail by the de Saint-Périers. In the sample studied, the breakdown by retouch is as follows:

Retouched blades	Both Sides	One Side	Partial
Fine	7	17	16
Heavy	23	43	16
Stepped	2	2	–
Scaled	36	68	42
Mixed	20	–	–

Besides being more frequent than in Early Noaillian series elsewhere, marginal retouch tends to be heavier and more invasive. The norm lies between heavy and scaled, the very fine scaled retouch typical of Late Noaillian series in the Dordogne being absent. Heavy and scaled marginal retouch is also used to form a series of symmetrical and asymmetrical points. Nine pieces in the series studied are of symmetrical foliate form (ibid., p. 86, fig. 39:11) and could well be termed *pointes à face plane*, though they lack the flat, invasive retouch characteristic of such pieces in the Solutrean. They average between 60 mm and 70 mm in length and are about 20 mm to 25 mm wide. More massive specimens are also present (ibid., p. 84, fig. 37:7). The term ''point'' for these artifacts, which include some Mousterioid pieces on flakes and flake/blades (ibid., p. 85, fig. 38:8), is somewhat inappropriate, since it seems clear, on the basis of the presence of asymmetrical pieces and others such as one made on a plunging flake (ibid., p. 86, fig. 39:14), that they are not armatures, but rather knives or scraping tools. They show no special treatment of the butt. The point is rarely sharp, but varies toward extreme forms of the blunt point end-scraper (itself ill developed in this level). Retouched points are a distinctive specialization of the Isturitz Noaillian.[39]

The tendency toward the point is expressed over several artifact types and is perhaps the characteristic that most notably distinguishes these Noaillian assemblages from those of the Périgord. Although the retouched point is most clearly expressed in the elongate leaf-shaped point and affiliated forms described above, it also appears as a feature characterizing the proximal end of burins (ibid., p. 102, fig. 49:4) and end-scrapers. On the latter, points very similar to those found on retouched blades are opposed to the scraping edge, especially on fan-shaped pieces. (Such pieces are not counted as combination tools.) Lastly, the tendency is expressed in the retouched edge burins made on pointed blades and even on dihedral burins—in which case one series of removals has removed a part of the marginal retouch. The fact that many of these ''points'' are manufactured at the proximal end of the blank, the bulb of percussion of which is not always removed, suggests that converging lines of marginal retouch were required rather than a point. It is possible that the point form, when it appears at the base of other tool types, may have been intended to facilitate hafting.

Discussion: Level IV. On the basis of the published descriptions of the Levels, it seems clear that Level IV of the de Saint-Périers must be equivalent to both Level C (above) and Level F-3 (below) of Passemard and *not*, as claimed by the de Saint-Périers (ibid., p. 10, n4), to his Level F-3 alone. It then might be that, since Passemard was able to divide the deposit, his description of the two assemblages would provide good evidence for trends of development within and between the levels. There are some differences, mostly concerning the bone and antler industry (Passemard 1924, p. 137). Gravette points, present in both levels, are noted as being larger in Level C (ibid., p. 136), and there are other minor differences in the flint industry. But Passemard's general conclusion is that the industry of Level C forms a developmental continuity with that of Level F-3 (Passemard 1944, pp. 37–38).

In 1967, H. M. Bricker had the opportunity to make a brief examination of the Passemard series from Levels F-3 and C in the Musée des Antiquités Nationales at Saint-Germain-en-Laye. The following comments are based on his observations. The assemblages of Levels F-3 and C are extremely similar, in terms of both tool type percentages and detailed typological characters. Both levels are certainly Noaillian and include the characteristic forms: Noailles burins, burin-points, modified truncation burins, and sagaies d'Isturitz. Both levels contain Gravette points with a high proportion of Vachons butt treatment. The main difference between the Passemard series and that of the de Saint-Périers lies in the proportion of Noailles burins, very low in the former and very high in the latter. Some sort of differential lateral distribution within the cave must be responsible for these differences. If Noailles burins are excluded from consideration, the assemblages from Levels F-3 and C of Passemard agree very closely in tool type frequency and typological details with that of Level IV of the de Saint-Périers.

The assemblage of Level IV differs from Early Noaillian assemblages of the Périgord to which it is typologically most similar in the following major respects:

a. A qualitatively superior technique for the production of blanks.

b. A much higher frequency of end-scrapers (37% of the core industry as against 11% in the Abri Pataud: Level 4: LOWER subdivision).

c. The rarity of blunt point end-scrapers.

d. The lower frequency of truncation burins of all types and the tendency toward larger forms of Noailles burins.

e. The rarity of break burins.

f. The exceptionally low frequency of truncated pieces.

g. A high incidence of marginal retouch.

h. Extensive use of marginal retouch to form fan-shaped end-scrapers, pointed butts of other tools including burins, special forms of retouched blades and flakes such as elongate, foliate *pointes à face plane*, and Mousterioid points, and to provide the edge from which burin blows were struck to make burins on pointed blades.

At least three of these differences (b, d, and e, and possibly f) might be attributed to inefficient collection by the excavators. The remaining variations (in spite of which the overall adherence of the assemblage to the Noaillian cultural tradition is very clearly apparent) do not appear to be due to seasonal factors (de Saint-Périer and de Saint-Périer 1952, p. 259). They may somehow be connected with the hunting of large numbers of horses and red deer in addition to reindeer, but their qualitative and quantitative nature argues for a more than purely economic differentiation. They suggest that the Pyrenean piedmont was occupied at this time by a

---

39. They are included with retouched blades in core industry statistics.

people kindred to those living in the Périgord but members of other social groupings and bearers of a variant of the Noaillian tradition that merits recognition as a separate regional facies.

Level III. The marked change in the nature of the deposits from Level IV to Level III is not paralleled by typological changes in the flint industry, termed "Aurignacien final" by the de Saint-Périers. The site was certainly less heavily occupied during the period of accumulation covered by Level III, but there is no apparent interruption of the occupation. Approximately one-half of the series was counted.

The same forms of end-scrapers (33.0%) are found as in the underlying horizon, and there is a similar incidence of fan-shaped and marginally retouched pieces. Other forms of scraper remain very rare. Backed tools (3.8%) show the same range of forms and size as in Level IV. Two Gravette points have square obverse truncations at the butt, a treatment also found at Laraux (Vienne) in Level 3. Backed tools were not localized within the level but were found sporadically over the whole excavated area. Burins retain their position as the most common tool class. Dihedral burins increase their representation to 32.4% of all burins as against 24.1% in Level IV (table 73). One-seventh have reduced burin edges. Among the truncation burins (29.0%), the Noailles burins remain dominant (20.8%) although sharply decreasing in frequency (42.7% of all burins, as against 58.6% in Level IV). Among other truncation burins there is no increase in the use of tertiary modification (de Saint-Périer and de Saint-Périer 1952, p. 41, fig. 17:5). Only one piece is classifiable as a Raysse burin. Burins on pointed blades are still present (ibid., p. 43, fig. 18:11). The Noailles burins are distributed as follows:

Noailles Burins	Single	Double	Triple
Small	69	32	1
Large	35	10	–
On break	8	3	–
On dihedral	2	–	–

This shows an increase in the proportion of large pieces and an overall decrease in the proportion of double burins.

Burin-points—still made mostly by the dihedral technique—break, and unretouched edge/end burins continue to be represented in small numbers. Truncated pieces (2.4%) are slightly more common in this level. Retouched blades increase from 10.5% to 12.8%. In contrast to retouched blades in the Périgord, there is no tendency toward an increase in the frequency of scaled retouch; the norm actually shifts in the direction of heavy retouch. Retouched points continue to be manufactured (ibid., p. 39, fig. 16:1).

The Level III assemblage is characterized by the retention of forms already present in Level IV. The special features characteristic of the facies remain constant, and even though the thickness of the levels must represent a considerable period of time, there is no sign of developments typical of the Noaillian of the Périgord. The absence of tools, partic-

ularly Raysse burins, characteristic of later phases of the Noaillian elsewhere, or of other non-Noaillian forms introduced from neighboring areas, suggests that during the period covered by Level III there was little contact with groups in other regions.

Level IIIa (including IIIb). The series described by the de Saint-Périers as "Solutréan moyen et typique" comes mainly from Level IIIa (including IIIb), but it also contains Solutrean pieces from the thin zone of limestone slabs and brown *limon* immediately above. Typologically, the series appears to be a mixture of Solutrean and Noaillian tools. The arbitrary division (de Saint-Périer and de Saint-Périer 1952, p. 36) of the thick clay deposit into Levels IIIa and III does not seem to have corresponded exactly with the break in the cultural succession. The de Saint-Périer's cut was deep enough in the clay to include some Noaillian material with the Solutrean of the upper part of the excavation unit. Thus, tools assigned to Level IIIa constitute a mixed series rather than a true assemblage, and only brief comments on the Noaillian tools are given here.

The Level IIIa series is much smaller than those of the underlying levels, containing a total of only 416 pieces and a core industry of 368 tools. There are only two backed tools, both Gravette point fragments (0.5% of the core industry). Noailles burins are common, forming 19.6% of the core industry and 76.6% of all burins. The trend toward increased size of Noailles burins continues into this level. As in the Périgord, but in a different cultural context, Noailles burins tend through time to approximate ordinary small truncation burins and lose their special characteristics. Few are notched.

Noailles Burins	Single	Double
Small	22	18
Large	18	14
On break	6	–

Raysse burins are altogether absent. There are four modified truncation burins (2.7% of all burins) and one burin-point (0.7% of all burins). Retouched blades continue their proportional increase to 17.4% of the core industry, the norm still lying between heavy and scaled retouch.

Solutrean types of point (mostly of laurel-leaf form) are of minor quantitative importance (6.3% of the core industry). There are four pieces which can be classified as willow-leaf points, but shouldered points are absent from the series.

Bone and Antler Tools from Levels IV, III, and IIIa. The bone and antler component was very fully described and illustrated in the site monograph and was not studied in detail by the present writer. The following discussion, based largely upon the literature, concentrates upon the most diagnostic artifacts.

Both Level IV and Level III are relatively rich in bone and antler tools, and all the forms found in both the Upper Périgordian and the Noaillian assemblages of the Abri Pa-

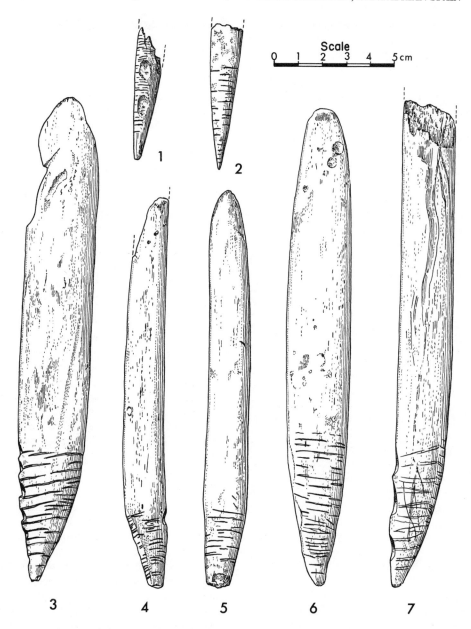

Figure 66.   SAGAIES D'ISTURITZ FROM THE GROTTE D'ISTURITZ: LEVEL IV (after de Saint-Périer and de Saint-Périer 1952, p. 126, fig. 66).

taud are also present at Isturitz, including pointed bones, smoothers, polishers, wedges, and compressers.

Isturitz is the type site of the sagaie d'Isturitz, of which about 150 (all broken except for a few with blunt points, which may well be reworked examples) were found in Level IV, where they are by far the most common type of armature. They show a range of forms, base treatments, and sizes identical to the Abri Pataud series. Pieces with notched bases, side bevel bases, asymmetrical, pointed, and blunt

base treatments are all present (fig. 66). They scarcely continue into Level III, where they are represented by only five examples, one of ivory.

Single-bevel-based armatures are the dominant type in Level III. There is considerable variation in their forms, but the modal type is about 15 cm long and 12 mm in diameter, with a 4 cm, usually striated, bevel (de Saint-Périer and de Saint-Périer 1952, p. 56, fig. 26:1). In Level III there are about 85 such pieces. A variant of this form, of which there are very few examples, may be of value as a horizon marker, correlating Level III with the Venus horizon of the Grotte des Rideaux at Lespugue (de Saint-Périer 1922); the central portion of the shaft above the bevel is flattened on one side and scored by deep incisions (de Saint-Périer and de Saint-Périer 1952, p. 56, fig. 26:9). Besides these types of armatures, conical-based pieces are present in both levels. In Level III some of these are grooved.

Tools of bone and antler are not numerous in Level IIIa. There are no clear examples of sagaies d'Isturitz. The dominant armature has a single bevel base, as in Level III. One kind, made of bone instead of antler, is not found in the underlying level, but is present in the Solutrean horizon at the Grotte des Harpons at Lespugue. This type together with three-eyed needles from Level IIIa should be attributed to the Solutrean increment.

The Isturitz armature series is important for cross-dating between the Pyrénées and the Périgord. The remainder of the bone and antler tool kit contains rare and interesting pieces but nothing else of such value for interpretation. Awls are very rare in all levels; the elongate type typical of the Abri Pataud Noaillian assemblage is present only in Level IV, where it is represented by two examples. Two pieces from Level III are ornamented with short parallel incisions (*marques de chasse*), one being perforated near the base. Pierced reindeer antlers, some decorated with cuts and striations, are present in Level IV (three pieces) and Level III (four pieces). (A pierced antler possibly of Noaillian manufacture occurred in the upper subdivision of the "Upper Périgordian" level at the Roque-Saint-Christophe.) Perforated tubes of bird bone, resembling musical instruments of recorder type, are present in both levels. They are without parallel from the Mesozoic plateau and plain region. A small polished bone object from Level IV, described by the authors as a spoon, having a flat rectangular end and a flattened oval shaft (ibid., p. 121, fig. 63:3), may perhaps be a headed awl with its point broken off. It is compared with a piece from the Grotte des Rideaux at Lespugue (ibid., p. 121, fig. 63:2).

Finally, it may be noted that the Isturitz bone and antler assemblages are characterized by a high incidence of pieces decorated with short parallel incisions, applied both to artifacts and to pieces that cannot be demonstrated to have had any utilitarian function. Such decoration occurs, though rarely, in Noaillian assemblages to the north.

Discussion. Unlike in the stone assemblages, developmental change is detectable and well marked in the bone and antler series, especially in the armatures. The change from sagaies d'Isturitz to bevel-based armatures has no parallel in the flint tool kits, which show very little development through the Noaillian horizons. At the Abri Pataud the opposite occurs; there are decided changes in the flint industry through time but little if anything that can be confidently termed developmental change in the bone and antler series. Typologically, the Isturitz series, especially that of Level IV, is closely related to Noaillian series from the eastern Mesozoic plateau region, with the majority of types held in com-

mon, and few regional specialities like the bone tubes. Even these have their parallel outside the region at the Abri Lespaux (inf., p. 307).

Use of the bone and antler series for cross-dating with the Mesozoic plateau region is difficult. There are two possible interpretations. The similarities between the bone and antler of Level IV at Isturitz and of the *whole* Noaillian sequence at the Abri Pataud might suggest that Level III (and, of course, IIIa) represents a Noaillian phase posterior to anything known from the north. On the other hand, it is possible that the similarities are inherited from a shared ancestral culture, and that the differences between Level III and Late Noaillian bone and antler series elsewhere indicate the divergence of contemporary cultures. It will be seen below that the first alternative is correct.

Chronology and Environment. In addition to the de Saint-Périers's description of the fauna, a supplementary study has been made by Bouchud (1951, 1952, 1963). Mme Leroi-Gourhan (1959) has analyzed the pollen, but the usefulness of this analysis is limited, since only one sample was taken from each of the levels recognized by the de Saint-Périers. "Thus, the analysis of Isturitz gives a series of points in time and not a continuous climatic curve" (ibid., p. 619). The various levels have been very tentatively assigned to different Würmian episodes by Alimen (1964, p. 334), whose interpretation was based upon the published data. Finally, there is a brief preliminary report (Laville and Thibault 1967) dealing with sedimentological observations; the results of the full analysis have not yet been published. Information given by the various sources is reasonably consistent, and in the paragraphs below it is summarized for the levels presently under discussion.

Level V. This level, containing an Aurignacian industry, was deposited during a time of intense cold, as evidenced by both the fauna and the pollen. The top 15 cm to 20 cm of this level, archaeologically sterile, are yellow clayey and sandy deposits, partly cemented and containing stalagmite zones. We have no information from pollen, fauna, or sediment analysis, but the presence of stalagmite and cementation suggests the possibility of a humid oscillation or period, perhaps broadly contemporary with the one registered at Pataud in Level 5 and elsewhere in the Périgord at the end of the Aurignacian and the beginning of the Upper Périgordian occupations.

Level IV. For purposes of establishing a relative chronology, the faunal and palynological information are of little help for this level. Mme Leroi-Gourhan (1959, p. 623) notes that Level IV represents the coldest and driest climate found in any level at Isturitz; what robs this finding of its utility is that we do not know from what part of Level IV the sample comes. The observations of Laville and Thibault are vital to an understanding of this part of the stratigraphy, but there is some uncertainty about just what levels they are referring to. Their "Upper Périgordian with Gravette points" and "Upper Périgordian with Noailles burins" levels must refer to Level IV of the de Saint-Périers, falling as they do between the "Aurignacien moyen" and the "Périgordien final." But the de Saint-Périers do not divide their Level IV into two neat units. Passemard does, however, and the two levels, Gravette and Noailles, of Laville and Thibault may refer to equivalents of Passemard's Levels F-3 (so-called Gravette) and C (Noailles). The "Level with Noailles burins" is characterized by very rounded éboulis and an important introduction of sand into the cave. In the underlying "Level with Gravette points," the éboulis blocks are much less altered. The authors conclude that at Isturitz, as at other sites in the Southeast of France, "a greater *ruissellement* and consequently a greater humidity characterize . . . the deposit contemporary with the Périgordian with Noailles burins" (Laville and Thibault 1967, p. 2366).

Levels III and IIIa. This thick clay level, subdivided arbitrarily and containing very different kinds of archaeological materials throughout its thickness, is distinguished from the underlying Level IV by a distinct stratigraphic break. The lower part (Level III), containing the "Final Aurignacian (= Périgordian)," was deposited under a cold, dry climate, witnessed by the pollen and the fauna. Laville and Thibault note that the éboulis in the "Final Périgordian" level are very angular, indicating a return to rigorous conditions after the oscillation visible in Level IV (upper part). Toward the top of the clay deposit, in Level IIIa, Mme Leroi-Gourhan notes a slightly humid amelioration. There is no relevant information about the fauna. It seems that the upper part of the clay, with the Solutrean industry, should be attributed either to the Würm III/IV Interstadial, the dating favored by Alimen, or at the very least to one of the "degressive oscillations" of the Würm IIIb recognized by Laville (1964a) at Laugerie-Haute (Dordogne).

In summary, then, we have two horizons that can be employed to relate the Würm sequence at Isturitz to the sequence in the Périgord: (a) the oscillation in the upper part of Level IV, the suggested equivalent of the Éboulis 3-4: Red deposition and the following weathering interval at the Abri Pataud; and (b) the oscillation or interstadial in Level IIIa, the suggested equivalent of terminal Würm III or Würm III/IV phenomena associated with the Solutrean at Laugerie-Haute (Dordogne). The Noaillian occupations at Isturitz appear during a period of cold climatic conditions sometime before the first oscillation, just as they do in the Périgord. How nearly contemporary the appearances are in the two different regions cannot be determined on the basis of the present evidence. The Isturitz Noaillian continues well after the oscillation, *a persistence which is not known for the Noaillian in the Périgord*. Given the occurrence of Noaillian forms in the base of Level IIIa, the Noaillian at Isturitz seems to persist until or almost until the end of the Würm III, and thus is probably contemporary with the Périgordian VI, Proto-Magdalenian, Aurignacian V, and possibly even the Lower and Middle Solutrean of the Les Eyzies region. These seem, at least, to be the most reasonable hypotheses on the basis of the evidence at hand. Publication of the detailed sedimentological analysis and radiocarbon dating are required to confirm or revise such conclusions.

The Noaillian in the Isturitz Vicinity

Noailles burins and Noaillian forms of end-scraper are present in small numbers in the Aurignacian industry of Level V, but the overall character of this assemblage is so completely different from that of the overlying Level IV that it is most reasonable to assume contamination of the underlying level. Here, as elsewhere, the Noaillian seems to be intrusive and, already at the time of its arrival in the western Pyrenean piedmont, a well-developed, specialized industry, differentiated from the facies characteristic of the Mesozoic plateau with which its arrival appears broadly contemporary. The Noaillian assemblage is generally similar to Early Noaillian phases elsewhere, although its divergence, whether the product of cultural drift, of other cultural factors, or of response to new environmental challenges, is sufficiently marked to justify its distinction as a separate facies of the culture. The differentiation is indeed such as might imply a fairly long period of separation or rapid cultural change *before* the first Noaillian occupation of the Grotte d'Isturitz.

THE AVENTIGNAN VICINITY (HAUTES-PYRÉNÉES)

Aventignan is situated more than 140 km east of Isturitz and 18 km SSE of Saint-Gaudens, near the boundary between the departments of Haute-Pyrénées and Haute-Garonne. It lies above the left bank of the Garonne River, here flowing north just before it joins the Neste at Montréjeau and turns east toward Saint-Gaudens. The vicinity lies at the boundary of the Primary rocks of the high Pyrénées, the Cretaceous limestone which extends along their northern edge, and the Tertiary rocks which here reach south along the Garonne and the Neste.

Grotte de Gargas (Commune d'Aventignan)

The Grotte de Gargas is a tunnel extending through a spur of rock overlooking the left bank of the Garonne with entrances to the north and west. The D. 26 road from Aventignan, 1.5 km to the northwest, runs beneath the site. The cave was first sounded by Garrigou in the 1870s. F. Regnault worked at the site at about the same time and subsequently published several minor articles (Regnault 1873, 1890, 1895). In 1911 and 1913, after their discovery of art in the cave, Breuil and Cartailhac undertook the excavations eventually published by Breuil and Cheynier (1958). The latter report forms the basis of the following summary.

The stratigraphy just inside the western entrance (Breuil and Cheynier 1958) includes over 7 m of clay containing quartzite pieces of Acheulian typology, successive levels of Mousterian (Level 2), Châtelperronian (Level 3), Aurignacian (Level 4), and finally two levels of "Upper Périgordian" beneath a stalagmite floor. The lower of these, Level 5, is a 30–40 cm-thick layer of coarse granitic sand probably introduced into the cave by water action. It contains unrolled "Upper Périgordian" and rolled Mousterian tools. The overlying Level 6 is a 15–30 cm occupation horizon with hearth debris.

Alimen (1964, p. 333) attributes the whole sequence from Levels 3 to 6 to Würm III, but the sediments have never been properly studied. The fauna of Level 6 has been examined by Bouchud (1958), who considers it indicative of a rigorous environment, but one which does not exclude the presence of forest nearby.

Materials from the Breuil and Cartailhac excavations are preserved in the Institut de Paléontologie Humaine at Paris and in the Muséum d'Histoire Naturelle at Toulouse.

Level 5. The small Upper Palaeolithic sample from this Level appears to be Upper Périgordian, containing no obviously Noaillian forms. If a true assemblage, it is important as the only example of an Upper Périgordian assemblage in the Pyrénées.

Level 6. The end-scrapers, mostly of small or medium size, include a large proportion of pieces with marginal retouch down one or both sides. Fan-shaped end-scrapers are common (Breuil and Cheynier 1958, p. 371, pl. XIV:222, 223, 225) and include the long pedunculate form (ibid., p. 371, pl. XIV:220, 221, 233). There are six *raclettes* and sixteen side-scrapers, the latter grading toward the Mousterioid point. There are round scrapers and some very short double end-scrapers (ibid., p. 371, pl. XIV:219). These types obviously resemble those of Isturitz Levels IV–IIIa.

The backed tools include Gravette points and backed bladelets. There are six large Gravette points, one with an atypical Vachons-style butt treatment (ibid., p. 365, pl. XI:147), better expressed on a broken and possibly reworked piece (ibid., p. 365, pl. XI:148). Obverse butt styles are also present. There are some very small backed bladelets or Micro-Gravette points and at least two small backed and truncated pieces.

Burins are the most abundant tool group. The frequency of dihedral burins is not stated. About 200 Noailles burins dominate the truncation burins almost to the exclusion of other forms (ibid., p. 369, pl. XIII:178–195, 198–201). They are often multiple and are very thin. Truncated pieces are not mentioned; it seems reasonable to infer that they are as rare here as at Isturitz. The retouched point is present (ibid., p. 371, pl. XIV:215) among the retouched blades.

Gargas is relatively rich in bone and antler tools, sharing many forms with Isturitz. A sagaie d'Isturitz found by Garrigou (Musée de Foix) presumably comes from this level. There is one conical-based armature. Grooved and bevelled points are absent. The assemblage compares well with Isturitz in other respects.

The high frequency of burins as a class and, specifically, the large proportion of small Noailles burins among them demonstrate that the Level 6 assemblage is predominantly Noaillian. The affinities of the Gargas assemblage to those of Isturitz are quite clear, confirming the existence of a South Aquitanian regional Noaillian facies. Dating of the series relative to the Isturitz sequence is impeded by the lack of

good quantitative data and by the small number of antler and bone armatures, which at Isturitz show the clearest developmental change. Neither the sedimentological nor the faunal evidence is sufficiently precise to permit exact correlation. All in all, the Gargas Noaillian assemblage is most similar to that of Isturitz Level IV.

THE LESPUGUE VICINITY (HAUTE-GARONNE)

At Lespugue, 47 km east of Tarbes and 14 km NNW of Saint-Gaudens, the Save River, flowing northeast from the Pyrénées to join the Garonne, has cut a gorge 300 m deep through the Petits Pyrénées. The site is situated at the edge of the Cretaceous limestone exposures, bordering the hills of the *molasse* immediately to the north.

Grotte des Rideaux (Commune de Lespugue)

The Grotte des Rideaux is ca 80 m above the Save River, immediately below the Château de Lespugue. The D. 9 *bis* departmental road runs beneath it along the river. René de Saint-Périer began his excavations there in 1911 and continued until 1914, resuming after the war in 1922, in which year he found the celebrated Venus figurine (de Saint-Périer 1922, 1923, 1924a, 1924b, 1924c). The front of the cave was closed off by a wall during the Middle Ages and the area behind it was very seriously disturbed. An undisturbed portion in the back gave the following stratigraphy (de Saint-Périer 1922, p. 362, fig. 1):

Level	Description
B (ca. 25 cm)	Modern humic deposit. Rockfall and local spread of stalagmite.
D (ca. 80 cm)	Black ashy level with some limestone blocks. The Venus figurine came from the upper part of this level. "Upper Aurignacian."
E ?	Clay with bones of bear, hyena, horse, red deer, and a bovid. Somewhere within it is a minor occupation horizon of undetermined cultural affinities. Bedrock not reached in excavation.

The Level D assemblage (table 74), consisting of only 48 pieces, is predominantly Noaillian and shows the same regional characteristics as are present at Isturitz, 150 km to the east. The end-scrapers (14 pieces of a core industry totalling 37) include a small, narrow, fan-shaped example with heavy marginal retouch down both sides. Seven Gravette and Micro-Gravette point fragments and a backed bladelet make up the backed tools. There are three single dihedral burins and one combined with an asymmetrical point. The eight truncation burins are, with one exception,

Table 74
FREQUENCY OF TOOL TYPES
FROM THE GROTTE DES RIDEAUX: LEVEL D ASSEMBLAGE (Saint-Périer collection)

Type	n
Ordinary End-Scraper	3
Irregular End-Scraper	1
Double End-Scraper	2
End-Scraper with Marginal Retouch	2
Blunt Point End-Scraper	2
Fan-Shaped End-Scraper with Marginal Retouch	1
End-Scraper on Flake	1
Atypical Nose-Ended Scraper	2
Rabot	1
Side-Scraper	2
Median Dihedral Burin	3
Truncation Burin: Convex	1 (TBu)
Single Noailles Burin on Truncation or Retouched Edge/End	4
Gravette Point	2
Micro-Gravette Point	3
Completely Backed Bladelet	3
Retouched Blade: Continuous Both Sides	1
Retouched Blade: Continuous One Side	1
Symmetrical Point	2
Asymmetrical Point	1
Solutrean Shouldered Point	1
Notched Piece	2
Denticulate Piece	1
Splintered Piece	1
Other: Disc with Two Patinas;	1
Asymmetrical Point with Flat Retouch over its Ventral Surface	1

Double Burins

   Double Noailles   3

Combination Tools

   DB + Asymmetrical Point   1

Total   49

all small Noailles burins, three of which are double. There are two retouched blades and no truncated pieces. Retouched points of the types found at Isturitz are represented by three examples. There is also one Solutrean shouldered point, identical to a piece from the Solutrean Level D of the nearby Grotte des Harpons (S. de Saint-Périer, personal communication).

For so small a lithic series, the bone and antler is extremely rich. It includes four sagaies d'Isturitz, eight single-bevel-based armatures of bone, two antler pieces with median flattening scored by deep incisions (exactly paralleled by pieces from Level III at Isturitz), and a small spatulate ivory object. There is also a well-finished polisher of long bone perforated at the base, again paralleling similar perforated pieces from Isturitz Level III. The remainder of the series includes gorges, perforated bone tubes, painted bones, and two antler wedges. A fragment of rib, perforated at one end, has two vipers engraved on it.

The small "Upper Aurignacian" series from the Grotte des Rideaux closely resembles the Isturitz III–IV assemblages in both stone and bone and antler tools and may be attributed to the same regional variant of the Noaillian cultural tradition. More precise cross-dating is not possible; the site is likely to have been frequented at several times during the period covered by Isturitz Levels III and IV. It is highly probable that the exquisite Venus figurine is of Noaillian manufacture; the many engravings from Isturitz prove that the southern Aquitanian Noaillians were excellent and productive artists, and the earliest Venus figurine found in a definite stratigraphic position in France, at the Abri du Facteur (Tursac, Dordogne), also comes from a Noaillian horizon. In my view, the Venus motif was introduced into Aquitaine by Noaillians at the time of their intrusion into the area.

THE CASSAGNE VICINITY (HAUTE-GARONNE)

Cassagne, 22 km east of Saint-Gaudens, is situated near the confluence of the Garonne and the Salat rivers. The village is 1 km east of the latter on the D. 69 road. It lies near the southern boundary of the Cretaceous limestone outcrops of the Petits Pyrénées. The topography resembles that of Lespugue, though less dramatic and more similar to the majority of vicinities in the Mesozoic plateau to the north.

Grotte de Tarté (or du Tarté) (Commune de Cassagne)

The Grotte de Tarté is situated in a low limestone cliff bordering a small side valley of the Salat, 1.5 km SSE of the village of Cassagne. It is 500 m to the northwest of the Grotte de Marsoulas and only 40 m distant from the Abri de Téoulé (inf., p. 303). In 1907, following exploitation for fertilizer and after excavations by Harlé (1893) and Darbas, J. Bouyssonie and Cartailhac undertook the excavations published by Bouyssonie thirty-two years later (J. Bouyssonie 1939). In later years, Casteret, Bégouën, Cazadessus, Thomson, and others also dug in the cave. Some deposits remained in situ, and new excavations were conducted in the early 1970s by Mme Suzanne Gratacos of Toulouse.

The archaeological horizons are limited to the first or main chamber and its two entrances. The stratigraphy, with level numbers added by the present author, is as follows (J. Bouyssonie 1939, pp. 180–181):

Level	Description
1	Minor rockfall, reaching almost to the vault of the cave, containing traces of a (possibly Neolithic) burial.
2	Disturbed deposits with a little archaeological material.
3	Sterile level.
4a and 4b (25 cm)	Two superposed archaeological levels not separated by sterile deposits. "Upper Aurignacian."
5 (60 cm)	Hard earth. Sterile.
6	Aurignacian with split-base bone points and some Mousterian pieces at the base, resting on cretaceous limestone bedrock.
–	Cretaceous limestone bedrock.

Reindeer is the dominant faunal element in all levels, followed by bovid and horse. Level 4a also contains bear, deer, boar, fox, and hare. Level 4b shows less variety but includes hyena. This faunal assemblage, generally comparable to Isturitz and Gargas, differs in the presence of wild boar, represented by one tusk.

Neither the selection from the Cartailhac and Bouyssonie series at the Institut de Paléontologie Humaine in Paris nor that part at the Muséum d'Histoire Naturelle in Toulouse (which seem to represent only a portion of the material described by Bouyssonie) allows a fuller interpretation to be made than that based upon Bouyssonie's report (1939).

Level 4b. The end-scrapers tend to be small and include many retouched examples (J. Bouyssonie 1939, p. 187, fig. 5:16). The fan-shaped form with retouched sides is present (ibid., p. 187, fig. 5:19, 20), as is a small, double, blunt point end-scraper (ibid., p. 187, fig. 5:14). Aurignacian forms are represented by a nose-ended scraper and an atypical carinate scraper, possibly a small blade nucleus.

Burins are the dominant tool group. Little information is given concerning dihedral burins. Marginal retouch seems common. Tertiary modification is perhaps present on some examples (ibid., p. 189, fig. 6:15). There are no busked burins. Noailles burins (ibid., p. 189, fig. 6:1, 2, 4) are present, as are larger forms on which the light working of the truncation should be noted (ibid., p. 189, fig. 6:14). An excellent example of a modified truncation burin is illustrated (ibid., p. 189, fig. 6:3). One burin (ibid., p. 189, fig. 6:11), although rather large, approaches the burin on pointed blade characteristic of Isturitz; it is also modified by tertiary retouch of the burin spall scar.

The backed tools, including Gravette points, are of some quantitative importance in the series. Truncated pieces are neither mentioned nor illustrated. The retouched point is present and also the shorter Mousterioid form.

Level 4a. The majority of the end-scrapers are unretouched (ibid., p. 191, fig. 8:31), but both broad and narrow fan-shaped pieces with retouched sides are represented (ibid., p. 191, fig. 8:33, 34). One end-scraper illustrated (ibid., p. 191, fig. 8:35) is a well-developed blunt point with retouched sides. Broader forms, including circular scrapers, may be considered as more typical of the Périgordian than of the Noaillian (ibid., p. 191, fig. 8:38).

Burins remain numerous and are said to include the same range of forms as in Level 4b. Among the burins illustrated are a dihedral burin on a retouched blade (ibid., p. 191, fig. 8:22) and a Noailles burin (ibid., p. 191, fig. 8:27). The other truncation burins would not be out of place in a Noaillian series.

Backed tools are abundant. Gravette points are present (ibid., p. 191, fig. 8:3, 5, 15) and include pieces with the Vachons butt style (ibid., p. 191, fig. 8:1). Small backed and truncated pieces are also included in the series (ibid., p. 191, fig. 8:2).

A point similar to those of Isturitz is illustrated (ibid., p. 191, fig. 8:18). Truncated pieces are not mentioned.

Bone and Antler. Level 4b is richer in bone and antler than 4a, though the latter includes one fragment of a sagaie d'Isturitz (ibid., p. 190, fig. 7:6). The lower level gave an atypical series including a split-base bone point, a double-bevel-based point, and a grooved point with butt treatment similar to that on a sagaie d'Isturitz (ibid., p. 190, fig. 7:16). The remainder of the series is banal.

The presence of a split-base point and of some Aurignacian scraper types in Level 4b indicates mixture with a minor Aurignacian horizon. The Noaillian materials are comparable to those of Gargas and Isturitz and belong to the South Aquitanian regional facies of the Noaillian culture.

Abri de Téoulé (Commune de Cassagne)

The Abri de Téoulé is situated 40 m downstream (northeast) of the Grotte de Tarté in the same cliff face. Most of the deposits were removed in three days by Thomson and Bégouën in 1924 (Thomson 1939), and all remaining material was excavated by Robert and others after World War II (Robert et al. 1952). The flint industry recovered indicates that there was only one occupation and that this was Aurignacian. There is, however, one sagaie base (Thomson 1939, p. 197, fig. 2b) with transverse striations and, apparently, lateral notches that appears to be a typical sagaie d'Isturitz (cf. de Saint-Périer 1952, p. 128). The significance of this piece, the exact provenience of which is not known, cannot be assessed.

THE SAINT-JEAN-DE-VERGES VICINITY (ARIÈGE)

Grotte de Saint-Jean-de-Verges (or Tuto de Camalhot) (Commune de Saint-Jean-de-Verges)

The Grotte de Saint-Jean-de-Verges is located in the limestone foothills of the Pyrénées 5 km north of Foix. The cave, 12 m long by a maximum of 7 m wide, opens to the southwest at an elevation of about 400 m. Excavations were carried out by Joseph and Jean Vézian between 1927 and 1934 (Vézian 1936; Vézian and Vézian 1966). The stratig-

raphy of the site, according to the latter publication, is as follows:

Level	Description
1 (ca. 30 cm?)	Horizontal level of éboulis and superficial debris from the hill-slope outside. Much disturbed by animal burrows.
2 (50 cm)	Brown earth with few stones and abundant humus material. Locally this level is a cone of éboulis introduced from outside through a window in the cave wall. In one area, Levels 1 and 2 cannot be distinguished, and a unitary recent level takes their place. In the latter are some human bones and Eneolithic artifacts.
3 (10 cm)	Light-colored clayey level with small stones (the summit of Level 4) containing a hearth level. Localized toward the entrance of the cave. "Périgordian V."
4 (70 cm–80 cm)	Reddish sandy clay with many small stones, becoming yellowish-white toward the top of the level. There are two hearth levels within this deposit, which is the main archaeological horizon. Aurignacian "I."
–	Bedrock.

Level 3 has been dated to $22,980 \pm 330$ B.P. (Gif-2942) and Level 4 to $24,200 \pm 600$ B.P. (Gif-2941) (Delibrias and Evin 1977, p. 219). As with other Gif, Gsy, and Lyons dates, these are unacceptably young in terms of the GrN dating framework.

Our brief comments are based upon the text and illustrations of the Vézian and Vézian monograph (1966). The series from Level 3 is extremely small, 203 pieces of which only 45 are retouched. The lithic assemblage consists of:

  10 end-scrapers

   2 carinate-like scrapers

   1 end-scraper plus burin combination tool

   5 burins

   8 Gravette points or fragments thereof

   4 backed bladelets

   7 retouched blades or fragments thereof

   3 splintered pieces

   2 perforators

   3 *divers*

Retouched blades are relatively numerous in the small series, and well-developed scaled marginal retouch seems to be present on at least some of the other tools (Vézian and Vézian 1966, p. 121, fig. 15:11, 13). One of the complete Gravette points (ibid., p. 121, fig. 15:7) appears from the drawing to exhibit the Vachons type of retouch at the butt. Among the burins is one clear Noailles burin (ibid., p. 123, fig. 17:5) on a small blade with a retouched truncation at the opposite end (unstruck burin?). Another piece (ibid., p. 121, fig. 15:11), a double burin, may well be a Raysse burin, judging from the drawing.

It is, of course, not possible to give a detailed interpretation of such a small assemblage. The most that can be said is that there is nothing in the Level 3 series that seriously argues against the presence of a Noaillian element.

OTHER SITES IN THE PYRENEAN FOOTHILLS

La Carane 3 (Commune de Foix) and Le Portel (Commune de Loubens) (Department of Ariège)

These sites are noted by J. Clottes (1974, pp. 76–77) citing Vézian (1964, 1966, 1972) in his useful summary of the Upper Palaeolithic of the French Pyrénées. La Carane 3, 10–15 km southwest of Saint-Jean-de-Verges and west of the Ariège river, is unexcavated. Four Noailles and one Raysse burin were found on the surface. The cave of Le Portel, about 10 km west of Saint-Jean-de-Verges, gave two Noailles burins in a very small series from Vézian's Couche B.

Grotte de Gatzarria (Commune de Suhare)

The Grotte de Gatzarria is a small cave in the Massif des Arbailles, a limestone foothill region of the Pyrénées, ca. 9 km south of Mauléon-Soule. Palaeolithic tools were discovered there in 1950 by P. Boucher, who carried out test excavations in the following years under the direction of G. Laplace. The latter's more extensive excavations, beginning in 1961, have revealed a stratigraphic sequence extending from the Mousterian, through the Châtelperronian and the Aurignacian, to an uppermost level of "Evolved Gravettian with Noailles burins" (Laplace 1966). Unfortunately, only traces of the latter archaeological level remain, and not much is known about the industry. It does, however, contain both Gravette points and Noailles burins.

Grotte de Lezia (or de Sare) (Commune de Sare)

The most southwesterly point yielding Noailles burins in Aquitaine appears to be the Grotte de Lezia, 11 km southeast of the Atlantic Ocean at Saint-Jean-de-Luz. Almost all the prehistoric deposits in the cave were removed decades ago

when an artificial lake was made, and the cave was otherwise altered to make a tourist attraction. Various investigators have reported the occurrence of Upper Palaeolithic tools from the cave. Noailles burins were found here by G. Laplace in a sandy level a few centimeters thick (Laplace, personal communication).

The Noaillian in Southern Aquitaine

The Noaillian assemblages of southern Aquitaine differ from those of the Mesozoic plateau and plain region in the typology of their stone artifacts, in greater numbers and variety of bone and antler tools, and in their art, seemingly richer and expressed in engraving on bone, stone, and antler. Without attributal analysis of lithic assemblages, for which new series from well-controlled excavations would be necessary, quantitative morphological differences can be only crudely estimated, but there are obvious qualitative differences between the two facies, centering in southern Aquitaine upon the retouched point and the application of convergent lines of heavy retouch to end-scrapers and burins. A more general difference is in the lack of development of the stone tool kit in this region, contrasting strongly with the sudden introduction of new burin types and changes in other tools characteristic of Early to Late Noaillian development in the Dordogne region to the north. In the Pyrenean foothills the lithic tool kit remains typologically Early throughout, although this interpretation, based upon the Isturitz sequence, may require revision as new evidence accumulates.

All assemblages from a wide area of the limestone Pyrenean foreland show a similar complex of characters, giving them coherence as a regional facies and differentiating them from other expressions of the Noaillian tradition. We term the facies "regional," rather than economic or seasonal, since the scant data available do not support the hypothesis of widely differing economic orientations in the south and in the Mesozoic plateau region. Closely related, but not identical, manufacturing norms are operative in the two regions, but, since comparable sequences are lacking, it is not possible to demonstrate that this southern Aquitanian region remained an interaction sphere throughout the period of Noaillian occupation.

Both the quality and the intensity of fieldwork in the Pyrénées have been less than in the Greater Périgord. There are fewer sites, and these are strung out along the limestone outcrops that fringe the northern Pyrénées, with no known outliers in the Tertiary hills to the north. In spite of the barriers to east-west movement through the region, only the site of Isturitz was definitely occupied intensively over a long period. Assemblages from other sites, with the possible exception of Gargas, are suggestive of temporary occupations, perhaps repeated irregularly over a considerable period. The population of the region seems to have remained very small throughout. Dating of the Noaillian development is hampered by the lack of radiocarbon measurements, but it can be approximated through the para-archaeological evidence and by cross-dating of types common to this and other regions. Although at most sites there is virtually no strati-graphic or environmental evidence of value for interpreta-tion, Isturitz suggests that the Noaillian occupation began in a period of rigorous conditions and continued through a milder and more humid interval into a subsequent cold phase. Comparison with the Abri Pataud sequence suggests that the Pyrenean Noaillian appears at approximately the same time as in the Greater Périgord, but that it persists through the oscillation represented at the Abri Pataud by the Éboulis 3-4: Red and ends at some time between the deposition of the Éboulis 3-4: Yellow and the top of the Abri Pataud sequence.

The presence of Vachons-style Gravette points in Isturitz Level IV is supporting evidence for the rough contempo-raneity of the start of Noaillian occupations in the Pyrénées and in the region to the north. In the absence of contem-porary Périgordian occupations, the regular association of backed tools with Noaillian assemblages argues that they form an integral part of the regional tool kit, whether ob-tained by diffusion from Périgordian groups, from Noail-lians to the north, or inherited from an ancestral culture. This conclusion is reinforced by the persistence of Vachons-style points into Level IIIa at Isturitz, for by this time they had already disappeared in the Périgord. Here as elsewhere there is no evidence that the Noaillian developed within the region. The culture was introduced by immigrants into an area either unoccupied or only occasionally visited by Pé-rigordians, who are as yet, and somewhat dubiously, rep-resented only by the small series from Level 5 at Gargas. Since the Pyrenean and Périgordian facies of the Noaillian are already differentiated at the time of their first appearance, it would seem that the proto-culture had already undergone a period of diversification before the incursion into Aqui-taine. Besides flint and antler tool types, there is reason to believe that Venus figurines were an element of this as yet hypothetical proto-culture.

THE NOAILLIAN CULTURE
IN CANTABRIAN SPAIN

Major C. R. McCollough has very kindly supplied the fol-lowing comment on his research (McCollough 1971) into the Upper Palaeolithic of Cantabrian Spain. His work sig-nificantly amplifies our knowledge of the Noaillian of the Pyrénées and confirms my interpretation of its dating. He writes as follows:

In her synthesis of the French Upper Palaeolithic se-quence de Sonneville-Bordes (1966, pp. 12–13) main-tains that the makers of the Périgordian Vc (Noaillian) did not cross the Pyrénées into Spain. The Spanish lit-erature tends to support this view, while David (1966, p. 552) alluded to a poorly published cave in the province of Vizcaya that supposedly contained a few Noaillian tools. This cave, Bolinkoba (Barandiarán 1950) was one of the sites considered in my survey of the Spanish ma-terials subsumed under the generic name Gravettian or Périgordian (McCollough 1971). The generic attribution masks the overwhelmingly Noaillian character of the Bo-linkoba Level VI industry, the first occupation of the cave. In fact, qualitative and quantitative comparisons with the Noaillian of Isturitz show that the samples may be con-sidered as coming from the same population, although the sites are 120 km apart. This realization prompted the analysis of the upper levels of Bolinkoba (V, IV, and III), and their assemblages likewise proved to be essen-tially Noaillian, with a few implements diagnostic as hori-zon markers of later industries—Middle/Upper Solutrean and Magdalenian "III." The crude dating indicators available demonstrate that the record of Noaillian occu-pation strikingly duplicates that of Isturitz and that Noail-lian traditions may have persisted in the western Pyrenean region, including the Spanish Basque provinces, for a very long period—from the time of the Würm IIIA/IIIB climatic oscillation, through the Würm IIIB stadial and III/IV interstadial, and well into Würm IV.

The Noaillian industry of Bolinkoba can be referred unquestionably to the Noaillian of Pyrenean Facies, and except in a few details it can be described within the framework of David's Isturitz analysis. The sagaie d'Is-turitz, Pyrenean retouched points, marginal retouch ap-plied to form blunt points on many tool types, and high proportions of Noailles burins and marginally retouched pieces support this contention, as does quantitative anal-ysis in terms of the core industries [table 75].

Backed blades and truncated blades are notably better represented here than at Isturitz, and there is no suggestion that the backed series (composed almost exclusively of Gravette points) represents a Périgordian component which was mixed with Noaillian materials upon excavation. Va-chons-style inverse thinning occurs in all levels and con-stitutes the most common type of butt modification (found on as many as one-third of all Gravette points in Levels VI and V); thus, as at Isturitz and numerous other French sites, the "Périgordian Vc" Vachons-style point is to be considered either an integral part of the Noaillian tool kit or an intrusive or "acculturative" element from contem-porary but essentially distinct Périgordian groups, the former being more likely in my opinion. "Aurignacian" end-scraper types made on Aurignacian blades and thick flakes and blocks constitute approximately 25% of the end-scraper series in each of the Bolinkoba levels, whereas they are practically absent at Isturitz. It is unlikely that there is mixture with an Aurignacian component at Bolin-koba, and Aurignacian end-scraper types are in fact well represented in all "Upper Périgordian" components in Spanish Cantabria, suggesting survivals of local Auri-gnacian technology throughout the area. The high pro-portions of retouched blades and marginal retouch on other tool types, noted as distinctive elements of the Is-turitz Noaillian, are exceeded at Bolinkoba, and I suggest that the normative application of scaled marginal retouch by Noaillian tool-makers of the western Pyrenean region is also rooted in Aurignacian technology.

Table 75

TYPE FREQUENCIES AND PERCENTAGES
OF THE CORE INDUSTRIES OF THE CUEVA DE BOLINKOBA: LEVELS VI–III

	Level VI		Level V		Level IV		Level III	
	n	%	n	%	n	%	n	%
End–Scrapers	179	28.8	46	25.8	104	28.2	69	21.9
Dihedral Burins	55	8.8	19	10.7	39	10.6	46	14.6
Truncation Burins	141	22.6	39	21.9	78	21.2	87	27.7
Truncated Blades	37	5.9	10	5.6	26	7.1	29	9.2
Retouched Blades	160	25.7	48	27.0	82	22.3	70	22.2
Backed Blades	49	7.9	16	9.0	33	9.0	12	3.8
Solutrean Types	2	0.3	–	–	6	1.6	2	0.6
N	623		178		368		315	
Noailles Burins	113	18.1	30	16.8	59	16.0	54	17.1
Raysse Burins	2	0.3	–	–	4	1.1	2	0.6
Retouched Points	20	3.2	3	1.7	7	1.9	6	1.9
Noailles Burins as a percentage of all burin edges	66.5%		62.4%		53.3%		45.4%	

Very minor indications of Noaillian occupation are found elsewhere in the Spanish Basque provinces—at the Cueva de Atxuri (Mañaria, Vizcaya, in the Bolinkoba locality), Cueva de Atxurra (Berriatúa, Vizcaya), and Cueva de Ermittia (Deva, Guipúzcoa)—and similar occurrences have been reported but not confirmed at a few other sites. The following tentative conclusions, based upon my examinations of these and other assemblages from the Spanish Basque provinces, can be proposed: (a) all materials assigned to the "Gravettian" in this region are almost certainly Noaillian; (b) wherever Solutrean tools are found, there are at least an equal number of examples of Noaillian technology; and (c) there is no major Solutrean occupation site in the Basque provinces.

Traces of Noaillian occupation are all but absent in the provinces of Santander and Asturias to the west, where the appropriate "Gravettian" stratigraphic position is filled by Upper Périgordian industries of strictly local character, which probably post-date the Würm IIIA/IIIB oscillation. The poorly-represented "Gravettian" horizons are succeeded here by a large number of rich Solutrean occupations.

These observations indicate that Noaillians occupied the focal areas on both sides of the western Pyrenean passes at least until the arrival of Solutrean groups from the north, which seems not to have occurred until the time of the Würm III/IV interstadial. The Noaillian presence may even then have discouraged Solutrean occupation in the Basque area, but interaction of the two groups is implied by the presence of full-blown, but regionally differentiated, Solutrean occupations farther to the west. The curious regional character of the Solutrean industries of Santander and Asturias can now be explained by the persistence throughout this period of a Noaillian "buffer zone" blocking the path of innovations originating in France.

Research in the important area of the Basque provinces is not yet highly enough developed to allow exhaustive testing of the hypotheses and tentative conclusions presented above, or to indicate what may have been the size and composition of the social groups involved. Bolinkoba stands curiously isolated as a significant occupation site in the interior highlands of the *westernmost* of the Basque provinces and would seem to be the base camp of a separate band rather than a seasonal or special-purpose camp of the same band which intensively occupied the site of Isturitz (cf. Campbell 1968). The minor Noaillian sites located between Bolinkoba and Isturitz, as well as those situated to the east of Isturitz in the Pyrenean piedmont, may reflect no more than seasonal or task-specific encampments, and the entire Noaillian of Pyrenean Facies represent two or perhaps three small bands of hunters whose central bases were at or near the sites of Bolinkoba, Isturitz, and Gargas. We are sorely in need of chronological, climatological, faunal, and fully reliable and representative artifactual data for sites in the southern part of the Noaillian culture area, which now includes the Spanish Basque provinces. Only new surveys and excavations, particularly in the Basque provinces where numerous minimally excavated Upper Palaeolithic sites still exist, can furnish such data and allow us to test the tentative social correlates which have been proposed and the hypothesis of unparalleled cultural lag involving the Noaillian of the trans-Pyrénées.

XIII

The Noaillian in the Low Riverine Plateaus

THE SAINT-QUENTIN-DE-BARON VICINITY (GIRONDE)

Saint-Quentin lies 23 km east of Bordeaux and 103 km west of Les Eyzies. It is situated on the plateau between the Dordogne and Gironde rivers, isolated from other vicinities that have given Noailles burins. This is lowland, all less than 100 m above sea level, formed of Tertiary marls, sands, and clays, with recent alluvium bordering the rivers. Isturitz lies 135 km to the SSW, but access to Saint-Quentin is easier along the Dordogne Valley (from which it is only 6.5 km distant at Moulon) than across the Landes and the watershed of the Adour and its tributaries.

Abri Lespaux (Commune de Saint-Quentin-de-Baron)

The Abri Lespaux lies in the Vallon de Bisquetan to the north of the Bordeaux-Castillon road (N. 136) in an outcrop of Oligocene (Stampian) limestone, exposed to the west. The site was discovered in 1943 by M. Krtolitza and excavated in the 1960s by M. Cousté and the discoverer (Cousté and Krtolitza 1961, 1965). The following comments are based upon the literature, on information kindly made available to me by the excavators, and on a brief inspection of part of the collections.

The shelter is some 7 m wide and 6 m deep. The following stratigraphy was recorded near its northern wall (Cousté and Krtolitza 1965):

Level	Description
6 (60 cm)	Humus. Gallo-Roman and Iron Age remains.
5 (40 cm)	Collapse of the vault. Large blocks overlying smaller éboulis containing sporadic ''Périgordian V'' (Noaillian) pieces.
4 (35 cm)	Light brown, coarse, sandy deposit. ''Périgordian V'' (Noaillian).
3 (40 cm)	Yellow to yellowish-red sandy sediment, in some places cemented, with much archaeological material and a major hearth
	scatter at base. ''Périgordian V'' (Noaillian).
2 (25 cm)	Grayish-yellow lens located in the rear of the shelter. ''Périgordian V''?
1	Yellow marly deposit formed by weathering of the bedrock. Sterile.
–	Oligocene (Stampian) bedrock.

The fauna of Level 3 consists mainly of reindeer; horse and bovids are of lesser importance.

A small series from Level 2 includes a few Gravette points, a *fléchette*, two Font-Robert points, and 15 Noailles burins. Detailed interpretation of this small series is not possible.

Level 3, directly overlying the former, is the major occupation horizon at the site. The assemblage, with over 650 pieces, is of Noaillian character. The end-scrapers appear Noaillian in their blanks and contour shapes; few are marginally retouched. There are 5–10% backed tools, including the Vachons-style Gravette point (ibid., p. 51, figs. 21, 22). There seem to be no backed and truncated pieces.

The burin component is dominated by the Noailles burin (ibid., p. 51, figs. 1–20), of which there are over 250 examples, as against about 150 dihedral burins. The former are, on inspection, indistinguishable from those of the Early Noaillian of the Périgord. The remainder of the truncation burins, perhaps 80 pieces, include about 15 Raysse burins and some modified truncation burins. No burin-points were noted.

The bone and antler tools include a number of pieces with cut notches, two headed pins, and a fragment of a sagaie d'Isturitz. There are also a grooved bone armature, three gorges, three pierced antler fragments, and a bone flute (Cousté and Krtolitza 1961, p. 30, fig. 6).

Level 4 has yielded about 100 pieces, including seven Noailles burins and two Gravette points. Bone and antler are virtually absent.

Sporadic pieces of the same industry (five Noailles burins) were found in the rubble of Level 5 and between the blocks fallen from the roof of the shelter.

The small series from Level 2 is suggestive of a mixture of Périgordian IV–V and Noaillian elements. The assemblages of Levels 3 and 4 pose other problems, none of which can be resolved with the data to hand. Both series are overwhelmingly Noaillian in character, and tool typology demonstrates a close relationship to the Noaillian facies found in the Greater Périgord. Raysse burins are present, and there are no characteristically Pyrenean flint types (the only artifact that might indicate contacts to the south is the bone "flute"). But the developmental sequence apparently is not that of the Mesozoic plateau region. The Level 3 assemblage is attributable to the Early Noaillian, although the presence of modified truncation and Raysse burins might indicate either that the site was occupied late in this phase, or—and this is perhaps more likely—that it was used occasionally over a longer period extending into Late Noaillian times. In either case it is surprising that Raysse burins were not found either in Level 4 or among the handful of pieces from Level 5. There are several possible explanations both for this and for the presence of backed tools in significant proportions in the assemblages, but given the isolated location of the shelter and the small size of the collections, we can only point out the apparent inconsistencies.

The Abri Lespaux, unique in its situation outside the limestone regions, is important in that it demonstrates that the Noaillians exploited, at least on occasion, the resources of the Aquitanian Plain. The site was discovered because its microenvironment resembled that of the region to the east, but it offers the hope that other sites, not necessarily caves or rock shelters, will eventually be found outside the "classic" limestone areas. Although it is unlikely that the concentration of sites in those areas is entirely an artifact of research, it may well be greatly exaggerated.

XIV

The Noaillian in Northern France

THE ARCY-SUR-CURE VICINITY (YONNE)

A belt of Jurassic and Cretaceous limestone outcrops along the northern border of the Massif Central and extends northeastward, reaching to the Ardennes and separating the Paris Basin from the valleys of the Saône and the Rhine. To the south, it merges into the Mesozoic plains of Aquitaine. Along its northern edge is a vicinity with assemblages problematically related to the Noaillian tradition.

Arcy-sur-Cure lies on the N. 6 road, 17 km northwest of Avallon. Two kilometers south of the village, the Cure River departs from its northerly course, turning sharply west and swinging back to the east before resuming its course toward Auxerre. Along the middle stretch of this bend, the left bank is bordered by cliffs honeycombed with caves and rock shelters. Among these are the Grotte du Renne and the Grotte du Trilobite. Beginning in 1946, Professor Leroi-Gourhan directed a campaign of excavations in the Arcy caves. A full bibliography of the Arcy-sur-Cure sites studied by Leroi-Gourhan is given in Leroi-Gourhan and Leroi-Gourhan (1964).

Grotte du Renne (Commune d'Arcy-sur-Cure)

The cave and its galleries extend almost 60 m into the cliff. The entrance, where the excavations have been concentrated, is now largely unprotected by a vault. The site has given a long sequence from the Mousterian to the "Gravettian"; only the latter levels are considered here. The description of the stratigraphy given below is a compilation from published data.

Level	Description
I	Humified portion of Levels II and III.
II, III (2–3 m)	*Éboulis secs.* Virtually sterile.
IV (10 cm)	Scattered artifacts in yellowish, pebbly, earthy deposit that entered the cave through a vent in the roof. "Gravettian" (Noaillian, probably largely derived from the directly underlying portion of Level V, and possible Proto-Solutrean).
–	Localized rockfall.
V	Two contemporary or near-contemporary occupation lenses within a matrix similar to that of Level IV and of the same origin (ibid., p. 55). "Gravettian" (Noaillian).
VI (55 cm–1 m)	Scatter of pieces in a thin pebbly horizon that is itself sandwiched within a yellowish earthy deposit similar to that above. "Gravettian" (Noaillian).
VII (40 cm?)	Three superimposed occupation lenses in platy éboulis lying within uncompacted, ochre-stained matrix. Aurignacian.
VIII–XIV	Châtelperronian (Périgordian I), "Post-Mousterian," and Mousterian levels.

Level VII is dated to 30,800 ± 250 B.P. (GrN = 1717) (Vogel and Waterbolk 1963, p. 166). There are no dates published for the overlying horizons. The definitive study of the "Gravettian" series is still awaited. Bailloud's (1953) description of those levels is extremely useful, although it does not cover material from later excavations at the site. His quantitative analyses of the 1953 samples are referred to below, but they are based upon a typology not easy to compare with the one used here. André Leroi-Gourhan has also given a brief description and excellent illustrations of the assemblages (Leroi-Gourhan and Leroi-Gourhan 1964).

Level VI. Burins comprised 52% of the small series in 1953, with truncation burins dominant and Raysse burins present (ibid., p. 54, fig. 19:9–10). Burin-points are represented, but not in high frequencies. End-scrapers are common (22%); the fan-shaped form with retouched margins is present. Backed tools are represented by one Gravette point with bidirectional backing (ibid., p. 54, fig. 19:2) and two backed fragments. Truncated pieces are fairly common, as are retouched and/or utilized blades. Blades with marginal retouch are rare. The class of *raclettes*, which according to Bailloud forms 12% of the assemblage, includes a wide variety of miscellaneous retouched pieces and is not limited to small, thin examples with continuous steep retouch around a large portion of their circumference. The bone and antler artifacts (not described) are stated to include pieces with parallel incisions. These recur in the overlying levels.

Level V. The assemblage now totals 845 retouched tools, and from figures quoted (ibid., p. 56), the frequency of burins can be calculated at 56.6%, that of backed tools at only 5.6%. The burins are mostly on truncations, and they include modified truncation burins, Raysse burins (apparently quite common), and many burin-points manufactured by the truncation technique (ibid., p. 57, fig. 21:9). Morphologically similar tools are made without the use of the burin technique by retouch alone (ibid., p. 57, fig. 21:10). Both kinds also appear at the neighboring Grotte du Trilobite. The end-scrapers (15% of the 1953 sample) are stated to be a varied class, including blunt point specimens (ibid., p. 58, fig. 22:2). The backed tools include approximately equal numbers of Gravette and Micro-Gravette points, in addition to several miscellaneous pieces (ibid., p. 57, fig. 21:3–7). Truncated pieces are present in lesser frequencies than in the underlying level, while retouched blades become more common, and marginal retouch is often applied to other tools. A pierced antler with engraved decoration is the most notable antler artifact.

Level IV. The assemblage is closely similar to that of Level V, differing quantitatively in a higher frequency of burins (71% in 1953) and a lower representation of backed tools (4%). A fragment of a point, with flat invasive retouch covering the dorsal surface, may indicate the presence of a Solutrean increment. It came from the uppermost part of the level.

These series will be considered further following description of closely comparable materials from the neighboring Grotte du Trilobite. Discussion of chronology is also postponed.

Grotte du Trilobite (Commune d'Arcy-sur-Cure)

The Grotte du Trilobite is located less than 20 m east of the Grotte du Renne in the same cliff. Parat's excavations in the front of the cave, undertaken between 1895 and 1898, revealed the following stratigraphy (Parat 1902):

Level	Description
6 (2 m)	Stony level. Neolithic.
5 (30 cm)	Magdalenian (and Solutrean?)
4 (1.50 m to 2 m)	Stony level in yellow, sandy clay matrix, partly disturbed by earlier workers. Proto-Solutrean?
Localized rockfall.	
3 (5–20 cm)	Thin, red occupation horizon. "Upper Aurignacian" (Breuil's (1918) determination).
2 (3 m)	Blocky éboulis at base, stony above, enclosed in a greasy clay matrix with discontinuous sandy lenses. Angles of rocks are sharp and unweathered. "Lower Aurignacian" of Breuil.
1 (70 cm)	Alluvial(?) deposits consisting of sand overlain by gray-green and yellowish clay. Sporadic Mousterian artifacts.

The faunal assemblages (David 1966, table 110) are too small for detailed analysis. Mammoth is present but rare throughout the sequence. Reindeer, horse, and cave bear are the most common animals, with reindeer overwhelmingly dominant in Level 3.

The Parat collection is now at the École Saint-Jaques at Joigny (Yonne). I was permitted to make a brief study of the series in 1965 and, during the day allotted to me, was able to count the assemblages of Levels 2 and 3 (tables 76 and 77).

Comparison of my counts with the numbers of tools recorded by Parat, and general differences between my observations of the Level 2 series (supposedly Aurignacian, but now containing an important number of Noaillian forms) and those of others who examined the collections a few years before me, lead to the strong suspicion that the Parat collection has suffered attrition and mixture during recent decades.[40] From the size of the pieces and the comparative rarity of broken specimens, it would seem that there was selection of *belles pièces*, either during or subsequent to the excavation. It is important that these cautions be borne in mind when considering the cultural affiliation of the assemblages.

Level 2. There is a definite Aurignacian increment in the large scraper series (41.9%). Backed tools are represented by four examples only. Burins form 40.2% of the core industry. Almost half are dihedrals (17.1%), including pieces with tertiary retouch modifying the burin edge (fig. 67:1). Modified truncation burins are present (fig. 67:2), together with two single Raysse burins (fig. 67:3, 4) and three others associated with other burins or on combination tools. There are no clear Noailles burins. The 12 burin-points are made by the truncation technique; they include examples made at the end of a long, deeply concave truncation (fig. 67:7). The same morphological, and very probably functional, type is also achieved by retouch alone without burination (fig. 67:6).[41] Truncated blades (6.0%) include burins reworked to make a small perforating tool.

The low frequency (8.5%) of retouched blades is misleading. Marginal retouch, ranging from scaled to heavy, is commonly applied to other tool types and over half the

---

40. Good illustrations and descriptions are given in Breuil (1918), but unfortunately there is very little quantitative information.

41. These pieces are counted with the burin-points.

Table 76

TYPE FREQUENCIES AND PERCENTAGES OF THE CORE INDUSTRIES
OF THE GROTTE DU TRILOBITE: LEVELS 2 AND 3 (Parat collection)

Tool Type	Level 2		Level 3	
	n	%	n	%
End-Scrapers	49	41.9	56	29.8
Dihedral Burins	20	17.1	16	8.5
Truncation Burins	27	23.1	92	48.9
Truncated Pieces	7	6.0	3	1.6
Retouched Blades	10	8.5	11	5.9
Backed Tools	4	3.4	10	5.3
N	117	100.0	188	100.0
Noailles Burins	1	0.9	1	0.5
Raysse Burins	2	1.7	1	0.5
Burin-Points	9	17.7	49	26.1

Table 77

TYPE FREQUENCIES AND PERCENTAGES
OF BURINS FROM THE
GROTTE DU TRILOBITE: LEVELS 2 AND 3
(Parat collection)

Burin Type	Level 2		Level 3	
	n	%	n	%
TBu	20	26.6	51	31.3
TBm	12	16.0	17	10.4
Noailles	2	2.7	1	0.6
Raysse	5	6.7	7	4.3
Burin-Point	12	16.0	60	36.8
DB	21	28.0	26	16.0
BB	3	4.0	1	0.6
N	75	100.0	163	100.0

end-scrapers. Perhaps fragments were not always collected. There are two retouched points, not similar to the Pyrenean types, but with flat invasive retouch covering much of the dorsal surface and, on one example, the proximal part of the main flake surface. Either or both may be strays from Level 4.

Level 3. End-scrapers drop to 29.8% of the core industry. No diagnostic Aurignacian types are present, but the same includes six flake scrapers, two of which are circular (Breuil 1918, p. 317, fig. 10:13). Backed tools are rare (5.3%), but Gravette points are present (ibid., p. 318, fig. 11:31–37). The burins (57.4%) include only 8.5% dihedral burins.

Modified truncation burins and Raysse burins (7 examples) are represented (fig. 67:8, 9). The most common form is the burin-point (26.1%), made either by the truncation technique (Breuil 1918, p. 320, fig. 13:43–53), or, in some cases, by retouch alone (ibid., p. 316, fig. 9:7–9). The truncation or the most concave line of retouch is consistently on the left. Unmodified truncation burins are also made on these long, curved, very oblique truncations.

Truncated blades are very rare (1.3%); the frequency of marginal retouch, in this level mostly heavy, is again underestimated by the frequency of retouched blades (5.9%). There are seven retouched points; on five the retouch is limited to the margins (ibid., p. 316, fig. 9:4, 8; fig 67:10), and on the remaining two it is more invasive. These pieces may be derived from the overlying Proto-Solutrean level.

Level 2 produced only four pointed bones and awl fragments, but there is a rich series of bone, antler, and ivory tools from Level 3; these include (data from Parat 1902):

34 fragments of armatures or rods of similar size

35 pointed bones and awls

1 smoother

2 polishers

1 pierced reindeer phalange

5 "needle" (gorge) fragments

several bone and antler fragments with engraved decoration

The armatures include the beveled base of an ivory piece and the lower portion of another with asymmetrically flattened and striated base. This piece is decorated along part of its right side with a half fishbone motif, identical to one from the Abri Pataud Noaillian assemblage. This motif also appears on an antler (armature?) fragment associated with a chevron design (ibid., p. 323, fig. 16:74). Bone armatures include the base of an elliptically cross-sectioned piece, resembling and striated like a sagaie d'Isturitz (ibid., p. 325, fig. 18:88). There is also the base of a smaller bevel-based bone armature.

There is one fragment of an elongated awl, and two headed awls, one worked out of a thick piece of long bone, the other thinner with a sculpted head (ibid., p. 325, fig. 18:94). Engraved pieces include an antler fragment with three raised longitudinal lines, a fragment of reindeer tibia with spaced parallel incisions, and an awl(?) fragment with shorter, more closely spaced incisions. Several horse mandibles are cut a few centimeters behind the canine and incised, and there is one fragment of long bone decorated with a realistic leaf design. This piece was not found *in situ* but was "authenticated" by Cartailhac.

Discussion of the Arcy-sur-Cure Assemblages

Bailloud (1953, pp. 342, 344) must be given the credit for recognizing the resemblance between the "Gravettian" assemblages of the Grotte du Renne, the comparable series at the Grotte du Trilobite, and the Late Noaillian assemblages from Pré-Aubert and Lacoste (near Brive, Corrèze). Full publication of the Grotte du Renne series will no doubt clarify their cultural attribution. The extent to which the Trilobite materials represent real assemblages is highly questionable. Although mixture may have occurred after excavation when the tools were in storage, Parat might not have recognized or distinguished all the stratigraphic divisions of the deposits. The evidence for this, an attempt (based on the published literature) to reconcile the stratigraphies at the two sites, is tenuous. Even though the two neighboring caves may often have formed part of the same encampment, the following correlation can be considered no more than suggestive. The best fit for the two sequences would seem to be what is diagramed below.

In this version, the mixture of Aurignacian and Noaillian elements in Trilobite Level 2 might be explained by the removal of two occupation horizons as one excavation unit. Level V at the Grotte du Renne and Level 3 at Trilobite may represent one settlement. Both the stratigraphy and the high degree of typological similarity between the assemblages support this view, although there is some proportional differentiation within the burin increment, and mammoth seems less important at Trilobite. Level 4 at Trilobite is characterized by numerous *pointes à face plane*, but it includes a number of the specialized burin types characteristic of Level 3. The unit is up to 2.50 m thick and may have included several occupations within it or at its base, one of which, represented at the Grotte du Renne by Level IV, was Noaillian.

It is clear that the *closest relationship* of the Renne "Gravettian" and the Trilobite "Upper Aurignacian" to assemblages of the Mesozoic plateau is with the *Late Noaillian*. This is indicated by the presence of modified truncation and Raysse burins and by burin-points made by the truncation technique. The absence, or virtual absence, of Noailles burins precludes an Early Noaillian phase attribution, although Raysse burins, at least at Trilobite, are less frequent than in Late Noaillian series of the Mesozoic plateau and plain, while the burin-point here attains a frequency and a degree of specialization unknown in Aquitaine. No doubt there are other differences that will appear when a more refined analysis has been made.

Interpretation of the nature of the differentiation of the definitely Noaillian elements from manifestations of the tradition in Aquitaine depends on firm relative or absolute dating. The Grotte du Trilobite can no longer supply this evidence; at the Grotte du Renne no radiocarbon dates are available for the "Gravettian" levels. Suggestions regarding relative dating can, however, be made on the basis of Arlette Leroi-Gourhan's palynological work (Leroi-Gourhan and Leroi-Gourhan 1964) at the Grotte du Renne. This shows a sudden climatic amelioration occurring within Level VII.

Grotte du Renne		Grotte du Trilobite	
Levels I, II, and III		Levels 6, 5, and most of 4	(Proto-Solutrean in 4)
Level IV and localized rockfall	Proto-Solutrean(?) and (? derived) Noaillian	Basal Level 4 and localized rockfall	Noaillian
Level V	Noaillian	Level 3	Noaillian
Level VI	Noaillian	Level 2	Noaillian and Aurignacian
Level VII	Aurignacian		
Levels VIII–XIV	"Châtelperronian," etc.	Level 1	Mousterian

Figure 67. VARIOUS TOOLS FROM THE GROTTE DU TRILOBITE (1:1)

LEVEL 2: 1: Dihedral burin with tertiary modification of the burin edge. 2: Modified truncation burin. 3, 4: Raysse burins. 5: Truncation burin (reworked). 6: Burin-point formed by retouch. 7: Burin-point.
LEVEL 3: 8: Mixed burin (Raysse + modified truncation). 9: Combination tool (Raysse burin + end-scraper). 10: Point.

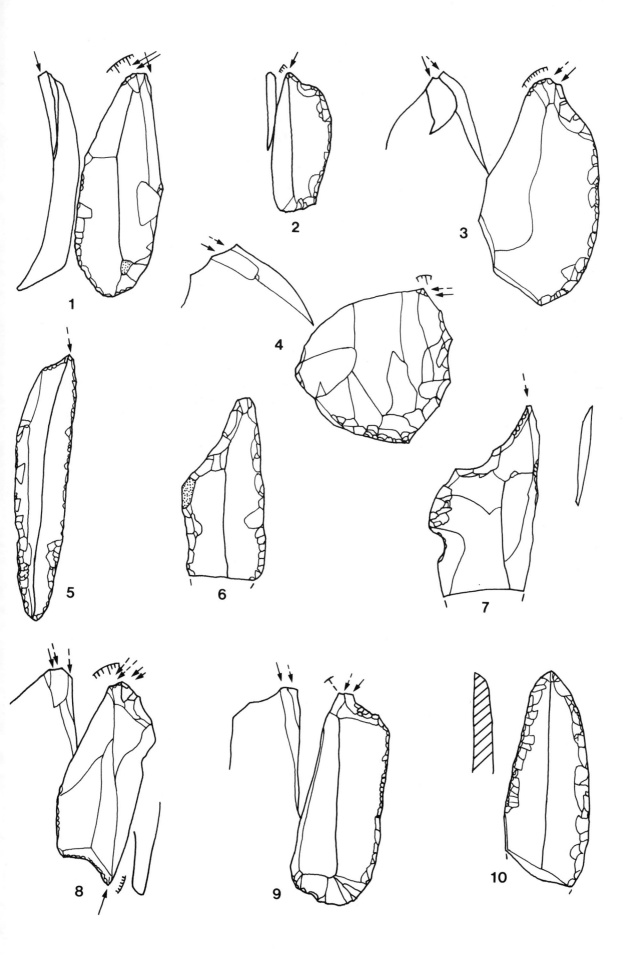

The frequency of arboreal pollen increases from less than 1% to a maximum of 18%, in which both cold-loving forms, especially pine, and deciduous trees, especially ash, are represented. This oscillation is followed by an equally rapid decrease in arboreal pollen to 1% around the Level VII/VI contact. In the lower part of Level VI, the frequency of arboreal pollen (almost entirely of cold-loving forms) increases again irregularly to 15%. After a decrease to below 2%, a secondary maximum of nearly 7% arboreal pollen is reached near the top of the level. The single sample from Level V shows 4% arboreal pollen. This sequence is interpreted as showing two periods of climatic amelioration, the first in Level VII being termed the ''Arcy Interstadial'' and the second, less-marked, double optimum equated with the ''Kesselt'' (ex-Paudorf) (cf. Girard 1976; Leroi-Gourhan and Renault-Miskovsky 1977). I would suggest on the evidence of the typology that this is wrong and that the sequence has been compressed into too short a time span. My alternative reading would correlate the first part of the second interstadial, represented in the lower part of Level VI, with the warm, moist period represented by the Périgordian IV of Abri Pataud Level 5 and there termed the Les Eyzies Oscillation (fig. 1). The subsequent cold episode then can be equated with Éboulis 4-5 and the lower part of Level 4, and the amelioration following with part at least of the Éboulis 3-4: Tan through Red sequence, i.e., the Tursac Oscillation. Unfortunately, since no information is available about the pollen of middle and upper Level V or Level IV at the Grotte du Renne,[42] the climatic trajectory cannot be reconstructed. However, the nature of the deposits and Leroi-Gourhan's reconstruction of their formation is strongly suggestive of relative mildness and the importance of colluvial processes. Unfortunately again, it is not recorded how precisely the thin Noaillian lens within Level VI fits into the climatic sequence, but I would hazard a guess that it is no earlier than the later part of the cold episode following the 15% arboreal maximum, and may be later than that. If this is the case, then the Level V and IV materials may well be roughly contemporary with Level 4a at the Abri Pataud.

The cultural relationships of the Renne and Trilobite Noaillian have been shown to lie rather with the Late Noaillian of the Mesozoic plateau and plain than with the Early Phase. It is conceivable but unlikely that they represent seasonal or functionally specialized sites of that grouping. It is more probable that the differentiation represents the fission of a group of southern Noaillians early in the Late Noaillian phase and perhaps simultaneously with the reduction of Noaillian territory that was occurring in the Greater Périgord region. The Arcy Noaillian, although the product of no more than a few brief visits to the Grottes du Renne and du Trilobite, may yet be taken as indicative of the existence of a third regional facies of the culture, and one that persisted at least as late as its putative ancestor.

---

42. The fauna of Levels VI–V has not yet been fully studied. Reindeer and mammoth are said to be the most common forms (Bailloud 1953, p. 344).

XV

The Noaillian in Provence and Italy

PROVENCE

In 1966 I predicted that a Noaillian ancestor would be found somewhere between the Carcassone gap and northwestern Italy (Liguria). It is very pleasing to report that such an ancestor may have been unearthed in the department of Var, where several sites have come to light through the excellent archaeological and sedimentological work of Gérard Onoratini and his colleagues (Onoratini 1975, 1976, 1982; Onoratini and Girard 1976; Escalon de Fonton and Onoratini 1976). In addition, Onoratini and da Silva (1978) have shown that a Noaillian occupation existed at the Grotte des Enfants at Grimaldi. This last-named site will be considered in the succeeding section on the Noaillian in Italy.

The Provençal sites will be treated very briefly since I have not seen the materials, which are, however, well and copiously illustrated in Onoratini's papers and especially his thesis (1982), to which the interested reader is referred. Although after a twenty-year gap I can no longer pick up stylistic details from illustrations and relate them to other materials, I am convinced that Onoratini has very clearly demonstrated the existence of a Noaillian facies in Provence that relates to both the Pyrenean and Greater Périgord facies of Aquitaine. He has also shown that it develops out of an industry characterized by backed blades and bladelets that is described as a "Périgordien IV provençal [or] méditerranéen," but which is quite distinct from the Upper Périgordian of the Périgord. The Provençal Noaillian itself evolves into a culture named the Arenian without any apparent break. The cultural continuity evident in this region thus contrasts very markedly with the Aquitanian sequences. Furthermore, Onoratini, through his sophisticated sedimentological analyses, has been able to place the Noaillian in a regional chrono-stratigraphic sequence that can be correlated with that of the Greater Périgord. The key site from this point of view is the Grotte no. 1 de la Bouverie, and this will be described first although the Noaillian is less well represented there than at Le Gratadis.

Grotte No. 1 de la Bouverie (Commune de Bagnols-en-Forêt, Var)

The site, first tested by Escalon de Fonton (1973), is a small cave with a narrow entrance that probably represents the back of a much larger site that has lost its roof through a major collapse. It has given a chronologically long but compressed sequence, subdivided by Onoratini (1976, p. 405) into four complexes of levels.

Complex D (Levels 1A to 1G) contains Late Arenian and Bouverian materials and dates from the end of Würm III (the Lascaux Interstadial) to the Bölling Oscillation. Complex C (Levels 1H1 to 2) contains Early Arenian materials. Its base, Level 2, is marked by a period of erosion followed by the deposition of a stalagmite horizon that is equated with the Bouverie Oscillation. Complex B includes the following levels:

Level	Approximate Thickness (cm)	Description
3	20	Medium-sized angular rock fragments (*cailloutis de grosse dimension*) in a yellow loam (*limon*) matrix with an eroded surface. "Post-Gravettien." This is the coldest period represented at the site and is equated with Würm IIIC2a.
4	5	Concretion. Latter part of the Tursac Oscillation.

Complex A continues the sequence:

Level	Approximate Thickness (cm)	Description
5A	8	Brown loam with pebbles. Surface eroded. Very cold conditions. "Périgordien V à Noailles."
5B	7	Medium-sized angular débris thinning toward the front of the site. 5B is the basal deposit in the rear. "Périgordien V à Noailles." Very cold conditions.
5C	Localized	Concretion indicating a climatic amelioration with marked humidity. Early part of the Tursac Oscillation.
6A	15	Rock fragments and pebbles affected by water action (*graviers et cailloutis lessivés*). "Périgordien 'IV.'" Relatively cold. Würm IIIc1.

Table 78
ALTERNATIVE CORRELATIONS OF PARTS OF THE ABRI PATAUD
AND GROTTE NO. 1 DE LA BOUVERIE SEQUENCES

Abri Pataud		La Bouverie			
		Correlation 1		Correlation 2	
Level 3 Éboulis 3–4: Yellow	Pér. VI	Level 3	Post-Grav.	Level 3	Post-Grav.
Éboulis 3–4: Red Level 4a	Term. No.	Level 4 Levels 5A and B Level 5C	(Concretion) Pér. V (Concretion)	Level 4	(Concretion) Tursac Osc.
Level 4	Noaillian	Level 6A	Pér. IV	Level 5A	Pér. V
Éboulis 4–5		Level 6B	Pér. IV	Level 5B	Pér. V
Level 5	Pér. IV	Level 6C		Level 5C	(Concretion) Les Eyz. or Salpet. Osc.
Éboulis 6–7 Level 6 and earlier levels?	Evolved Aur.	Level 6D	Pér. Sup.	Level 6A Level 6B and Levels 6C and D?	Pér. IV Pér. IV

6B	5	Rock fragments in ashy gray matrix (localized). "Périgordien 'IV'." Relatively cold. Würm IIIc1.
6C	5	Concretion. Localized at the entrance of the cave. Salpetrian Oscillation or Interstadial.
6D	8	Basal gravel and pebbles. "Périgordien supérieur." Part of Würm IIIb.
–		Rhyolite bedrock.

In his "Essai de corrélations," Onoratini (1976, p. 450), making use of information from Laville's publications, correlates his Post-Gravettian with the Périgordian VI of Laugerie-Haute. Since in both cases these cultures are found in deposits indicative of very cold conditions that succeed a period of marked climatic amelioration, this would appear very reasonable and a fair baseline from which to approach the interpretation of the underlying levels. Neither in the 1976 paper nor in his thesis (1982) does Onoratini make reference to Farrand's (1975) work at the Abri Pataud. However, it would seem that one of the two alternative correlations shown in table 78 is most likely to be correct. Their implications are very different. Correlation 1, which compresses four levels into the Tursac Oscillation including a cold phase (Levels 5A and B) for which there is no evidence at the Abri Pataud, would deny the possibility that the Provençal Noaillian is ancestral to that of Aquitaine. Correlation 2 can be objected to on the grounds that the Les Eyzies Oscillation is represented by only localized formation of calcite (and perhaps the *lessivage* of Level 6A), but is other-

wise more persuasive. Correlation 2 allows the Périgordian V of Provence to be ancestral to that of Aquitaine. There are no radiocarbon dates, and we therefore must appeal to the cultural evidence before coming to a tentative conclusion.

The cultural materials from the relevant levels at La Bouverie are extremely few; an inventory of Levels 6D through 4 is given in table 79. Onoratini's diagnosis of cultural continuity is supported by study of his illustrations (1976, figs. 12–17; 1982, vol. 2, pp. 69–74, 76–79). In Levels 6A through 6C we are clearly not dealing with a classic Périgordian IV. The Noaillian of Levels 5A and B includes only one convincing Noailles burin (Onoratini 1976, p. 431, fig. 17:4). We may note the use throughout of flat inverse retouch at both point and butt of Gravette and Micro-Gravette points, and, in Levels 5A and 5B, of fan-shaped endscrapers formed by retouch and of points formed by retouch that would be quite at home in an Isturitz Noaillian series. But attribution of these assemblages to cultures depends primarily on the evidence of other sites. In the case of the "Périgordian IV," this appears better represented at the Station des Gachettes (Var), a site that has produced a series of 114 retouched tools (Onoratini 1982, vol. 1, pp. 94–95 and vol. 2, pp. 64–67).[43] For the Noaillian we turn to the Station du Gratadis.

Station du Gratadis (Commune d'Agay, Var)

The site is located on an old terrace between two streams. The occupation horizon is an old surface (*sol de tassement*)

43. Onoratini (ibid., vol. 1, p. 94) also notes the existence of a Noaillian open site 100 m away.

Table 79
INVENTORY OF LEVELS 6D THROUGH 4 OF THE GROTTE NO. 1 DE LA BOUVERIE
(de Sonneville-Bordes/Perrot type list)

Type	Level					
	6D	6B	6A	5B	5A	4
1. Simple End-Scraper	1	1	3	–	3	1
2. Atypical End-Scraper	–	–	2	–	–	1
3. Double End-Scraper	1	2	2	–	–	–
4. Ogival End-Scraper	–	1	1	–	1	–
5. End-Scraper on Retouched Blade	–	3	1	2	1	–
7. Fan-Shaped End-Scraper	–	–	–	1	1	–
8. End-Scraper on Flake	–	–	1	–	–	1
17. End-Scraper + Burin	–	1	3	–	1	–
18. End-Scraper + Truncation	1	–	–	–	–	–
23. Perforator	1	–	–	–	1	–
24. Bec	1	1	–	–	–	–
27. Median Dihedral Burin	–	–	–	2	2	–
28. Asymmetrical Dihedral Burin	–	1	–	–	–	–
29. Lateral Dihedral Burin	–	–	2	1	–	1
31. Multiple Dihedral Burin	–	1	–	–	1	1
30. Break Burin	–	1	3	–	1	–
34. Truncation Burin: Straight	–	–	1	–	–	–
35. Truncation Burin: Oblique	–	–	–	–	1	–
36. Truncation Burin: Concave	–	–	–	1	1	–
40. Multiple Truncation Burin	–	–	1	1	–	–
42. Noailles Burin	–	–	–	1	2	–
41. Mixed Burin	–	–	1	–	2	–
48. Gravette Point	3	2	5	1	1	–
50. Micro-Gravette Point	–	1	12	3	1	4
85. Backed Bladelet	1	2	3	–	5	5
57. Shouldered Piece	–	–	2	1	–	–
65. Retouched Blade: Continuous One Side	–	2	1	–	1	–
66. Retouched Blade: Continuous Both Sides	–	–	1	–	2	–
93. Point Formed by Retouch	–	–	–	1	1	–
74. Notched Piece	–	–	1	1	–	2
75. Denticulate Piece	1	–	–	–	–	–
77. Side-Scraper	–	2	–	–	–	–
Total	10	21	48	18	30	16

Source: Onoratini 1976, pp. 451-452.

Table 80

THE CORE INDUSTRIES FROM THE STATION DU GRATADIS: LEVEL 2 AND SURFACE SERIES

	Level 2 (in situ)		Surface	
Tool Type	n	%	n	%
End-Scrapers	12	7.3	52	22.9
Dihedral Burins	5	3.0	20	8.8
Truncation Burins	121	73.3	56	24.7
Truncated Pieces	3	1.8	5	2.2
Retouched Blades[a]	3	1.8	16	7.0
Backed Tools	21	12.7	78	34.4
N	165	99.9	227	100.0
Noailles Burins	107	64.8	37	16.3
Burins plans	–	–	6	2.6
Points Formed by Retouch	–	–	3	1.3
Total Inventory	186		268	

Source: Onoratini 1982, vol. 1, pp. 98-99.

Note: The great difference between the two series in relative frequencies does not appear to be a matter of differential collection and is not easily explained. Perhaps different parts of the site were sampled.

a. Includes points formed by retouch.

underlying ca. 30 cm of sandy clay (Onoratini 1982, vol. 1, p. 81 and vol. 2, p. 22). Initial surface collections produced 145 tools including 27 Noailles burins (Onoratini and Girard 1976). Subsequent excavations gave 186 tools, of which no less than 107 are Noailles burins (table 80), and increased the surface sample to 268 (Onoratini 1982, vol. 1, pp. 98–99 and vol. 2, pp. 81–97). The Noailles burins are quite typical, and there are also burins with tertiary modification of the burin edge and at least two candidates for Raysse status (ibid., vol. 2, p. 93:2, 7). Fan-shaped end-scrapers and points formed by retouch are also present as are, among the small series of backed pieces, examples with flat inverse, Vachons or Vachons-like, working of the ends. There appears to be no reason to doubt Onoratini's diagnosis of the industry nor of his correlation of it with Levels 5A and B at La Bouverie, at least in general terms. Whether the abundance of Noailles burins here and their near absence at La Bouverie is a function of time or of the location of the Bouverie sample in the dark back of a once larger site, or of some other cause, cannot be determined. A significant feature of the Gratadis series is the presence of types characteristic of both the Pyrenean and Greater Périgord facies of the Aquitanian Noaillian.

Station de la Cabre (Commune d'Agay, Var)

This is another open site, situated similarly to Gratadis from which it is just over two km distant to the southwest. The site, on which I have little information, has given Middle Palaeolithic, Noaillian, and Neolithic materials. The Noaillian series, totalling 73 tools and including 10 Noailles burins, once misattributed to the Magdalenian by Pistat and Vassy in 1920, has been restudied by Onoratini (1982, vol. 1, p. 101).

Station du Maltemps (Var)

Onoratini (1982, vol. 1, p. 102) makes brief mention of this open site, located about 4 km WSW of Gratadis and again on an old terrace. Four characteristic Noailles burins, 48 flakes, and a blade were recovered from a bulldozer cut.

Discussion

Recent work in the Department of Var has demonstrated the presence of a flourishing Noaillian facies that appears to represent a stage in an ongoing cultural development that begins with a Provençal Périgordian and continues through Arenian and Bouverian stages to the end of the Pleistocene. The new finds are of the greatest importance for understanding the Noaillian of other areas, and their dating within the last glacial sequence is critical.

If Correlation 1 between the Abri Pataud and La Bouverie

is accepted, and if we also accept Onoratini's attributions of the Bouverie: 5A and 5B, Gratadis, and Cabre collections to the same Noaillian facies, then the Noaillian of the Greater Périgord must be earlier. If this is the case, then the similarities between the Provençal facies and those of Aquitaine are to be explained in terms of diffusion, quite possibly both from the Périgord and the Pyrénées, and a Noaillian ancestor must be sought elsewhere. If, on the other hand, Correlation 2 is correct or approximately correct, then we may see the Provençal Noaillian facies developing *in situ* from a culture analogous to but typologically quite distinct from the classic Périgordian IV or its "Bayacian" ancestor. The Provençal Noaillian comes to possess forms that, following a westward migration, were to be elaborated differentially by Pyrenean and Greater Périgord Noaillians. I believe this to be the most economic hypothesis, especially since, as we shall see in the next section, there exists in Campania in southern Italy another Noaillian facies that is, according to radiocarbon dates, contemporary with the Noaillian of the Greater Périgord. Migration or diffusion from an area central to the known Noaillian distribution rather than from the fringes is more likely on general grounds, gives the best fit with the typological evidence, and cannot be shown to conflict with the chrono-stratigraphic record as this is presently known.

ITALY

Recent excavations at the Grotta della Cala near Salerno raise to seven the number of Italian sites from which Noailles burins have been reported. The Grotta della Cala assemblages are also the only ones of any size to have been fully described (Palma di Cesnola 1971). Laplace (1964b) has published inventories for six other assemblages, but without discussion of their typology. I had the opportunity to inspect parts of the materials from two of these sites in 1964. They and the Grotta della Cala series are briefly described below, the evidence from the remaining sites, including the Grotte des Enfants, is summarized, and I conclude with a general discussion of the Italian evidence.

Riparo Mochi (Grimaldi, Liguria)

The Riparo Mochi is situated in the "Balzi Rossi," red rocks of Cretaceous limestone just above the shore of the Mediterranean, directly beneath the village of Grimaldi, and a few hundred meters from the Franco-Italian frontier. At the start of the excavations the ground surface was 27.21 m above sea level. Work at the site was begun by Professor A. Mochi and A. C. Blanc just before World War II and was continued after the war by Blanc and L. Cardini, who took over the excavations after Blanc's death in 1961. The site is to be published by Cardini and Laplace, the latter being responsible for the typological analyses of the materials.

The shelter has no overhang remaining. The following description of the stratigraphy is based upon the excavation of 1949. A. C. Blanc (1938) also describes the levels.

Level	Description
A (60 cm)	"Epi-Périgordian" (now considered a facies of the Romanellian), characterized by microlithic triangles.
B (40 cm)	Earthy matrix, with fewer stones than in the underlying levels. Some cementation and stalagmitic concretions. Virtually sterile.
C (60 cm)	Scattered occupation materials in a deposit similar to that of B but with more stone inclusions. "Upper Aurignacian" (Laplace's Final Typical Périgordian or Gravettian).
D (1.8 m)	Deposit similar to the overlying levels but lacking concretions and with a higher percentage of limestone fragments of maximum diameter greater than 10 mm. There are some definite charcoal or ash-stained lenses within the body of the deposit. "Upper Périgordian" (Laplace's Typical Périgordian or Gravettian).
E (25 cm)	In this and the underlying levels (F, G), more than half the deposit is made up of limestone fragments. Virtually sterile.
F to I (ca. 6 m)	Succession of levels containing Aurignacian, "Lower Périgordian," and Mousterian industries.
–	Bedrock not reached.

The fauna is rare and nondiagnostic (Piero Cassoli, personal communication).

Three major phases are represented in the sedimentary sequence. The Mousterian occupation of Level I is likely to have taken place in a period of variable but relatively mild conditions, although more rigorous than those of the present; this may be tentatively correlated with a part of the Stillfried A complex (Würm I and II in French terms). The increased percentages of cryoclastic debris in Levels H to E are likely then to represent all or part of the Würm III stadial, with Level D coming at the end of this period. Palynological evidence (Renault-Miskovsky 1972, pp. 184–86; Leroi-Gourhan and Renault-Miskovsky 1977) shows a marked amelioration contemporary with the "Typical Aurignacian" and this is correlated with the Arcy Interstadial. Palynological evidence is lacking for the upper strata, however Level D precedes an interval of more temperate conditions, indicated by a decrease in frequency of limestone fragments and a possible increase in humidity in Levels C and B. The Romanellian occupation may be much later.

Thus, although precise relative dating is out of the question on the basis of present evidence, Level D with its Noailles burins may be broadly contemporary with Noaillian manifestations in Provence and Aquitaine and is placed in the Tursac Oscillation by Onoratini (1976, p. 450).

The thick Level D was excavated by a combination of arbitrary units and hearth levels. In making his inventories, Laplace (1964b, table II) divides the materials into three series: Level D: LOWER, MIDDLE, and UPPER (table 81).[44]

When Professor Cardini and Baroness Blanc kindly allowed me to inspect the collection at the Instituto di Paleontologia Umana (Rome) in 1964, the artifacts had not been unpacked or sorted by types or levels. The following impression of the Level D assemblage may therefore require substantial revision in the light of future publications.

The Level D assemblage is made on somewhat irregular blades with complicated dorsal ridge patterns. The end-scrapers are small, the median length being estimated at about 3 to 4 cm. Arc contours are rare, irregular contours very common. There are some rounded arc contours and others with a slight tendency toward shouldering or toward the blunt-point type. Marginal retouch is present on a significant proportion of end-scrapers. There are also a number of miscellaneous carinate forms and a few flake scrapers.

The backed tools fall into two groups: backed and, in Laplace's terminology, "marginally backed." The latter group consists of Dufour or Dufour-like bladelets with very light backing that grades into steep, fine marginal retouch. Obverse backing is by far the most common form, although inversely worked pieces are also present. The backed points range in size from very small pieces similar to the Dufour bladelets, 2–3 cm in length, to a few much larger examples, one of which must have measured at least 8 cm in its unbroken state. Several are in the 5–7 cm range, the majority probably being less than 5 cm long. Backing on these pieces is heavier and bidirectional backing is common. A few pieces have retouch at the butt, either obverse or inverse, tending to truncate the butt obliquely. Flat retouch at either butt or point is also present. There is one example of Vachons-style butt treatment on a piece measuring 6.5 cm in

length. Without detailed analysis of the series, it is difficult to relate it to backed tools from either the French Périgordian or Noaillian assemblages. In size, the backed tools are comparable to a Périgordian VI Gravette point series, but they differ in the much lighter backing applied to them. The Dufour bladelets in particular have no parallels in Périgordian IV or VI assemblages. Size also serves to differentiate the series from Périgordian IV samples, as does the absence of many of the typical butt treatments. In general, the association of Dufour bladelets and true backed bladelets demonstrates that the series is quite different from any known Périgordian assemblage from France.

The dihedral burins are mostly small and irregular, with a high proportion of angulated and curved edges. Dihedral burin-points are absent, but in other respects the series is, on inspection, quite similar to the Abri Pataud: Early Noaillian samples. The same is true of the Noailles burins, which in size, shape, and technique are indistinguishable from Early Noaillian series of the Périgord. Other truncation burins, many of which resemble Noaillian burins in their overall morphology, are approximately as frequent as Noailles burins within the sample. Tertiary modification of the burin edge is present on a small proportion of pieces, and there is one Raysse burin. Truncated pieces are rare, showing no specially marked characteristics.

In general terms, there appears to be considerable stylistic similarity between the Riparo Mochi: D and the Var Noaillian materials. Many of the same forms are present, including the Dufour-like bladelets, but a detailed attributal comparison of the actual series and not merely of illustrations is required before typological relationships can be established with any certainty. The quantitative evidence will be considered below.

Grotte des Enfants (Commune de Grimaldi, Liguria)

The Grotte des Enfants is located only a short distance from Riparo Mochi in the same line of cliffs, the Balzi Rossi, and just on the Italian side of the frontier. Excavations at the site began in 1858, but the site is best known from the work of Villeneuve and his colleagues (1906–1919). Onoratini and da Silva (1978) have restudied the materials from the upper *foyers* (G through C), which they regard as reasonably uncontaminated though biased toward larger tools by poor collection techniques. *Foyer* H, which, according to Onoratini and da Silva, contained a Mediterranean Périgordian IV assemblage, is unfortunately among the mixed series. *Foyer* G is attributed by them to the Noaillian and overlying horizons to the Early Arenian and Bouverian. Thus Onoratini sees the same cultural sequence here as in the Var. The copious illustrations bear him out, the Noaillian materials showing a very similar range of types that include Noailles burins, Raysse or Raysse-like burins, shouldered pieces among the relatively few backed blades, end-scrapers

---

44. Core industry statistics as presented below for Italian series are not exactly comparable to those of French series. Laplace (1964a) and his followers enumerate all tools whether they form part of mixed, triple, or quadruple burins, or combination tools. The frequencies of burins and end-scrapers thus appear higher than they would if the series had been inventoried according to the de Sonneville-Bordes/Perrot list. The extent of the distortion can be roughly assessed, since Palma di Cesnola (1971) provides sufficiently detailed data for the Grotta della Cala assemblages to be enumerated in either manner. In comparison to French series, figures for end-scrapers are overestimated by 1–2%, dihedral burins by 1–2%, truncation burins by up to 6%, but more usually by about 3%, and truncated pieces by less than 1%. In contrast, retouched blades are underestimated by 2–3% and backed tools by up to 6%, but generally by 2–3%.

Table 81
CORE INDUSTRIES OF THE RIPARO MOCHI: LEVEL D SERIES

Tool Type	LOWER		MIDDLE		UPPER	
	n	%	n	%	n	%
End-Scrapers	41	14.7	44	17.5	58	15.8
Dihedral Burins	26	9.4	26	10.4	32	8.7
Truncation Burins	20	7.2	44	17.5	63	17.1
Truncated Pieces	2	0.7	6	2.4	10	2.7
Retouched Blades	32	11.5	34	13.5	59	16.0
Backed Tools	157	56.5	97	38.7	146	39.7
N	178	100.0	251	100.0	368	100.0
Truncation Burins with Stop-Notch	7	2.5	15	5.1	30	8.2

Source: Recalculated from Laplace 1964b.

Note: The frequency of "truncation burins with stop-notch" (Laplace's type B9) greatly underestimates the number of Noailles burins.

on retouched blades (among which are fan-shaped examples), and points formed by retouch. The quantitative evidence is, given the sampling techniques, of very dubious value (table 82) and shows no similarity to the Riparo Mochi: D statistics. Nevertheless, in view of the obvious qualitative parallels, I believe it quite likely that the series are related, perhaps very closely. Pending a full-scale comparison of the Var, Grotte des Enfants, and Mochi materials, I would accept the implications of Onoratini's research, that the Var and the Franco-Italian border area are—during the latter part of the last glacial—part of the same culture region, within which a relatively uniform cultural development took place (see Onoratini 1982, vol. 1, pp. 198–206).

Grotta della Cala (Marina di Camerota, near Salerno, Campania)

The Grotta della Cala lies a few meters from the beach on the southwest side of a limestone hill, known locally as Il Poggio. The Grotta del Poggio and the Poggio shelter, both of which have given rich Mousterian materials, lie respectively 90 and 60 meters west. The cave consists of an outer and an inner chamber separated by a narrow bottleneck. It measures about 30 m deep and is 12 m wide at the mouth, its widest point. The surface of the deposits is at 9 m above sea-level but was originally higher, as can be seen from breccia adhering to the cave wall. Excavations, beginning with tests in 1966 and 1967 and subsequently continued on a larger scale, have been conducted only in the outer chamber (Palma di Cesnola 1971). The stratigraphy is described as follows:

Level	Description
A–L (95–135 cm)	Historic period, Bronze Age, and Epi-Gravettian levels.
M (20–50 cm)	Reddish-brown, loamy-sandy (limoso-sabbioso) deposit with some cementation and less compacted lenses with bone fragments. Evolved Epi-Gravettian.
N–P (0.30 cm)	Firmly cemented brown-gray level with thin, localized brownish lenses. Evolved Epi-Gravettian.
Q (40–70 cm)	Unconsolidated mass of archaeological remains with a little dark brown, sandy-loamy matrix. Gravettian.
β (15 cm)	Stalagmite with an intercalated lens of dark brown soil (βI–III). Gravettian.
R–T (1.0–1.10 m)	Mousterian horizons with intercalated beds of stalagmite.
U (?)	Firmly cemented marine conglomerate.

The Grotta della Cala has provided the only absolute dates for Italian assemblages with Noailles burins. Three radiocarbon dates were run by the Florence laboratory on burnt bone samples from Level Q, which was excavated in six arbitrary subdivisions numbered I to VI from top to bottom.

Table 82
THE CORE INDUSTRY
OF THE GROTTE DES ENFANTS: *FOYER* G

Grotte des Enfants:
Foyer G

Tool Type	n	%
End-Scrapers	59	33.1
Dihedral Burins	26	14.6
Truncation Burins	30	16.9
Truncated Pieces	18	10.1
Retouched Blades[a]	25	14.0
Backed Tools	20	11.2
N	178	99.9
Noailles Burins	5	2.8
Flat-Faced TB	present	
Points Formed by Retouch	14	7.9

Source: Onoratini and da Silva 1978.

a. Includes points formed by retouch.

The dates are as follows:

Q I–III	25,300 ± 2,400 B.P.	(F 5/6/7)
Q IV	25,800 ± 2,500 B.P.	(F 8)
Q V–VI	27,000 ± 1,700 B.P.	(F 9/10/11)

According to Palma di Cesnola (1976, p. 82), "Une élaboration des mêmes données au point de vue statistique (C. M. Azzi et al. 1973) aurait reculé ces dates en les portant à 28,000–27,000 B.P. environ, avec une marge d'erreur en plus ou en moins également forte." In spite of their large standard deviations, the dates are internally consistent and cover the period suggested for the main Noaillian occupation (Level 4) at the Abri Pataud. Provisionally at least the Level Q materials must be accepted as contemporary with Noaillian manifestations in France.

Among the fauna of Levels βI–III to N are *Bos*, *Cervus*, *Capreolus*, *Capra ibex*, and *Sus scrofa*. Neither in βI–III nor in Q is there evidence of exploitation of marine resources or of terrestrial mollusca.

The assemblages of Levels βI–II and Q are the only ones as yet described. The relationship of the small series from βI–II to the materials from the overlying levels is unclear (table 83).

Palma di Cesnola describes the typology of Level Q globally and then shows how quantitative trends and differentiation within the six arbitrary subdivisions of the horizon argue for its apportionment into two archaeological units: Qa, equivalent to subdivisions QI through QIII; and Qb, equivalent to QIV through QVI. It is not easy to determine how this division is reflected in artifact morphology, especially as de Cesnola is using Laplace's (1964a) classification, which does not correspond either to that of de Sonneville-Bordes or to my own. As at the Riparo Mochi, the technique of blank production is poor; a large proportion of pieces is made on small flakes, and the blades tend to be irregular with complex dorsal ridge patterns.

The end-scrapers (Qb = 8.7%, Qa = 18.2%) include significant numbers of pieces classed as nosed and carinate scrapers, though few approximate the thick, chunky types typical of the Aurignacian. Well-made pieces on long blades are rare and the modal end-scraper is made on a flake between 6 and 3 cm in length. End-scrapers on retouched blades or flakes are common; among them are found fan-shaped and pointed pieces identical to examples from the Noaillian levels of Isturitz (e.g., Palma di Cesnola 1971, p. 281, fig. 6:1, 3, 6). There are also 39 points, including

Table 83
THE CORE INDUSTRIES OF THE GROTTA DELLA CALA: LEVELS βI–II AND Q

Tool Type	βI–II n	Qb n	%	Qa n	%
End-Scrapers	4	101	8.7	94	18.2
Dihedral Burins	7	160	13.8	51	9.9
Truncation Burins	2	473	40.6	134	26.0
Truncated Pieces	3	49	4.2	29	5.6
Retouched Blades	11	149	12.8	124	24.0
Backed Tools	16	231	19.9	84	16.3
N	43	1163	100.0	516	100.0

Source: Recalculated from Palma di Cesnola 1971.

specimens of the Mousterioid (ibid., p. 296, fig. 11:2) and foliate forms characteristic of the Noaillian of the French Pyrénées.

Burins dominate the Qb series (54.4%) but are rather less important in Qa (35.9%). Truncation burins are almost three times as frequent as dihedrals in both units. There are also dihedral burins with stop-notches. Among the truncation burins the ratio of flakes to blades is 7:4, and of 550 truncation burins (excluding transverse examples and the unique piece with a stop-notch) only five are longer than 6 cm; 247 are between 6 and 3 cm; and 298 are less than 3 cm long. Judging from the illustrations they are—in their range of forms, as in size—very similar to burins from Early Noaillian assemblages in France. Besides the one Noailles burin with a stop-notch from the main excavation, there are others from test soundings (ibid., p. 276, fig. 4:1, 2, 4). Many of the small truncation burins without stop-notches could, and in a French assemblage would, be classed as Noailles (ibid., p. 273, fig. 3:7, 9, 10; p. 276, fig. 4:5–10). Others would be quite at home in the same cultural context (ibid., p. 273, fig. 3:3–6; p. 278, fig. 5:1–8). One piece (ibid., p. 273, fig. 3:2) might be a Raysse burin.

The truncated pieces generally resemble the truncation burins in size and morphology. Retouched blades are usually characterized by invasive (*profondo*) retouch, but the classification employed does not distinguish between scaled and other types of invasive or heavy retouch.

While the end-scrapers, points, and truncation burins prove a cultural linkage between the assemblages of Level Q and Early Noaillian series from France, the backed tools are testimony to the extent of the differentiation of the industries of the two areas. Of 158 points, all but nine are less than 3 cm long. Backing is indifferently uni- or bidirectional, and 27 points are partially backed or shouldered. Tips, butts, and the edge opposite the backing often show obverse or inverse retouch. There are 30 pieces on which the retouch is more invasive and flatter, "fino al invadere qualche volta l'intera superficie disponibile dell'estremità apicale o, contemporaneamente, di quella apicale e basale (vedi punta des Vachons)" (ibid., p. 290–291). None of these pieces is illustrated, but, given the size of the points, it is unlikely that they resemble Vachons-style Gravette points very closely. In addition to the backed points, there are seven backed bladelets and 12 shouldered pieces, all less than 3 cm long, and four pieces—three being fragments—which are both backed and truncated. Although the Dufour type of Riparo Mochi seems to be absent, the backed tool component of Level Q is equally difficult to relate to any Aquitanian Upper Périgordian phase. The relationship if any is distant and generalized.

Other Sites

Noailles burins are known from three additional sites in Tuscany and from two in Latium. A typical notched example is present in a small series of about 30 retouched tools from

the Grotta del Golino, Talamone, a cave in a rocky promontory on the Mediterranean coast 135 km northwest of Rome (Graziosi 1928). The open-air site of Laterina, near the village of the same name in the Arno Valley, 30 km southeast of Florence, produced a larger series that has been inventoried by Laplace (1964b, table 2). The Noailles burins are typical, but I am unable to comment on the backed tools since a part of the assemblage, stored at the Instituto di Paleontologia of Florence University, had been mislaid at the time of my visit. Quantitative features of the assemblage will be discussed below. Noailles burins and other "Upper Périgordian" types were also recovered from Massacuiccoli in the Versilian marshes southwest of Viareggio (A. C. Blanc 1937). In Latium a Noailles burin is reported from the "Upper Périgordian" level of Riparo Blanc, at Monte Circeo, south of Rome (Cardini and Taschini 1958–1961), and at least one other from Levels 7–8 at the unpublished site of Palidoro, Rome. Laplace (1964b, table IV) has counted the Palidoro series and classified them as Evolved Tardigravettian. This attribution, at least as regards Levels 6 and 7–8, is disputed by Palma di Cesnola (1971, p. 318n). Their core industries are set out together with that of Laterina in table 84.

Discussion

Exegesis of the Italian materials would require greater knowledge of the Upper Palaeolithic of the area than I command.[45] I will consider below only their relevance to an understanding of the French Noaillian.

The three dates from the Grotta della Cala, Level Q, are evidence of the contemporaneity of that Level with the Early and Late, though not necessarily the "Terminal," phases of the Noaillian of the Greater Périgord. The extreme rarity of Raysse burins in Italy strongly suggests that there were no direct relationships between Italy and the Greater Périgord after the Early phase and it seems probable that this conclusion can be extended to cover all Aquitaine.

The Italian materials taken as a whole differ quantitatively from the French in the much higher frequencies of backed tools, larger proportions of retouched blades, and correspondingly lower—in some cases much lower—proportions of truncation burins. Most similar to the French Noaillian is the earlier (Qb) series from the Grotta della Cala, not, as might have been expected, one of the three from the Riparo Mochi. Differentiation within the Italian group of assemblages is very marked. The series from the lower part of Riparo Mochi, Level D, has many more backed tools and fewer truncation burins than any other. The proportion of truncation burins increases in the middle subdivision, which differs little from the upper except in the latter's higher proportion of truncation burins with stop-notch. This trend may be continued in the quantitatively similar Laterina se-

---

45. The reader is referred to Palma di Cesnola's (1976) survey of the Italian Upper Palaeolithic for an up-to-date summary.

Table 84

THE CORE INDUSTRIES OF LATERINA AND PALIDORO: LEVELS 8-7 AND 6

| | Laterina | | Palidoro | | | |
| | | | Level 8-7 | | Level 6 | |
	n	%	n	%	n	%
End-Scrapers	17	12.4	30	24.0	30	24.8
Dihedral Burins	6	4.4	11	8.8	15	12.4
Truncation Burins	19	14.9	26	20.8	25	20.7
Truncated Pieces	10	7.3	6	4.8	4	3.3
Retouched Blades	24	17.5	33	26.4	33	27.2
Backed Tools	61	44.5	19	15.2	14	11.6
N	137	100.0	125	100.0	121	100.0
Truncation Burins with Stop-Notch	17	12.4	1	0.8	0	0.0

Source: Recalculated from Laplace 1964b.

ries. (It should be noted that while the proportion of truncation burins with stop-notch increases from bottom to top of Level D, their frequency relative to other truncation burins changes much less.) The Grotta della Cala: Qb series is distinguished from those of the Riparo Mochi by having relatively many more truncation burins and many fewer backed tools. Retouched blades increase at the expense of truncation burins in the Qa series, which, in its turn, most resembles those of Palidoro, Levels 8–7 and 6. There is a suggestion here of chronological ordering within the northern (Ligurian and Tuscan) sites and within those from Latium and Campania, but the two groups cannot be situated in time relative to each other.

We may conclude by saying that the Italian assemblages with Noailles burins also resemble the Early Noaillian of Aquitaine in other members of the truncation burin class, in the technology of blank production, and in the end-scrapers. There are detailed parallels to the Pyrenean facies in the presence of fan-shaped end-scrapers on retouched blades and of Mousterioid and foliate points. These similarities are at the same time too precise and too varied to be attributable

to a limited process of diffusion, although the presence of backed points with invasive retouch on the ventral surface of the butt both in Italy and in Provence does lead to the question whether Vachons-style treatment of Gravettes diffused from Périgordians to Noaillians (or vice versa) or was independently developed by both. The quantitative importance of backed blades in the Italian Noaillian, while it cannot be attributed to specific connections with the Aquitanian Upper Périgordian, renders it unlikely that a migration, whether from east to west or west to east, can explain the relationships between the Noaillian industries of Italy and Aquitaine. Therefore, pending fuller understanding of the Italian Upper Palaeolithic sequence, the assemblages that have given Noailles burins in peninsular Italy are best attributed provisionally to an *areal* variant of the Noaillian tradition, derived with that of Aquitaine from a common ancestor. Recent work in the French Department of Var has resulted, as discussed above, in the discovery of a good candidate for ancestral status in the form of a Noaillian facies that may extend as far as the Franco-Italian border area.

XVI

Reports from Other Areas

EASTERN FRANCE

Five truncation burins from the Upper Périgordian D-1 horizon at the rock shelter of La Colombière, Poncin (Ain), are described as "of reduced dimensions tending toward the Noailles type" (Movius and Judson 1956, p.106). Movius makes it clear that these are not typical examples, and they lack specific Noailles characteristics. The relationships of the D-1 horizon to the Périgordian of Aquitaine is not fully understood, but there appears to be no reason to connect it with the Noaillian development proper.

BELGIUM

J. Verheyleweghen (1956, cited in Tixier 1958, p. 642) has reported the presence of Noailles burins from two sites at Lommel in the province of Limbourg. Reference to the report of Hamil-Nandrin, Servais, and Louis (1935) on these sites does not support this attribution. Noailles burins are not mentioned in the text and are not illustrated. The assemblages are clearly Epipalaeolithic. Any resemblance of the truncation burins to Noailles burins is the coincidental product of convergence.

Convergence may also be invoked in the case of a few tools, including a piece misclassified as a sagaie d'Isturitz, from the sites of Engis, Trou Magrite, and Goyet that are claimed by Otte (1977, p. 266 and fig. 11:13–17) as traces of the Périgordian Vc.

ENGLAND

Garrod (1926, fig. 35:10) reported a Noailles burin from the site of Mother Grundy's Parlour, Creswell Crags, Derbyshire. The piece is a small truncation burin without special Noailles characteristics and forms part of an Epipalaeolithic Creswellian assemblage.

CZECHOSLOVAKIA

Noailles burins were reported from Czechoslovakia by the Abbé Breuil (1924, p. 582 and fig. 10:16–20). During a museum tour of the C.S.S.R. in 1965, the present writer studied a large number of Upper Palaeolithic assemblages but found no trace of these tools. Neither did the Czechoslovakian workers know of any Noailles burins or any other Noaillian tool types from their so-called Eastern Gravettian (Pavlovian) or other Upper Palaeolithic industries. The tools illustrated by Breuil are again small truncation burins, lacking specific Noailles characters.

In summary, the distribution of the Noaillian appears to be limited to those areas already treated, though this is not to deny the possibility of more distant, indirect contacts as are, for example, suggested by the presence of Venus figurines in Central Europe and farther to the east.

XVII

The Noaillian Tradition:
Time-Space Systematics and Reflections on Method

The participation of the Noaillian in the Upper Périgordian tradition of Aquitaine can no longer be maintained. Its distinctiveness has been conclusively demonstrated at the Abri Pataud, Isturitz, and several other sites, including a large majority of those excavated by modern techniques that have been comprehensively published. Attributal and quantitative analyses combine to show that the Noaillian industry expresses technologically, functionally, and stylistically peculiar but, in any one region, coherent characteristics. No evidence has been adduced by others or appears from the data available to support the alternative view, that the differentiation of assemblages characterized by high frequencies of Noailles or Raysse burins is the product of activity-related specialization within the Upper Périgordian. This hypothesis, based it would seem entirely on data from the Greater Périgord, also flies in the face of the evidence from other regional and areal facies of the Noaillian in the Pyrenean foothills, Arcy-sur-Cure, Provence, and Italy (fig. 68). On the other hand, this same "cultural trifurcation" theory of the Périgordian V finds support in the currently received view of the place, or rather places, of the Noaillian within the Last Glacial sequence (Laville et al. 1980). If, as they suggest, the (Early) Noaillian of La Ferrassie is contemporary with the Périgordian VI of Laugerie-Haute and the (Late) Noaillian increment of Flageolet 1:4, and if all these levels postdate the Late Noaillian of the Abri Pataud, then the reconstruction proposed in this monograph is nonsense. I have attempted in the preceding chapters to show that this is not the case and that Laville's interpretation of the evidence can be revised and levels recorrelated to show the development of the Périgordian IV in the Les Eyzies Oscillation, the appearance of assemblages characterized by Font-Robert points and *éléments tronqués* shortly after, and the intrusion of the Noaillian in the latter part of the succeeding cold phase, continuing into the Tursac Oscillation (fig. 1). Although much more can and no doubt will be said on this question, the tests of my hypothesis of Noaillian independence proposed in chapter IX have been run and have failed to result in its rejection. Furthermore, evidence from other regions and areas—whether palaeoenvironmental, as in southern Aquitaine and Provence, or based on

isotopic dating as at the Grotta della Cala—appears to confirm the approximate contemporaneity of the appearance of the early Noaillian throughout its broad area of distribution. However unsatisfactory it may be to base an interpretation of the cultural sequence upon the internal evidence of typology rather than upon some exterior form of dating, I submit that a classification based upon descriptive attribute analysis of series that embody a high stylistic information content, provides, in conjunction with intrasite stratigraphy, a less imprecise means of correlating assemblages and deposits than current sedimentological or other palaeoenvironmental studies. This is true perhaps only for the area and period under consideration. No doubt the pendulum will swing back, as it did decades ago in the case of the Lower and Middle Palaeolithic of Northern France. Why it should be so today is beyond the scope of the present discussion.

The absolute dating of the Noaillian is far from certain. The Abri Pataud date of 27,060 ± 370 B.P. (GrN-4280) for the MIDDLE-1 subdivision fits reasonably well with dates for the underlying Périgordian IV: 26,600 ± 260 B.P. (GrN-4477), 27,660 ± 260 B.P. (GrN-4662), and 28,150 ± 225 B.P. (GrN-4634), and for the overlying Périgordian VI: 22,780 ± 140 B.P. (GrN-4506) and 23,010 ± 170 B.P. (GrN-4721). Dates processed earlier from the same horizons are younger, i.e., Périgordian IV: 23,600 ± 800 B.P. (W-151) and 24,000 ± 1,000 B.P. (W-191); Périgordian VI: 18,470 ± 280 B.P. (GrN-1864) and 21,540 ± 160 B.P. (GrN-1982). Coincidentally, these dates are in fair agreement with other Noaillian dates from Facteur, Laraux, and Saint-Jean-de-Verges, and a series for the Font-Robert horizons at La Ferrassie. But the agreement is indeed—unless some systematic error is involved—coincidental. The older series of GrN dates is to be preferred (Waterbolk 1971, p. 29), and, taking it as a standard frame of reference, the Noaillian of the Abri Pataud should center around 27,000 B.P. Its duration is largely a matter of guesswork, but a best estimate might be 27,500 for the initial occupation of Level 4: LOWER and 26,250 for the deposition of the Terminal Noaillian increment of Level 4a. All three dates from the Grotta della Cala fall within this range at one standard deviation, although we are far from being able to

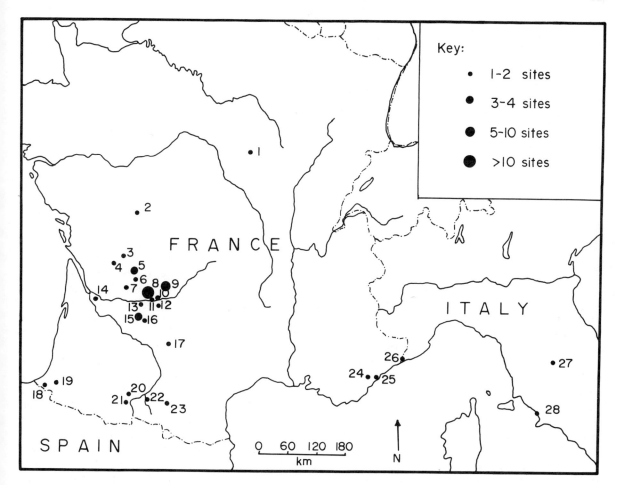

Figure 68. MAP SHOWING THE DISTRIBUTION OF VICINITIES/SITES IN FRANCE AND
NORTHERN ITALY THAT HAVE GIVEN NOAILLIAN MATERIALS. Key: 1, Arcy-sur-Cure
vicinity, Yonne; 2, Laraux, Vienne; 3, Vilhonneur vicinity, Charente; 4,
Les Vachons, Charente; 5, Brantôme vicinity, Dordogne; 6, Périgueux
vicinity, Dordogne; 7, Solvieux, Dordogne; 8, Les Eyzies vicinity, Dordogne; 9, Brive-la-Gaillarde vicinity, Corrèze; 10, Cantelouve, Dordogne;
11, Flageolet 1, Dordogne; 12, Roc de Combe and Pechialet, Lot; 13, Combe-
Capelle and Termo-Pialat, Dordogne; 14, Lespaux, Gironde; 15, Gavaudun
vicinity, Lot-et-Garonne; 16, Roc de Cavart, Lot-et-Garonne; 17, Bruniquel
vicinity, Tarn-et-Garonne; 18, Sare, Basses-Pyrénées; 19, Isturitz, Basses-
Pyrénées; 20, Lespugue, Haute-Garonne; 21, Gargas, Hautes-Pyrénées; 22,
Cassagne vicinity, Haute-Garonne; 23, Saint-Jean-de-Verges, La Carane 3
and Le Portel, Ariège; 24, La Bouverie, Var; 25, Le Gratadis, La Cabre,
and Maltemps, Var; 26, Grotte des Enfants, Liguria (Italy), and
Riparo Mochi, Liguria (Italy); 27, Laterina, Toscana (Italy); 28, Talamone,
Toscana (Italy).

determine the duration of the various, probably regional, facies of the Noaillian in Italy. In Provence, the tradition seems to develop from a somewhat earlier "Périgordian IV" *sensu lato* and to continue, perhaps influenced by events elsewhere, through a series of cultural stages that persist to the end of the Pleistocene. In the Basque provinces of France and Spain, at Isturitz and at sites studied by McCollough, the Noaillian carries on as a recognizable cultural entity through the Tursac Oscillation and at least into Solutrean times, though it may have contributed to the heritage of even later cultures. At Arcy-sur-Cure a specialized Late Noaillian facies may also persist later than that of the Périgord.

We see, then, the Noaillian developing in eastern Provence and spreading at about the same time east into Italy and west to Aquitaine. The incursion into the latter area is likely to have come in two or more thrusts through the Carcassonne gap, whence Noaillian groups would have fanned out, some along the northern Pyrenean foothills, a region at that time sparsely inhabited or uninhabited, others northwest to the Mesozoic plateau and plain. In this region, arguably the richest in game and other resources, the Noaillians must have found themselves in contact, if not quite necessarily in competition, with Upper Périgordians and possibly also, if the Aurignacian IV of La Ferrassie is contemporary with the Périgordian IV of the Abri Pataud, with remnant Aurignacian groups about to become the losers in their millennial strife (Bricker 1978). It is this circumstance that renders the Greater Périgord sequence the most complex and interesting.

Leaving the vexed question of the epi-Aurignacian aside, I propose the following paradigm for the Upper Périgordian/Noaillian sequence in the Mesozoic plateau and plain (table 85):

Noaillian immigration occurred here after the appearance of Font-Robert points and after *éléments tronqués* had become a quantitatively significant part of the Upper Périgordian tradition. It also overlaps with a Périgordian phase characterized by the presence in significant numbers of Vachons-style Gravette points. Within the Greater Périgord facies, Noaillian assemblage typology and composition varies, at least in the Early and Late phases, primarily as a function of time rather than of synchronic cultural or activity-related differences. A period of stability (exaggerated perhaps by the effects of natural and cultural formation processes) is followed by an apparently, though not quite certainly, sudden change in technology and in typology. In the Late phase, Raysse burins begin to be manufactured in quantity, largely replacing the eponymous Noailles burin, which becomes steadily less distinct as a type. Other tools display less marked but nonetheless definite changes at this time. Once the transformation is achieved, the Noaillian enters a second phase of typological stability. Although the stratigraphic evidence of the Abri Pataud might admit an interval between the phases, no assemblage satisfactorily fills the putative gap in the developmental sequence. The

change, even if it appears exaggeratedly brusque at the Pataud, must have occurred over a relatively short time span and for no immediately obvious reason. The Terminal phase is much less well known, but there are strong suggestions of Périgordian influence.

It is usually possible to attribute assemblages from the Greater Périgord to one or another Noaillian phase, but, in the absence of intrasite stratigraphy, finer relative dating is not normally possible. The weak expression of directional trends, whether qualitative or quantitative, is one contributory factor. Different series may also represent widely differing durations and intensities of occupation. Suggestions of relative intraphase dating are sometimes forthcoming from sites where occupations have been finely subdivided or are likely to have been brief.

Although the pre-Terminal Noaillians relied mainly on armatures of organic materials, backed tools occur in percentages generally not exceeding 6% of the core industry in all assemblages (excepting Plateau Baillart, where they are lacking). Especially in view of their presence in Provence and in the Italian areal variant, there is reason to believe that a knowledge of backed tool manufacture formed part, although in Aquitaine an unimportant part, of Noaillian technology. For various reasons Périgordian artifacts, including stylistically characteristic backed tools, are found in Noaillian series. One or two examples of such types could have come to be associated in any number of ways and where larger numbers are in question their presence is often due to mixture of levels by natural causes or careless excavation (or excavation techniques conditioned by the belief that the Noaillian formed part of the Périgordian tradition). In at least one case, at the Abri Pataud, the Noaillians themselves dug down into Périgordian IV deposits and by so doing incorporated earlier tools into their own debris. In view of the quantities of evidence from the Abri Pataud that Upper Palaeolithic peoples were accustomed to modify their camp sites in various ways, it is remarkable how few such instances have been recorded from other sites. There are, however, a limited number of sites at which controls are good enough for such agencies to be, if not entirely discounted, at least discredited. In these, cultural factors may be invoked to account for the associations. Further consideration of this question is best postponed to the final chapter where we introduce a hitherto missing element: information on developments within the Périgordian tradition and their reaction to Noaillian intrusion. For the moment we will turn instead to emphasize the contrast between the nature of Noaillian typological development and change farther to the south.

Noaillian development in the Pyrénées has been directly studied only at Isturitz and, by McCollough, at Bolinkoba. The sequence here differs quite markedly from that of the Greater Périgord. Moving into the region from the east, the Noaillians may have found relict groups of Aurignacians or a country empty of human life. The Périgordian presence suggested by the Gargas materials does not imply permanent

Table 85

PARADIGM PROPOSED FOR THE UPPER PERIGORDIAN/NOAILLIAN
SEQUENCE OF THE MESOZOIC PLATEAU AND PLAIN

| Perigordian | | | Noaillian | |
Crucial Assemblages	Phase	Phase	Crucial Assemblages	
Pataud: 3; Laugerie-Haute: B	VI	-	-	
Flageolet 1:III; Roc de Combe: 1	?	Terminal	Les Jambes: 2 and 3	
Vachons 1 and 2:4	"Vc"	Late	Pataud: 4: UPPER and MIDDLE-1; Raysse: 4; Bassaler-Nord: 4	
Vachons 1 and 2:3; Ferrassie: J, K (Peyrony), D2-E4 (Delporte); Laraux: 5	Va+b	Early	Pataud: 4: MIDDLE-2 and LOWER; Facteur: 10-11; Gavaudun: 2	
Pataud: 5; Gravette: Jaune, Noire, and Rouge	IV	-	-	

settlement in the area, nor were the makers of those tools necessarily related at all closely to the Périgordians of the Greater Périgord. Interaction between the Pyrénées and the latter region appears to have been minimal, and there is no evidence of an Early to Late typological development in the Pyrenean stone tool kit. Gradual changes are detectable, and there is some turnover in the organic component of the assemblages, but it is the overall continuity of the Pyrenean Noaillian facies over an immense span of time that most requires explanation. A topography favoring isolation and an economy less dependent upon reindeer as the staple prey— and thus more stable—may have contributed to the persistence of Noaillian hillbillies in the Basque provinces of France and Spain at least into what, farther north, were Solutrean times. This is, after all, an area still characterized by the retention of a unique cultural identity that reaches back into prehistory. Vachons butt styles are a common feature of Gravette points found at Isturitz and Bolinkoba and are present at other sites. In the absence, so far as is known, of contemporary Périgordian groups in the region, it would seem probable that the style either developed from inversely retouched forms of butt present in the Provençal proto-culture and/or that this is, as Bricker (1973, p.1793)

has suggested, a true horizon style linking the Noaillian and Périgordian traditions.

In northern France, we have argued that the events that led to the appearance of an apparently late and very specialized Noaillian facies at Arcy-sur-Cure included a divergence within the Greater Périgord Later Noaillian phase, followed by northward migration around the fringes of the Massif Central. Fuller publication of the Grotte du Renne materials perhaps may require modification of this interpretation. It is conceivable, for example, though I think very unlikely, that these minor occupations might represent the summer hunting camps of Noaillians accustomed to winter in the Mesozoic plateau and plain.

Since others are in a better position than I to contribute to understanding of the Noaillian of Provence and Italy, I will not rehearse the conclusions drawn regarding these different facies, but will conclude this chapter with a few remarks concerning the typological approaches employed in this study.

Descriptive attribute analysis has proved itself more capable than Bordian quantitative analysis of demonstrating the differentiation of an Upper Palaeolithic tradition and of tracing its development. The critical difference between the two approaches is that the former directly monitors the expression and interaction of variables within tool classes. Bordian method does this indirectly by the imposition of a typological grid, the subdivisions of which are not necessarily comparable from one assemblage to another. Attribute analysis also makes it possible to define more precisely the loci of stylistic and functional differentiation and to distinguish them from, say, mechanical contingencies or the effects of economizing raw material. It was by no means clear, for example, when I began this project, whether the different burin techno-types were expressions of function or of style (cf. Clay 1976). Until the factors contributing to variability at the level of the tool are understood, there can be little hope of inferring its cultural significance.

The simple form of attribute analysis employed required as equipment only tools that are within the competence of any handyman to use: a slide rule and an electric calculator, plus time well spent in getting to know the artifacts. It took me three weeks before I suddenly realized what the Noaillians were doing with Raysse burins and why, but at that moment there was a thrilling flash of communication across the millennia. Although computerization of data management, various forms of cluster analysis, and more advanced statistics would have speeded up and improved the typological analyses, they are no substitute for thought; neither do I believe that they would have led to any substantive changes in conclusions. There are many parts of the world where an electric calculator is the archaeologist's most sophisticated technical aid, and there are real advantages in an analytical approach that does not require more advanced facilities.

Attribute analysis is undoubtedly time-consuming, and it is therefore encouraging to find that it is not always necessary. Quantitative analysis of assemblages in terms of a type list designed specifically to bring out those characteristics of assemblages that attribute analysis has shown to be of relevance to the problem at hand effectively manages information loss while generating evidence compatible with that produced by more detailed studies. Attribute analysis, it seems, is of most value at the level of intraregional variation. The Pyrenean and Greater Périgord Noaillian facies are sufficiently distinct for the approach to be superfluous in their comparison. Another area in which attribute analysis has proved of some value is in distinguishing mixed assemblages, as for example at Masnaigre and, rather less convincingly, in the disputed case of the Abri Pataud Level 4a series. On the question of demonstrating borrowing of traits and acculturation, the method has perhaps not had a fair test. The Laraux: 3 series, with its apparently out-of-phase Noaillian and Périgordian increments, remains problematic.

On a broader scale, although Noaillian influence on the Périgordian VI seems likely to have led to a greater reliance on organic armatures and changes in their technique of manufacture, reflected in truncation burin typology and frequencies, this remains a matter of intuition rather than demonstration.

Although more evidence could have been accumulated by investigation of those items in the tool kit that have been but lightly touched upon or ignored, it is legitimate to base certain kinds of interpretation upon the cluster of core industry tool classes that are both common and highly characterized by retouch and/or burination. On the other hand, there can be no doubt that no self-respecting archaeologist today would pay so pitifully little attention to core reduction techniques and to debitage. In analyses of the horizontal distribution of artifacts within lenses (which will be attempted in a later volume in the Abri Pataud series), these and the remaining tool types will be taken into consideration.

Much remains to be done; that more could not be achieved is in part due to imperfections in the excavation of many sites and subsequent treatment of artifacts that invalidate in advance some kinds of analyses of the assemblages affected and would render specious their conclusions. But, even in the optimal situation where excavation is of the highest standard and there are no problems of sample size, the potential of purely typological evidence must depend upon the precision of those ancillary disciplines that provide the archaeologist with his chronological and ecological framework. Although there are many years of analysis and reanalysis facing Palaeolithic specialists, it may not be too much to suggest that typology has reached a point where, to progress further in certain kinds of cultural inference, archaeologists require more para-archaeological information than geologists, paleontologists, and palaeobotanists are currently able to provide. In the present instance the typologically defined phases of the Noaillian of the Greater Périgord are more refined than the units of the Last Glacial chronostratigraphic sequence. Instead of basing our interpretation upon independent lines of evidence, we have been compelled to rely largely on typology to set up a cultural sequence in terms of which cultural manifestations can be considered. Circularity of argument becomes, to a certain extent, inevitable. If the limits of chronological ordering through environmental reconstruction are reached before those of typology, this interdisciplinary obstacle will come to hinder the drawing of cultural inferences from archaeological data as much or more than any other factor. For, even in the Palaeolithic, culture may change faster than climate.

XVIII

Noaillians and Périgordians

My intentions for this final chapter are limited. Following a brief summary of what is known about the biome of the period, I will discuss Upper Périgordian and Noaillian economy, especially as revealed by Bouchud's and Spiess's studies of the faunal remains from the Abri Pataud. These sections provide a background and justification for revision of my earlier interpretation of gross features of Noaillian social structure (David 1973). Lastly, in the light of Harvey M. Bricker's (1973) major work on the Upper Périgordian, I will attempt to sketch a picture of Noaillian-Périgordian interrelationships and of their implications for the two cultures.

THE BIOME

The following description of the environment of Upper Périgordian and Noaillian times focuses on the Les Eyzies region and is drawn largely from the work of Farrand, Bouchud, Donner, Wilson, and Drury (in Movius, ed., 1975) and from Spiess (1979), whose *Reindeer and Caribou Hunters: An Archaeological Study* makes an important contribution to this archaeologist's understanding of caribou and reindeer biology, ethology, and zooarchaeology, and also of man-caribou relations in the ethnographic present. My serious disagreements with his interpretations of the Pataud data will be discussed in the following section.

During the last glaciation the climate of southwestern France was significantly colder and drier than that of today. There was a much-increased incidence of cold, dry winds from the east and northeast, especially during the winter months. Lows moved in less often from the Atlantic and, because of reduced evaporation, brought less rain with them. At the glacial maximum—ca. 18,000 B.P.—mean July temperatures are estimated to have been some five degrees Celsius lower than at present (i.e., ca. 15°) (Gates 1976), but would have been rather warmer than this for most of the Périgordian IV and Noaillian periods. Wilson (1975, p. 185) suggests mean winter temperatures of around zero Celsius. She continues:

It must, however, be realized that there would be considerable local variation. On north-facing slopes temperatures would be somewhat lower, especially in the summer,

and it is likely that snow would lie on these slopes for considerable periods of the summer months. The landform suggests that the average cloud cover would probably be less than in the Massif at present. The consequent high insolation would result in day temperatures, especially on the south-facing slopes in summer, being high as in the Massif at present—with summer values of 25–30° C (76–85° F) being frequent.

Under such a regime, which allowed valley glaciers to penetrate no closer than 115 km to Les Eyzies, snow cover is unlikely to have been heavy even in winter.

Reconstruction of the vegetation is hampered by lack of both macrobotanical and pollen evidence. At the few sites where palynological studies have been made, samples were often taken at chronologically widely spaced intervals and all too frequently gave very small numbers of pollen. Such sampling effects leave individual sequences and, *a fortiori*, correlations between sites open to question. They may, for example, be responsible for the conflict between the Pataud pollen results and other climatic indicators, the Périgordian IV period wrongly appearing colder than that of Levels 1–4 (Donner 1975; p. 170, table 2).

During the last glaciation plant communities existed in the Les Eyzies region that have no parallel today, even in those parts of the Massif Central near the tree line which might be expected to be the most similar. Drury infers (1975, p. 192) that:

. . . the Périgordian IV and Noaillian Periods cover an interval during which climatic changes resulting in snowfields in the mountains were relatively ineffective in the lowlands. These climate shifts moved species now abundant at the higher levels a few hundred vertical feet toward the outer apron of the Massif . . . In the rich topography and truncated climatic gradients of the Late Pleistocene, local topographic differences made species of plants grow together (pines, oaks, grasses, spruce, birch, and arctic heaths) which we would now consider to have major climatic significance.

However, the general consensus appears to be that the plateau uplands and foothills would have supported a parkland and steppe flora, with perhaps rather scrubby trees and also shrubs more common in the deep-cut, sheltered valleys. Species represented in the Pataud pollen counts include principally oak and pine, but with (for example, in the single Level 4 sample) ash and juniper and, represented by single grains, six other species including the warmth-loving walnut.

The fauna of Upper Périgordian and Noaillian times was varied (table 86), although it should be emphasized that reindeer accounts for between 85% and 98% of the "*débris osseux*" in the Pataud levels and grossly similar frequencies at most other Greater Périgord sites. Bouchud (1975, pp. 144–145), noting the possible disturbing influences of hunters' choices, has used the relative frequencies of herbivores other than reindeer as climatic indicators, with conclusions not dissimilar from Farrand's. In Drury's (1975, p. 192) view such changes suggest "small fluctuations resulting in only local changes in the less common species . . ." His "overall conclusion is that habitat variety and favorable climatic conditions made ideal circumstances for support of a varied herbivore supply upon which Upper Palaeolithic man thrived." It can, however, be argued that both Drury and Wilson have exaggerated the variety and density of game available. There do appear to be periods in the record, for example those represented at the Pataud by the Éboulis 3-4: Red and some other éboulis horizons, during which there is very little evidence indeed of human occupation in the Greater Périgord. Bouchud's statistics, summarized in table 86, would at first sight appear to indicate an overwhelming reliance upon reindeer, with only occasional, opportunistic kills of other animals. I have previously argued that overspecialization on reindeer may have been an important factor in Upper Palaeolithic cultural dynamics. This view is hotly disputed by Spiess (1979), to whose work on the economy represented by the Abri Pataud faunal series we now turn.

UPPER PÉRIGORDIAN AND NOAILLIAN ECONOMY

In my earlier paper (1973), I suggested on the basis of ethnographic analogies that different activities are likely to have contributed to Noaillian subsistence in the following range of proportions:

Gathering of plants and small land fauna	6–25%
Hunting and trapping	76–85%
Fishing (including shellfish and sea mammal hunting)	6–15%

These estimates are for the whole year and, depending upon the seasonalities of occupations and upon preservation, are not likely to be proportionately expressed in the materials from a single occupation horizon. We have in fact from the Abri Pataud no direct evidence of gathering, nor for the collecting of shellfish or for sea mammal hunting. In spite of good preservation, the evidence for fishing is also very limited: the Noaillian gorges, together with small numbers

of salmon or salmonid vertebrae in the Noaillian and Périgordian VI (but not apparently in the Périgordian IV). Nor has the record at any other site suggested that fishing was more than a very subsidiary contributor to subsistence. The direct evidence on subsistence is in fact almost entirely limited to the remains of the land mammals hunted. Information on flint variety and on the exotic molluscs present in various levels is of course also of economic significance.

Knowledge of the biology and ethology of the herbivores on which man preyed is a key element in the reconstruction of subsistence. Spiess has made a valuable contribution in this area and I accept, and will not repeat, his inferences (1979, see especially pp. 234–235 and Appendix A) on the likely seasonal groupings and movements of all the animals *except* the reindeer. Reindeer, he suggests, would have wintered in the deep-cut valleys before spreading out and forming small localized groups in and around scattered calving grounds in the hilly country from Sarlat and Montignac west to the edge of the low riverine plateaus. Given the sometimes high summer temperatures estimated, it appears more likely that the prevailing trend in spring and summer would have been easterly and upward toward the edges of the ice sheets. Certainly the evidence from Abri Lespaux and from the Brive locality indicates that herds were, over the course of the year, to be found in a wide range of habitats that included the coastal plain. On the other hand, Spiess is surely right in castigating my earlier suggestion that major fall and spring migrations would have been the critical economic focus for Upper Palaeolithic man, and thus primarily responsible for the formation and maintenance of regional bands. It now appears much more likely that reindeer migrations were less highly patterned, never involved huge aggregations of herds, and took place over distances that rarely exceeded a hundred kilometers or so between their farthest points.

Seasonality of occupation has been studied at very few sites and mainly by Bouchurd, who (1975) states that the Abri Pataud was occupied in all months of the year, but Spiess (1979, pp. 67–84, 97–100) has shown that his interpretations of the reindeer antlers and teeth upon which the claim is based are almost certainly wrong. Spiess's own claim, that the whole of the Upper Palaeolithic record at the Abri Pataud can be referred to late fall, winter, and early spring occupation, is equally dubious. His argument is based upon only 42 individual pieces of evidence, 18 of which—the fetal long bone and antler data—are biased toward the detection of kills of that period. Several levels and many subdivisions of levels produced no clues to seasonality, and although no evidence of summer and early fall occupations has come to light (with the exception perhaps of the salmonid vertebrae), it is not impossible that cultural processes may be partly responsible. While Upper Palaeolithic man was certainly less fastidious than ourselves, rotting faunal remains may have been differentially cleared from the living area in warmer months in order to combat insect and parasite infestation. Thus while Spiess has successfully demonstrated that the site was repeatedly occupied in the colder months of the year, summer occupation cannot be excluded.

Spiess's suggestion that in the latter season groups moved to camps in the open is well taken but, for the moment at least, remains speculation. I am inclined to wonder, for example, whether generally north-facing Laugerie-Haute beneath its tall cliffs would have made an attractive winter residence.

According to Spiess (1979, p.184), at the Abri Pataud, "Over 96.5% of their food (for an average over the more than 15,000-year span) came from five species, in the following order of importance: large bovines as a group (*Bos* and *Bison*), reindeer-caribou, horse and red deer." This surprising conclusion is based upon his estimation of MNI from a series of what he terms "living floors," i.e., levels and lens complexes that he believes were laid down over a relatively short span of time. These include the Level 3: Main occupation and much of Level 4: Lower (his "0-2 living floor"), but no sample drawn from Level 5. The MNI are "maximal" in that as far as possible side, size, age, and sex were taken into consideration in their calculation. In working out the meat and fat contribution to the diet, Spiess assumes that each individual identified represents a whole animal available to the occupants of the area sampled. I fear that his estimates are thoroughly misleading, misrepresenting the numbers and proportions of animals killed during the period(s) of occupation of a living floor perhaps by several orders of magnitude. His analyses (see especially 1979, pp. 182–183) pay only passing attention to natural and cultural formation processes; he also effectively ignores the implications of the facts that the excavated area represents only part of a vast site, and that the faunal series studied by him do not include contemporary materials from the talus. Thus for his estimates of man-days of occupation to offer, in his words, "a picture realistic enough to use in reasoning about the factors which cause variation in the archaeological record," we must accept numerous assumptions including the following. Almost every animal killed and eaten by the inhabitants of the "living floors" (and no other) is represented by at least one distinctive bone, tooth, or antler. The whole animal was eaten without wastage and only by those members of the group associated with the living floor, or equivalent amounts of food but no distinctive bones were exchanged with other site occupants. Natural and cultural processes were so similar between living floors that the results of the MNI studies are comparable.

I do not believe that we can afford such cavalier assumptions, a view shared by Binford (1980) in a hard-hitting but fair review of Spiess's work. However, rather than argue on purely methodological grounds, it is preferable to present data. One of the units studied by Spiess is the Level 4: "0-2 living floor." It is not entirely clear which excavation units were included (cf. Spiess 1979, p. 207; Movius 1977, pp. 65–74), but it must represent at least one-half of the Level 4: Lower deposits within the main excavation and have contained a similar proportion of the faunal remains. Perusal of table 87 suggests that:

1. Spiess's sample is simply inadequate for his pur-

poses. Either he has studied only part of the collection, or he is much less capable than Bouchud of identifying faunal remains or much more conservative in his attributions to species (or subfamily). This must generally reduce potential MNI.

2. Spiess attributes a lower proportion of the material to reindeer and a higher proportion to horse than does Bouchud. This could be due to sample error.

3. There are substantial and obviously highly significant differences in the ratios between the numbers of "*débris osseux*" and "identifiable bones" of the various animals and their contributions to MNI. Thus, according to Spiess, each reindeer brought to the site is represented by 6.2 identifiable bones and the only large bovine by a single piece. (Other fragments were identified as *either* large bovine or horse.)

4. Spiess's sample and procedures are heavily biased against the detection of individual reindeer. This is partially but by no means wholly due to his failure to control for the logarithmic relationship between MNI and sample size (see Grayson 1979 and references cited therein).

5. If the MNI are even approximately correct, we have suggestive evidence of differential treatment of the various prey species that could be confirmed or denied by study of the element counts by species. However, if there was differential treatment of prey species, it becomes somewhat ludicrous to suppose that the one identifiable large bovine bone, in this case a second phalange, represents 770 kg of meat and fat (see Spiess 1979, p. 214, table 6.13).

If Spiess had used procedures similar to those of Binford (1978) or Lyman (1979) for calculating available meat yield from individual skeletal elements, the contribution of reindeer would be seen to be overwhelming. Thus Spiess's estimates of both absolute and proportional contributions to the diet of the various prey species are thoroughly untrustworthy. Furthermore, using MNI and meat weight data to calculate contributions to the diet in the 0-2 living floor series (an attempt made difficult by errors in his table 6.14), we find (table 88) that reindeer made the most important contribution. The same is true of 3: Main where their contribution is approximately 38%. Both the Noaillian and the Upper Périgordian samples therefore differ from his characterization of an average Upper Palaeolithic economy. Presumably the Aurignacian does also, and the average is of little meaning except that departures from it appear to demonstrate that the Upper Palaeolithic occupations cannot be treated as a unitary phenomenon.

Spiess (1979, pp. 220–226) offers a number of checks on the validity of his estimates. Variation of samples from average rates of bone deposition and cataloged tool deposition per estimated man-day is limited, but says nothing about the validity of the estimates *per se*. Another check involves a comparison of the Abri Pataud average of 0.7

Table 86

NUMBERS OF FRAGMENTS (*débris osseux*) OF SKELETAL PARTS FROM THE UPPER PÉRIGORDIAN AND NOAILLIAN LEVELS IN THE MAIN EXCAVATED AREA OF ABRI PATAUD

Level		Reindeer *Rangifer* n	%	Other Game Animals (excluding carnivores) Bos/Bison	Equus/Bos/Bison	Equus	Elephas	Sus	C. elaphus	Capreolus	C. ibex	Rupicapra	Lepus	Total	Other Salmonid fish	Birds	Carnivores
Level 3	n	2080	85.2	71	155	66	–	1	19	1	24	10	14	361	15	7	14
	%			19.7	42.9	18.3		0.3	5.3	0.3	6.6	2.8	3.9	100.1			
Éboulis 3–4	n	1803	92.0	26	45	26	–	–	31	5	7	–	16	156	1	2	7
	%			16.7	28.8	16.7			19.8	3.2	4.5		10.3	100.0			
4: UPPER	n	8484	95.7	35	97	27	–	1	140	32	18	12	16	378	3	1	11
	%			9.3	25.7	7.1		0.3	37.0	8.5	4.8	3.2	4.2	100.1			
4: MIDDLE	n	4314	95.6	25	70	30	–	–	52	4	2	10	4	197	–	1	1
	%			12.7	35.5	15.2			26.4	2.0	1.0	5.1	2.0	99.9			
4: LOWER	n	2701	89.9	54	114	54	–	–	45	6	7	22	2	304	–	–	2
	%			17.8	37.5	17.8			14.8	2.0	2.3	7.2	0.7	100.1			
Éboulis 4–5	n	392	84.8	6	3	2	–	–	50	–	2	7	–	70	–	–	–
	%			8.5	4.3	2.9			71.4		2.9	10.0		100.0			
5: UPPER	n	6913	97.7	18	46	8	1	–	54	4	7	6	17	161	–	3	7
	%			11.2	28.6	5.0	0.6		33.5	2.5	4.3	3.7	10.6	100.0			
5: MIDDLE	n	4779	97.2	6	29	14	2	–	34	–	4	2	49	140	–	6	62
	%			4.3	20.7	10.0	1.4		24.3		2.9	1.4	35.0	99.9			
5: LOWER	n	7402	97.8	3	48	14	1	–	34	6	12	3	49	170	–	36	119
	%			1.8	28.2	8.2	0.6		20.0	3.5	7.1	1.8	28.8	100.0			

Source: Bouchud 1975, p. 120, table XXXII.

Note: Percentages of reindeer are based on total samples of reindeer plus other game animals (excluding carnivores). *Capreolus* has since been reassigned by Spiess (1979, pp. 280–282) to either *C. ibex* or *Rupicapra*. Microfauna are not included in the table.

Table 87

COMPARISON OF NUMBERS OF SKELETAL FRAGMENTS (*DÉBRIS OSSEUX*) OF GAME ANIMALS
(EXCLUDING CARNIVORES) IDENTIFIED BY BOUCHUD (1975) FROM LEVEL 4: LOWER
WITH THE NUMBERS OF "IDENTIFIABLE BONES" IDENTIFIED BY SPIESS (1979)
FROM HIS "0-2 LIVING FLOOR"

	Bouchud 4: LOWER n *débris osseux*		Spiess 0-2 Living Floor "identifiable bones"		Spiess MNI	n "identifiable bones" / MNI
	n	%	n	%		
Reindeer	2701	93.4	161	87.5	26	6.2
Large Bovine	54	1.9	1	0.5	1	1.0
Horse	54	1.9	11	6.0	3	3.7
Red Deer	45	1.6	2	1.1	1	2.0
Roe Deer[a]	6	0.2	1[b]	0.5	0	–
Ibex	7	0.2	4	2.2	1	4.0
Chamois	22	0.8	2	1.1	1	2.0
Hare	2	0.1	2	1.1	1	2.0
Total	2891	100.1	184	100.0		

a. Identification denied by Spiess and reattributed to ibex and/or chamois.
b. Small bovid.

lithic tools deposited per estimated man-day with a figure of 0.34 from a Dorset Eskimo house in Labrador. The relevance of this comparison is dubious since: (a) the sites are qualitatively very different and the samples have presumably suffered different rates of attrition over vastly different time periods; (b) the Eskimo house was completely excavated; and (c) the numbers of cataloged "lithics" are partially dependent upon cataloging practices that probably differed at the two sites.

In another and, to Spiess, the most convincing check, he compares—using Bouchud's figures since the latter's "postcranial counts are more expert than my own" (Spiess 1979, p. 226)—the number of reindeer-caribou *fragments* of skeletal parts from various levels with the comparable figures from Kangigugsuk, a protohistoric interior Eskimo site in northwest Alaska, at which an MNI of 276 was based on a simple count of mandibles. His reasoning goes (ibid., p. 226), "that if the MNI from the Abri Pataud are approximately correct, and one such MNI, for example in Level 14, is 15 (5.8% of 276), then the average *Rangifer* skeletal recovery rate in Level 14 ought to be about 5.8% of that at Kangigugsuk. Average rates are used because of chance variation in preservation in small, fragmentary samples." The primary flaws in this argument are that: (a) he is working with fragments rather than skeletal elements so that differential breakage will affect the results; and (b) he has not controlled for sample size. Amusing and ingenious, there-

fore, but scarcely a check. And why are mandibles not included in the comparison?

Spiess's inferences regarding hunting techniques are to an extent dependent upon his MNI estimates. He suggests for example that since large numbers of reindeer were not found, the Upper Palaeolithic hunters were not operating massive caribou drives. Apart from MNI, the composition of the samples as he reconstructs them suggests random culling of the total reindeer population, which is as consistent with drives as with the other techniques suggested (ibid., p. 203): "thrusting or throwing spear from ambush, stalking by single or small groups of hunters, or self-acting traps like snares, pitfalls or nets . . ." Games can be played with Spiess's figures to show that medium-scale drives are in fact quite likely to have taken place. Caribou skins may be supposed to have been required, as well as meat and fat and other byproducts. The best skins are those taken in September-October, a period during which Spiess believes that the 3: Main people were at the site, and during which they would have obtained a large majority of the skins required for clothing, bags, rawhide, hut coverings, and the like. Spiess (1975, p. 209) interprets 3: Main "as possibly two cold season occupations by a group averaging seven persons." If we were to assume that they would have required a number of skins comparable to minimum estimates from the arctic (see Spiess 1979, pp. 29–30), that they did not have kayaks, and that 10% of skins were not renewed annually, a requirement of ten skins/person/annum is not unreasonable. Thus over a two-year period they would have had to kill 140 reindeer, or 70 in each September-October period. The MNI which, it is suggested, represents kills eaten during these periods and through two winters, is only 40. A lot of caribou are apparently being killed and either not being eaten or at least not contributing their bones to the Pataud series. And to kill such numbers of caribou would seem likely to have required at least medium-scale drives and considerable manpower. The best reason to deny the existence of large-scale drives is still surely the ethological and environmental data adduced by Spiess, strongly suggesting that reindeer were probably too dispersed for large-scale drives to have been possible.

We conclude, therefore, that Spiess's reconstruction of seasonality is questionable and that until serious attention is paid to the factors that, in any particular level, may have distorted numbers and proportions of animals, his MNI calculations and inferences derived from them are more likely seriously to mislead than to provide the high resolution view of segments of the Palaeolithic past for which Spiess is seeking.[46] The radiocarbon dating and sedimentation rate estimates for the Upper Périgordian and Noaillian occupations at the Abri Pataud, combined with the large quantities of bone debris, to my mind convincingly indicate occupation durations that are at least two orders of magnitude greater than those proposed by Spiess, that is, decades or centuries.

My extended criticism of Spiess is, I hope, warranted, but it should not be construed as denying the importance of his contributions, which open the way to much more sophisticated (and demanding) studies of Upper Palaeolithic faunal series and consideration of their implications. For the moment, however, our interpretation of Upper Périgordian and Noaillian economy must, I believe, rely rather on gross counts of faunal remains and on other sorts of data, such as site distributions and varieties of flint used, interpreted in the light of ethnological, biological, and environmental data considered in an analogical frame. I therefore suggest that in the Greater Périgord dependence upon reindeer was indeed very great for most occupations known, and that except at certain sites, for example Les Vachons where horse and large bovines predominate, big game other than reindeer was only rarely killed. If we may generalize from the Isturitz data, the Pyrenean Noaillians, whether by choice or necessity, practiced a more balanced big game procurement strategy. This may indeed have contributed to the extraordinary persistence of the facies (David 1973, pp. 298–299).

Unfortunately the data on seasonality do not at present permit reconstruction of annual movements, and even were they more complete, the known site distribution, heavily biased toward caves and rock shelters in limestone country, is perhaps unlikely to be fully representative. The study of flint varieties might be expected to give indications of possibly seasonal movements. Only samples of nuclei have been systematically studied from this perspective (see ch.

V; Bricker 1975), whereas tools are more likely to be informative. The data available indicate that all but a tiny fraction of the flint used by Noaillians at the Abri Pataud came from nearby, a pattern similar to that of the Périgordian VI. In the Périgordian IV, however, significant quantities of Maestrichtian flint is presumptive evidence of the collection of raw materials probably from the area north and east of Bergerac. Flint variety thus fails to support, though it can scarcely be said to invalidate, a hypothesis of Noaillian and Périgordian VI seasonal movements.

---

46. Major factors are summarized below. I am grateful to Peter McCartney and Margaret Glass for their assistance in preparing this listing and for several useful arguments.

A. Differential introduction of faunal remains into the site.
  1. Transport and butchering constraints.
  2. Storage technology and practices (e.g., boneless smoked meat brought to the site).
  3. Distribution of parts of kills *between* sites.
  4. Collection (scavenging) of faunal remains by man for tool manufacture, architecture, fuel, etc.
  5. Noncultural introduction of fauna (e.g., burrowing rodents).
  6. Noncultural introduction of faunal remains (e.g., by erosion or by carnivore accumulation).
B. Differential removal of materials from the site.
  1. Refuse disposal to offsite locations (including "housekeeping," differential seasonal and ritual disposal of remains).
  2. Tool manufacture and curation.
  3. Erosion.
  4. Scavenging from the site by animals including man.
C. Differential destruction at the site.
  1. Butchering and processing, including comminution of bones.
  2. Use of bones as fuel.
  3. Disposal of bones by burning.
  4. Chemical and physical attrition by natural processes.
  5. Carnivore and other biological attrition.
D. Differential distribution within the site.
  1. Refuse disposal practices.
  2. Food and byproduct distribution and redistribution within the site.
E. Differential archaeological recovery.
  1. Collection bias (e.g., screen size).
  2. Unrepresentative sampling of site area.
  3. Varying stratigraphic resolution causing problems in determining precise associations.
F. Analytical problems.
  1. Logarithmic relationship of sample size and MNI.
  2. Varying ratios of identified to unidentifiable remains for different animals.
  3. Variable expressions of criteria used in MNI studies (e.g., sex, age, side).
  4. Variability in body part representation (and thus of degree to which individuals can be treated as contributing to the diet).
  5. Variability in the competence of analysts, availability of comparative collections, etc.

Table 88
MEAT YIELDS CALCULATED FOR THE "0-2 LIVING FLOOR" SERIES

Animal	Meat Yield (kg)	%
Reindeer		40.5
11(?) calves of the year	242	
3 yearlings	99	
12 two-year-olds and over	642	
Red Deer		6.7
1 adult	162.5	
Horse		19.3
1 subadult	82.5	
2 adults	385	
Large Bovine		31.7
1 adult	770	
1 Ibex	22	0.9
1 Chamois	19	0.8
1 Hare	2	0.1
Total	2426	100.0

Source: Spiess 1979, tables 6.13 and 6.14.

NOAILLIAN SOCIETY

Spiess (1979, p. 247) quite rightly chides me for my use of ethnographic analogies in the 1973 paper. I agree with him that we should "not expect macroband-sized groups [i.e., regional bands] dependent upon caribou drives in the early Upper Paleolithic of southwestern France." Regional bands, represented archaeologically by the Greater Périgord and Pyrenean facies, do appear to have existed, and may indeed have aggregated, as he suggests, at some time in the summer when exchange, socializing, and other activities could be supported for a time by drives of larger ungulates, together with gathering and, perhaps, some fishing. Greater biotic diversity is likely to have led to reduced seasonal variation in group size as compared with Arctic caribou hunters such as the Nunamiut, with the local band composed of several families remaining as a unit for considerable periods, breaking up into groups of one or two families when food was scarce.

Large-scale occupations such as those found at the Abri Pataud, Laugerie-Haute, La Gravette, Gavaudun, and Isturitz may well represent local bands. Indeed, if Spiess is correct in postulating a winter concentration of ungulates in the deep valleys of the Les Eyzies region, this appears a very reasonable inference. Unfortunately, we lack information on faunal density, the most critical factor affecting the aggregation of the human predators.

When, however, Spiess (1979, p. 249) states that "we cannot guess at macroband sizes or linguistic-cultural area size," then he is surely wrong, at least for the Noaillian. The regional facies described in the body of this monograph imply relatively intense and continuing interaction within facies boundaries—and a marked drop off beyond them—such that changing isochrestic patterns of material culture were maintained throughout the area covered by the facies. There was, however, very little contact between facies, and similarities between their artifact suites are best explained by reference to common cultural origins. If the facies, as I now believe, represents the regional band, their integration could still have been maintained without annual aggregation. Rather, frequent exchanges of personnel between local bands, reflecting variation in local resources, changes in social relations, the requirements of mating, etc., may have been sufficient.

Thus, with important modifications of scale, I hold to the view of Noaillian society set out in more detail in 1973. Since that date, however, Bricker's (1973) vitally important thesis has appeared, permitting for the first time an evaluation of Noaillian relationships with the Périgordians and of the differences between the societies. It should be emphasized that the term "Périgordian" is here used strictly, referring to the variety of the larger complex of "Gravettian" industries characterized by backed blades that is stylistically typical of the Périgord and some nearby regions. Finally, then, we may move to a brief consideration of intercultural relationships in the Greater Périgord during this segment of the Upper Palaeolithic.

NOAILLIANS AND PÉRIGORDIANS

The period lasting from the early Périgordian IV, at about 29,500 B.P., to the end of the Périgordian VI, at approximately 22,250 B.P., is one for which we have exceptionally tight control over typological variety and distributions. This gives us a better opportunity to investigate cultural continuity, change, and intercultural relations than for any comparable period in the Western European Upper Palaeolithic sequence.

The Bayacian phase of the Upper Périgordian, characterized by an abundance of *fléchettes*, begins at or near the end of a cold and moist climatic phase and develops into the classic Périgordian IV with Gravette points (Bricker 1976) in the succeeding long, mild, and humid period that has been dubbed the Les Eyzies Oscillation by Farrand (1975; Movius 1977). This oscillation is succeeded ca. 28,000 B.P. by a cold, dry episode during which Font-Robert points and *éléments tronqués* (backed and truncated blades) are added to the Périgordian inventory, and it is during this phase that Noaillians first enter the Southwest of France (fig. 68).

During the Early Noaillian phase, there are contemporary developments in the Périgordian tool kit: *fléchettes* and Font-Robert points disappear, and *éléments tronqués* become far less common. They are replaced by increasing frequencies of a type previously present in small numbers, the Vachons-style Gravette point, characterized by flat inverse treatment of the butt. I have called this phase the Périgordian Vc. It is after the inception of the Périgordian Vc and during a time of climatic amelioration that the change from Early to Late Noaillian takes place, apparently suddenly. Some time afterward, during the exceptionally well marked Tursac Oscillation or Interstadial, the Noaillian disappears, probably before 26,000 B.P.

We have very little information about cultural developments during the maximum of the Tursac Oscillation, which is marked at some sites by a cessation of deposition, at others by gullying and erosion; but with the sudden return of cold, moist conditions at 24,000, we begin to pick up traces of the Périgordian VI, in which there are further developments in the backed blade and other tool classes. This phase persists through another period of major cold into a third milder pedogenetic interval, ending at around 22,250 B.P. This ends the Upper Périgordian sequence of the Greater Périgord, and in the following cold phase a seemingly new culture appears, the Proto-Magdalenian.

It would appear that in the Greater Périgord Périgordians and Noaillians coexisted for over a millennium and that the two societies practiced indistinguishable economies. If this indeed is the case, then we are in the presence of a phenomenon that would seem to confound the principles of cultural materialism, for surely that theory teaches us to expect that within a relatively brief period one society would either out-compete the other or that a fusion of ethnic identities would take place. The coexistence of the Périgordian V and the Noaillian thus becomes a test of cultural materialist theory.

Where two or more groups practicing closely similar economies live in proximity one to the other, there appears always to be a frontier, often disputed or fluctuating, between them. At times when competition is reduced for whatever reason, there may be a tendency for voluntary exchange of personnel and a lessening of cultural differentiation. If, on the other hand, there is pressure on resources, expression of ethnicity is likely to be emphasized (Hodder 1980). Where two or more ethnic groups are sympatric, then we always find that their economies are in some way complementary, and that the societies are exploiting different resources within their environment. Normally, the societies interact, usually with greater or lesser exploitation of one by the other [e.g., the Bantu-Pygmy "wayward servant" pattern (Turnbull 1965), the exploitation of Hutu and Twa by a Tutsi pastoralist elite (Maquet 1961), or the less unequal and more fluid interrelations of Dorobo and Maasai-speakers on the Leroghi plateau of northern Kenya (Hodder 1980, pp. 87–104)]. In other cases, two cultures may occupy territories that overlap, however this need not mean that the same resources are being exploited in the same place by both peoples at the same time. We may cite here the contrasting pastoralist adaptations of the Fulani and Moors of the Mauretania-Mali border area, between whom there is little interaction and less competition. I know, however, of no cases where for periods of many generations two societies practicing identical economies are able to survive in the same territory while maintaining their cultural identities. Did this in fact occur in the Upper Palaeolithic of southwestern France?

Let us first close a few loopholes. It might be suggested that Périgordians, presumed descendants of Western Classic Neanderthals, and Noaillians were different types of man between whom there were genetic barriers. This unlikely proposition is in any case clearly irrelevant since we are discussing not nature but culture, and, given that both populations were of the subspecies *Homo sapiens sapiens* with psychologies that can have differed relatively little from our own, it is inconceivable that diffusion and acculturation would not have taken place. Indeed, we shall see that it did, though not to any great extent until toward the end of the period in question. Second, it might be argued that the two populations maintained themselves at so low a level that there was no competition between them. This will not work either since: (a) some competition was surely inevitable even if representatives of the two groups met only occasionally; and (b) since human breeding populations of less than 300–500 are chronically unstable (Sauvy 1969), it is extremely improbable that both would have survived in the same region for 1000 years or more. Third, a gross inadequacy of the archaeological record might be invoked: the sample is simply too small and too fragmentary for us to address these questions. While admitting the manifold imperfections of the record, this argument can be dismissed. For example, research over the past 100 years has resulted in the identification of over 40 sites in the Greater Périgord that have given Noaillian materials, and although several of these represent no more than find spots, and others mixed series, sufficient sites have been excavated to have repeatedly produced evidence of one or more occupations that can and have been subjected to detailed and meaningful analysis, at least of their artifactual assemblages. Biases there certainly are, both in the range of microenvironments sampled and in the types of site represented, but the sample is nonetheless substantial.

It would seem, therefore, that if we are to rescue cultural materialism, we must be able to prove at least one of the following propositions.

The first pair deals with our cultural interpretation of the record:

1. The Noaillian and Périgordian industries do not represent ethnic groups but, say, activity variants within the same culture, or

2. Granted ethnicity is being expressed in the industries, the economies practiced were either

   a. Complementary, or at least

   b. Different to the point that competition was systematically averted.

The second pair of propositions takes issue with our control of the chrono-stratigraphic record:

3. The problem as such does not exist. Apparent sympatry is a product of a lack of resolution of the time scale. This is so long that both cultures could have made temporary use of the Greater Périgord without ever coming into contact.

4. It might be argued conversely that we are falsely inflating the time span of Périgordian and Noaillian sympatry, that this was in fact a very brief phenomenon, resolved, as might be expected, by the rapid disappearance of one of the cultures and/or by its submergence in the other.

I shall briefly discuss these propositions in order. The first is one of the alternative views taken by Laville, Rigaud, and Sackett (1980). Their interpretation fails to take into consideration the existence of a probable Noaillian ancestor in Provence, or of a distinctive regional facies of the Noaillian (and the absence or near absence of the Périgordian V) in the Pyrénées, and of another in the Arcy-sur-Cure locality in the department of Yonne—let alone the presence of a separate but contemporary areal variant of the Noaillian in Italy (fig. 68). Furthermore, their reading of the chrono-stratigraphic record of the Périgord is misleading; it is not true as they claim (ibid., fig. 8.2) that, for example, the Périgordian VI of the Abri Pataud is contemporary with the Early Noaillian of the Abri du Facteur and earlier than the Late Noaillian increment in the Flageolet 1 series. On the contrary, the assemblages of both traditions show an ongoing typological development. Given the marked stylistic differences identified by attribute analysis, the argument that we are in the presence of two cultural traditions becomes overwhelming.

Proposition 2, that the economies were either complementary or at least different, is more difficult to handle since study of faunal remains has generally been limited to the identification of species, usually without quantification. The Abri Pataud data cited earlier in this chapter do not support it, nor is there any patterned difference in economy between the two cultures.

While we can fairly safely say that complementarity of economic adaptation is extremely unlikely, since at the Abri Pataud the Périgordian IV and the Périgordian VI faunal collections (both from periods when there were no Noaillians present) are remarkably similar to those of the Noaillian, we cannot to our full satisfaction demonstrate that the Noaillian and Périgordian economies were to all intents and purposes identical. It remains a remote possibility that even though they hunted the same prey, they might have contrived to do so in different, nonconflicting ways.

The third proposition, that sympatry is an illusion caused by our inability to read the archaeological record, can be dismissed. At several well- or relatively well-excavated sites where there is little likelihood of mixture of levels by the excavators, including the Abri Pataud, Flageolet 1, Roc de Combe and Les Jambes in Dordogne, Les Vachons in Charente, and Laraux in Vienne, characteristically Noaillian and Périgordian tools are associated in levels that must have been laid down over quite short periods of time. It is not always possible to determine whether these associations are the result of more than one occupation, the residues of which subsequently became incorporated into the same thin stratum, or whether they result from intercultural diffusion of types or episodes of more generalized acculturation. However this may be, these series are sufficient to demonstrate an at least partial sympatry of the two traditions that, according to the typology of the series in question, can be shown to have occurred in both the Early and Late, and also in the shadowy, less well-represented, Terminal Noaillian phase.

Proposition 4, which claims that the Noaillian period lasted not for over a millennium but only for a much shorter period is, perhaps curiously, one of the more difficult to rebut. The chronology suggested is, as stated above, based upon the large GrN series from the Abri Pataud. Its essential correctness is argued (although I have slightly modified their interpretations) by Waterbolk (1971) and by Movius (1975, 1977); dating of the last part of the sequence is also supported by GrN dates from Laugerie-Haute. Nevertheless, there is only one acceptable date for the Noaillian of the Greater Périgord, and only two for the Périgordian IV. We have, therefore, to rely partially upon estimation of the time span implied by the sediments which, at the Abri Pataud, appear to cover the full time range of the Noaillian in the Périgord. This is fraught with difficulties, briefly discussed by Farrand (1975, pp. 51–52), who suggests a mean site sedimentation rate of 55 cm per 1000 years. The main Noaillian level (Level 4) averages, according to the same author, 26.8 cm in thickness, but this excludes the Terminal Noaillian occupation of Level 4a above, which adds about another 15 cm. The combined figures would suggest that the Noaillians made use of the Abri Pataud over a period of 760 years, a figure which, while only about half that suggested above, is surely enough to rebut the proposition.

Does, then, the dismissal of all four propositions mean that we have overthrown the mighty, if inelegant, theoretical edifice that is cultural materialism? Certainly not! I will argue below that, quite apart from an initial premise that well may not stand up to prolonged inspection, it would be unwise to accept the arguments presented without further understanding of the societies behind the industries and of their probable demographic characteristics. Such data are prerequisite to the investigation of cultural dynamics.

Comparative evidence from North America suggests that Noaillian population in the entire Southwest of France is likely to have averaged something on the order of 750–1250 individuals, perhaps at times reaching 2000 or more (David 1973). Halving these figures gives a reasonable estimate of the population of the Greater Périgord. Local bands now appear the most effective social unit, although the regional band is reflected in the archaeological facies. Also clear from a study of assemblage typology and of site distribution is that the Late Noaillians of the Vézère Valley, though perhaps not those closer to the territorial boundaries, retained or were able to recreate a cohesive social identity despite what well may have been a significant population reverse at the end of the Early phase (fig. 62). This may have been caused by a catastrophic collapse of animal resources, following which it would have taken some time, marked at the Abri Pataud by an interval of much less intense occupation or even abandonment, for the population to build up again to archaeological visibility, by which time they were practicing a Late Noaillian style and technology (David 1973). It can be unequivocally stated that, unless an improvement in core reduction technique is taken as evidence of contact with Périgordians, Early to Late Noaillian development was not due to Périgordian influence or pressure. The converse, as Bricker (1973) has shown, is most definitely not true.

Périgordian V assemblages contemporary with the Early Noaillian, while remaining Périgordian, tend to show idiosyncratic features in many tool classes including the backed blades. Change is less patterned whether by time or by space. Furthermore, it is perhaps at this time that an isolated Upper Périgordian with Font-Robert points appears at the Gisement Brun, near Roanne, to the east of the Massif Central.

Upper Périgordian sites are many fewer than Noaillian. There are a maximum of seven sites at which classic Périgordian IV occupations have been positively identified, and all are in the Dordogne except for one, the Grotte de Noailles, in Corrèze. The population must have been very small and may have consisted of only two local bands. In the Périgordian Va+b and early Vc there are still many fewer sites of this tradition that have produced evidence of occupations of any importance, and moreover these are scattered through at least six departments (fig. 69). It is difficult to escape the conclusion that Périgordian society was severely disrupted by the Noaillian intrusion and that the Périgordians became dispersed in small groups, local bands, and household clusters that could keep up only minimal contact with each other around the periphery of a more unitary and homogeneous Noaillian territory, focused on the lower Vézère Valley around Les Eyzies.

Bricker (1973) gives the same designation (his "time e" series) to Périgordian assemblages classed by me as Vc that are contemporary with the Late and Terminal Noaillian phases and which precede the Tursac maximum, and to those that continue into and through the subsequent cold, i.e., the Périgordian VI. Understanding of this whole period is hampered by poor dating and lack of attribute data on some critical Périgordian assemblages (especially the Corbiac series). From a Noaillian perspective, I see a marked concentration of sites in the Vézère and perhaps the Isle valleys, including in the former the Brive vicinity in Corrèze (fig. 62). Late Noaillian occupation appears to have been short-lived elsewhere. Furthermore, there is much more evidence of actual or potential interaction with Périgordians, and this appears to proceed progressively inward from the margins toward the center of Noaillian tribal territory. In the Terminal phase it reaches right into the Les Eyzies vicinity.

The difficulty here is composite: some critical series such as those from Les Jambes, La Chèvre: 2–5, and Pataud: 4a are either poorly dated or very small, or have question marks attached to them for other reasons. It is indicative that whereas Bricker regards several of these series as Noaillian, strongly influenced by the Périgordian, I read much of the data as suggesting admixture. The fact that the evidence is not good enough to allow a firm decision is, however, for present purposes irrelevant. Either way it is clear that during the Late phase Noaillian dominance in the Dordogne began to be strongly challenged and that by the Terminal phase the Périgordians are effectively reasserting control. Possibly the Noaillians may have retreated upriver to a refuge in the Planchetorte valley near Brive.

The typology of the backed blades of this period is especially interesting in that in several aspects they hark back to those of the Périgordian IV. They also show less inter-assemblage variability. The Vachons-style Gravette point is, Bricker suggests, a true, if long-lived, horizon marker present in both cultures. The evidence of Périgordian end-scrapers and burins is less clear, but for the latter category he argues for some direct trait diffusion from Noaillians to Périgordians. The inference is as yet speculative but still strong that the Dordogne heartland is being recolonized by Périgordians from beyond the former Noaillian frontier, from Charente, and perhaps from an area in the Dordogne itself around Bergerac—the Corbiac and Rabier series—which he suggests may have been a Périgordian refuge. The industrial traditions of these Périgordians appear to have been maintained relatively unaffected by Noaillian impact, and I predict that once the assemblages are fully studied we will be able to document a reconvergence of Périgordian cultural norms and a reintegration of their society.

The end product of this recolonization process is the Dordogne Périgordian VI, itself represented at few sites and of limited distribution. In this phase backed blade and endscraper traditions are further developed, and are associated with exceptionally strong evidence of the incorporation and reworking of Noaillian ideas. These are apparent in a florescence of the truncation burin and bone and antler tool kit quite strange to the earlier Périgordian, and also in iconography. Here I refer to the Venus motif, an ideological trait introduced by Noaillians into the Greater Périgord.

In conclusion let us return to the question of cultural materialism. Whereas in the first part of this section I treated the Noaillian and Périgordian of the Greater Périgord from a normative cultural perspective as unitary traditions, and was able to make a case for overthrow of the theory, in the second I have (albeit perfunctorily) exploited assemblage variation as evidence of contrasting and developing sociocultural patterns. My initial question—how was it that cultures practicing identical economies were able to coexist sympatrically for a millennium?—was far too simple. Industrial traditions may, even in the Palaeolithic, mask much socio-cultural variety. A small Périgordian population, perhaps already near the minimum for assured survival, was thrown into disarray by the invasion of a larger, more vigorous society. Several dispersed Périgordian groups no doubt did become socially and/or physically extinct. These may have included the occupants of the Gisement Brun over the Massif besides others who remained in close contact with the Noaillians. Others again, remaining in the west but beyond the Noaillian frontier (and, incidentally, in areas that have been far less intensively searched for Palaeolithic sites) subsequently took advantage of a Noaillian population reverse to press inward, progressively and selectively adopting aspects of Noaillian culture, toward that prime territory, the Vézère Valley around Les Eyzies, that had earlier been the focus of Aurignacian and Périgordian IV occupations and that perhaps was for much of the Upper Palaeolithic a preferred reindeer wintering area or stood at the confluence of a number of migration routes traveled by the herds as they fled the heat of summer for the pastures around the icefields, and through which they retreated in the fall. The Syndicat d'Initiative had right on its side when it baptized Les Eyzies "La Capitale de la Préhistoire."

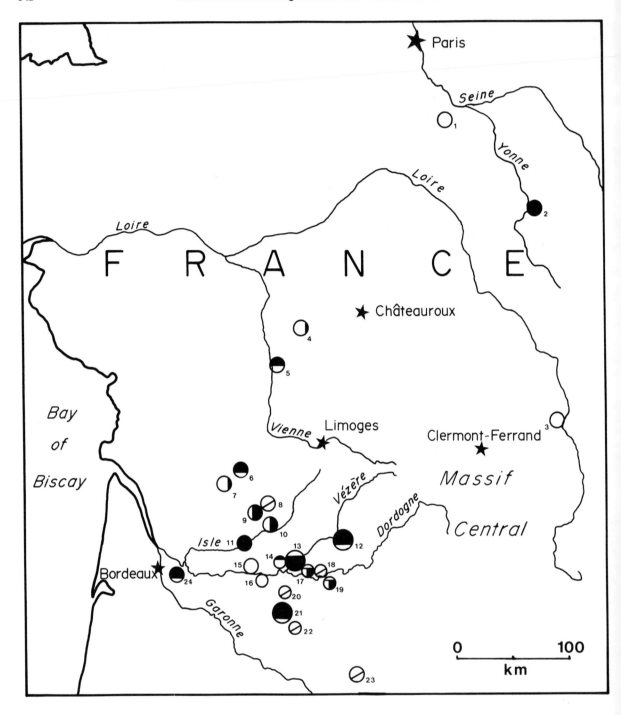

Figure 69. MAP SHOWING THE DISTRIBUTION IN THE GREATER PÉRIGORD AND NORTHERN
FRANCE OF SITES/VICINITIES WITH NOAILLIAN AND PÉRIGORDIAN V-VI MATERIALS.
Key: Noaillian = black; Périgordian = white. The infilling of the circles
gives a crude indication of Noaillian-Périgordian relationships at particular
sites/localities. At site 19, for example, characteristically Noaillian and
Périgordian materials are found together in lower levels (whether as a
result of natural or cultural processes), and there is a Périgordian
occupation above. Circles with a diagonal bar indicate that the data are
too poor to permit even such diagrammatic expression of relationships.

		Phases Represented	
Sites		Périgordian V-VI	Noaillian
1.	Cirque de la Patrie	V/VI	–
2.	Renne and Trilobite	–	Late (Arcy facies)
3.	Brun	Va+b	–
4.	Roches de Pouligny	Va+b	?
5.	Laraux	Va+b	Early
6.	Ragoût and Chasseur	Va+b	Early
7.	Vachons	Va+b, Vc, VI	Early
8.	Bonhomme, Durand-Ruel	V	Early
9.	Chèvre	–	Late (+ Terminal?)
10.	Jambes and Petit-Puyrousseau	Vc	Terminal
11.	Solvieux	–	Early and Late
12.	Brive locality (10 sites)	Va+b	Early and Late
13.	Les Eyzies locality (13 sites)	Vc, VI	Early, Late, Terminal
14.	La Ferrassie	Va+b	Early
15.	Corbiac	V/VI	–
16.	Rabier	V/VI	–
17.	Flageolet 1	Va+b, VI	Early and Late
18.	Cantelouve	?	Early?
19.	Roc de Combe and Péchialet	Va+b, VI	Early
20.	Combe-Capelle and Termo-Pialat	Va+b?	Early?
21.	Gavaudun locality (5 sites)	Va+b?	Early and Late
22.	Roc de Cavart	–	Early?
23.	Battuts and Rouset	Va+b?	Early (and Late?)
24.	Lespaux	Va+b	Early

References

Alaux, Jean-François
1963– "L'abri gravettien des Forges," *Travaux et*
1964 *Recherches de la Fédération Tarnaise de Spé-*
léo-Archéologie, no. 2, pp. 25–37.
1964– "Note sur quelques pièces périgordiennes de
1965 la Grotte de Rouset, Commune de Larroque
(Tarn)," *Travaux et Recherches de la Fédéra-*
tion Tarnaise de Spéléo-Archéologie, no. 3,
pp. 36–39.
1965– "Burins du type 'Le Raysse' de l'Abri des
1966 Battuts, Penne (Tarn)," *Bulletin de la Fédéra-*
tion Tarnaise de Spéléo-Archéologie, no. 4,
pp. 48–52.
1967 "Burins du type 'Le Raysse' de l'Abri des
Battuts (Tarn)," *Comptes Rendus des Séances*
Mensuelles, Bulletin de la Société Préhisto-
rique Française, vol. 64, no. 8, pp. 242–247.
1967– "Note préliminaire sur l'abri périgordien des
1968 Battuts (Tarn)," *Travaux et Recherches de la*
Fédération Tarnaise de Spéléo-Archéologie,
no. 5, pp. 37–42.
1969 "Note préliminaire sur l'abri périgordien des
Battuts (Tarn)," *Bulletin de la Société Pré-*
historique Française, vol. 66, no. 1, pp. 10–
15.
1973 "Pointes de la Font-Robert, en place, dans le
Périgordien à burins de Noailles de l'abri des
Battuts (Commune de Penne, Tarn)," *Bulletin*
de la Société Préhistorique Française, vol. 70,
pp. 51–55.

Alimen, Henriette
1964 "Le Quaternaire des Pyrénées de la Bigorre,"
Mémoire pour Servir à l'Explication de la Carte
Géologique de France. Paris, Imprimerie Na-
tionale.

Andrieu, P., and J. Dubois
1966 "Travaux récents á la Grotte eponyme de
Noailles (Corrèze)," *Comptes Rendus des Sé-*
ances Mensuelles de la Société Préhistorique
Française, vol. 63, no. 5, pp. 167–180.

Arambourou, Robert, and Paul E. Jude
1964 *Le Gisement de la Chèvre à Bourdeilles (Dor-*
dogne). Périgueux, Imprimerie Magne.

Azzi, C. M., L. Bigliocca, and E. Piovan
1973 "Florence radiocarbon dates I," *Radiocarbon*,
vol. 15, no. 3, pp. 479–487.

Bailloud, Gérard
1953 "Note préliminaire sur l'industrie des niveaux
supérieurs de la Grotte du Renne, à Arcy-sur-
Cure (Yonne)," *Bulletin de la Société Préhis-*
torique Française, vol. 50, pp. 338–345.

Balout, Lionel
1956 "L'Abri du Chasseur, au Bois-du-Roc, Commune de Vilhonneur (Charente). Note préliminaire," *Congrès Préhistorique de France,*
Comptes Rendus de la 15ième Session, Po-
itiers-Angoulême, 1956, pp. 199–205.
1957 "Un gisement martyr: l'Abri André Ragout,
au Bois-du-Roc (Vilhonneur-Charente)," *Bul-*
letin de la Société Préhistorique Française,
vol. 54, pp. 51–53.
1958 "L'Abri André Ragout, au Bois-de-Roc (Vilhonneur-Charente). Fouilles de 1957," *Bul-*
letin de la Société Préhistorique Française,
vol. 55, pp. 599–627.
1959 "Grottes et abris sous roche de Vilhonneur
(Charente)," *Actes du Congrès des Sociétés*
Savantes, Bordeaux, 1957, pp. 13–25.
1965 "Grottes et abris paléolithiques—le Bois-du-
Roc: Abri André Ragout," *Bulletin de l'As-*
sociation Française pour L'Étude du Quater-
naire, 2e Année, nos. 4–5, pp. 237–242.

Barandiarán, José Miguel de
1950 "Bolinkoba y otros yacimientos paleoliticos en
la Sierra de Amboto (Vizcaya)," *Cuadernos*
de Historia Primitiva, vol. 5, no. 2, pp. 73–
112.

Bardon, Louis, Amédée Bouyssonie, and Jean Bouyssonie
1906 "La Grotte de Font-Robert (Corrèze)," *Congrès*
Internationale d'Anthropologie et d'Archéo-
logie Préhistorique, Comptes Rendus de la 12e
Session, Monaco, 1906, vol. 2, pp. 172–184.
1908 "La Grotte de la Font-Robert, près Brive (Corrèze)," *Bulletin de la Société Scientifique, His-*
torique et Archéologique de la Corrèze, vol.
30, pp. 315–331.

1910   "La Grotte Lacoste, près Brive (Corrèze),"
        Revue de l'École d'Anthropologie, vol. 20, pp.
        28–40, 60–71.

1924a   "Stations préhistoriques de Planchetorte. II.
        La grotte préhistorique de Pré-Aubert, près Brive
        (Corrèze)," *Bulletin de la Société Scientifique,
        Historique et Archéologique de la Corrèze*,
        vol. 46, pp. 141–158.

1924b   "Stations préhistoriques de Planchetorte. III.
        Complément sur d'autres grottes préhisto-
        riques de Planchetorte," *Bulletin de la Société
        Scientifique, Historique et Archéologique de
        la Corrèze*, vol. 46, pp. 159–171.

Bardon, L., J. Bouyssonie, and A. Bouyssonie
1903   "Un nouveau type de burin," *Revue de l'École
        d'Anthropologie de Paris*, vol. 13, pp. 165–
        168.

1904   "Monographie de la Grotte de Noailles (Cor-
        rèze)," *Revue de l'École d'Anthropologie*, vol.
        14, pp. 283–294.

1905   "Monographie de la Grotte de Noailles (Cor-
        rèze)," *Bulletin de la Société Scientifique, His-
        torique et Archéologique de la Corrèze*, vol.
        27, pp. 65–84.

1906   "Grattoir caréné et ses dérivés à la Coumba-
        de-Bouitou," *Revue de l'École d'Anthropo-
        logie*, vol. 16, pp. 410–412.

1920   "La grotte préhistorique de Pré-Aubert, près
        Brive (Corrèze)," *Revue Anthropologique*, vol.
        30, pp. 177–189.

Barrère, Pierre, Robert Heisch, and Serge Lerat
1959   *France de demain: la région du Sud-Ouest*.
        Paris, Presses Universitaires de France.

Binford, Lewis R.
1980   *Nunamiut ethnoarchaeology*. New York, Aca-
        demic Press.

1979   "Review of Spiess, 1979," *American Anthro-
        pologist*, vol. 82, pp. 628–631.

Blanc, Alberto C.
1937   "Nuovi giacimenti paleolitici del Lazio e Tos-
        cana," *Studi Etruschi*, vol. 11, pp. 273–304.

1938   "Nuovo giacimento paleolitico e mesolitico ai
        Balzi Rossi di Grimaldi," *Rendiconti della
        Accademia Nazionale dei Lincei*, vol. 28, pp.
        107–113.

Blanc, Séverin
1948   "Grotte de la Chèvre, au Francilloux, Com-
        mune de Bourdeilles (Dordogne)," *Gallia*, vol.
        6, pp. 395–397.

Bordes, François
1968   "La question périgordienne," in *La Préhis-
        toire: problèmes et tendances*, pp. 59–70. Paris,
        CNRS.

Bordes, François, and J. Labrot
1967   "La stratigraphie du gisement de Roc de Combe
        (Lot) et ses implications," *Bulletin de la So-
        ciété Préhistorique Française*, vol. 64, no. 1,
        pp. 15–28.

Bouchud, Jean
1951   "Étude paléontologique de la faune d'Istu-
        ritz," *Mammalia*, vol. 15, pp. 184–203.

1952   "Les oiseaux d'Isturitz," *Bulletin de la So-
        ciété Préhistorique Française*, vol. 49, pp. 450–
        459.

1958   "La faune de la Grotte de Gargas (Haute-Py-
        rénées)," *Bulletin de la Société d'Histoire Na-
        turelle de Toulouse*, vol. 93, pp. 383–390.

1963   "L'évolution du climat au cours de l'Auri-
        gnacien et du Périgordien d'après la faune,"
        in *Aurignac et l'Aurignacien*, Louis Méroc,
        ed. (*Bulletin de la Société Méridionale de Spé-
        léologie et de Préhistoire*, vols. 6–9, 1956–
        1959), pp. 143–153.

1964   "Étude sommaire de la faune du gisement de
        la Chèvre," in R. Arambourou and P. E. Jude,
        *Le Gisement de la Chèvre à Bourdeilles (Dor-
        dogne)*, pp. 115–120. Périgueux, Imprimerie
        Magne.

1966   *Essai sur le renne et la climatologie du Paléo-
        lithique moyen et supérieur*. Périgueux, Im-
        primerie Magne.

1968   "L'Abri du Facteur à Tursac (Dordogne). II.
        La faune et sa signification climatique," *Gal-
        lia-Préhistoire*, vol. 11, pp. 113–121.

1975   "Étude de la faune de l'Abri Pataud," in *Ex-
        cavation of the Abri Pataud, Les Eyzies (Dor-
        dogne)*, H. L. Movius, Jr., ed., American
        School of Prehistoric Research, Bulletin no.
        30, pp. 69–153. Peabody Museum, Harvard
        University.

Boule, Marcellin
1896   "La Grotte d'Isturitz (Basses-Pyrénées),"
        L'Anthropologie, vol. 7, pp. 725–726.

Bourlon, Maurice
1911   "Essai de classification des burins. Leur modes
        d'avivage," *Revue Anthropologique*, vol. 21,
        pp. 267–278.

1913   "Station préhistorique de Masnaigre, Com-
        mune de Marquay (Dordogne)," *Revue An-
        thropologique*, vol. 23, pp. 254–268.

Bouyssonie, Amédée, Jean Bouyssonie, and Louis Bardon
1910   "La Grotte Lacoste, près Brive (Corrèze),"
        Bulletin de la Société Scientifique, Historique

et Archéologique de la Corrèze, vol. 32, pp. 217–249.

1939   "La grotte des Morts," *Bulletin de la Société Scientifique, Historique et Archéologique de la Corrèze*, vol. 61, pp. 131–142.

Bouyssonie, Jean
1923   "Station préhistorique aurignacienne de Bos-del-Ser, près Brive (Corrèze)," *L'Association Française pour l'Avancement des Sciences, Comptes Rendus de la 47e Session, Bordeaux*, pp. 617–622.

1939   "La Grotte de Tarté," *Mélanges de Préhistoire et d'Anthropologie offerts par ses Collègues, Amis et Disciples au Professeur Comte H. Bégouen*, pp. 179–194. Toulouse.

1948   "Un gisement aurignacien et périgordien, Les Vachons (Charente)," *L'Anthropologie*, vol. 52, pp. 1–42.

Bouyssonie, Jean and André Cheynier
1961   "Quelques nouvelles observations sur la Grotte Lacoste (Corrèze)," *Bulletin de la Société Scientifique, Historique et Archéologique de la Corrèze*, vol. 83, pp. 131–134.

Bouyssonie, Jean, and P. Perol
1960   "La station préhistorique de Raysse et sa Grotte Fouillade, avec Solutréen," *Bulletin de la Société Scientifique, Historique et Archéologique de la Corrèze*, vol. 82, pp. 33–42.

Bouyssonie, Jean, and Denise de Sonneville-Bordes
1957   "L'Abri No. 2 des Vachons, Gisement aurignacien et périgordien, Commune de Voulgézac (Charente)," *Congrès Préhistorique de France, Comptes Rendus de la 15ieme Session, Poitier-Angoulême, 1956*, pp. 271–309.

Breuil, Henri
1907   "La question aurignacienne: étude critique de stratigraphie comparée," *Revue Préhistorique*, vol. 2, pp. 173–219.

1918   "Études de morphologie paléolithique. III. Les niveaux pre-Solutréens de Trilobite," *Revue Anthropologique*, vol. 28, pp. 309–333.

1924   "Notes de voyage paléolithique en Europe Centrale. II. Les industries paléolithiques du loess de Moravie et Bohème," *L'Anthropologie*, vol. 34, pp. 515–552.

1927   "Oeuvres d'art paléolithiques inédites du Périgord et art oriental espagnol," *Revue Anthropologie*, vol. 38, pp. 101–108.

1929   "Gravures aurignaciennes supérieures de l'Abri Labattut, à Sergeac," *Revue Anthropologique*, vol. 29, pp. 147–151.

1958   "Les fouilles de Breuil et de Cartailhac dans

la Grotte de Gargas en 1911 et 1913," *Bulletin de la Société d'Histoire naturelle de Toulouse*, vol. 93, pp. 341–382.

Breuil, Henri, and André Cheynier
1958   "Les fouilles de Breuil et Cartailac dans la Grotte de Gargas en 1911 et 1913," *Bulletin de la Société Méridionale de Spéléologie et de Préhistoire*, vol. 5 (1954–1955), pp. 341–382.

Bricker, Harvey M.
1973   *"The Périgordian IV and related cultures in France."* Ph.D. dissertation, Harvard University.

1975   "The provenience of flint used for the manufacture of tools," in *Excavation of the Abri Pataud, Les Eyzies (Dordogne)*, H. L. Movius, Jr., ed., American School of Prehistoric Research, Bulletin no. 30, pp. 194–197. Peabody Museum, Harvard University.

1976   "La contribution de l'Abri Pataud à la question bayacienne," *Congrès Préhistorique de France, Comptes Rendus de la 20e Session, Provence, 1974*, pp. 48–52. Issoudun, Imprimerie Laboureur.

Bricker, Harvey M., and Nicholas C. David
1984   *Excavation of the Abri Pataud, Les Eyzies (Dordogne): Périgordian VI (Level 3) Assemblage*. American School of Prehistoric Research, Bulletin no. 37. Peabody Museum, Harvard University.

Broglio, Alberto, and Piero Leonardi
1963   "Les industries leptolithiques pré-aurignaciennes, aurignaciennes et gravettiennes en Italie," in *Aurignac et l'Aurignacien*, Louis Méroc, ed. (*Bulletin de la Société Méridionale de Spéléologie et de Préhistoire*, vols. 6–9, 1956-1959), pp. 93–102.

Brooks, C. E. P.
1949   *Climate Through the Ages*. 2nd edition. London, Ernest Benn.

Brun, Victor
1865   "Découvertes de l'âge anté-historique faites à Bruniquel (Tarn et Tarn-et-Garonne)," *Congrès Archéologique de France, Comptes Rendus des Séances Générales tenues à Montauban, Cahors et Guéret, 32e Session*, pp. 17–37.

Butzer, Karl W.
1964   *Environment and Archaeology*. Chicago, Aldine.

Capitan, Louis, and Denis Peyrony
1912   "Station préhistorique de la Ferrassie, Com-

mune de Savignac-le-Bugue.'' *Revue Anthropologique*, vol. 22, pp. 29–50.

Cardini, L., and Mariella Taschini
1958– "Campagno di scavo al Riparo Blanc in lo-
1961   calità Cava di Alabastro al Monte Circeo,''
       Quaternaria, vol. 15, pp. 353–354.

Cartailhac, Emile
1903   "Les stations de Bruniquel sur les bords de
       l'Aveyron,'' *L'Anthropologie*, vol. 14, pp. 129–
       150.
1906   *Les Grottes de Grimaldi (Baoussé-Roussé)*, vol.
       2, fasc. 2, Archéologie. Monaco, Imprimerie
       de Monaco.

Célérier, Guy
1967   "Le gisement périgordien supérieur des
       'Jambes,' Commune de Périgueux,'' *Bulletin
       de la Société Préhistorique Française*, vol. 64,
       pp. 53–68.

Célérier, Guy, Henri Laville, and Claude Thibault
1967   "Étude sédimentologique du gisement préhis-
       torique des Jambes à Perigueux,'' *Bulletin de
       la Société Préhistorique Française*, vol. 64,
       pp. 69–82.

Champagne, F., and R. Espitalié
1967   "La stratigraphie du Piage,'' *Bulletin de la
       Société Préhistorique Française*, vol. 64, pp.
       29–34.

Charbonnier, Olivier
1962   "L'abri aurignacien des Roches, Commune de
       Pouligny-Saint-Pierre,'' *L'Anthropologie*, vol.
       66, pp. 469–484.

Clay, R. Berle
1976   "Typological classification, attribute analysis,
       and lithic variability,'' *Journal of Field Ar-
       chaeology*, vol. 3, pp. 303–311.

Clarke, David L.
1968   *Analytical Archaeology*. London, Methuen and
       Co.

Clottes, Jean
1974   "Le Paléolithique supérieur dans les Pyrénées
       françaises,'' *Cahiers d'Anthropologie et
       d'Écologie humaine*, vol. 2, nos. 3-4, pp. 69–
       88.

Cocchi, Piero
1952   "Nuova stazione litica all'aperto del paleoli-
       tico superiore nel Valdarno,'' *Revista di Scienze
       Preistoriche*, vol. 7, pp. 87–107.

Coiffard, Joseph
1914   "Station des Vachons. Commune de Voul-
       gézac (Charente),'' *L'Association Française
       pour l'Avancement des Sciences, Comptes
       Rendus de la 43e Session, Le Havre*, pt. 5, pp.
       623–627.
1922   "Station des Vachons, Abri 2,'' *L'Association
       Française pour l'Avancement des Sciences,
       Comptes Rendus de la 46e Session, Montpel-
       lier*, pp. 492–494.
1937   "L'Aurignacien en Charente,'' *Bulletin de la
       Société Archéologique et Historique de la
       Charente*, pp. 113–128.

Couchard, Jean, and Denise de Sonneville-Bordes
1960   "La Grotte de Bassaler-Nord, près de Brive,
       et la question du Périgordien II en Corrèze,''
       L'Anthropologie, vol. 64, pp. 415-437.

Coulonges, L.
1949   "Le gisement paléolithique de Cavart, Lot,''
       L'Anthropologie, vol. 53, pp. 558–560.
1963   "Magdalénien et Périgordien post-glaciaire: la
       grotte de la Borie-del-Rey (Lot-et-Garonne),''
       Gallia-Préhistoire, vol. 6, pp. 1–29.

Coursaget, J., and J. Le Run
1966   "Gif-sur-Yvette natural radiocarbon measure-
       ments I,'' *Radiocarbon*, vol. 8, pp. 128–141.

Cousté, R., and Yovan Krtolitza
1961   "La flute paléolithique de l'Abri Lespaux à
       Saint-Quentin-de-Baron (Gironde),'' *Bulletin
       de la Société Préhistorique Française*, vol. 58,
       pp. 28–30.
1965   "L'Abri Lespaux (Commune de Saint-
       Quentin-de-Baron) et la question du Périgor-
       dien en Gironde,'' *Revue Historique et Ar-
       chéologique du Libournais*, vol. 33, pp. 47–
       54.

Coutier, Léon
1925   "Grotte des Rochettes, près de Saint-Léon-
       sur-Vézère,'' *L'Association Française pour
       l'Avancement des Sciences, Comptes Rendus
       de la 49e Session, Grenoble*, pp. 482–483.

Coutier, Léon, and M. Emetaz
1926   "Station des Rochettes. Transition moustério-
       aurignacienne,'' *Bulletin et Mémoires de la
       Société Anthropologique de Paris*, vol. 7, pp.
       147–148.

Dance, S. Peter
1975   "The molluscan fauna,'' in *Excavation of the
       Abri Pataud, Les Eyzies (Dordogne)*, H. L.
       Movius, Jr., ed., American School of Prehis-

toric Research, Bulletin no. 30, pp. 154–159. Peabody Museum, Harvard University.

Daniel, Raoul
1935   "Notule sur une gravure magdalénienne de l'abri de Saint-Antonin (Tarn-et-Garonne)," *Bulletin de la Société Préhistorique Française*, vol. 32, pp. 512–515.
1968   "Le Roc de Cavart, commune de Montcabrier (Lot)," *Bulletin de la Société Préhistorique Française*, vol. 65, pp. 60–62.
1969   "Les burins de Noailles du Fourneau du Diable, Commune de Bourdeilles (Dordogne)," *Bulletin de la Société Préhistorique Française*, vol. 66, pp. 16–18.

Daniel, Raoul, and Beatrice Schmider
1972   "L'abri Durand-Ruel près Brantôme (Dgne) et ses problèmes stratigraphiques," *Gallia-Préhistoire*, vol. 15, pp. 323–337.

David, Nicholas C.
1966   "The Périgordian Vc.: an Upper Palaeolithic culture in Western Europe." Ph.D. dissertation, Harvard University.
1970   "Périgordian Vc regional facies: an attempt to define upper palaeolithic ethnic groups," *7e Congrès Internationale des Sciences Préhistoriques et Protohistoriques, Prague*, vol. 1, pp. 323–326.
1972   "On the life span of pottery, type frequencies, and archaeological inference," *American Antiquity*, vol. 37, no. 1, pp. 141–142.
1973   "On upper palaeolithic society, ecology, and technological change: the Noaillian case," in *The Explanation of Culture Change. Models in Prehistory*, Colin Renfrew, ed., pp. 277–304. London, Duckworth.

David, Pierre
1930   "Station des Vachons, commune de Voulgézac (Charente). Fouilles de 1922, 1923, 1924. Abri de l'Oeuil de Boeuf," *Société Linnéenne de Bordeaux, Procès-verbaux de la séance du 22 janvier 1930*, sep., 7 pp.

Delage, Franck
1937   "L'abri des Merveilles à Castelmerle (Sergeac, Dordogne)," *Congrès Préhistorique de France, Comptes Rendus de la 12e Session, Toulouse*, pp. 577–608.

Delibrias, Georgette, and Jacque Evin
1980   "Sommaire des datations 14C concernant la préhistoire en France. II. Dates parues de 1974 à 1978," *Bulletin de la Société Préhistorique Française*, vol. 77, pp. 215–224.

Delporte, Henri
1956   "Stratigraphie de l'abri du Facteur ou de la Forêt à Tursac (Dordogne)," *Bulletin de la Société d'Études et de Recherches Préhistoriques, Les Eyzies*, vol. 6.
1957   "L'industrie périgordienne de l'abri du Facteur ou de la Forêt, à Tursac (Dordogne)," *Bulletin de la Société d'Études et de Recherches Préhistoriques, Les Eyzies*, vol. 7, pp. 24–37.
1958   "Observations nouvelles à l'abri du Facteur (Tursac)," *Bulletin de la Société d'Études et de Recherches Préhistoriques, Les Eyzies*, vol. 8.
1959   "Un nouvelle statuette paléolithique: la Vénus de Tursac," *L'Anthropologie*, vol. 63, pp. 233–247.
1961a   "Note préliminaire sur la station de la Rochette: le Périgordien supérieur," *Bulletin de la Société d'Études et de Recherches Préhistoriques, Les Eyzies*, vol. 11, pp. 39–49.
1961b   "Les niveaux aurignaciens de l'Abri du Facteur à Tursac, et l'évolution générale de l'Aurignacien en Périgord," *Bulletin de la Société d'Études et de Recherches Préhistoriques, Les Eyzies*, vol. 11.
1962   "Étude paléo-topographique d'un habitat du Périgordien supérieur," *Bulletin de la Société Préhistorique Française*, vol. 49, pp. 345–353.
1968   "L'abri du Facteur à Tursac (Dordogne). I. Étude générale," *Gallia-Préhistoire*, vol. 11, pp. 1–112.
1976   "L'organisation du Périgordien supérieur en France et ses rapports avec le Périgordien d'Europe centrale," in *Périgordien et Gravettien en Europe, Colloque XV, 9e Congrès, Union Internationale des Sciences Préhistoriques et Protohistoriques, Nice*, Bohuslav Klima, ed., pp. 7–65.

Delporte, Henri, and Guy Mazière
1977   "L'Aurignacien de La Ferrassie. Observations préliminaires à la suite des fouilles récentes," *Bulletin de la Société Préhistorique Française*, vol. 74, pp. 343–361.

Delporte, Henri, and Alain Tuffreau
1972–1973   "Les industries du Périgordien supérieur de La Ferrassie," *Quartär*, vol. 23/24, pp. 93–123.

Donner, Joakim J.
1975   "Pollen composition of the Abri Pataud sediments," in *Excavation of the Abri Pataud, Les Eyzies (Dordogne)*, H. L. Movius, Jr., ed., American School of Prehistoric Research,

Bulletin no. 30, pp. 160–173. Peabody Museum, Harvard University.

Drucker, P.
1955   *Indians of the Northwest Coast.* New York, Natural History Press.

Drury, William H.
1975   "The ecology of the human occupation at the Abri Pataud," in *Excavation of the Abri Pataud, Les Eyzies (Dordogne)*, H. L. Movius, Jr., ed., American School of Prehistoric Research, Bulletin no. 30, pp. 187–193. Peabody Museum, Harvard University.

Escalon de Fonton, Max, and Gérard Onoratini
1976   "Les civilisations du Paléolithique supérieur en Provence littorale," in *La Préhistoire française*, H. de Lumley, ed., vol. 2, pp. 1145–1156. Paris, CNRS.

Evin, J., G. Marien, and C. Pachiaudi
1979   "Lyons natural radiocarbon measurements VIII," *Radiocarbon*, vol. 21, pp. 405–452.

Farrand, William R.
1975   "Analysis of the Abri Pataud sediments," in *Excavation of the Abri Pataud, Les Eyzies (Dordogne)*, H. L. Movius, Jr., ed., American School of Prehistoric Research, Bulletin no. 30, pp. 27–68. Peabody Museum, Harvard University.

Féaux, Maurice
1878   "Station préhistorique de Petit-Puyrousseau (Commune de Périgueux)," *Bulletin de la Société Historique et Archéologique du Périgord*, vol. 5, pp. 38–44.
1905   *Catalogue des collections préhistoriques du Musée de Périgord.* Périgueux, Joucla.
1912   "La station du Petit-Puyrousseau, Commune de Périgueux," *Bulletin de la Société Historique et Archéologique du Périgord*, vol. 39, pp. 458–460.

Garrod, Dorothy A. E.
1926   *The Upper Palaeolithic Age in Britain.* Oxford, Oxford University Press.

Gates, W. L.
1976   "Modeling the Ice-Age climate," *Science*, vol. 191, pp. 1138–1144.

Gaussen, Jean, and James R. Sackett
1976   "Les structures d'habitat au Paléolithique supérieur dans le Sud-Ouest de la France," in *Les structures d'habitat au Paléolithique su-*

périeur, Colloque XIII, 9e Congrès, *Union Internationale des Sciences Préhistoriques et Protohistoriques, Nice*, André Leroi-Gourhan, ed., pp. 55–83.

Gay, H.
1880   "L'homme des temps préhistoriques dans la vallée de la Couze," *Bulletin de la Société Scientifique, Historique et Archéologique du Périgord*, vol. 2, pp. 427–431.

Gérard, R. de
1883   "Station préhistorique de Cantelouve," *Bulletin de la Société Historique et Archéologique du Périgord*, vol. 2, pp. 427–431. (Not consulted; cited in Denise de Sonneville-Bordes, *Le paléolithique supérieur en Périgord.*

Girard, M.
1976   "La végétation au Pléistocene supérieur et au debût de l'Holocène dans les Alpes, le Jura, le Bourgogne et les Vosges," in *La Préhistoire française*, Henry de Lumley, ed., vol. 1, pp. 517–524. Paris, CNRS.

Girod, Paul
1906   *Les stations de l'âge du renne dans les vallées de la Vézère et de la Corrèze. Stations solutréenes et aurignaciennes.* Paris, J. B. Baillière et Fils.

Grayson, Donald K.
1979   "On the quantification of vertebrate archaeofaunas," in *Advances in archaeological method and theory*, M. B. Schiffer, ed., vol. 2, pp. 200–237.

Graziosi, Paolo
1928   "La grotta di Talamone," *Archivio per l'Antropologia e l'Etnologia*, vol. 58, pp. 122–152.

Hamal-Nandrin, J., J. Servais, and M. Louis
1935   "Nouvelle contribution à l'étude du préhistoire dans la Compigne limbourgeoise (Belgique)," *Bulletin de la Société Préhistorique Française*, vol. 32, pp. 175–203.

Harlé, Edouard
1893   "La grotte de Tarté, près de Salies-du-Salat (Haute Garonne)," *Bulletin de la Société d'Histoire Naturelle de Toulouse*, vol. 27, pp. 23–24.

Harrison, G. A., J. S. Weiner, J. M. Tanner, and N. A. Barnicot
1964   *Human Biology: an Introduction to Human*

Evolution, Variation and Growth. Oxford, Clarendon Press.

Hauser, Otto
1911   *Le Périgord préhistorique*. Le Bugue, G. Rejou.

Helm, June
1968   "The nature of Dogrib socio-territorial groups," in *Man the Hunter*, Richard B. Lee and Irven DeVore, eds., pp. 118-125. Chicago, Aldine.

Herskovits, Melville A.
1948   *Man and his Works*. New York, Alfred A. Knopf.

Hodder, Ian
1980   *Symbols in Action*. Cambridge, Cambridge University Press.

Jalut, G.
1976   "La végétation au Pléistocene supérieur et au debût de l'Holocene dans les Pyrénées," in *La Préhistoire française*, Henry de Lumley, ed., vol. 1, pp. 512–516. Paris, CNRS.

Klaatsch, H., and Otto Hauser
1910   "*Homo aurignacensis hauseri*. Ein paläolitischer Skelettfund aus dem unteren Aurignacien der Station Combe Capelle, bei Montferrant (Périgord)," *Prähistorische Zeitschrift*, vol. 1, pp. 272–358.

Kroeber, Alfred L.
1939   *Cultural and Natural Areas of Native North America*. University of California Publications in American Archaeology and Ethnology, no. 38. Berkeley.
1948   *Anthropology* (revised edition). London, Harrap.

Lalanne, J. G., and Jean Bouyssonie
1941–   "Le gisement paléolithique de Laussel. Fouilles
1946   de Dr. Lalanne," *L'Anthropologie*, vol. 50, pp. 1–163.

Laplace, Georges
1958–   "Recherches sur l'origine et l'évolution des
1961   complexes leptolithiques. Le problème des Périgordiens I et II et l'hypothèse du synthétotype . . . ," *Quaternaria*, vol. 5, pp. 153–240.
1964a   "Essai de typologie systématique," *Annali dell'Università di Ferrara* (n.s.). Sezione 15, Paleontologia Umana e Paletnologia. Supplemento 2 al vol. 1.
1964b   "Les subdivisions du Leptolithique italien: étude

de typologie analytique," *Bulletino di Paletnologia Italiana* (n.s. 15), vol. 73, pp. 25–63.
1966   "Les niveaux castelperronien, proto-aurignacien, et aurignaciens de la Grotte Gatzarria à Suhare en Pays Basque (fouilles 1961–1963)," *Quartär*, vol. 17, pp. 117–140.

Laville, Henri
1964a   "Recherches sédimentologiques sur la paléoclimatologie du Würmien récent en Périgord," *L'Anthropologie*, vol. 68, pp. 1–48.
1964b   "Étude géologique," in *Le Gisement de la Chèvre à Bourdeilles (Dordogne)*, R. Arambourou and P. E. Jude, pp. 121–128. Périgueux, Imprimerie Magne.
1968   "L'abri du Facteur à Tursac (Dordogne). IV. Étude sédimentologique du remplissage," *Gallia-Préhistoire*, vol. 11, pp. 133–145.
1969   "Le remplissage des grottes et abris du Sud-Ouest de la France," *Études Françaises sur le Quaternaire, Bulletin de l'Association Française pour l'Étude du Quaternaire*, pp. 77–80.

Laville, Henri, and Jean-Philippe Rigaud
1973   "The Périgordian V industries in Périgord: typological variations, stratigraphy and relative chronology." *World Archaeology*, vol. 4, no. 3, pp. 330–338.

Laville, Henri, Jean-Philippe Rigaud, and James R. Sackett
1980   *Rock Shelters of the Périgord. Geological Stratigraphy and Archaeological Succession*. New York, Academic Press.

Laville, Henri, and Claude Thibault
1967   "L'oscillation climatique contemporaine du Périgordien supérieur à burins de Noailles, dans le Sud-Ouest de la France," *Comptes Rendus de l'Academie des Sciences de Paris, Série D*, vol. 264, pp. 2364–2366.

Leroi-Gourhan, André
1961   "Les fouilles d'Arcy-sur-Cure," *Gallia-Préhistoire*, vol. 4, pp. 3–16.

Leroi-Gourhan, Arlette
1959   "Résultats de l'analyse pollinique de la grotte d'Isturitz," *Bulletin de la Société Préhistorique Française*, vol. 56, pp. 619-624.
1968   "L'abri du Facteur à Tursac (Dordogne). III. Analyse pollinique," *Gallia-Préhistoire*, vol. 11, pp. 123-132.

Leroi-Gourhan, Arlette, and André Leroi-Gourhan
1964   "Chronologie des grottes d'Arcy-sur-Cure," *Gallia-Préhistoire*, vol. 7, pp. 1-64.

Leroi-Gourhan, Arlette, and Josette Renault-Miskovsky
    1977   "La palynologie appliquée à l'archéologie:
            méthodes, limites et résultats," in *Approche
            écologique à l'homme fossile*, H. Laville and
            J. Renault-Miskovsky, eds., *Supplément au
            Bulletin de l'Association Française pour l'Étude
            du Quaternaire*, no. 47, pp. 35-49. Paris,
            Université Pierre et Marie Curie, Laboratoire
            de Géologie I.

Le Tensorer, Jean-Marie
    1981   *Le Paléolithique de l'Agenais*. Université de
            Bordeaux I, Institut du Quaternaire, Cahiers
            du Quaternaire, No. 3. Paris, CNRS.

Lyman, R. L.
    1979   "Available meat from faunal remains: a con-
            sideration of techniques," *American Antiq-
            uity*, vol. 44, no. 3, pp. 536–546.

MacCurdy, George G.
    1931   "The Abri des Merveilles at Castelmerle near
            Sergeac (Dordogne)," *American School of
            Prehistoric Research*, Bulletin no. 7, pp. 12–
            23. Peabody Museum, Harvard University.

McCollough, Major C. R.
    1971   "Périgordian facies in the Upper Palaeolithic
            of Cantabria," Ph.D. dissertation, University
            of Pennsylvania.

Maquet, J.
    1961   *The Premise of Inequality in Ruanda*. London,
            Oxford University Press.

Monméjean, E., François Bordes, and Denise de Sonneville-Bordes
    1964   "Le Périgordien supérieur à burins de Noailles
            du Roc de Gavaudun (Lot-et-Garonne),"
            L'Anthropologie, vol. 68, pp. 253–316.

Movius, Hallam L., Jr.
    1966   "The hearths of the Upper Périgordian and
            Aurignacian horizons at the Abri Pataud, Les
            Eyzies (Dordogne), and their possible signif-
            icance," *American Anthropologist*, vol. 68,
            pp. 296-325.
    1975   "A summary of the stratigraphic sequence,"
            in *Excavation of the Abri Pataud, Les Eyzies
            (Dordogne)*, H. L. Movius, Jr., ed., American
            School of Prehistoric Research, Bulletin no.
            30, pp. 7–18. Peabody Museum, Harvard Uni-
            versity.
    1977   *Excavation of the Abri Pataud, Les Eyzies
            (Dordogne). Stratigraphy*. American School
            of Prehistoric Research, Bulletin no. 31. Pea-
            body Museum, Harvard University.

Movius, Hallam L., Jr., ed.
    1975   *Excavation of the Abri Pataud, Les Eyzies
            (Dordogne)*. American School of Prehistoric
            Research, Bulletin no. 30. Peabody Museum,
            Harvard University.

Movius, Hallam L., Jr., and Nicholas C. David
    1970   "Burins avec modification tertiare du biseau,
            burins-pointe et burins du Raysse à l'Abri
            Pataud, Les Eyzies (Dordogne)," *Bulletin de
            la Société Préhistorique Française, Études et
            Travaux*, pp. 445-455.

Movius, Hallam L., Jr., Nicholas David, Harvey M. Bricker,
and R. Berle Clay
    1968   *The Analysis of Certain Major Classes of
            Upper Palaeolithic Tools*, Hugh Hencken, ed.
            American School of Prehistoric Research,
            Bulletin no. 26. Peabody Museum, Harvard
            University.

Movius, Hallam L., Jr., and Sheldon Judson
    1956   *The Rock-Shelter of La Colombière. Archae-
            ological and Geological Investigations of an
            Upper Périgordian Site near Poncin (Ain)*.
            American School of Prehistoric Research, Bul-
            letin no. 19. Peabody Museum, Harvard Uni-
            versity.

Onoratini, Gérard
    1975   "La station du plein air de la Cabre (Var),"
            *Bulletin du Muséum d'Histoire Naturelle de
            Marseille*, vol. 35, pp. 259–269.
    1976   "La grotte de la Bouverie (Var)," *Congrès
            Préhistorique de France, Comptes Rendus de
            la 20e Session, Martigues, 1974*, pp. 349-458.
    1982   *Préhistoire, sédiments, climats du Würm III à
            l'Holocene dans le Sud-Est de la France*.
            Université de Droit, d'Economie et des Sci-
            ences d'Aix-Marseille, Faculté des Sciences et
            Techniques de St. Jerome. C.N.R.S. E.R. 46.
            Mémoire I, 2 vols.

Onoratini, Gérard, and J. da Silva
    1978   "La Grotte des Enfants à Grimaldi. Les foyers
            supérieurs," *Bulletin, Musée d'Anthropologie
            Préhistorique de Monaco*, vol. 22, pp. 31–71.

Onoratini, Gérard, and G. Girard
    1976   "La station du plein air de Gratadis (Var),"
            *Congrès Préhistorique de France, Comptes
            Rendus de la 20e Session, Martigues, 1974*,
            pp. 459-472.

Nougier, L. R.
    1954   "Essai sur le peuplement préhistorique de la
            France," *Population*, vol. 19, pp. 241–274.

Palma di Cesnola, Arturo

1971   "Il gravettiano evoluto della grotta della Cala a Marina di Camerota (Salerno)," *Rivista di Scienze Preistoriche*, vol. 26, no. 2, pp. 259–324.

1976   "Le leptolithique archaique en Italie," in *Périgordien et Gravettien en Europe, Colloque XV, 9e Congrès, Union Internationale des Sciences Préhistoriques et Protohistoriques, Nice*, Bohuslav Klima, ed., pp. 66–99.

Paquereau, Marie-Madeleine

1970   "Flores et climats paléolithiques dans le Sud-Ouest de la France," *Revue de Géographie Physique et de Géologie Dynamique*, vol. 12, pp. 109–116.

1976   "La végétation au Pleistocène supérieur au début de l'Holocène dans le Sud-Ouest," in *La Préhistoire française*, Henry de Lumley, ed., vol. 1, pp. 525–530. Paris, CNRS.

Parat, Alexandre

1902   "Les grottes de la Cure. XXI. La grotte du Trilobite," *Bulletin de la Société des Sciences Historiques et Naturelles de l'Yonne*, vol. 56, pp. 49–99.

Passemard, E.

1924   *Les stations paléolithiques du Pays Basque et leurs rapports avec les terrasses d'alluvions*. Bayonne, Bodiou.

1944   "La caverne d'Isturitz en Pays Basque," *Préhistoire*, vol. 9, pp. 1–96.

Peyrony, Denis

1908   "Station du Ruth, près Le Moustier (Dordogne). Superposition du Solutréen à l'Aurignacien," *L'Association Française pour L'Avancement des Sciences, Comptes Rendus de la 37e Session, Clermont-Ferrand*, deuxième partie, pp. 689–691.

1909   "Station préhistorique du Ruth, près Le Moustier (Dordogne)," *Revue de l'Ecole d'Anthropologie*, vol. 19, pp. 156–176.

1932a   "Les gisements préhistoriques de Bourdeilles (Dordogne)," *Archives de l'Institut de Paléontologie Humaine*, Memoire 10.

1932b   "Les abris Lartet et du Poisson à Gorge d'Enfer (Dordogne)," *L'Anthropologie*, vol. 42, pp. 241–268.

1933   "Les industries 'aurignaciennes' dans le bassin de la Vézère," *Bulletin de la Société Préhistorique Française*, vol. 30, pp. 543–599.

1934   "La Ferrassie. Moustérien, Périgordien, Aurignacien," *Préhistoire*, vol. 3, pp. 1–92.

1939   "Fouilles de la Roque-Saint-Christophe,"

Bulletin de la Société Historique et Archéologique du Périgord, vol. 66, pp. 248–269, 360–387.

1941   "Station préhistorique de Fongal," *Bulletin de la Société Historique et Archéologique du Périgord*, vol. 68, pp. 166–175.

1943   "Le gisement du Roc de Combe Capelle," *Bulletin de la Société Historique et Archéologique du Périgord*, vol. 70.

1946   "Une mise au point au sujet de l'Aurignacien et du Périgordien," *Bulletin de la Société Préhistorique Française*, vol. 43, pp. 232–237.

1949   "Le Périgord préhistorique," *Publications de la Société Historique et Archéologique du Périgord*, Périgueux.

Peyrony, Elie

1934a   "Les burins dans le gisement préhistorique de la Forêt, Commune de Tursac (Dordogne)," *L'Association Française pour l'Avancement des Sciences, Comptes Rendus de la 58e Session, Rabat*, pp. 185–187.

1934b   "Le gisement de la Forêt, Commune de Tursac (Dordogne)," *Congrès Préhistorique de France, Comptes Rendus de la 11e Session, Périgueux*, pp. 424–430.

Pittard, Eugène

1912a   "La préhistorique dans le vallon de Rebières," *Congrès Internationale d'Anthropologie et d'Archéologie Préhistorique, Comptes Rendus de la 14e Session, Genève*, pp. 363–405.

1912b   "L'outillage de la station aurignacienne 'Les Rebières II' (Station Durand-Ruel)," *Congrès Internationale d'Anthropologie et d'Archéologie Préhistorique, Comptes Rendus de la 14e Session, Genève*, pp. 450–478.

1912c   "Outillage microlithique de la station aurignacienne Durand-Ruel (Vallon des Rebières)," *Congrès Internationale d'Anthropologie et d'Archéologie Préhistorique, Comptes Rendus de la 14e Session, Genève*, pp. 479–488.

Pradel, Louis

1959a   "Le niveau de Noailles d'Oreille d'Enfer, Commune des Eyzies-de-Tayac (Dordogne)," *Bulletin de la Société Préhistorique Française*, vol. 56, pp. 228–235.

1959b   "Le périgordien II de la Grotte des Cottés (Commune de Saint-Pierre-de-Maille, Vienne)," *Bulletin de la Société Préhistorique Française*, vol. 56, pp. 421–427.

1965   "L'abri aurignacien et périgordien des Roches, Commune de Pouligny-Saint-Pierre (Indre)," *L'Anthropologie*, vol. 69, pp. 219–236.

1966   "À propos du burin du Raysse," *Comptes*

Rendus des Séances Mensuelles de la Société Préhistorique Française, vol. 63, no. 2, pp. 47–49.

Pradel, Louis, and A. Chollet
1950 "L'abri périgordien de Laraux, Commune de Lussac-les-Châteaux (Vienne)," *L'Anthropologie*, vol. 54, pp. 214–227.

Pradel, Louis, and J. H. Pradel
1966 "La station paléolithique du Raysse, Commune de Brive (Corrèze)," *L'Anthropologie*, vol. 70, nos. 3-4, pp. 225–253.

Ragout, André
1935 "Gisement de l'Abri du Chasseur à Vilhonneur (Charente)," *Congrès Préhistorique de France, Comptes Rendus de la 11e Session, Périgueux*, p. 431.
1939– "Un proto-harpon aurignacien," *L'Anthropo-
1940 logie*, vol. 49, pp. 679–701.

Regnault, Félix
1873 "Fouilles dans la grotte de Gargas," *Congrès Préhistorique de France, Comptes Rendus de la Congrès Scientifique de France*, p. 369.
1890 "Fouilles dans les grottes de Gargas et de Malarnaud," *L'Association Française pour l'Avancement des Sciences, Comptes Rendus de la 19e Session, Limoges*, vol. 2, pp. 410–411.
1895 "Foyers paléolithiques de la grotte de Gargas," *L'Association Française pour l'Avancement des Sciences, Comptes Rendus de la 24e Session, Bordeaux*, vol. 1, pp. 315–316; vol. 2, pp. 781–786.

Renault-Miskovsky, Josette
1972 "Contribution à la paléoclimatologie du midi mediterranéen pendant la dernière glaciation et le post-glaciaire, d'après l'étude palynologique du remplissage des grottes et abris sous-roche," *Bulletin du Musée d'Anthropologie Préhistorique du Monaco*, vol. 18, pp. 145–210.

Rigaud, Jean-Philippe
1969 "Note préliminaire sur la stratigraphie du gisement du 'Flageolet-1-' (Commune de Bézenac), Dordogne," *Bulletin de la Société Préhistorique Française, Comptes Rendus des Séances Mensuelles*, vol. 66, no. 3, pp. 73–75.
1976 "Données nouvelles sur le périgordien supérieur en Périgord," in *Périgordien et Gravettien en Europe, Colloque XV, 9e Congrès, Union Internationale des Sciences Préhisto-*

riques et Protohistoriques, Nice*, Bohuslav Klima, ed., pp. 53–65.
1976 "Les structures d'habitat d'un niveau de Périgordien supérieur du Flageolet-1 (Bézenac, Dordogne)," in *Périgordien et Gravettien en Europe, Colloque XIII, 9e Congrès, Union Internationale des Sciences Préhistoriques et Protohistoriques, Nice*, Bohuslav Klima, ed., prétirage, pp. 93–102.

Rivière, Emile
1906 "Trente-sept années de fouilles préhistoriques et archéologiques en France et en Italie," *L'Association Française pour l'Avancement des Sciences, Comptes Rendus de la 35e Session, Lyon*, pt. 2, pp. 773–798.

Robert, Romain, George Malvesin-Fabre, and L. Michaut
1952 "Nouvelles découvertes à la grotte de Téoulé (Haute-Garonne)," *Bulletin de la Société Préhistorique Française*, vol. 49, nos. 1–2, pp. 81–90.

Sackett, James R.
1982 "Approaches to style in lithic archaeology," *Journal of Anthropological Archeology*, vol. 1, no. 1, pp. 59–112.

Saint-Périer, René de
1922 "Statuette de femme stéatopyge découverte à Lespugue (Haute-Garonne)," *L'Anthropologie*, vol. 32, pp. 361–381.
1923 "La dernière statuette stéatopyge paléolithique," *Revue Anthropologique*, vol. 33.
1924a "Les fouilles de 1923 dans la grotte des Rideaux à Lespugue," *L'Anthropologie*, vol. 34, pp. 1–15.
1924b "Résultats des fouilles en 1923 dans la grotte des Rideaux à Lespugue (Haute-Garonne)," *L'Anthropologie*, vol. 34, pp. 290–291.
1924c "La statuette féminine de Lespugue (Haute-Garonne)," *Bulletin de la Société Préhistorique Française*, vol. 21, pp. 81–84.
1936 "La grotte d'Isturitz. II. Le Magdalénien de la grande salle," *Archives de l'Institut de Paléontologie Humaine*, Mémoire 17.

Saint-Périer, René de
1965 "Réflections sur le Paléolithique supérieur d'Isturitz," in *Miscelánea en homenaje al Abate Henri Breuil*, E. Ripoll-Perello, ed. Barcelona, Disputación Provincial de Barcelona, Instituto de Preistoria y Arqueologia, vol. 2, pp. 319–325.

Saint-Périer, René de, and S. de Saint-Périer
1952 *La grotte d'Isturitz. III. Les solutréens, les*

aurignaciens et les moustériens. Archives de l'Institut de Paléontologie Humaine, Mémoire 25.

Sauter, Marc R.
1946   "Les industries moustériennes et aurignaciennes de la station paléolithique du 'Bonhomme,' vallon des Rebières (Dordogne)," *Cahiers de Préhistoire et d'Archéologie*, vol. 2.

Sauvy, A.
1969   *General theory of population*. London, Weidenfeld and Nicolson. (Original publication in French by Presses Universitaires de France, 1966.)

Schiffer, Michael B.
1976   *Behavioral Archaeology*. New York, Academic Press.

Schmider, B.
1969   "Contribution à l'étude du Périgordien supérieur de la Rochette (Dordogne)," *Gallia-Préhistoire*, vol. 12, pp. 259–271.

Siret, Louis
1933   "Le coup de burin moustérien," *Bulletin de la Société Préhistorique Française*, vol. 30, no. 2, pp. 120–127.

Sonneville-Bordes, Denise de
1953   "Le Paléolithique supérieur du plateau Baillard à Gavaudun (Lot-et-Garonne)," *Bulletin de la Société Préhistorique Française*, vol. 50, pp. 356–364.
1954   "Esquisse d'une évolution typologique du Paléolithique supérieur en Périgord: défense et illustration de la méthôde," *L'Anthropologie*, vol. 58, pp. 197–230.
1955a   "La question du Périgordien II," *Bulletin de la Société Préhistorique Française*, vol. 52, pp. 187–203.
1955b   "À propos du Périgordien," *Bulletin de la Société Préhistorique Française*, vol. 52, pp. 597–601.
1955c   "À propos du Périgordien II," *Bulletin de la Société Préhistorique Française*, vol. 52, pp. 663–665.
1955d   "La grotte de Chanlat et la question du Périgordien II," *L'Anthropologie*, vol. 59, pp. 357–360.
1960   *Le Paléolithique supérieur en Périgord*, 2 vols. Bordeaux, Delmas.
1966   "L'évolution du Paléolithique supérieur en Europe occidentale et sa signification," *Bulletin de la Société Préhistorique Française*, vol. 63, pp. 3–34.

Sonneville-Bordes, Denise de, and Jean Perrot
1954   "Lexique typologique de Paléolithique supérieur. Outillage lithique. I. Grattoirs. II. Outils solutréens," *Bulletin de la Société Préhistorique Française*, vol. 51, pp. 327–335.
1955   "Lexique typologique de Paléolithique supérieur. Outillage lithique. III. Outils composites, perçoirs," *Bulletin de la Société Préhistorique Française*, vol. 52, pp. 76–79.
1956a   "Lexique typologique de Paléolithique supérieur. Outillage lithique. IV. Burins," *Bulletin de la Société Préhistorique Française*, vol. 53, pp. 408–412.
1956b   "Lexique typologique de Paléolithique supérieur. Outillage lithique. V. Outillage à bord abattu. VI. Pièces tronquées. VII. Lames retouchées. VIII. Pièces variées. IX. Outillage lamellaire, pointe azilienne," *Bulletin de la Société Préhistorique Française*, vol. 53, pp. 547–559.

Spiess, Arthur E.
1979   *Reindeer and caribou hunters: an archaeological study*. New York, Academic Press.

Thomson, Basil
1939   "L'abri aurignacien de Téoulé, pres Tarté (Haute-Garonne)," *Mélanges de Préhistoire et d'Anthropologie offerts par ses Collègues, Amis et Disciples au Professeur Comte H. Bégouen*, pp. 195–200. Toulouse.

Tixier, Jacques
1958   "Les burins de Noailles de l'abri André Ragout, Bois-de-Roc, Vilhonneur (Charente)," *Bulletin de la Société Préhistorique Française*, vol. 55, pp. 628–644.

Turnbull, Colin M.
1965   *Wayward Servants*. New York, Doubleday.

Vergne, Alban
1929   "Les stations préhistoriques de Gavaudun: l'Abri Peyrony," *Revue de l'Agenais*, vol. 56, pp. 137–149.

Verheyleweghen, J.
1956   "Le paléolithique final de culture périgordienne du gisement paléolithique de Lommel (Province de Limboug, Belgique)," *Bulletin de la Société Royale d'Anthropologie et de la Préhistoire*. (Not consulted; cited in J. Tixier, "Les burins de Noailles de l'Abri André Ragout . . . ," 1958, p. 642.)

Vézian, Jean
 1972   "La grotte du Portel, Commune de Loubens
         (Ariège)," *Bulletin de la Société des Études
         et Recherches Préhistoriques, Les Eyzies*, vol.
         21, pp. 88–102.

Vézian, Joseph
 1936   "Les quartzites taillés de la station aurigna-
         cienne de Saint-Jean-de-Verges (Ariège),"
         *Congrès Préhistorique de France, Comptes
         Rendus de la 12e Session, Toulouse-Foix*, pp.
         689–692.

Vézian, Joseph, and Jean Vézian
 1966   "Les gisements de la grotte de Saint-Jean-de-
         Verges (Ariège)," *Gallia-Préhistoire*, vol. 9,
         pp. 93–130.

Villeneuve, L. de, M. Boule, R. Verneau, and E. Cartailhac
 1906–   *Les grottes de Grimaldi (Baoussé-Roussé)*.
 1919   Monaco, Imprimerie de Monaco.

Vogel, J. C., and H. T. Waterbolk
 1963   "Groningen radiocarbon dates IV," *Radio-
         carbon*, vol. 5, pp. 163–202.
 1967   "Groningen radiocarbon dates VII," *Radio-
         carbon*, vol. 9, pp. 107–155.

Waterbolk, H. T.
 1971   "Working with radiocarbon dates," *Proceed-
         ings of the Prehistoric Society*, vol. 37 (2),
         pp. 15–33.

Willey, Gordon R., and Philip Phillips
 1958   *Method and Theory in American Archaeology*.
         Chicago, Chicago University Press.

Wilson, Joan F.
 1975   "The Last Glacial environment at the Abri
         Pataud," in *Excavation of the Abri Pataud,
         Les Eyzies (Dordogne)*, H. L. Movius, Jr.,
         ed., American School of Prehistoric Research,
         Bulletin no. 30, pp. 174–186. Peabody Mu-
         seum, Harvard University.